THE PRACTICAL ENCYCLOPEDIA OF

pregnancy, babycare & nutrition for babies & toddlers

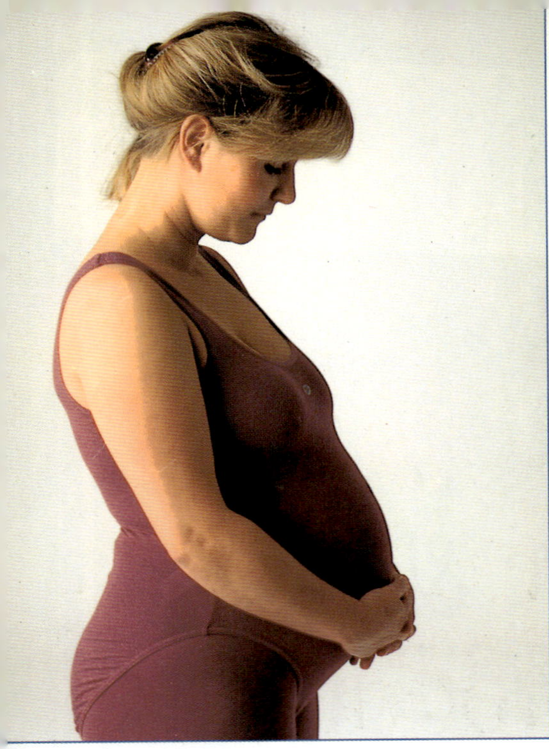

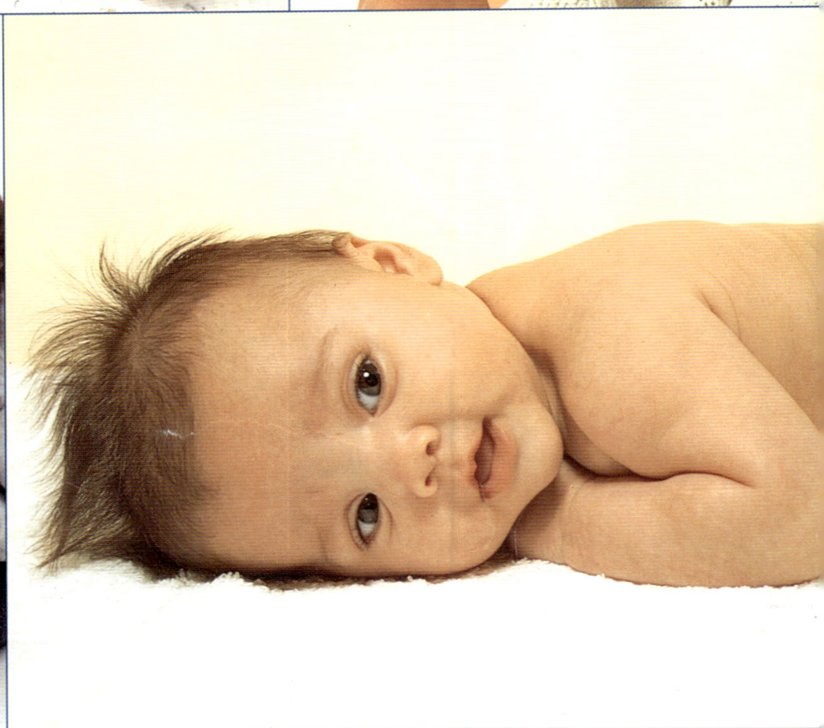

THE PRACTICAL ENCYCLOPEDIA OF pregnancy, babycare & nutrition for babies & toddlers

ALISON MACKONOCHIE
AND
SARA LEWIS

HERMES HOUSE

A very special thank you to Robin for his unfailing support, to Lucy and Kate, without whom we would not have had Christmas, and to Dominic for just being himself. (AM)

CONTENTS

This edition is published by Hermes House

Hermes House is an imprint of Anness Publishing Ltd
Hermes House, 88–89 Blackfriars Road, London SE1 8HA
tel. 020 7401 2077; fax 020 7633 9499; info@anness.com

A CIP catalogue record for this book is available from the British Library.

Publisher: Joanna Lorenz
Project Editors: Casey Horton, Nicky Thompson, Judith Simons, Emma Wish, Rebecca Clunes
Editor: Elizabeth Longley
Designers: Bobbie Colgate Stone, Sue Storey
Jacket Design: DW Design, London; Axis Design
Special Photography: Alistair Hughes, John Freeman
Additional Photography: Carin Simon
Illustrations: Ian Sidaway
Home Economists: Sara Lewis, Jacqueline Clarke, Petra Jackson
Stylist: Judy Williams
Hair and Make-up: Bettina Graham

Previously published as two separate volumes, *The Practical Encyclopedia of Pregnancy & Babycare* and *Cooking for Babies and Toddlers*

10 9 8 7 6 5 4 3 2 1

NOTES FOR RECIPES

Standard spoon and cup measures are level.

Large eggs are used unless otherwise stated.

Printed and bound in China

INTRODUCTION

Being a parent is the most important and responsible role that you will ever have. And it begins long before the birth of your child. By making sure that you and your partner are both healthy before conception, you will be giving your baby the best possible start in life. Once you have conceived, and your pregnancy is confirmed, you will want to do everything you can to ensure that you are doing the best thing for your developing baby.

Understanding what is happening during your pregnancy and how your baby is developing will help you to cope with both the physical and emotional changes that you are likely to experience. Part One of this book guides you through your pregnancy. To keep things simple, a new topic is discussed for each week of your pregnancy. Do remember, though, that every pregnancy is different and many of the topics mentioned will be relevant throughout the baby's development and not just for the week in question.

Preparing for the coming baby can be stressful so do make the time to relax. Yoga is a good method of getting in shape and easing tension at the same time.

Thankfully the days when you had to give birth lying in bed, on your back, are gone. Today, you and your partner can usually choose where and how you give birth. Although this is good news, you may find it difficult to know what would be best for you. Once you know about the available options you can then make informed decisions.

Toys are a baby's way of finding out about the world, and discovering that their actions have an effect on things around them.

As the end of the nine months draws near, it is natural to be concerned about the approaching birth. Sometimes fear about how you will cope can overshadow what is the most miraculous event you are ever likely to encounter. By preparing yourself for labor and understanding what will happen, both you and your partner will be able to make the most of this unique experience.

Once your baby is born, your role as a parent begins in earnest. You are now responsible for the care and well-being of this person. This can seem rather daunting as your baby will expect you to be on call whenever she wakes. Coping with tiredness, a new lifestyle, and the demanding baby can be overwhelming so it is important that you look after yourself.

Your body went through enormous changes during pregnancy and labor, and a post-partum care routine, combining exercise, healthy eating, and relaxation, will help you look your best. You will soon develop a routine that suits both you and your baby but at first you may need some help.

Left: Babies enjoy feeding themselves, and a banana, packed with essential vitamins, makes the ideal snack. Opposite: Your new baby will soon respond to the people around her – with a specially big smile reserved for you.

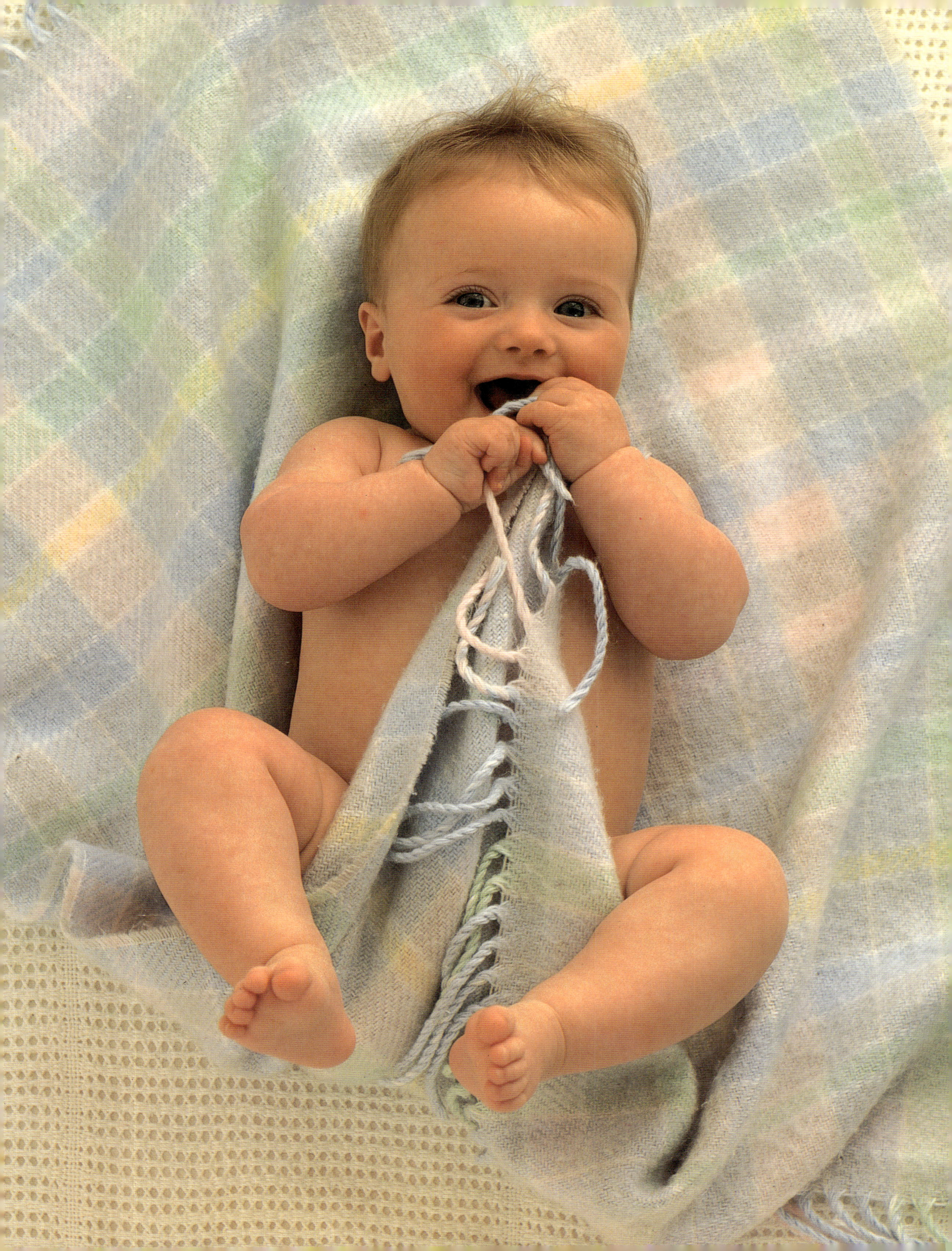

A toddler should still have about a pint of milk a day, but he is now grown up enough to drink from his own cup rather than a bottle.

Part Two guides you through the necessary daily babycare routines. So, whether you are concerned about feeding, bathing or changing diapers, you'll find help and practical advice in the section. A baby isn't all hard work and, if you use the time you spend each day on babycare to play with and to get to know your baby, you'll find that even the chores can be a pleasure!

Your baby's health and development are extremely important and as a parent you will be concerned about what to do if your child is ill or injured in any way. The chapters on first aid and illness are designed to be a quick reference guide to help you cope with emergencies and know when you should call the doctor.

When your baby celebrates her first birthday you will look back and marvel at how much she has learned in this first year. Part Three explains, month by month, how your baby will progress during the first twelve months. Each month she will grow stronger, learn to control her movements, and start to understand the world around her. Do remember that this is only a guide and that every child develops at his own rate.

So that you will be able to help and encourage your child, the final chapters of this section look in more detail at the development of your child's senses and explain how she learns to walk and talk. Play and social behavior are also an integral part of your child's development.

The right food is, of course, the basis of health, and providing a balanced diet can be one of the most challenging aspects of babycare. Nutritional needs change dramatically over the first few years, and you need to be aware of your baby's requirements – at every meal. Children eat four or five times a day so Part Four concentrates on the practical aspects of food.It provides sound nutritional advice on what foods you should introduce at each stage of development, and which are best avoided. Time-saving tips are included, along with guidance on common food problems: hygiene, fussy eating, and going vegetarian.

A baby chair on the floor will keep your baby safe while allowing him to see all of the activity going on around him.

This section also provides more than 200 recipes, each fully illustrated and set out in a step-by-step style. From first purées for a baby to fun meals for a fussy two-year-old, the recipes are easy to follow and perfectly designed to meet the nutritional needs of your child. There is a special section on cooking for all the family, helping you to adapt a single recipe so that it can feed a baby, a toddler, and their parents.

Even when she is accepting solid foods, your baby still needs her bottle; settle down and enjoy this quiet time with her.

Tips such as these help make life easier, taking the stress out of deciding what to eat, showing the simple steps required to prepare a meal, and perhaps preventing food fads from becoming an overwhelming problem. They help you to concentrate on the important things in life: sharing a pleasant meal with your family and enjoying their company.

This book has been written by two experienced mothers, drawing on their own first-hand knowledge. The aim is to give you a comprehensive source of information and, most important of all, the reassurance that you are doing everything "right." We hope you find it a helpful companion during your pregnancy and your baby's first year.

Above: Toddlers learn how to interact with others of their own age and build the basic skills for friendship.
Left: As you eat together, praise your baby for good behavior. This will encourage good table manners later.

PART ONE

PREGNANCY

PREGNANCY IS A VERY SPECIAL TIME for both you and your partner. Knowing what is happening to you and your growing baby during the weeks ahead will help you both to enjoy this exciting period in your lives. Starting with pre-pregnancy care, this book explains how conception takes place and then looks at pregnancy and your baby's development week by week. Many of the issues raised will be relevant throughout your pregnancy and not just during the week in which they are first mentioned, so do read it all.

It is normal to experience some minor discomforts during pregnancy and you will want to know how to cope with them. More serious problems can occasionally occur, and it is important to recognize the symptoms so that you will know when immediate medical treatment is required. The birth is something you may feel anxious about and it will help you if you understand the choices available in both prenatal care and childbirth. By being informed you will be able to choose the type of care and birth that is right for you.

As your body adapts to the changes that pregnancy brings, you will begin to prepare yourself physically, emotionally and practically for parenthood. A well-balanced, healthy diet is essential for both your well-being and that of your baby. Exercise has an important part to play too, not just in keeping you fit but also in preparing your body for the birth. Looking good will help you to feel good, so you should take special care of your physical appearance throughout your pregnancy. Knowing how to select the right clothes to suit your changing shape and how to use makeup to emphasize your best features will help you to feel confident and make your pregnancy an even more enjoyable experience.

PREPARING FOR PREGNANCY

Once you have decided that you want to have a baby, you and your partner should concentrate on getting yourselves fit and healthy before you try to conceive. Ideally, you should begin preparing for pregnancy at least three months before conception so that you can be sure that your child will get the best possible start in life. If your pregnancy is unplanned, then start taking extra care of yourself as soon as you suspect that you might be pregnant. This may involve some basic changes in your lifestyle.

There is evidence that suggests that smoking by either partner can delay conception, so if you or your partner smoke you should stop now. In addition, smoking during pregnancy will put the baby at risk and can also affect your well-being; giving up before conception will benefit you and your child.

Alcohol can inhibit fertility, so both you and your partner should avoid drinking alcohol while trying to conceive. Once you are pregnant alcohol can restrict fetal development and could even cause malformation. Since there is no safe limit for alcohol during pregnancy it is better to give it up altogether.

MEDICATION

Fertilization and the early development of a baby are controlled by delicately balanced chemical processes in the body. Additional chemicals entering your body as medication can upset this development, so if possible you should avoid taking any medicines before conception and during pregnancy. If you are on long-term medication, you will need to talk to your doctor about your options. Medicines that are available over the counter, natural remedies and vitamin supplements should also be avoided, unless they have been recommended by your doctor.

Oral contraceptives rely on chemically-produced hormones to control fertility. If you are taking the pill, change to a barrier method, such as the condom or diaphragm, for three months before trying to conceive. This allows your body to clear itself of synthetic hormones and to re-establish its own cycle.

IMMUNIZATIONS

An unborn baby exposed to rubella (German measles) during its early development can be born severely handicapped. Don't assume that because you were vaccinated in your teens, or you have had the infection, that you are automatically immune. Ask your doctor to give you a blood

Before trying for a baby, both partners should get fit by walking and other exercise.

Salmon is ideal as part of a balanced diet, because it is low in fat but full of vitamins.

By doing regular stretching exercises at home, or at an organized class, you will strengthen yourself for pregnancy.

As your legs have to carry more weight during pregnancy, try to do regular daily exercises such as running in place to build them up.

test to check. If you are not immune you can be vaccinated, but you should not get pregnant until the vaccine virus has cleared from your blood, which takes about three months. If you have been given vaccines for tropical diseases, you should also wait for three months before getting pregnant.

Nutrition and exercise

A well-balanced, healthy diet that contains reasonable daily amounts of carbohydrate, protein, fat, minerals, and vitamins is essential for both your well-being and that of your baby. Everything you eat will also become your unborn child's nourishment, and what you store before pregnancy is important for early fetal development when all the major organs are formed.

One of the B vitamins, folic acid, helps prevent neural tube defects (NTD), such as spina bifida, in unborn babies. It is recommended that all women planning a pregnancy should increase their average daily intake to 0.6 mg by taking a 0.4 mg supplement before attempting conception, and during the first 12 weeks of pregnancy. This is the time when your baby's organs and body systems are forming.

Regular exercise, such as brisk walking or swimming, is important if you are to maintain a healthy lifestyle. Exercise will help you get fit before conception and, as your pregnancy progresses, it will strengthen muscles in your lower back, stomach, and legs, which will help your body cope better with the demands of pregnancy.

THE FIRST TRIMESTER

WEEKS 1–4: CONCEPTION

During the first half of the menstrual cycle two chemical substances called hormones are released from special glands into the bloodstream. One hormone stimulates the process that results in the production of an ovum, or ripe egg. The other hormone stimulates the endometrium, or lining of the uterus (womb), to thicken in readiness to receive a fertilized ovum. About two weeks from the end of your menstrual cycle the work of the first hormone is completed and you ovulate; that is, a ripe ovum is released from one of your ovaries. Conception occurs if your partner's sperm fertilizes this ovum. This usually takes place in the fallopian tube that connects the ovary to the uterus. The fertilized ovum completes its journey to the uterus, where it implants into the thickened uterine lining. Once this process occurs the cervix increases slightly in width and becomes softer, and a thick mucous plug seals off the uterus to protect it from infection. After two weeks, if there has been no conception, the thickened uterine lining is shed and menstruation takes place.

AFTER FERTILIZATION

The fertilized single-cell egg multiplies into two, then four cells, and it continues multiplying so that by about day seven, when it reaches the uterus, it has grown into a ball of over 100 cells with a fluid-filled cavity. This ball, called a blastocyst, has two layers: the outer one becomes the placenta, while the inner one forms the embryo, which develops into your baby.

The embryo is made up of three layers of tissue, each of which forms separately. The outer layer develops into the nerves and skin; the middle layer forms the bones, cartilage, muscles, circulatory system, kidneys, and sex organs; and the inner layer becomes the respiratory and digestive systems.

The placenta is the unborn baby's life-support system. It is attached to the lining of the uterus and separates the developing baby's circulation

You and your body

You won't be aware of the changes that are happening inside your body during these early weeks, although it is possible that you may experience very slight bleeding at the time when your next period would have been due. Usually the first indication that you are pregnant will be a missed period.

Female reproductive organs

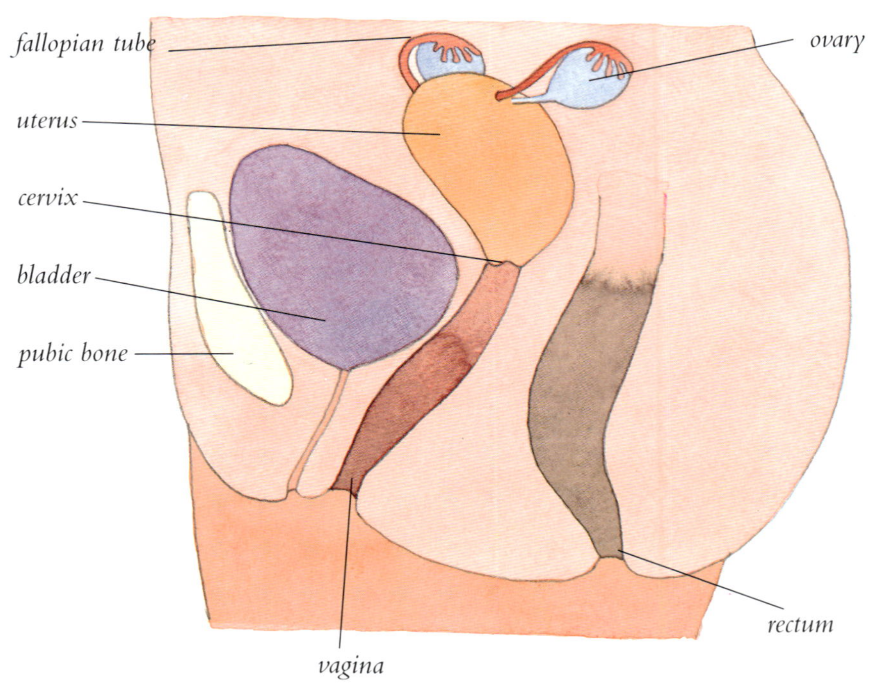

If an egg in the fallopian tube is fertilized by a sperm, it will embed itself into the lining of the uterus. If not, it is shed down through the cervix and out through the vagina.

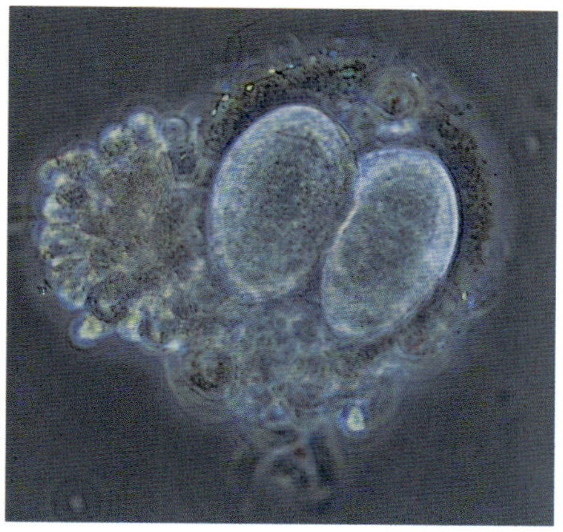

This fertilized egg now has two cells called blastomeres and is the primitive embryo. It will multiply to over 100 cells.

An enlarged sperm and ovum

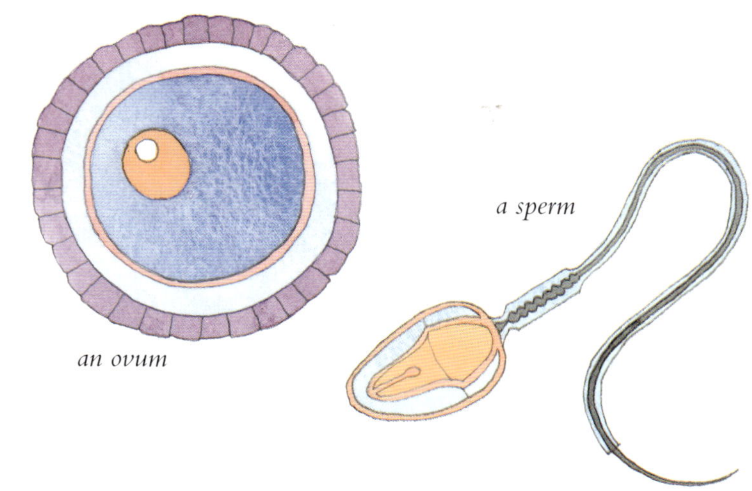

A sperm and an ovum are tiny. A man ejaculates about 500 million sperm, while a woman usually produces one ovum half-way through her menstrual cycle.

from its mother's. It allows oxygen and food, as well as protective antibodies, to pass from the mother along the umbilical cord to the baby. The placenta isn't fully formed until the end of the 12th week of pregnancy when it is able to take over the production of the pregnancy hormones estrogen and progesterone, from the ovaries.

Within the uterus, the embryo is contained in the amniotic sac. This is filled with fluid in which the developing child will float until birth. The amniotic fluid offers protection from any external pressures.

Male reproductive organs

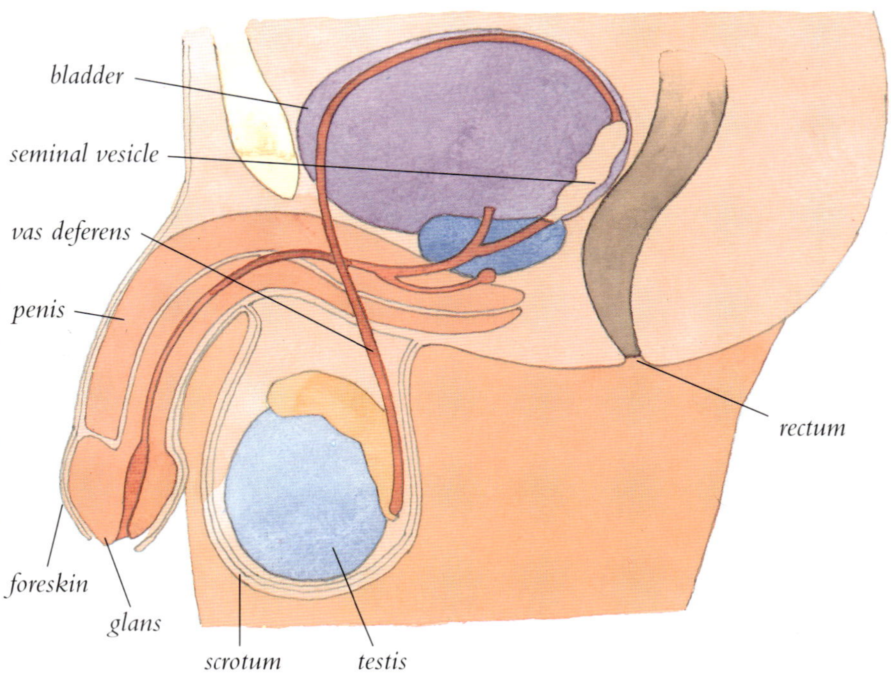

Sperm mature in both testes. When a man is sexually aroused, the penis becomes erect and the outlet from the bladder into the ejaculatory duct is closed leaving it free for sperm.

THE BABY'S SEX

A child's sex is determined by the father's sperm at the time of conception. Sperm carry either an X or Y chromosome while the egg has only an X chromosome. If a Y-chromosome sperm fertilizes the egg, the baby will be a boy. If the sperm carries an X chromosome, the baby will be a girl.

Trimesters

Pregnancy lasts approximately 40 weeks and is calculated from the first day of your last period, although conception will probably not have taken place until around two weeks after this. Pregnancy is divided into three parts known as trimesters. The first covers weeks 1–13, the second trimester weeks 14–26, and the third trimester week 27 until birth.

WEEK 5: CONFIRMING PREGNANCY

Your growing baby

Although the embryo is only just visible to the naked eye, the spinal column and brain have already begun to grow and a blood vessel has developed which will become the heart. The embryo is ⅛ in long.

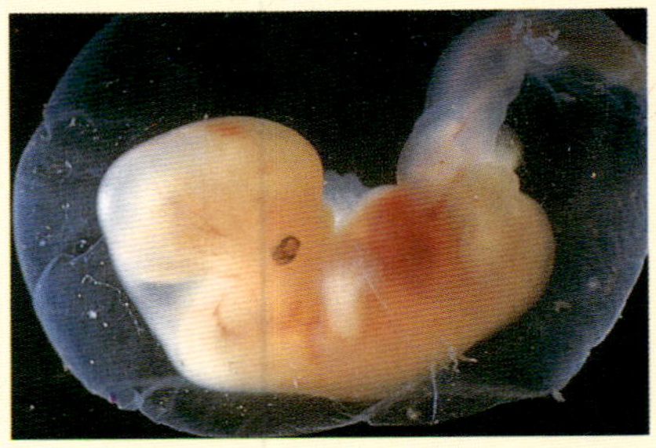

Pregnancy can be confirmed by means of a simple test that measures the levels of the pregnancy hormone human chorionic gonadotrophin (HCG) that are present in your urine. The test can be carried out as soon as you reach the day that your next period should have started. Your doctor or family planning clinic will do the test, or you may prefer to perform a home test yourself using one of the kits available from the pharmacist. Ensure that you choose a kit that will give an accurate result this early. Although many modern home-testing kits state that you can test your urine at any time, you may wish to use an early morning sample because this urine will contain the highest concentration of HCG.

If the result is positive, you must make an appointment to see your doctor so that he or she can make arrangements for your prenatal care and the birth.

If you're lucky, you'll experience no nausea in pregnancy and continue exercising as normal.

EARLY SYMPTOMS

Some women experience all the early symptoms of pregnancy, while others sail through the first weeks without any feelings of discomfort.

- Your body is having to work hard to adapt to the demands of pregnancy, so you may feel overwhelmingly tired. Try to get as much rest as possible. You will find that sitting with your feet up for even half an hour will help.
- Your breasts may tingle or feel tender, rather as they do before a period; your nipples will appear darker and more prominent and the veins will be more noticeable. You should wear a good support bra from now until after your baby is born.
- You may experience a strange metallic taste in the mouth, which

You and your body

This is the first week that you will be able to confirm that you are pregnant.

To confirm a pregnancy, you can do a test with a kit from a pharmacist, but ensure you choose one that is suitable to use for a test at five weeks.

can be accompanied by an aversion to certain foods and tea and coffee.

• A feeling of nausea, or even actual vomiting in the morning or at any time during the day, is quite usual. It is often worse when your stomach is empty, so have a few light crackers before you get up in the morning. During the day try eating six high-carbohydrate meals, such as pasta, potato, and bread. Avoid rich or fatty foods.

• Finally, as the enlarging uterus presses on your bladder you may need to urinate more frequently.

DATING THE BIRTH

Once your pregnancy is confirmed, you will want to know your baby's likely date of birth. You can calculate an estimated date of delivery (EDD) by counting 40 weeks from the first day of your last period. But you should remember that since you don't know the exact date of ovulation this EDD is approximate. At about 10 weeks the fetal heartbeat can be measured with a Doppler device.

Estimated date of delivery

JANUARY	1	2	3	4	5	6	7	8	9	10	11	12	13	14	15	16	17	18	19	20	21	22	23	24	25	26	27	28	29	30	31	JANUARY
OCTOBER	8	9	10	11	12	13	14	15	16	17	18	19	20	21	22	23	24	25	26	27	28	29	30	31	1	2	3	4	5	6	7	NOVEMBER
FEBRUARY	1	2	3	4	5	6	7	8	9	10	11	12	13	14	15	16	17	18	19	20	21	22	23	24	25	26	27	28				FEBRUARY
NOVEMBER	8	9	10	11	12	13	14	15	16	17	18	19	20	21	22	23	24	25	26	27	28	29	30	1	2	3	4	5				DECEMBER
MARCH	1	2	3	4	5	6	7	8	9	10	11	12	13	14	15	16	17	18	19	20	21	22	23	24	25	26	27	28	29	30	31	MARCH
DECEMBER	6	7	8	9	10	11	12	13	14	15	16	17	18	19	20	21	22	23	24	25	26	27	28	29	30	31	1	2	3	4	5	JANUARY
APRIL	1	2	3	4	5	6	7	8	9	10	11	12	13	14	15	16	17	18	19	20	21	22	23	24	25	26	27	28	29	30		APRIL
JANUARY	6	7	8	9	10	11	12	13	14	15	16	17	18	19	20	21	22	23	24	25	26	27	28	29	30	31	1	2	3	4		FEBRUARY
MAY	1	2	3	4	5	6	7	8	9	10	11	12	13	14	15	16	17	18	19	20	21	22	23	24	25	26	27	28	29	30	31	MAY
FEBRUARY	5	6	7	8	9	10	11	12	13	14	15	16	17	18	19	20	21	22	23	24	25	26	27	28	1	2	3	4	5	6	7	MARCH
JUNE	1	2	3	4	5	6	7	8	9	10	11	12	13	14	15	16	17	18	19	20	21	22	23	24	25	26	27	28	29	30		JUNE
MARCH	8	9	10	11	12	13	14	15	16	17	18	19	20	21	22	23	24	25	26	27	28	29	30	31	1	2	3	4	5	6		APRIL
JULY	1	2	3	4	5	6	7	8	9	10	11	12	13	14	15	16	17	18	19	20	21	22	23	24	25	26	27	28	29	30	31	JULY
APRIL	7	8	9	10	11	12	13	14	15	16	17	18	19	20	21	22	23	24	25	26	27	28	29	30	1	2	3	4	5	6	7	MAY
AUGUST	1	2	3	4	5	6	7	8	9	10	11	12	13	14	15	16	17	18	19	20	21	22	23	24	25	26	27	28	29	30	31	AUGUST
MAY	8	9	10	11	12	13	14	15	16	17	18	19	20	21	22	23	24	25	26	27	28	29	30	31	1	2	3	4	5	6	7	JUNE
SEPTEMBER	1	2	3	4	5	6	7	8	9	10	11	12	13	14	15	16	17	18	19	20	21	22	23	24	25	26	27	28	29	30		SEPTEMBER
JUNE	8	9	10	11	12	13	14	15	16	17	18	19	20	21	22	23	24	25	26	27	28	29	30	1	2	3	4	5	6	7		JULY
OCTOBER	1	2	3	4	5	6	7	8	9	10	11	12	13	14	15	16	17	18	19	20	21	22	23	24	25	26	27	28	29	30	31	OCTOBER
JULY	8	9	10	11	12	13	14	15	16	17	18	19	20	21	22	23	24	25	26	27	28	29	30	31	1	2	3	4	5	6	7	AUGUST
NOVEMBER	1	2	3	4	5	6	7	8	9	10	11	12	13	14	15	16	17	18	19	20	21	22	23	24	25	26	27	28	29	30		NOVEMBER
AUGUST	8	9	10	11	12	13	14	15	16	17	18	19	20	21	22	23	24	25	26	27	28	29	30	31	1	2	3	4	5	6		SEPTEMBER
DECEMBER	1	2	3	4	5	6	7	8	9	10	11	12	13	14	15	16	17	18	19	20	21	22	23	24	25	26	27	28	29	30	31	DECEMBER
SEPTEMBER	7	8	9	10	11	12	13	14	15	16	17	18	19	20	21	22	23	24	25	26	27	28	29	30	1	2	3	4	5	6	7	OCTOBER

Find the first day of your last period on the white bands; the date on the tint band below is your EDD.

WEEK 6: PRENATAL CHOICES

If you haven't already, now is the time to select a practitioner to care for you before and during the birth. In the U.S., most babies are still delivered in a hospital by an obstetrician-gynecologist, though many women are increasingly opting for the services of a certified nurse-midwife. Another choice is the maternity center, which is staffed with nurse-midwives and has one or more physicians on call in case difficulties arise. If you choose to have a midwife assist with the birth, you may still want to see an obstetrician-gynecologist for part or all of your prenatal care.

Women choose a midwife over an OB-GYN for a number of reasons, but two of the most common are the desire for a more natural, less medicalized birth, and the feeling that midwives offer greater sympathy for both physical and emotional issues than most physicians. Before making any decisions, of course, you should consult your health insurance plan to determine which services are covered, and to what extent.

If you have reason to believe that yours may be a high-risk pregnancy, you may want to consider yet another option – a high-risk specialist. Factors that could lead to a pregnancy being classified as high-risk include certain chronic medical conditions (such as diabetes or lupus), previous pregnancy losses, or advanced maternal age (though more and more older women are having healthy, normal pregnancies). A high-risk specialist, also known as a perinatalogist or maternal-fetal specialist, can act as a consultant to your own

You and your body

If you are suffering from morning sickness, you may find that the smell of certain things, such as tobacco smoke or frying food, brings on the sickness or makes it worse. The texture of your skin may become dry and flaky, or you may break out. Now is the time to start thinking about your prenatal care, and the type of birth you want.

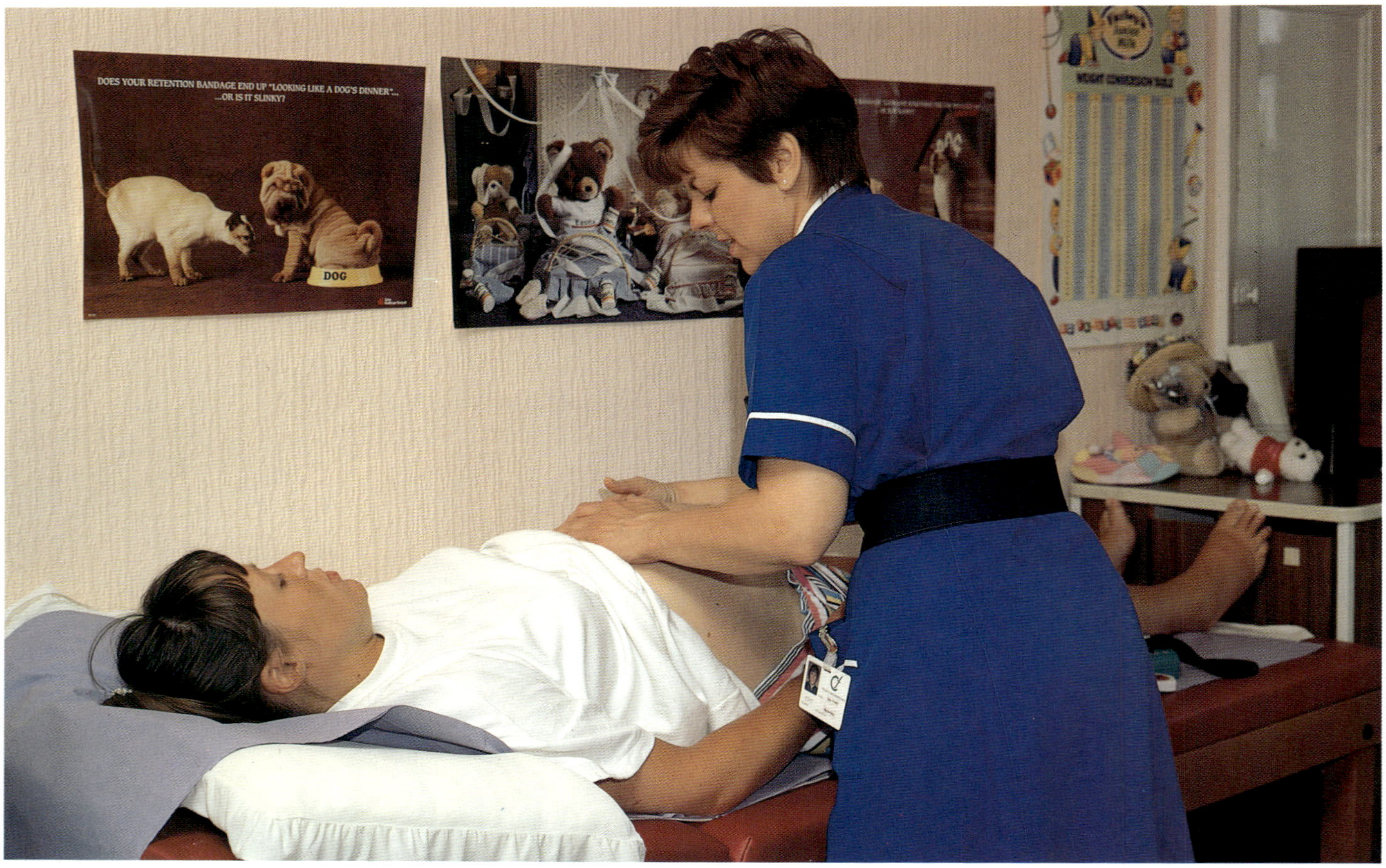

In a home birth, a midwife will often palpate your abdomen, to feel the top of the uterus (fundus).

doctor or alternatively function as your primary caregiver.

If for any reason your pregnancy becomes "high-risk" as it progresses, you can bring in a specialist at any stage. One advantage to being treated by this kind of practitioner is that it offers the anxious mother increased interaction with her doctor and an enhanced sense of control over her pregnancy. It's helpful, too, to remember that most so-called high-risk pregnancies result in the birth of healthy babies.

The actual care you get will be similar wherever you receive it, because all prenatal care is designed to ensure that you and your unborn baby remain healthy during pregnancy.

These days, the best pattern of prenatal care for a healthy woman is considered to be no more than nine prenatal appointments. If you have any concerns between these appointments, you can telephone your doctor or midwife for advice.

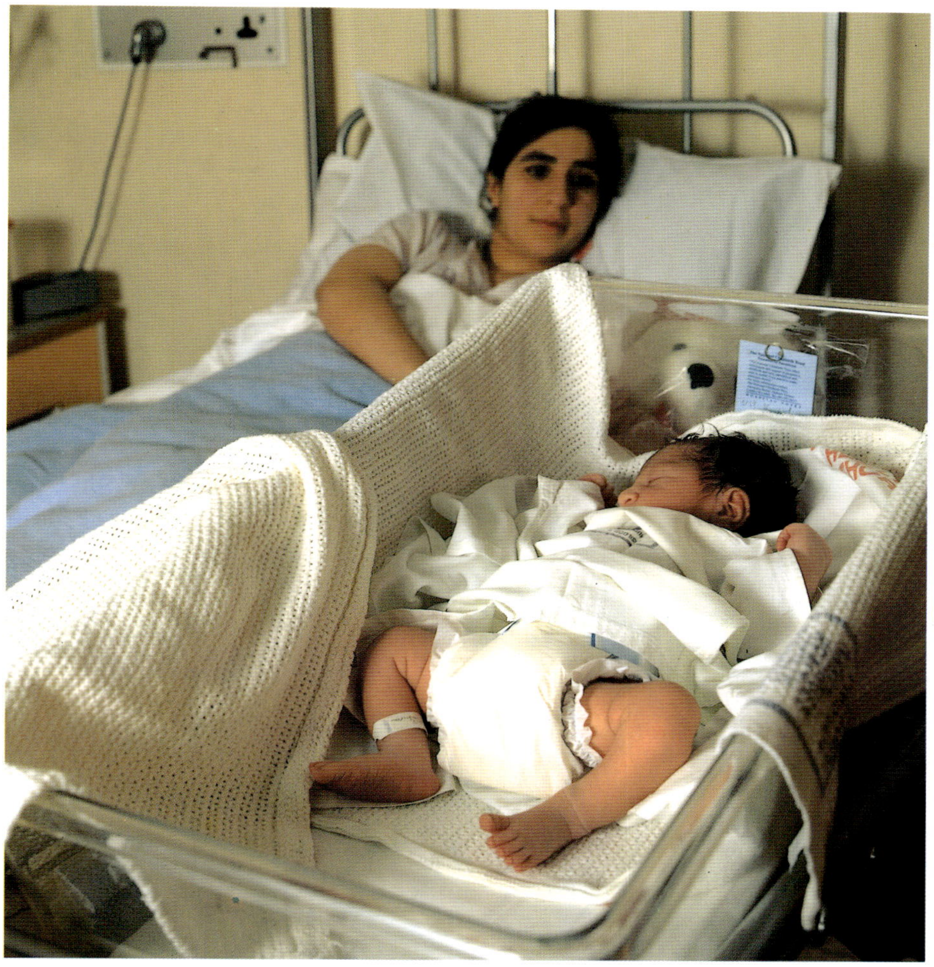

You will usually spend between two to three days in the hospital when you give birth, depending on your delivery.

Home birth

A home birth means you give birth in the familiar surroundings of your own home under the supervision of a midwife. If you want to deliver your baby in this way, you will need to talk to your doctor to see whether there are any medical reasons why this isn't advisable. Home births, though relatively common in Europe and Great Britain, are still extremely rare in this country.

Hospital birth

Most women still prefer a hospital birth because they feel safer knowing that there will be experts on hand to help if there are any complications. Also, if the baby needs special care this will be available almost immediately. Although hospitals are no longer the dictatorial places they used to be, and most try to cater to parents' wishes, not all of them are able to offer every type of birth. You will need to find out what facilities your hospital offers. Often your doctor will be affiliated with a certain hospital and will direct you there. Most hospitals offer childbirth education classes which include a tour of the labor and birthing rooms and the nursery. It is very important to check your insurance plan as there are varying types of coverage for semi-private and private rooms, anaesthesia and length of stay. Many insurance companies allow only one overnight hospital stay for a vaginal delivery with no complications, but offer follow-up home care. Before making your decision talk to other mothers who have had their babies there recently.

Your growing baby

The heart has now formed in the chest cavity and is beginning to beat. By the end of this week the stalk connecting the embryo to the placenta will have begun to grow into the umbilical cord and blood vessels will have started to form. The embryo is now about the size of your little fingernail and its movements can be picked up by ultrasound scan. The head has the beginning of the eyes, ears, and mouth and there are tiny buds which will become arms and legs.

WEEK 7: POSSIBLE PROBLEMS

Although the majority of pregnancies go without a hitch, sometimes serious problems do occur and special care is needed. Complications can usually be resolved with monitoring, but occasionally the pregnancy comes to an end. Although the following conditions are not likely to affect you, you should be aware of their symptoms:

Preeclampsia (pregnancy-induced hypertension) This is a high blood pressure condition that is sometimes associated with a reduction in the quality of placental function. If preeclampsia is left untreated it can cut the oxygen flow to the fetus and put it at risk; the fetal growth rate may also be affected. Symptoms include elevated blood pressure, protein in the urine and, occasionally, headache. You will be tested for signs of preeclampsia at each prenatal visit. In the early stages preeclampsia may be treated with complete bedrest or medication under medical supervision. Later in the pregnancy, if the condition is severe, it may become necessary to induce the birth. The mother's blood pressure will soon return to normal. If the condition is left completely untreated it can develop into eclampsia, which can be fatal for both the mother and the child. Today, this condition is extremely rare, and most cases don't occur until at least the twentieth week.

Bleeding in early pregnancy
Bleeding or spotting from the vagina is known as a threatened miscarriage. It is possible to bleed quite heavily and not miscarry or do any harm to the baby. All bleeding in pregnancy must be taken seriously, however, and you should report it to your doctor immediately. Your doctor is likely to carry out an internal pelvic examination and arrange for you to have an ultrasound scan to see whether the baby is developing normally. Providing everything is all right you will probably be told to rest until the bleeding stops.

Ectopic pregnancy This occurs when the fertilized egg implants itself in one of the fallopian tubes rather than in the uterus. If it is undetected, the growing baby even-

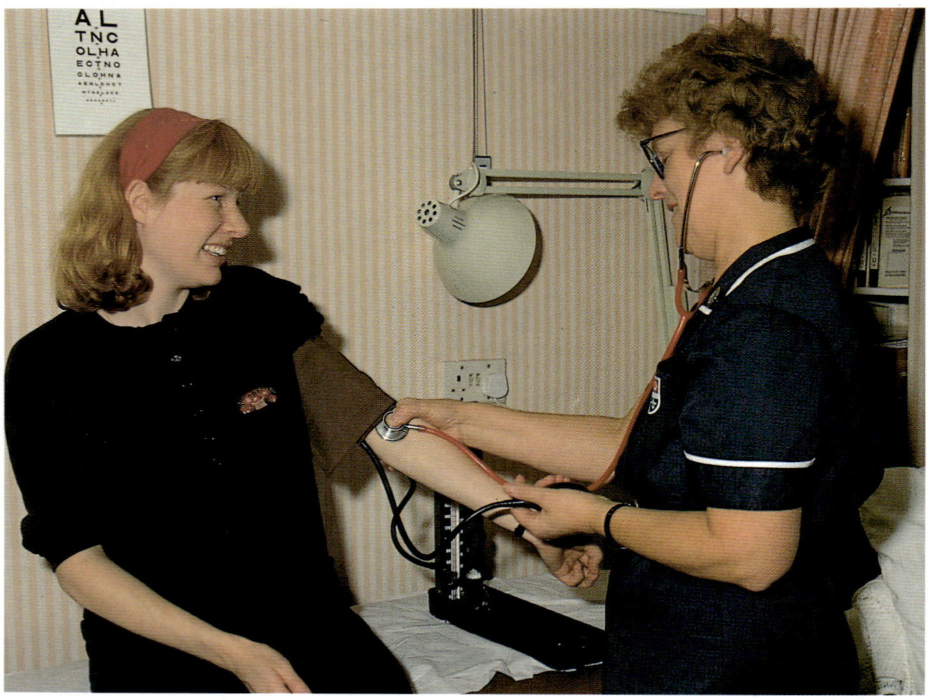

Regular blood pressure checks are essential at prenatal visits to detect preeclampsia.

You and your body

You may feel dizzy or even faint if you stand for too long or you are in a crowd. Overwhelming exhaustion can also be a problem now, so make sure you get plenty of rest. If you don't feel like making love at the moment don't worry; this is quite normal and you may find that your sex life is better then ever in the second trimester.

Your growing baby

The unborn baby is now known as a fetus and is about ½ in long. The nostrils, lips, tongue, and teeth are beginning to form and the arms and legs are growing. The lungs are beginning to develop and the intestines, spine, and the brain are now almost fully developed.

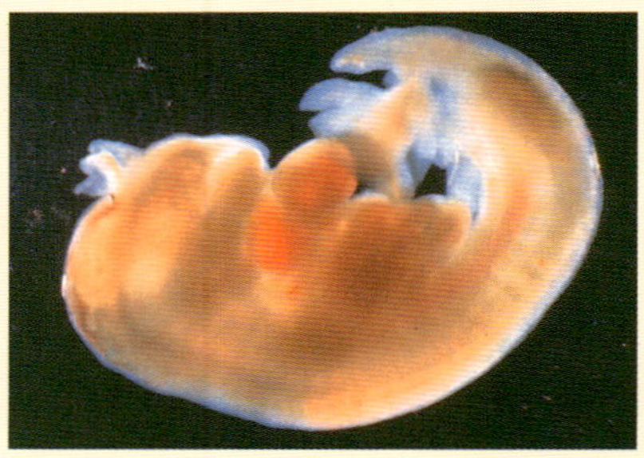

tually ruptures the tube, which causes severe pain. Immediate surgery is required to terminate the pregnancy, and this often means losing the fallopian tube as well. In extreme cases the ovary may also have to be removed. If the other ovary and fallopian tube are healthy, there is no reason why another successful pregnancy should not take place.

If the ectopic pregnancy is discovered early enough, a drug can be given that causes the embryo to be reabsorbed by the body; this prevents the fallopian tube from bursting. Symptoms of an ectopic pregnancy include pain in the side of the abdomen, vaginal bleeding, and fainting.

Miscarriage The most common time for miscarriage is during the first three months of pregnancy, although losing a baby at any time before the 24th week is described as a miscarriage. Some miscarriages occur for no known reason. Known causes of miscarriage include hormonal problems, disease or infection, abnormalities of the uterus, or an incompetent cervix. If this last condition is known to exist, it can be dealt with by a surgical suture that will be removed before the EDD.

Although it is unlikely that sexual intercourse will cause miscarriage, women who have experienced bleeding early in their pregnancy or who are known to have a tendency to miscarry are usually advised by doctors not to have intercourse for the first 12 weeks, until their pregnancy is well established.

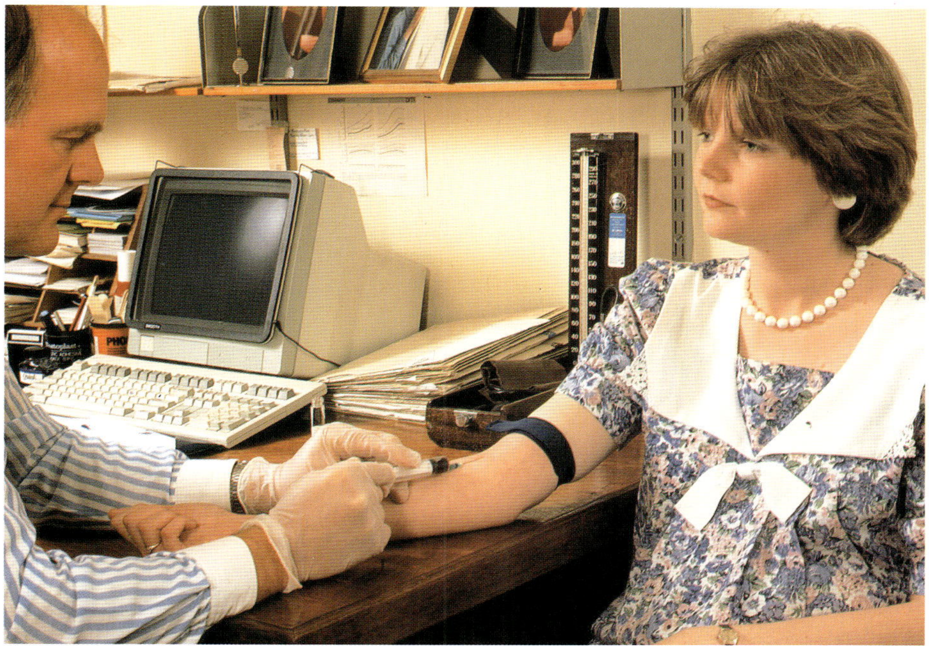

You will have a number of blood tests throughout your pregnancy but these are no cause for alarm. The tests are simply a means for your doctor to make sure that you are progressing normally and not experiencing any problems.

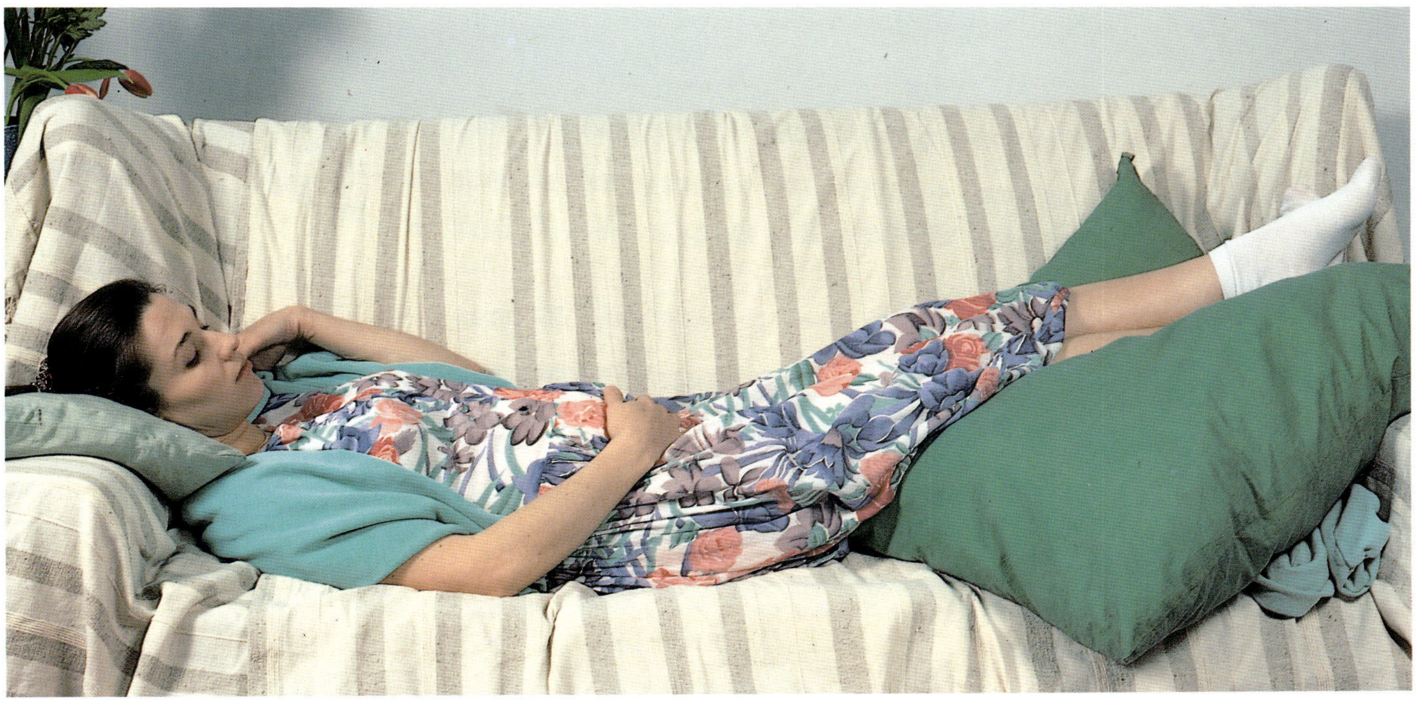

You may start to feel very tired in these early weeks, so get plenty of rest and make sure your feet are propped up.

WEEK 8: ROUTINE TESTS

Your first prenatal check-up will usually take place between eight and 12 weeks, and will almost certainly be the most thorough of all your prenatal visits. You will be asked a lot of personal questions about your health, family medical history, and possibly even about your and your partner's jobs and living accommodations. All this information is required to build up a picture of you and your pregnancy so that any potential risks can be spotted and help can be offered where it is particularly needed.

If you have any questions or worries about your pregnancy, this is a good time to discuss them. It's easy to forget to ask something important when there is so much to take in at one time, so it may be helpful to write down a list of things that you want to know about before you attend the exam.

Routine tests

Certain tests are carried out during pregnancy to ensure that both you and the fetus are progressing well. Some of these will be repeated at each prenatal visit; others will only be carried out at the initial exam.

Blood pressure This will be taken at each visit. Increased blood pressure could develop into preeclampsia, which could endanger both you and the fetus.

Urine You will be asked to give a sample of urine at each prenatal visit. This will be tested for any infections that may require some treatment, as well as for sugar, protein, or the chemical substances known as ketones. Sugar in the urine could be a sign of diabetes; protein may indicate the onset of preeclampsia; and ketones may indicate that your kidneys are being adversely affected by your progressing pregnancy.

Weight gain during pregnancy

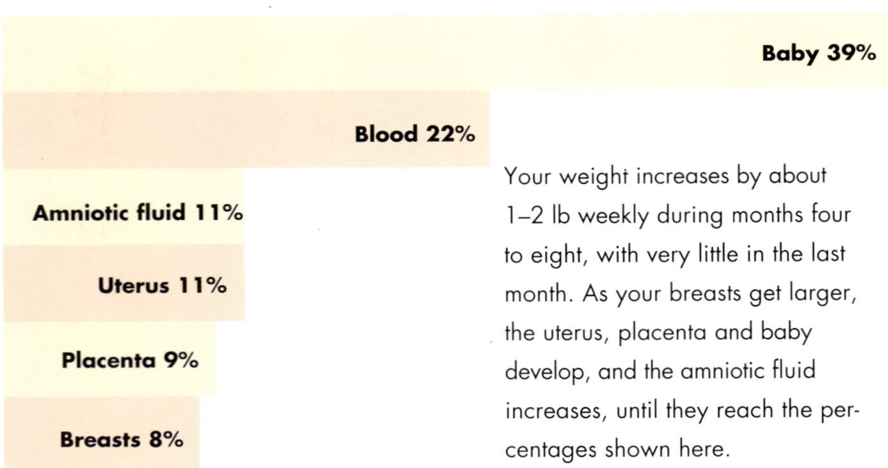

Your weight increases by about 1–2 lb weekly during months four to eight, with very little in the last month. As your breasts get larger, the uterus, placenta and baby develop, and the amniotic fluid increases, until they reach the percentages shown here.

The amount of weight that you will gain during pregnancy varies, depending on your height and size, but can be as much as 40 lb.

You and your body

The changes to your body are becoming more noticeable as your breasts and nipples enlarge and become sensitive. Your vagina changes from light to dark pink, and you may notice an increased vaginal discharge.

It is time for regular monitoring of your pregnancy.

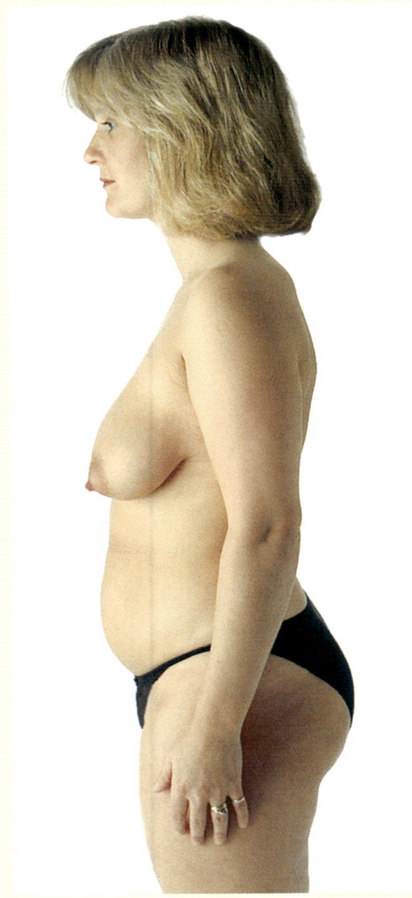

Weight Your weight will almost certainly be monitored regularly to see how the baby is growing. You can expect to gain anything from 20 lb to 40 lb during your pregnancy, with most of this extra weight going on after the 20th week. A sudden increase in weight could be an indication of preeclampsia.

Height You will be measured at your first appointment because your height gives a rough guide to

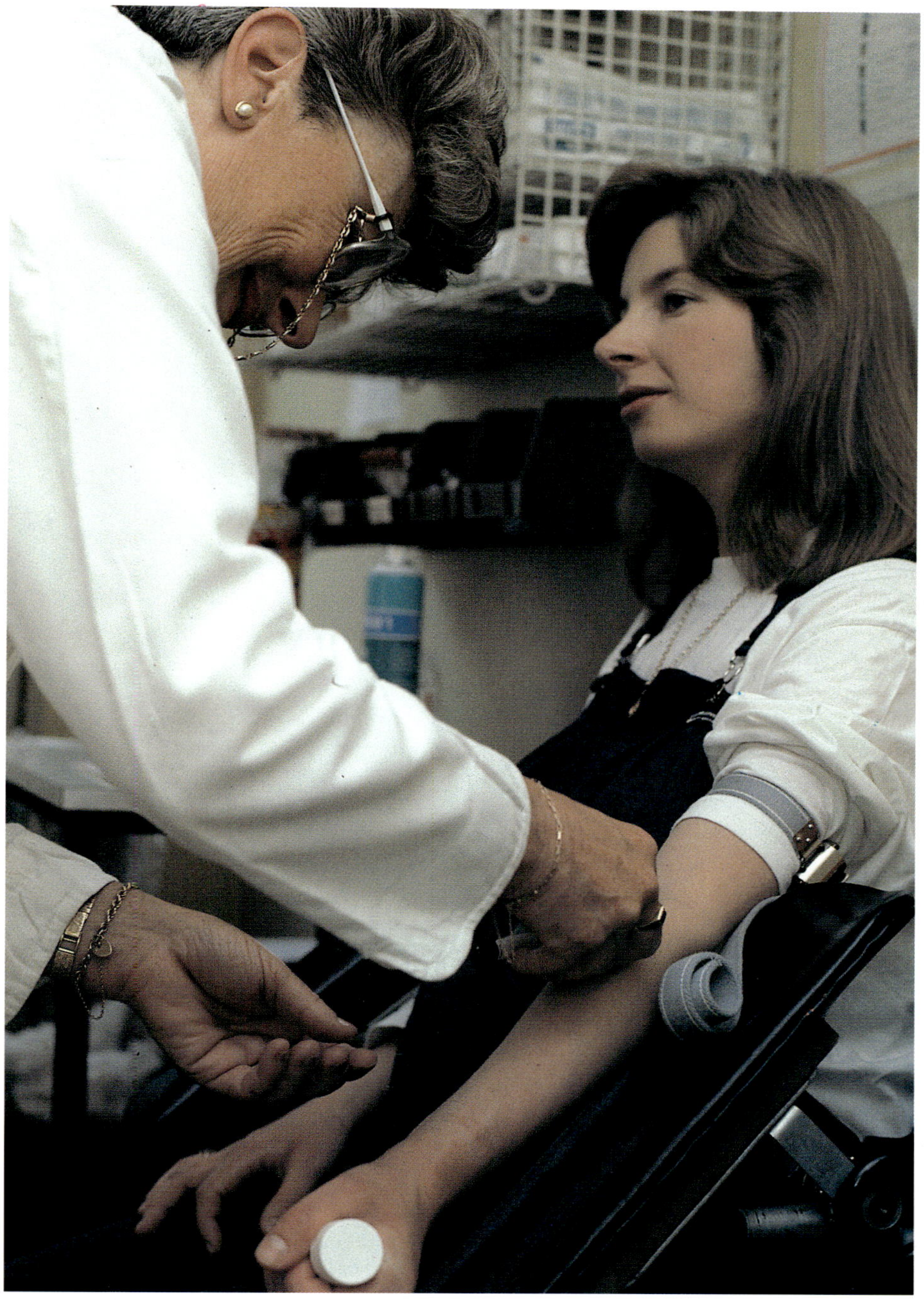

At your first prenatal check-up, a blood sample will be taken to find out your blood group and type, and to make sure you're not anemic or carrying a virus such as hepatitis B. You will have blood tests regularly through your pregnancy.

the size of your pelvis. If your pelvis is too small to accommodate your baby's head at the birth, then a Caesarean delivery may well be indicated. It is worth noting, however, that the size of most babies is in proportion to the mothers who are carrying them.

Blood tests At your first appointment you will be asked to give a blood sample to confirm your blood group and to find out if you are Rh negative or positive. Your blood will also be checked to see if you are anemic and if you are immune to rubella (German measles). Other tests are also carried out to detect any serious conditions that could affect the development of your baby, such as syphilis and hepatitis B. If you are of Afro-American descent, they will probably test for sickle-cell disease. Blood-testing for the HIV or AIDS virus is not routinely done at hospitals, except by special request of the mother.

Internal examination You may have an internal examination at your first visit. This is to check for any abnormalities of the vagina, cervix, or the uterus. If you haven't had a cervical Pap smear during the last three to five years you may well be given one.

Wrists and ankles These will be checked at each visit for any noticeable swelling, or edema, caused by fluid retention, since these signs could possibly indicate that the mother has preeclampsia.

Palpation The doctor or midwife will palpate, that is press, your abdomen to feel the top of the uterus (fundus). He or she will then feel down toward the pelvis to check the size of the fetus and the way it is lying in the uterus.

Your growing baby

The fetus is now about 1 in long, which is 10,000 times bigger than at conception. All the major organs are present, although still developing. The ears and eyes have formed and the skin covering the eyes will eventually split to form the eyelids. The middle ear, which controls balance as well as hearing, is also developing. The heart is now pumping with a regular beat, and blood vessels can be seen. As the arms and legs grow longer, the fetus begins to move around and starts to kick, although it is still too small at this stage for you to be able to feel it or detect any movement.

WEEK 9: SPECIAL TESTS

Your growing baby

The face is now developing well and the mouth and nose are now clearly visible. The limbs continue to grow rapidly and the fetus measures about 1¼ in.

Your blood will have been tested at your initial appointment to determine your blood group and to establish its Rh status. The Rh status of your blood depends on whether or not it possesses the Rh factor. If the factor is present, your blood is Rh-positive, if it is absent, your blood is Rh-negative. Most people's blood is Rh-positive.

If both you and the baby's father are Rh-negative, there is no problem. Complications only occur when the father's blood is Rh-positive and yours is Rh-negative. The unborn baby may acquire the Rh factor from its father, which can result in its blood being incompatible with yours. This can lead to a serious or even fatal illness for the baby before, or after the birth. Fortunately, this rarely affects a first pregnancy and it can be prevented in subsequent pregnancies by injections of Rhogan, an antibody that may be given during pregnancy and again within 72 hours of a baby being delivered.

SPECIAL TESTS

There are a number of prenatal tests that are used in special circumstances and usually only when there is some fear of genetic abnormality. They include:

Amniocentesis If you have a family history of genetic abnormalities such as Down's syndrome, cystic fibrosis, or spina bifida, or your blood shows a high or exceptionally low AFP (alpha-fetoprotein) level, you will be offered an amniocentesis, usually at around 16–18 weeks. This test is also offered to all women over 35 years of age because they have a higher risk of having a Down's syndrome baby. Guided by ultrasound scan, a long hollow needle is inserted through the wall of the abdomen and the uterus to draw out a sample of amniotic fluid. This is then tested for abnormalities. You will get the results in about four weeks. The test carries a small risk of miscarriage.

In an amniocentesis test the fetus's position is checked by ultrasound, before amniotic fluid is taken by a needle from the uterus.

Triple/double test This blood test is carried out at 16 weeks to measure the levels of three substances produced by the mother and the placenta. The levels change during pregnancy and a higher level could indicate that the baby may have Down's syndrome or spina bifida. The test cannot confirm that the baby is affected but it does indicate whether further tests, such as amniocentesis, are required. Not all doctors use the triple test; some offer the double test, where two substances are measured; others don't offer the test routinely, but you can ask to have it done.

Chorionic villus sampling (CVS) CVS is done at around 11 weeks to test for Down's syndrome or other genetic or chromosomal abnormalities. A fine tube is passed into the

You and your body

You will start putting on weight at this stage of your pregnancy. Your gums are becoming softer and thicker because of hormone changes so you will need to pay special attention to oral hygiene. Brush your teeth more frequently to avoid the risk of infections.

You should now familiarize yourself with some of the other prenatal procedures and tests that you can expect as your pregnancy progresses.

Brush your teeth and gums regularly.

uterus to remove some of the cells from the tissue that surrounds the baby. The cells are then tested, and the results are usually known within one to two weeks. The advantage of CVS is that if the baby is found to have a problem and you want a termination it can be done early in pregnancy. However, there is a slightly higher risk of miscarriage with CVS than with amniocentesis.

Cordocentesis Very rarely done in the U.S., this test is administered to confirm diagnosis of chromosomal abnormalities and other handicaps, plus diseases such as rubella and toxoplasmosis. A hollow needle is inserted through the abdomen into the umbilical vein, close to the placenta, and a sample of the baby's blood is withdrawn. It is only performed after 18 weeks when the blood vessels are large enough. Results are usually known within about 48 hours.

GENETIC COUNSELING

If you are worried about the possibility of your children inheriting a disease or handicap, you can talk to a genetic counselor who is specially trained to help people with a family history of genetic disorders. Counseling is usually based on details of any genetic diseases that run in the family. A chromosome analysis from a blood sample may also be used. The counselor will be able to explain the likelihood of future children being affected by the genetic disorder and also about any tests that can be carried out. It is a good idea to have this discussion before attempting to get pregnant so that you know what is involved. Otherwise, tell your doctor that you want to see a genetic counselor when your pregnancy is confirmed.

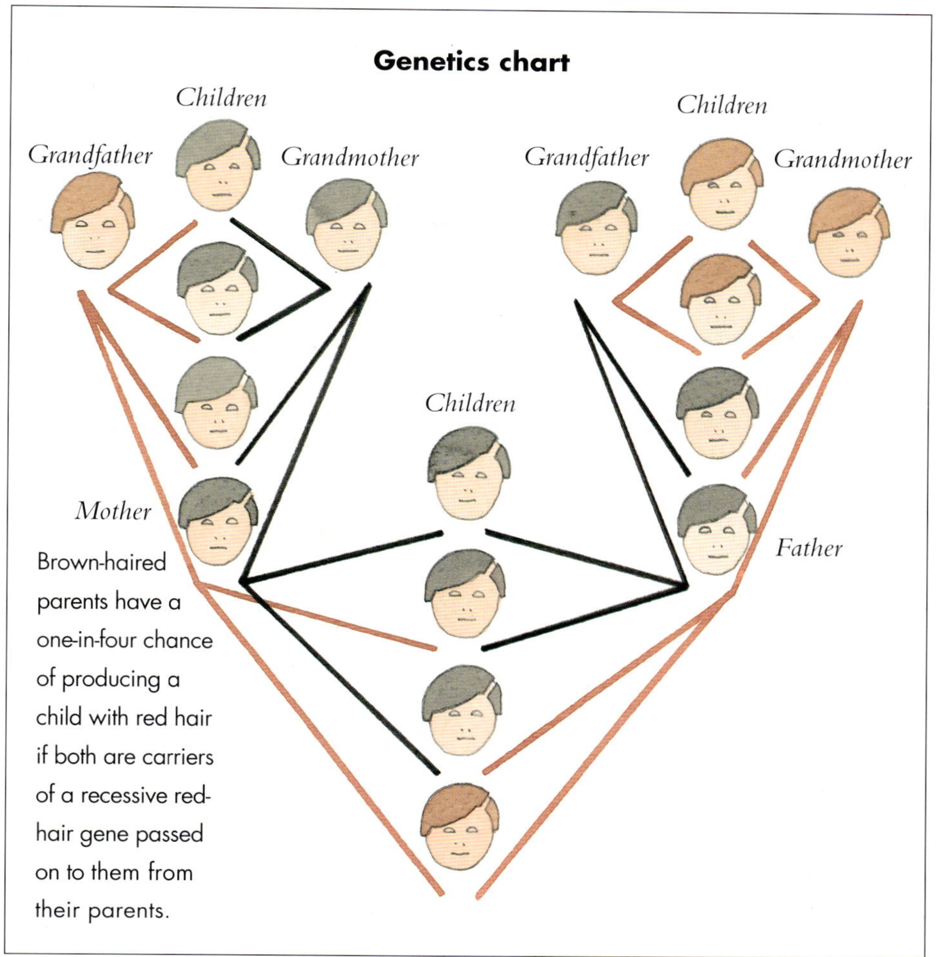

This genetics chart shows how red hair that is inherited through a recessive gene can miss a generation, but has a high chance of reappearing in the third generation. This can also apply to some inherited diseases.

If your family has a history of a genetic disorder, you can talk to a genetic counselor who will discuss with you and your partner the likelihood of your baby having a problem.

WEEK 10: HORMONES/ HORMONAL CHANGES

Hormones play an important part during pregnancy and labor. The prime source of the hormones related to pregnancy are the ovaries during the early stages, and then the placenta once it is established at around 12 weeks. These hormones dictate how fast the fetus grows and are responsible for the changes in your breasts and body. They also ensure that your labor occurs at the right time.

High levels of the hormone called human chorionic gonadotrophin (HCG) circulate in your body during the first 12 weeks of pregnancy. They are responsible for any emotional changes, feeling tired, nausea, and vomiting.

Hormones and your emotions

Pregnancy can produce a number of conflicting emotions, ranging from feelings of pure joy to bouts of black depression. It is quite natural to feel like this as you adjust to your changing role and come to terms with the fact that your life will never be quite the same again. You may find that you start worrying about whether you are ready for motherhood, or the effect that a new baby may have on your established relationship with your partner.

You may also find that mood swings, often brought on by the hormonal changes going on in your body, cause petty arguments between you. So it is most important

Your growing baby

The external ears are now visible on the head, which is growing fast to make room for the brain. The fetal body is elongating and its fingers and toes are clearly defined but are still joined with webs of skin. At this stage of your pregnancy, the fetus is now about 1¾ in long and weighs around ¼ oz.

You and your body

There is an increase in the amount of blood that is circulating in your body, which may cause you to feel warmer than usual. Your uterus is now the size of a large orange and your changing shape may mean that you are more comfortable in loose-fitting clothes that do not restrict you.

Other changes are also taking place in your body. Although these are not always physically obvious, they are in fact the result of shifts in your body's chemistry.

As you experience hormonal changes in your body you may find you become irritable and anxious. Discuss any of your worries with your partner who can talk things through with you and reassure you.

As your emotions are probably confused now, don't brood over heightened squabbles with your partner, but make up quickly.

If you find you're getting very tense, try practicing relaxation techniques on your own, or some deep breathing exercises.

Keep a personal record

Now that your pregnancy is confirmed and you have started planning your prenatal care and the type of birth you want to have, you may like to keep a record of your feelings and the physical changes that occur during your pregnancy. Useful things to include would be:

- Date of your last period, so that you can calculate your estimated delivery date (EDD) and then compare it with the actual birth date.
- Prenatal checks throughout your pregnancy.
- Prenatal tests and their results, along with the dates you were given them.
- The dates of scans which show your baby's development.
- Any foods that disagree with you, perhaps giving you indigestion.
- Ailments related to your pregnancy such as morning sickness and varicose veins.
- Your weight gain throughout the pregnancy.
- Your baby's first movement.
- Any drugs and medication including pain-relieving drugs during labor.

to make time to talk to each other so that you can both voice your feelings and share any worries or anxieties.

Ask your doctor to explain

It can often be difficult to remember everything that you are told at a check-up, so make notes of what your doctor tells you and don't be afraid to ask for an explanation of medical terms. Also write down any queries you may have beforehand, so that you don't forget to ask your doctor. The doctor will try to ensure that you understand the tests that you are being given.

WEEK 11: COMMON DISCOMFORTS

You and your body

Any sickness should start to fade and you will begin to feel less tired than in the preceding weeks. You should start to think seriously about prenatal classes because they can get booked up quickly. Ask friends for referrals, or inquire at your doctor's office about local classes.

As your body prepares itself for birth, you may experience some physical effects. These are perfectly normal, can usually be dealt with easily, and should not leave any long-lasting effects, but knowing the reason for a complaint can often help in dealing with it.

Backache This can occur at any time, but usually happens when you try to compensate for your baby's weight by leaning backward which puts a strain on the lower back's muscles and joints. Try to avoid lifting heavy objects, bend with your knees bent, wear flat shoes, and always sit with your back well supported.

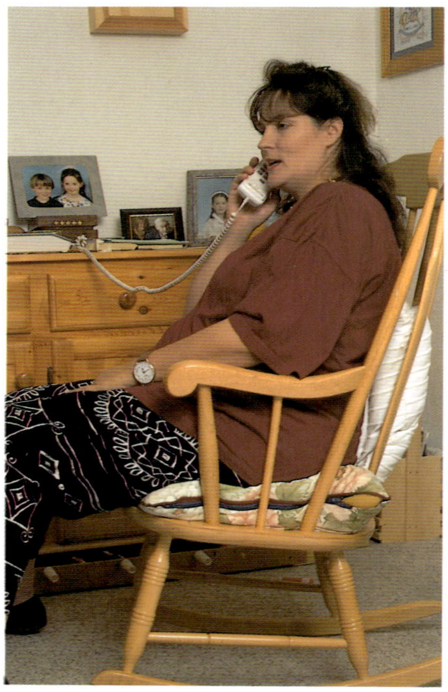

Your back is now more vulnerable, so support it with a cushion when you sit down.

Bleeding gums Hormonal changes can cause a build-up of plaque on your teeth, which can lead to bleeding gums. It is important to pay special attention to oral hygiene and to avoid snacking on sweets and sugary drinks. Dental treatment is especially important now so have at least two check-ups during this time.

Leg and foot cramps You may have a sudden sharp pain in your legs and feet, often at night. Try pulling your toes upward toward your ankles and rub the affected muscles. Regular gentle exercise will help prevent cramps.

Constipation Some of the extra hormones produced in pregnancy can cause the intestines to relax and become less efficient. Eating plenty of fruit, vegetables and fiber, and drinking water will help constipation.

Fainting You may feel faint if you stand for too long or get up too quickly. This happens because not enough blood is getting to your brain; if the oxygen level gets too low you may actually faint. Try to rise slowly from either sitting or lying positions and, if you are standing, sit down and lower your head toward your knees.

Hemorrhoids These are a form of varicose vein that appear around the anus. They can be very uncomfortable as they are itchy and may even

Eating a high-fiber diet can help prevent painful constipation in pregnancy.

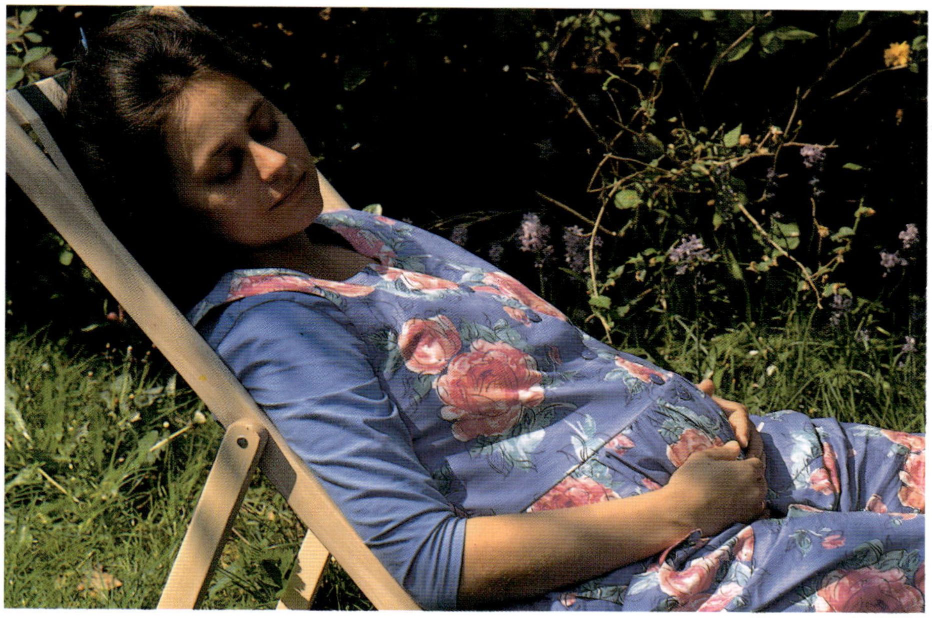

Your growing baby

Most of the major organs are formed, so the most vulnerable time will be over by the end of this week. The fetus is now relatively safe from any congenital abnormalities and infections, excepting rubella.

The external genitals have formed, along with either the ovaries or the testicles. The heart is now pumping blood to all the major organs of the body. The fetus weighs around ½ oz and is now about 2⅛ in long.

Although you may now be feeling less tired than in the early weeks, you should still rest as much as you can.

bleed slightly. If left untreated they can become prolapsed, which means they protrude through the anus, causing a good deal of pain. Eating high-fiber foods will keep your stools soft so that you don't have to strain, which puts pressure on hemorrhoids. An ice pack wrapped in a soft cloth, or a witch hazel compress, will bring relief, or you can buy a specially formulated hemorrhoid preparation from the pharmacist. Hemorrhoids usually disappear within a couple of weeks of the birth.

Vaginal discharge An increase in vaginal discharge during pregnancy is quite normal as long as the discharge is clear and white. If it becomes colored, smells, or makes you itchy, you may have developed an infection, such as yeast, which will need treatment.

Take some gentle, regular exercise with your partner as this will help to prevent leg cramps and keep you feeling fit.

WEEK 12: HEALTHY EATING

The fetus gets all the nourishment it needs to grow from what you eat, so it is important to maintain a good diet throughout pregnancy. To achieve a healthy balanced diet you need to eat foods containing reasonable amounts of starchy carbohydrate, protein, fat, minerals, and vitamins each day. Starchy carbohydrates are found in bread, cereals, pasta, rice, and potatoes; they provide energy, vitamins, minerals, and fiber. Meat, fish, eggs, nuts, beans, peas, and lentils supply protein and minerals. Milk and dairy products such as hard cheese and yogurt will give you protein, vitamins, and calcium. Fresh fruit and vegetables and well-washed salads are good sources of minerals and vitamins. Folic acid can be found, along with other vitamins, in green leafy vegetables, fruit, nuts, bread, and rice.

If you are a vegetarian, you will need to increase your milk intake to at least 1 pint a day of either pasteurized milk or fortified soy milk, or the equivalent in cheese, yogurt, and dairy products.

Vegans will need to discuss their diet with a qualified dietitian as they could be deficient in calcium, iron, and vitamin B_{12}, which is found in foods of animal origin. Try to avoid eating sugary snacks and carbonated drinks and keep "junk" foods to a minimum. Cut down on your caffeine intake from drinks like tea, coffee, chocolate and cola; try drinking bottled water and diluted fruit juices as alternatives.

You and your body

You can expect to put on about one-quarter of your pregnancy weight between now and week 20. You may be beginning to feel more energetic and generally better than during the past few weeks. You should consider telling your employer at this time that you are pregnant.

Meanwhile, look at your lifestyle and be sure that your diet includes a sensible range of foods – for you and the unborn baby.

Eat plenty of fruit when pregnant as it is a good source of minerals and vitamins.

Cut down on your caffeine levels and drink more diluted fruit juices.

A grain salad will give you plenty of fiber.

Vegetables are important in your pregnancy diet as they are low in fat and contain minerals, vitamins and folic acid in leafy varieties.

Use olive and light vegetable oils.

YOUR WEIGHT

Although you need extra energy during pregnancy to meet the needs of the developing fetus, and to store fat ready for breastfeeding later, you are not likely to need special energy foods. If you were an acceptable weight for your build before pregnancy, the only extra calories you should need are during the last three months when you eat around 200 extra calories a day. However, if you were overweight or underweight your weight gain will need monitoring, and a special diet may be necessary. Ask a professional for advice.

Your growing baby

The fetus's heart is beating at between 110 and 160 times a minute and its chest is beginning to rise and fall as it practices future breathing movements. Features are becoming more clearly defined and fingers and toes are now fully formed, with tiny nails beginning to grow. The fetus can suck its thumb and it swallows amniotic fluid and passes it back as urine. The amniotic fluid is completely replaced every 24 hours. The fetus is now about 2½ in long and weighs ¾ oz.

WEEK 13: THE HEALTH PROFESSIONALS

You and your body

Your uterus is enlarging at a noticeable rate and you will be able to see the first signs of a visible belly. Your nipples have become darker and the blue veins in your breasts are a lot more obvious.

Now that you are at the end of the first trimester and your pregnancy is visible, you should start to familiarize yourself with some of the professionals with whom you will regularly be interacting.

During pregnancy, and after the birth, a number of different people will be involved in your care. How many you see will depend on where you are having your baby and the kind of prenatal care that is being offered. The type of professionals involved in your prenatal and postpartum care will be the same wherever you are having your baby.

Obstetrician-gynecologist (OB-GYN) In America, most women will receive their primary care, both before and during childbirth from an OB-GYN. Your doctor may be in private practice on his own, work with a partnership of other doctors, or be part of a health-maintenance organization (HMO). If there is more than one doctor involved in the practice, you should determine whether your care will be given by one primary physician or whether you will be treated by a number of different doctors, since this will certainly be a factor in your choice of practitioner.

It is more and more common in group practices for two or three OB-GYNs to take on patients in a rotation, so that each patient sees each doctor three or four times during the pregnancy. The doctors usually share similar opinions about procedures, medication, and treatments, but it is advisable to query each about your birth plan. The doctors divide up each 24-hour period so one is always on call, with the result that you will be assured of a familiar doctor when your time comes. Though perhaps it is preferable to see one doctor all the way through your pregnancy, if that doctor is off duty or away on vacation when you actually go into labor there is a chance that you might well end up with a complete stranger at your bedside.

Certified nurse-midwife An increasing choice among women looking for less medicalized, more personal births, a nurse-midwife has been trained to be an expert in pregnancy and labor. She can offer prenatal care, or you can see a physician for prenatal care and utilize the midwife during labor and delivery. When considering a midwife, make sure to ask if she is associated with a physician; this can be very important if any risks develop during pregnancy or childbirth.

Some midwives work in a kind of group practice called a maternity center, which is generally associated with one or more physicians who are called on for consultations when it is necessary. Maternity centers offer not only full prenatal care but facilities for labor and delivery. Be aware, however, that you may have to be transferred from the maternity-center to a hospital should your birth

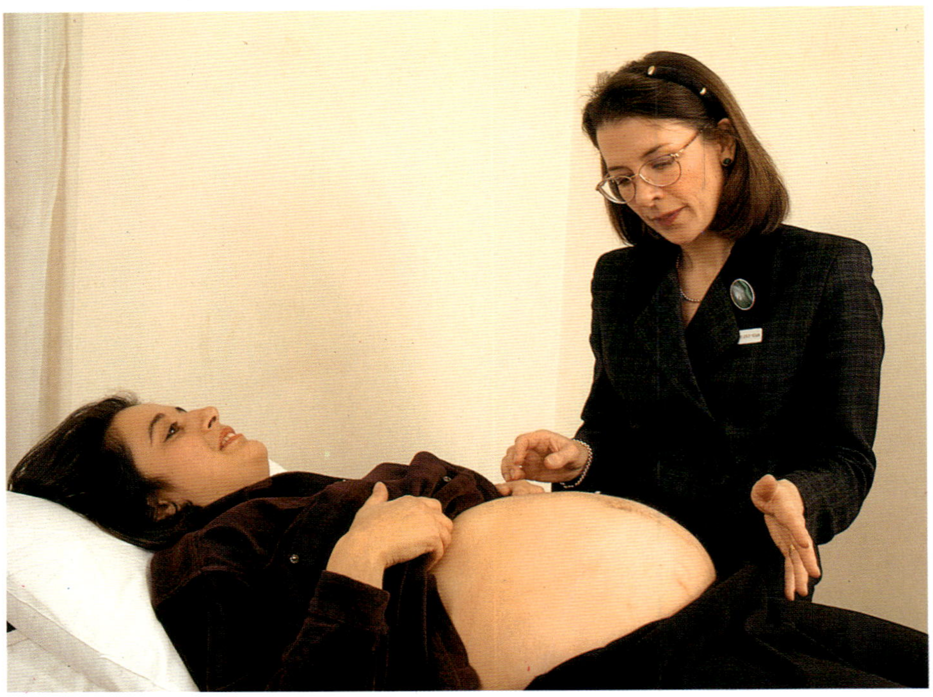

As your pregnancy progresses you may be examined by an obstetrician who specializes in birth and child care. She will advise on your baby's development and discuss any problems.

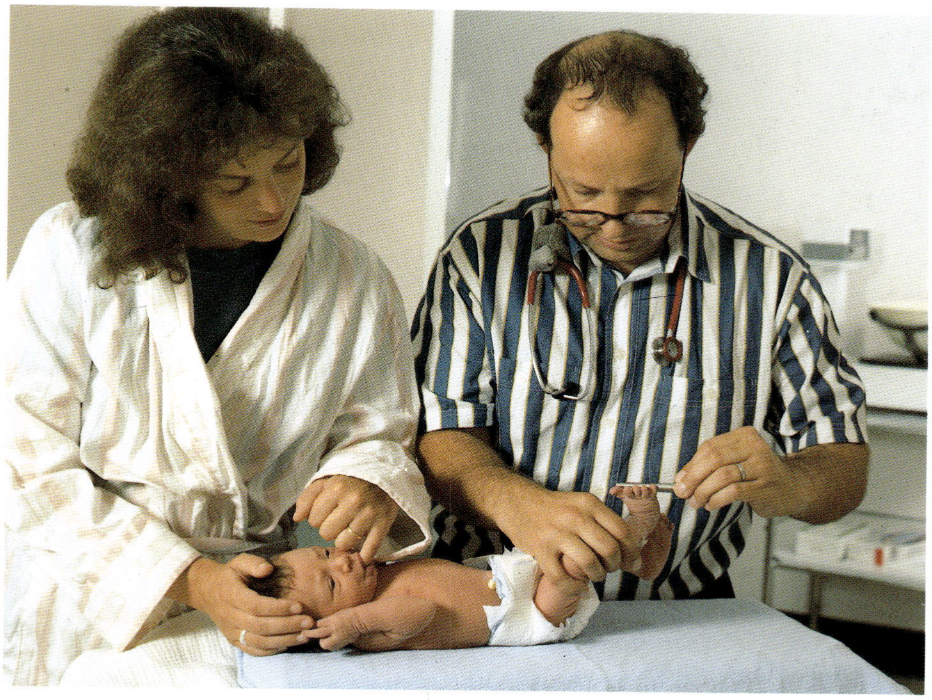

Your growing baby

The fetus is now 3 in long and weighs 1½ oz. The bone marrow, liver, and spleen have now taken over production of blood cells. The bones are developing and the teeth are in place. The fetus may already be practicing lip movements to develop the muscles needed for the sucking reflex after the birth.

The pediatrician will perform several checks on your baby after birth. Here he is checking that the newborn's foot reflex works correctly.

be considered or become high-risk.

Most hospitals have a group of midwives who are available to attend labor and delivery in the hospital rooms. If you want to use a midwife this can be the best of both worlds as you will have the hospital's technology to call on if any complications suddenly arise.

High-risk practitioner Also known as neonatalogists or maternal-fetal specialists, these physicians work with women whose pregnancies have been labeled "high-risk." They may consult with a woman's regular OB-GYN or actually take over as the primary physician. If you have reason to believe that your pregnancy is in the high-risk category, you may well want to consider consulting a specialist in the early weeks at the beginning of your pregnancy.

Pediatrician This is a doctor who specializes in caring for babies and children. Your baby will have a complete check-up by a pediatrician soon after the birth.

After your baby's birth his navel will need to be checked to ensure that it is healing.

THE SECOND TRIMESTER

WEEK 14: SEX DURING PREGNANCY

To be able to enjoy sex it is important to know that making love cannot harm the developing fetus. It is well protected in the uterus by the amniotic fluid and membranes, and the uterus itself is sealed with a plug of mucus, which stays in place until just before the birth. Even deep penetration is safe, but it should of course be gentle so that it doesn't cause discomfort.

Many women find that the middle months of pregnancy are a sensual and even erotic time. Physical changes, such as the increase in the size of your breasts, can actually serve to heighten your interest in sex, which in turn leads to an increase in sexual pleasure. Your genitals may also appear bigger and the pressure from the growing baby can actually make them more responsive. Some women find that they experience orgasm for the first time during pregnancy, while others come to orgasm much more quickly.

Experiencing orgasm is perfectly safe; in fact it can be considered to be beneficial since the uterus often remains hard and firm for several minutes afterward. This is similar in effect to the Braxton Hicks, or practice, contractions you experience toward the end of your pregnancy that prepare the uterus for the birth of your baby.

You may of course find that you feel a lessening of desire during pregnancy, or even a complete loss of interest in sex. These feelings are not uncommon, but they can cause unnecessary stress between you and your partner if they are not brought out into the open and discussed.

You and your body

You are now beginning the second trimester when you should start experiencing what is known as mid-pregnancy bloom. You will be feeling better about everything; if your sex drive has diminished over the last few months it will probably return and sex may be better than ever.

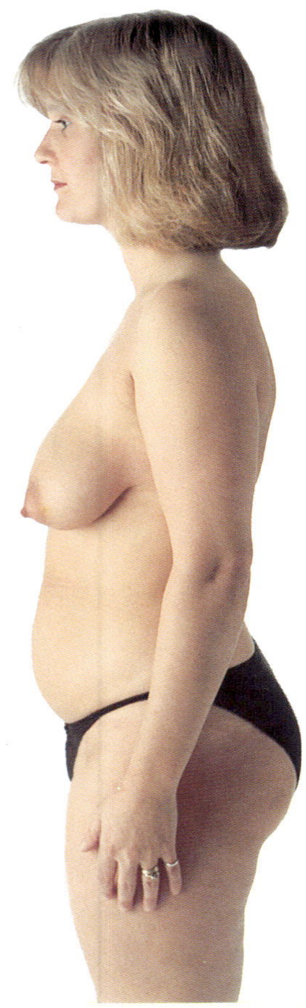

If you don't feel much like making love in early pregnancy, still cuddle your partner and show him lots of affection.

Your partner may feel that he is being rejected, so it is important to find alternative ways of giving each other love and reassurance.

DIFFERENT WAYS TO MAKE LOVE

It is important that you and your partner show each other physical affection during pregnancy, but this does not always have to involve sexual intercourse. You may find as your pregnancy progresses that you want lots of cuddles and other signs of affection from your partner without actually having sex. Men often find this hard to understand as they tend to link such physical contact with intercourse. Explain to your partner how you feel so that together you can find other ways of expressing your love for each other.

Try experimenting with different forms of sex play that don't necessarily end in penetration, so that you can still make love even if you don't feel like intercourse. Take time to find out what you both enjoy and don't be afraid to tell your partner what you do and don't like.

Often during the middle months of pregnancy, you can start to feel more sensual and show renewed interest in sex.

Stroking, massage, mutual masturbation, and oral sex are some alternative ways of making love that you can both enjoy and that may at times be more appropriate than full intercourse.

As you grow larger you'll find some positions for lovemaking more comfortable than others. Experiment with positions that keep your partner's weight off you.

USING SEX TO INDUCE LABOR

Sex can sometimes be a way of inducing labor. Your partner's semen contains a hormone called prostaglandin, which will help to soften the cervix in preparation for birth. Lovemaking will also stimulate the cells in the cervix to secrete their own prostaglandins; this too may help bring labor on.

Breast stimulation in late pregnancy sometimes produces quite strong contractions which are thought to help prepare the way for labor by softening and drawing up the cervix. It has been discovered that stimulating nipples can reactivate a labor that has halted – something that your partner might like to remember.

Your growing baby

The fetus is beginning to look human as the chin, forehead, and nose become more clearly defined. It can now turn its head around and even wrinkle its brow. The fetus may even respond to external stimulus by actually moving away when the doctor or midwife examines your abdomen. The fetus is now 3½ in long and weighs about 2 oz.

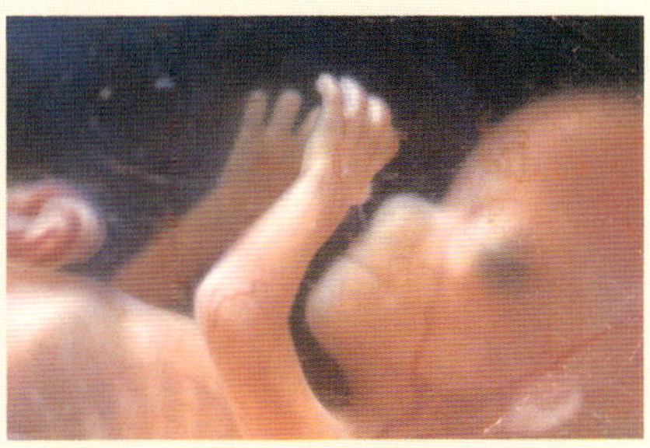

WEEK 15: HEALTH AND SAFETY

You may hear about risks during pregnancy. Some are valid, others are based on misinformation.

If you work with dangerous substances such as chemicals or in a job that requires you to do heavy lifting, you could be risking your health and the health of your child. Your employer must offer you an alternative job if yours is a recognized risk. If you are concerned about risks at work talk to your doctor, your employer, or union representative.

A common concern among working women is that sitting all day in front of a VDT screen such as a computer terminal or word processor will harm the developing fetus. The most recent research shows no evidence of this being a risk, but you may need to have your microwave checked out for any minor radiation leaks, although with modern equipment these are very unlikely.

Recent evidence has shown that there is no risk to the growing fetus for women who regularly use computer terminals. However, move around often to minimize backache.

You and your body

Your heart has enlarged to cope with the increased amount of blood circulating in your body and the fetus's need for oxygen, and has increased its output by 20 percent. You will be feeling more energetic than before and now is a good time to take a vacation before the birth.

HEALTH HAZARDS

While you are pregnant you should avoid unpasteurized milk and products made with unpasteurized milk; pâté made from meat, fish, or vegetables; soft and blue vein cheeses; pre-cooked poultry; and prepared salads (unless they are washed thoroughly) because of the risk of listeria.

Listeria monocytogenes is the bacterium which causes listeriosis in humans and animals. Animals that carry the bacterium are likely to infect the milk they produce and the meat that is produced from them. The bacterium is usually destroyed during the pasteurization of milk and milk products. However, if food is contaminated and then refrigerated the bacteria will continue to multiply. Listeriosis can also be spread through direct contact with animals that are infected.

Toxoplasmosis is a disease that occurs in both humans and animals. It can be extremely dangerous if it is contracted during pregnancy because it may cause miscarriage or severe fetal abnormality. The disease is spread to humans by eating undercooked or raw meat and through coming into contact with cat feces. As it is quite possible to have the disease without knowing it, you should have a blood test to find out whether

Your growing baby

The fetal skeleton is developing well and its legs are now longer than its arms. The hair on its head is becoming thicker and it has eyelashes as well as eyebrows. The fetus can probably hear now and the amniotic fluid makes an excellent sound conductor, so it will be able to hear your stomach rumbling and your heart beating as well as the sound of your voice. The fetus is 4¾ in long and now weighs 3½ oz.

or not you have immunity. If you are immune, you definitely cannot infect your baby.

If you find that you are not immune, you should take a number of precautions throughout your pregnancy. Avoid any meat that has not been cooked thoroughly and wash your hands, cooking utensils, and surfaces after preparing raw meat. Wash fruit and vegetables to remove all traces of dirt. Avoid unpasteurized goats' milk and goats' milk products. Finally, always wear rubber gloves when gardening and wash your hands well afterward. Put covers on your children's sand boxes in the yard to prevent any cats from getting in them and using them as litter boxes. Finally, always wear some rubber gloves when handling used cat litter, and remember to wash your hands and also the gloves when you have finished.

Above: Hard cheeses are safe to eat in pregnancy. However, make sure you only eat hard-boiled eggs and drink pasteurized milk to avoid Listeria monocytogenes. *Right: Always wear some gloves when gardening during pregnancy as toxoplasmosis can be caught from cat feces.*

Food safety

Avoid putting yourself at risk during pregnancy by taking the following precautions with food.

- Wash all fruit, vegetables, and salads, including any pre-packaged salads, thoroughly.
- Don't eat raw or undercooked meat.
- Eggs must be well cooked and all dairy products should be pasteurized.
- Avoid eating any soft, imported cheeses such as Brie and Camembert, blue-vein cheeses, and those that are made from goats' and sheep's milk because of the risk of listeria.
- Don't eat liver and liver products, such as pâté and liverwurst. They contain high levels of vitamin A, which is toxic in excessive amounts.
- Avoid shellfish.
- Keep your refrigerator below 41°F and don't refreeze any previously frozen foods.
- Pay special attention to hygiene in the kitchen.
- Don't eat food that is past its expiration date.

WEEK 16: SCANS/TWINS

At around 16 weeks you may be offered an ultrasound scan so that you can see your baby for the first time. A scan can be carried out at any stage of pregnancy, but is usually offered between 16 and 20 weeks.

The procedure is completely painless. High-density sound waves are used to create a picture of your baby in the uterus, and you will be able to see this on a screen. The best pictures are obtained when you have a full bladder so you will be asked to drink a lot of fluid beforehand.

You lie on a table and your stomach is lubricated so that the person performing the scan can pass the scanner smoothly across it. The picture that appears on the screen may not be very clear, so ask the sonographer to explain the rather indistinct images to you, if you are unsure of anything that you are seeing.

The fetus's age can be determined from a scan; it also shows up most abnormalities of the head and spine that may have occurred and will detect the presence of twins. The exact position of the placenta and the fetus can be seen, so if there are any problems, for example when the placenta is situated very low down, extra care will be taken throughout your pregnancy.

TWINS

There is about a one in 80 chance that you and your partner will conceive twins. However, you are more likely to give birth to twins if you have a history of them in your, or your partner's, family.

Identical twins come from one egg which, once fertilized, then splits into two separate cells. Each of the cells then grows into a separate fetus, but they usually share the same placenta. Because identical twins originally came from the same cells they are always the same sex and look like each other.

Non-identical twins, also known as fraternal twins, are the result of two eggs being fertilized by two different sperm at the same time. Each fetus has its own placenta and the sexes of the babies may differ.

Fraternal twins usually don't look any more alike than brothers and sisters who are born years apart.

You and your body

You may feel your baby's first movements around this time. These early movements are like a fluttering, bubbling sensation. You may notice the beginning of *Linea nigra*, a dark line that appears down the center of your abdomen. This will disappear after the birth.

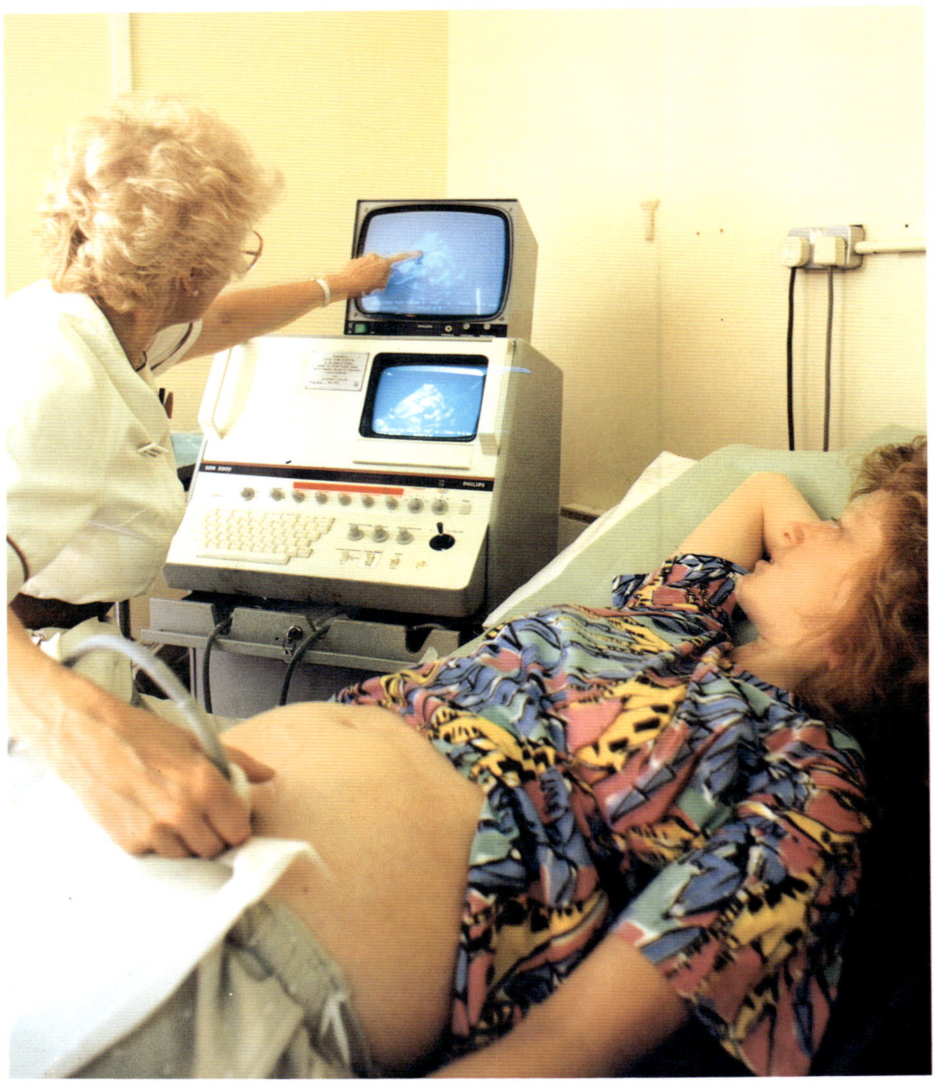

An ultrasound scan may be carried out around your 16th week of pregnancy. It will show up abnormalities in your baby and also indicate the presence of twins.

The arrival of twins can come as a shock. Get your partner to help as much as he can and you will soon find that you both start bonding with them.

The joy of having twins is that as they grow up they will learn to play with each other.

Your growing baby

The fetus will be moving around frequently now, although you may have only just started to feel these movements. The body will become covered in a fine downy hair called lanugo. It is possible to tell a baby's sex now through an ultrasound scan, though scans aren't 100-percent effective as predictors of gender. The fetus is 6¼ in long and weighs 5 oz.

Twins in the womb

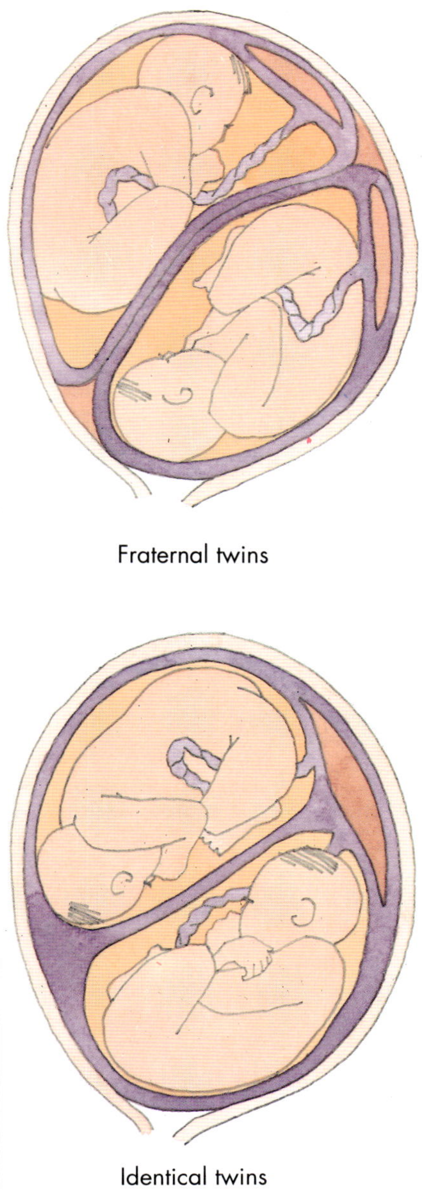

WEEK 17: YOUR PREGNANCY WARDROBE

You will find that loose ordinary clothes, in a bigger size if necessary, will see you through most of your pregnancy. A few basic garments that are interchangeable will help you achieve a variety of looks. Buy skirts and slacks with elasticated waists, baggy shirts, and big T-shirts in natural fibers such as cotton. Choose underwear with some cotton content for softness and absorbency and maternity tights or stockings to give your legs support. As your breasts are likely to increase in size rapidly during the early months of pregnancy, it makes sense to buy a well-fitting support bra early. This will prevent your breasts from sagging which will help them to return to their normal shape once the baby is born.

A baggy cardigan worn over a skirt with an elasticated waist helps conceal your belly.

A loose-fitting pants suit with a long jacket can look and feel good in pregnancy.

You and your body

Your waistline will have completely disappeared and you may have begun to develop stretch marks. Bleeding gums may be a problem, so if you haven't had a dental check-up now is the time to go. If you work, you should start thinking about when you intend to leave and whether you will want to return.

Your growing baby

All your baby's limbs are now fully formed as well as the skin and muscle. Its taste buds are beginning to develop so that it will be able to distinguish sweet from non-sweetened fluid. The fetus is now about 7 in long and weighs around 6½ oz.

Maternity benefits

Once your pregnancy is confirmed, you should make inquiries about your maternity benefits. If you work you may qualify for maternity leave from your employer. You may be allowed to take time off work to attend prenatal classes. Your obstetrician or midwife will help or advise if you are unsure of what to do. Check your health-insurance policy to determine what benefits are and aren't covered. Under the new Family Leave act all companies with over 50 employees must grant 12 weeks of unpaid leave, except to those in the top 10% income bracket (they assume you are too essential to take up that much time so it's discretionary). Negotiate leave and compensation early to avoid any confusion.

Front-opening dresses won't be restricting, and can be useful for breastfeeding.

If your feet ache take off your shoes inside your home, but be careful on polished surfaces.

Front-opening clothes are comfortable to wear in both early and late pregnancy, as they expand with you.

You can still stay fashionable by wearing a larger size of leggings over your belly, which can be concealed with a long, loose T-shirt.

WEEK 18: LOOKING YOUR BEST

You may find that your hair behaves in a rather unpredictable way while you are pregnant. Hormone changes mean that your hair may appear thicker than usual, or in some women the opposite happens and the hair loss increases so that the hair looks thinner. Dry hair may become even drier and oily hair more greasy. Whichever condition applies to you, just wash your hair using a mild shampoo. If your hair tends to be very dry, use a good conditioner after every wash and, if possible, allow it to dry naturally rather than using a hair dryer.

Dry hair will need extra conditioning during your pregnancy because it becomes drier as your hormones change.

Pregnancy hormones can affect the color and texture of your skin. Uneven patches appear and dark-skinned people may even get a butterfly-shaped patch of pigmentation across the face known as "the mask of pregnancy." A heavier foundation will help hide these marks and a UVA sun screen will prevent any further increase in pigmentation. Pregnancy "bloom," which is caused by an increase in the tiny blood vessels under the surface of the skin, can be toned down with green cream or powder. It is a good idea to use hypoallergenic skin-care products as your skin may be particularly sensitive at this time.

Try using hypoallergenic skin-cleansing products on your skin as it will be particularly sensitive at this time.

FLUID RETENTION

Your body retains more water than usual during pregnancy, so your hands and feet may become slightly swollen and you may find that your eyes get puffy and your face looks fuller. The best solution is to get as much rest as possible, sitting with your feet higher than your heart, as this will help reduce the swelling in your feet and ankles. While you are resting, place some cotton pads soaked in witch hazel, or slices of cucumber, on your eyes. This will soothe them and reduce any puffiness. You can disguise a fuller face by applying blusher below the cheekbones and blending a darker shade of foundation along your jawline. Alternatively, you can draw attention away from your face by wearing a colorful scarf or a chunky necklace around your neck.

Try not to be too critical of your changing looks during pregnancy; many other people will consider that this new, softer look to your appearance makes you seem altogether younger and healthier.

You and your body

You should be able to feel the fetal movements quite clearly now. Your nose may become blocked as pregnancy causes the membranes inside the nasal passages to swell. You may also notice an increase in vaginal discharge. You will find that there are several physical changes besides the predictable weight gain.

Your growing baby

The skin is still wrinkled because the fetus hasn't started to gain body fat and is very active. It is becoming aware of sounds outside the uterus and you may be able to feel it jumping at unexpected noises. The fetus is now around 8½ in long and weighs about 8 oz.

With extra care you can transform your face from looking tired and pale in pregnancy (left) to attractive and striking (right). A concealing foundation masks any pigmentation marks, mascara and soft eye shadows can highlight your eyes, and a vivid lipstick can emphasize your mouth.

WEEK 19: EXERCISE

Regular, gentle exercise has an important part to play in keeping you fit during pregnancy and will help you get back into shape after the birth. Remember, if you ever feel faint, light-headed or breathless while you are exercising you must stop immediately. If you haven't been exercising regularly, start swimming, or take up yoga or walking as they can all be done at a gentle, rhythmic pace that can be adapted to suit each stage of your pregnancy. If you find it easier to follow an exercise routine you can do at home, never include sit-ups or exercises that involve raising the legs when you are lying down as these could damage the abdominal muscles. It is important to stop and relax between exercises and to make sure that your breathing always remains at a controlled rate.

You and your body

You have started to put weight on your buttocks, hips, and thighs as well as your abdomen. Tiny veins may start appearing on your face. These are very small broken blood vessels which are caused by circulation changes. They will disappear after the birth.

Toning your breasts

1 *Hold arms at breast level with hands loosely clasping opposite arm. Tighten grip and hold briefly, then relax.*

2 *Still keeping your hands clasped, raise them to eye level and tighten your grip and hold, then relax.*

3 *Lower your arms to your waist, tighten and hold, then relax. Repeat this sequence several times.*

Feet exercises

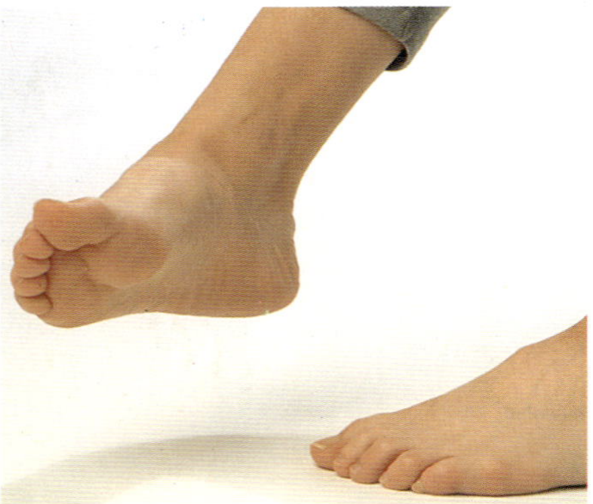

1 *To loosen ankles, sit down with feet flat on the ground. Lift one foot at a time and circle ankle five times in both directions.*

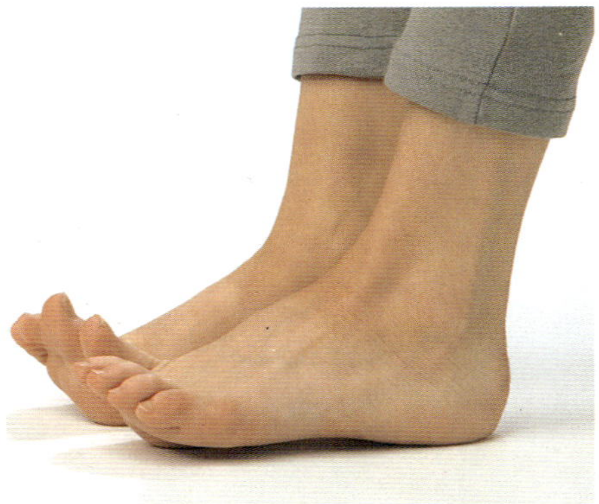

2 *To tone the feet, place your feet flat on the floor. Now lift your toes up as far as you can and hold briefly, then relax.*

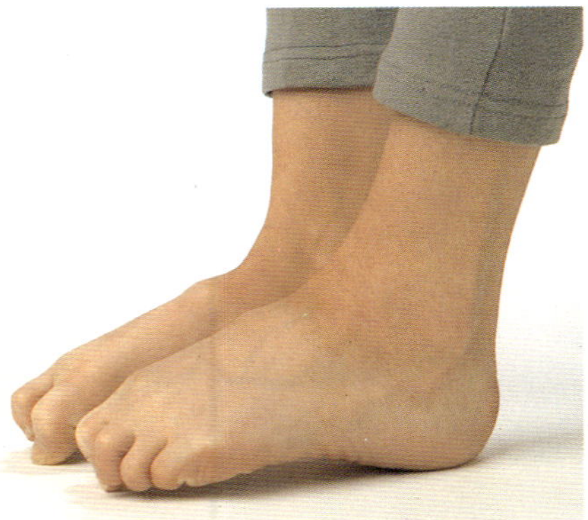

3 *Now clench your toes hard, hold for a few seconds, then relax again. Repeat this technique, and Step 2, 10 times.*

Taylor sitting and squatting exercises

1 *To loosen the groin and hips and stretch the inner thighs, sit with the soles of your feet together. Holding ankles, bring your pelvis and feet together by moving your hips toward your feet.*

2 *This is a good position for labor. Squat down keeping a straight back; try to put your heels down placing your weight evenly. Press your elbows against your thighs stretching the inner groin and thighs.*

Tummy toning exercises

1 *Put a folded towel or pillow under your head and lie with your knees bent and your feet flat on the floor. Press the small of your back down on the floor.*

2 *Slowly extend both your legs in front of you until they are both completely straight, but still keep your back pressed well down onto the floor.*

3 *Draw one knee up and then the other, without lifting your back off the floor. Relax your legs until straight; repeat five times.*

Your growing baby

The fetus is starting to put on weight and its rapid rate of growth has begun to slow down. The baby teeth have developed in the gums and the buds for the permanent teeth are beginning to form. The fetus is around 9 in long and weighs about 10 oz.

WEEK 20: SKIN CARE/CRAVINGS

You and your body

Your uterus is enlarging quite rapidly now so that you look pregnant. Your navel may be flattened or pushed out and it will stay this way until after the birth. Heartburn may start to become a problem because the uterus is starting to push against your stomach.

Your breasts are likely to increase by as much as two bra sizes during pregnancy, so you will need to make sure that they are well supported so that they do not sag and become uncomfortable. Small bumps may appear in the skin around your nipples. These are sebaceous glands that secrete sebum, a fatty lubricant. As your pregnancy progresses, your nipples grow softer and gentle massage will help make them supple and ready for breastfeeding. Your breasts may leak a yellow fluid called colostrum, which will form a crust on the nipples. You will need to wash and dry them gently and thoroughly at least twice a day.

Your nails are made of protein and are affected by the hormonal changes taking place in your body. Usually they grow longer and stronger during pregnancy, but occasionally pregnancy will cause them to split and break. If this happens, keep them short and protect them by wearing gloves when you are doing rough jobs or when you immerse your hands in water.

Check your bra size by measuring around your ribcage. For cup size measure around your bust at its fullest.

If the elasticity of your skin becomes overstretched as you put on weight, you may develop stretch marks. These usually appear on the breasts, stomach, and the tops of the thighs as thin, reddish lines. There is little you can do to avoid them, but keeping your skin well moisturized, and being careful not to put on too much extra weight, will help minimize them. Stretch marks fade to thin silvery lines after the birth.

Your nails may be brittle during pregnancy so keep them short to stop them splitting.

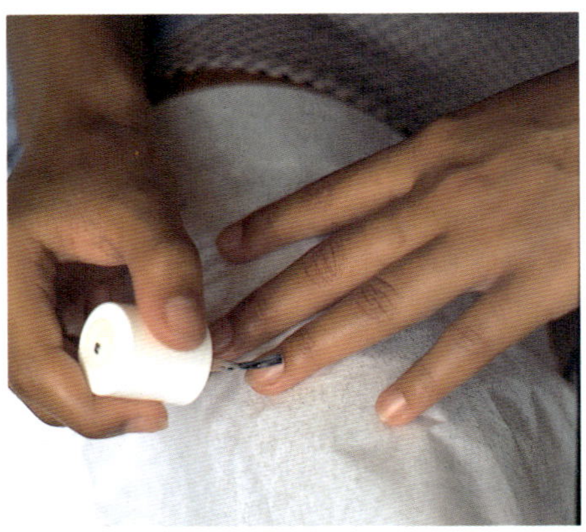

Paint on a nail strengthener to keep your nails strong at this time.

Varicose veins can be caused by pregnancy hormones or, later in pregnancy, by the uterus pressing down and obstructing the flow of blood from the legs to the heart. Although not serious, they can lead to aching or sore legs. Try to avoid standing for long periods and put your feet up whenever possible to ease any discomfort. Walking will help the blood flow; put on support tights or stockings when you get out of bed in the morning to give your legs more support. Varicose veins usually disappear soon after the birth.

CRAVINGS

No one is sure why some pregnant women have cravings while others don't. Doctors disagree about them; some are sympathetic while others doubt that they actually exist. If you desire a certain food there is no reason why you shouldn't indulge yourself within reason, but make sure that you don't exclude other more nourishing foods as a result.

Above: Your legs may ache more with the increased weight you're carrying, so try massaging them with a pleasant body lotion. Right: You can't prevent stretch marks from appearing on your stomach, but rubbing in lotion may help to reduce them.

Your growing baby

Vernix, a white greasy substance, is starting to form over the fetus's skin to protect it from the amniotic fluid. This usually wears off before the birth, but sometimes traces of it can be seen. At this stage in your pregnancy the fetus weighs around 12 oz and measures about 10 in.

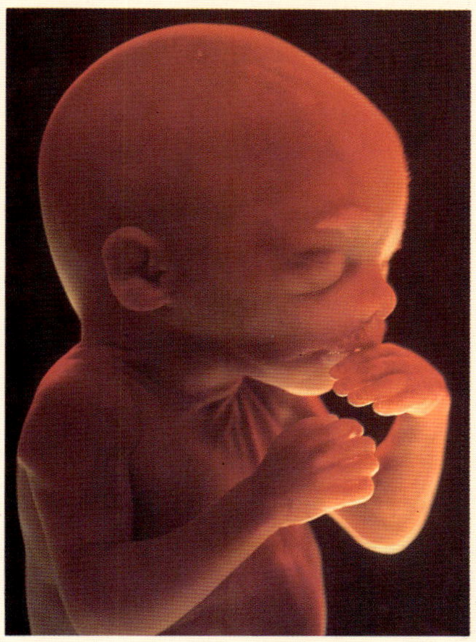

WEEK 21: MINOR COMPLAINTS

You and your body

You should be able to see your abdomen ripple as the fetus moves. You may be feeling slightly breathless as your expanding ribcage pushes upward, giving your lungs less room. You will probably be feeling energetic so now is the time to tackle things such as planning the baby's room.

By now you may be experiencing some of the minor problems that occur later in pregnancy. These include:

Heartburn This is a strong burning feeling in your chest that often happens during the last few months of pregnancy. It is usually worse when lying down. Hormones cause the valve at the top of your stomach to relax, which allows stomach acid to pass back into the esophagus, causing a burning sensation. Avoid eating spicy and fatty foods. Eating small, but frequent meals may help reduce heartburn. Sleeping propped up at night and drinking a glass of milk before you go to bed may also help ease the discomfort. Your doctor may prescribe an antacid if the problem regularly keeps you awake at night. If you buy an over-the-counter remedy always tell the pharmacist that you are pregnant because some of the remedies available are not suitable for use during pregnancy or breastfeeding.

If you are suffering from heartburn, try drinking a glass of milk before you go to sleep at night.

Insomnia Sleeplessness often becomes a problem as your pregnancy progresses because you find it difficult to get comfortable, and you have to make frequent trips to the bathroom. Vivid dreams can also be a problem at this time. A bath followed by a warm drink at bedtime will help you relax. It is important to find restful sleeping positions, so use lots of pillows to support your abdomen when you lie on your side. You could also try practicing some relaxation techniques.

Insomnia can be a problem in later pregnancy. If you can't sleep, try supporting your tummy on pillows to make yourself more comfortable.

Itching This often occurs on the areas of skin around the belly and is sometimes accompanied by a rash. Calamine lotion should help relieve the itching and since it is usually caused by sweating, wearing loose clothes made of natural fibers can help prevent it. Severe itching during the last three months of pregnancy could be a warning of pregnancy cholestasis – a rare but potentially dangerous liver disorder – and you should consult your doctor.

Edema (swelling) This occurs in the feet and ankles and sometimes

Your growing baby

The fetus is very active now and you will probably be able to feel it kicking quite eas ly. If this disturbs you at night, stroke your tummy and talk to the fetus because it may be soothed by the sound of your voice. The fetus is now around 11 in long and weighs about 14 oz.

the hands because your body is retaining more fluid than normal. By the end of the day this fluid tends to gather in your feet, especially if the weather has been hot or you have been doing a lot of standing. Try to sit or lie with your feet up whenever you can, as this will help reduce the swelling. Wear support hose and comfortable shoes during the day and avoid standing for long periods. You should always tell your doctor about any swelling that you experience as it may possibly be a sign of preeclampsia.

Fatigue The extra weight you carry during late pregnancy can make you feel more tired than usual. It is important to build some regular rest periods into your day when you can sit down with your feet up. If the fatigue you are experiencing feels excessive, you may be suffering from anemia. Make sure you are getting plenty of iron in your diet by eating lean red meat, whole grains, dark green leafy vegetables, nuts, and legumes. If the feeling still persists then ensure you consult your doctor.

Above: You may well be feeling more energetic than usual at this stage in your pregnancy, but don't forget to give yourself time to sit down and rest.

Below: If your ankles start to swell when you have been on your feet for a while, lie down on the floor with your head supported by a pillow and your feet propped up on several pillows.

WEEK 22: RELAXATION AND MASSAGE

It is important to be able to relax, both mentally and physically, during pregnancy because this will help you to rest. Knowing how to make your body relax during labor will allow you to work with the contractions rather than against them.

Physical relaxation Start by getting comfortable and make sure that every part of your body is supported. Then concentrate on tensing and relaxing individual parts of your body. Start at your toes and work gradually upward to your head and then back down to your toes again. By the time you have finished this exercise you should be feeling nice and loose.

Mental relaxation This requires deep concentration so you need to be completely comfortable and in a quiet place where no one will disturb you. Empty your mind and concentrate on your breathing. Breathe in deeply and hold your breath for a few seconds before letting it out slowly. Once you have established a steady pattern of breathing you should make sure that all your muscles are relaxed, then allow your mind to float away. One way to do this is to imagine that you are floating gently on calm water under a clear blue sky, in tranquil surroundings.

You and your body

Your lower ribs are starting to cause you pain as they get pushed outward by your growing baby and your expanding uterus. Your ribcage rises by a small amount as it is pushed upward. To minimize the discomfort, try sitting up as straight as you can or lifting your arms above your head. This is an ideal time to investigate the different methods that you can use to ease discomfort now and during labor and birth.

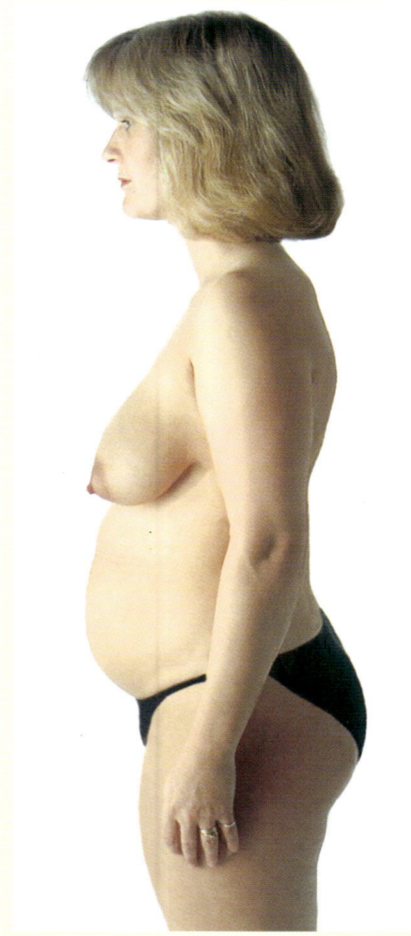

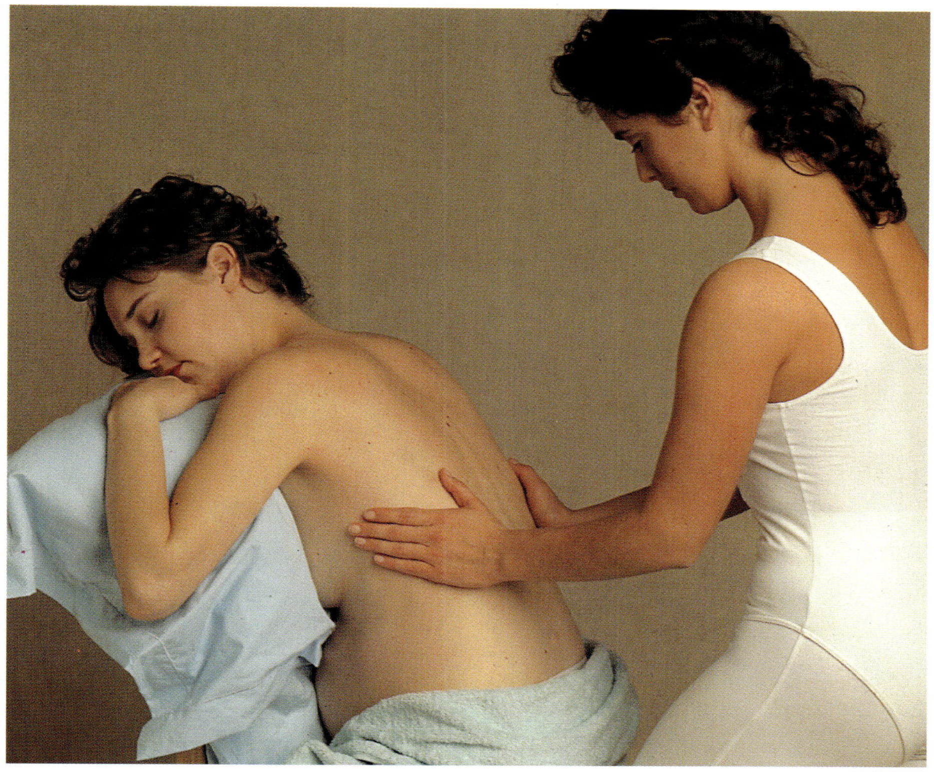

OTHER TECHNIQUES

Massage is an excellent way of relieving tension. It is best done on bare skin, but if you find your skin is particularly sensitive, it can be carried out through a thin cotton nightgown. Massage strokes should be firm, smooth, and rhythmic.

Aromatherapy massage uses essential oils that are added to a carrier oil before being applied to your skin. Certain essential oils can be dangerous during pregnancy because they may trigger uterine contractions, so you must always get qualified professional advice. Many aromatherapists will not treat a pregnant woman at all. Most of those who will treat expectant mothers will do so only after the sixth month of pregnancy. One effective blend is mandarin oil well diluted (i.e. a maximum solution of one percent: no more than 10 drops of oil to 50 ml carrier oil) in a sweet almond carrier oil. A well-diluted solution of true lavender, jasmine, and rose in sweet almond oil is also thought to be beneficial during labor and birth.

In acupuncture tiny needles are used to stimulate meridian points situated on the body's energy lines with the aim of rebalancing the energy flow. The treatment can help backache, but some points on the body are thought to stimulate uterine contractions, so it is important to visit a qualified practitioner and let him or her know that you are pregnant.

Above: If you are suffering regularly from backache, having a soothing massage from a qualified practitioner can help. With an aromatherapy massage, make sure she chooses oils that will not affect the baby.

Below: Regular massage on your legs may help to relieve any aches and pains that you are experiencing.

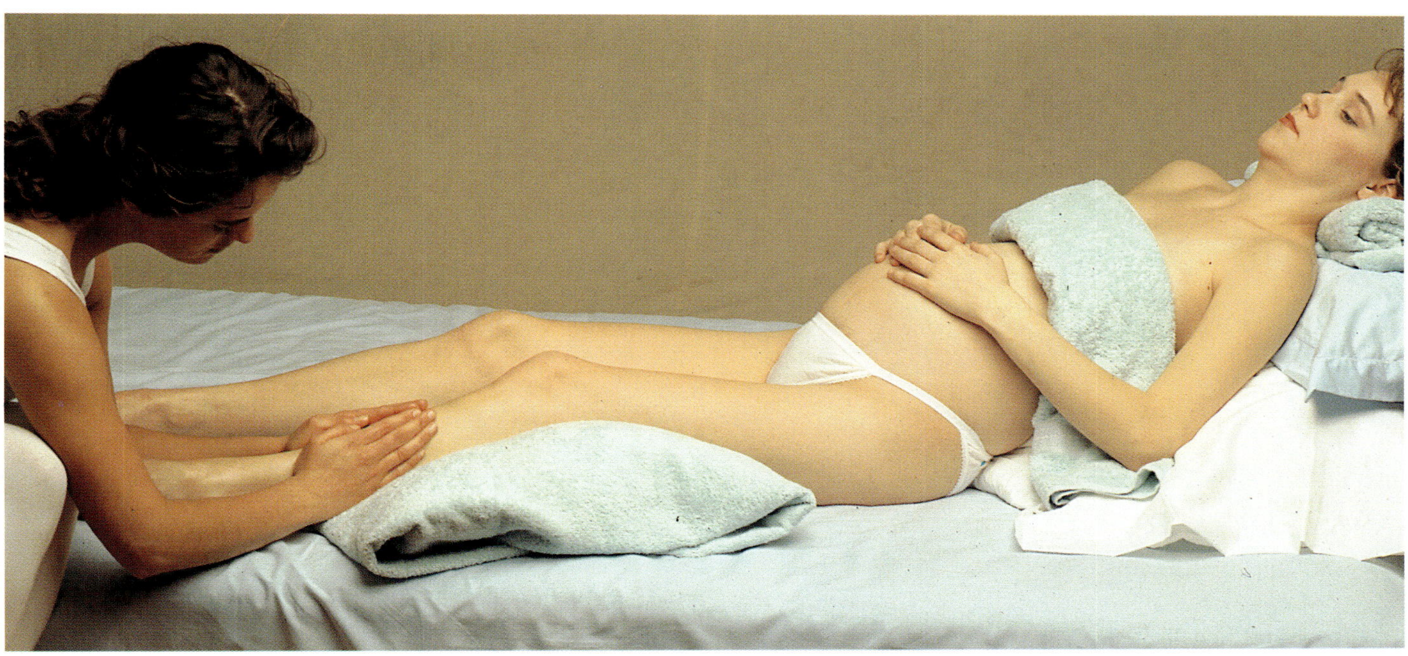

WEEK 23: PREPARING THE BABY'S ROOM

You and your body

The baby can now be felt through your abdominal wall and the doctor will palpate your abdomen to see how the baby is lying. You may occasionally feel a pain that is rather like a stitch down the side of your stomach. This is the uterine muscle stretching and it will go away after you have had a rest.

This is a good time to think of practical things like planning the baby's room. Whether you have a spare room which you are going to turn into a baby's room, or you intend to make a corner for your baby in your own bedroom, you should start getting it ready now while you still have the energy.

Before you begin you will need to take into consideration the shape and size of the area so you can decide how much furniture and baby equipment will comfortably fit into it. You should also check whether there are enough electrical sockets; that there is sufficient heating and that the ceiling or wall lights are where you want them. Major changes such as rewiring or putting in another radiator are better done before you start to decorate or carpet the baby's room.

Babies enjoy looking at bright, primary colors and big, bold patterns so choose a colorful paint and paper; washable materials will make it easier to keep the walls looking bright and fresh. Decals, borders, pictures, and mobiles can be used very effectively to brighten up a plain background if you are reluctant to commit yourself to a color scheme until you know your baby's sex.

Rugs and polished floors look nice but are unsuitable because of the risk of slipping on them while holding the baby. Any flooring needs to be warm underfoot and non-slip. Sealed cork tiles are ideal because they are warm and any spills can be wiped up without damage to the floor. Fitted carpets and carpet tiles are suitable alternatives, but don't buy expensive carpet because it will probably need replacing after a relatively short time.

An overhead light with a dimmer switch or a specially designed baby's room light is very useful for night feeding as it gives out a soft comforting glow that won't startle either of you too much in the middle of the night. A nightlight will provide enough illumination for you to check on your sleeping baby, but you will need a brighter light for diaper changing and general care. Avoid any lamps with trailing cords that you could trip over, and fit all unused electrical sockets with a safety cover.

Planning the baby's room can be enjoyable. You can start to buy some outfits in advance, but remember that you will often be given baby clothes when your baby is born.

FINISHING TOUCHES

The room where the baby sleeps must be draft-proof so cover any windows with thick, lined curtains. These will not only keep out the cold but will also keep the morning light from waking your baby during the summer. Windows need to be

fitted with childproof locks and the curtains should be out of reach of the crib. Never place the baby's crib under a window or near radiators. Young babies cannot regulate their own temperature so they need to be kept in a comfortably warm environment at around a constant 65°F. A special baby's room thermometer or a thermostat fitted to the radiator will help ensure that you maintain the room temperature.

Babies actually require very little in the way of furniture. Somewhere to sleep, a dresser or chest to keep clothes in, and a place for changing and storing toiletries and diapers, as well as a chair for you to sit in while you are feeding or rocking the baby, is all that you really need for the first few months. All baby's room furniture should be sturdy enough that it can't be pulled over when babies are older and using it for support as they begin to pull themselves up onto their feet.

If you buy secondhand furniture, make sure that any paint or varnish is non-toxic and lead-free. Also check that there are no broken bits to harm your baby. Unless you're sure that the crib conforms to current safety standards, don't buy it.

Your growing baby

The fetus is beginning to look as it will at birth, with the head much more in proportion to the body. In a boy, the scrotum is now well developed and in a girl the ovaries already contain several million eggs. (These will reduce to around two million at birth and will continue decreasing until puberty is reached.) The fetus is around 12¼ in long and weighs approximately 15½ oz.

When decorating your baby's room, bear in mind that babies like bright, primary colors. They also love pretty mobiles.

A basket can by kept by or near your bed, and your baby can sleep in it for up to three months.

WEEK 24: BABY CLOTHES AND EQUIPMENT

You and your body

You will noticeably be putting on weight, perhaps as much as 1 lb per week. Your feet and legs may start to feel the strain of carrying this extra weight, so make sure that you wear comfortable shoes and that you get plenty of rest.

Start planning what you need to buy for your baby so that by the birth you will at least have purchased the major items. If you leave everything until the end of the pregnancy, you may be too tired to enjoy shopping for your baby.

Only buy a few basic first size or newborn garments as your baby will probably rapidly outgrow these. Also, most baby clothes are sized by the approximate age and height of the child and you won't know the size of your child until she is born.

Choose some well-designed baby clothes, which will make your life easier and allow you to dress and undress your baby with the minimum of time and fuss. Clothes with elastic necks or a shoulder fastening will let you slip clothes over the baby's head easily, and snaps up the inside of legs of rompers or stretchies will help to ease the regular diaper changing that is necessary.

Your new baby will probably go through as many as three changes of clothes a day, so it is a good idea to check the washing instructions on any garment before you buy. These instructions will tell you how best to care for each garment so that you can see whether it is easy-care, or if it will require a lot of attention.

A baby's layette: a hat, undershirt, stretchie, mittens, booties, diaper and a cardigan.

BABY'S TRANSPORT

Before you decide on a carriage, stroller or combination, you need to consider your lifestyle and the various methods of transport you will be

Baby transport

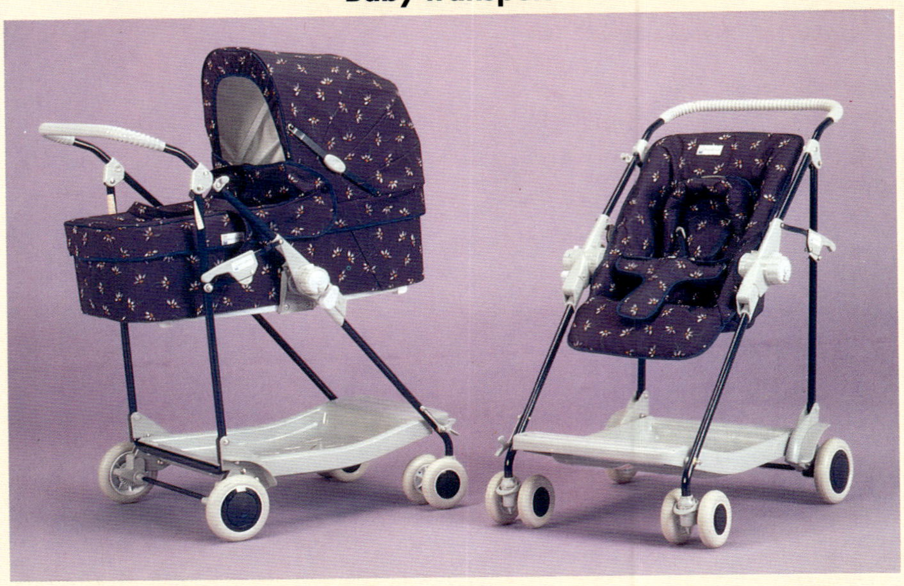

Transportation choices include a carriage (left) or a folding stroller (right).

A traditional carriage is sturdy with plenty of space to carry shopping. It is probably the best option if you walk everywhere and you are planning to have another child fairly quickly. Generally, carriages are unsuitable for cars unless they are fitted with a detachable body.

A folding stroller with a reclining seat can be used from babyhood through to toddler stage. Choose one that is light enough to carry on and off public transportation.

A stroller that converts to a carriage is especially useful, as is a lightweight umbrella stroller.

A folding stroller with a package shelf can be very useful when you go shopping with your baby.

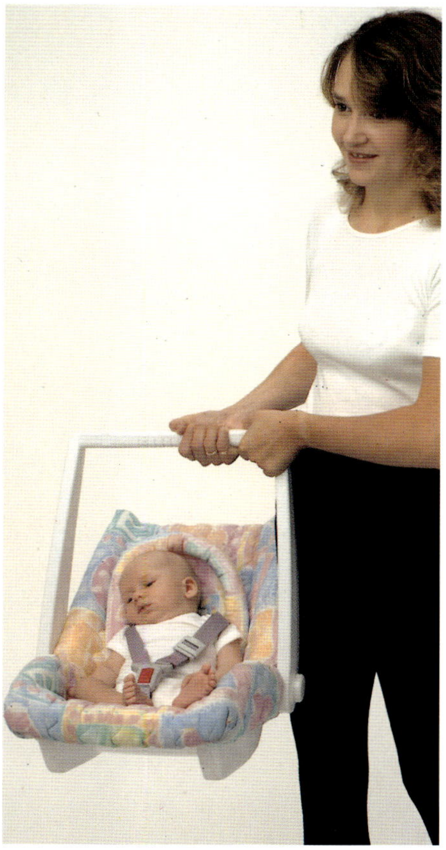

A car seat carrier is easily transported and can be bought in different sizes to suit the age of your baby.

using regularly. You also need to think about where it will be stored when not in use. Once you have selected the type most suitable to your needs, see if the store you order it from will keep it for you until after the baby is born.

When buying a car seat, you can choose between an infant carrier, which is suitable from birth to six months, or a combination seat, which is suitable from birth to around four years. Both types are held securely in place using the existing car seat belts.

EQUIPMENT

Whether you buy a crib, basket, or bassinette will probably depend on where your baby is going to sleep and how much space you have available. If the baby is going to sleep in your room at first and you haven't much space, think about buying a crib later.

However, when you do purchase a crib make sure that the new mattress you get to go in it is firm. It should also fit snugly into the base of the crib.

You need to have at least six sheets and several lightweight blankets for the crib and another six sheets and at least three more blankets for your carriage or stroller. You may want to include a crib bumper and comforter as well.

Your growing baby

Vigorous movements followed by periods of quiet will start to occur as the fetus develops its own waking and resting periods. The pattern that develops now may well continue after the birth so it's a good idea to monitor it for a few days to see how it compares with the sleep pattern once the baby is born. The heartbeat can be heard with an ordinary stethoscope and the fetus can hear you clearly when you speak. It is now around 13 in long and weighs about 1 lb.

A two-level high chair can be used in the higher position when your baby is young (left) and in the lower position (above) when he is older. Always make sure you strap him in securely.

WEEK 25: FEEDING CHOICES

Now is the time to start thinking about how you are going to feed your baby. Whether to breast- or bottle-feed is a personal and emotional decision and one that you need to feel completely happy about. Before you make up your mind talk it over with your partner and your doctor, and get some first-hand experiences from other mothers.

Breastfeeding

Breast milk is the best possible food for your baby because it contains everything he or she needs in the right proportions, and it changes as the baby grows. It contains antibodies which will help protect the baby and it is easily digestible so less likely to cause stomach upsets. Breast-fed babies are also less likely to develop conditions such as eczema and asthma and are less prone to getting some infections.

Breastfeeding has advantages for you as well. Not only is breast milk free and always on "tap," at the correct temperature, it also releases hormones that encourage the uterus to shrink back to its original size more quickly. It uses up calories too, so it will help you get your figure back.

During pregnancy the skin around your nipples will appear darker and raised sebaceous glands will appear as little bumps in the areola, the dark area surrounding the nipple. As your pregnancy progresses the nipples will grow softer. You can help make them more supple by gently massaging them. Take extra care washing and drying your breasts toward the end of pregnancy when they may leak a little, and avoid using soaps that have a drying effect on the skin. You may find that you need to use breast pads to prevent your clothes from getting stained.

Breastfeeding is the best way to nourish your baby, but bottle feeding with formula can be gradually introduced as he gets older, and can be given by both partners.

You and your body

You should be looking rosy-cheeked and healthy because of the increase in blood circulation under the skin. Pressure from the growing uterus on the bladder means that you need to make frequent trips to the bathroom. Leg cramps, heartburn, and backache are often problems now.

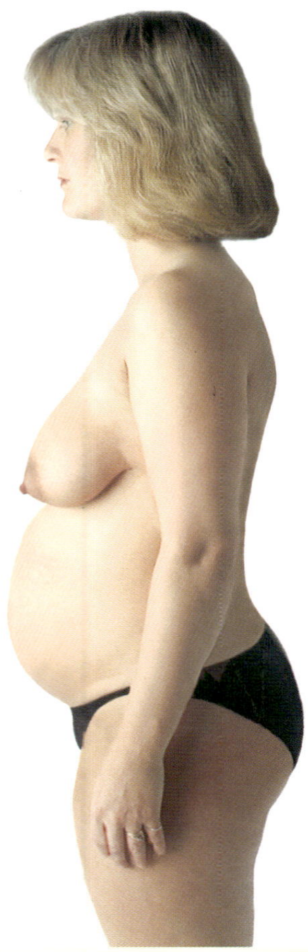

Breast milk is free so the only additional cost involved at first is for nursing bras and breast pads. Choose cotton, front-opening nursing bras, with adjustable straps and fastenings because the size of your breasts will change. Wait until after your 30th week of pregnancy before buying a nursing bra – one that fits you then should fit you after the baby is born.

If you want to be able to express

milk you will also need a couple of bottles and nipples, sterilizing equipment, and possibly a breast pump.

BOTTLE-FEEDING

Formula has been specially produced for bottle-fed babies. It contains the right balance of vitamins and minerals that a baby needs to thrive. Formula has more protein than breast milk, which means that it takes longer to digest. There are a number of brands to choose from and most are based on cows' milk, although alternatives are available that are designed for children who require special diets for medical reasons. If you use powdered formula, it is very important to follow the instructions because too much or too little can be harmful. The baby will gradually settle into a routine but until then you will need to respond to his or her hunger just as you would if you were breastfeeding.

One of the main advantages of bottle-feeding is that you and your partner can share the feeding between you, so that you can both use the time when you are feeding to get to know your baby.

Hygiene is very important when you bottle-feed because your baby is not getting protection from the antibodies that he or she would have from breast milk. You will need to take particular care in washing and sterilizing bottles and nipples. There are several ways of sterilizing feeding equipment and it is important to choose the method that best suits your needs.

As well as formula you will need at least six bottles and nipples, with caps, a sterilizing unit or container, a bottle brush, and you may also find that a bottle warmer is useful for the night feeding.

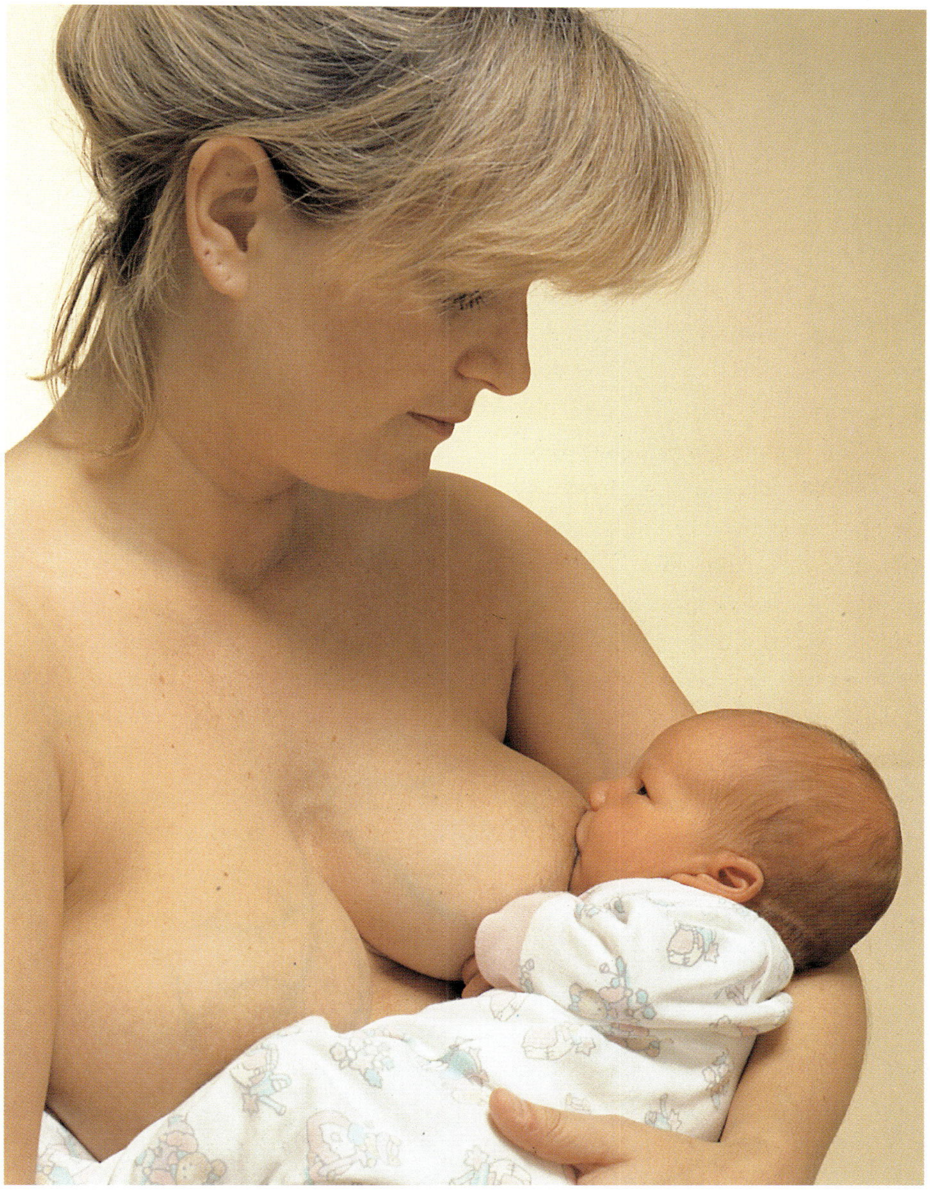

Breastfeeding can help you bond with your baby, and the milk will give her everything she needs, including protection against infection.

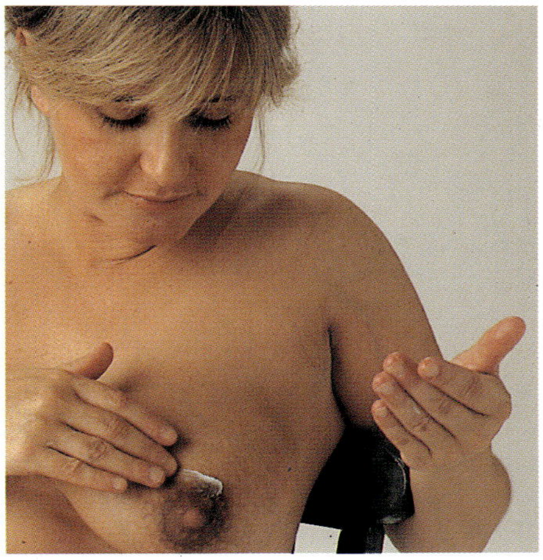

Massaging your nipples in pregnancy will make them more supple for breastfeeding.

Your growing baby

The fetal brain cells continue to develop and become more sophisticated and the bone centers are beginning to harden. The fetus actively practices breathing, inhaling and exhaling amniotic fluid, as more air sacs develop in the lungs. When too much amniotic fluid is swallowed, you may feel a hiccup. The fetus is now about 13½ in long and now weighs around 1¼ lb.

WEEK 26: CHILDBIRTH CLASSES

You should be about to start childbirth classes. You may choose one or more of these. Childbirth classes show you practical techniques such as relaxation, breathing, and postures for labor and birth. The teacher can answer any questions you may have during the last few months of your pregnancy and will be able to give you information on the birth. Your partner will be welcome at most classes and you will find that they are a good way of meeting other pregnant women and sharing mutual anxieties. Childbirth classes also allow you to feel more in control of a process that can otherwise seem rather daunting.

WHAT THE CLASSES TEACH

Today, most childbirth classes teach a series of techniques gleaned from a number of different approaches, including the Lamaze and Bradley methods, though both Lamaze and Bradley practitioners continue to offer courses in their own specific disciplines. Lamaze classes emphasize the teaching of certain positive responses to the stresses of labor and delivery, including the use of panting and patterned breathing; the Bradley method, on the other hand, stresses more natural breathing methods, as well as the efficacy of good diet and regular exercise.

In almost all classes, you will learn about the stages of labor and will be

You and your body

If you are working you need to decide the date when you are going to stop and inform your employers. Though many women continue working virtually up until the delivery is due, others find that time off before the birth is practical and restorative. If you haven't started taking regular exercise you should do so now, because this will help prepare your body for the rigors of labor.

Active birth classes

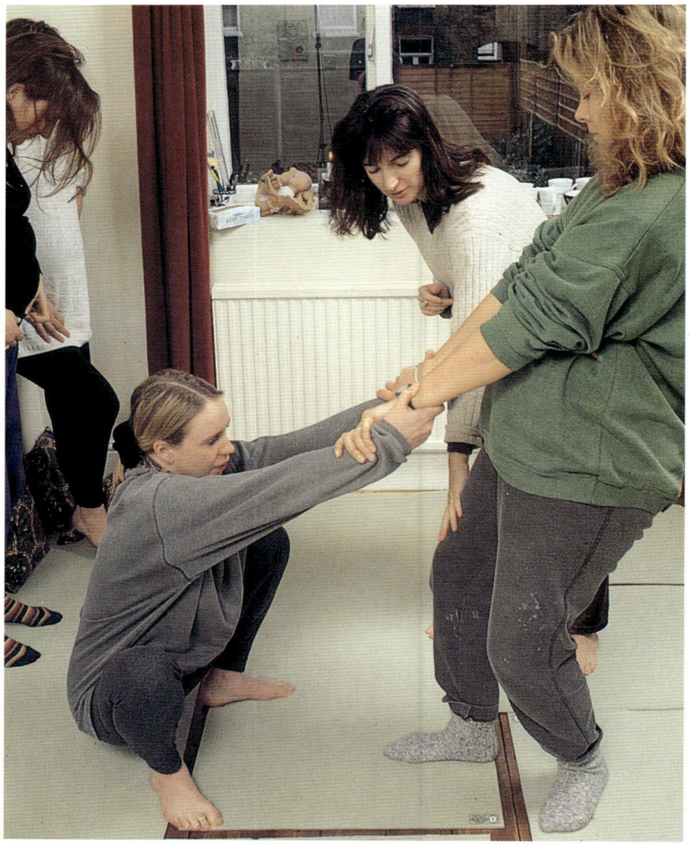

taught appropriate responses in each phase. You will probably learn relaxation techniques to calm you before and during labor, and your partner will almost certainly be expected to act as a full and caring participant during labor. (If your partner is leery of participating, you can usually choose another person to act as your support.)

In addition, most childbirth classes will give you information about the various methods of pain relief that are available, medical and otherwise, and should also arm you with sufficient information so that you can make an educated decision when the time comes.

When choosing a class, speak to your doctor or midwife, as well as to friends who've already gone through the process of childbirth education. If at all possible, make sure that the classes are small and personal. Do ask to sit in on a class before making a final commitment so that you see what is involved.

BREATHING TECHNIQUES

Controlled breathing is important during labor and you need to practice the breathing exercises you will be taught at your classes. In general, breathing needs to be slow and smooth with deep breaths, inhaled through your nose and exhaled through your mouth. A long slow breath at the beginning of each contraction will help oxygenate your blood and this may help relieve any pain caused by the lack of oxygen to the muscles of your uterus. Oxygen is also carried in the blood flowing through the placenta into the umbilical cord, so if you do not get enough, your baby will suffer a shortage too.

During contractions you will be concentrating on each outward breath as this will help you to relax your muscles. It will be important not to over-breathe during the second stage of labor, because this may make you feel dizzy and lightheaded.

If you do find yourself needing to breathe more quickly then you should concentrate on making each breath as light as possible.

Your growing baby

Although still appearing rather scrawny, the fetus is beginning to accumulate fat under the skin. This fat will help regulate body temperature now and after the birth. The fetus is around 13$\frac{3}{4}$ in long and weighs approximately 1$\frac{1}{2}$ lb.

Gentle yoga-based exercises are ideal preparation for labor and help you to get ready physically and emotionally, so that you are in tune with the demands on your body. They should always be done under qualified supervision. Exercises include going down into a squatting position (far left and left) in anticipation of labor; massage, which particularly helps if you've got sciatica (below left), and stretching to ease pressure at the base of the spine (below right).

THE THIRD TRIMESTER

WEEK 27: CHOICES IN CHILDBIRTH

Now that you have entered the third trimester you should start planning the kind of birth that you want. If you are having a hospital birth, you will need to discover what facilities are available and then try to plan the birth around them. Although nowadays hospitals do try to accommodate a mother's wishes, not all are able to offer every type of birth. If you want an active or water birth, you will have to find out whether it is possible to arrange at your hospital. If you are having a home birth then having an active birth is easier to arrange. However, you need to remember that if any complications do occur during labor any decisions that you make now may have to be changed to suit the circumstances.

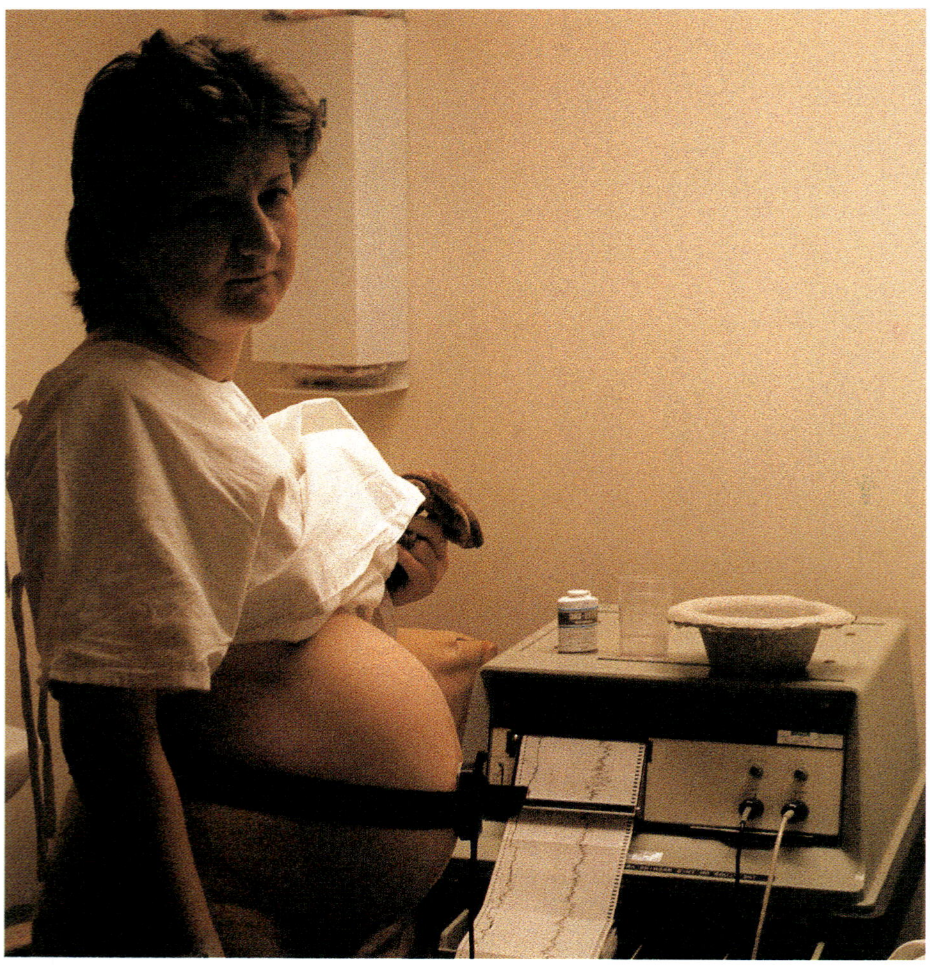

When you give birth in a hospital, special straps might well be put around your belly to attach you to a monitor that checks the strength of your baby's heartbeat.

You and your body

You will be getting noticeably larger and will have put on weight around your chest as well as your breasts. Make sure that you are wearing the correct size of maternity bra. Avoid lying on your back too much because this may make you feel faint, as the enlarged uterus presses directly against blood vessels.

NATURAL CHILDBIRTH

This is when you go through labor and birth without any of the medical procedures that often alter the natural rhythm of labor. Natural childbirth involves the use of breathing and relaxation techniques and sometimes homeopathic remedies.

WATER BIRTH

More popular in Europe than in the U.S., water birth involves spending part of your time in a birth pool, filled with warm water, and giving birth either outside the pool or in the water. The warm water eases contractions, and helps you to relax. Although there is no evidence to prove an increased risk of complications if you have your baby in the water, you should still talk to your doctor before planning to do this.

ACTIVE BIRTH

This means that you are free to move and walk about during labor. Keeping mobile allows the contractions to be more effective. Being in an upright position helps the baby's circulation and encourages the baby to rotate into the best position for

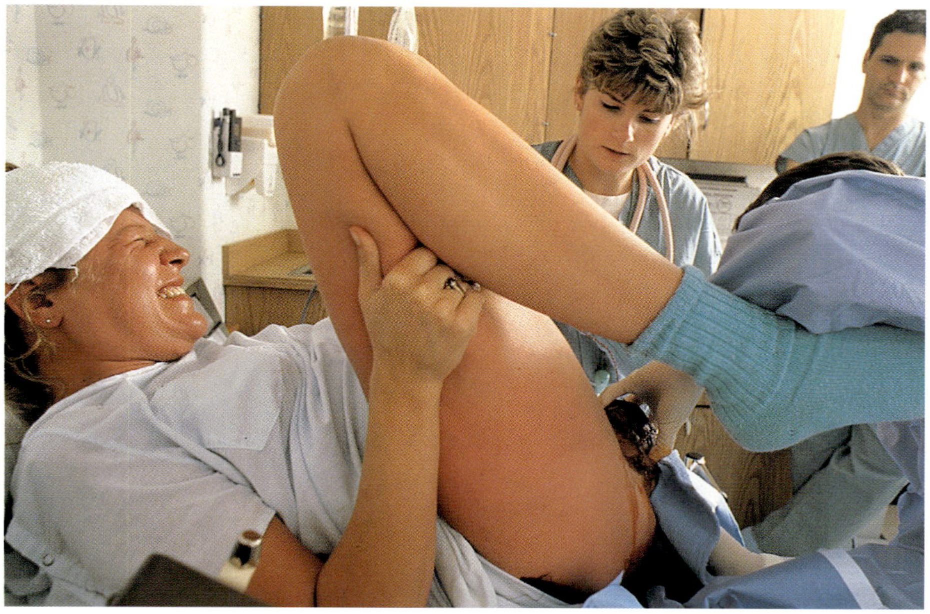

In a natural birth you go through labor without painkillers, using only relaxation methods and maybe homeopathic treatments.

delivery. Gravity aids the baby's descent, and giving birth in a squatting or kneeling position increases the size of the pelvic outlet.

HIGH-TECH BIRTH

Labor is controlled by medical methods such as induction, where labor is started artificially using chemical substances, or the waters are broken manually. Painkilling drugs are used and an epidural or spinal block to deaden pain may be administered. Epidurals, because of their general safety, are also used increasingly during childbirth.

CAESAREAN BIRTH

This is when the baby is delivered through an incision that is made through the wall of the abdomen into the uterus. It is done under a general anaesthetic, or sometimes with an epidural or spinal block. If an epidural or spinal block is used you will be awake during the delivery, although a screen is placed across your body so that you don't actually see what is happening. You will be given your baby to hold as soon as it is born. After the birth, the incisions are stitched and you will be kept in hospital for about five days. A Caesarean may be chosen if the reasons that make it necessary are evident before labor begins. This is known as an elective Caesarean. If it is decided on after labor has started, it is known as an emergency Caesarean. Reasons for a Caesarean include abnormal presentation of the baby (that is, not head-first toward the cervix), fetal distress where the baby suffers from lack of oxygen, and a high blood pressure condition in the mother.

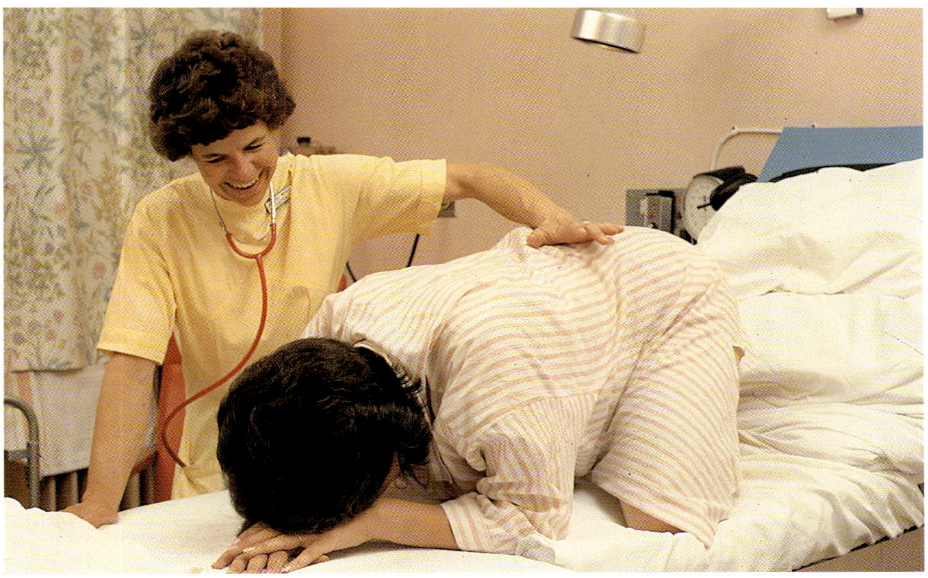

An active birth involves moving around in labor and adapting different positions that will help your baby's descent.

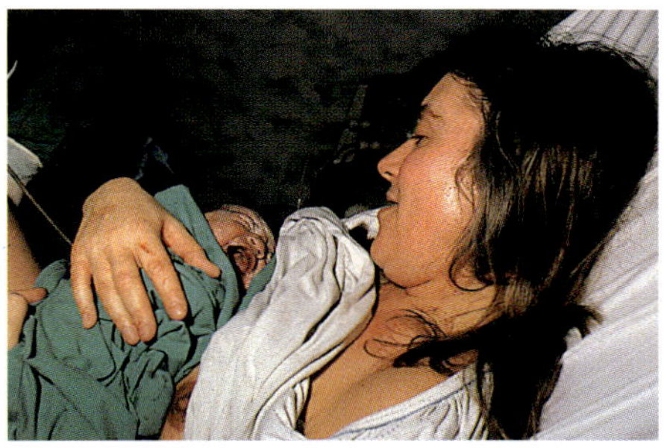

When you hold your newborn baby in your arms all the hard work of labor will seem worthwhile.

Your growing baby

The fetus's eyes are open and it will be able to see light through the skin of your abdomen. It will have started to practice sucking and may even be able to suck its thumb or fist. The fetus is now about 14¼ in long and weighs about 1¾ lb.

WEEK 28: THE BIRTHPLAN

You and your body

Your breasts are producing colostrum, the fluid which precedes breast milk. If your breasts are leaking put breast pads or folded tissues inside your bra. If you have a prenatal appointment you will probably have a second blood test to check for anemia. If you are anemic, iron supplements may be offered.

You may find it useful to draw up a birthplan – a written set of instructions for your doctor or midwife outlining what procedures you prefer – and which you would like to avoid. Even if there are still things concerning labor or the birth about which you are undecided, writing out a plan will help you focus on the type of birth you want. It will also give you the opportunity to discuss the birth in detail with your partner.

When drawing up your birthplan it is important to remember that there is no right or wrong way to give birth. Your plan should reflect what you feel is right for you, while taking into account your medical history as well as the facilities available at the place where you are going to have your baby.

A birthplan is a guide to how you would like things to be, but in the event of a problem this ideal may become totally impractical so you will need to be flexible. Once you have finalized your birthplan ask for a copy to be kept with your notes so that the doctor or midwife who attend you during labor have it on hand when necessary. You should also keep a copy for yourself so that your birth partner can refer to it when he wants to.

BIRTH PARTNER

Although your partner will be encouraged to be with you during labor, you may prefer to have another woman as your actual birth partner, especially if your partner is worried that he may not be able to cope

Write a birthplan with your choices.

Birthplan checklist

The following questions will help you prepare your own birthplan.

- Whom do you wish to have with you during labor – your partner, your mother, a friend? You can choose more than one birth partner.
- Can your birth partner remain with you if you have to have a Caesarean or forceps delivery?
- Do you want to be free to move around during labor, or would you rather be constantly monitored while staying in bed?
- Are there special facilities such as a birthing pool or bean bags available to you?
- Is there any special position you want to use for the birth?
- Do you wish to wear your own clothes during labor and the birth?
- Would you like music, soft lighting, massage or other therapies to help you cope with getting through labor?
- How do you feel about pain relief? If you want to manage without any, you will need to make sure that everyone knows. If you want pain relief which sort do you want?
- Are you prepared to have an episiotomy if it is required, or would you rather tear naturally?
- Do you want your baby placed straight onto your abdomen or do you want him or her cleaned up first?
- Are you going to breast-feed? If so, do you want to put your baby to the breast immediately?
- Do you want an injection to help deliver the placenta or would you prefer to wait for it to be delivered naturally after the birth?
- How soon after the birth would you like to go home, assuming that there are no complications?

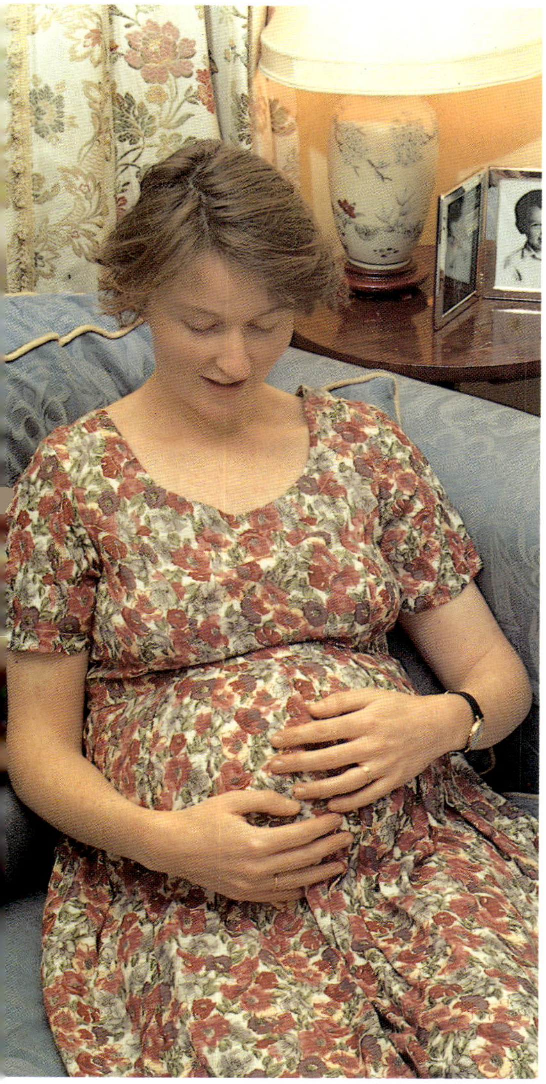

Once you've made your birthplan and put your feelings about your baby's birth in writing, you will feel happier.

with seeing you in pain. Whatever you finally decide, make sure that you talk about it together so that there are no misunderstandings later and so that you don't get upset about the final choice.

Your growing baby

Now fully formed, the fetus would be viable if it were born at 28 weeks, although the body systems are still very immature. The heart is beating at a rate of around 150 beats a minute. The fetus weighs around 2 lb.

If your partner is worried about being with you during a long or painful labor, talk it through with him and make your feelings known if you're counting on his support.

WEEK 29: SPECIAL CARE

You and your body

You will probably be able to feel the fetus's buttocks and feet as it moves around. The fetus will be putting pressure on your stomach and diaphragm now and you will need to sit down and rest more often.

If you suffer from a medical condition or blood disorder your pregnancy will require careful managing. Your doctor will need to monitor your progress and you may have to have special prenatal checks. If there is a possible problem, you may be offered another ultrasound during the last trimester, which will clearly show the fetus's breathing movements, how it is lying, and the position of the placenta.

Anemia is caused by an abnormally low level of iron in your red blood cells and is treated with iron supplements. You can build up your body's store of iron by eating a diet which includes red meat, whole grains, dark green leafy vegetables, nuts, and legumes. Liver is not recommended because of the high levels of vitamin A, which could be toxic. A second blood test is done in late pregnancy to check for anemia.

Kidney infection is usually caused by bacterial infection and you should contact your doctor if you think you have a kidney infection. Symptoms are pain, frequent urination accompanied by a burning sensation, and occasionally blood in the urine. Other symptoms you may experience include back pain, high fever, chills, nausea, and vomiting.

Placenta previa is a rare condition which usually occurs when a woman has had more than one child. The placenta is situated low in the uterus so that it blocks, or partially blocks, the cervix. The pressure of the fetus on the placenta may cause painless bleeding any time after 28 weeks. If this happens, you may have to stay in the hospital until after your baby is born. If the obstruction is particularly severe, your baby may need to be delivered by Caesarean.

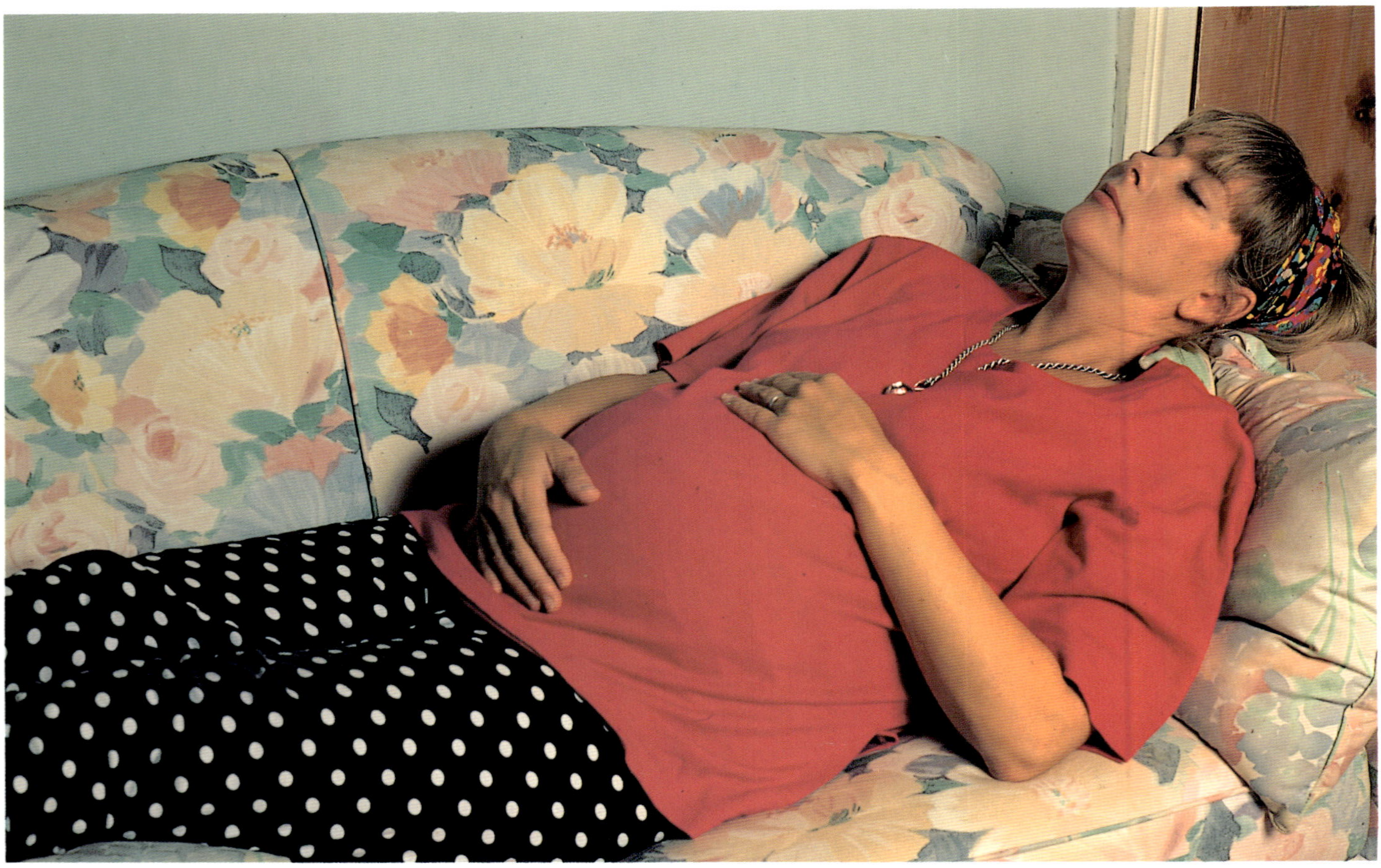

As your baby starts to put pressure on your stomach, you'll need to lie down more often to rest.

If the weather is pleasant, you might well prefer to take your regular rests in the garden, but remember to support your legs.

Abruptio placentae is when part of the placenta comes away from the wall of the uterus causing some abdominal pain and bleeding. You should call the doctor immediately. The fetus could be at risk if a large part of the placenta has separated, because it will be deprived of necessary oxygen and nutrients. Sometimes a blood transfusion is necessary and in late pregnancy the baby may be delivered by Caesarean. If only a small part of the placenta has separated, you will need to have complete bedrest until the bleeding has stopped.

Placental insufficiency occurs when the placenta doesn't function efficiently and the fetus grows more slowly than normal because of lack of nourishment. If this happens, you will be told to rest so that the blood flow from the placenta to the fetus can improve. A urine test will also be taken to see whether the health of the fetus is being affected and whether induction is going to be necessary for the birth.

Your growing baby

The fetus is filling almost all the space in your uterus and its head is now more or less in proportion with the rest of the body. The eyebrows and eyelashes are now fully grown and the fetus has quite a lot of hair which is still growing. The eyes, which can now open and close, are beginning to be able to focus properly. The fetus weighs around 2¼ lb and is about 15 in long.

WEEK 30: TRAVEL/BACKACHE

There is no reason why you shouldn't travel during pregnancy, but during the later stages you should check with your doctor if you are going abroad. Airlines may not be willing to take you once you are past 28 weeks because of the risk of a premature labor occurring.

If you want to fly you will need to check with the airline before you buy a ticket; the airline may insist on a medical certificate stating that it is safe for you to travel. If you wish to visit a country where immunization is required, you will have to get medical advice because some vaccines should be avoided completely during pregnancy.

You will probably want to avoid long car journeys toward the end of pregnancy because you may find them uncomfortable. When traveling by car it is important to wear your seatbelt so that it fits neatly across your thighs and above your abdomen, but not across the middle. If the belt was worn across your body it could possibly cause damage to your baby if you were involved in a car accident.

BACKACHE

This can be particularly troublesome during the last months of pregnancy. Hormones have softened your ligaments and the additional weight you are carrying inevitably puts a strain on your stomach muscles, which in turn puts strain on your back muscles. If the backache you are suffering is particularly severe, always check with your doctor because backache can indicate the presence of a kidney infection.

Don't fasten your seatbelt over your belly as your baby could be damaged in a accident.

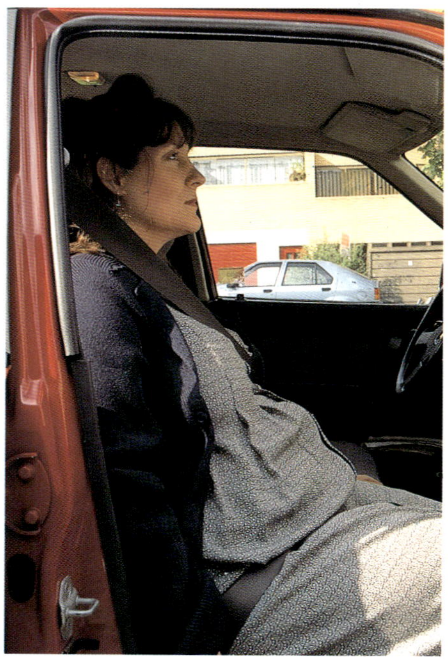

Fasten your seatbelt under your belly and across your thighs to protect your baby.

You and your body

You will feel larger and clumsier now and your movements will be slower. It is important to try to maintain good posture to prevent backache. You may have problems sleeping and become a bit breathless if you walk too fast or climb stairs.

Ease upper backache by lying flat on a firm surface with pillows under your head and knees. Lower backache can be helped by kneeling on all fours, with your back straight and your hands and knees well apart, then dropping your head and arching your back. Repeat this exercise several times.

You can help to avoid backache by wearing low-heeled shoes and trying not to hollow your back when you are standing. When you sit down, put a cushion in the small of your back; when you get out of a chair, push yourself right to the edge before attempting to stand up.

A firm mattress will help when you are lying down; when you get up from the lying position, roll over onto your side and then push yourself slowly up. If you have to bend down, always bend your body from the knees and then squat down to pick up anything from the floor.

Your growing baby

The fetus is beginning to move about less vigorously now because it has less space to move around in the uterus. To get comfortable it is likely to adopt a curled-up position with arms and legs crossed. The fetus is now about 15½ in long and weighs around 2½ lb.

Bending in pregnancy

1 *In later pregnancy particularly, bend your knees, not from the waist, and pick up the object when you are squatting.*

2 *As you get up from the squatting position, keep your back straight and lift up the object at arm's length.*

3 *As you gradually become upright, straighten your bent knees without making any jerky movements.*

How to relieve backache

1 *To relieve painful aches in your lower back in pregnancy, try this exercise. Kneel down on the floor on all fours with your back straight, your head facing down, and your hands and knees spaced well apart.*

2 *Drop your head right down and arch your back to stretch out the painful muscles, hold for several seconds, then release, raising your head again. Repeat the exercise several times for the best relief.*

WEEK 31: DEALING WITH DISCOMFORT

The fetus is getting quite big and will be putting pressure on your diaphragm, which may mean that you are now finding it more difficult to breathe. This breathlessness should pass once the fetus's head drops into the pelvis and becomes engaged in a few weeks' time. Try sitting and standing as straight as possible, and put some extra pillows behind your shoulders when you are in bed.

You are likely to need a larger size bra toward the end of pregnancy and the one that you buy now should fit you after the baby is born. If you are intending to breastfeed, buy a front-opening nursing bra that will be suitable to wear both now and after the birth.

Choose a bra with wide adjustable straps and fastenings and that has a broad supportive band under the cups. Make sure that the cups fit comfortably and do not gape under the arms. Buy one made from cotton or a cotton blend that will be more comfortable to wear, and allow your skin to breathe properly, particularly in hot weather.

Braxton Hicks contractions

During pregnancy you will experience contractions that may be uncomfortable but are not usually painful. These are known as Braxton Hicks contractions, which tighten the muscles of the uterus about every 20 minutes throughout pregnancy, although you have probably not been aware of them during the early months. In the last weeks of pregnancy these contractions become more noticeable as they begin to prepare the uterus for labor by drawing up the cervix and making it thinner. When you have these

You and your body

Breathlessness may be more of a problem now, especially if you overdo things. Try to get as much rest as possible and slow down any exercise regimen to a pace that suits you. If your breasts feel uncomfortable when you go to bed, wear a maternity or specially designed sleep bra at night.

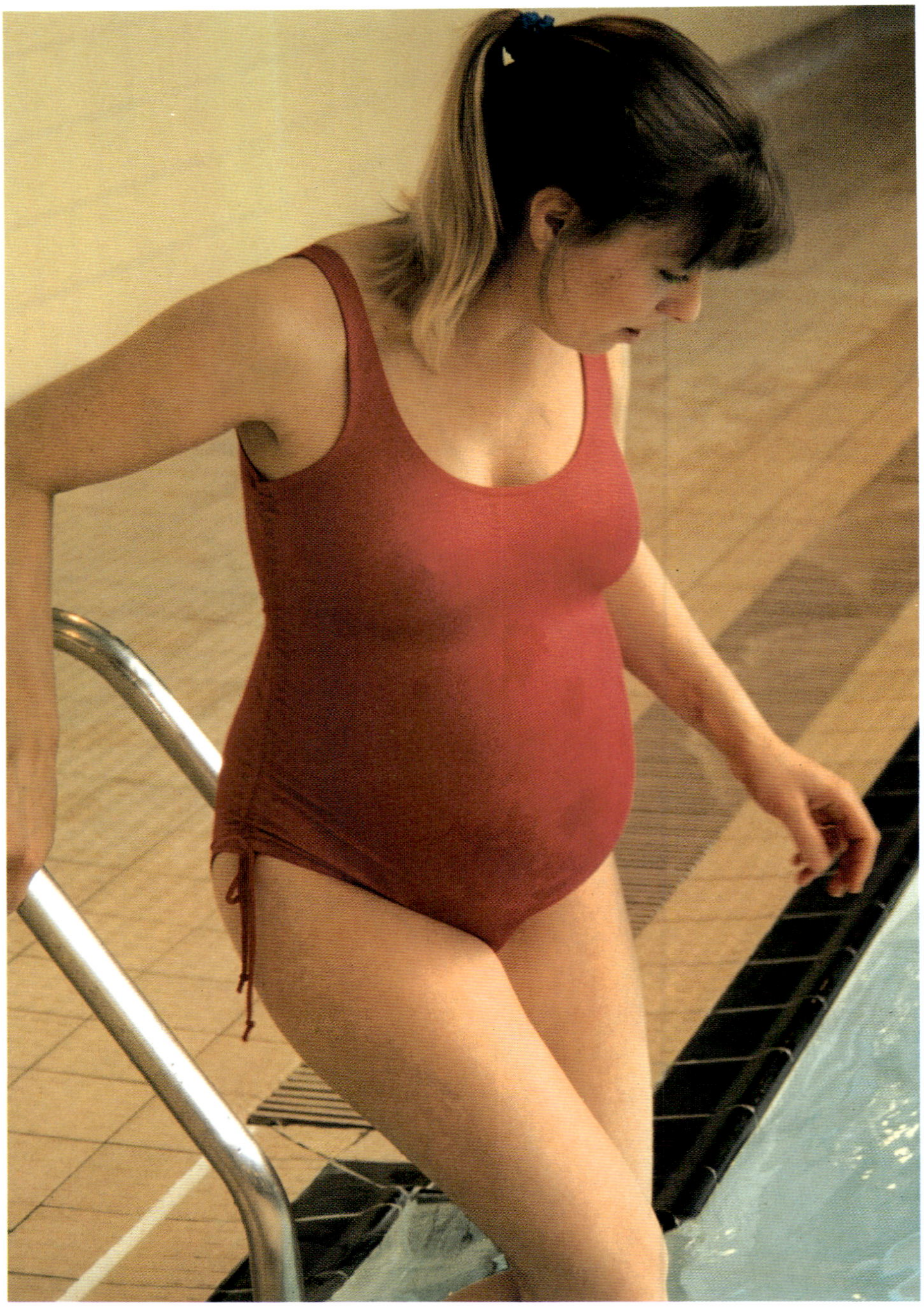

Exercise like swimming, where you are supported in the water, will keep you fit in late pregnancy. It will also relieve backache as the swimming motion will stretch the back muscles.

contractions, practice your breathing techniques for labor.

Kick counts

You can check on your baby's well-being by keeping a count of the fetal movements. If there is any concern about the fetus's development you may be asked to keep a kick chart recording the first 10 movements each day. For your own peace of mind you should be aware of these movements so that if for any reason they become less frequent, or even stop altogether, you will notice immediately. If you are ever concerned about lack of movement, seek some medical advice immediately because it could indicate some trouble with the fetus.

As your pregnancy progresses and the fetus gets bigger it has less room to maneuver, so movements will be more noticeable, but less frequent. By the end of your pregnancy the fetus will probably move between 10 and 12 times in a 12-hour period.

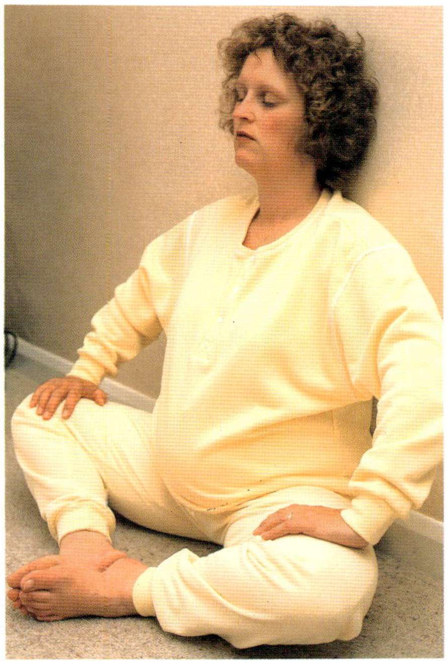

Try sitting in a yoga position with your back straight to alleviate the pressure your baby is putting on your diaphragm.

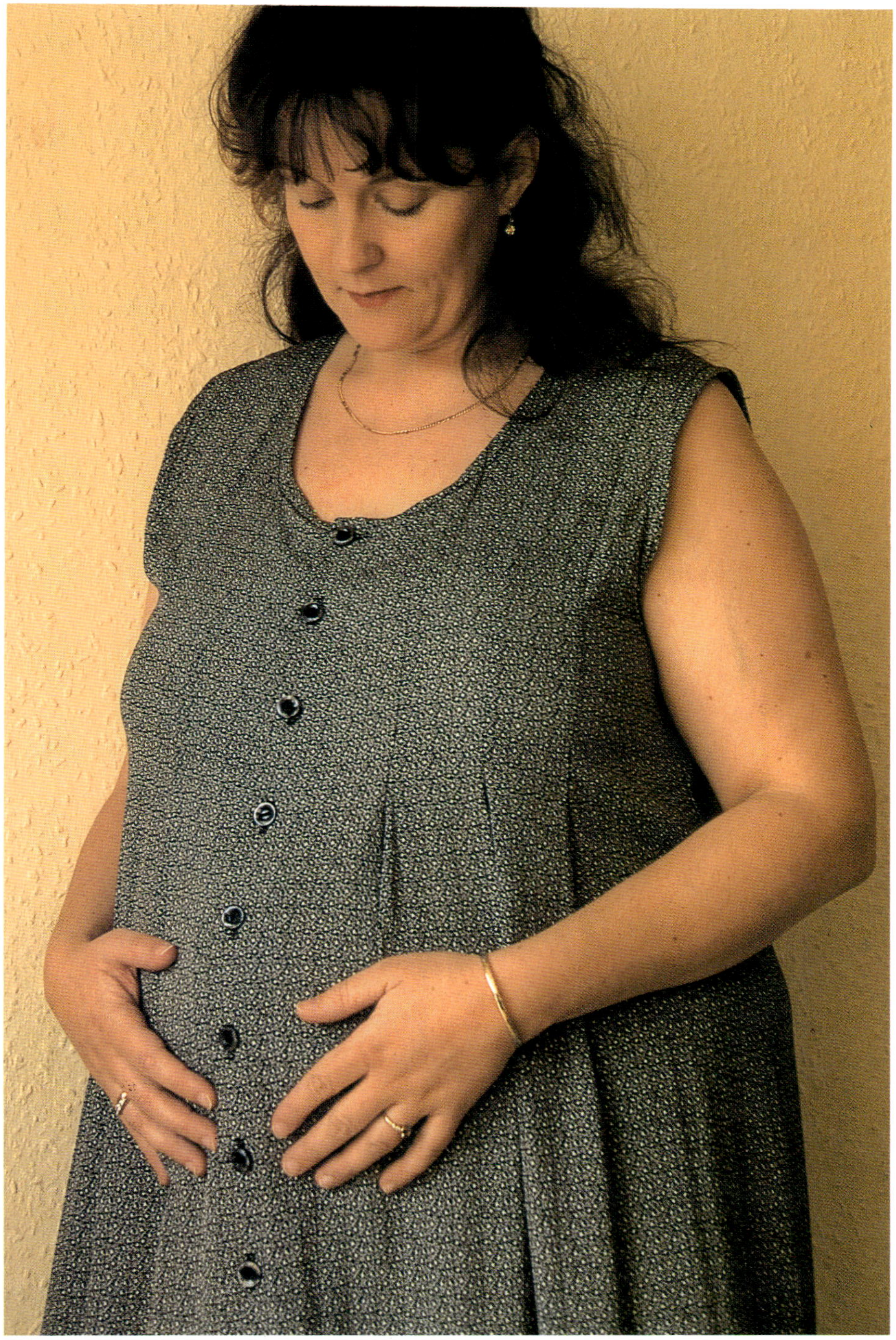

Keep a kick count of your baby's movements on a chart, so that you can monitor any noticeable changes and seek medical help if you feel it is necessary.

Your growing baby

The organs are almost completely developed, apart from the lungs which are still not fully mature. The brain is still growing and the nerve cells and connections are now working. A protective sheath is developing around the nerve fibers so that messages travel faster, enabling the fetus to learn more. It can feel pain and will move if prodded and you can feel it jump at loud noises. The fetus is around 15¾ in long and weighs about 3 lb.

WEEK 32: POSITIONS FOR LABOR

It is a good idea to practice some of the positions that will help you through the different stages of labor. During the first stage you should try to stay upright and keep active. Being upright will make your contractions stronger and more efficient. It will also allow gravity to keep the baby's head pressed down, which will help your cervix to dilate faster so that labor is speeded up. Remaining active will give you more control over labor so that you should feel less pain. If you are lying down, your uterus presses on the large blood vessels running down your back and this can reduce the blood flow through the placenta to and from the baby. If you feel you want to lie down during labor, try to position yourself on your side rather than on your back.

COPING WITH CONTRACTIONS

You should aim to give the fetus as much room as possible in your pelvis and the best way to achieve this is by keeping your knees well apart and leaning forward so that the uterus tilts away from your spine. During the first-stage contractions it may help to lean against your partner, or if you prefer you can kneel down resting your arms and head on a cushion on the seat of a chair. If you find being upright tiring, try kneeling on all fours. This allows you to keep the weight of the fetus off your lower back. By the time your contractions are coming every few minutes you may want to adopt a squatting position, or you could try kneeling forward onto a pile of cushions or a bean bag with your legs wide apart. It may help if your partner massages your back while you are in this position.

When you reach the second stage you'll want to find a comfortable position for the birth. If you lie on your back you will literally have to push the baby uphill. If you remain upright your abdominal muscles will work more efficiently as you bear down, and gravity will help the baby out. Try squatting, supported on both sides, or with your partner supporting you from behind, so that your pelvis is at its widest and you have control over the pelvic floor

You and your body

If you work, you may have left by now or will have a date when you are going to leave. Enjoy the last weeks of your pregnancy and spend time singing and talking to your baby. You may find the fetal movements uncomfortable now that it is so much bigger. Occasionally, you may feel its feet getting stuck under your ribs.

Labor positions

1 *Relax on all fours by flopping forward onto a pile of cushions or a bean bag to give the fetus as much room as possible in the pelvis. Your partner can help by massaging your back.*

2 *Take the weight of the baby off your spine by kneeling on the floor on all fours with your arms and legs wide apart. Keep the small of your back flat and not hollowed.*

Your growing baby

The fetus is now very energetic and it will have periods of extreme activity, and you will feel it twisting and turning. As it continues to grow it will have less and less room to move in, so it will soon settle, probably in the head-down position, ready for birth. The fetus measures about 16 in and weighs about 3½ lb.

which you will need to relax. Kneeling with your legs wide apart and supported on both sides is another good position for pushing.

Once you have tried these positions, experiment with others that you feel may be right for you during labor. Try them on the floor, on the bed, leaning on or against furniture, or using your partner for support. This way, when you are in labor, you will already know how to get into positions that are comfortable for you and that will help you cope with contractions.

Partner support

1 *Practice using your partner for support during labor by leaning back against him, allowing him to take your weight.*

2 *Stand with feet well apart and lean on your partner, putting your head on your arms to ease pressure on your uterus.*

3 *Kneel on all fours with your forearms on the floor and your knees spread wide so that your abdomen is hanging between them. It can help to rock backward and forward in this position.*

4 *In this squatting position, your pelvis is wide open and the baby's head is pressed down. You may find that it helps to place your hands on the floor to give yourself some support.*

WEEK 33: EMOTIONS IN LATE PREGNANCY

It is not just your body that is going through great changes while you are pregnant. Your whole way of life is changing and this can lead to conflicting emotions, especially during the last few months. You may wonder how you are going to cope with all the new responsibilities and be concerned about your baby – whether it will be born perfect in every way. Vivid dreams are common at this time and can be upsetting, especially if they are about the birth or babies. You may even feel occasionally that the whole thing has been a ghastly mistake and that you want to go back to the way things were before you became pregnant. Don't worry, all these feelings are quite normal.

It helps to talk about your fears and concerns, either to your partner or to a close friend who has had similar feelings. Childbirth classes are also a good place to discuss these worries, especially as you will be with other women who are experiencing the same emotions. If you find that talking about it doesn't help and that anxiety is taking over your life, discuss how you feel with your midwife or doctor.

YOUR PARTNER

It is easy to forget that an expectant father is also going through emotional changes as he comes to terms with impending parenthood. He doesn't have any outward sign of the change that is about to occur in his life, but that doesn't mean he isn't feeling the same concerns as you. He also has additional worries about you and how you will cope during labor; he may even secretly fear for your safety during the birth. If he is now solely responsible for providing financially for you and the baby he may be feeling considerable stress.

Make time to talk to each other about your feelings and try to ensure that these last weeks before the birth are special for you both. Share the preparation for the birth so that each of you is involved in what is going to happen. Plan some treats where you can be alone together, such as a special dinner at a favorite restaurant, a trip to the theater, or a weekend away at a hotel. By making time for yourselves you are less likely to have misunderstandings that could lead to hurt and disappointment.

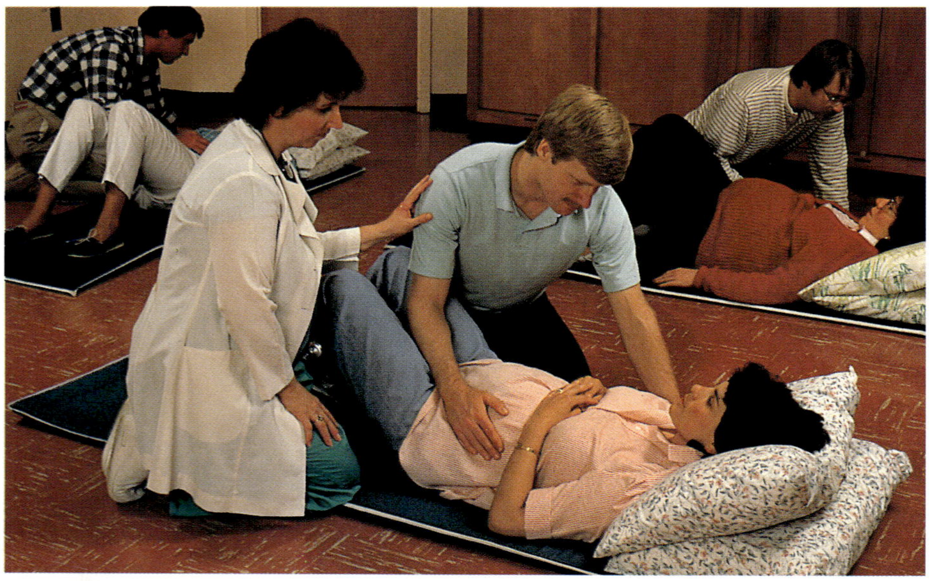

At childbirth classes you learn what to expect in labor and the different positions you can adopt. Your partner is usually expected to come with you and find out how he can help.

You and your body

Your weight gain should have slowed down. If it hasn't and you are still gaining more than 2¼ lb a week, you should check with your doctor that everything is all right.

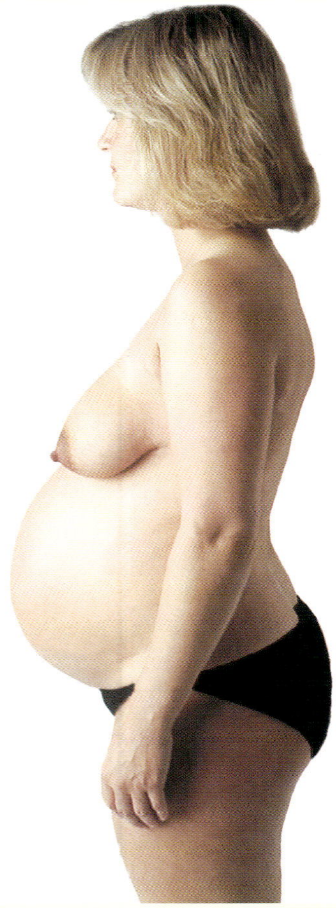

Your growing baby

The fingernails are fully formed although the toenails are not quite so advanced. The vernix covering the skin has become thicker. The lungs are almost fully developed and the fetus will be practicing breathing in preparation for the birth. It measures around 16½ in and now weighs about 4 lb.

Let an older child feel your belly, and talk to him or her about their new brother or sister, so they can get used to the idea of a new family member.

OTHER CHILDREN

If you have other children you may have told them about the new baby early on in your pregnancy. Very young children will need to have it explained to them over and over again, because the concept of a new baby is hard for them to grasp. Older children will probably be very excited and will enjoy being involved in any preparations you are making for their brother or sister.

How children react once the baby has arrived depends a lot on their age and personality, as well as their relationship with you. A preschool child may react by misbehaving for a period in an attempt to get your attention. A toddler, who has recently been potty trained, may start wetting or soiling him- or herself again. Both age groups may start waking at night. Use common sense and tact to minimize any problems. Talk to your children about the new baby, encourage their help and involvement when he or she has been born but always make sure that they have time with you on their own.

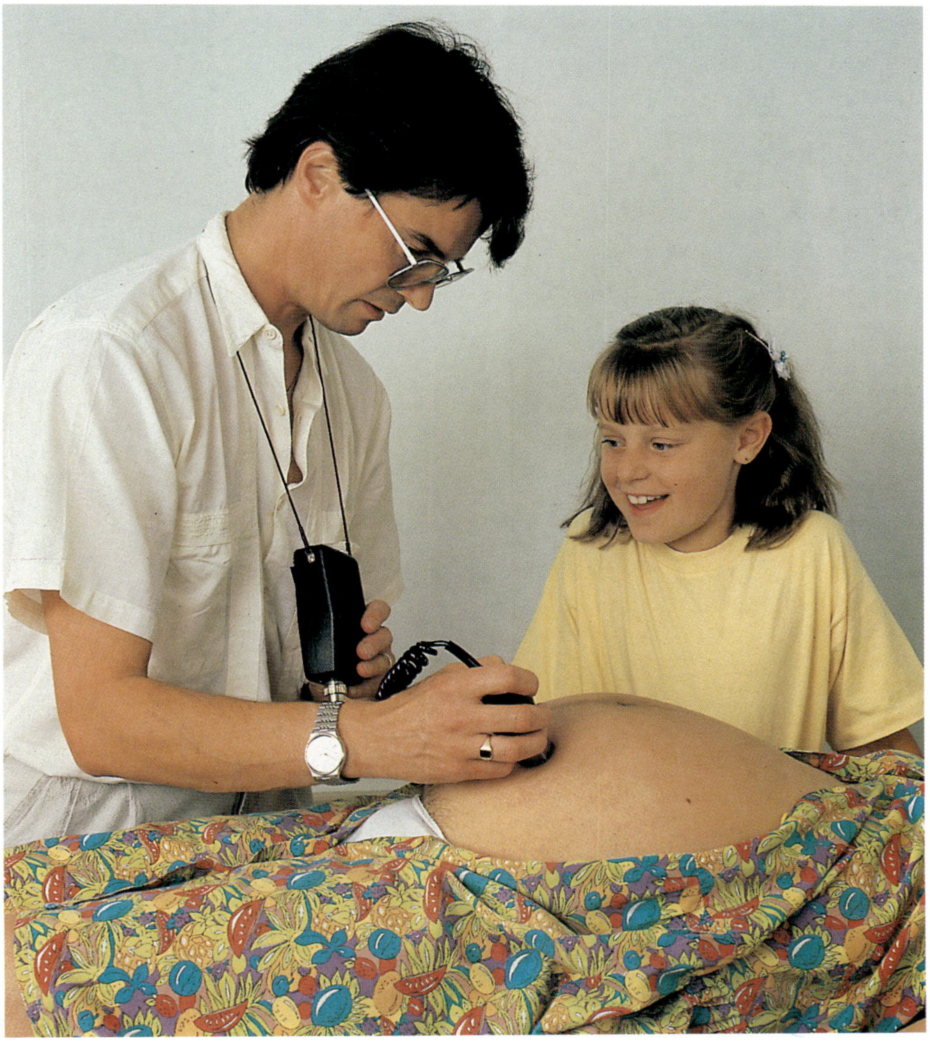

When your doctor checks your baby's heartbeat, let any older children be present if they are interested.

WEEK 34: OLDER FIRST-TIME MOTHERS

If you are 35 or over, you will probably have been offered an amniocentesis because of the higher risk of fetal abnormality. The amniotic fluid will have been screened for a number of chromosomal disorders, which include Down's syndrome and spina bifida. Of course, you are not obliged to have this test, but many mothers prefer to do so because they find it reassuring.

It is important that you attend all your prenatal checkups so that a close check can be kept on you and the unborn baby all through the pregnancy. The risk to the baby during labor and birth does increase somewhat with rising maternal age, but many different factors affect labor, including the general health of the mother during pregnancy. Although nearly 70 percent of women over 30 have normal deliveries, there is a slightly greater risk of complications during labor for women who are over the age of 35. On the other hand, because older mothers tend to have a higher socioeconomic status and more education than younger mothers, their prenatal care is generally better.

BIRTH AND THE OLDER MOTHER

Most older women go full term, and if you are between 30 and 34 there is no reason why you shouldn't have a natural birth. If you are 35 or over, or if there is a suggestion that your baby may be small, you may have to have continuous monitoring. This may also be necessary if there is a likelihood of a prolonged labor, or if the waters, when they break, show some sign of staining. This means that you will be unable to move around freely. But this is a very small price to pay for having a normal, healthy baby.

You and your body

Your blood pressure may be slightly elevated and you will probably be told to take things easy. Swelling of the hands and feet could also be a problem so get as much rest as possible, preferably with your feet up.

Seeing her baby on an ultrasound scan can be very reassuring for an older mother.

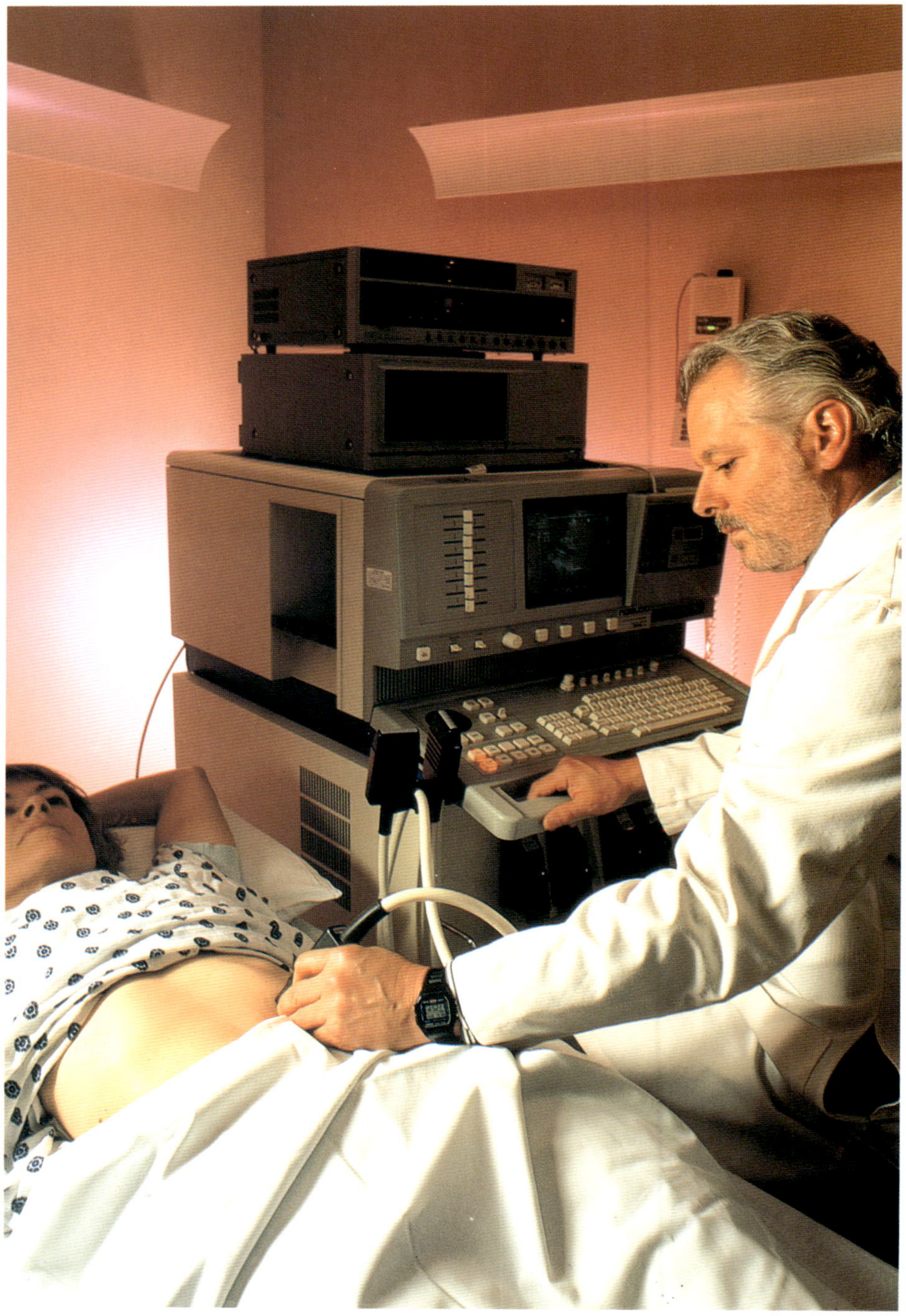

Babies born to older mothers have a slightly greater chance of being born preterm. This is sometimes because of the failure of the placenta, which means the baby is no longer getting sufficient oxygen and nourishment. If this happens you may have to have a labor induced delivery, or you may be offered a Caesarean section.

Your growing baby

The weight gain continues to increase. The eyes respond to bright lights and the fetus will start to practice blinking; eyebrows and eyelashes are fully developed. A boy's testicles will have descended into the groin. The fetus is 17 in long and now weighs about 4½ lb.

Right: As time progresses, you will find you need more rest with your back supported.

Below: The doctor will talk about your baby and may give you a printout of your scan.

WEEK 35: FINAL PREPARATIONS

You and your body

Discuss any worries you may have about labor and birth with your doctor or midwife. You will be feeling tired and even a little fed up, so try to get as much rest as you can. Pay special attention to your diet: you will be needing another 200 calories a day during these last weeks. Some practical planning now can save time and forestall anxiety at the time of labor and delivery.

Even though your baby is not due for some weeks, you should be ready in case he or she decides to put in an early appearance. Check the baby's room and make sure all the sheets and blankets have been washed and aired. Sort out all the baby clothes and put the ones you will want immediately after the birth in your hospital bag.

It's a good idea to stock up on nonperishable goods and to fill the freezer. This will save you from having to do a lot of shopping over the next few weeks and will allow you more time with the baby when you first come home.

Make sure you know where your partner is going to be over the next few weeks; if he is out and about you may want to consider renting a beeper so that you can keep in constant touch. Keep your car filled with gas and make sure that you both know the quickest route to the hospital. Have a list of emergency numbers, including a local taxi firm, beside the telephone.

THE HOSPITAL

Pack what you want to take to the hospital several weeks before the delivery date; keep the bag where you can easily get it when the time comes. Remember that there are three separate aspects to consider: labor, your hospital stay, and going-home clothes for you and the baby.

You should bring any personal items that will make life more comfortable for you during labor. Include anything from a cassette player and your favorite music to a washcloth and massage oils. You might want to pack a deck of cards or even a bottle of champagne (check with your doctor on this). Leave some room for last-minute items such as an ice pack for backache and even a snack and drink for your partner. Don't forget to put your birthplan right at the top so that you can give this to the doctor when you arrive at the hospital. It is

It is a good idea to buy vegetables and other food that can be cooked and frozen in preparation for when you return from the hospital.

You might need to get to the hospital quickly, so have your bag packed and keep a local taxi number close by.

It is sensible to pack a small bag for your brief stay in the hospital well in advance in case you have to leave in a rush. Don't forget some clothes for your new baby to wear.

sensible to pack things for labor separately, since you will want to be able to get to them quickly.

How much you pack for the hospital depends on your planned length of stay after the birth. The hospital may issue a list of the items that you will need to bring with you. But if it doesn't, ask your doctor or midwife whether you need to take in baby clothes and diapers, or contact the maternity unit direct. If aren't too tired, you might want to write cards to your friends and relatives announcing your baby's arrival, so remember to include birth announcement cards, your address book, and stamps. You may also want to bring along a camera or possibly a camcorder to take photographs or a film of your baby.

You will need clothes for you and the baby when it's time for you to return home. It is sensible to pack a small bag now with all the items you think you'll want for your return journey; you can either bring it with you or your partner can bring it later. Remember that although you will feel considerably slimmer than you were before the birth, it takes quite a while before you get your figure back, so your going-home outfit will still need to be loose and comfortable to wear.

Your growing baby

The fetus is putting on weight each day and now fills most of the uterus, so you may find it uncomfortable when it starts to move around. The fetus now does body rolls rather than the more energetic movements it was able to make when it was smaller. It is now about 17½ in long and weighs around 5 lb.

WEEK 36: DISCOMFORTS IN LATE PREGNANCY

You and your body

You will be able to feel the top of your uterus just below your breastbone. This can make breathing uncomfortable and you may suffer from pain in your ribcage. Your prenatal checks will be weekly from now on.

As you find getting around more difficult and everything generally more of an effort, you may become irritable over the smallest things. You will be impatient for your baby to arrive, and concern about the impending birth and worries about how you will cope with being a parent can make you short-tempered, especially with your partner. Tell him how you are feeling so that he understands why you are being so irritable and perhaps not giving him as much attention as usual.

Aches or pains around your pubic area, in your groin, or down the inside of your legs can be caused by your baby's head pressing on the nerves, or by your pelvic joints beginning to soften in preparation for labor. Pain under your ribs is caused by the expanding uterus pushing the ribs up. These aches and pains are not serious, but they can be quite uncomfortable. Sitting or standing as straight as you can, or stretching upward, will help ease most of these discomforts, although you may find lying down better for relief of pelvic pain. If you get severe pain in your abdomen, or if you suffer any abdominal pain that is also accompanied by vaginal bleeding, you must get in touch with your doctor at once.

It is quite common to suffer from heartburn and nausea toward the end of pregnancy. This is caused by the enlarged uterus pressing on your stomach. It often helps to eat small

Soaking in a warm bath can help to relieve any aches and pains you are suffering.

meals at frequent intervals, rather than two or three big meals a day.

PRENATAL CHECK-UP

An internal examination may be carried out to check the size of your pelvis. If there is any concern about the size of your pelvis in relation to your baby's size, or there is some other reason for the baby's delivery not being straightforward, a Caesarean may be discussed. If this is thought to be necessary, the doctor at the hospital where the delivery is to take place will explain the medical procedures that will be used.

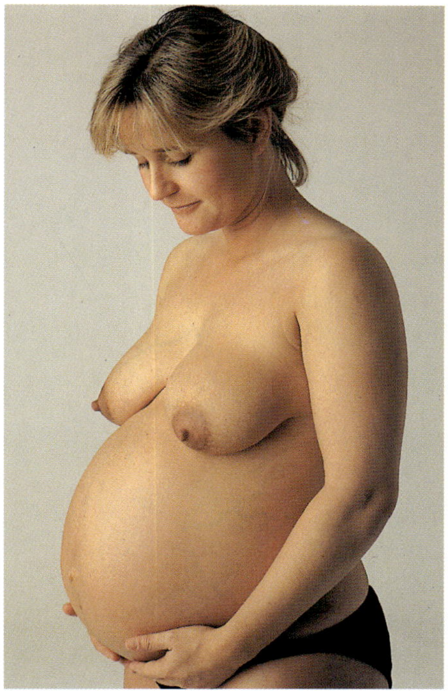

As your baby increases in size, you may begin to find breathing uncomfortable and get some pain in your ribcage.

Your growing baby

The nervous system is maturing and the fetus is getting ready for birth by starting to practise breathing movements, sucking, and swallowing. It is now about 18¼ in long and weighs around 5½ lb.

In this late stage of pregnancy you will probably be able to feel the top of your uterus which is now positioned just below your breastbone.

WEEK 37: AS BIRTH APPROACHES

Between weeks 36 and 38 the baby's head is likely to "engage." This is when it settles downward, deep in your pelvis ready for the birth. You should feel some relief from the pressure in your abdomen when this happens which is why it is sometimes referred to as "lightening." You will start to feel less breathless now because the baby is no longer putting any pressure on your diaphragm and your lungs.

If this is not your first baby, but your second or third child, the head may not engage until you actually go into labor.

This is probably the last time for a while that you will have time to yourself, so make the most of it and rest often.

Your growing baby

The lanugo, the fine hair that covers the fetus's body, is beginning to wear off. The fetus has started to produce a hormone called cortisone which will help the lungs to become fully matured so that they are ready to cope with breathing once it is born. The fetus will be practising breathing although there isn't any air in its lungs yet. The fetus is now about 18½ in long and weighs around 6 lb.

PREMATURE AND TWIN BIRTHS

If the baby is born before 37 weeks it will be described as being preterm or premature. Most premature babies are cared for either in the regular nursery or in a neonatal intensive care unit. Babies are given expert care and attention in these facilities,

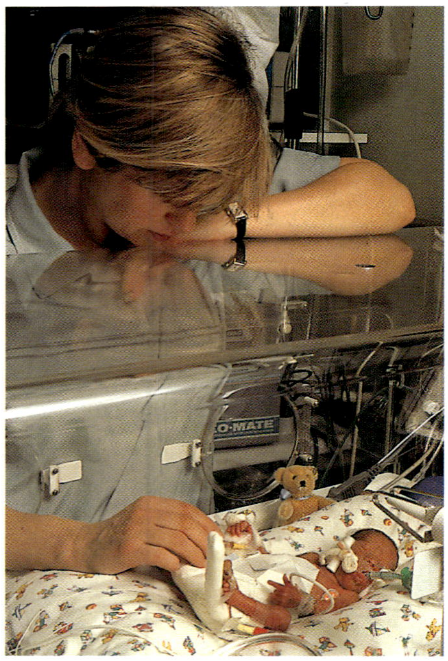

With modern technology even babies as young as 24 weeks can survive in the neonatal intensive care units.

so that even those that are born as young as 24 weeks have a reasonable chance of survival.

If you are giving birth to twins, the labor doesn't usually take any longer than if you are giving birth to a single baby.

Because twins tend to be smaller babies, the labor and birth can often be easier and less painful to endure. Once the birth canal has been stretched to allow one baby to be born, the second baby will usually be born quite quickly afterward. If twins share the placenta, they will both be born before it is delivered. Even if they are fraternal twins and each has her own placenta they will usually be born first, although occasionally one baby is born, followed by its own placenta, before the second baby arrives.

You and your body

Your baby could arrive at any time from now until the end of week 42, so check that you have everything organized. You will probably be able to visit the hospital about now and see where you are going to give birth. Don't be afraid to ask questions if there is anything you don't understand about hospital procedures.

Sometime between now and the birth, you may experience a sudden burst of energy, known as the nesting instinct. Don't overdo things and decide to spring-clean your whole house. Remember that you will shortly need all your energy reserves for the exhausting demands of labor.

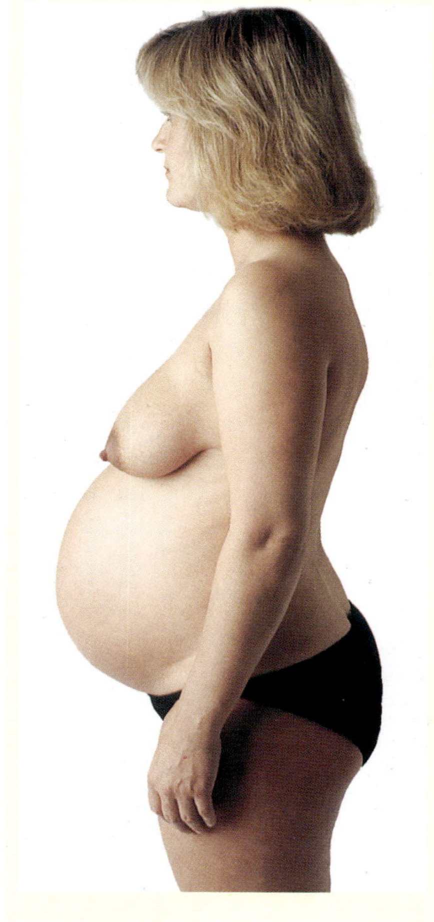

As the birth approaches, it is a good time for you and your partner to start making a list of names that you both like.

WEEK 38: INDUCTION/PAIN RELIEF IN LABOR

You and your body

You will notice that the fetus is moving about less now that it is head down in the uterus. You may be feeling tired and rather depressed about the waiting so try to keep busy.

Sometimes labor has to be started artificially because of a problem such as preeclampsia, bleeding, diabetes, or you are well past your due date and the placenta is no longer working efficiently. Induction involves several techniques:

Artificial rupture of the membranes (ARM) This involves puncturing the amniotic sac in which the baby is sealed so that the increased pressure on the cervix causes the contractions to become much stronger.

Pitocin drip A hormone that stimulates contractions, known as oxytocin or, more commonly, by its trade name Pitocin, is administered – generally by intravenous drip – to help contractions remain constant and steady. This may lead to stronger contractions than you would otherwise have had.

PAIN RELIEF

You will have been told about the various forms of pain relief at childbirth classes. If you want to have a completely natural birth make sure that this is marked clearly on your birthplan and inform the medical staff who will be attending you during labor.

Remember that you can always change your mind later if you find coping with the pain too difficult. If you have decided to opt for some form of pain relief, there are a number of options you can choose from:

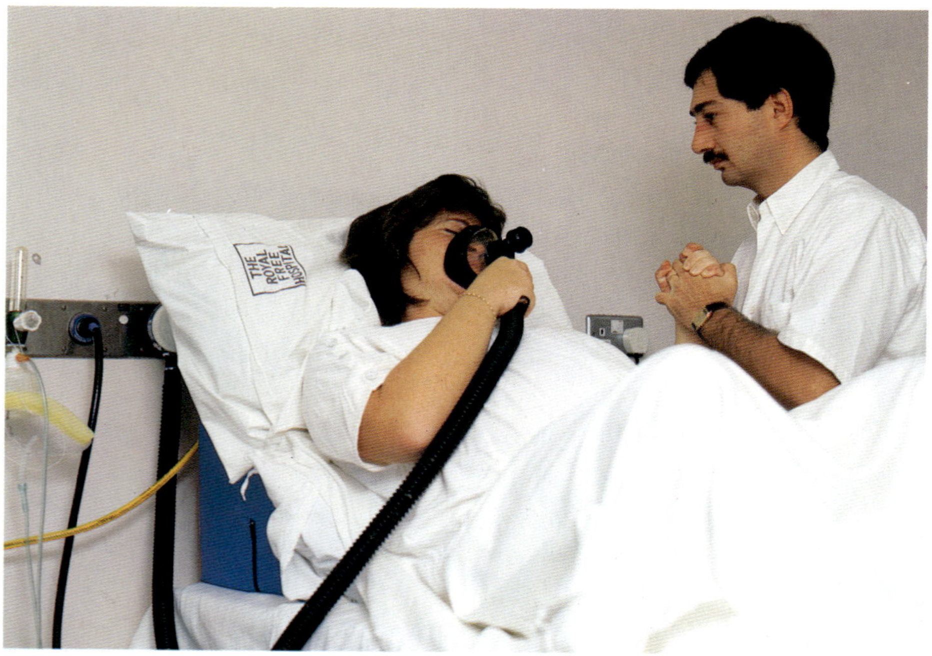

In the past oxygen and nitrous oxide were given for pain relief during contractions. This method is seldom used today.

Injections Drugs like meperidine hydrochloride (Demerol) can be given during the first stage of labor. They will help you relax and relieve pain but they can affect the baby, making him sleepy at birth.

"Gas and air" (Entonox) A mixture of oxygen and nitrous oxide that is breathed in through a mask and takes the edge off pain. The gas is processed in your lungs so it doesn't affect the baby. This procedure, however, is now becoming increasingly uncommon.

Epidural A local anaesthetic is injected into the space between your spinal column and the spinal cord, numbing the nerves that serve the uterus. It may also numb your leg nerves, making it hard for you to move around the hospital. An epidural may also be used if a Caesarean delivery is performed because it allows the mother to stay awake, but be pain free, while her baby is being delivered.

An anaesthesiologist is needed to give an epidural injection, which takes around 30 minutes to set up, and then usually requires topping up every hour and a half.

Other, less common, blocks may also be administered. These include the pudendal block, which is given in the perineum or around the vagina to ease the pain of delivery, and the spinal or low spinal block, in which the anaesthetic is injected straight into the spinal fluid.

Alternative pain relief Both of the alternative therapies – acupuncture and hypnosis – can be used to relieve pain during childbirth, but if you are having a hospital birth you will need to get permission so that you can have a private practitioner with you during labor.

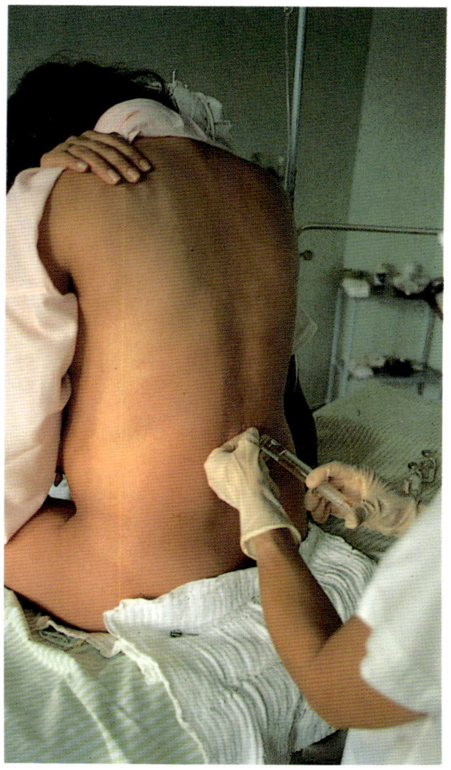

An epidural injection into the spinal area helps deaden the nerves around the uterus.

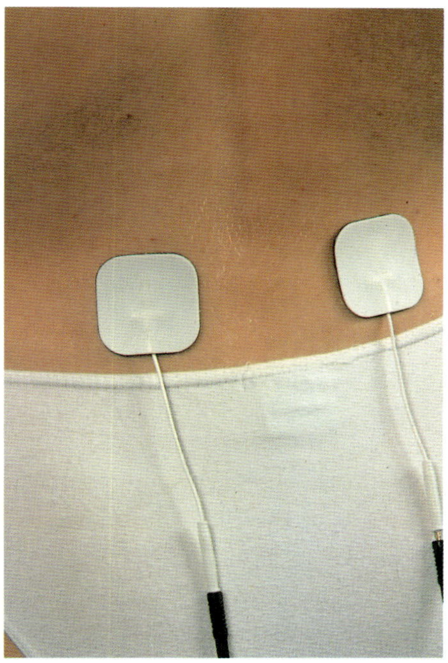

In Europe, pads from a TENS machine can be put on your back to ease labor pains.

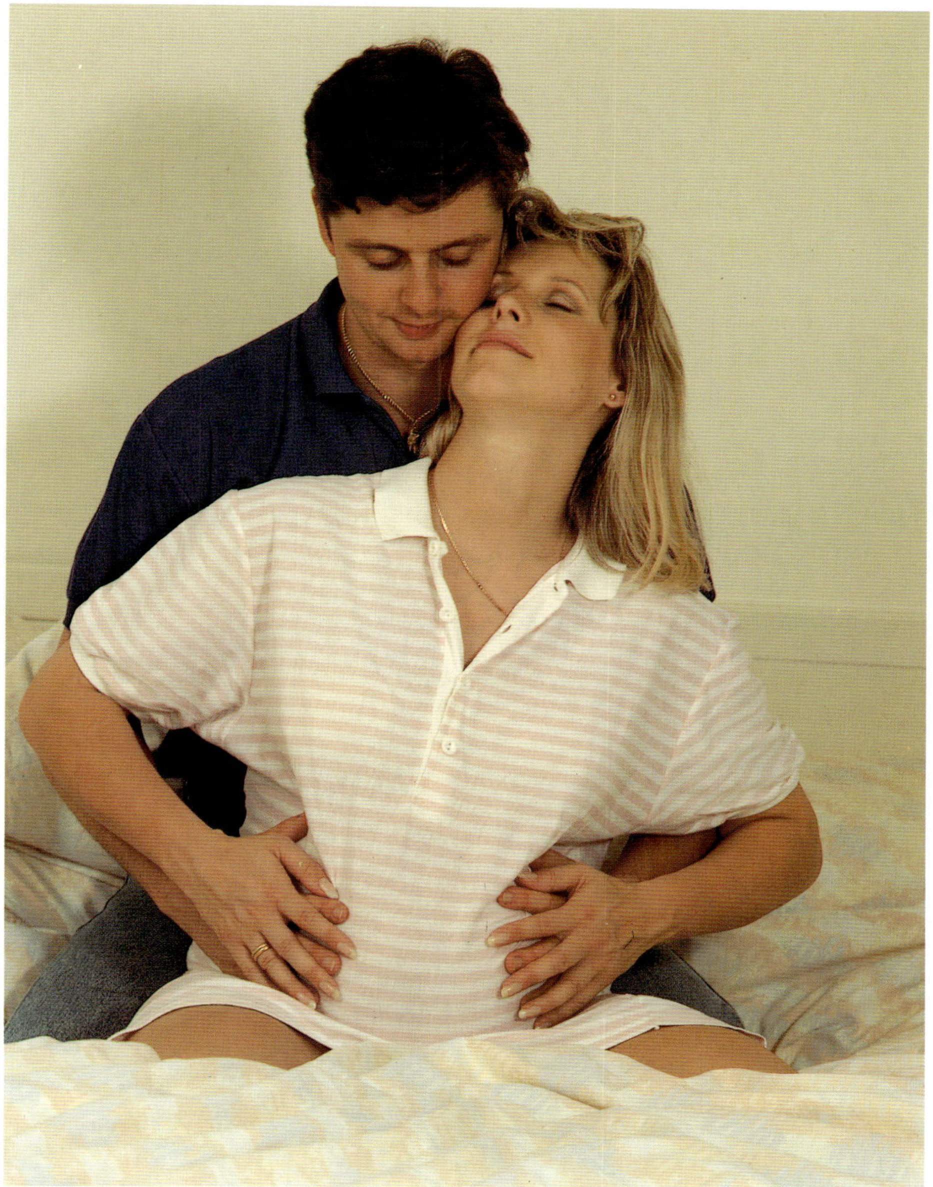

At the most painful times in your labor, lean on your partner for support and encouragement. He can also massage your back if it is really painful.

Used in the correct way by a professional practitioner, massage, aromatherapy, and reflexology can all help to ease the pain and discomfort experienced in labor. You should get some expert advice from the relevant associations and then talk to your doctor before the birth if you intend to use any of these special techniques during your labor.

Your growing baby

The fetus has put on some fat so that it now appears more rounded and its skin has a pinkish look. The hair may be as long as 2 in and the nails already need cutting. The vernix, which has been protecting the skin of the growing fetus from the amniotic fluid, is beginning to dissolve. At this stage of your pregnancy, the fetus measures about 19 in and weighs around 6½ lb.

WEEK 39: COMPLICATIONS DURING BIRTH

The ideal position for your baby to be born is with its head lying down with its back against your abdomen. This way it has less distance to rotate in the birth canal. Sometimes a baby is in an abnormal position which can make birth more complicated, but this does not necessarily mean that it can't be born in the normal way.

An occipito posterior position means that the baby is lying with its back toward your back and, if it fails to turn, will be delivered normally, but will be born face up. This way of lying often leads to what is known as a "back labor."

In a deep transverse arrest, the baby's head partially rotates in the birth canal and then becomes stuck with its face toward one side. The baby will need to be helped out.

Disproportion means that the baby's head is too big for your pelvis. Rarely, a scan will be done to decide whether there is enough room for a normal delivery to take place. If there isn't, your baby will probably be born by Caesarean.

Birth positions

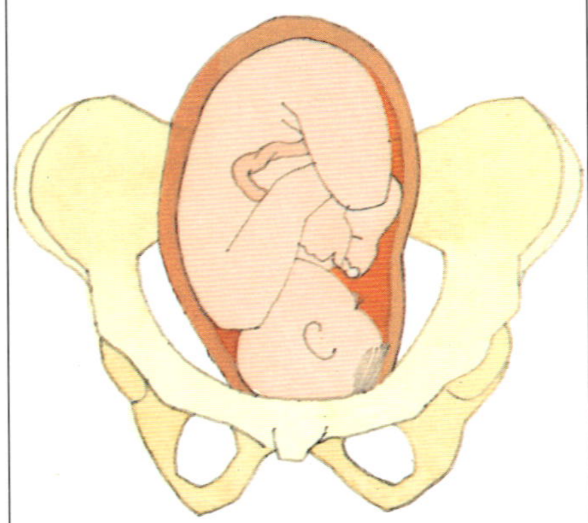

A normal birth

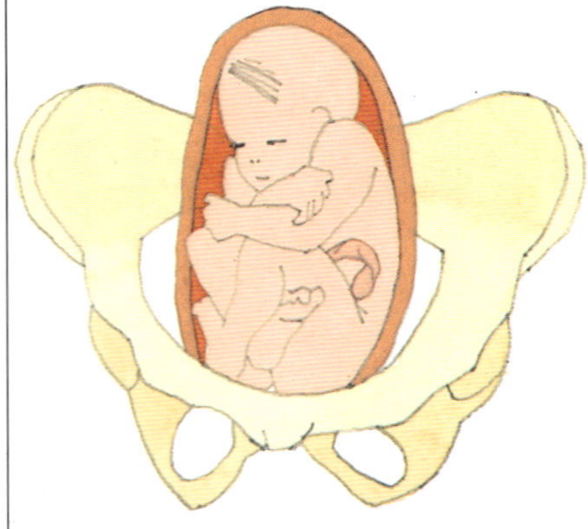

A breech birth

BREECH BIRTH

A small number of babies don't turn around in the normal way in the last few weeks of pregnancy. This means that their feet or buttocks would be delivered first so the birth canal will not have been stretched sufficiently when the head, the largest part of the baby's body, is then ready to be born.

Doctors have different opinions about the best way of delivering a breech baby; some insist that a Caesarean is the safest method, others believe that birth should take place under an epidural, and some think that if the mother remains mobile throughout the first stage of labor the baby will manage to get itself into a good position for the actual birth. It may then be helped out by using forceps or by the vacuum extraction method.

You and your body

The waiting is nearly over and you will probably be feeling both excited and apprehensive. You may be having quite strong Braxton Hicks contractions as the cervix softens in readiness for the birth. Although you may be feeling heavy and weary, don't simply sit around waiting for something to happen. Keep up your social life and talk to other friends from your childbirth classes who are at the same stage as you.

FORCEPS DELIVERY

In a forceps delivery, your legs will be put up in stirrups and then the forceps, which are like a pair of large, shallow metal spoons, will be inserted into the vagina and cupped around the baby's head. The doctor helps the baby out while you push.

VACUUM EXTRACTION

Vacuum extraction is sometimes used instead of the forceps method. With this technique the doctor places a suction cup on the baby's head and the baby is then sucked out as you push down hard with each contraction.

If the birth canal is not going to be big enough for the baby's head and there is a risk that the perineum may tear, a small cut may be made in this area under local anaesthetic.

Your growing baby

The fetus is now able to function on its own, although it is still getting nourishment from the placenta. The fetus is in position for the impending birth and is now about 19¼ in long and weighs around 7 lb.

This type of incision is called an episiotomy and is stitched after the birth, again under local anaesthetic.

Fetal monitoring

This keeps a check on the unborn baby's heartbeat during labor and birth. Monitoring can be done the low-tech way by simply placing a stethoscope against the patient's abdomen, or through electronic fetal monitoring (EFM).

There are two types of EFM and they both give a continuous readout of the baby's heart and uterine contractions; if the EFM method is used then you are having a high-tech birth.

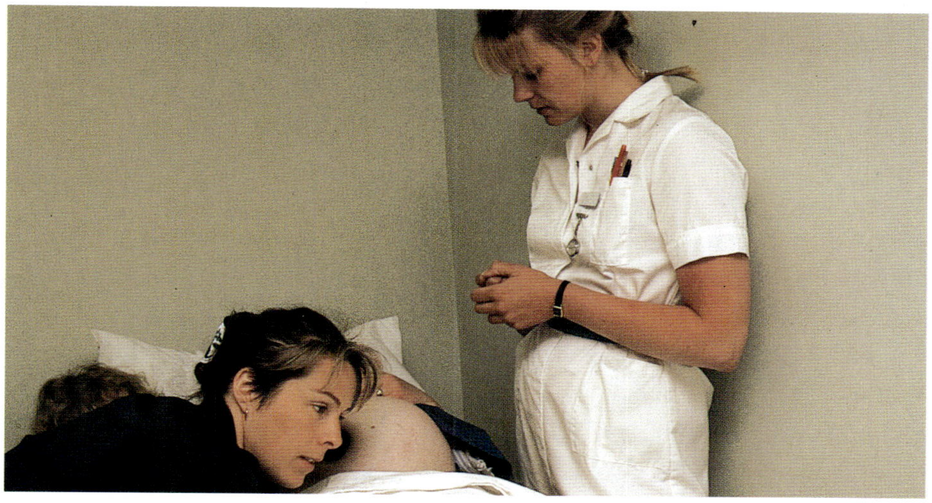

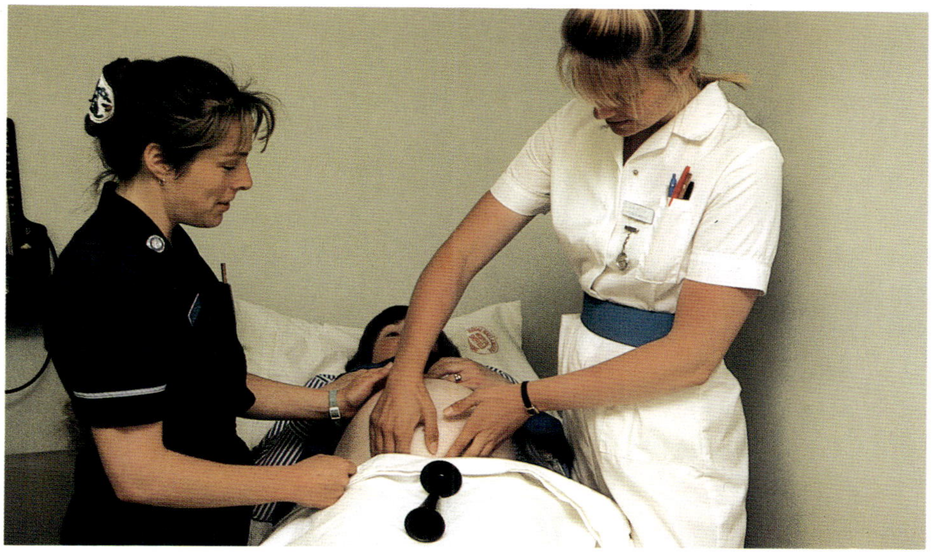

There are two different methods of fetal monitoring. The basic method is to listen to the fetal heartbeat using a fetal stethoscope (top right). The position of the baby will also be checked at the same time (right). Electronic fetal monitoring (EFM) (below) involves placing a belt around your belly which is attached to a monitor. This gives a continuous readout of the baby's heart.

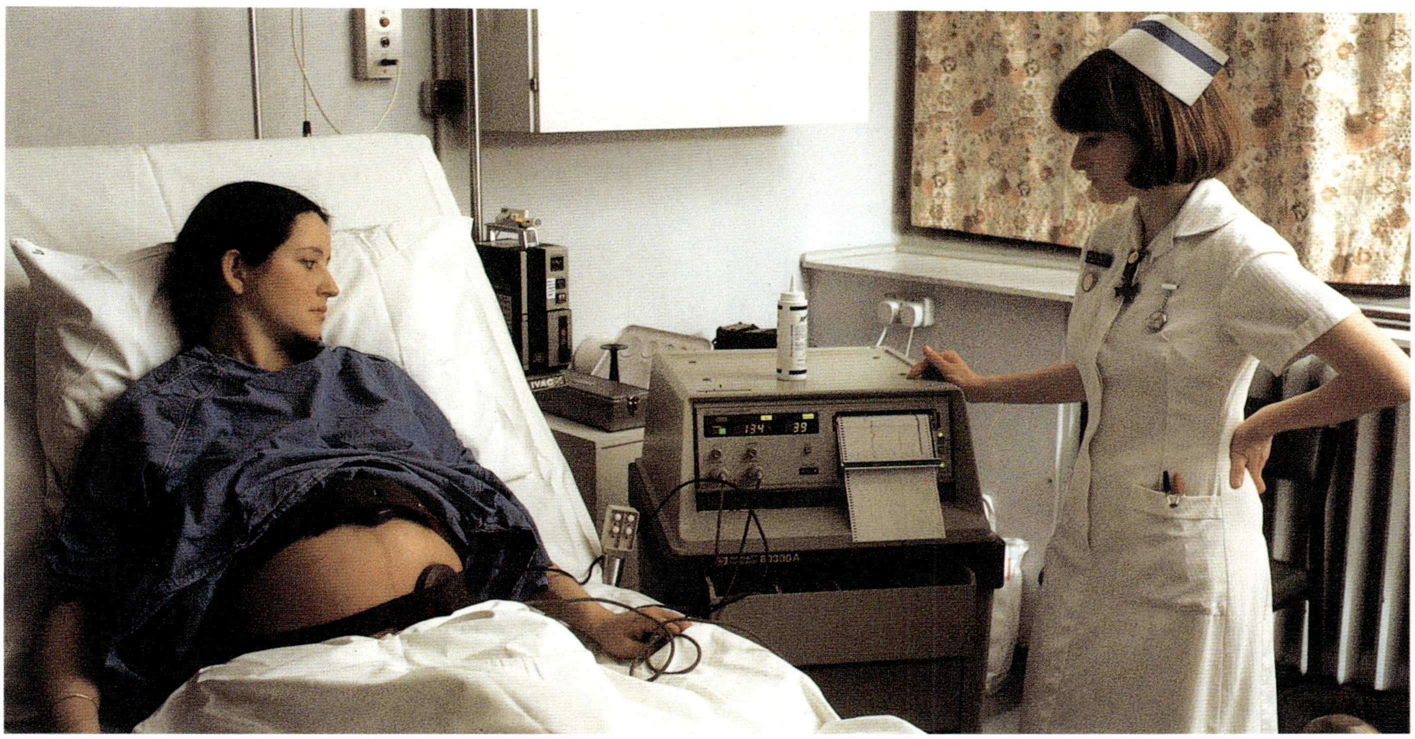

WEEK 40: LABOR AND BIRTH

It is unlikely that you won't recognize the beginnings of labor as the signs, when they come, are generally unmistakable. There are three main indications that labor is about to start, or has started, and they can occur in any order. Once one or more of these has occurred you should let your doctor or midwife know immediately:

A show The protective plug, which sealed the cervix at the neck of the uterus, comes away and passes down the vagina. It usually appears as a small amount of bloodstained mucus. A show occurs before labor starts or during the first stage.

Waters breaking The membranes of the amniotic sac in which your baby has been floating break, causing either a trickle or a sudden gush of clear fluid from the vagina. If the fluid is yellow, greenish, or brown in color you will need to go to the hospital immediately because the baby may be in distress. Your waters can break hours before labor starts or when it is well underway.

Contractions The regular tightening of the muscles of the uterus occurs throughout labor. During the first stage, the contractions thin out and dilate the cervix from closed to 10 cm open; in the second stage they help to push the baby down the vagina and after the birth they then deliver the placenta (afterbirth). For most women they feel rather like bad menstrual cramps. Contractions may be also be accompanied by uncomfortable backache, sickness, and some diarrhea.

Your growing baby

Your baby is lying curled up, head down, in the fetal position with legs drawn up underneath and waiting to be born. He or she now measures about 19¾ in and weighs around 7½ lb.

You and your body

You will probably be impatient for labor to start as you approach your EDD. If nothing has happened by your due date try not to be too disappointed; only around five percent of babies actually arrive on the date they were expected. Keep yourself busy and make plans for each day so that you are not just sitting and waiting for something to happen. Once you are close to your EDD you may feel more confident wearing a sanitary napkin just in case your waters break.

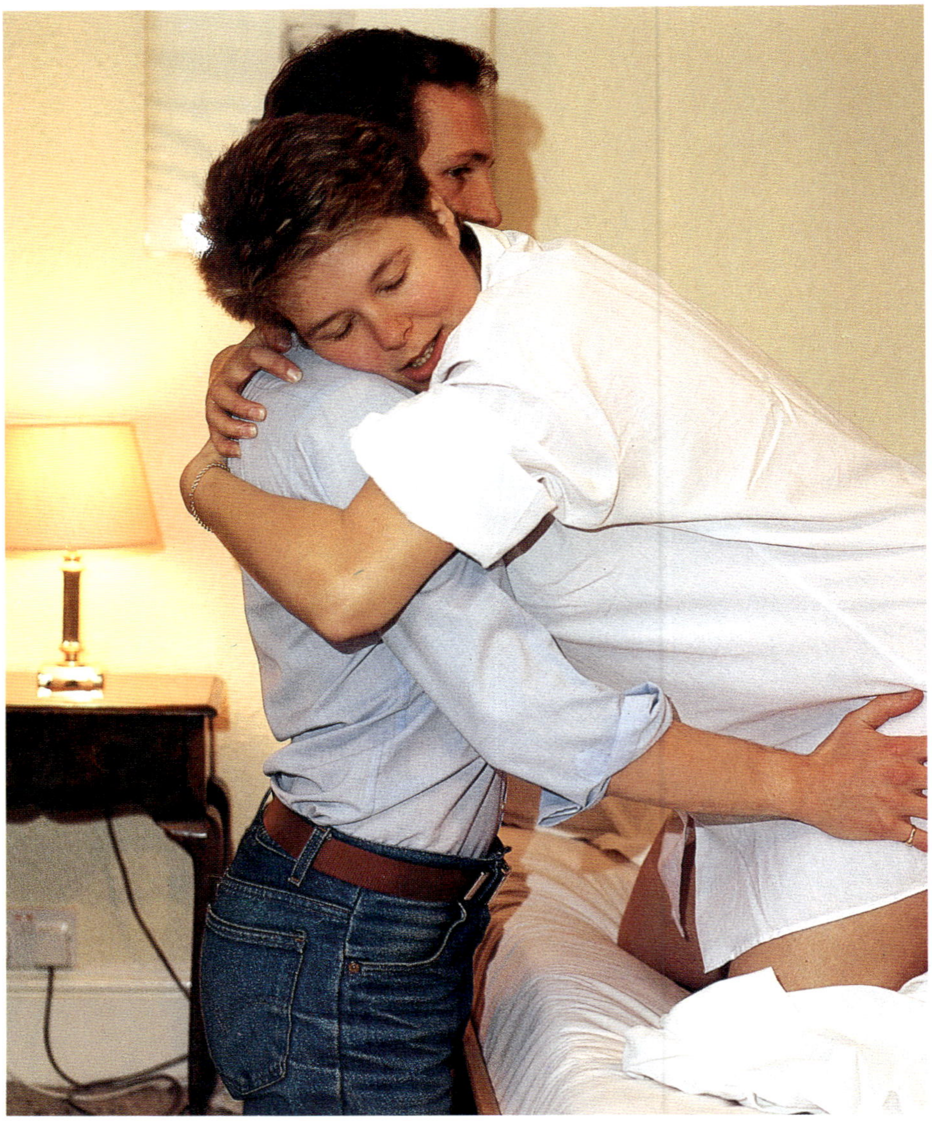

During the first stage of labor, you can involve your partner by leaning and holding onto him for comfort and also physical support.

Your partner can help and encourage you when you're on all fours to keep the weight of the baby off your back in an active birth.

STAGES OF LABOR

The first stage: There are three stages of labor and the first is usually the longest, lasting generally from 12 hours upward for a first baby. Contractions, which may have started off as mild and infrequent will, by the end of the first stage, be very strong and coming close together. Once they are coming regularly

Tips for labor

- Keep active for as long as you can during the first stage of labor.
- Don't be on your own: get your partner, mother or a friend to stay with you once labor has started.
- If your waters break check that the fluid is clear: yellow, greenish, or brown fluid could mean that your baby is in distress and you should go to the hospital immediately.
- Try different positions to help you cope with the pain of contractions.
- Ask for pain relief if you need it.
- Get your birth partner to make sure your wishes are known to whoever is delivering your baby. You may be too busy coping with contractions to explain clearly what you want.
- Put your baby to the breast soon after the birth. This will stimulate your milk supply and help to speed up the delivery of the placenta.

every 10 minutes, or are each lasting for around 45 seconds, you should start getting ready to go to the hospital, or call the midwife if you are having your baby at home. When you get to the hospital, or the midwife attending you at home arrives, you will be examined to see how far your cervix has dilated and your blood pressure will be checked.

Although you will be able to carry on fairly normally for quite a lot of the first stage you should have someone with you. It is advisable to eat very little once labor has begun in case you need an emergency anaesthetic for any reason and to avoid being sick.

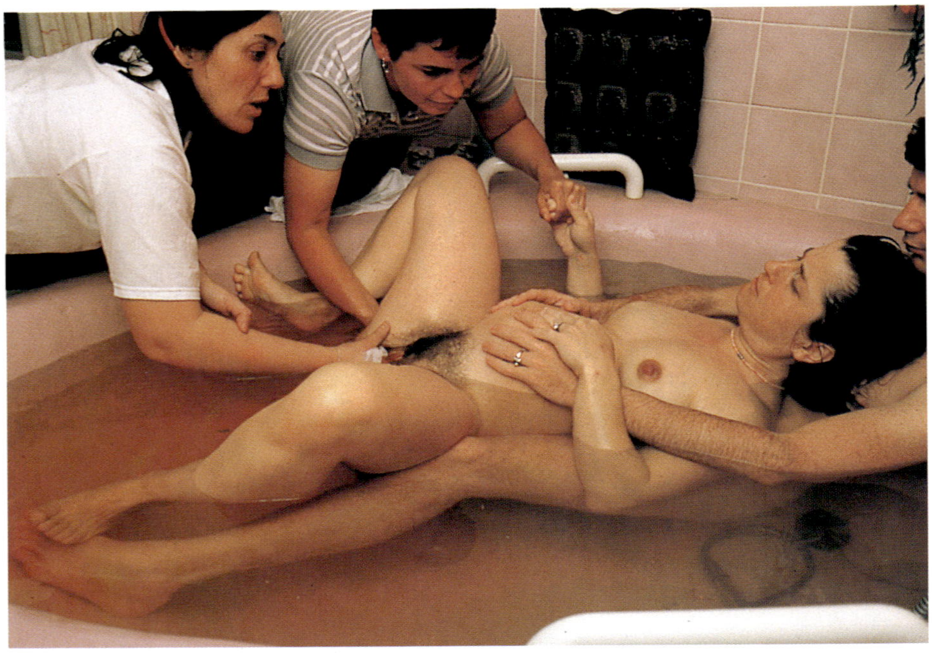

With a water birth, still uncommon in the U.S., contractions can be eased by the warm water. Your baby can be delivered in the water or outside.

If you have your baby in the water, he will be given to you immediately after the birth for you and your partner to cuddle.

Toward the end of the first stage you will go into what is known as the transitional stage which can last for anything up to an hour. During this transitional period your baby moves down the birth canal and you will feel pressure on your back which may make you want to start pushing, even though the cervix is not fully dilated. By using the breathing techniques you have been taught you will be able to control this urge.

The second stage: Once the cervix is fully dilated and you start pushing the baby out you have entered the second stage. It can last for as little as half an hour or for as long as two hours or more. Once the baby's head is visible to the doctor or midwife she will tell you to start pushing. When the head reaches the vaginal opening you will be told to pant in short breaths so that the head can be delivered as slowly as possible. This allows the skin and muscle of the perineum to stretch so that the head can be born. If tearing seems likely an episiotomy, a small cut in the perineum, the area between the vagina and anus, may be given. Once the head is born your baby's body will follow quickly.

When your baby is delivered it may be lifted onto your stomach for you to see it. The umbilical cord will be clamped and cut and the doctor or midwife will check the baby to make sure that he is all right and breathing properly. You may want to put your baby to the breast, and you'll certainly want to admire him or her with your partner and welcome your child into the world.

Above: A doctor holding a newborn baby boy, with the umbilical cord still attached, at a home delivery.
Right: With a Caesarean the baby is delivered through an incision. It is performed when there are risks from natural childbirth.

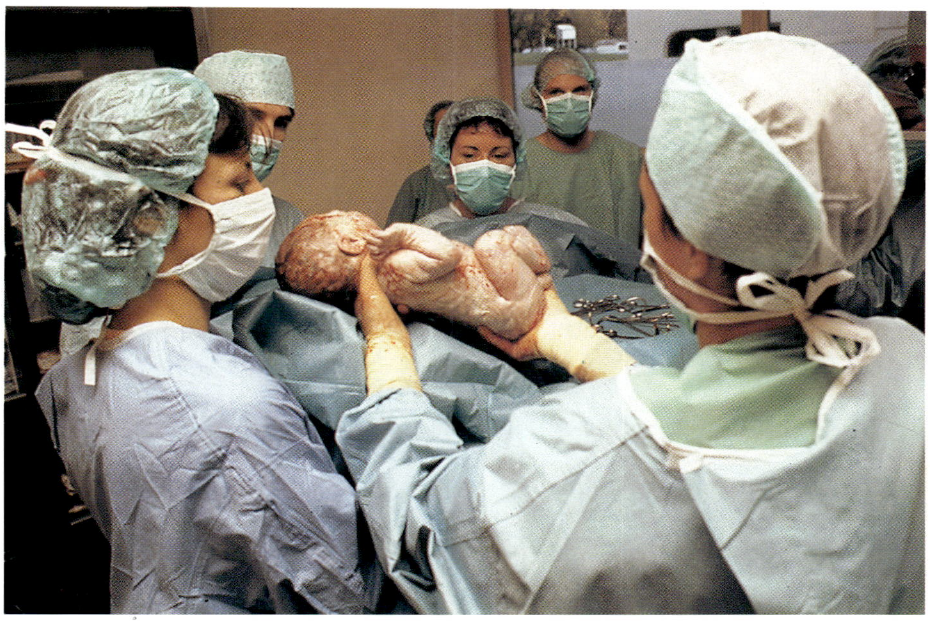

The third stage: The final stage of labor is the birth of the placenta, which usually takes less than half an hour. You may be given an injection to speed up the delivery. The midwife will check to see that the placenta is whole and that nothing has been left inside you. If you have had an episiotomy it will be stitched up.

PART TWO

BABYCARE

A NEW BABY can seem rather overwhelming, especially if this is your first experience of motherhood. Suddenly you are responsible for the care and welfare of a very demanding little person who needs looking after almost 24 hours a day. If you have never fed, bathed or changed a baby you need to learn how to carry out these daily routines. This section looks at basic babycare and explains, in simple terms, everything that you are likely to need to know about caring for your baby during the first year of his life.

It is important to take care of yourself too, especially in the days after the birth, so your post-partum care is described at the beginning of this section.

Feeding your baby should be a special time for you both, regardless of whether you are breast- or bottle-feeding in the early months. But when things go wrong, or your baby doesn't feed in the way you expect, it can be difficult to know what to do. Breast- and bottle-feeding are discussed here, along with the latest information on when and how to introduce first foods.

When your child seems unwell it is quite natural to be concerned. Knowing what to do and when you need to call the doctor comes with experience. In the meantime the section on common childhood ailments such as coughs, colds, teething and illness tells you how to relieve discomfort and when you should seek medical help. There is also a comprehensive first aid section which explains exactly what you should do if your child has an accident.

Caring for your baby will take up a great deal of your time during the first year, so use the daily routines of bathing, feeding and changing as a time to get to know and enjoy each other.

POST-PARTUM CARE

Although your new baby will probably give you intense emotional satisfaction, you may well be physically uncomfortable. Your body has gone through many changes during pregnancy and it will take a while for it to return to its pre-pregnancy state.

Six weeks or so after the birth your doctor will examine you to make sure that everything is returning to normal; this also gives you a chance to discuss any worries you may have. The doctor will take your blood pressure and check a sample of your urine. Your breasts and abdomen will be examined and the doctor will make sure that any stitches have healed properly. You will probably have an internal examination to check the size and position of your uterus and you may have a Pap test if one is due.

If your baby was born in the hospital, a doctor or midwife will probably talk to you about contraception before you go home. Alternatively, you can discuss this at your first check-up. Don't take any risks; to avoid getting pregnant again you should use contraception as soon as you resume intercourse with your partner. While breastfeeding may prevent conception, it is by no means a dependable safeguard.

If you were not immune to rubella (German measles) during your pregnancy, you may be offered the immunization before you leave the hospital or at your six-week check-up. Ask your doctor if you are at all unsure about your immunity.

YOUR BODY

Immediately after the birth your breasts will produce colostrum, a high-protein liquid full of antibodies. Then, after the pregnancy hormones decline, your main milk supply should come in around the third or fourth day. At this time the breasts swell, feel hard, and can sometimes be painful. Bathing them with warm water is soothing, and letting the baby have frequent feeding will also help. This initial swelling subsides after a few days as both you and your baby get used to feeding. However, if you have decided to bottle-feed, your breasts will remain full for a few days until they gradually stop producing milk. Your breasts will probably never be quite as firm as they were before pregnancy, but a well-fitting support bra and exercise will help greatly.

After delivery your abdomen will probably be quite flabby and wrinkled because of slack muscles and stretched skin. Gentle post-partum exercises will help tighten up your abdominal and vaginal muscles, so make time to do them every day. If you feel you're not disciplined enough to exercise on your own, consider joining a post-partum class.

Following the birth you will have a vaginal discharge which is known as lochia. This will be like a very heavy period for a few days, with the flow gradually getting lighter until it disappears within a few weeks. Use maternity pads or large sanitary napkins to absorb the discharge because there is a risk of infection if you use tampons in the early weeks after the birth. Your

Your newborn will find your physical presence very reassuring during the first days after the birth. She will also find your smell comfortingly familiar.

Post-partum exercises

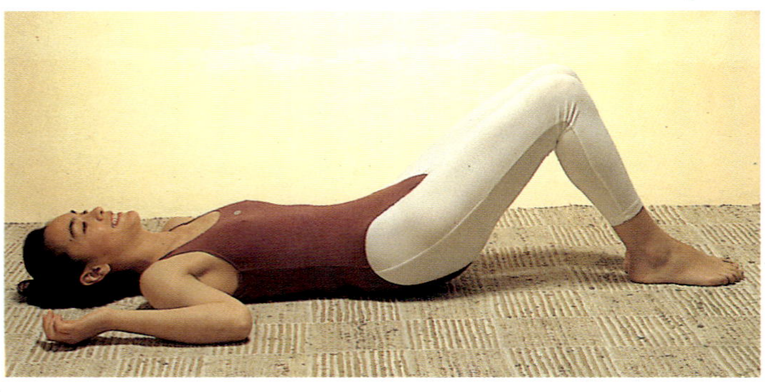

Pelvic floor: Lie flat on the floor with your legs drawn up and slightly apart. Close the back passage by drawing it in, hold for the count of four, then relax. Do as often as possible.

Tummy toner: Sit up with knees bent and feet flat on the floor. Fold arms in front. Lean back until you feel the abdominal muscles tighten, hold, then sit up and relax. Repeat several times.

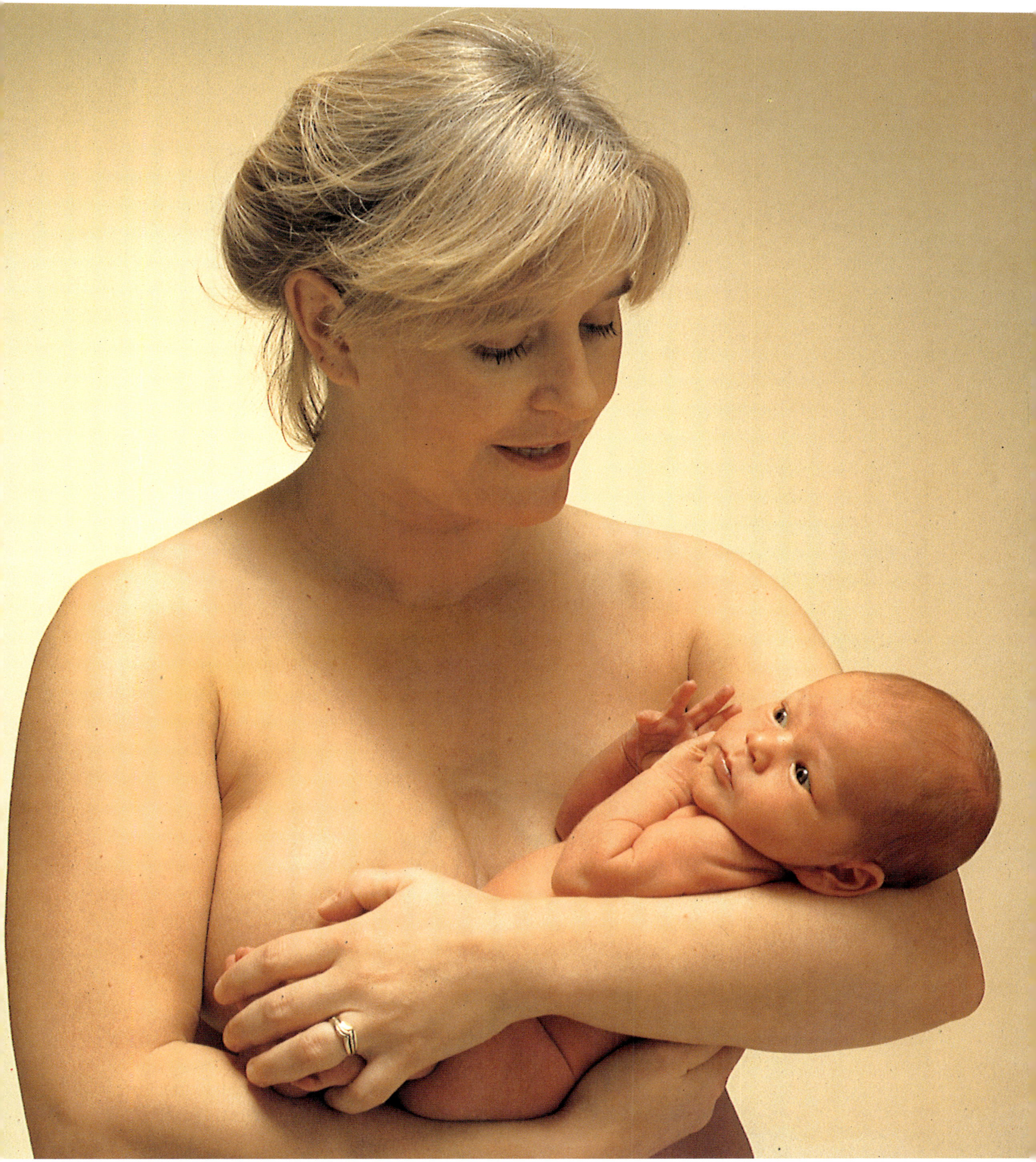

1 *Curl-ups: This exercise will help strengthen your vertical abdominal muscles. Lie on your back with a pillow under your head, your knees bent and your feet flat on the floor.*

2 *Pull in your abdominal muscles and, raising your head, stretch your arms toward your knees. Hold for a count of five and then relax slowly. Repeat several times.*

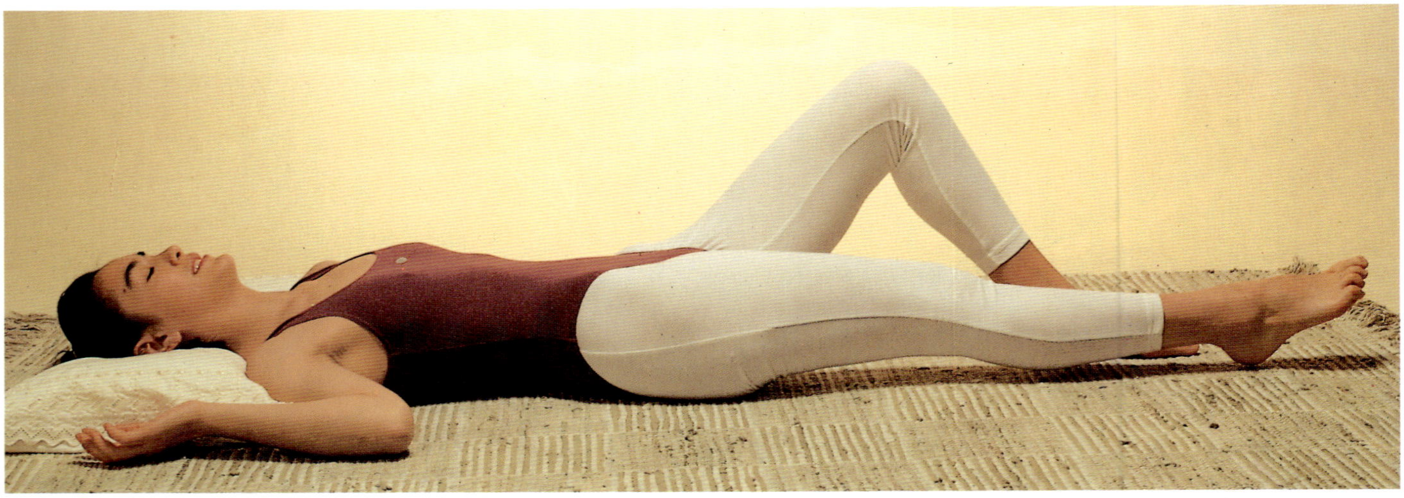

Leg slide: Lie with your head on a pillow with the small of your back pressed against the floor and your knees bent. Gently slide one leg away from your body until it is fully extended, keeping the small of your back pressed against the floor for as long as you can. Slowly draw the leg back toward your body and then repeat with the other leg. Do this several times.

uterus will take about six weeks to return to its original size. If you are breastfeeding you may feel it contract as you feed the baby.

If your perineum (the skin between the vagina and anus) was bruised during labor, or if you had stitches, you will find that anything that puts pressure on the area painful. Soreness can be soothed with an ice pack (or ice cubes wrapped in a washcloth) held against the perineum or by Sitz baths (ask your doctor). Try drying the area with a hand-held hair dryer, set on cool, rather than with a bath towel. Do not put the dryer too close to your skin, or use it in the bathroom. Adding a cup of salt to the bath water will also help the stitches to heal.

Getting back into shape

Despite losing the combined weight of the baby, the placenta, and the amniotic fluid, you will still be heavier than you were before you became pregnant. You may even find that you have to continue to wear maternity clothes for a short while. As your uterus shrinks during the six weeks following the birth you will lose more weight, but you will need to watch your diet to regain your pre-pregnancy shape. Try to eat regularly and healthily and don't be tempted, because you're short of time, to snack on foods containing empty calories such as sweets and sodas. If the weight isn't disappearing as fast as you'd like, ask your doctor for advice. Do not attempt any diet now or while breastfeeding – this would just increase stress as your body is trying to regain its equilibrium. Doing exercises will help you get

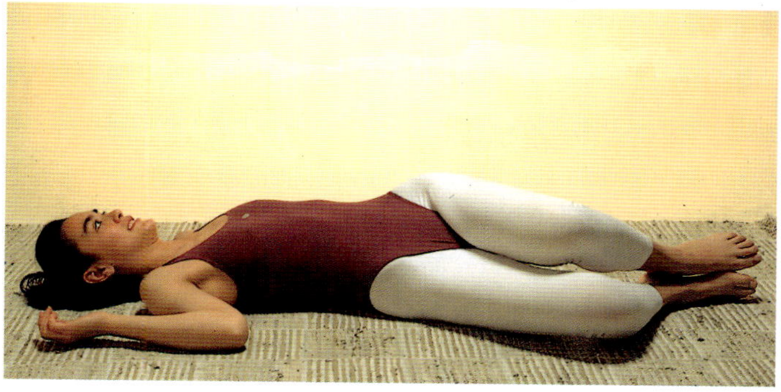

1 *Waist trimmer: Lie on the floor with your arms away from your side, with your knees bent and feet flat. Pull in your abdominals and, with knees together, roll over to the right. Bring your knees back to the middle and pause.*

2 *Rest briefly, then pull in your abdominals again and roll your knees to the left, then back to the middle and pause. Keep your shoulders flat on the floor as you roll from side to side. Repeat six times and work up to 20.*

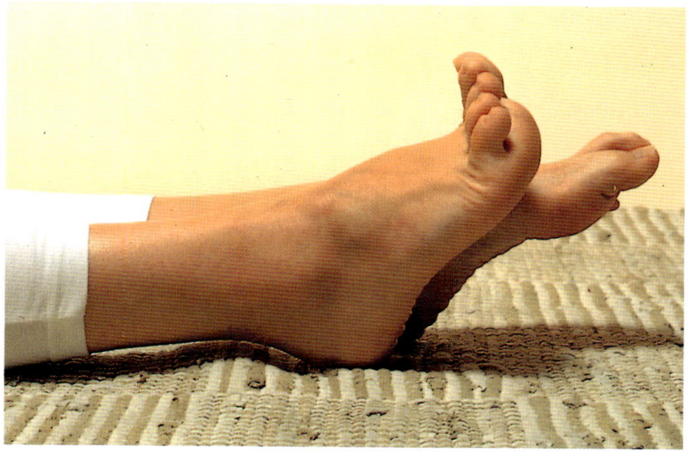

1 *Foot exercises: These will help improve your circulation and are especially important if you are confined to bed. Lie with your legs straight and knees together and bend and stretch your feet.*

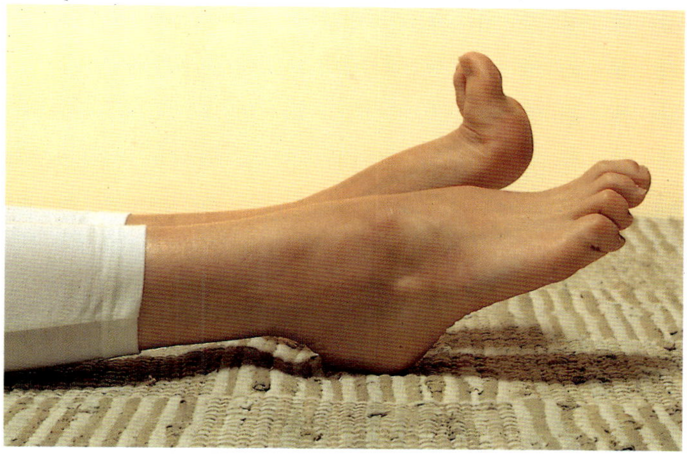

2 *Flex one foot, pulling the toes up toward you while pointing the other foot away from you. Repeat, alternating the feet. Do this exercise quite briskly for about 30 seconds.*

Post-partum depression

Two or three days after the birth you may suddenly feel very tearful and depressed. This is commonly called the "baby blues," or the milk blues, because it usually coincides with the milk coming into your breasts. These feelings are caused by all the hormonal changes that are going on in your body and should disappear after a few days. If they don't go away, however, you need to talk to your doctor. You may be suffering from post-partum depression (PPD) which, if left untreated, can go on for several months. Symptoms of PPD include feeling unhappy as well as irritable and exhausted, yet unable to sleep. You may also lose all interest in food, or find yourself eating too much and then feeling guilty afterward. PPD is one of the most common problems following childbirth and it is likely that it is related to the huge hormonal changes that take place at the time of the birth, but it is still unclear as to why it affects some women so badly but not others. If you think you are suffering from PPD, don't feel ashamed about it and don't ignore the symptoms. You are in need of help and the sooner you ask for it the sooner you will begin to feel better and able to cope with your life again. Post-partum depression is a common condition. Many women are affected by it, and it needs to be treated early on, not just ignored in the hope that eventually it will just go away on its own.

your figure back, get you moving again, and make you feel fitter. Those for strengthening the pelvic floor are among the most important post-partum exercises. The pelvic floor muscles support the bladder, uterus, and rectum, so it is vital that their tone is restored after being stretched during childbirth.

Fatigue and relaxation

Fatigue goes hand in hand with being a new mother, but you need rest to help your body recover from childbirth. It is tempting to use the baby's sleep times to catch up on chores, but do try to have a nap or proper rest at least once during the day. You and your child are more important than housework, so find ways to cut down the work. Accept offers of help and, if no one volunteers, don't be afraid to ask people.

Another way to cope with fatigue or stress is relaxation, so try using the prenatal relaxation exercises to help you now. For a real treat, ask your partner to give you a massage using a specially formulated oil before you go to sleep. Baths are generally not recommended until after bleeding stops.

Hair and nails

The condition of your hair is likely to change during this time. It may become more greasy, or the opposite may happen and it will become noticeably drier than before. You may also suffer an increase in hair loss or your hair may seem a lot thicker than it did before you became pregnant. Whichever condition applies to you, wash your hair using a mild shampoo and avoid rubbing or brushing oily hair too much as this will only stimulate the sebaceous glands to produce more oil. Dry hair should be conditioned after every wash and, if possible, allowed to dry naturally.

Your nails are made of the same tissue as your hair, so if you are having problems with one you are likely to have problems with the other. These are due to fluctuating hormone levels and as soon as these settle your hair and nails will return to normal. Meanwhile, include enough protein and B vitamins in your diet because these will help improve the condition of both your hair and nails.

Above: Eating regularly and healthily will help you to regain your pre-pregnancy shape.

Left: When bleeding has stopped, a lazy bath with a few drops of oil, such as lavender, will help you to relax.
Below: A stimulating rub with a loofah brush or mitt will help remove dead cells on the skin's surface, and will stimulate the circulation.
Below right: Try using some unscented soap or a soapless cleansing bar if your skin is very itchy.

CARING FOR YOUR NEWBORN

You may find the first weeks at home with your new baby quite difficult, especially if you are still feeling weak and emotionally down. Don't get upset if the house is a mess; it is much more important for you to spend time with your baby than to do housework. If you are still in your nightgown at lunchtime don't worry; your baby will not care and it is how he or she feels that matters most at the moment.

Your newborn will seem fragile at first, but is actually quite tough. It is natural to be worried about how to pick your new baby up and hold him without hurting him in any way. Before you pick up your baby make sure that you have his head and neck supported with one hand, then slide the other hand underneath his back and bottom to support the lower part of his body before lifting. Hold your baby firmly against you, either cradled against your chest with one arm still supporting the head and the other holding the bottom and lower back, or cradled in your arms with your baby's head lying in the crook of one arm while your other arm supports his back and legs. Always keep any movements gentle so that you don't hurt or frighten your baby.

The newborn at delivery

As soon as the baby is born it will be assessed on the five points of the Apgar Score: heart rate, respiratory rate, color, activity, and response to stimulation. The baby will be given a maximum of two points for each category, so if he is pink, active, and responsive the score is 10. The Apgar Score is usually done twice – one minute after birth and five minutes after birth – and it may be done again later if there are any problems.

Your baby will also be weighed and measured by the doctor and will probably receive a dose of vitamin K, by injection, to prevent a rare bleeding illness which occasionally affects newborn babies. Vitamin K is given by injection to very premature babies or those who have had a traumatic birth.

After the birth, the umbilical cord will be cut and a plastic clamp placed about ½–1 in from the infant's body. Over the next few days the cord will shrivel up and after about a week it will drop off completely. During this

A newborn baby boy's genitals may appear rather big in proportion to the rest of him. This will correct itself after a few days.

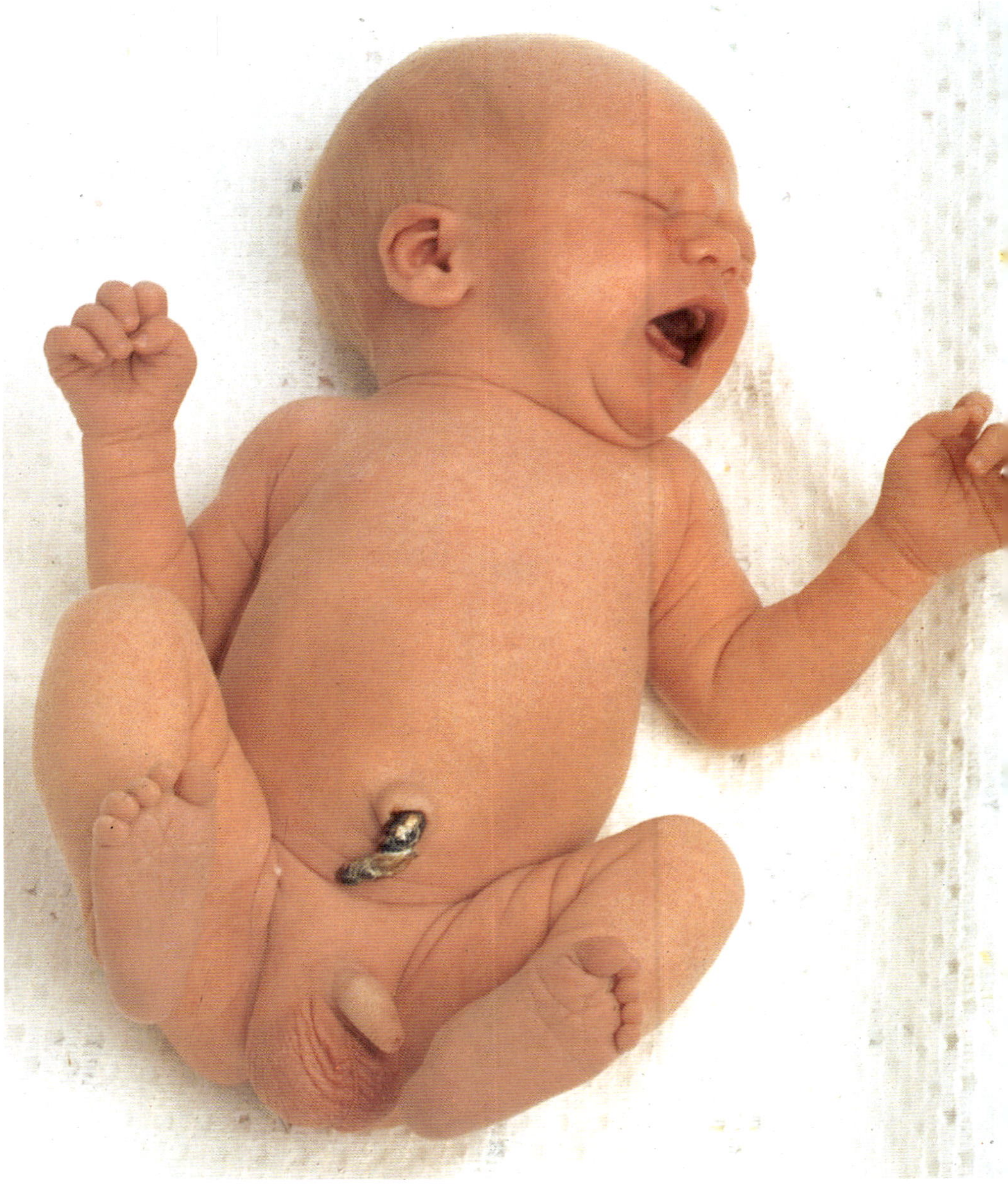

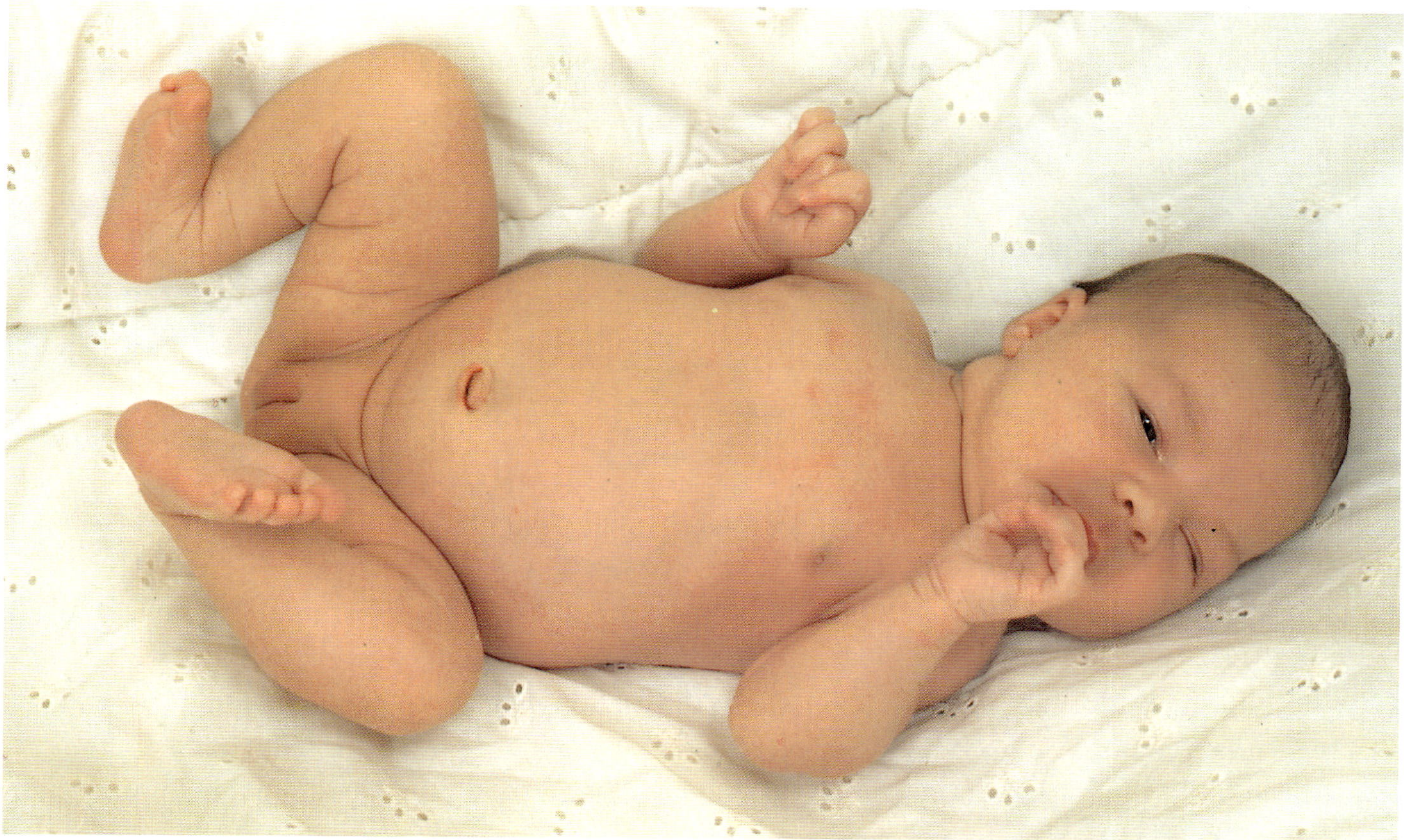

A newborn baby loses the stump of her umbilical cord usually within the first few days after the birth.

time the area around the cord should be kept dry and clean to avoid the risk of infection. Apply alcohol to the base of the cord with each diaper change, but avoid the tender abdominal skin. Try to let the air get to the healing navel as much as possible so that moisture from wet diapers doesn't affect it.

Your baby has soft spots known as fontanelles on the top of the head. These are the spaces between the skull bones, where they have not yet joined. There is usually a large one on top of the skull and a smaller one farther back. They will gradually fuse over the next two years or so. The fontanelles are covered with a tough membrane to protect the brain and you should never press them hard. If you notice a bulge or the skin seems

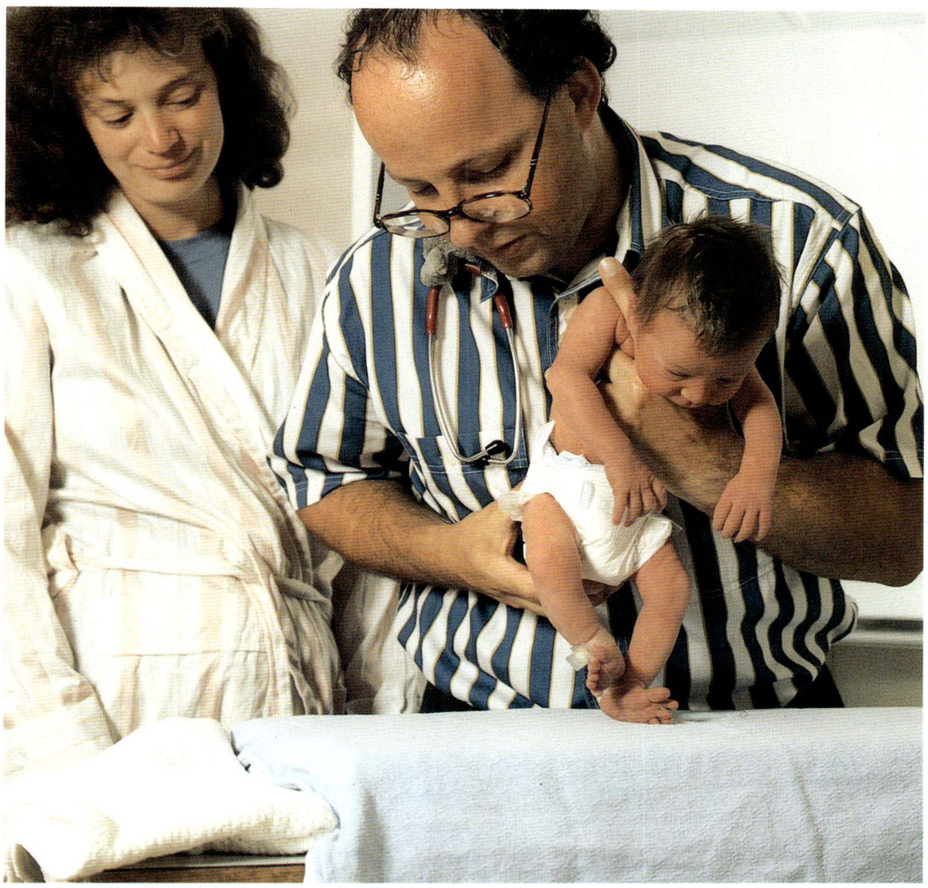

Sometime during the first couple of days your newborn baby will be given a complete physical examination to check that all the organs and limbs are functioning correctly.

very tight over the fontanelles you should get in touch with your doctor immediately.

Some babies are born with a lot of hair, others arrive almost bald. Any first hair that a baby has will fall out within a couple of months, but this will be replaced with new hair growth. The new hair may be a different color.

Most Caucasian babies are born with eyes that appear to be blue-gray in color. This is because melanin, the body's natural pigment, is not present in the eyes until some weeks after birth. Babies with brown or black skins may have brown eyes at birth. If your baby's eyes are going to change color this will gradually happen over a period of weeks or even months. Although a new baby may cry quite a bit during these early weeks there probably won't be any tears. Some babies don't produce

Babies often scratch themselves accidentally with their nails when they are very young. Cotton mitts will stop your newborn from catching her face with her fingernails.

How to hold your new baby

1 *Pick up your newborn baby by sliding one hand under his neck and head and then placing the other hand under his back and bottom to support his body.*

2 *Lift your baby so that he is cradled against your chest with one arm supporting the head and the other holding the lower back. Holding him close to your body will make him feel secure.*

Right: Touch is very important to a newborn and a gentle massage with a special baby oil can be soothing.

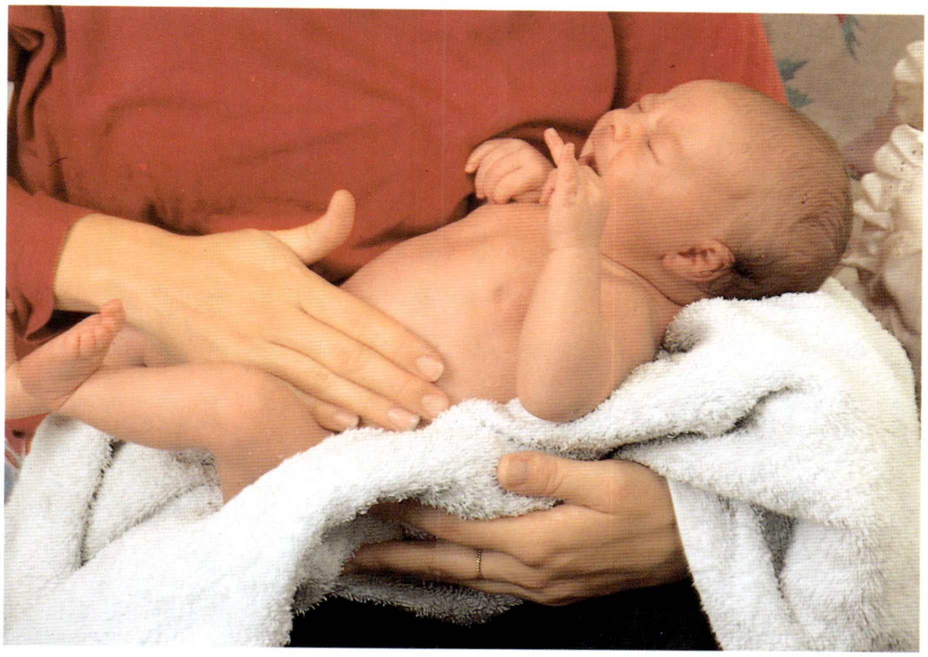

tears until they are six months old – this is not a cause for concern.

Slightly swollen or bloodshot eyes are common in newborn babies. This is caused by pressure from the birth and will disappear within a week or two. The muscles controlling a new baby's eye movements are still very weak so he may look slightly crosseyed at first. After a month or so the muscles will have developed sufficiently for the eyes to work together. However, even when looking crosseyed, a baby can focus on things up to 8–10 in away, so hold your face close when you are feeding or talking.

Enlarged genitals and breasts are common in both boys and girls when they are first born. In some cases the breasts may even ooze a little milk and baby girls can have a slight vaginal discharge. This is caused by your hormones, which are still in your baby's bloodstream. In a few days these effects will disappear.

GENERAL HYGIENE

Young babies often object noisily to being undressed and immersed in a bath full of water, so don't feel you have to bathe your baby every day if the infant is unhappy about it. A top and bottom wash every other day is quite sufficient until you both feel more comfortable. Always start by washing the baby's face with warm water using cotton balls or soft washcloths. Never use any kind of soap on the baby's face or near his eyes. If you wipe the eyes, use separate cotton balls for each one and start from the inner corner wiping outward. A baby's ears and nose are self-cleaning

Above: Your baby's fingernails will grow quickly and you will need to keep them short to keep him from scratching himself. You may find it easier to cut the nails while your baby is asleep.

so never try cleaning inside them with cotton balls or swabs. Just gently remove any visible mucus or wax. Once you have washed his face you will need to lift up his head and clean the folds of his neck, making sure that you dry the area carefully afterward. Using another piece of cotton, wash between all your baby's fingers and then dry both his hands carefully.

When you have finished the top half you need to remove his diaper, wiping away any solid matter before gently cleaning his bottom. You can use lotion to do this, or some warm water. Once the area is dry, you can apply a barrier cream to help prevent diaper rash.

Cradle cap is very common in the early months and can sometimes continue for a while. Dry white or yellow scales form a crusty cap on the scalp. Rub olive oil, baby oil, or

Cleaning your baby

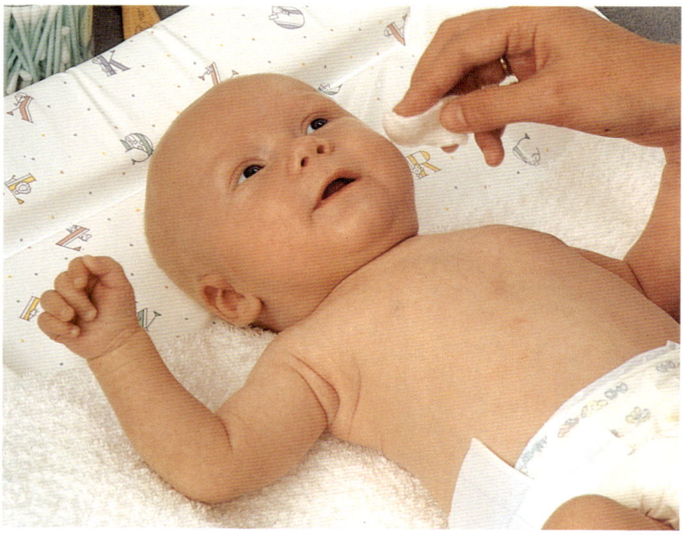

1 *Undress your baby down to his diaper. Using water, and several pieces of cotton, gently wash his face. Never use any kind of soap on your baby's face or near his eyes.*

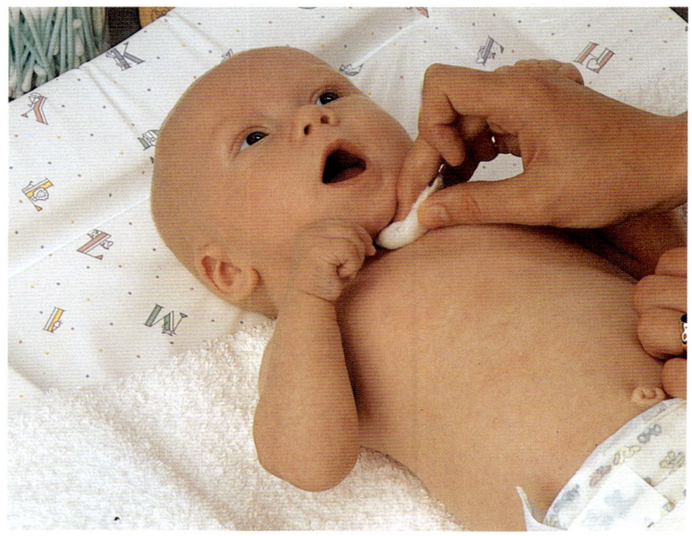

2 *Take a piece of cotton and gently lift his chin so that you can wash in the folds of his neck. When you have finished, use another piece of cotton and carefully dry between the folds.*

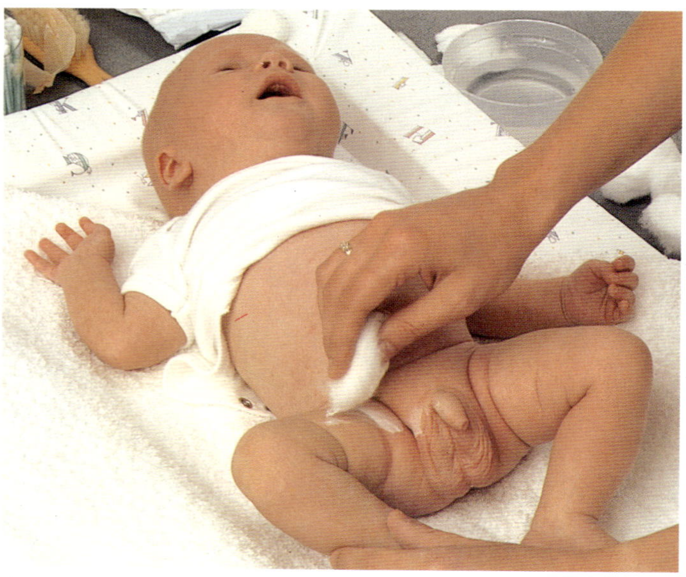

5 *Gently wipe his bottom area with lotion or damp cotton making sure that you clean in all the folds and creases of his legs.*

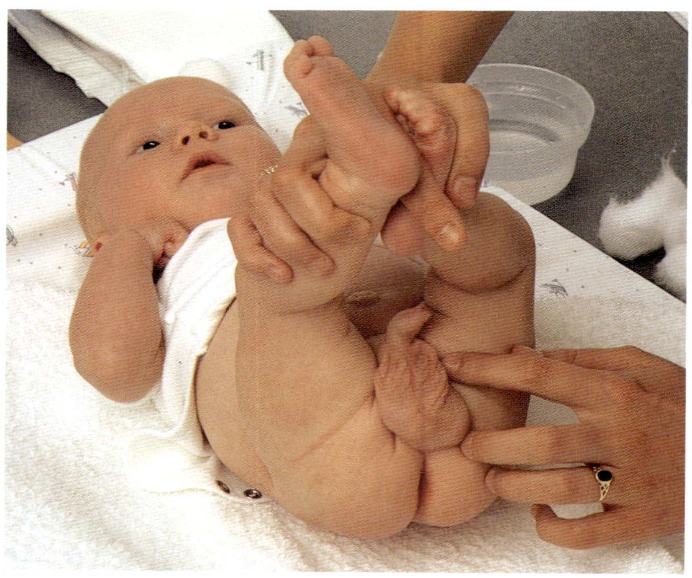

6 *Once you have dried the diaper area, apply a small amount of barrier cream to help prevent diaper rash.*

a specially formulated treatment into the scalp and then comb out the loosened flakes. Wash your baby's head afterward with baby shampoo and dry thoroughly. As soon as the condition is under control you will only need to do this once a week. Cradle cap is unsightly but otherwise benign. It usually disappears by the time a baby reaches about eight or nine months.

A young baby's nails will grow very quickly and if not cut can cause scratches, especially on his face. You should keep his fingernails and the toenails short by cutting them straight across with a pair of blunt-ended scissors. If your baby objects to this procedure, or you find it difficult to cut his nails while he is constantly wriggling about, try doing it while he is fast asleep or get someone else to hold him steady while you quickly cut his nails.

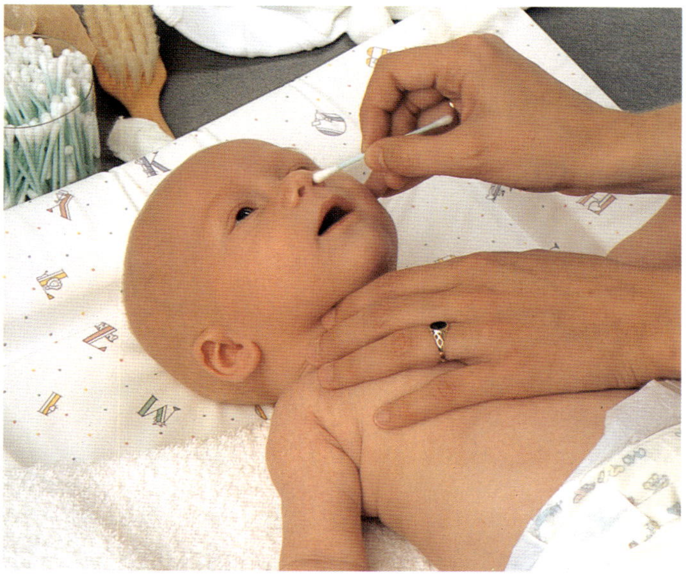

3 *Your baby's ears and nose are self-cleaning, so don't be tempted to clean inside them with cotton swabs. Take a dampened cotton swab and carefully remove any visible mucus from his nose.*

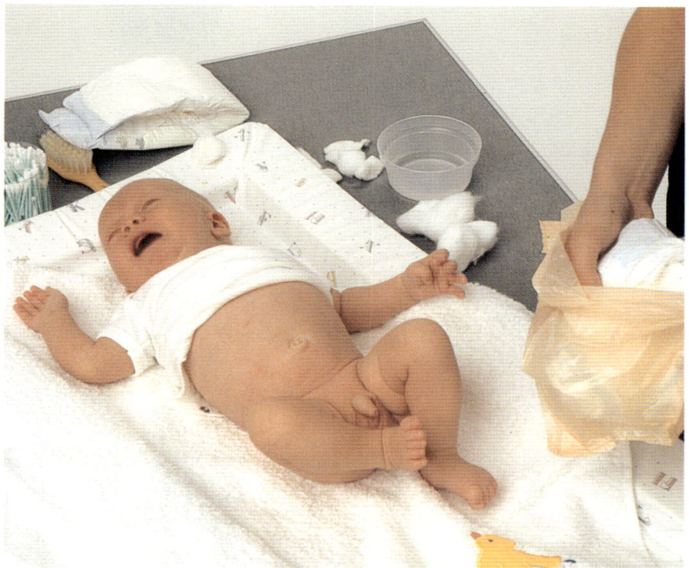

4 *Put your baby in a clean undershirt and then remove his diaper, wiping away any solid matter with a clean corner before placing the dirty diaper in a bag.*

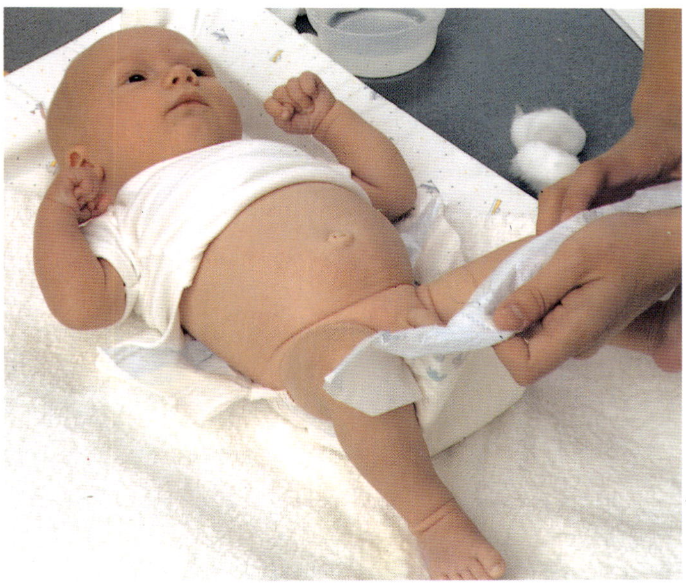

7 *Now that your baby is clean and dry he is ready to have his diaper put on. Place the diaper under his bottom and draw it up carefully between his legs.*

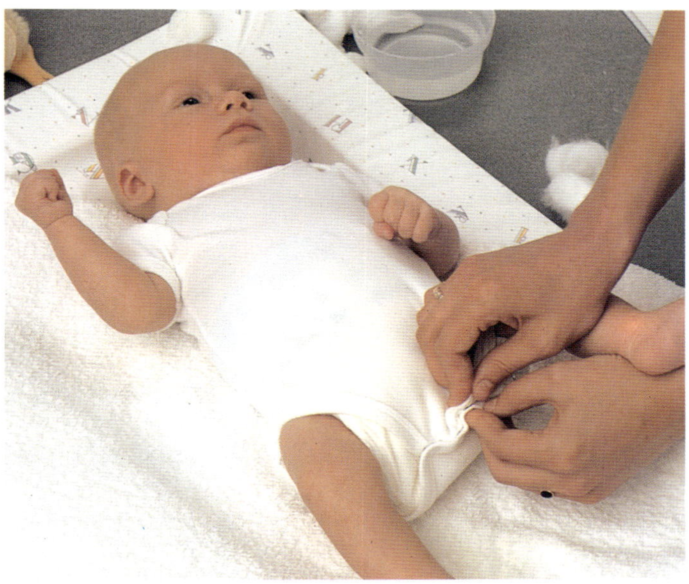

8 *Fasten the diaper securely and once it is firmly in place pull down your baby's undershirt over the top of it. He is now clean and ready to be dressed again.*

BREASTFEEDING

Breastfeeding is the ideal way to feed a baby because breast milk is a baby's natural food containing all the required nutrients in the right proportions for the first months of life. But like any new skill, breastfeeding has to be learned and you may find it more difficult than you expected. Don't give up though, because breastfeeding really is best for your baby and for you and, once it is established, it can be a real pleasure. If you are having problems, talk to your doctor about it.

Ideally, you should put your baby to your breast as soon after birth as possible. The sucking will start a reaction that leads to the release of the hormones that cause both the milk to be manufactured in the breast and the let-down reflex, which allows the milk to pass through the breast to the nipple.

Immediately after the birth and for the first few days, the breasts

Getting your baby latched on

Hold your baby in a comfortable position. Offer her the breast making sure that her mouth is open wide enough.

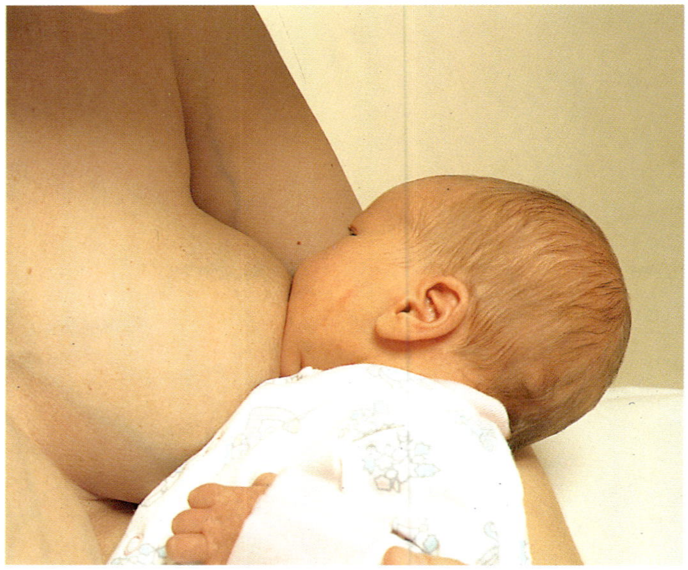

Make sure that your baby's body is in a straight line with your breast so that she doesn't have to turn her head to feed.

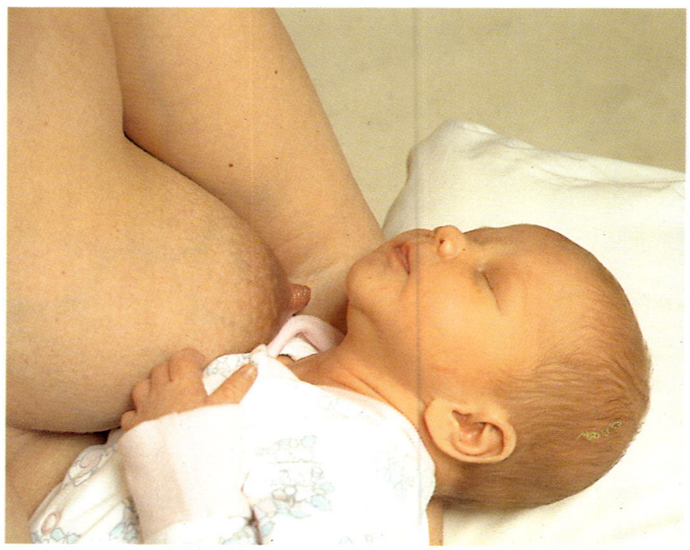

Allow your baby to feed from one breast for as long as she wants. She will let you know when she has had enough.

produce colostrum, a high-protein liquid full of antibodies. This is followed by the actual milk coming in, which often makes the breasts feel heavy and uncomfortable. This discomfort will soon wear off once breastfeeding has become established.

At the first stage of a feeding your baby gets foremilk from the breast; this has a high water content to satisfy thirst. Foremilk is followed by calorie-rich hindmilk which satisfies your baby's hunger and helps her to grow. To make sure that your baby always gets the hindmilk, you should allow her to feed for as long as she wants from one breast before you offer her the other one. If your baby has had enough when she has finished feeding from one breast, remember to start with the other breast at the next feeding.

Your breasts produce milk in response to your baby's feeding, so the more your baby feeds the more milk you will produce. By letting your infant feed for as long as she wants you should be able to produce the amount of milk that is needed.

FINDING THE BEST POSITION

Finding the position that best suits both you and your baby is one of the most important factors for successful breastfeeding, so don't be afraid to experiment. Immediately after the birth, when you are still sore, you may find that sitting on a low chair with plenty of soft cushions is more comfortable than sitting in bed. You can raise your knees slightly by resting your feet on a low stool, or put a pillow on your lap to raise your baby and cushion your abdominal muscles.

Hold your baby so that her body is in a straight line with your breast so that she does not have to turn her head to feed. Sit up straight and lean

Breastfeeding techniques

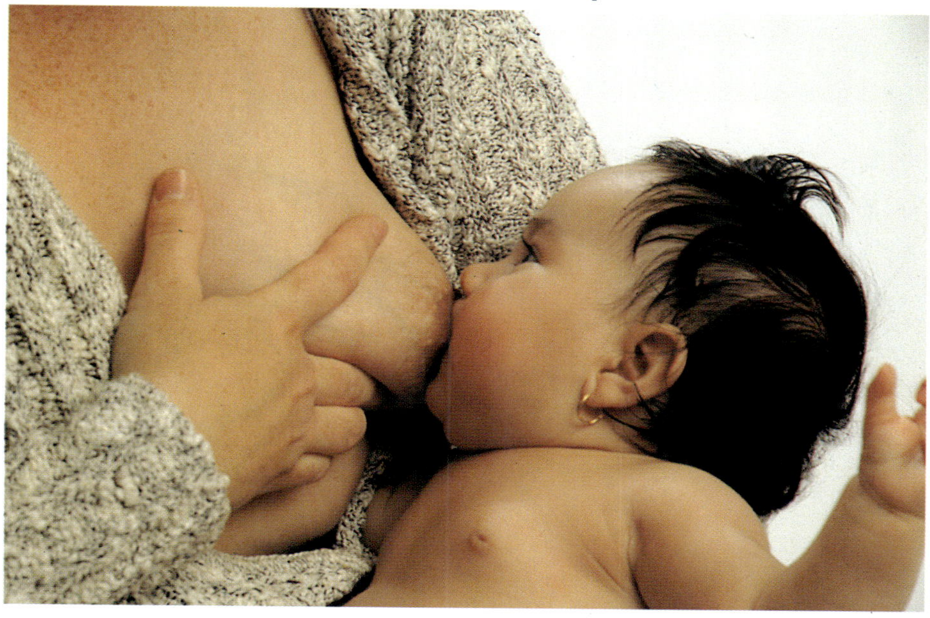

Aim the nipple toward your baby's nose and allow her to take it into her mouth herself. When supporting your breast try not to apply pressure which can block the milk ducts.

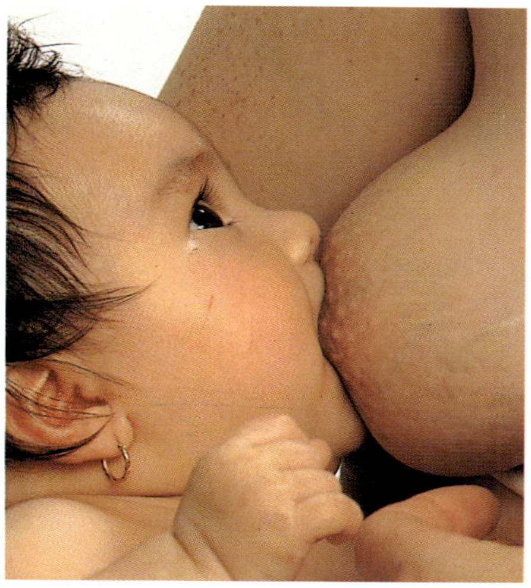

Your baby may try to hold your breast or simply clench and unclench her fists while feeding. Her ears will move as she swallows.

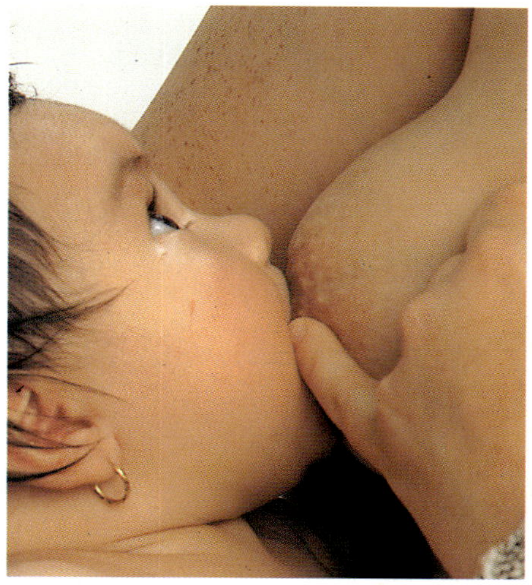

When you want to remove your baby from the breast, insert a finger into her mouth to release the suction.

Advantages of breastfeeding

- Breast milk is designed especially for babies and it contains all the nutrients your baby needs. It is always available, at the right temperature, and it is free.
- Breast milk is easy for your baby to digest, so she is less likely to suffer stomach upsets and constipation.
- Breast milk contains antibodies which will help protect your baby against some infections.
- Breast-fed babies are less likely to develop allergies.
- Breast-feeding will help you get your figure back more quickly.

To bring up any gas, either during the feeding or once she has finished, lay your baby across your knees and stroke her back gently.

You may prefer to burp your baby by sitting her upright on your knee, supporting her head, and gently patting her back.

slightly forward so that the nipple drops into your baby's mouth. Make sure that she is then properly latched onto the breast. This means that your baby takes as much as possible of the areola (the dark area surrounding the nipple) into her mouth, along with the nipple. The milk ducts lie just under the areola and your baby's sucking action on these effectively draws the milk from the breast. You may well be told to check that your baby's nose is not pushed against your breast, making it hard for her to breathe. However, if your baby is positioned properly, she will be able to breathe easily.

There is no set pattern for feeding. Some babies want to be fed every hour, others can happily go for two to three hours before requiring a feeding. Your baby will let you know when she is hungry and your milk supply will be regulated by supply and demand.

EXPRESSING MILK

Expressing milk allows someone else to feed your baby with your breast milk. You can express milk with your hands or you may find it easier to use a breast pump. The best time to express is when you have the most milk, which is either in the morning or, once your baby has dropped her night feeding, it may be in the evening. Milk can be expressed from your breast and kept in a sterile container in the refrigerator for up to 48 hours, or it can be frozen and kept for up to six months. Any feeding equipment or containers you use must be sterilized.

BREASTFEEDING PROBLEMS

If you are concerned that you are not producing enough milk, breastfeeding more often will automatically increase your supply, so don't be afraid to let your baby suck for as long as it is comfortable.

You may have a sleepy baby who needs to be awakened for a feeding. If your baby needs encouragement, gently brush her mouth with your nipple but don't force it into her mouth. Your baby may fall asleep at the breast after a feeding but this only means that she is contented, well fed and doing all right.

Breastfeeding may hurt during the first few weeks because your milk supply has to become established and your nipples are not yet used to your baby's sucking. If the discomfort persists, however, then the positioning of your baby on the breast may not be right and you should experiment. Also check that your baby is latched on properly. If not, your baby may just be sucking the nipple which means she won't be getting enough milk and the more she sucks the more painful it will actually become for you.

You may experience engorged breasts. This is when your breasts become over-full and painful. Feeding your baby frequently will help and you can ease the swelling by bathing your breasts with warm water or having a hot bath. Smooth out some milk with your fingers, stroking the breast downward toward the nipple.

If you experience a shooting pain when your baby sucks, you may have a cracked nipple. If your baby is in the correct position even if your nipples are sore, they shouldn't hurt when you are feeding, so check your positioning. Keep sore nipples clean and dry and let the air get to them as much as possible. A nipple shield that fits over your nipple may help, but don't wear it for more than a day or two. Occasionally sore nipples can be caused by thrush (yeast) in a baby's mouth. If you think this may be the case, discuss the problem with your doctor.

Finally, some nursing mothers can develop a condition called mastitis. This is an infection of the milk ducts and your breast will be inflamed, hot, and flushed in places. Bathing your breast in warm water, or holding a cold washcloth against it, will help to ease any discomfort. You may also need a course of antibiotics to clear up the infection, so consult your doctor.

Sore, cracked nipples and mastitis are usually caused by your baby sucking just the nipple. Make sure your baby takes the nipple and surrounding area well into her mouth when she is feeding.

Breastfeeding equipment

Although no equipment is essential, there are some items that will make life easier, such as nursing bras. There are other things that you may require if you decide to express milk so that you can bottle-feed occasionally. You will need:

- At least two well-fitting cotton nursing bras that allow access to a large area of the breast when your baby is nursing.
- Breast pads for use inside the bra to absorb any leaks of milk.
- Nipple shields to protect your sore nipples.
- Breast shells to fit over the nipple and collect excess milk.
- Breast pump, bottles, and nipples.
- Sterilizing equipment if you intend to express breast milk.

Breast milk can be expressed by hand, or using a manual breast pump like this. Electric pumps are also available.

Various accessories may help with breastfeeding. Breast pads will absorb any leakage, freezer bottles can be used to freeze breast milk, and nipple shields will protect sore nipples.

BOTTLE-FEEDING

If you decide to bottle-feed you should be content with your decision. Do not feel guilty, or think that you are giving your baby second best. Such feelings will only take away the pleasure you should get from feeding your baby. Make the most of each feeding by settling comfortably and giving your baby all your attention.

FORMULA

Formula has been specially produced to provide all the vitamins and minerals your baby needs. Most formula is made from cows' milk, which has been specially treated to make it easily digestible, and its nutritional quality is as near to that of breast milk as possible. There are several brands to choose from and your doctor will be able to advise you. If your baby is known to have a lactose intolerance, or there is a very strong family history of allergies that are connected to cows' milk, you may be advised to use an alternative to regular formula. Often this is a soy-based milk, but others are available. It is important that these alternatives are only introduced if recommended by your doctor.

Formula is available in powdered form, which is made up with cooled boiled water. It is important to follow the instructions on the can or package because the amounts have been carefully calculated to make sure that a baby gets the correct balance of nutrients. Never be tempted to add more powder than is recommended because feedings that are too strong can be harmful to your baby. Ready-prepared formula is also available. This is usually more expensive than powdered formula but it's useful when you are out with your baby.

HOW TO BOTTLE-FEED

Prepare the formula according to the instructions, making up enough for 24 hours. Store the bottles in the refrigerator until needed and make sure that any unused formula is

Feeding equipment

All feeding equipment needs to be kept scrupulously clean at all times. Bottles and nipples should be washed out immediately after use and then sterilized thoroughly before you make up the next batch of formula. You will need to have:

• Enough bottles, nipples, and caps to enable you to make up feedings for a 24-hour period.

• Sterilizer – there are four main ways of sterilizing feeding equipment: boiling – in a pot on top of the stove for 25 minutes; using an electric steam sterilizer; utilizing a microwave steam sterilizer, or boiling on the stove.

• Bottle brush for cleaning inside all the bottles.

• Bottle warmer – this is an optional piece of equipment, but it can be very useful to have, especially when you are doing night feedings.

A bottle warmer is useful at night.

Sterilizing equipment for bottles.

A microwave steam sterilizer.

Feeding should always be a special time for a baby as it helps him bond with the people closest to him. Here a father takes his turn at bottle-feeding.

Burping is something a father can do whether you breast- or bottle-feed.

An older baby may prefer to hold the bottle himself, but he will still need to be cuddled and you should check that the nipple is always full of milk.

thrown away after this time. Never reuse leftover milk because it is a potential breeding ground for bacteria. Some babies are quite happy to take their bottles at room temperature but if yours prefers warm milk, heat the bottle either in a normal bottle warmer, or by standing it for a short time in a pot of hot water. Always remember to test the temperature of the milk on the inside of your wrist to make sure that it isn't too hot before giving the bottle to your baby to drink.

Check that the milk is coming through the nipple at the right speed. If your baby is having to work hard to get the milk, the flow is too slow and you need a nipple with a bigger hole. If, on the other hand, your baby seems to be gulping a lot and the milk is leaking out of the corner of his mouth, the flow is too fast and the nipple should have a smaller hole. If the nipple flattens while you are feeding, pull it gently out of the baby's mouth to release the vacuum, then insert it again.

All your baby's feeding equipment must be thoroughly washed before sterilization.

Chemical sterilizing (a traditional method still used in Europe)

1 *After washing the equipment fill the sterilizing unit with cold water.*

2 *Add sterilizing tablets to the water. Put the bottles, nipples and caps in the unit.*

3 *Check bottles are filled with water, then place tray in unit. Leave for time specified.*

Electric steam sterilizer

1 *Wash and rinse the feeding equipment and then place it in the sterilizing unit.*

2 *Add water, taking care to follow the manufacturer's recommendations.*

3 *Place lid on unit and switch on. The steam destroys any bacteria present.*

Making up formula

1 *Fill the bottle with the correct amount of cooled boiled water. Never use water that has been boiled more than once.*

2 *Measure the required amount of formula, leveling off each scoopful with the back of a knife.*

3 *Add powdered formula to the bottle. Never add extra formula as this can make the mixture too concentrated and could be harmful.*

4 *Secure nipple and place lid on bottle. Shake until the powder has dissolved. Check the milk temperature before giving it to your baby.*

You may want to encourage feeding by stroking the nipple across your baby's mouth. Once his mouth has opened, place the nipple between his lips and your baby should start sucking. Keep the bottle tilted so that formula fills the nipple completely and your baby doesn't suck in air, which can cause gas. Never leave your baby to feed from a bottle on his own because he could vomit and choke. Don't add solids such as cereal to the bottle as this could cause your baby to choke.

The amount of milk your baby needs at feedings will change as he gains weight. At first he may take only a couple of ounces but this will increase. Your doctor can help you to assess his progress.

Gas can sometimes be a problem, so try stopping halfway through a feeding and burp your baby by holding him against your shoulder, or propping him up on your lap while you rub his back. You may want to do this after the feeding is finished as well. The baby may bring back a small amount of milk during or after a feeding; this spitting up is quite normal. If vomiting becomes frequent or violent, you need to consult your doctor.

INTRODUCING SOLIDS

Once milk alone no longer satisfies your baby you will need to start introducing solids into her diet. This can be any time between four and six months of age – in general, babies younger than this shouldn't be put on solids. Your baby will let you know she is still hungry by wanting more after the feeding is finished. A baby may also begin to demand feeds more often and if she normally sleeps through the night, you may find that she starts waking up early wanting to be fed.

Breast milk and formula give babies all they require for the first six months so you don't have to worry if your baby seems satisfied with milk alone until this age.

HOW TO START

By six months of age, your baby needs the additional nourishment provided by solids, and she also needs to learn how to eat. First solids are really just tasters to get a baby used to different textures and flavors; the main nourishment will still come from breast milk or formula. The first food should be bland and smooth, like rice cereal mixed with formula or breast milk. To begin with offer a small amount on the tip of a clean spoon, halfway through a feeding, once a day. Once your baby has accepted this, you can introduce a small amount of fruit or vegetable purée, for example, banana, potato, or carrot (with no added salt or sugar), mixed with formula or breast milk.

As soon as your baby has got used to taking solids off a spoon, you can begin to introduce new foods and other solids at a second meal. If your baby obviously doesn't like the taste of something don't force matters. Try another food and reintroduce the rejected food at a later stage. At first the baby will simply try to suck anything off the spoon. But it won't take long to master getting the food off the spoon and into the back of her mouth. Once your baby can do this she will be able to cope with lumpier textures, so you can begin to mash rather than purée food. Your baby will then also be able to appreciate a wider variety of tastes and textures.

ADVANCED FEEDING

By six to nine months, you can introduce food combinations such as baby cereal and fruit or sweet potato and peas – make sure, though, that peas are well mashed. Food can be lumpier and more solid so that it encourages your baby to start chewing. Try mincing or mashing the food with a fork.

At nine months and over, your baby is likely to be on three meals a day as well as milk, unsweetened diluted fruit juice, or water. Giving your child food at grown-up meal-

Making your own purée

1 *Steam the fruit or vegetable until it is thoroughly cooked and soft, then place it in the food mill or blender.*

2 *Without adding any sugar or seasoning, blend to a smooth consistency then remove a portion for your baby.*

3 *Pour the remaining purée into an ice-cube tray to freeze in baby-size portions. Label and use within one month.*

times will encourage her to learn social skills by watching others. As her appetite grows you can gradually increase the amount given at each meal. Offer finger foods such as slices of peeled apple, and banana; this will encourage her to feed herself. Always stay with your child while she is eating in case of choking.

As with younger babies, don't force unwanted foods; your child may simply not be ready for that particular taste. Don't ever fight over it. Take the food away, but don't offer alternatives or provide snacks between meals or let the child fill up on drinks, especially non-nourishing drinks, such as lemonade.

THE VEGETARIAN BABY

The principles of weaning are the same as for a non-vegetarian baby with the first solids being cereal, puréed fruit, and vegetables. However, vegetarian diets tend to be high in fiber and too much fiber is not suitable for young babies to absorb easily. And it can also interfere with the absorption of minerals such as calcium and iron. So your child will require a combination of cereals, milk, and vegetables which contain the right balance of energy and other nutrients for healthy growth. The diet will also need to include iron-rich foods such as dried fruit, fortified breakfast cereals, bread, lentils, eggs and green leafy vegetables. Vitamin C helps the absorption of iron from vegetables so you should give fresh orange juice, fresh fruit, or raw vegetables with every meal.

A vegan diet excludes milk and all dairy products, as well as meat and fish, and it may be unsuitable for young babies. If you are considering a vegan diet it is essential that you

Equipment

First foods need to be puréed, preferably using a blender or liquidizer, although a strainer and spoon will achieve the same results. As your baby gets older and is able to cope with lumpier foods you can use a fork to mash the food. Your baby should have his or her own feeding utensils, which you will need to keep very clean.

To prepare and feed your own puréed foods you will need:

- Blender or liquidizer.
- Unbreakable bowl, spoon, and feeding cup.
- Bib (preferably two or three) and several washcloths.
- Ice-cube tray or similar for freezing small portions of purée.

Use an unbreakable bowl, plastic teaspoon and feeding cup when weaning your baby.

A blender or strainer will purée first foods. Freeze baby portions in an ice-cube tray.

Left: By eight months a baby will be enjoying finger foods. At first he will examine the food, squashing it between his fingers as he explores its texture. Right: Once he's examined the food he will probably concentrate on trying to get it into his mouth.

Below right: Using both his hands to help him, he eventually manages to get the food into his mouth. These are the very early stages of how a child learns to feed himself.

talk to your pediatrician before beginning to wean your baby onto some solid food.

BABY FOODS

You can make your own first foods by puréeing ripe fruit or vegetables. Remove the skin and any seeds or pits, then boil, steam, or microwave until thoroughly cooked. Allow the cooked fruit or vegetable to cool, then purée. Fruits with seeds such as strawberries will need to be strained. Make a batch of purée, and freeze in small portions for convenience. Reheat thoroughly before use and allow it to cool before giving it to your baby. When your baby is older and has progressed to lumpier, mixed foods she can eat the same foods as you, but remove a small portion for your baby before you add any seasoning or sugar.

Warming food for babies in a microwave is not recommended because it can result in uneven heating which could scald the child's mouth. If you have to use a microwave, stir the food well after cooking to ensure the even distribution of heat and allow it to stand for at least one minute. Check the temperature again before offering the food.

The alternative to homemade

Choking

If your baby chokes while eating try to hook out the obstruction with your finger (being careful not to push it further in) while gently slapping the child on the back. If this doesn't work, lay your baby face downward with her chest and abdomen lying along your forearm and your hand supporting her head. Then slap the infant gently on the back to dislodge the obstruction.

baby food is to choose from the prepared baby foods that are widely available. One of the main advantages of prepared baby foods is that they are quick and convenient. They have been formulated to make sure that, in conjunction with breast milk or formula, a baby receives a nutritionally balanced diet. Available in jars, there are commercially prepared baby foods available for each stage of weaning. Check the labeling for the age range for which it is suitable and, if you wish, whether it is acceptable for a vegetarian diet.

Introduce new combinations of prepared baby food with the same care as you would homemade food. Different food combinations contain several ingredients, some of which may be new to your baby. Always place the amount you require in a dish rather than feeding straight from the jar. The digestive substances in your baby's saliva can find their way from the feeding spoon into the container, which can make any remaining food unsuitable for another meal. Once jars are opened, they should be stored covered in the refrigerator and kept for up to 48 hours.

Always feed your baby her food using a plastic spoon. Keep the dish away from her until she learns not to put her hands in it.

FOODS TO WATCH

You must think carefully about the foods you introduce to your baby's diet. Some must be avoided altogether; others simply need special care in their preparation.

High-fiber foods Babies and young children shouldn't be given high-fiber foods such as bran because their digestive systems are too immature to cope with them.

Salt Never add salt to any food that your baby is going to eat. An infant's system can't cope with more salt than is found naturally in food. Remember too that some products, such as potato chips, are usually quite salty, so you need to be aware of any salt intake from these foods.

Sugar Sugars occur naturally in fruit and vegetables so you should never add sugar to your baby's food or drinks as this can lead to tooth decay and obesity. Some manufacturers' prepared foods may contain sugars, so read labels: sugars may be listed as glucose, sucrose, dextrose, fructose, maltose, syrup, honey, or raw/brown sugar. Avoid honey for the first year.

Additional fats Babies shouldn't have much additional fat added to their food – although the occasional pat of butter added to mashed potato will do no harm.

Nuts Never give whole nuts to a child under five years of age because of the risk of choking. Nuts that are finely ground may be given to children over six months.

Spices Strong spices such as chilies, ginger, and cloves are not suitable to be given to babies.

Eggs Not recommended during the first year. Since eggs can cause allergic reactions, start with well-cooked, easy-to-digest yolk. Eggs should always be cooked until solid.

FOOD ALLERGY

If either you or the baby's father have a family history of food allergies, eczema, asthma, or hayfever, your baby may have an intolerant reaction to the following foods: wheat, oats, and barley cereal; citrus fruits, eggs, nuts, and fish; dairy products, including cows', goats' and sheeps' milk. Intolerance to cows' milk is usually the result of an allergy to one of the proteins in milk or an intolerance of lactose (milk sugar). When you buy commercially manufactured food, always check the ingredients for any foods that may cause an allergic reaction.

Drinks, other than breast milk or formula, should be given in a feeder cup from the age of six months.

At around one year a baby will be able to manage finger food and a feeder cup without help. Never leave your baby alone when he is eating in case he chokes. Give drinks at the end of a meal or they will fill your baby up before eating.

Vitamin drops

If you are breastfeeding, it is recommended that vitamin supplements are also given to children from the age of six months. These vitamin supplements are usually given to children to supplement their diet up to the age of five. As a matter of course, most pediatricians will prescribe vitamins for children when they think that the time is right, though not all doctors believe in their efficacy.

Symptoms of food intolerance or allergy include diarrhea, vomiting after eating, or occasionally blood in stools. In extreme cases the reaction can be a generalized blotchy skin rash which occurs within an hour or so of eating the food. Your child's lips may become swollen, the eyes puffy, and breathing a little wheezy. If breathing becomes restricted you will need to get medical help immediately. The blotchiness and swelling will disappear quickly but it should always be reported to your doctor. Extreme responses to an allergy are rare, but if they do occur you should avoid that particular food.

If your child shows an intolerance to any food it is important that you seek advice from your doctor. It may be that you need to change some of the food in your child's diet, but this should always be done with the advice of a health professional.

MILK AND OTHER DRINKS

As the amount of food increases, your baby's intake of milk will decrease. However, the recommendation is at least 1 pt of breast milk or formula a day, up to one year.

So-called "second-stage" milks have been produced to help meet the nutritional needs of growing babies from six months to two years. They contain more iron than other milks, plus a mix of other nutrients.

In the past cows' milk was introduced into the diet at around six months, but it is now thought that it is not suitable until the baby is at least one year old. This is because cows' milk is low in vitamins like C and D, and is particularly low in iron, all of which your baby needs for healthy growth. After one year whole milk should be given to the under-fives because it provides energy, protein, and calcium, even though it has more saturated fat than breast milk or formula.

Reduced-fat milks are not suitable for babies as they are low in calories and vitamins. Skim milk should not be given to a child until he is at least two years of age, though most doctors recommend part-skim at this point. Always check with your pediatrician first.

If your baby seems thirsty and you are still breastfeeding, your milk will provide all the liquid needed. Otherwise, offer cooled, boiled water between feedings after the age of four weeks. Try giving your baby these additional drinks from a teaspoon; this will make the idea of a spoon seem familiar before you start weaning him onto solids. From the age of six months onward, any drinks other than breast milk or formula should be offered to your baby from a feeder cup.

Any water you give your baby needs to be boiled and cooled until the child is at the age when you no longer need to sterilize feeding equipment. Only ever use boiled water or bottled water sold specifically for babies – never make up a feeding with, or offer your baby, bottled mineral water.

DIAPERS

Diapers are produced in a variety of types, styles, and sizes, but the basic choice is still between disposable and cloth diapers. Ideally, you should decide which type of diaper you are going to use before your baby arrives. You will need to take into account a number of factors: your lifestyle, the amount of time and money you have available, and the type of washing and drying facilities you will be using.

CHANGING

Whichever diaper you choose, the techniques required for changing and cleaning a baby's bottom are the same. You should change your baby whenever he is wet or dirty. The number of changes may vary from day to day, but generally you will have to change your baby first thing in the morning, after each feeding, after a bath, and before bed at night. Get everything you need together before you start so that there is no reason to leave your baby unattended while you are changing the diaper. Make sure that the room where you are changing your new baby is warm and free from drafts. Lie your baby on a folded towel or changing mat, placed on the floor, a table, or on the bed, making sure that a

---

Folding cloth diapers/Triple absorbent fold

This is particularly good for newborn babies because it makes a small, neat shape while giving extra absorbency between the legs.

1 *Fold the diaper into four sections with the two folded edges nearest you and to your left.*

2 *Pick up the top layer by the right-hand corner and pull it out to make a triangle.*

5 *Fold these layers over again to make a thick central panel.*

6 *Place a diaper liner over the top of the central panel.*

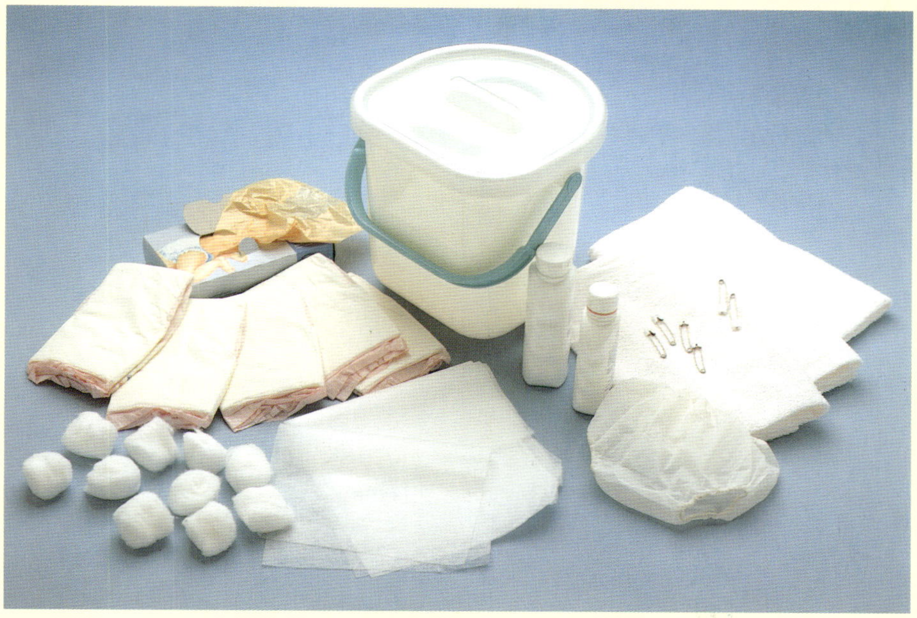

Changing equipment:

- Changing mat or towel.
- Clean cloth diaper, diaper liner, pins, plastic pants. Or a disposable diaper.
- Baby lotion or wipes, cotton.
- Bowl of warm water.
- Diaper ointment (optional).
- Pail for dirty diaper or a plastic bag for a disposable diaper.

3 *Turn the diaper over.*

4 *Fold the vertical edge into the middle by a third.*

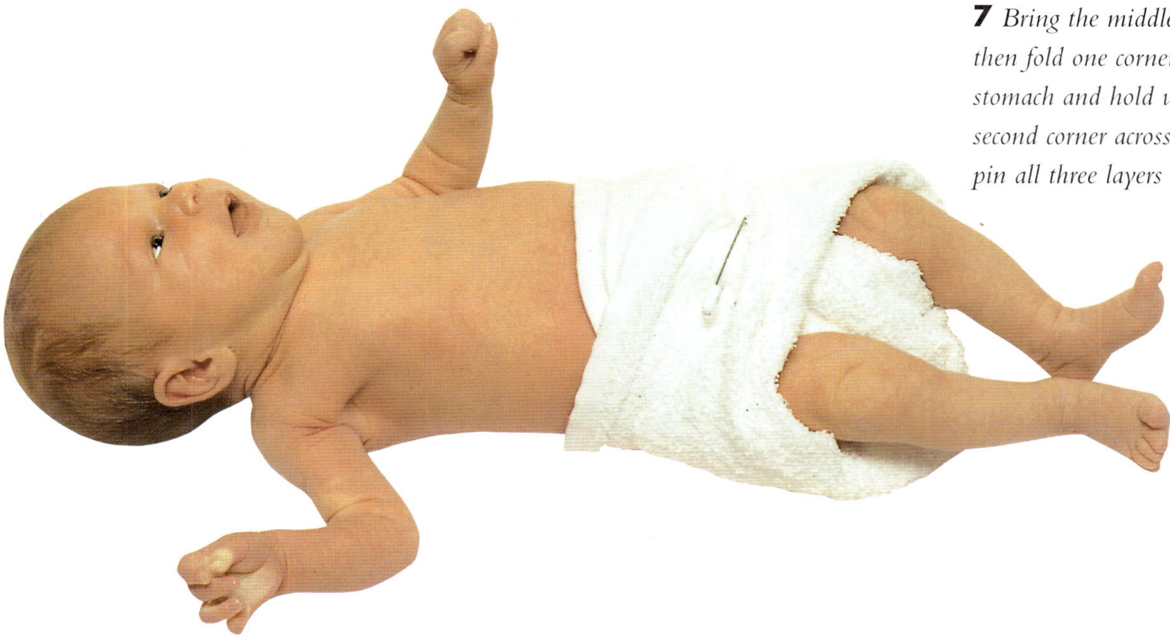

7 *Bring the middle fold between the legs, then fold one corner across your baby's stomach and hold while you bring the second corner across. Pull taut and then pin all three layers together.*

Kite fold

This is suitable from about three months onwards. You can adapt the size of the diaper by varying the depth when you fold the point up, before positioning the liner.

1 *Lay the diaper out flat in front of you so that it is in a diamond shape with one of the corners nearest you.*

2 *Fold the sides into the center so that you form a kite shape with the diaper.*

5 *Bring the diaper up between the baby's legs and carefully fold one side and then the other into the middle. Secure the diaper with one pin in the center for a small baby and two pins, one on either side, for a bigger baby.*

---

wriggling infant cannot roll off if you are changing the diaper on a raised surface.

Remove the soiled diaper. Then clean your baby's bottom thoroughly, wiping away any solid matter with a clean corner of the used diaper, or with a damp tissue or cotton soaked in warm water. A baby wipe, or some baby lotion, can be used to finish cleaning the area. Once you have dried your baby's bottom, you can apply a little specially formulated ointment to protect the skin. Then put on a clean diaper.

WHAT'S IN A DIAPER?

You may find the diaper of your new baby is stained dark pink or even

3 *Fold the point at the top down toward the center so that there is a straight edge along the top.*

4 *Fold the bottom edge up toward the center, adjusting the fold so that the diaper is the correct size for your baby.*

red. This is because the urine of newborns contains substances called urates. Your newborn's immature bladder cannot hold urine for very long so he may urinate as frequently as 20 times in every 24 hours. This will gradually lessen.

Your baby's first stools will be a blackish-green color because the meconium from your amniotic fluid is still working its way out of his system. Once feeding begins, the stools will change to greenish-brown and then to a regular yellowish-brown color. The number of stools passed will vary from baby to baby, although bottle-fed babies tend more toward constipation.

DISPOSABLE DIAPERS

There is no doubt that disposables are more convenient than cloth diapers. They are quick and easy to put on and remove and they don't require washing, which is a strong consideration when you think about the extra washing your baby is likely to produce without even including diapers. Their main disadvantages are that they are more expensive to buy than their cloth counterparts and, despite their name, are cumbersome to dispose of. Environmental concerns, too, have caused a number of states to consider banning them. Most end up being wrapped and put in the trash.

Alternatively, there are a number of portable units available which will wrap and seal the dirty diaper in strong film, so that they can be stored for a number of days and then be disposed of in bulk.

Disposables work by allowing moisture to soak through a top sheet into an absorbent filling, which is protected on the outside by a waterproof backing. They come in a wide range of shapes and sizes and most are also available in boy/girl styles. Most disposables have elasticized legs to ensure a snug fit, and reusable tapes so that you can check whether the diaper needs changing and adjust the leg size. Disposables need to be checked frequently because many of them are so good at keeping your baby dry that you may forget to change them.

CLOTH DIAPERS

These are a once-only buy which makes them more economical than disposables. Cloth diapers come in a variety of absorbencies and qualities. As a general guide the more absorbent the diaper the more expensive it is, so buy the best you can afford. The diaper can be folded in a number of different ways to fit your baby. It is held together with special pins and covered with reusable plastic pants to prevent leakage. One-way liners can be placed inside the diaper to help keep your baby dry; this method also has the added advantage of allowing you to flush any stools down the toilet with

Putting on a cloth diaper

Cloth diapers can be folded in a variety of ways to suit the age and sex of your child.

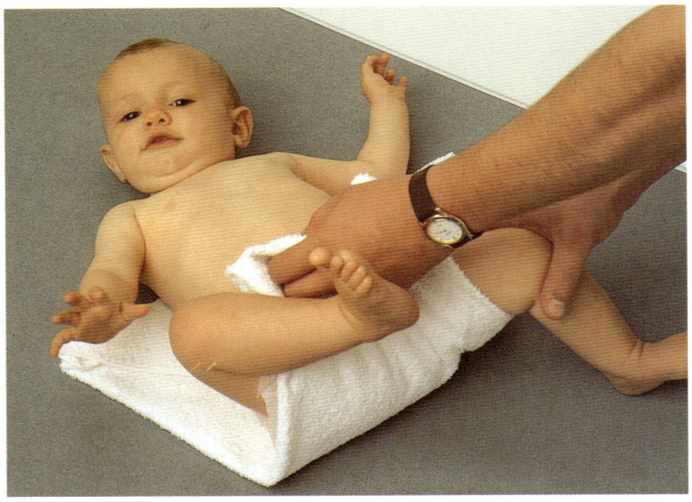

1 *Fold diaper and place a liner in the center. Lay your baby on the diaper with top edge at waist. Now bring diaper up between her legs.*

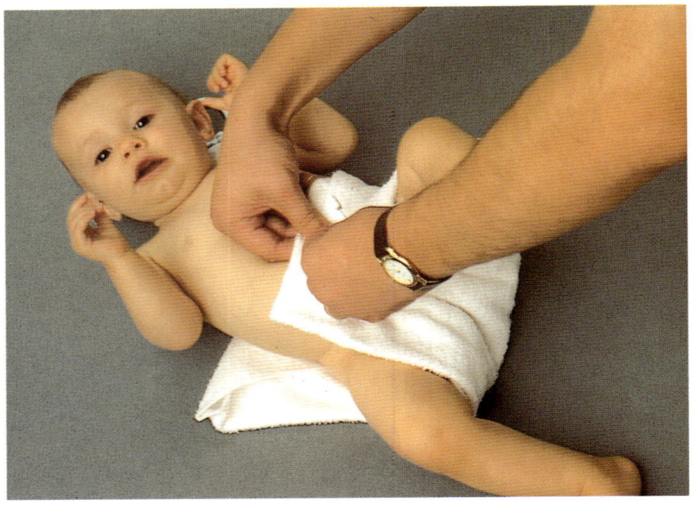

2 *Holding the diaper in place, fold one side over the central panel and secure with a diaper pin.*

3 *Fold the other side into the middle and secure. Always keep your finger between the diaper and your baby's skin when inserting the pin so that there is no risk of pricking your baby.*

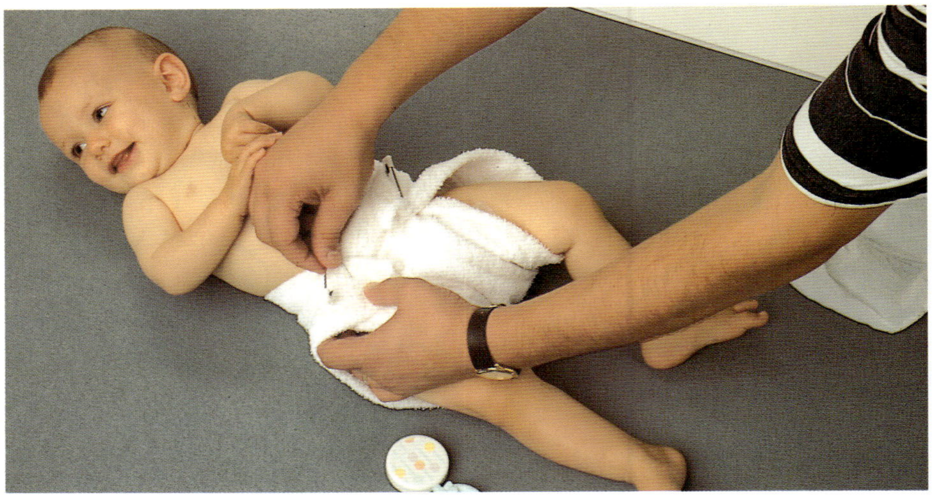

4 *Once the diaper is securely in place you may want to put on a pair of protective plastic pants. Try not to get cross if your baby wets her clean diaper immediately and you have to start all over again.*

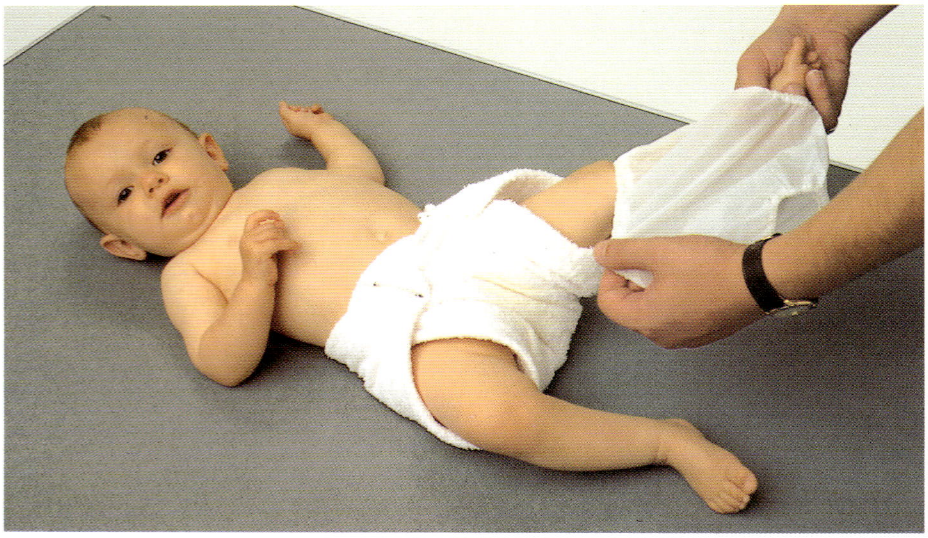

the minimum of bother and mess.

When working out the price of cloth diapers you first need to take into consideration the extra cost of detergent, the electricity used for washing and drying them, plastic pants, diaper liners, and pins. Cloth diapers are harder work to use than disposables because they need continual washing, so a reliable washing machine and tumble dryer will make life much easier and more convenient for you. The diapers will also need to be well washed and dried thoroughly. Then they should be aired before being reused.

SHAPED WASHABLE DIAPERS

These wash like cloth diapers but are shaped like disposables with re-sealable fastenings and elasticized legs. They come in various sizes, and have a waterproof backing.

CONVENIENCE AND HELPING THE ENVIRONMENT

The choice of diaper is influenced by environmental considerations. Disposable diapers are a great convenience for busy parents, but there are hidden costs to the environment. Some manufacturers of disposables try to minimize the bulk of their products without cutting down their efficiency. This uses fewer natural resources for materials, but some portion of the diaper still will not break down completely after being discarded. Cloth diapers would therefore seem more environmentally friendlier to use, but you must first assess the cost of energy resources and the impact on the environment of all the detergent needed to wash all the used diapers.

If you choose to go with cloth diapers instead of disposable ones, using a diaper service can make your life a great deal easier. For a fee (and sometimes a hefty one), the diaper service will pick up all the soiled diapers and replace them with some clean ones.

DIAPER RASH

Whichever diaper you choose, it is unlikely that your baby will get through the diaper years without experiencing a diaper rash at some time. The key to avoiding the problem is cleanliness and frequent diaper changes, so that urine and feces don't remain in contact with the skin too long. Allow your baby to spend some time naked each day; this will help keep the skin clear. Diaper rash is sometimes caused by the yeast fungus, and if so an anti-fungal cream will be needed, so consult your doctor if the rash persists.

Putting on a disposable diaper

Disposable diapers are available in a variety of shapes, sizes and absorbencies. Always select the size that is recommended for your baby's weight.

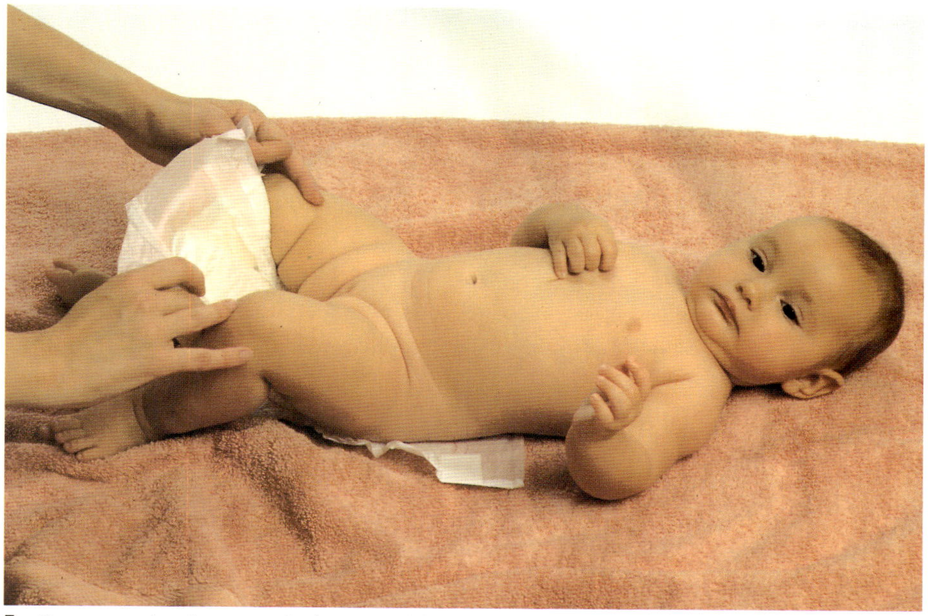

1 *Open out the diaper with the re-sealable tabs at the top. Lay your baby on the diaper so that the top aligns with her waist. Bring the front of the diaper up between her legs.*

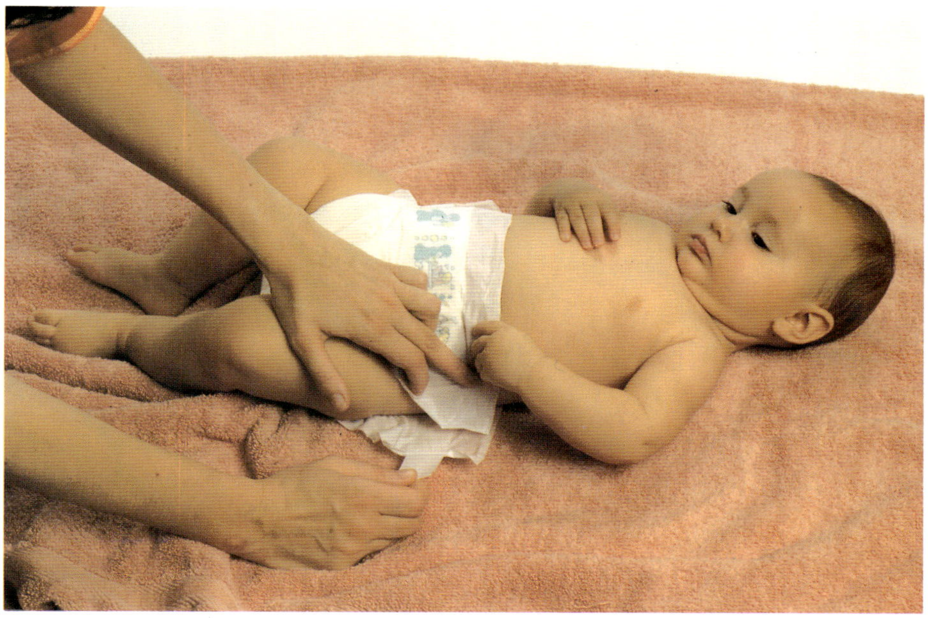

2 *Smooth the front of the diaper so that it fits snugly around your baby's waist. Pull the adhesive tabs firmly toward the front of the diaper and fasten them to secure.*

DRESSING YOUR BABY

There are clothes to fit every size of newborn, from the tiny premature baby to the bouncing 10-pounder. Most baby clothes are sized by the approximate age and height of the child. Your baby probably won't require a great number of newborn clothes and may well grow into the next size within a matter of weeks – some babies are even big enough when born to bypass the newborn size entirely.

Dressing and undressing your newborn can be difficult enough without having to worry about doing up complicated fastenings, so keep first clothes simple and save buttons and bows until later. Choose well-designed baby clothes that allow you to dress and undress your baby with the minimum of fuss. Look for garments that have wide, stretchable necks so that you can slip them over baby's head easily. Stretchies that have fastenings up the inside leg will allow you to change a diaper without having to remove all your baby's clothes. "Onesie" undershirts, which fasten between the legs, will prevent your baby from getting cold around the middle and are ideal if you dress your baby in separates.

If you have a girl you may well be tempted to put her in dresses from the beginning, but dresses are not practical everyday wear for a young baby. They ride up and can be uncomfortable to lie on, they will allow drafts in around her middle, and they get in the way when she is starting to crawl. It is better to save them for special occasions or for when she's older. Lacy jackets and shawls are best avoided too, as little fingers can get caught in the holes.

As your baby grows, colorful rompers and overalls can take the place of stretchies. They are versatile and are suitable for both boys and girls. Rompers, which are really stretchies without feet, are easy to wear as they allow your baby freedom of movement. When you buy overalls make sure that they have generous turn-ups and adjustable shoulder straps so that you get the maximum wear out of them.

When the weather is warm, babies need to be dressed in clothes that will keep them comfortably cool, and you should always cover their heads with a sun hat if you are out and about. Outerwear for cold days should be roomy enough to fit easily over everyday clothes.

Easy-care fabrics

Your baby is quite likely to go through as many as three or four changes a day so it makes sense to buy clothes made in easy-care fabrics that will wash and wear well. Choose natural fabrics as these are best for warmth and also for absorbency. Pure cotton clothing is ideal for your baby's underwear and also for her stretchies, but note that government regulations about fire retardancy have nearly made cotton sleepwear a thing of the past.

Whether you are machine or hand washing garments, always follow the instructions on the labels so that your baby's clothes retain their shape, color, and texture. Avoid using any harsh detergents as these may irritate your baby's skin. It is important that all clothes are well aired and completely dry before being put away.

Footwear

It is very important that a baby's toes are never restricted by tight footwear. Check regularly that stretchies, leggings, and tights have enough room in them for the baby to wiggle her toes. Socks, booties, and tights that have shrunk or been outgrown should be discarded. The same care should be taken with tight collars, cuffs, mittens and also gloves.

Your baby will not need proper shoes until she is walking and her feet need protection from the hard ground. If you do put your child in soft shoes before this, these should be made from a lightweight breathable material such as cloth or very soft leather and they must be flexible enough for you to feel her toes through them.

When you come to buy your baby's first shoes always have them fitted at a shop that offers a special fitting service for children. Both your baby's feet should be measured for length and width. If you can afford them, shoes with leather uppers are best. It is essential to check regularly that the shoes still fit and have not become too tight.

For a first layette you will need:

- 3 baby gowns.
- pair of scratch mittens.
- shawl.
- 7 stretchies.
- 2 pairs of booties or socks.
- 4 vests or onesies.
- warm outer wear for chilly days.
- sun hat.

How to dress your newborn

Dressing and undressing a newborn can seem difficult at first. Always dress a newborn baby on a flat surface so that you have both hands free.

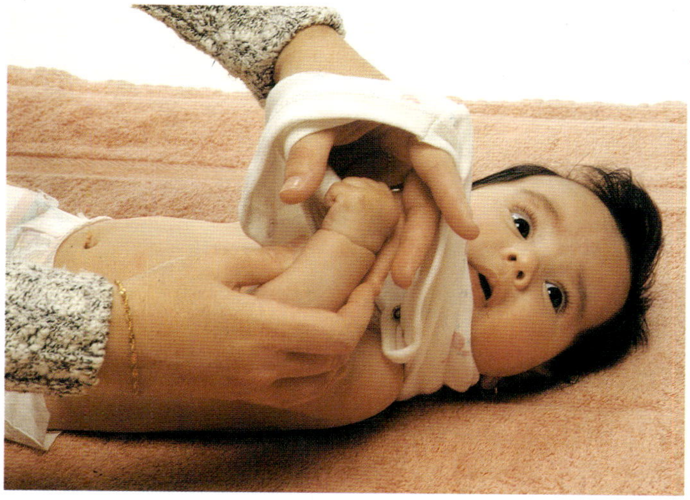

1 *Put the "onesie" over your baby's head, raising her head slightly. Then widen one of the arm holes with your hand.*

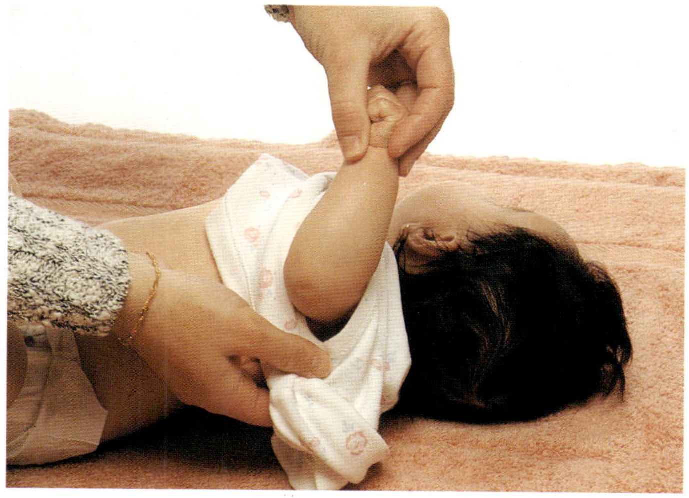

2 *Using your other hand, gently guide the arm through the sleeve. Repeat with the other arm.*

3 *Place your hand under your baby's bottom and pull down the back of the onesie.*

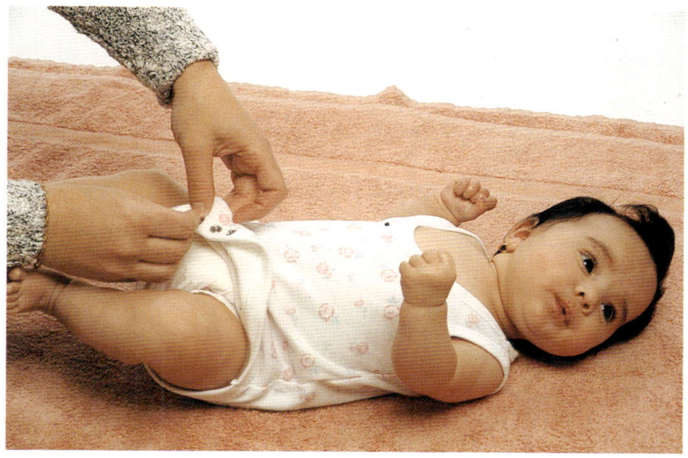

4 *Do up the snaps between the legs and make sure that the onesie isn't too tight anywhere when fastened.*

5 *Scrunch up the leg of the sock and then hold it wide as you ease it over your baby's foot.*

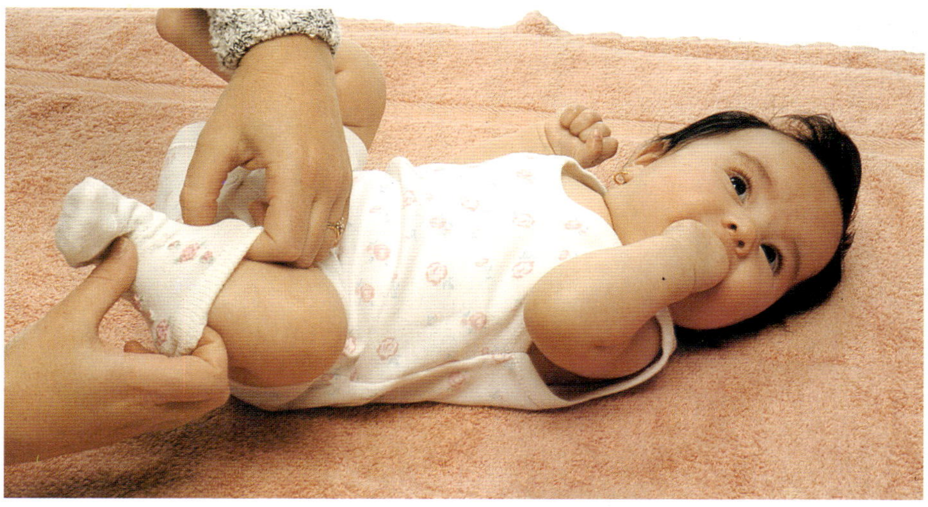

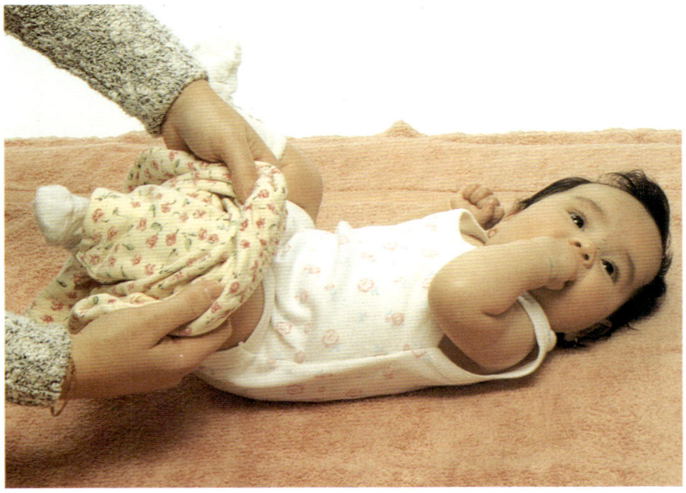

6 *Gently place one foot in the pant leg and then the other and pull the pants up.*

7 *Place your hand under your baby's bottom and lift so that you can pull the pants up over the diaper.*

8 *Adjust the pants and make sure that the onesie is smooth and that there are no puckers that could be uncomfortable to lie on.*

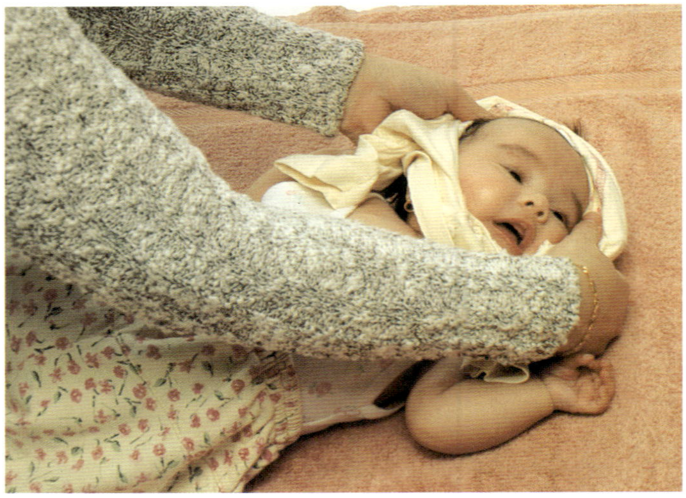

9 *Hold the neck of the T-shirt wide as you slip it over your baby's face and then pull it down over the back of her head.*

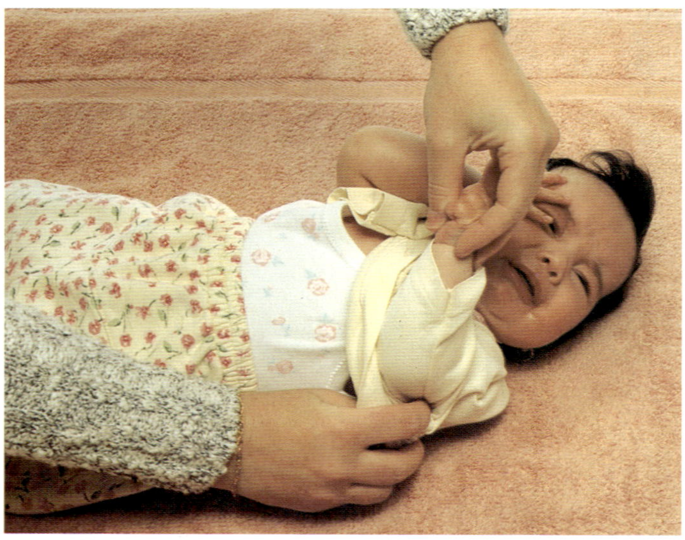

10 *Gently ease your baby's arm through the T-shirt's sleeve and then pull the sleeve down.*

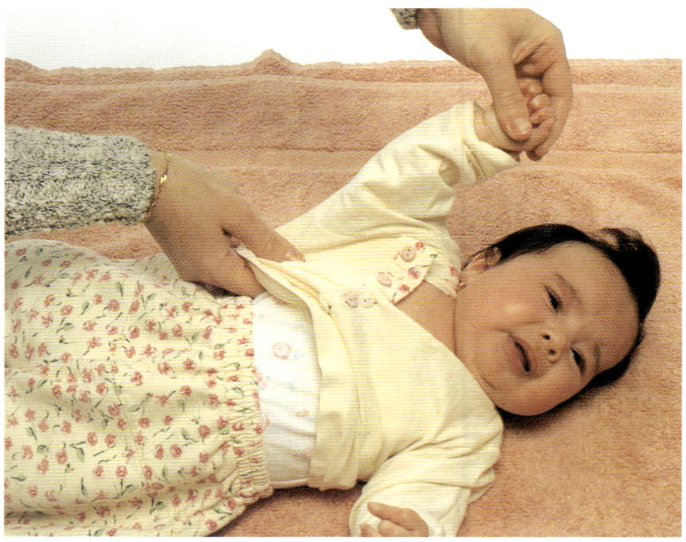

11 *Put her other arm into the sleeve, then pull down top and tuck into her pants. Your baby is now ready to face the day!*

An all-in-one stretchie with leg fasteners is ideal for a new baby. The leg opening allows you to change the diaper easily without having to remove any of her clothes.

Rompers and a top are ideal for an older baby and are practical for both boys and girls. The romper straps hold the rompers in place even when your baby is being very active and will help prevent gaps occurring around the middle.

A more mobile baby will be happiest in pants that will protect her legs as she learns to walk. Make sure the pant legs clear the floor so that she doesn't trip.

Choose clothes carefully

You will be surprised at how quickly your baby grows during the first 12 months. Select clothes that will mix and match and allow some room for growth. Once she begins to crawl, your baby will need sensible easy-care clothes that will withstand endless washing. Make sure that neck openings are large enough and that garments are easy to unfasten for quick diaper changes. Not all clothes have to be practical; it is nice to buy a couple of special outfits that can be used for parties and days out too.

Dresses look pretty, but are not really practical everyday wear for very young babies or once your baby becomes mobile. Keep dresses for those special occasions.

Rompers with short sleeves made in natural fibers are ideal for the summer. Synthetic fibers don't allow the skin to breathe properly and may make your baby feel hot and uncomfortable.

Babies don't need proper shoes until they have started to walk. Soft shoes like these are perfect for little feet in the meantime.

BATHING

When you bathe your baby you need to get all you require together before you start. It helps if you can keep all the diapers, pins, pants, and toiletries either in a changing bag or box. A diaper pail is essential because you'll need somewhere to put the dirty diaper and used wipes. A second pail is also useful for dropping the dirty clothes into as you undress the baby. Any clean clothes and towels should be well aired before you begin and the room where you undress your baby should be warm (a minimum of 70°F) and draft-free.

When babies are tiny it is easier to bathe them in a baby bath on a stand, or one that fits into the big bath. This way they will be at a comfortable height for you to hold them. Before undressing your baby, fill the bath with warm water, putting the cold in first then the hot, and mix well. Add any bath preparation at this stage. Test that the water is at the right temperature. A special bath thermometer will give you an accurate temperature reading or you can just use your elbow.

For bathing you will need:

- Bowl of warm water, absorbent cotton and cotton swabs (optional) to clean your baby's face before bathing (see cleaning your baby).
- Baby bath.
- Changing pad.
- Bath towel.
- Baby shampoo.
- Baby powder (optional).
- Diaper changing equipment and a clean diaper.
- Clean clothes.

1 *Wrap your baby firmly in a towel. Test the temperature of the bath water again then, having tucked his legs firmly under your arm, hold your baby's head over the bath, supporting his neck and back with your hand.*

2 *Wet his head and apply a mild baby shampoo. Wash the hair with gentle circular movements, keeping the water and shampoo well away from his eyes. Once washed, rinse off the shampoo and lift your baby back onto your knee and towel his hair dry.*

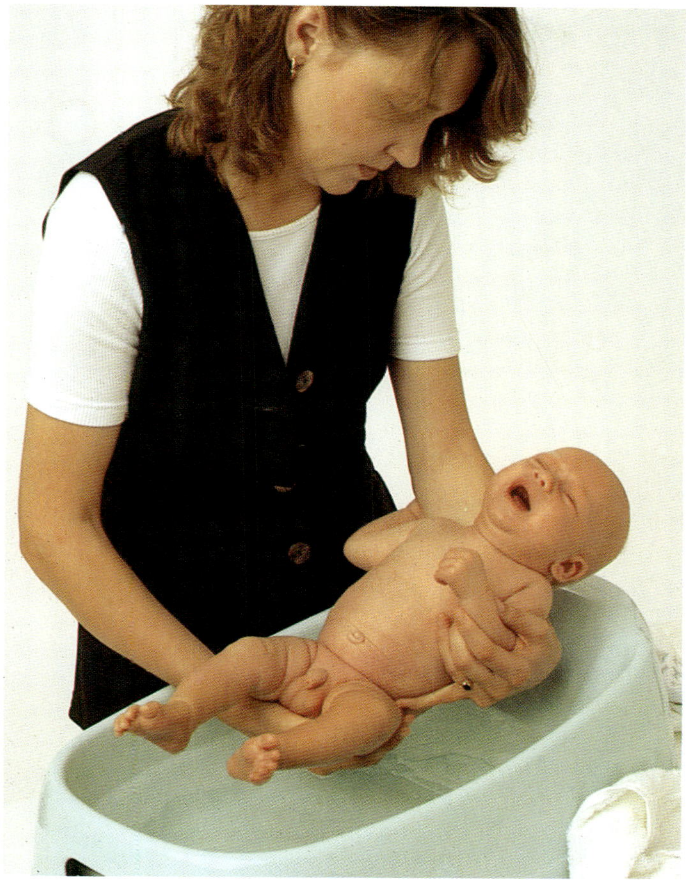

3 *Lift your baby gently into the bath, supporting his head and back on your arm, while holding the arm that is the farthest away from you.*

4 *This leaves your other hand free to wash under his arms and in all the folds and creases. When you have finished, lift your baby out of the bath and into a warm towel.*

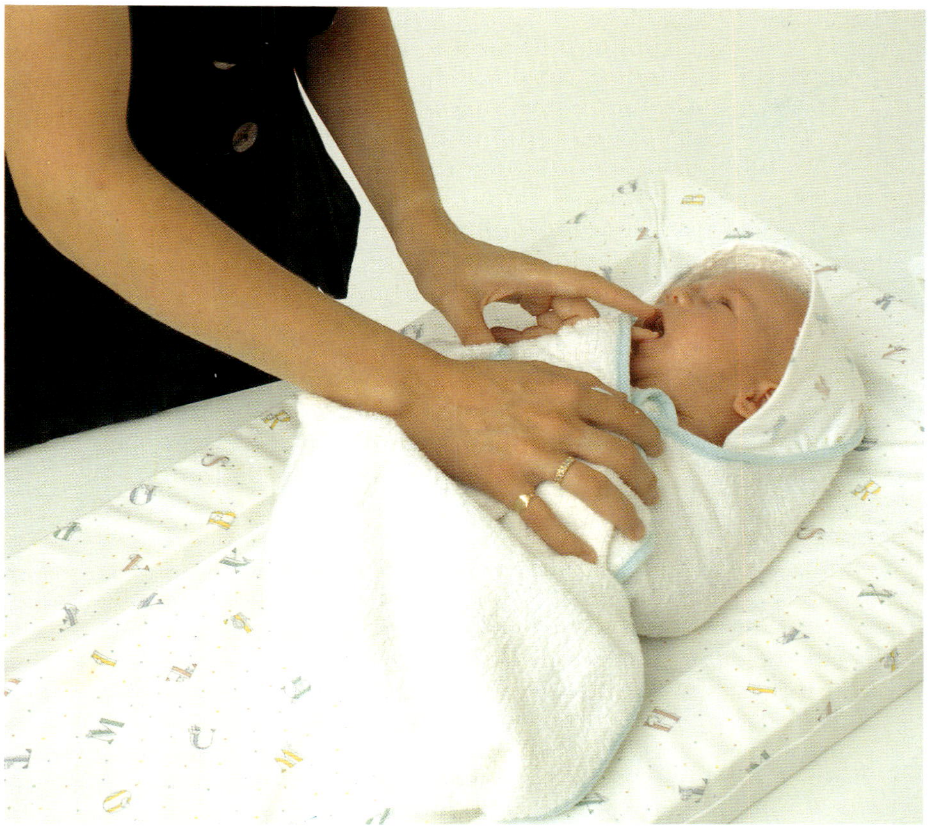

5 *Once you have dried your baby, you may want to apply some baby powder. Put a little powder on your hands and then rub it onto the baby's body, making sure you close the lid tightly after use. Don't sprinkle it on straight from the container in case it gets into your baby's mouth or eyes. It can be dangerous for young infants to inhale powder into their lungs.*

You may find it easier to bathe a very young baby in a baby bath. Some of these have their own stand; others, like the one above, fit over a big bath.

A sponge inlay that fits snugly into the bottom of the bath will prevent your baby from slipping, and will make it easier for you to hold him.

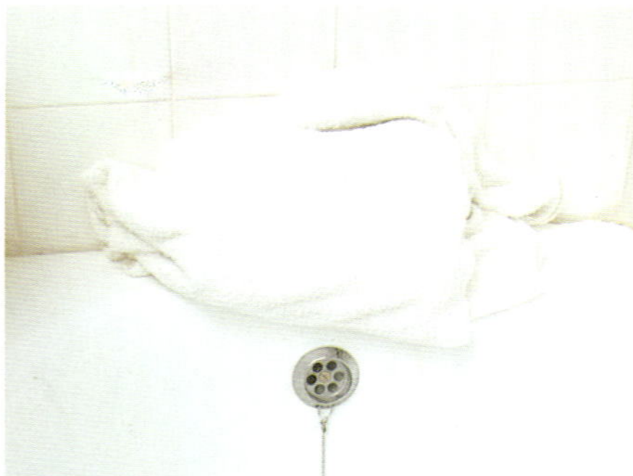

Once your baby is old enough to be bathed in the big bath you should cover the taps with a folded towel before putting him in the bath. This will prevent him from accidentally burning himself on the hot faucet.

An older baby will be happy to spend time in the bath if he has bath toys to play with. Containers that can be filled and emptied and toys that float and bob about will give hours of fun and entertainment.

Safety notes

Never leave your baby or toddler alone in the bath. It only takes a few seconds for a child to drown in as little as 2 in of water.

- When drying or dressing your baby never leave him unattended on a raised surface. He could easily roll off and hurt himself.
- Always check the temperature of the bath water before putting your baby in the bath.
- If you bathe your child in a conventional large bath, place a cover over the taps so that he can't burn himself. A folded towel will do.
- Use a non-slip bath mat in the bath.
- Always put the cold water in first when running the bath.
- If you are using a bath and stand, make sure that it is sturdy and secure before lifting your baby into it.

Above: Your child may enjoy sharing his bath with others, or he may prefer to have a bath alone. If you are intending to bathe two or three children together it is often easier to put the smallest into the bath first and then let the others join him one at a time.

Right: Not all children enjoy spending time in the bath. If one child is unhappy about bathtime don't force him to stay in longer than he wants. Always stay in the bathroom with your children so that you can be sure that they are safe.

SLEEPING

Your new baby has no understanding of day and night so during the first weeks of her life she will sleep and wake at random. You may find that she sleeps for 20 hours out of every 24 or for only 12 hours out of 24. Whatever pattern your baby adopts, she will be getting as much sleep as she needs.

Average sleep pattern

Birth	17 hours in every 24	
	Day	**Night**
3 months	5 hours	10 hours
6 months	4 hours	10 hours
9 months	3 hours	11 hours
12 months	2 hours	11 hours

Your baby's biological clock will dictate when she is ready for sleep in the evenings and this is a good starting point for establishing a regular bedtime. From the very beginning you should make the hour before bed quiet and relaxing. You may choose this time to give your baby a bath, and you will certainly want to feed and change your baby before putting her down in the crib. It's best to let your child learn to fall asleep on her own, so avoid rocking her to sleep. During the first three months your baby may sleep better if swaddled in a blanket or sheet – this will prevent tiny limbs from jerking and twitching. These sudden involuntary movements often wake a very young baby. As your child gets older she will begin to settle on her own and you can help by providing things for amusement, such as a mobile and crib toys. Follow the same routine every night so that the baby gradually begins to associate the crib with night-time and sleep.

Your baby will enjoy being outside from an early age. Keep her out of direct sun in the shade and have the hood up to protect her from drafts.

A baby's room needs to be warm – around 65°F – so that the child doesn't wake up cold in the night.

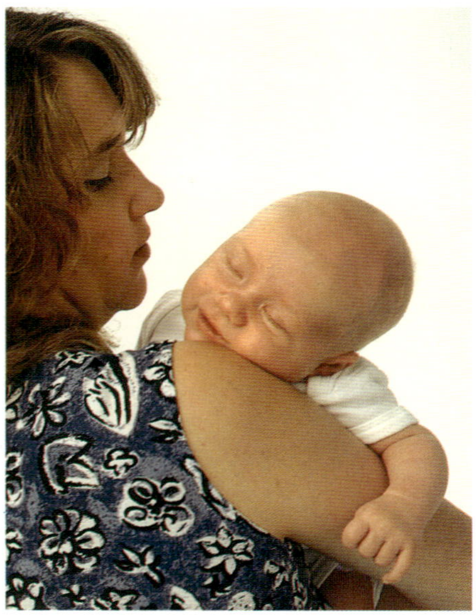

Try not to let your baby fall asleep before putting him in his crib as he may wake feeling distressed if you are not there.

Crib death

All parents are worried about the possibility of crib death, technically known as Sudden Infant Death Syndrome (SIDS). Although the chance of this happening to your baby is remote, it is sensible to take a few simple precautions that are known to reduce the risk.

• Make sure that your baby sleeps either on her back or side, with the lower arm forward to stop the child from rolling onto her stomach.

• Keep your baby warm, but not too warm. Check her temperature regularly by feeling the back of her neck or tummy, and use several lightweight blankets so that you can add or take them away to adjust the temperature.

• Don't use a duvet or baby nest because these could be too warm for your baby.

• Do not smoke near your baby and keep him out of a smoky atmosphere.

• If your baby seems unwell, take him to the doctor immediately.

• Try, if you can, to breast feed. It is believed to help reduce the risk of crib death.

• Research is being carried out into the possible link between chemicals found in mattresses and crib death, but as yet no proven link has been found. However, you can safeguard your baby by making sure that his mattress is kept clean, dry and well aired.

• Make sure your baby's room is well ventilated. Leave the door ajar or a windown open (but ensure that the baby is not in a draft.) Don't leave room heaters on at night. The temperature should be around 65°F.

Bedtime tips

- Encourage your baby to sleep while there are background noises going on. This way she won't expect silence at bedtime.
- Put a selection of toys in the crib to provide amusement if she wakes early.
- Make night feedings as quick and quiet as possible, keeping the lights low and changing the baby first. Don't do anything stimulating.
- Put the baby down to sleep in the crib at night so that she comes to associate it with sleep.
- Wrap up a newborn baby firmly so that she feels secure.

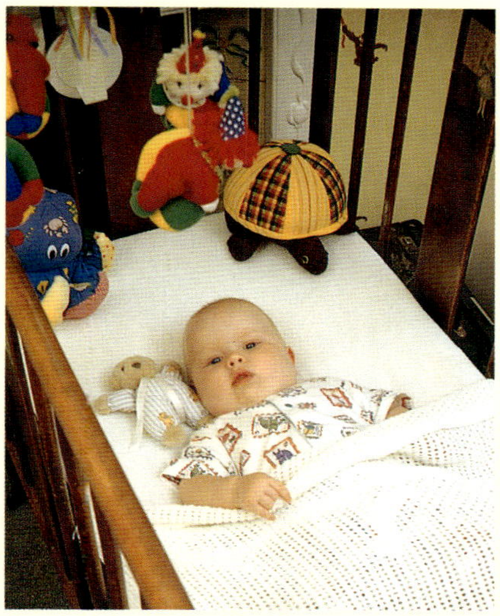

An older baby will enjoy looking at a mobile when he is awake in his crib.

Put your baby down to sleep in a onesie, diaper, and stretchie and cover her with a sheet and several layers of blankets. You can check for body warmth during the night by feeling the tummy or the back of the neck, then you can add or take away blankets accordingly. If your baby seems worried by the dark, leave a nightlight on near the crib.

You can help your infant develop a better sleeping pattern by encouraging her to be more awake during the day. Stimulate your baby by talking and playing with her in the daytime when she is awake. Keep feeding and changing down to a minimum amount of time during the night so that your baby learns that this is not a time for being sociable.

Above: If your baby prefers to sleep on her side, make sure her lower arm is in a forward position to stop her from rolling onto her stomach.
Below: Check your baby's body warmth regularly at night, and remove some blankets if she feels too warm.

CRYING

Your response to your child's crying and the way you comfort him can influence the bond that grows between you. There is no risk of spoiling your child by responding to his cries. It is impossible to give a young baby too much love. By going to your baby you will be showing him that you care and this in turn will help to form a deep, loving relationship between you.

WHY BABIES CRY

Babies cry for a lot of different reasons and you need to understand what makes your baby cry so that you can provide comfort. Your newborn may cry a lot because this is the main means of communicating with you. The infant needs to be able to let you know that the world he is now in is a strange and sometimes frightening place. Once he has adapted to the new environment and you have developed a routine that takes account of his likes and dislikes, the amount of crying will gradually start to decrease.

Hunger is the most common cause of crying and you will soon learn to recognize when your baby is hungry. The first action is to feed on demand – a very young baby may need feeding about every two or three hours.

Being too hot or too cold can also make a baby cry. A young baby can't regulate his own temperature and he can easily become too hot or too cold, so it is important to keep a check on an infant's temperature. You should make sure that your baby's room is kept at a constant 65°F. Wet or dirty diapers do not cause crying except when the wet diaper gets cold.

Your new baby will probably hate being undressed, even in a warm room. This is because the feel of clothing on the skin creates a secure feeling, so when it is removed the infant cries. Keep undressing to a minimum in the first few weeks. Sponge rather than bathe your baby so that you only need to remove a bit of clothing at a time. When you do undress him completely, wrap him in a towel to give him a feeling of security.

Pain is a definite cause of crying, but it may be hard for you to locate the cause of the actual pain. If you

Crying cures

- Movement soothes a baby so try rocking him or walking around holding him on your shoulder.
- Put your baby in a bouncing seat that will move very gently.
- Push him backward and forward in the carriage.
- Put the baby in his car seat and go for a drive.
- Talk, sing, or croon soothingly.
- Put on the radio or TV or turn on the vacuum cleaner.
- Distract the baby with a noisy toy.
- Play a tape of calm music.
- Carry a young baby next to your body in a sling.

Not being allowed to do what he wants, when he wants, can lead to a child's tears of frustration.

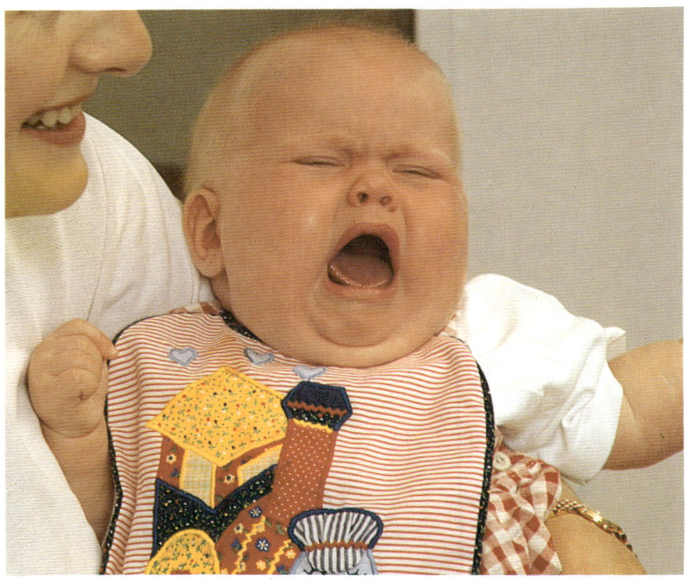

Waiting for a bottle to cool down can be tiresome and can lead to angry tears from a hungry baby.

can, remove the source of the pain – for example an open diaper pin. If you can't find a reason for the pain, don't just leave your baby to cry; pick him up and comfort him. Stay with your baby until he is completely calm. If your baby seems feverish or just generally unwell, always seek medical advice.

Any baby will normally start crying when he is tired. If you think that this is the cause, put your child down to sleep in a dimly lit, warm room. If necessary, rock or sing a soothing song to him until he has completely calmed down and starts to become sleepy.

Tiredness is a common reason for tears before bedtime.

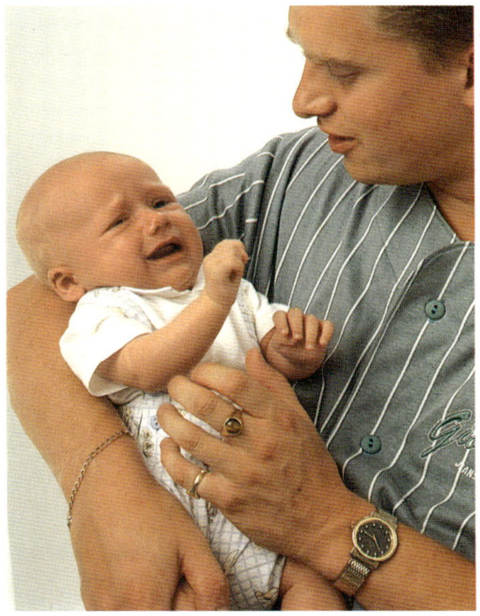

The discomfort of gas after a feeding can cause a baby's tears.

Sometimes it all gets too much for a young child and the only way to show his feelings is to scream.

COLIC

Young babies sometimes have prolonged periods of crying during the day which are frequently attributed to colic. These crying spells often take place around the time of the evening feeding, although they can happen at any time of day. Colic, if it is going to occur, usually starts within the first three weeks after birth and normally lasts until around three months, although it can go on for longer. It generally stops as abruptly as it starts, having caused your baby no harm.

Although no one knows exactly what colic is, or what causes it, many doctors believe that it is a type of stomach ache that occurs in spasms, and makes the baby draw up her legs in pain. The pattern of crying would indicate cramp-like pains; the baby is miserable and distressed, then calms down for a few minutes before starting to scream again. This may continue for several hours at a time, which can become very wearing and upsetting for both of you.

POSSIBLE CAUSES

Colic has been blamed on many things and it is certainly worth investigating all the possibilities if your baby suffers from it. Since colic affects both bottle- and breast-fed babies the method of feeding is not thought to be the cause. However, if you are breastfeeding it could be something that you are eating that is causing the problem. Try cutting out of your diet anything you have eaten during the previous 24 hours that you think might have affected your baby. It has been suggested that the amount of feedings offered – both too little and too much – could be to blame, or that the milk, if bottle-feeding, could be too hot or too cold, or the feedings too weak or too rich. Remember, when you make up a bottle it is essential to follow the manufacturer's instructions.

Other possible causes are constipation, diarrhea, indigestion or intestinal cramps. Vigorously crying babies are almost always healthy, but if your baby looks pale or ill, seek medical advice.

There may also be a link between tension and colic, which can lead to a chain reaction. The end of the day is usually a busy time in a household and you may be tired and tense as you try to prepare the baby for bed, clean up, and get a meal ready. Your baby is sensitive to your moods and may respond to tension by crying which, of course, increases your anxiety, with the result that the crying becomes prolonged and ends when you are both exhausted.

WHAT TO DO

There is no reliable treatment for colic and, although there are some medicines available you should always consult your doctor before attempting to give them to your baby. On a practical level you can rearrange your day by preparing the evening meal earlier, so that you have time to spend comforting your baby during this crying period. Although there is little you can do to ease your baby's discomfort completely, holding him against you, so that there is gentle pressure and warmth on her stomach, and rubbing her back soothingly may be of some help. Try to share the comforting with your partner to spread the strain, and remember that colic doesn't last for more than a few months so, although it is awful at the time, it will not last forever.

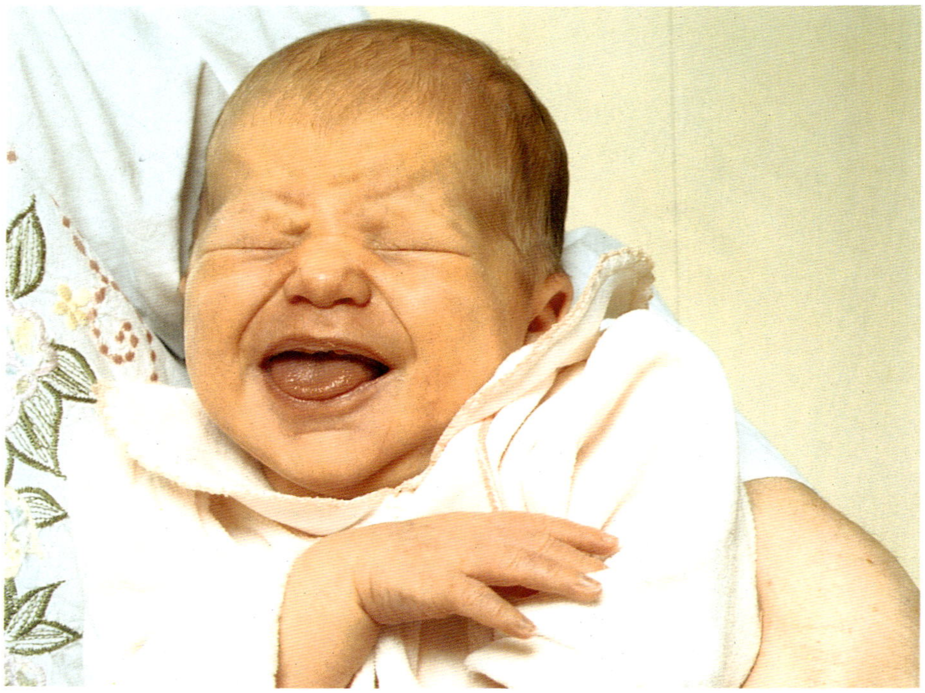

Colic can start as early as three weeks and may last until your baby is three months old. Be patient; it will pass and it won't do your baby any harm.

TEETH

At around six months your baby's first teeth will start to emerge and by the age of two and a half all 20 first teeth will usually have appeared. Every tooth has two parts: the crown, which can be seen in the mouth; and the root, which anchors

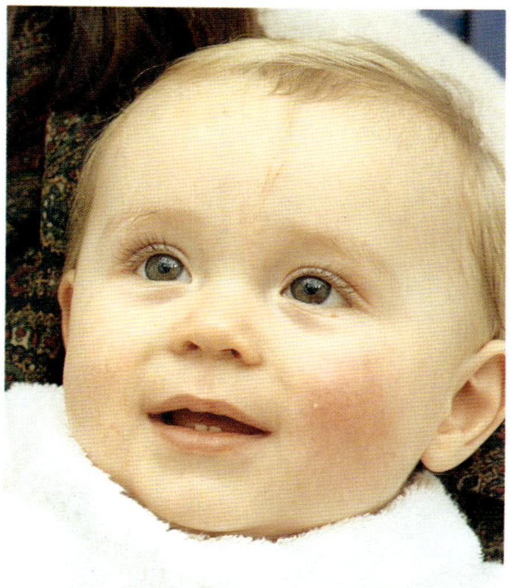

Your baby's first teeth will start to emerge when he is around six months old, and you should start to clean them as soon as they appear in the gums.

the tooth to the jaw. The outside of the tooth is made of enamel which protects the crown and provides a strong surface for chewing. Because the enamel is not fully formed when the teeth first come through, calcium and other minerals are required over the next six to 12 months to strengthen it. These minerals are found in the saliva and plaque in your child's mouth and, under normal conditions, will steadily accumulate in the teeth. But calcium and phosphates in the enamel frequently come under attack from acids that are formed by the bacteria living in plaque. These bacteria use carbohydrates, such as sugar, to generate the acid.

Your baby needs carbohydrates, but food and drink containing a lot of simple sugars such as sucrose, fructose, and glucose will speed up the production of the acids which can damage

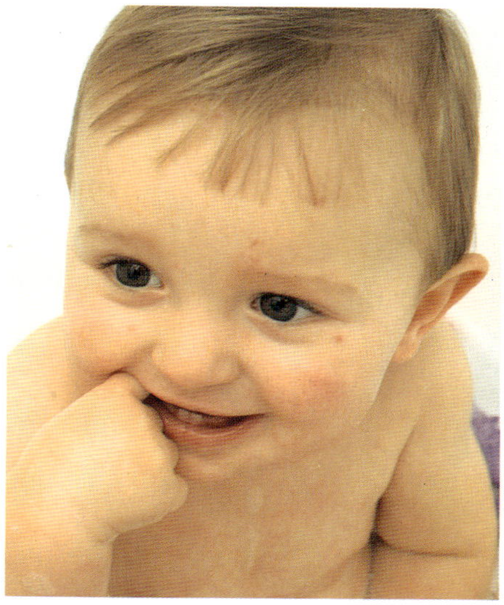

When he is teething your child will chew anything, even his fingers. Try offering him finger foods, such as a stick of raw carrot as something different to chew on.

teeth. It is not just the amount of sugar she eats that affects your child's teeth, it is also the frequency of her consumption of sugary food and drink. Drinks taken slowly, or sugary foods eaten over a long period of time, keep the sugar content of the

Chewing and biting on things is often one of the first signs of teething in a baby, and this may occur some weeks before any teeth appear.

Before you start trying to brush your baby's teeth, it is a good idea to let him play with his toothbrush so that he becomes familiar with it and does not cause a fuss when you put it in his mouth.

Your child will find it good fun attempting to brush his own teeth from a very early age.

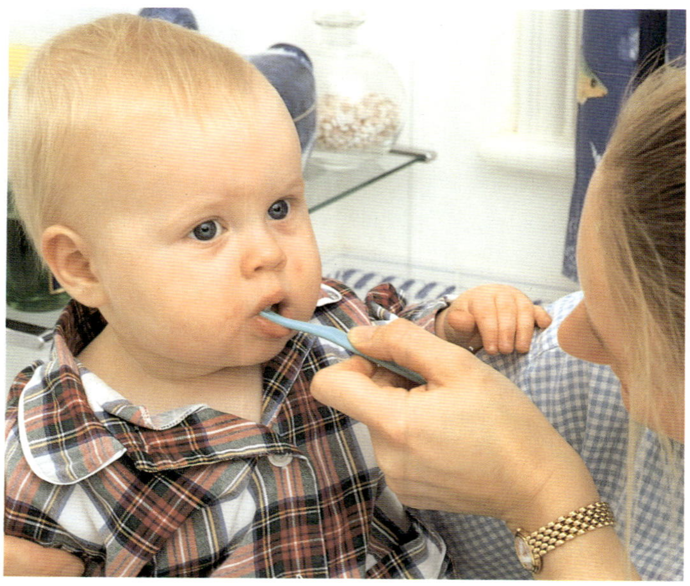

You will need to clean your child's teeth until he is old enough to do it himself. A fluoride toothpaste will help protect his teeth and gums.

mouth high, which means that calcium and phosphates are being removed for longer and less time is available to replace them. Generally, the lower the sugar content of food and drink the better they are for the teeth because it is the total sugar levels, not just added sugar, that counts. This is why you should never add sugar to your baby's food or drinks and you should always dilute concentrated drinks and give them in a trainer cup rather than a feeding bottle.

Cleaning teeth

As soon as your baby's first teeth appear, you should clean them every morning and night. Cleaning the teeth at night, before bed, is especially important because the flow of protective saliva decreases when your baby is asleep, which means that any sugar in the mouth allows the plaque to stay acidic for a prolonged period. In the morning, brushing your baby's teeth will help to remove any build up of plaque that has occurred during the night.

The main point of cleaning teeth is to remove as much plaque as possible, and toothpaste does this with the aid of abrasives; there are toothpastes specially formulated to be suitable for young children. A pea-sized amount of toothpaste on the brush is all that is required to clean a mouth full of teeth. You'll probably find it easiest at first to use your finger wrapped in a soft cloth and then, when your baby has got used to the idea of having his teeth cleaned, you can start to clean his teeth with a soft baby toothbrush.

Since the introduction of fluoride toothpastes, children's teeth have been healthier. Fluoride, which is present in most toothpastes, works by making the enamel stronger against attack from plaque. The amount of fluoride children should use varies according to their age and the fluoride levels already present in the water.

As your child starts to get teeth she will experiment with the chewing action on her favorite toys.

The dentist

Take your baby with you when you go for your own dental check-ups so that he will become familiar with the dentist and his office. By getting your child used to having his teeth inspected before he needs treatment, he will then experience no alarm at the thought of going to the dentist. A child usually won't need to have an actual dental check-up until he is about three years of age, when your dentist will check to see that the teeth are developing properly. The dentist will also be able to advise you about any special protective treatments available for your child.

Cleaning your young baby's new teeth at bedtime is essential to prevent the build-up of plaque as he sleeps.

IMMUNIZATION

Diseases such as measles, mumps, whooping cough, rubella (German measles), diphtheria, tetanus, polio, and Hemophilus influenza type b (a cause of meningitis) can be very serious and, in very young children, can be fatal. Immunization offers long-lasting protection against these diseases. If you are concerned about your child having the immunizations, or are worried about allergic reactions, or because there is a family history of convulsions, don't just decide not to have your child immunized, discuss it with your doctor.

The triple vaccine or DPT, which immunizes against diphtheria, whooping cough (the P in DPT stands for pertussis – the medical name for whooping cough) and tetanus, is usually given as one injection at two months, four months, and six months of age. Hib vaccine, which protects against two of the forms of bacterial meningitis is also given with the DTP injection. Polio vaccine is usually given by mouth in three doses at the same time as these injections. With all of these it is important to complete the course of three doses to ensure the maximum immunity. MMR immunizes against measles, mumps, and rubella and is given in one injection – normally between 12 and 15 months.

A test for tuberculosis (TB) will generally be given to your baby when he is one year old. The tuberculin test is virtually painless.

Hepatitis B vaccine prevents the baby from contacting this viral infection, which can cause liver cirrhosis and liver cancer, in infancy and later in life. All mothers should be screened for Hepatitis B during pregnancy. If you test positive your infant should have the vaccine and Hepatitis B immune globulin immediately after birth, then be vaccinated again at one to six months of age. Consult your doctor about when your baby should be vaccinated, depending on your circumstances.

SIDE-EFFECTS

Many parents worry about possible side-effects of these vaccines, especially from the whooping cough vaccine and MMR. However, research shows that the risk of harmful complications from any of the vaccines on the schedule is very small. A child is much more at risk from the diseases themselves than from immunization.

After any immunization your child may feel a bit off-color for a while and may even run a slight temperature. It is quite normal for the skin around the site of the injection to become red and sore or slightly swollen. But if you are at all worried about your child you should contact your doctor.

Any side-effects from the triple vaccine are usually mild. Your baby may be slightly feverish and appear unhappy for up to 24 hours after the injection. Very occasionally a convulsion occurs as a result of the fever, but this is over very quickly and has no lasting effect. The whooping cough part of this vaccination is the one that most parents worry about, but the latest research suggests that there is no proven link between the vaccine and brain damage. The Hib vaccination has similar side-effects to the triple vaccine: some redness and swelling at the injection site and slight fever and irritability.

The MMR immunization has no immediate side-effect, but some children develop a mild fever and rash seven to ten days after the injection; others sometimes get a very mild form of mumps. Neither of these reactions are infectious.

If your baby is feverish or acutely unwell or has had a severe reaction to an earlier immunization, you should not have her immunized again without consulting your doctor. Remember to tell the doctor who is doing the immunization if your baby is taking medication or if she has a severe allergic reaction to eggs. If the baby is vomiting or has diarrhea it is better to put off giving the polio vaccine until she is better.

THE DISEASES

Immunizations have developed over the years and many diseases that were formerly feared are no longer threats. This is the result of a sound

At 2 months:		***At 4 months:***	
Diphtheria	}	Diphtheria	}
Whooping cough	}DPT one injection	Whooping cough	}DPT one injection
Tetanus	}	Tetanus	}
Hib/Meningitis C	}one injection	Hib/Meningitis C	}one injection
Polio	}usually by mouth	Polio	}usually by mouth

immunization program applied to virtually all children. Often parents are vague about the actual disease themselves, so it is worth familiarizing yourself with the symptoms:

Diphtheria starts with a sore throat and then quickly develops into a serious illness which blocks the nose and throat, making it difficult and sometimes nearly impossible for a child to breathe. It can last for weeks and can often be fatal.

Tetanus is caused by germs from dirt or soil getting into an open wound or burn. It attacks the nervous system causing painful muscle spasms. Immunization has made it rare, but there is still a real chance of getting it and it can be fatal.

Whooping cough is a highly infectious disease which causes long bouts of coughing and choking. These bouts can occur up to 50 times in one day and the cough can last two to three months. Whooping cough can cause convulsions, ear infections, pneumonia, bronchitis, and even brain damage. It can prove fatal, especially in children who are under one year of age.

Bacterial Meningitis develops rapidly and can cause serious illness within a few hours. If left untreated seizures can occur followed by loss of consciousness leading to coma and in some cases it can be fatal. Even when children recover there is a risk of long-term problems such as deafness and epilepsy.

Polio attacks the nervous system and causes muscle paralysis. If it affects the breathing the sufferer will need help to breathe and could even die. Thankfully, polio is rare in most western countries because of immunization, but there is still a risk of contact with the disease through foreign travel, which is why immunization is still important. Adults should check to see if they need a polio booster when they take their baby for immunization.

Measles can be much more serious than people think because it is the disease most likely to cause encephalitis (inflammation of the brain). It begins like a bad cold with a fever and then a rash appears, often accompanied by a bad cough. Measles can cause convulsions, ear infections, bronchitis, and pneumonia; it can sometimes be fatal.

Mumps is usually a mild illness, but it can have serious complications which affect both boys and girls, and it can cause permanent deafness.

Rubella (German measles) is a mild disease, but one which can harm an unborn baby if a woman catches it when she is pregnant. The risk is particularly high during the first four months of pregnancy. Babies whose mothers get rubella during pregnancy can be born deaf, blind, and with heart and brain damage.

Tuberculosis (TB) usually affects the lungs; symptoms include a cough, fever, or night sweats. Children are vulnerable and develop TB meningitis more often than adults.

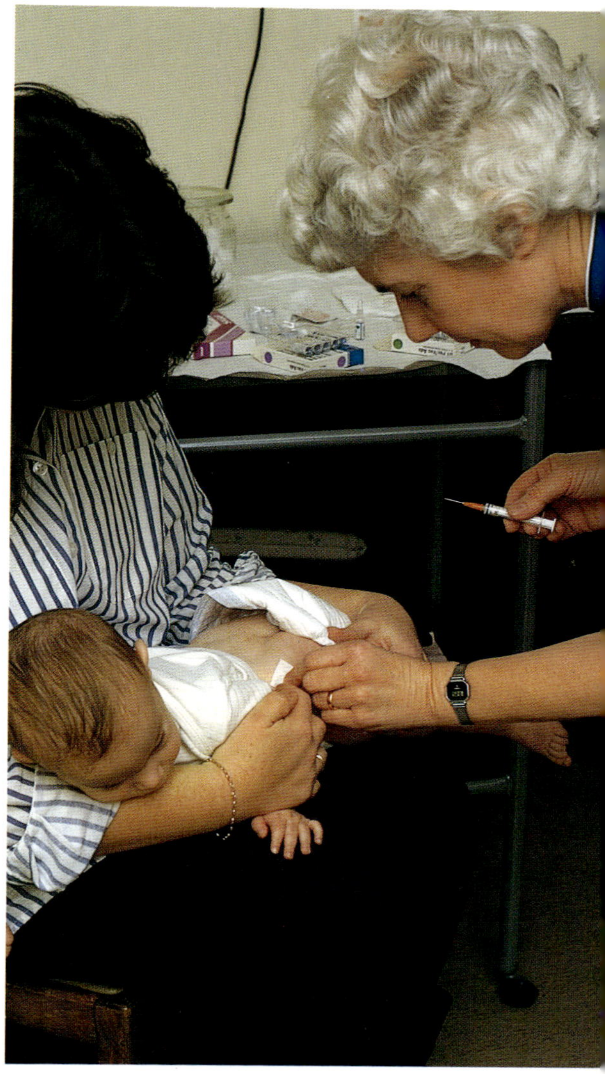

At two months your child will be given his first immunizations. Although they may cause some momentary discomfort it will all soon be forgotten with a cuddle.

Immunization timetable*

**Your doctor will advise you of the hepatitis B vaccination schedule*

At 6 months:		**At 12-15 months:**		**At 15-18 months and 4-6 years (pre-school booster):**	
Diphtheria	}	Measles	}		
Whooping cough	}DPT one injection	Mumps	}MMR one injection	DTP	}one booster injection
Tetanus	}	Rubella	}		
Hib/Meningitis C	}one injection	Hib/Meningitis C	}one injection	Polio	}usually by mouth
Polio	}usually by mouth	TB	}skin prick		

CHILDHOOD ILLNESSES

Knowing what to do when your child is ill and when you should call the doctor is something that comes with experience. Common symptoms that indicate that your child is unwell include vomiting, diarrhea, or a high temperature. These may be accompanied by unusual behavior such as listlessness, refusing to eat, and crying for no apparent reason. However, it is not always easy to tell when a very young baby is unwell so you should trust your instincts – you know your baby better than anyone. Signs indicating that a baby is ill and that you should call the doctor include refusing feedings, a fit or convulsion, extreme drowsiness, difficulty in breathing, severe diarrhea, vomiting, high fever and the appearance of unusual rashes.

Dealing with illness

Fever occurs when the body temperature rises above normal and is usually caused by an infection. If your child is feverish he will need a lot of cold fluids to drink and possibly a dose of acetaminophen syrup to bring his temperature down (aspirin should not be given to children under the age of 12, unless specifically prescribed by your doctor).

If your child is very feverish, keep him in bed and cool him down. This can be done by sponging him all over with tepid water, then covering him with a light sheet and making sure that he drinks plenty of liquids. Alternatively, put a cool fan next to the bed – but safely out of reach.

The easiest way of detecting feverish illness is by taking your child's temperature. This can be done by using a clinical thermometer which is placed under your baby's arm, or in the groin – older children can hold it under their tongue. Alternatively, you can hold a fever strip on your child's forehead. Whichever method you use, make sure that you start with a low reading. A clinical thermometer should have the mercury shaken down close to the bulb. A normal temperature is 98.6°F for an adult, but a child's can vary between 96.8°F and 99.5°F. You must phone your doctor if the temperature goes over 102°F, or if it remains above normal for more than two days.

Medicines for young children usually come in liquid form and can be given to them by dropper, or by using a specially designed spoon; older children can manage with an ordinary spoon. It is important that you know what the medicine is, what it does, and the correct dosage before you give it to your child. If you are in any doubt, check the details with your pharmacist.

You are the best person to judge whether your child is unwell as you know him better than anyone else. As you become more experienced as a parent you will know whether you need to call the doctor. If you are unsure, it is always better to seek medical advice.

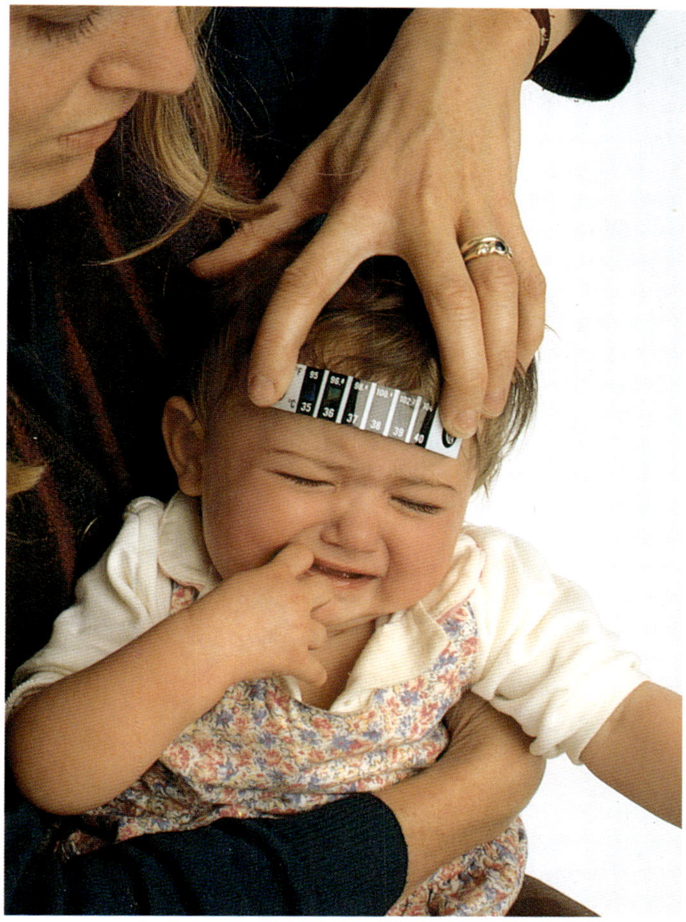

It may be easier to take a young baby's temperature using a fever strip. Place the strip on your child's forehead and hold it there for 15–20 seconds to get the necessary reading.

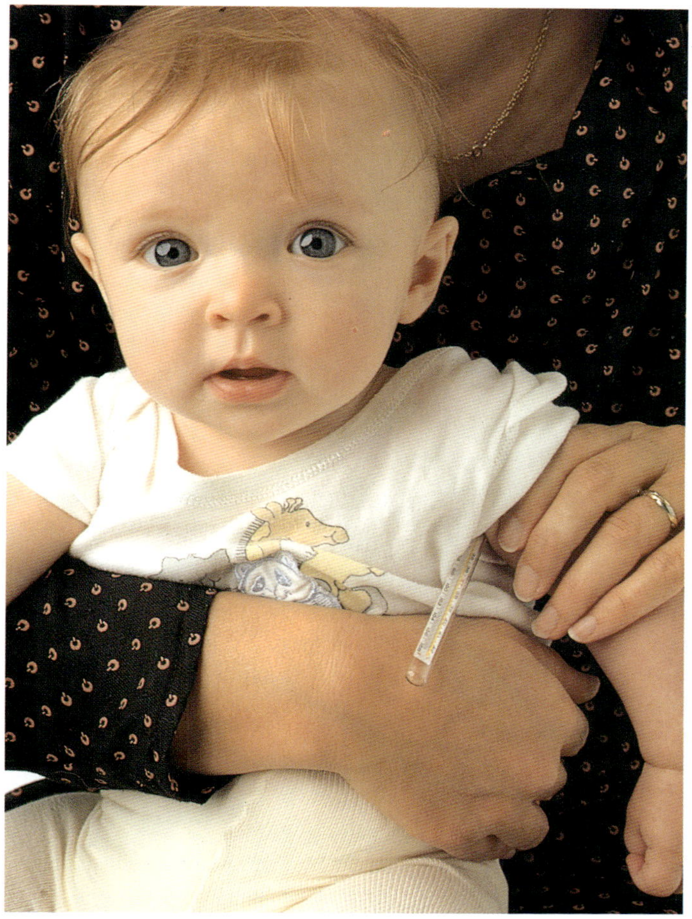

A more accurate way of taking a temperature is with a clinical thermometer. Place it under your child's arm, in the armpit, and hold it in position for two or three minutes.

Specific conditions:

Coughs and colds

Colds are caused by air-borne viruses, not bacteria, so antibiotics can't be used to help relieve the symptoms. If your child is suffering from a blocked or runny nose, you may need to buy a nasal decongestant or your doctor may prescribe some nose drops, particularly if the cold is hindering your baby's feeding. Always seek advice from your doctor if a cold is affecting your child's breathing. It is better to be safe than sorry.

Irritating coughs can often occur with a cold, but before giving your child any type of cough medicine be sure that you consult first with your pediatrician for advice.

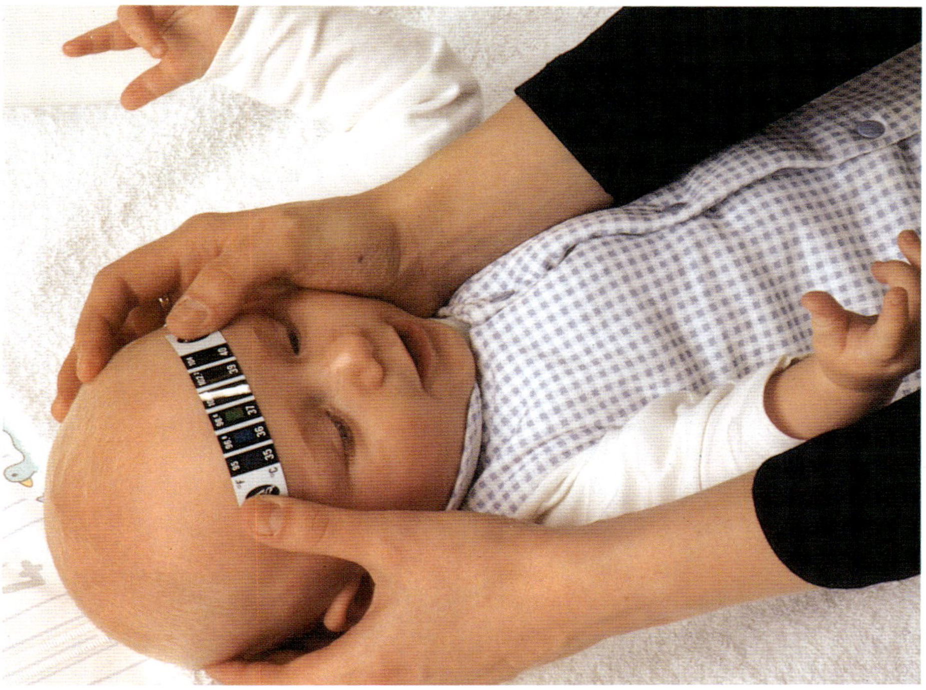

Although a fever strip is not as accurate as a thermometer it is useful for a quick assessment. It will show a raised temperature so that you can take the appropriate action.

Medicines for young children usually come in liquid form and can be given on a teaspoon. Sit your baby on your knee and hold his hands out of the way as you spoon the medicine into his mouth.

If your child appears hot and feverish you can help to cool him down by wiping his forehead with a washcloth that has been wrung out in cold water.

Ear infections

Problems with a child's ears often accompany a cold. One of the first signs is if your baby starts pulling at one of her ears, which might appear red, but she may also just cry a lot and seem generally unwell. Acetaminophen syrup will help relieve the pain, but an antibiotic may also be needed to clear up any infection, so consult your doctor for advice. Do not take your child swimming with an ear infection

Constipation and diarrhea

If a child is having difficulty passing stools because they are hard, the problem is most likely to be constipation. A change in diet will be necessary. Including more water, fruit, vegetables, and fiber will help solve the problem. If the problem still continues to persist, a mild laxative may be required. Consult your pediatrician for advice.

Diarrhea is the frequent passing of loose, watery stools. If a baby is being bottle-fed or being weaned, you should omit one or two milk feedings and solids and offer plenty of clear fluids instead, including an oral rehydration mixture if the loose stools continue. Breast-fed babies can continue milk feedings as normal.

You should contact your doctor if the diarrhea persists after a period of 12 hours, or if it is accompanied by vomiting because the baby could become dehydrated.

Teething

The first signs of teething in a young child are often a red area on his cheek, excessive dribbling, and he starts chewing on his fingers. A teething gel, containing a local anaesthetic, will help to give some relief, but you will need to watch out for any sign of allergic reactions to the gel. These can include a noticeable reddening or swelling of the gums.

Vomiting

If your baby starts to vomit frequently or violently, and if there is any other sign of illness, you should always contact your doctor immediately as young babies can very quickly become dehydrated if they start vomiting.

Older children can vomit once or twice without suffering any lasting effect. Give your child plenty of clear fluids to drink and don't bother about trying to offer him any tempting food until he is feeling better.

CHILDHOOD DISEASES

There are a number of diseases that affect most children. If treated promptly, they pose no serious threat and will probably give immunity to the sufferer. The key thing for the parent is to recognize the condition as close to its onset as possible and take the appropriate action.

German measles (Rubella)

This is usually a mild illness that causes few problems. It is rare for a child to get German measles in the first six months if the mother has had the infection or has been immunized. The incubation period is 10-21 days and the virus is spread through the coughing and sneezing of an infected person. It is infectious from the day before the rash appears and for two days after its appearance. It is very important to keep your child away from any woman who might be pregnant if you suspect German measles because it can seriously damage an unborn baby.

Symptoms: The first sign is usually a rash that starts on the face and then spreads to the trunk. The spots are pink, pinpoint in size, separate (not blotchy), and are not raised above the level of the skin. The rash is not

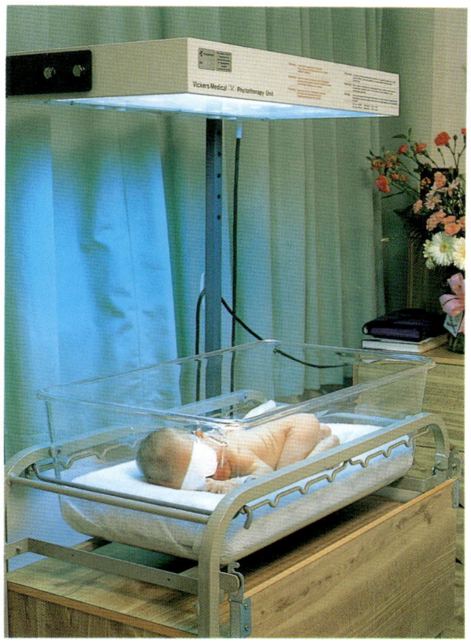

Some babies are born with slight jaundice, a yellowing of the skin, which may need treatment with ultra-violet light. It is normally carried out in the post-partum ward.

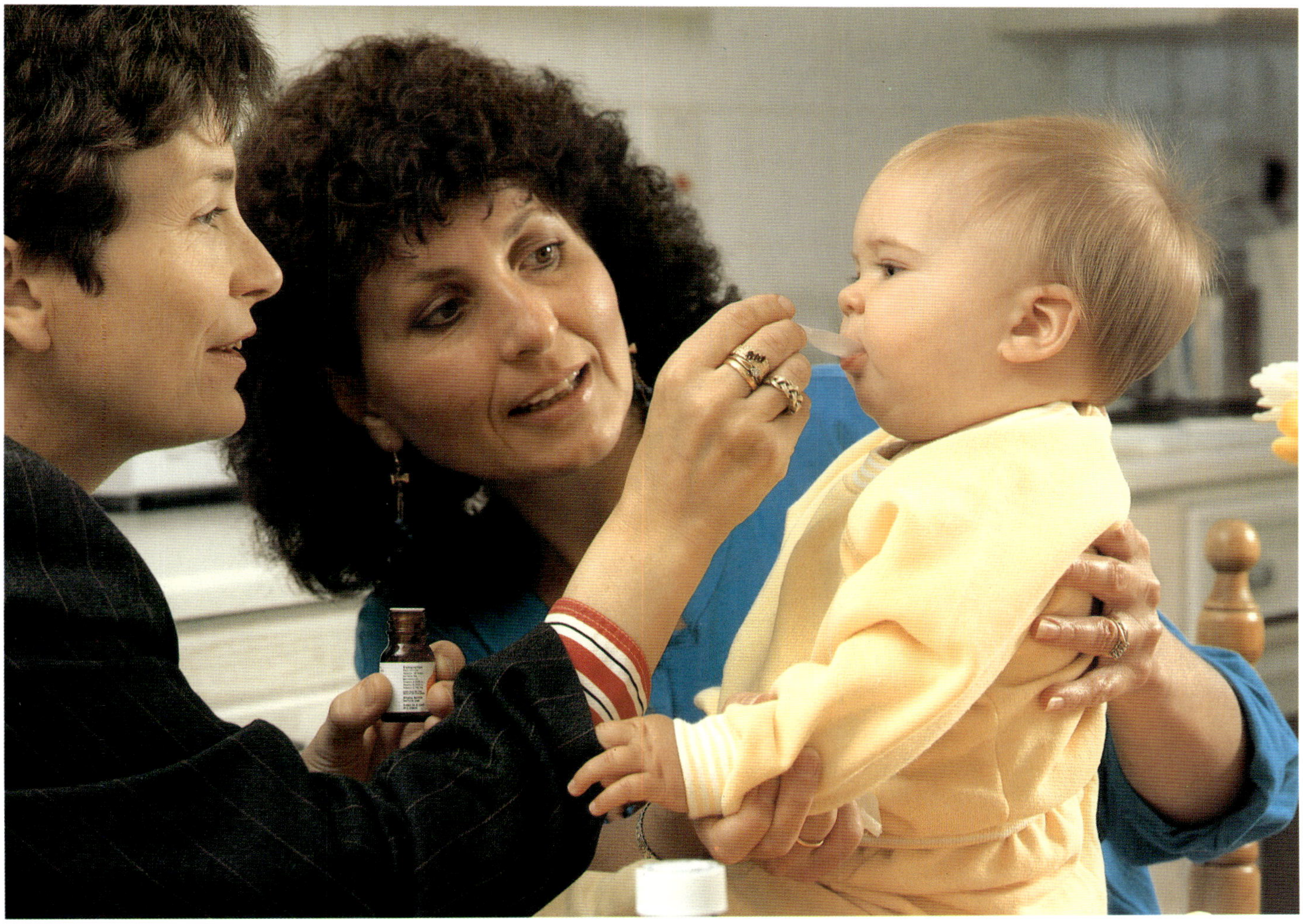

The polio vaccine will probably be given to your baby on a spoon at the same time as he has his other injections.

itchy and lasts for only two or three days. It may be accompanied by a slightly runny nose and a little redness around the eyes and swollen glands in the neck, the back of the head, and behind the ears. These may remain swollen for a few days.

Treatment: Check your child's temperature at least twice a day and give plenty of fluids if the temperature is at all raised.

Call the doctor: If you think your child has German measles, contact your doctor to confirm it. Do not take your child to the doctor's office because of possible contact with a pregnant woman.

MEASLES

It is rare for a child under six months to get measles if the mother had measles as a child, because the mother's immunity is passed on to the baby. The incubation period is 10-15 days and your child is infectious about six days before the rash appears and for five days afterward. The virus is spread through droplets from the nose and throat of an infected person.

Symptoms: The first symptoms are a slightly raised temperature, runny nose, cough, redness of the eyes, lethargy, and loss of appetite. Two or three days later white spots about the size of a pinhead, with a surrounding red area, can be seen on the inside of the cheeks. These last for a few days then a blotchy, slightly raised, red rash appears behind the ears and on the face and then spreads to the chest during the next 24 hours. By the third and fourth day it will have spread over the arms and legs and will have reached the feet. The rash is not itchy but it will be accompanied by a high temperature. As the rash fades, the temperature falls.

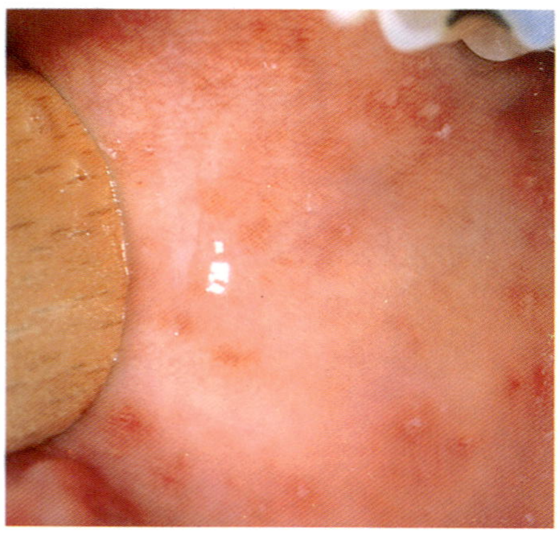

One of the first signs of measles are Koplik's spots which appear inside a child's cheeks. The spots are small and red and have a white center.

Treatment: Bring the fever down. If your child's eyes become crusted, wipe them gently with absorbent cotton dipped in warm water. Your child can get out of bed as soon as she is feeling better.

Call the doctor: If your child is no better three days after the rash develops; if the child's temperature rises very rapidly; if earache or breathing difficulties develop.

MUMPS

This affects the glands in the neck and in front of the ears and causes swelling. Sometimes mumps causes inflammation of the testicles, but this is rare in boys before puberty. Mumps is unlikely to affect a baby under the age of six months. The incubation period is 12-21 days. Mumps is spread by droplet infection and it is infectious from two days before the swelling appears and until it disappears.

Symptoms: Pain and swelling in one or both of the parotid glands which are situated just in front of the ears. The swelling makes the face appear puffy and reaches its maximum in about two days. It subsides within about five days.

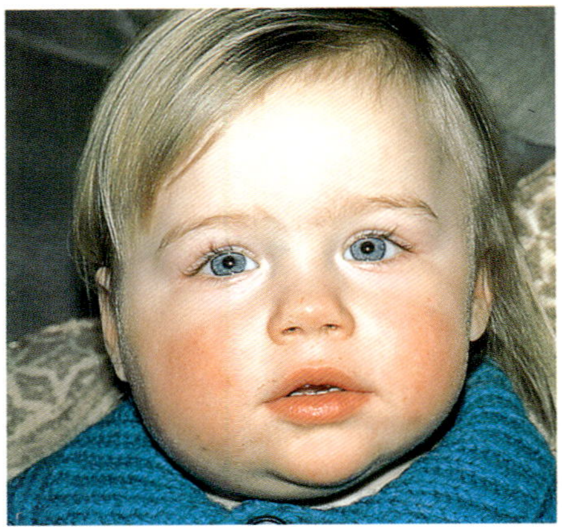

With mumps, your child's face will become swollen and he may find it hard to swallow. Make sure he drinks plenty of liquids and give him Jell-o and ice cream to eat.

Treatment: Give a suitable painkiller to reduce discomfort. Offer easy-to-swallow foods such as ice cream and Jell-o and plenty of liquids, but avoid acidic drinks. If opening the mouth is painful, try getting her to drink through a straw. Warmth will help to soothe the swelling, so heat a soft cloth and hold it gently to her cheeks.

Call the doctor: If your child develops bad pains in her stomach or, if a boy, has a red testicle. Your doctor should be told if you suspect that your child has mumps.

WHOOPING COUGH

This can occur at any age and is one of the most serious common infectious diseases. The incubation period is 7-10 days and the germ is spread through droplet infection. A child is infectious from about two days before the onset of the cough until about three weeks later.

Symptoms: Whooping cough starts with a slight cough and sneezing and is often mistaken for an ordinary cold. It develops into severe bouts of 10-20 short, dry coughs which occur during the day and night – these are often worse during the night. In children over 18 months of age a long attack of coughing is followed by a sharp intake of breath which may produce the crowing or whooping sound. Not all children develop the whoop. During bad bouts of coughing your child may vomit, become red in the face and sweat. The cough can last for two to three months.

Treatment: Stay with the child during her coughing fits because these are distressing and she will need you to comfort her. Try lying her face-down across your lap while she coughs. Sleep with her at night when the cough is at its worst. Keep a bowl near her in case of vomiting and clean it afterwards with disinfectant so that the infection isn't spread. Try to keep your child entertained to distract her from coughing.

Call the doctor: Immediately if you suspect that your child has whooping cough. The doctor may prescribe a cough suppressant and an antibiotic. A very young baby may need to be admitted to the hospital if the coughing is affecting breathing.

CHICKEN POX

This is a highly infectious but usually mild disease in childhood (it can be serious if it occurs during adulthood). It is caused by one of the herpes group of viruses and is transmitted through direct contact with an infected person. The incubation period is 14-21 days and it is most infectious before the rash appears, which makes it difficult to isolate an infected child from others.

Symptoms: Chicken pox often starts with a fever, which may be accompanied by a headache and is then followed by a rash. Sometimes the only sign is the rash, which appears mainly on the trunk and then spreads to the rest of the body and may even occur in the mouth. The rash consists of small red spots that quickly turn into itchy blisters. These gradually dry to form crusts which can remain for a few weeks. New spots appear in batches so an area may be covered in both crusty spots and new blisters. Scars only occur if the spots are scratched or if they become infected. Your child is infectious to other children until new blisters have stopped appearing, which normally takes about one week.

Treatment: Treat any fever as previously described. Keep your child's nails very short to prevent him from scratching and infecting the spots. Apply calamine lotion to help reduce the itchiness. A handful of bicarbonate of soda added to a cool bath will also ease itchiness.

Call the doctor: If the itchiness is really causing a serious problem or if any of the spots have become infected or are very painful.

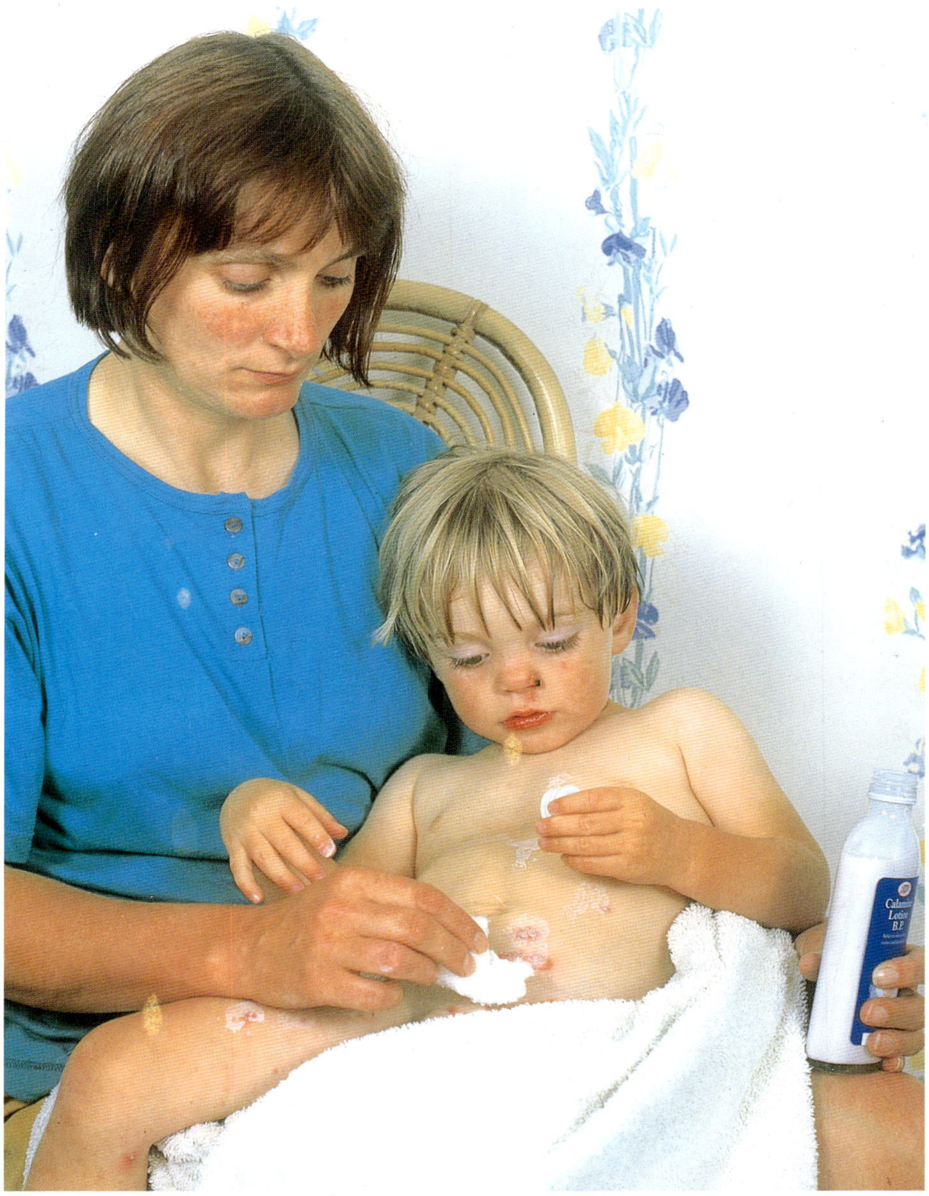

Your child will probably feel miserable if he has chicken pox. Try to prevent him from scratching the spots as this will lead to scarring. Applying some calamine lotion to the spots will help reduce the itchinesss and irritation.

LEARNING WITH TOYS

Playing with toys is important in children's development because through play they learn about themselves and the world in which they live. During the first few months your child isn't capable of manipulating objects so he learns through sight, sound, and touch. A young baby likes to see things from close up and will enjoy objects that are colorful and that move or make a noise. A baby doesn't need a lot of toys because in these early months you will be his best plaything and your baby will be endlessly fascinated by your face and will study it during feeding. Sing and talk to your baby because, even though he can't understand, he will love the sound of your voice. As your baby gets older he will start imitating you and making different sounds. Encourage him by playing games such as Pat-a-cake or singing "Old MacDonald had a farm" and getting him to help with the animal noises. Your child may be able to remember simple concepts too, such as putting things in and taking them out of a container. Bath toys will give a lot of pleasure as your baby learns the fun of playing in water.

Toys will help your child learn to develop new skills, and they offer stimulation at each stage of development. For example, a very young baby will gain a lot from a simple carriage toy; he can see it, touch it, suck, and smell it and by doing so will be discovering a number of new sensations. It won't take long to learn that a toy pushed out of the carriage will just disappear. By performing this trick over and over again your baby will start to realize that he can make things happen that influence his world.

In the first year, toys can be used to help a child to learn hand and eye coordination, recognition, and then crawling and walking. As a child gets older, toys become useful props in imaginative games that teach him how to communicate with others, and help him to discover different aspects of life.

A baby will enjoy a play mat that offers her different textures to play with. She will also be fascinated by the bright colors and bold designs featured on the mat.

An activity gym will keep a baby amused from a young age. At first he will just look at the hanging objects, but he will soon start to reach for the toys.

Left: An activity center is always fascinating to a young baby and this one can be used as a walker too. Toys that will help your child to balance as she begins to pull herself up and then take her first steps will give her confidence.

Below: Although there are many attractive, well-designed toys available, don't be surprised if your baby decides that a wooden spoon and a metal pan are her favorite play things.

There are so many toys to choose from that it's often difficult to decide which ones are right for a child at any particular stage. You should always buy the correct toys for the age of your child. Toys designed for an older child may well have loose parts on which a baby could choke. You should check all the toys a child plays with regularly to make sure that there are no loose or broken parts that could hurt him.

Your young baby will like looking at a toy hung from the carriage or above the crib.

Toys for 0-6 months

- Mobile
- Rattle
- Soft toys
- Baby mirror
- Squeaker
- Baby gym
- Play mat

Toys for 7-12 months

- Cloth or board books
- Big ball
- Soft blocks
- Cups
- Bath toys
- Pop-up toys
- Musical toys
- Push-along toys

This rollaball can be rolled along and will help your baby's hand/eye coordination.

Simple toys that are colorful, tactile and chewable will interest a young baby.

As your baby learns to coordinate his hands, he will like to hold and feel toys that are easy to handle. This frog also has a baby-safe mirror. Your baby will be fascinated by his own reflection.

A play telephone with push buttons that make different noises will intrigue your baby and keep him amused for hours.

This colorful activity octopus has eight different textured tentacles for your young baby to grasp and pull at. The caterpillar can be bent into different positions.

Your older baby will enjoy playing with different-sized, colored stacking cups.

This stacker has different colored rings to help an older baby recognize colors and learn how to stack the rings.

This shape sorter offers your child the opportunity to explore different shapes as well as colors.

Once your baby can sit unaided he will enjoy toys such as this train that he can push along the floor.

A simple shape sorter will give your older baby hours of entertainment as he discovers how to put the squares into the holes and then watch them drop inside.

All babies enjoy an activity center and one that can be fixed to the side of the crib will keep your baby amused when you put him down for a rest.

Pull-along toys will develop and encourage your baby's mobility. They will also help him gain confidence as he learns how to push and pull the toy back and forth along the length of the floor.

BABY MASSAGE

Touch is an important part of your baby's physical and emotional growth, and massage is an ideal way of extending your natural inclination to caress and cuddle your baby. Massage has been used on babies in India and Africa for hundreds of years, not only to help form a bond between mother and baby, but also as a means of relieving colic, helping the digestive system, and making the developing muscles supple. It is thought that gentle stroking encourages the abdominal walls to relax, which helps to alleviate gas and ease colicky pain; massaging the young limbs will also help to strengthen them.

There are a number of specific massage techniques that can be learned, but initially your instinctive touch will be enough, just as long as you are gentle and don't try to manipulate your baby's limbs. You need to be sensitive to your baby's moods and should only massage her when she is content, perhaps between feedings or after a bath. Before you undress your baby for massage, make sure that the room is very warm and draft-free – this is important because babies lose their body heat 10 times more quickly than adults.

Remove any rings or bracelets before you begin and make sure that your fingernails are short and that there are no jagged edges that could scratch or irritate your baby. Relax your hands by stretching and shaking them, then warm them up by rubbing them together. Place a small amount of baby oil on your hands and, with your fingertips, gently massage the baby's skin using light, rhythmic movements. Start at the head and gradually work down to the feet.

Remember, a newborn needs only a feather-light, extremely gentle touch, and you must be careful when stroking the head and around the still-healing navel. The tiny infant will naturally revert to the fetal position, so you shouldn't try to straighten out her arms and legs too much. As your baby gets older you can start to apply a slightly firmer touch, using the whole of your hand in the massage. When you have finished and your baby is dressed, allow her to have a nap if that is what she seems to want.

Massaging tips

- Don't attempt to massage your baby if she is tired, hungry, or cranky.
- Allow yourself plenty of time so that the massage is not hurried or stressed.
- Get everything you need ready before you begin.
- Don't massage for more than 10 minutes or your baby will start to become bored.
- Talk or sing to your baby during the massage so that it is a pleasurable experience.
- If your baby isn't enjoying the massage, stop immediately and try again another time.

How to massage your baby

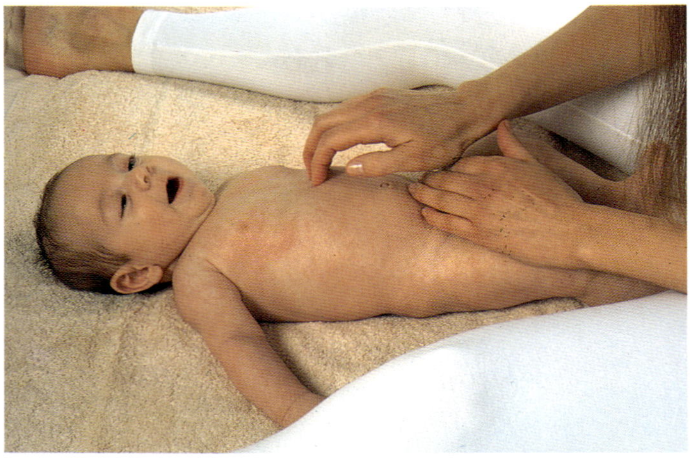

1 *Your baby will love the feel of massage. Place him on a towel in a warm room. Take some warmed baby oil into your hand and lightly massage his chest with circular movements.*

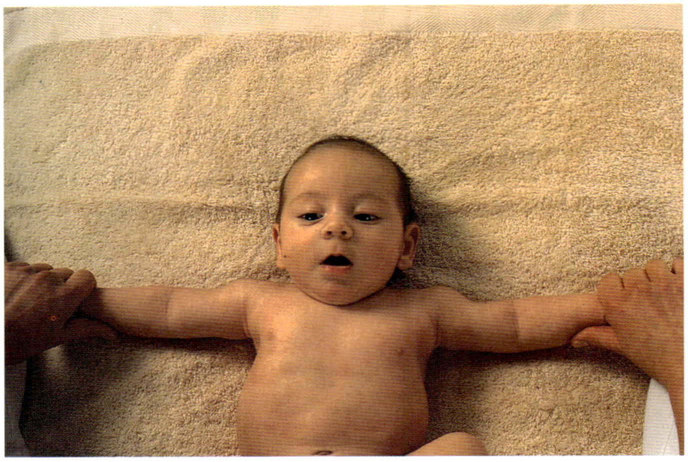

2 *Move on to the arms. Hold your baby's hand in one hand and with the other squeeze down his arm from the shoulder to the wrist. Repeat three times and then work on the other arm.*

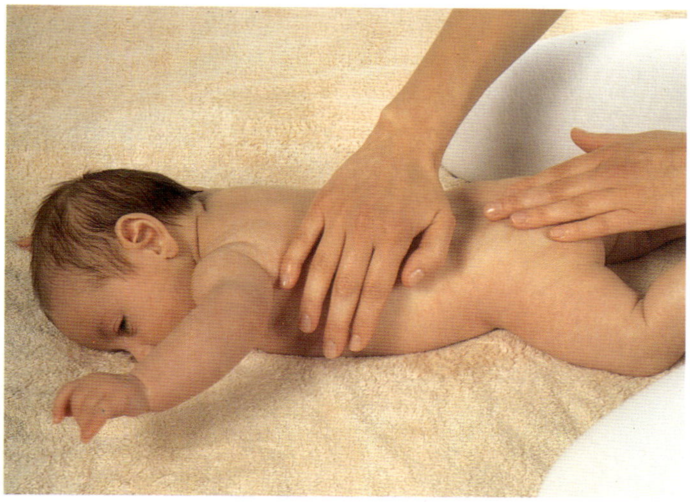

3 *Turn him onto his stomach and, with a hand on each side of his body, massage him from his bottom up to his shoulders, crossing your hands from side to side. Work down again and repeat.*

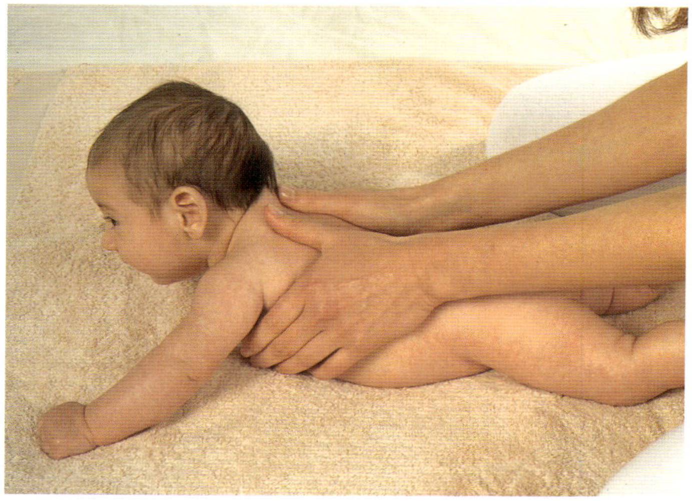

4 *Placing your hands on either side of his shoulders, bring your thumbs together and gently massage around your baby's neck and shoulders with a circular movement.*

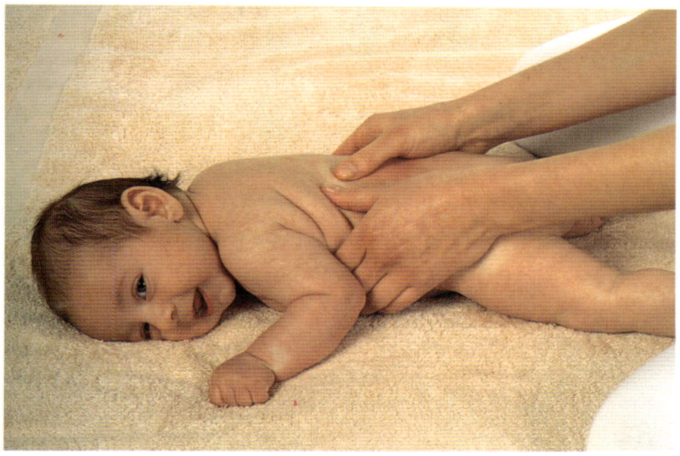

5 *Move both your hands down to your baby's left-hand side and softly knead his skin for a short time between your fingers. Repeat on his right-hand side.*

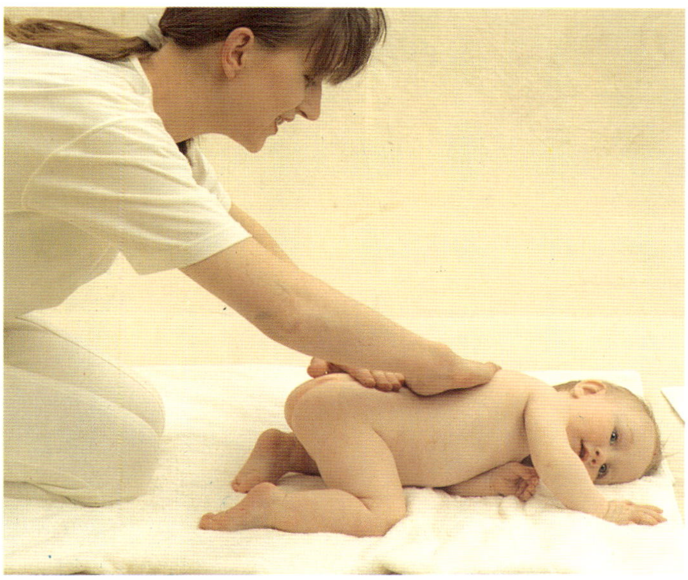

6 *Move your hands into the center of your baby's back and do some light kneading movements with your fingers up and down the length of his spine.*

To finish your baby's massage, make some soft circling strokes with both hands up and down the back.

TRAVELING WITH A BABY

The secret of successful traveling with children, no matter how long or short your journey, is careful planning. Young children are surprisingly adaptable, so providing that you take the essentials – food, diapers, and a favorite toy or two – your child should be quite happy to go with you.

The car is probably the easiest form of transport with a baby as you can use it as a kind of nursery on wheels, packing into it everything that you and your child are likely to require. Prepare a survival kit for the journey before you set off and keep it where it is easily accessible. The kit should include spare diapers, a change of clothes, baby wipes, changing equipment, and a mat or towel. If you are bottle-feeding or giving solids, you will also need to include some feedings plus some feeding equipment.

From birth your child should travel in the car in an approved car seat suitable for his age and weight. These seats must be fixed securely and used properly to obtain maximum protection for your child in the event of an accident.

An older baby will need to be kept amused on the journey and the easiest way to do this is with a selection of toys. Choose toys that have been specially designed for use in the car, or ones that have suction pads that will stick on the window or the back of the front seat. These are better than loose toys, which you may find you have to retrieve each time they are dropped.

Try to make the journey as relaxed as possible by checking the route before you set out and allowing extra time to get there. This way you won't arrive late and anxious because you've had to make a number of unscheduled stops. If you are going on a long journey consider traveling at night. If you are fortunate, your child will be soothed by the motion of the car and will sleep for at least half the journey.

If the journey you are taking involves public transportation, you will need to be selective about what you take with you as you'll have to transport your luggage as well as your baby. Take a similar survival kit to the one already mentioned, but make sure it is packed into an easy-to-carry holdall. If possible, take a lightweight stroller, which you can fold with one hand, leaving the other free, or put your baby in a baby carrier, either strapped on your front if he is still very young, or on your back if he is old enough to sit up on his own.

If you are booking a seat on a train, bus, or plane, always mention the fact that you are traveling with a young child when you arrange your ticket and ask for the most convenient seating accommodation available. If the train or bus station has a lot of steps to be negotiated ask one of the staff to help you, or find out if there is an elevator close by that you can use.

Some airlines have sky cribs and others will allow you to take a stroller onto the plane as hand luggage. They may even allow you to use your car seat (if it is a suitable type) as a restraint for your child. Ask the airline or your travel agent what facilities are available for babies and older children before you set off.

Whichever method of transport you use, always shield your child from the sun, and make sure that any exposed skin is protected by a high-factor sunscreen. Keep your baby as comfortable as possible by putting him in clothes that are loose and easy to change. A number of layers of fairly thin clothing are best as this will allow you to add or take away a layer depending on how warm it is. Cars can get very hot in the summer, with the temperature creeping up considerably without you realizing it, so keep a constant check on your child while traveling.

Once your baby can support his head, you can put him in a carrier on your back. But always make sure that it is a comfortable fit.

A baby sling is an ideal way for either parent to carry a young baby, both inside the house, or when they are out and about.

KEEPING YOUR CHILD SAFE

Although there is no such thing as a completely safe home, many accidents can be prevented by taking a few safety precautions. High-risk areas can be made safer by installing devices that have been specially designed to prevent your child from getting into danger.

HALL, STAIRS AND LANDING

The most common accident in these constantly used corridor areas is a child falling down the stairs, so keep staircases blocked off at both the top and bottom.

What you can do:

- Ensure that there is no loose floor covering or any trailing wire at the top of the stairs on which either you or a child could trip.
- If you have carpet on the stairs make sure that it is securely fitted and in good repair.
- Make sure that the gaps between the stair rails are no more than 4 in so that a child's head cannot get stuck between them.
- Fix gates at the top and bottom of the stairs to prevent young children from having access to them.
- Check that the lighting is good, so that there is no risk of tripping on some unseen object on the stairs.
- Fit safety glass to any glass doors in these areas.
- Make sure that the front-door latch and letterbox are out of reach.

Stairs can be hazardous for your child and should ideally be blocked off top and bottom. Teach him to hold on to the rails or wall to keep his balance.

LIVING ROOMS

These rooms are more difficult to keep safe because the environment is constantly changing as people come in and out and items are moved. Frequent safety checks are needed because the danger areas change as your child becomes more mobile. Try looking at the room from your child's level. One of the biggest dangers in the living area is fire.

What you can do:

- Install a circuit-breaker
- Install smoke alarms throughout your home.
- Fit all fireplaces with guards.
- Use electrical plug socket covers to prevent a child from poking something into the socket.
- Unplug portable heaters when they are not in use.
- Make sure that all fabrics and upholstery are made from fire-resistant materials.
- Keep matches, lighters and cigarettes out of reach and regularly empty ashtrays.

A safety gate is an essential piece of baby equipment. Fitted to the top or bottom of the stairs it will prevent your baby from climbing the stairs and falling. Placed across a doorway it will keep your child out of a room, such as the kitchen, where he could be in danger.

As your baby becomes more mobile he will use anything he can hold on to when pulling himself up. Once he is standing, things that were safely out of the way while he was still only sitting or crawling can now be reached.

Ideally, don't smoke at all!
• Fit safety protectors to the corners of tables and cupboards.
• Use placemats instead of tablecloths so that your child can't pull things off the table on top of her.
• Place all ornaments and breakables out of reach.
• Check the floor regularly for small objects that could be swallowed.

KITCHEN

This is potentially the most dangerous room in the house for a young child. The most common accidents to occur in the kitchen are scalds from hot water, burns from stoves, and poisoning from cleaning products.
What you can do:
• Keep the doorway blocked with a safety gate so that your child can't get in unnoticed.
• Put all sharp objects, such as knives, well out of reach of children.
• Fit safety catches to all low-level cabinets, drawers, refrigerator, and also the freezer.
• Shield controls on the stove front.
• Cook on the back burners of the stove with all the pan handles facing inward.
• Never leave containers of hot liquid, such as cups or pots of coffee, where your child can reach them.
• Make sure that all household chemicals and cleaning materials are kept out of reach and that their lids are always tightly screwed on.

Kitchen cabinets have a fascination for most young children. Safeguard your child by fitting cabinets with safety catches so that he can't open them.

BATHROOM

Among the most common accidents to happen in the bathroom are scalds from hot water, falls in the bath or shower, poisoning from medicines, and cuts from razors, scissors and broken glass.
What you can do:
• Make sure that all medicines and other dangerous objects, such as razors, are locked away in a cabinet that is placed out of easy reach of a child.
• Use a non-slip mat in the bottom of the bath to prevent your child from slipping.
• Fit a lock to the toilet seat.
• Make sure that your child cannot reach the bathroom window by climbing on the toilet or the bath.
• Always run cold water into the bath before adding hot water and then check the temperature before putting your child into the tub.
• Make sure the hot water thermostat is not too high. The water should not be above 90°F.
• Hang a towel over the taps to prevent a child from burning herself.
• Check that a child can't reach the door lock and lock herself in.

NURSERY

This is the one room where a child will spend time alone, so regular

Equipment

• Always make sure that any equipment you buy conforms to the safety regulations established by the U.S. government.
• Only use equipment for the age of the child it has been designed for.
• Second-hand equipment needs to be checked thoroughly to make sure that it is safe.
• Always use safety straps when you put your baby in a carriage, stroller, highchair, or bouncing seat.
• Never put a bouncing seat on a raised surface because your baby's active movements could easily make it fall off.
• When traveling in a car, always put your baby in a car seat approved for the child's weight and age.
• Use child locks on the doors.
• Don't leave your child alone in the car, even if she is firmly strapped into her seat.

safety checks need to be carried out as your child grows and becomes more adventurous.

What you can do:

- Make sure that your baby's crib and mattress conform to safety standards and that the mattress fits snugly into the crib base.
- If your child sleeps in a bed, always use a bed barrier and make sure there is a safety gate fitted at the top of the stairs.
- Use a crib light, nursery light, dimmer, or plug light to give your child reassurance at night and to allow you to look in on her without causing any disturbance.
- Install a monitor so that you can listen to your child.
- Place a thermometer in the nursery to help you keep a check on the temperature. The room needs to be around 65°F.
- If you, or your partner, must smoke, protect children from coming into contact with cigarette smoke, which could put them at risk from coughs, chest infections, and even SIDS. There is also some evidence linking passive smoking with the development of childhood asthma.
- Fit any windows with locks.
- Make sure you place the crib or bed away from the window.

OUTSIDE

Many accidents happen outside the home. Even if you have your own yard you should never leave a young child outside unattended.

What you can do:

- Keep all garden tools and chemicals locked away.
- Fit locks to garden sheds and garage doors.
- Make sure that the gate to the road outside is secure.
- Never leave a child unattended near a swimming pool, whether it is filled or not.
- Make sure that the surface under any play equipment is safe for children to fall on.
- Cover up any standing water.

A bouncing seat can be used from around three weeks, and your baby will enjoy reclining back in the soft fabric. He will quickly learn that by kicking his legs hard he can make the seat bounce.

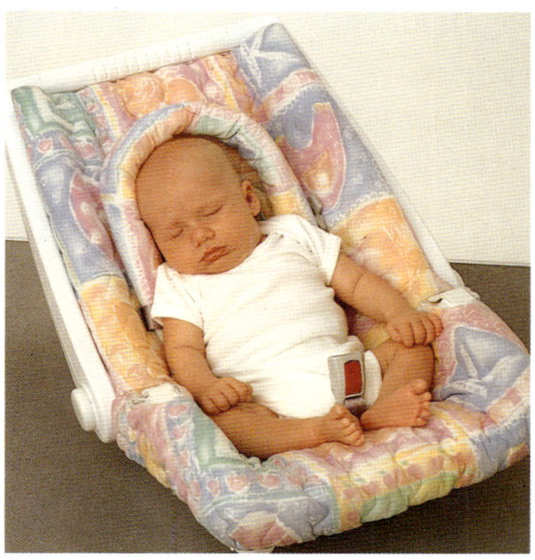

Many infant carriers double as car safety seats for at least the first six months. They are usually light and portable so that a newborn will fit into them snugly.

The rear-facing infant carrier can be fitted on both the front passenger seat and the rear seat. The seat is held in place in the car with any approved three-point adult seat belt.

FIRST AID

Many accidents can be dealt with when and where they occur. Adults with a sound knowledge of first aid can not only calm a distressed child, but they can also help to limit the effects of an accident, aid recovery, and could save a child's life. First of all you need to assess the situation and establish whether basic first aid is sufficient to treat the injury, or whether you think professional help might be required.

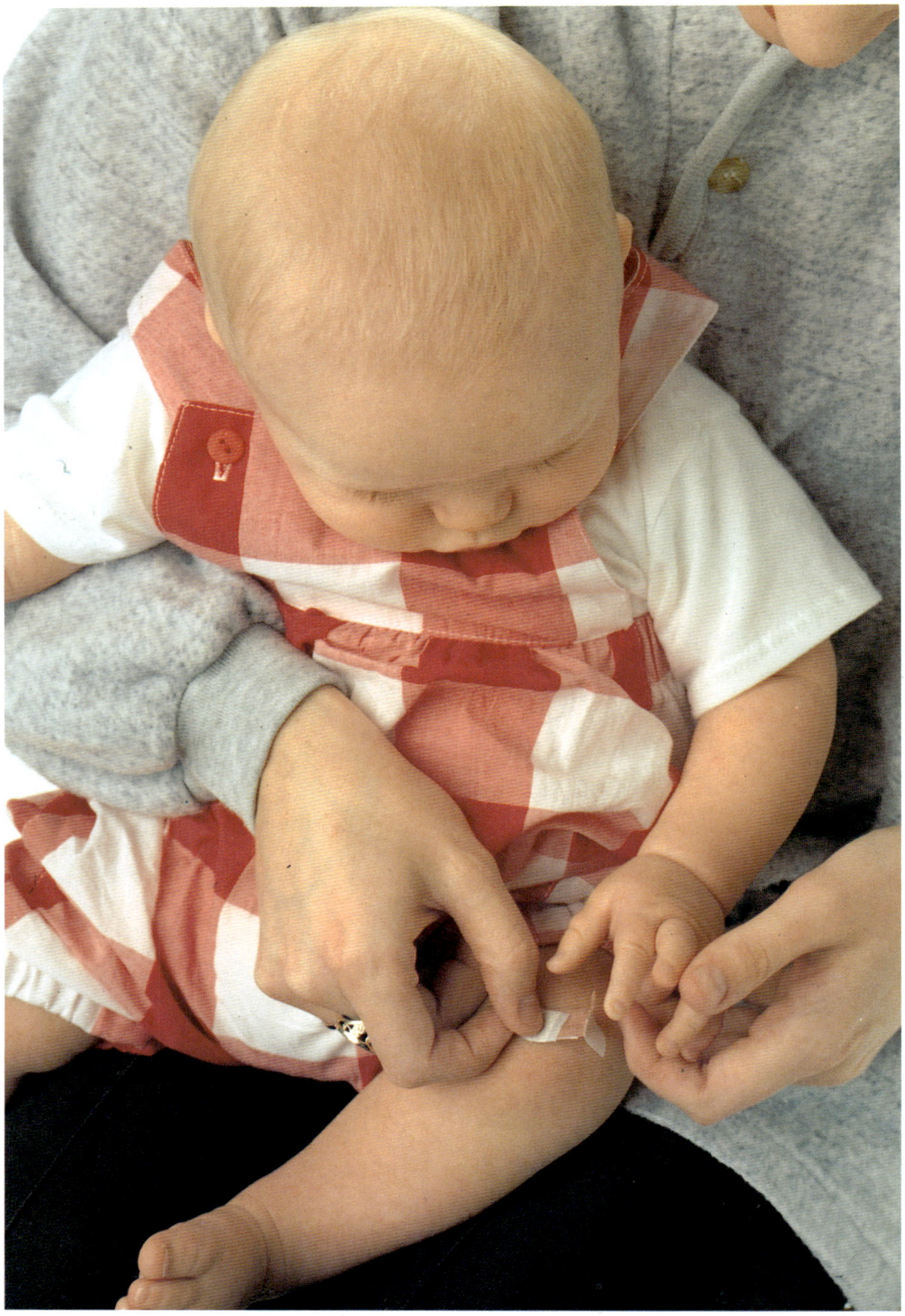

Any minor cuts that a young baby suffers usually an be dealt with on the spot from your first aid kit.

GETTING MEDICAL HELP

If your child is unconscious or you think that he may have suffered spinal injury – after a fall, for example – always call for emergency assistance. If there is even a small possibility of spinal injury, do not attempt to move your child as this could cause severe damage. The best thing you can do is to keep your child warm, still, and calm until help arrives.

Time is of the essence in dealing with an emergency case that requires immediate medical attention.

Should you need to get your child to the hospital urgently, and he can be moved safely, it may be quicker to take him there yourself. If possible, find someone else to drive, so that you can sit with your child in the back seat and give first aid if required. Although it is difficult, it is most important that you try to remain calm and to reassure your child.

If you are unsure where the nearest hospital emergency department is, however, or have no suitable transport, then you should call for an ambulance; the driver will quickly take you to the nearest suitable hospital.

If you fear that your child has injured his neck or back, call for help and do not move him unless he is in immediate danger. If your child must be moved, you need extra pairs of hands to help turn him onto his back in one movement while holding his neck, shoulders and hips steady.

BREATHING

If your child has stopped breathing, start resuscitation at once and continue until breathing resumes. Get someone else to call for help.

Mouth-to-mouth resuscitation:

1 Position – lay your baby or child on his back on a firm surface.

First aid kit checklist

It is important to have a fully stocked first aid kit in your home and you should also carry a basic kit in the car. You can buy ready-made kits, or you can make up your own by buying the items separately and storing them in an airtight container, out of the reach of children. You should check the contents regularly and replace items as they are used, so that you will always be ready for an emergency. Your home first aid kit should contain:

- absorbent cotton
- cotton balls
- sterile gauze dressings
- sterile eye pad
- roll of 2 in gauze bandage
- crepe bandages
- triangular bandage
- safety pins
- surgical tape
- scissors
- blunt-ended tweezers
- acetaminophen syrup
- antiseptic solution or wipes
- calamine lotion
- clinical thermometer or fever strip
- doctor's telephone number
- details of your nearest hospital emergency room

2 Clear his airway – tilt his head on its side and remove any obstruction from the mouth with your fingers.

3 Open his airway – if your child is unconscious the airway may be blocked or narrowed, making breathing difficult or impossible. With a baby, tilt his chin using one finger. With a child, place one hand on the forehead, pushing his head backward while you tilt his chin gently with the other hand.

4 Check breathing – once his airway is open he may breathe spontaneously. Place your ear near the mouth and look along the body for movement. If there is no breathing after five seconds, give artificial respiration.

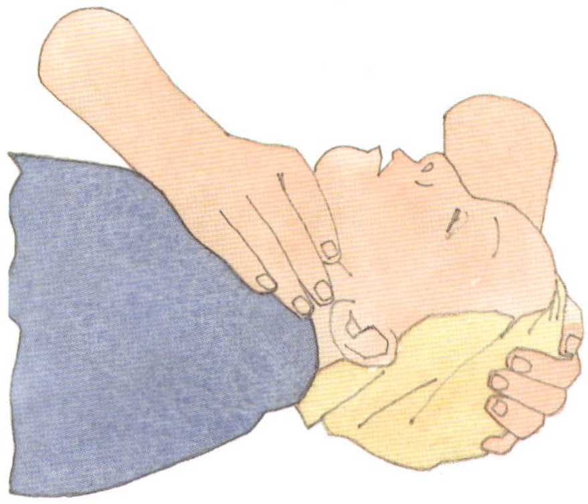

5 With a baby, take a breath through your mouth, cover his nose and mouth with your lips and breathe gently into his lungs until the chest rises. With a child, tilt his head back and bring the chin forward. Pinch his nostrils, take a deep breath and seal your lips around the child's mouth. Blow steadily until his chest rises.

6 Monitor recovery – your child's chest should rise as you blow air into the lungs, and fall when you take your mouth away. Look for this each time you raise your head to take a new breath of air. The first two

breaths should be given quickly, then continue at one breath every three seconds. Keep this up until a medically qualified person can take over.

If your child's chest fails to rise the airway may not be fully open, so readjust the position of his head and jaw and try again. Check a baby's pulse on his upper arm. With a child, check the pulses in his neck or groin. If the heart is not beating, external chest compression is needed.

CARDIOPULMONARY RESUSCITATION (CPR) If your baby is under one year old and you can't feel a pulse or hear a heartbeat, start chest compressions:

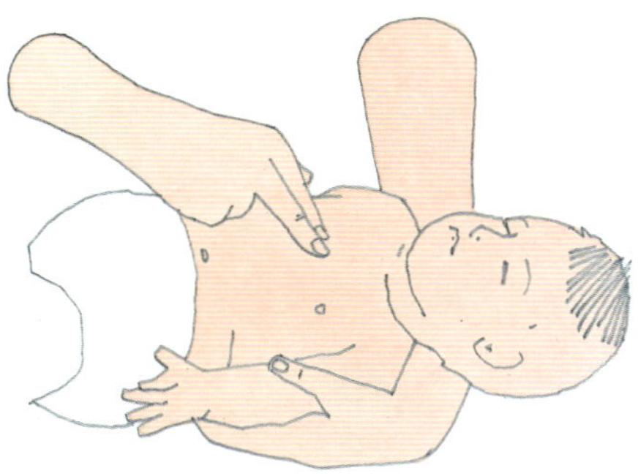

1 Place two fingers on the middle of your baby's breastbone, just below the nipples. (Use the heel of your hand on an older child.)
2 Press your fingers ½ in into his chest five times in three seconds, making the compressions smooth and rhythmic.
3 Give a breath into his lungs and then five more chest compressions.
4 Continue with five compressions followed by one breath until the heart starts beating, or emergency help arrives.
5 Check every few minutes to see if the heart has started beating. When it does start you must stop the chest compressions immediately.
6 Continue with artificial respiration until your baby begins to breathe on his own.

UNCONSCIOUSNESS AND THE RECOVERY POSITION

If a baby is unconscious but breathing, cradle him in your arms, tilting his head so that his airway is kept open, and phone for medical help. An older child should be put in the recovery position. This prevents your child's tongue from slipping back into his throat and obstructing his airway, and avoids choking if he vomits. Put your child into this position if unconscious, but still breathing:
1 Lie your child on his back, face turned toward you, keeping the chin pulled down.
2 Place the arm nearest you at right angles to his body, elbow bent, with the palm upward.
3 Fold the arm farthest-away over your child's chest with the back of his hand against his opposite cheek.
4 Lift the farthest knee, keeping this foot flat on the ground.
5 Keeping your child's hand pressed against his cheek, pull on the thigh farthest away from you, to roll him toward you.
6 Tilt your child's head back with his hand supporting it. Adjust his upper leg so that it supports his body.

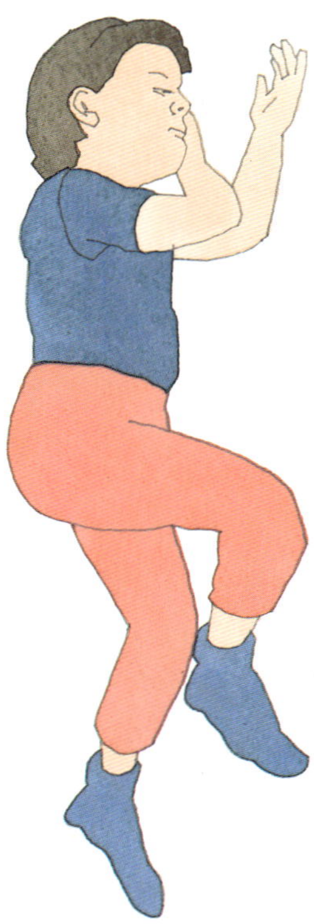

7 Cover the child with a blanket and stay with him until help arrives, checking constantly for breathing and heartbeat.

CUTS AND SCRAPES

You should seek medical help if there is a serious risk of infection, even with small wounds. But treat minor wounds yourself:
1 Clean the wound and surrounding area under running water.
2 Use an antiseptic cream or lotion to reduce the risk of infection.
3 Apply a dressing once the surrounding area is dry.

Never:
- use a tourniquet.

Larger, more serious wounds must be treated immediately to control the bleeding and to minimize the risk of infection. Once the blood flow has been stemmed you should take your child to the hospital:
1 Control any severe bleeding by applying direct pressure to the wound. If possible use an absorbent sterile dressing.
2 If the wound is on an arm or leg, raise and support it.
3 Cover the wound with a sterile dressing and then attach it firmly with adhesive tape to help control the bleeding.

BURNS AND SCALDS

Burns are caused by dry heat like flames and hot electrical equipment. Scalds are the result of wet heat, such as steam or boiling water. There is always a risk of infection with both burns and scalds because of the damage they do to the skin.
1 Cool the damaged area of skin under running cold water for at least 10 minutes.
2 Try to remove anything that might constrict the area if it swells,

for example, rings or tight clothing.

3 Cover with a sterile dressing.

4 Always seek medical advice for all minor burns and scalds.

Never:

- apply butter, oil or grease to the damaged area.
- burst any blisters.
- use adhesive dressings or tape.
- remove anything that is sticking to the burn.

BRUISES AND SWELLING

If your child falls and hits himself, or receives a blow, bleeding may occur under the skin that causes swelling and discoloration. This should fade over about a week. You should hold a cloth that has been wrung out in cold water, or wrapped around an ice pack, to the bruised area for about half an hour to help reduce the swelling.

STRAINS AND SPRAINS

A strain is a tear or rupture of a muscle which causes swelling and discomfort. However, a sprain is more serious because it involves damage to the joint itself or the ligaments that surround it. Symptoms of a sprain include swelling, acute pain, and restricted movement. Both strains and sprains require the same treatment:

1 Avoid any activity that may overstrain the injured area until the swelling has gone down. Do not massage the injury because this may cause further damage.

2 Cool the injury with a cold pack, a bag of ice wrapped in a towel, or a cold, wet towel. This will reduce the pain and control inflammation.

3 Use a bandage to apply gentle compression to the injured area. This will give support and help to lessen inflammation.

4 Raise and support the injured area as this will help reduce swelling.

APPLYING A BANDAGE

Select the width of bandage appropriate to the area to be covered.

1 Support the injured limb while you are bandaging.

2 Start below the injury site, and wrap the bandage around the limb, using a spiral action, overlapping by two-thirds each time.

3 Secure with a safety pin or some adhesive tape.

4 Check to make sure that the bandage isn't restricting the circulation.

5 Bandage injured joints by wrapping the bandage around the joint in a figure-eight pattern, overlapping by two-thirds each time.

Never:

- bandage too tightly because this can affect the circulation. If the fingers or toes of the bandaged limb are cooler or darker than the other limbs the bandage is too tight. It should be removed and then reapplied, fixing it in position more loosely.
- ignore a limb injury. Always seek medical help if the leg is too painful to take your child's weight, if he is not using his arm, or if any swelling hasn't gone down after 48 hours.

BROKEN BONES

Technically, a broken or cracked bone is a fracture. All fractures should be treated with great care because any undue movement could cause further damage:

1 Keep your child still and cover with a coat or blanket.

2 Remove anything that might constrict any swelling around the injured area.

3 Get medical assistance.

BITES AND STINGS

Bites from mosquitoes and gnats or stings from wasps and bees can be extremely painful, causing hard, red, swollen lumps which itch intensely. A small number of people are allergic to wasp and bee stings. If your child appears to be having difficulty breathing as the result of a sting you must seek medical help immediately. In ordinary circumstances:

1 If the stinger has been left in the skin, remove it with tweezers, taking care not to squeeze the poison sack because this would force the remaining poison into the skin.

2 Apply a cold compress to the site for quick relief from pain.

3 Massage sting-relief cream into the affected area for longer-term relief.

EYE INJURIES

Eyes are delicate organs that can be damaged very easily, so immediate first aid treatment is required if an injury occurs:

- Remove any foreign object from your child's eye using a damp piece of cotton. If you can't do this or the pain remains after the removal, cover the eye with a clean pad, and then take your child to the hospital.
- If your child's eye has been injured by a blow, apply a sterile dressing, and take him to the hospital for immediate treatment.
- Chemicals that are splashed into the eye should be washed out completely by flooding the eye with some clean, cold water for at least 15 minutes. Then cover the damaged eye with a clean pad and get your child to the hospital.

CHOKING

This happens when a foreign object gets lodged in the throat and obstructs the airway.

For a baby:

1 Lay your baby face downward, with the chest and abdomen lying

Choking

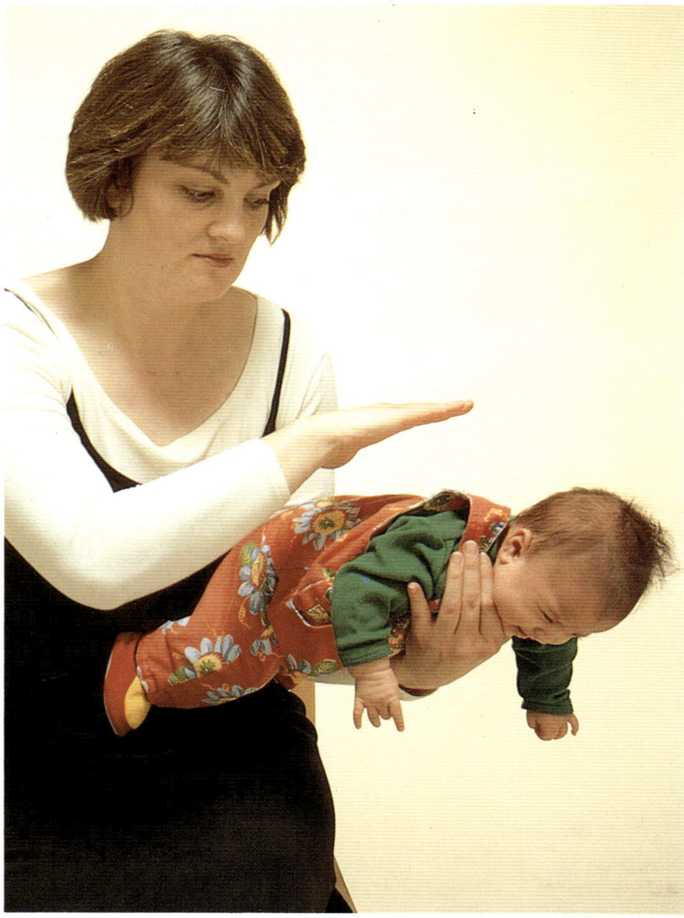

If your baby is choking, you will need to take immediate action. Lay a young baby face down with her chest and abdomen lying along your forearm with your hand supporting her head. Slap her gently on the back several times.

With an older baby or toddler the action would be slightly different. You will need to lay her horizontally, with her head facing downward. To remove the obstruction, slap her firmly between the shoulder blades.

along your forearm and your hand supporting his head.

2 Slap him firmly between the shoulder blades four times. If your baby or child doesn't start to breathe again normally once the blockage is completely removed, call for an ambulance immediately.

For a child:

1 Lay your child across your knee, with his head down, and slap him sharply and firmly between the shoulder blades four times.

2 If the above fails to remove the blockage, use your finger to try to hook out the object, taking care not to push it farther down your child's throat.

CROUP

Croup is a noisy barking cough that may be accompanied by fever and, in severe cases, your child may breathe with a wheezing or grunting noise. Croup can be quite frightening for both you and your child, so it is very important to stay calm and to reassure him. To help remedy the situation:

- Treat simple croup with warm drinks and acetaminophen syrup to bring down any fever.
- Ease severe croup by getting your baby or child to inhale steam from a kettle, or sit in the bathroom with the hot shower tap on or near wet towels over a radiator. Make sure that he cannot scald himself on the source of the steam.
- If your child is very distressed or is having trouble breathing or swallowing, call your doctor immediately, or alternatively take him straight to the nearest hospital.

DROWNING

If possible get your child out of the water immediately, otherwise you will need to give emergency first aid in the water.

1 Empty your child's mouth and, if his breathing has stopped, start to give CPR. Do not attempt to remove any water out of your child's stomach or from his lungs.

2 If you carry your child, keep his head lower than the rest of his body to reduce the risk of him inhaling any water.
3 Lay him down on a coat or blanket. Open the airway and check his breathing and pulse.
4 Once your child is breathing normally again, remove all his wet clothes and cover him with some warm, dry ones. Give him a reviving hot drink.
5 Always take him to the hospital for a thorough examination, even if she appears to be fine and to have completely recovered.

ELECTRIC SHOCK

Most electrical accidents occur in the home, so it is vitally important to ensure that household appliances are wired correctly and kept out of the reach of young children. Severe injuries and even death can result from electric shock. But if a shock does still occur:
1 Switch off the current and pull out the plug before touching the child. If this is not possible, use something wooden, such as a broom handle or chair that will not conduct the electricity, to move him right away from the power source.
2 Check his breathing and heartbeat. If your child is unconscious, immediately place him in the recovery position.
3 Treat any burns.
4 Cover your child to keep him warm and reassure him by talking to him calmly.
5 Phone to get emergency medical assistance immediately.
Never:
• touch your child until the power source has been turned off.
• apply water to a burn that occurs from an electric shock while your child is still attached to the source of the electricity.

NOSEBLEEDS

Bleeding often follows a blow to the nose, or may occur as a result of blowing the nose too hard. Sometimes there is no apparent reason for the nosebleed. The flow of blood can be quite heavy, which can be frightening, although it is not usually a serious problem:
1 Sit your child upright with him head positioned slightly forward. Putting the head back can sometimes cause choking and cause some discomfort.
2 Get your child to breathe through his mouth while you pinch the soft part of his nose firmly for 10 minutes until the flow of blood slows down and stops.
3 If your child's nose is still bleeding, hold a very cold cloth or an ice pack wrapped in a cloth to his nose for a couple of minutes, then pinch her nose again.
4 Try to ensure that your child avoids blowing his nose for several hours after a nosebleed has finally been staunched.

POISONING

This occurs when harmful substances are inhaled or swallowed. It is important to keep all such substances out of reach of young children. Always be on the alert and see that your child does not eat any poisonous berries or plants in the garden, or when you are out in the countryside. If you suspect poisoning, call for emergency medical assistance and then take immediate action:
1 Check breathing and be ready to start CPR if necessary.
2 If your child is breathing, but is unconscious, place him in the recovery position and phone for help.
3 Never give him anything to eat or drink without first consulting a physician for advice.
4 Keep the bottle or container the poison was in, or a similar berry or fruit to take to the hospital. This will enable the medical staff to administer the correct antidote to your child as fast as possible.
Never:
• try to give fluids to your child if he is unconscious.
• try to induce vomiting. This can be extremely dangerous as the poison could find its way into his lungs and cause severe damage to these organs as well as endangering his breathing.

SHOCK

Severe bleeding, burns, and even fear can bring about a state of shock. You can recognize shock by an extreme loss of color along with cold and clammy skin. The child may also be shivering and sweating at the same time. This may be accompanied by rapid breathing and dizziness, and possibly by vomiting. Shock often occurs after a major accident, so all casualties must be treated for shock, even if they are not showing any of these symptoms. In extreme cases shock can be fatal, so it requires some immediate action and should always be taken seriously:
1 Lay your child down on his back and make sure that his breathing isn't restricted.
2 Loosen any restricting clothing at his neck, chest, and waist. Then cover your child with a blanket or a coat, but take care not to allow him to overheat.
3 Try to get your child to remain still and to be calm while you seek medical help.

PART THREE

THE FIRST YEAR

YOUR NEWBORN arrives in the world a helpless, totally dependent baby, yet, with your help, within a year she will have learned all the basic skills that she needs to build on for her future growth and development. This section takes you, month by month, through the first year of a child's development. It is, however, important to realize that your child is unique, so there is little point in comparing her with others in anything other than a general way at this stage.

You will want to help and encourage your child as she masters each new skill. Understanding how she learns to talk, crawl, walk and play will enable to you to assist her at each stage. The five senses - hearing, vision, taste, smell and touch - are all extremely important from the time your child is born. As each sense develops, your child will be discovering something new about the world in which she's living.

Being able to participate in this fascinating time in your child's life is a very special privilege. You will be part of the most exciting process in the world: the development of your child from a helpless baby to a confident, independent toddler.

NEWBORN

Your newborn baby will probably look wrinkled and slightly blotchy at first. When he is born his skin may have a bluish tinge and the legs may even be a different color from the rest of his body. This will only last for a short time, until oxygen from the lungs has had time to reach the bloodstream. You may also find patches of dry skin. Eyes may be reddish and slightly swollen and your baby may still be covered with vernix, the greasy white substance that has been protecting the skin from becoming waterlogged by the amniotic fluid. There may also be a covering of lanugo, fine hair that covers the shoulders, upper arms, and legs.

Your baby's head may look too big for his body. It is usually about one-quarter of the total body length and it may be a slightly odd shape because of the pressure that was put on it during the birth. His features may also appear slightly flattened from being squeezed through the pelvis. Your baby's head may be covered with very thin hair or have a thick thatch that stands up on end.

Milestones

Your child is immediately able to:

- Hear and respond to noises.
- Focus on objects that are within 8–12 in.
- Grip your finger tightly.
- Suck vigorously.
- Make walking movements when held on a hard surface.
- Turn toward you when you stroke his cheek.

An increase in female hormones from the placenta just before birth affects both boys and girls and your baby's genitals may be enlarged and breasts may appear slightly swollen.

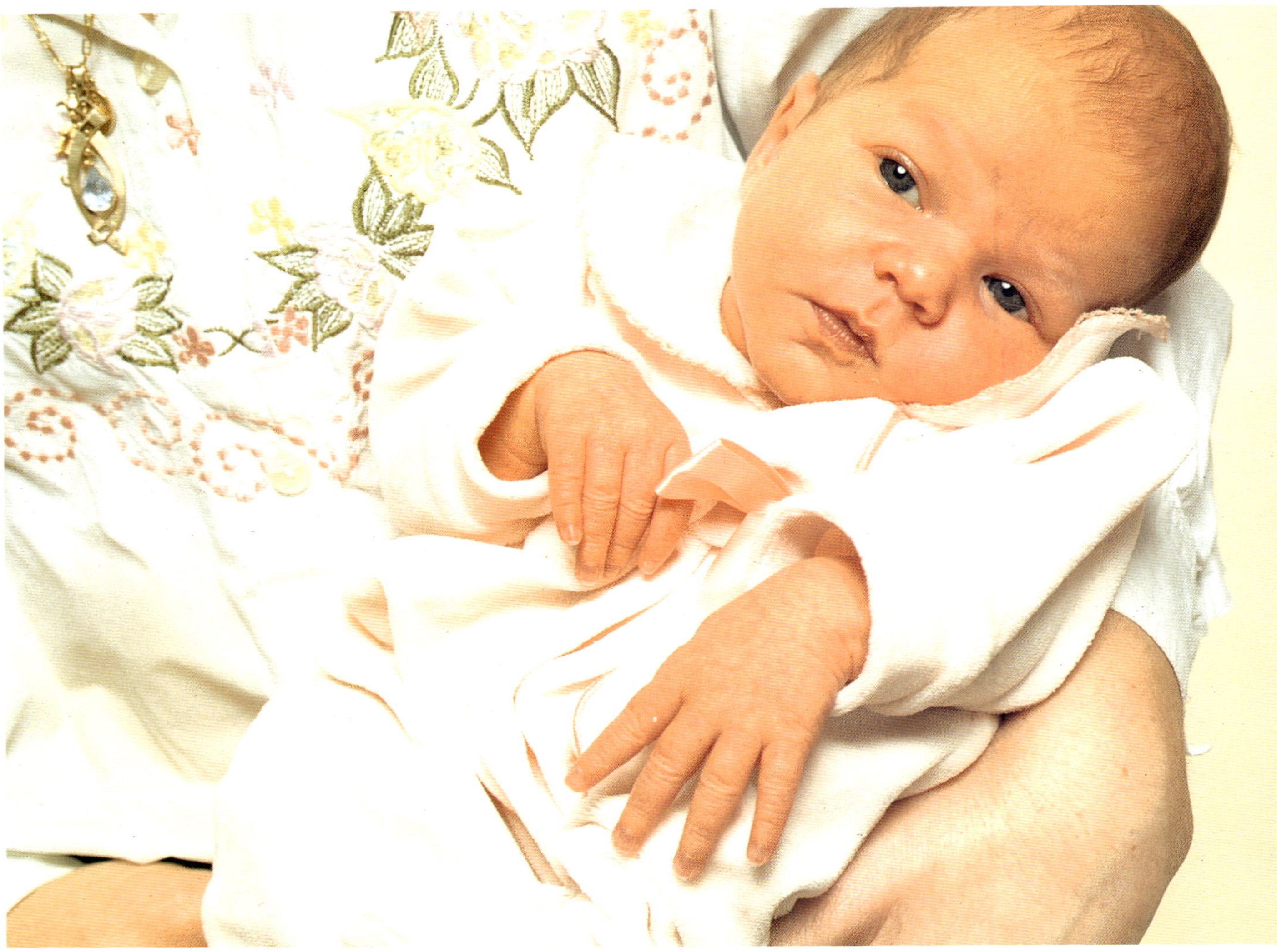

When a baby is born he can be between 18–22 in long and weigh anything between 5½–10 lb.

It is quite usual for the breasts of both boys and girls to have a milky discharge; girls may have a slight vaginal discharge as well. All these features will disappear over the next few weeks.

SIZE

Although the average weight of a baby at birth is 7½ lb, wide variations occur so, assuming that your baby was born around the estimated date of delivery (EDD), it could weigh anything between 5½-10 lb. Your baby's weight is determined by a lot of factors, including your size and the size of your partner, how much weight you put on in pregnancy, and your general health.

Your baby is quite likely to lose weight during the first week. This is because it takes a little while for regular feeding to become properly established. Once an infant is feeding well his weight should remain stable for a couple of days and then, within seven to 10 days, he will regain his birth weight. A baby's weight gain is one of the easiest ways of telling whether he is thriving.

The average length of a newborn infant is between 19-20 in, but as with weight, this can vary, although most babies are somewhere between 18-22 in long.

REFLEXES

A baby is born with a number of reflexes. The rooting reflex means that your child's mouth automatically searches for your nipple; grasping is seen when your baby demonstrates a surprisingly strong grip. When on his back, your baby may adopt the tonic neck reflex – the head is turned to one side and the arm and leg on that side are extended while the opposite ones are flexed. A loud noise or the sensation of falling causes the startle or Moro reflex: the newborn extends legs, arms, and fingers, arches the back and throws the head back and then draws back the arms, fists clenched, into the chest. All these initial reflexes will gradually diminish over the next weeks and months as voluntary movements take their place.

In addition to these reflexes, every baby is born with the ability to suck, swallow, and gag so that they can start to feed as soon as they are born. The gagging reflex prevents a baby from choking on too much liquid and allows the child to get rid of any mucus that may be obstructing his airways.

Your newborn will probably hiccup and snuffle a lot at first. Hiccups occur because the baby's breathing rhythm is still rather jerky. They don't hurt, or even particularly

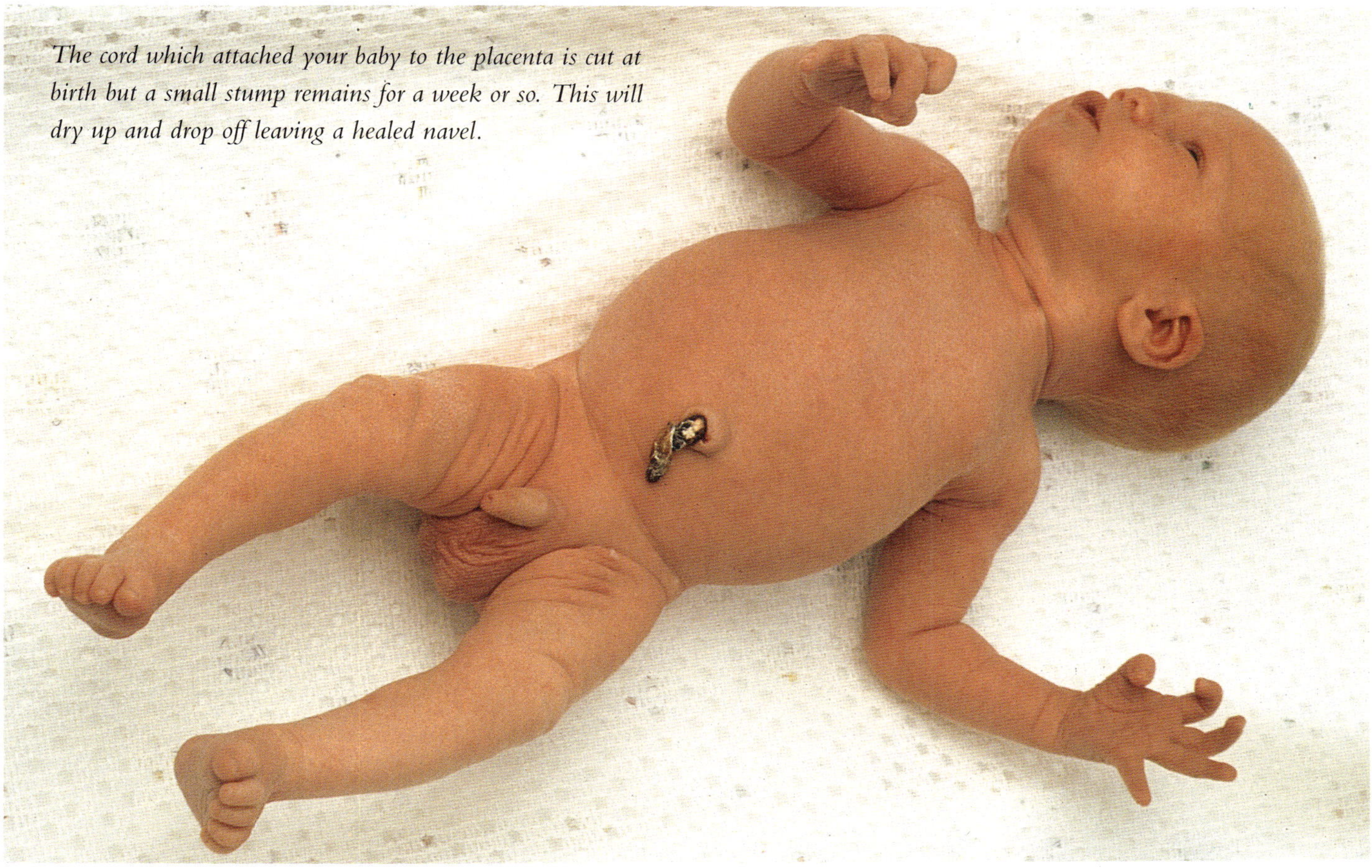

The cord which attached your baby to the placenta is cut at birth but a small stump remains for a week or so. This will dry up and drop off leaving a healed navel.

bother them in fact, so you need not worry about them at all. Your baby will also make some snuffling noises. This is from learning to breathe through his nose and because the nasal passages are still very small. As the nose gets bigger the snuffling will stop.

All babies are sensitive to bright lights when they are born and this may make them sneeze when they first open their eyes. This is because the light stimulates the nerves in their nose as well as their eyes. Sneezing is also a way of helping to clear out the nasal passages and it will prevent any dust from getting into the baby's lungs.

CRYING

Your baby may make his first cry as soon as his chest has been delivered; others wait until they have been born or until they start to breathe normally. These first cries are often not much more than a whimper and the full-bodied cry follows later. A baby may look red and angry while crying, but this is normal. Crying is a baby's way of communicating as well as a means of exercising his lungs.

Hunger is the main reason for a newborn to cry, but being lonely, wet, or tired may also make a baby cry. Some babies cry because they don't like being undressed, others when they are immersed in water. Some babies are more easily upset than others so they cry more. You will quickly learn to recognize why your baby is crying and the best way to soothe him.

NEWBORN TESTS

The first test your baby will be given is the Apgar test. The scores are recorded at one minute after birth and then again at five minutes and they reflect your newborn's general condition. Babies who score between 7 and 10 are in good to excellent condition, those who score between 4 and 6 are in fair condition, but may need some resuscitative measures. Babies who score under 4

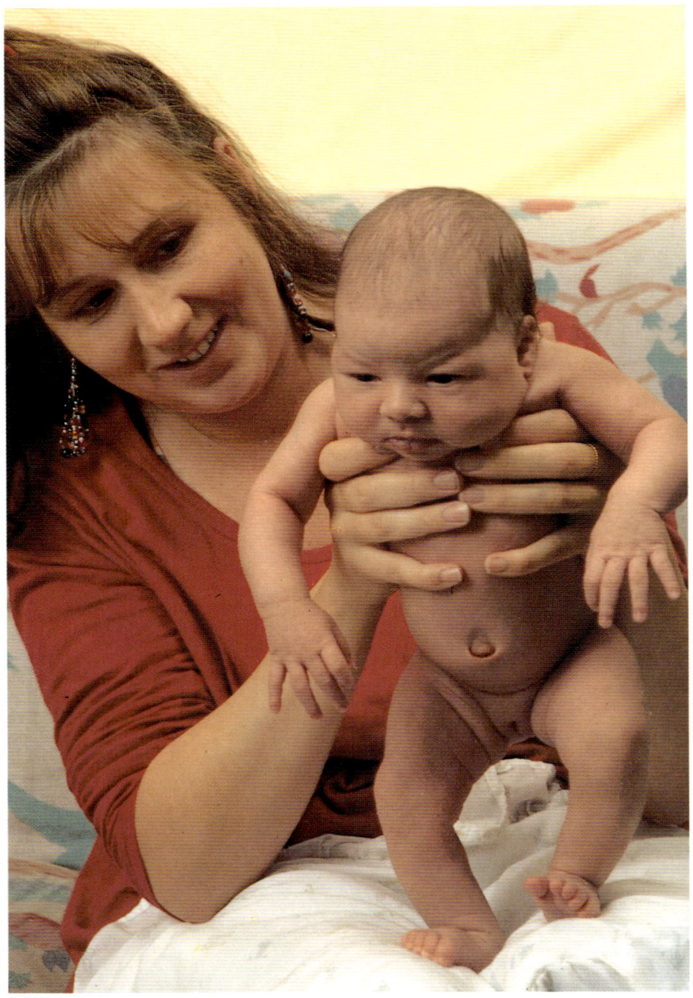

A newborn baby might initially have a stepping reflex, but this will soon be replaced by voluntary movements.

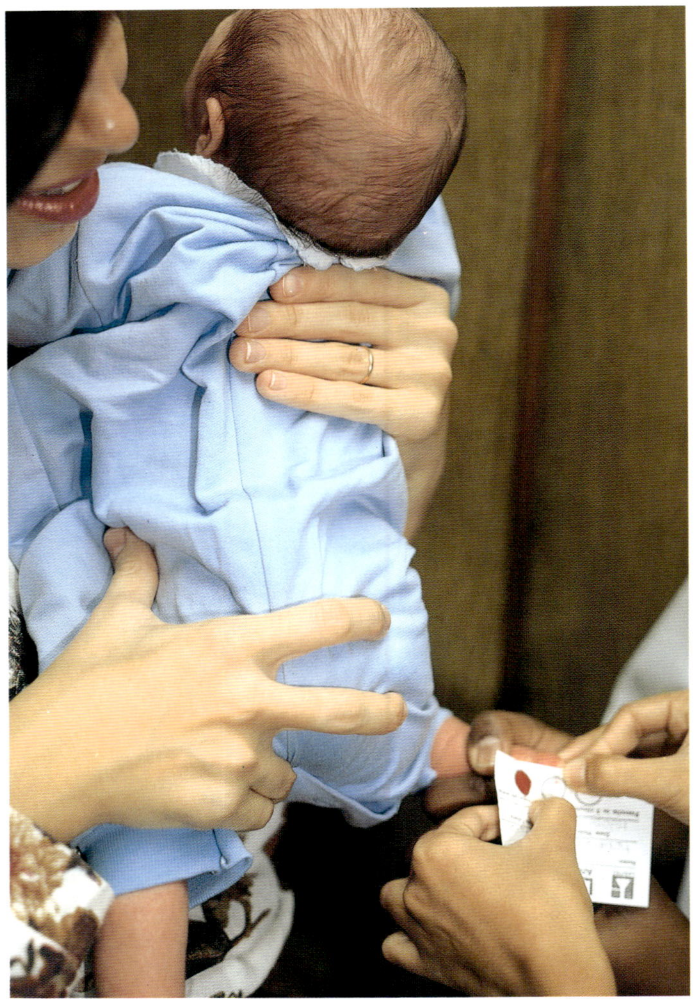

Before a baby is discharged from the hospital he will be given the Guthrie test to test for phenylketonuria, a rare mental disease.

Apgar table

Score	**0**	**1**	**2**
Appearance (color)	pale or white	body pink, extremities blue	pink
Heart rate	not detectable	below 100	over 100
Grimace (reflex irritability)	no response to stimulation	grimace	cough, sneeze
Muscle tone	flaccid (no or weak activity)	some movement of extremities	moving
Respiration (breathing)	none	weak, gasping, irregular	crying, regular

will need some immediate emergency treatment.

Sometime during the first 24-48 hours your baby will be thoroughly checked. A doctor will check your baby's head circumference, the fontanelles, and the roof of the mouth to see if there are any abnormalities. The doctor will listen to the heart and lungs and feel your baby's abdomen to check that the internal organs such as kidney, liver, and spleen, are the right shape and size. The genitals are also checked for abnormalities and, if your baby is a boy, the doctor will look to see that both testicles have descended. Hips will be checked for possible dislocation and all the limbs will be inspected to see that they are the right length and are moving correctly. The doctor will run his thumb down the baby's spine to make sure that the vertebrae are in place. The baby's reflexes will also be checked.

The Guthrie test is usually done before discharge from the hospital. This involves a blood sample being taken from the baby's heel. This sample is then tested for phenylketonuria (PKU), a rare disease that causes severe mental retardation to affected people and hypothyroidism.

SPECIAL CARE

If your baby is born several weeks early, the birth weight is low, or your child needs extra care for any other reason, he may be put in the Special Care Nursery (SCN). Here the infant will be monitored so that he gets all the special treatment required. It can be distressing to see your baby in a special care unit, especially if he is surrounded by an array of strange equipment. Ask the staff to explain what the equipment is for and why your baby needs it. Try to spend as much time as you can with your baby in special care because, even if you can't pick him up and hold him, your baby will be able to hear your voice and it will soothe him. You will probably be able to touch your baby through the side of the isolette.

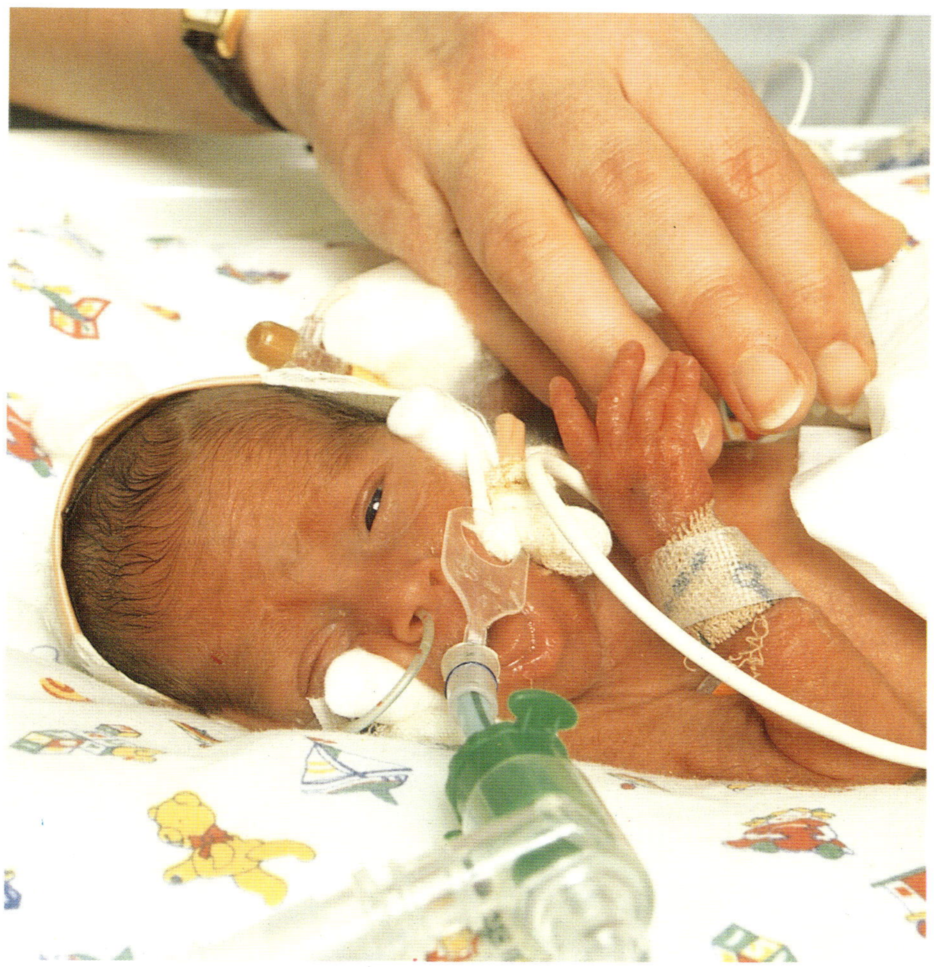

If your baby is born early, he may have to go into the Special Care Nursery. Don't be afraid to ask about all the equipment he is attached to, and let him know you are there by touching and talking to him.

ONE MONTH

Your baby's movements are still dominated by the primary reflexes so when placed on her back your infant will adopt the tonic neck reflex posture, with her head to one side and the limbs on that side extended while the ones on the other side are flexed. If you place your baby on her stomach her head will turn to one side, then your baby will pull her knees under the abdomen and hold her arms close to her body, with her hands curled into fists. The fingers and toes will fan out when she straightens her arms or legs. If you hold your baby to stand on a hard surface she will press down and make a forward walking movement.

Although your baby was born with vision and can see colors and shapes at close range, her sight is still immature. Images that offer a high contrast and simple patterns, for example black lines on a white background, are easier for a baby to understand than paler, more complicated designs. Hold your baby upright or in a half reclining position

Milestones

Your child may be able to:

- Lift her head briefly while lying on her stomach.
- Focus on your face while feeding.
- Respond to a small bell being rung by moving her eyes and head toward the source of the sound.
- Follow with her eyes an object that is moved in an arc about 6–10 in away from her face.
- Turn her head toward you when you speak to her.

Even at this early age your baby will be interested in things around him.

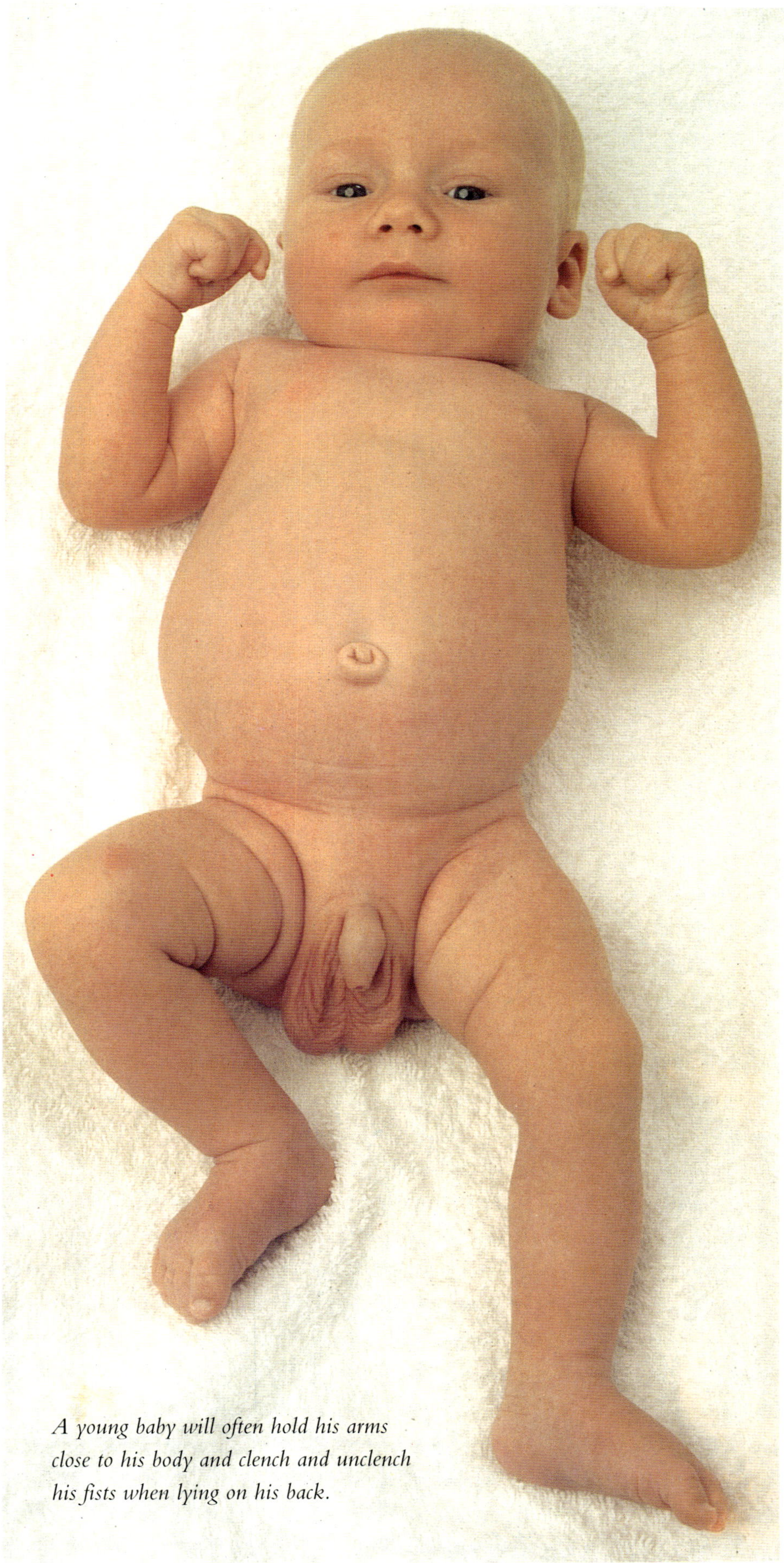

A young baby will often hold his arms close to his body and clench and unclench his fists when lying on his back.

if you are showing her something; this will help to keep the child's interest and will stop her from dropping off to sleep. Crib books, with bold patterns and shapes that attract very young eyes, placed where a baby can see them, will help develop visual powers.

Babies can recognize their mother's smell from the earliest days and your baby will be able to distinguish between the smell of your breast milk and that of any other mother. She can also tell the difference between the smell of formula or cows' milk and your milk.

MINOR BLEMISHES

Occasionally babies may be born with some minor skin blemishes. These are usually harmless and require no treatment; they disappear on their own as the skin matures.

Milia are tiny white spots on the face, caused by blocked oil glands. They should fade after a few days.

Stork bites or angel kisses are red marks that occur around the back of the neck, on the eyelids, or across the bridge of the nose. They usually disappear during the first few months.

Strawberry marks are raised red marks that sometimes appear in the days after the birth and they may grow rapidly during the first few weeks. These usually disappear after about six months, although they can sometimes last until the child is much older. Treatment may be required if the mark has not disappeared by the time your child is in his teens.

Port wine stains are red or purple marks that are usually found on the face and neck. These are permanent and will require treatment once your child is older.

Urticaria, or nettle rash has a raised white center surrounded by an

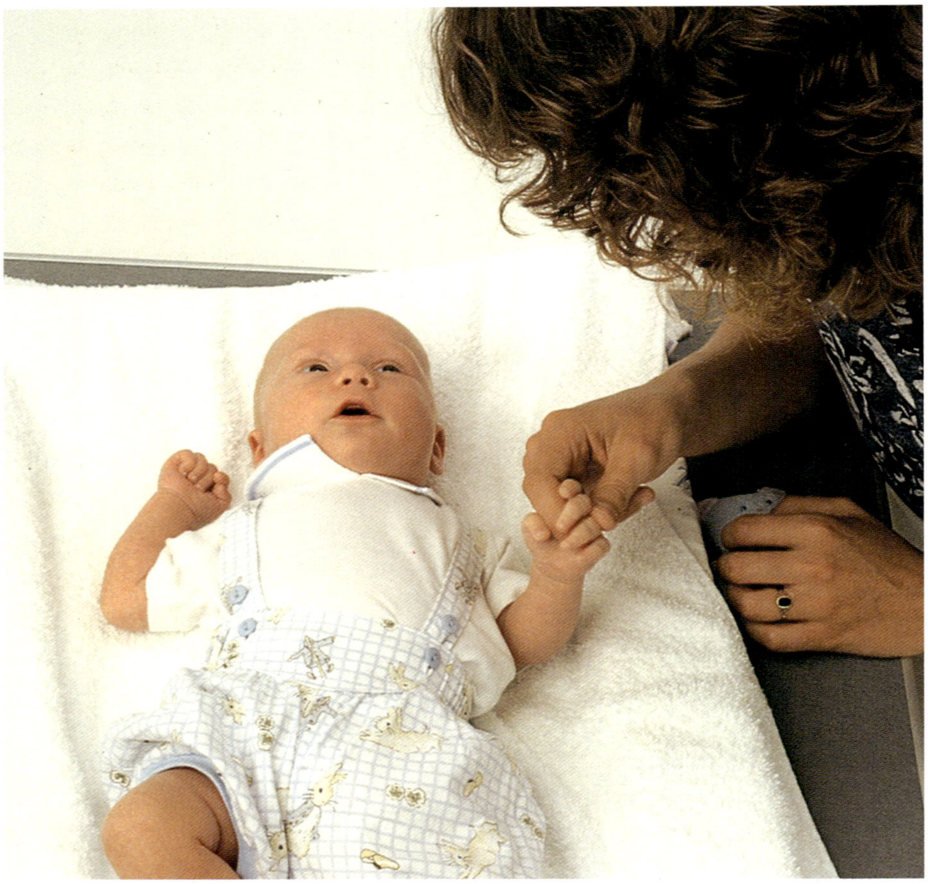

When you are changing your baby, always make time to play and talk to him. This will make him feel secure and at ease.

inflamed red area and quite commonly occurs during the first weeks. This rash doesn't require any treatment and will usually clear up after the first month.

INFECTION

Thrush is a fungal infection that produces white patches on the baby's tongue, the roof of her mouth, and in her cheeks. It can be caught from unsterilized nipples and pacifiers or from the mother if she was suffering from vaginal thrush (yeast) at the time of the birth. Thrush can also appear on the baby's bottom as a red rash that spreads from the anus over the buttocks. Oral thrush is treated with anti-fungal drops and thrush on a baby's bottom needs to be treated with antibiotic cream. Both can be obtained from your doctor.

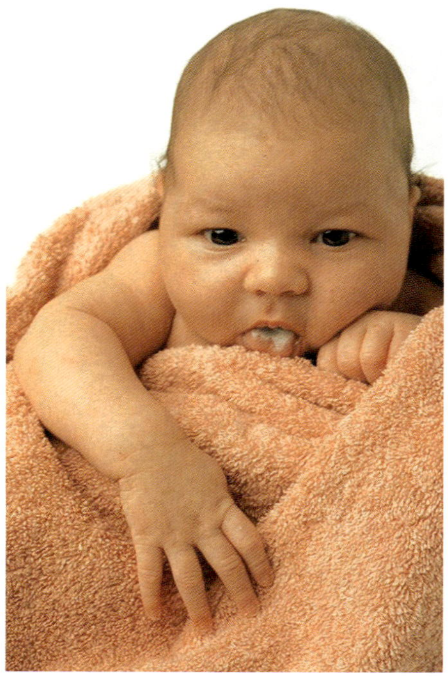

Above: White patches on the tongue are one indication that your baby has thrush. This is easily treated.

FRESH AIR

A baby needs fresh air so if you have a yard or secure outside area and the weather is warm enough you can let your infant sleep outside in the carriage from the first week or so providing that the child is well covered up and away from drafts. When it is hot, use a canopy rather than the carriage hood so that the air can circulate, and make sure that the carriage is in the shade. When outside, protect your baby from cats and

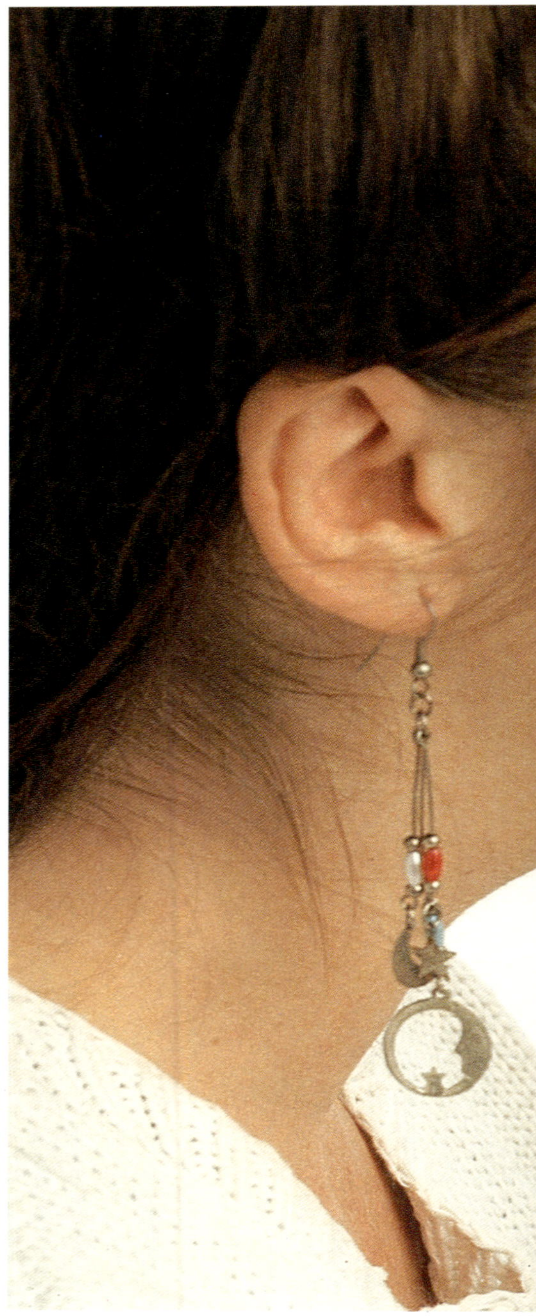

insects with a fine mesh carriage net. If you have no place to leave the baby outside, put her in the crib and open the window to let fresh air into the room. Don't leave a baby in her crib or carriage for too long when she is awake because she will get bored. Babies need other activities to stimulate them as well as exercise.

Taking your baby on outings in a baby sling or carrier is another way of giving your baby fresh air and a convenient way for you to carry her if you don't want to push a carriage. Your baby will enjoy being close to you and will be able to see the world from a different viewpoint.

NOISE

There is no need to tiptoe around or to get people to whisper while your baby is asleep. If you do, it could mean that your baby won't be able to go to sleep if there is any noise and will wake at the least little sound, which can cause sleep problems when your child is older. A very young baby will quickly learn to sleep through the everyday noises that go on in a home, such as the television and vacuum cleaner. Sudden loud noises may wake your baby, but reassurance and a cuddle should soon settle her down again.

When newly born your baby's vision is not well developed, so hold her up to talk to her and let her focus on your face.

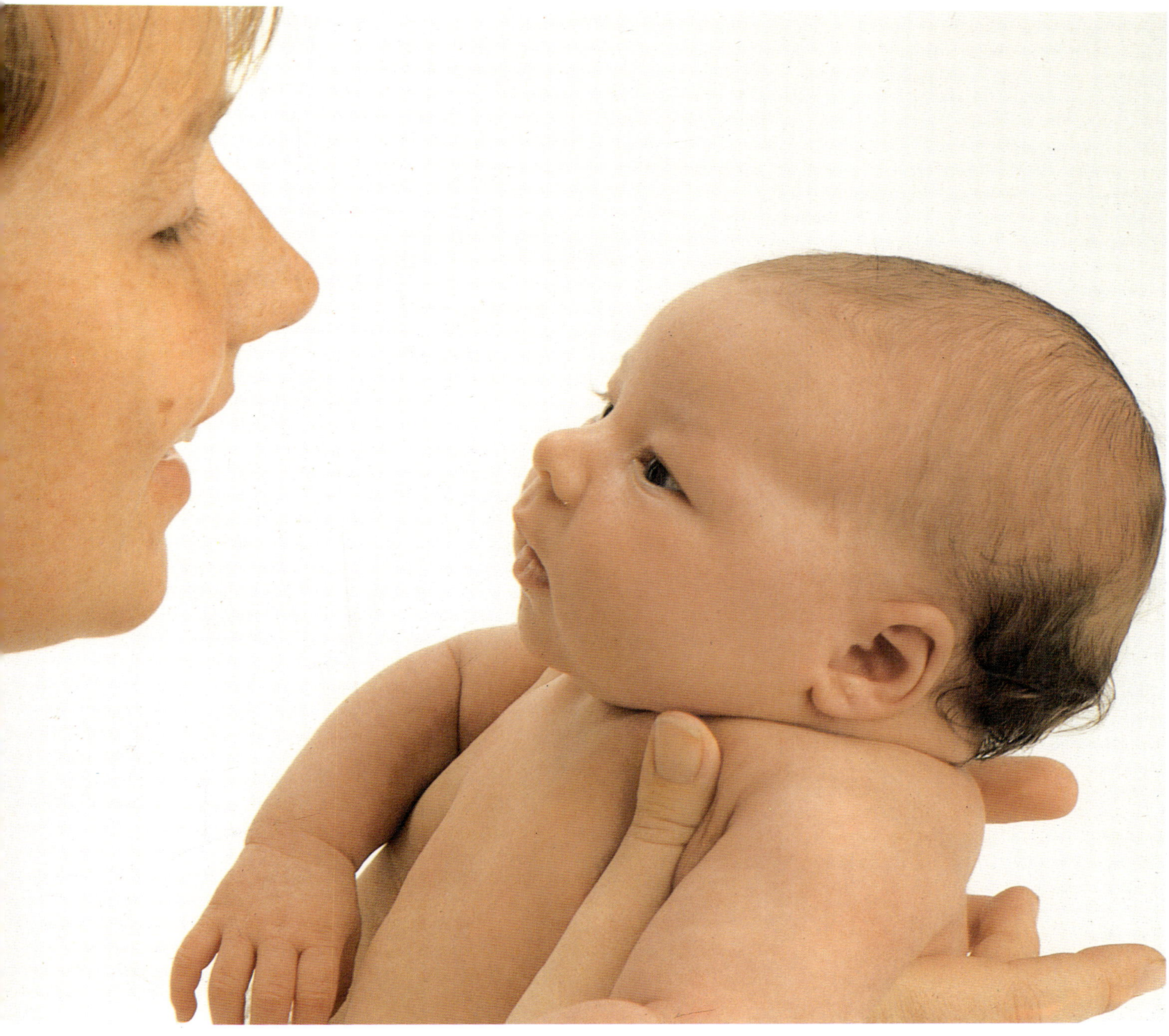

TWO MONTHS

Your baby is developing quickly and, although you may not realize it, he is already trying to talk to you by making a number of vowel sounds and throaty gurgles. At first it may not seem as though these noises are actually directed at you because your baby will enjoy practicing these vocal exercises as much for his own benefit as for yours. Each new noise is helping your baby discover which combinations of throat, tongue, and mouth actions make which sounds. As your baby masters each new sound you will begin to notice that he uses them to communicate vocally with you.

Crying

Your baby now stays awake for longer periods between feedings and is usually more awake in the evenings. It is quite likely that your baby will use some of this extra waking time to cry. Of course not all babies are the same and yours may cry very little, but on average babies usually cry for two to three hours a day and much of this takes place in the evening. Very often this is blamed on colic, thought to be a type of stomach or abdominal ache occurring in spasms, which makes a

Milestones

Your child may be able to:

- Smile.
- Begin to make cooing noises.
- Lift his head 45° when lying on his stomach.
- Grasp a rattle for a few seconds if one is put in his hand.
- Follow an object that is moved in a 180° arc above his face.

At two months, your baby will start to smile at you and will turn her head to follow objects moved above her head.

baby draw up his legs in pain as he screams. No one knows exactly what colic is, but if it is going to occur it usually starts within the first three weeks of birth and lasts until around three months, although it can go on longer. There is no reliable treatment for colic and, although there are some medicines available, you should always consult your doctor before giving them to your baby.

Colic isn't always the cause of excessive crying; some babies cry for no obvious reason for some time each day. If your baby does this you may be able to offer comfort by rocking, letting him suck, or by distracting him with a toy. Don't leave

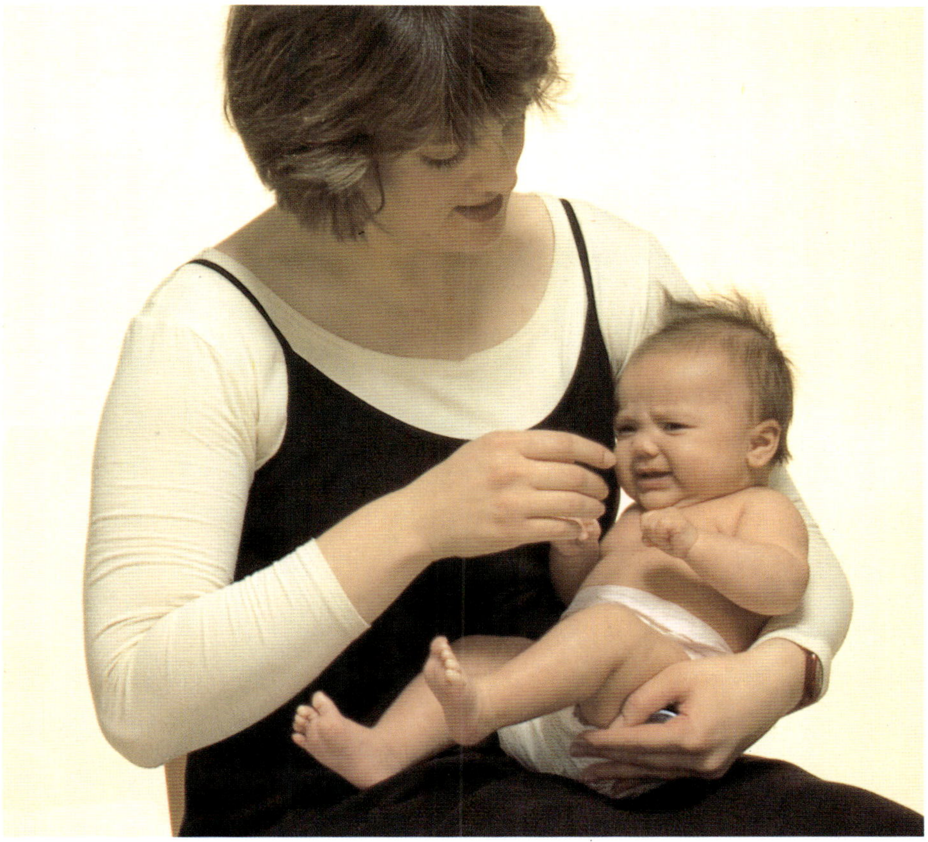

When you support your baby in a sitting position, she can hold her head up for a minute.

Holding and cuddling your young baby is an important part of her getting to know you.

him to cry for more than a few minutes; at this age crying is the only way to let you know that he is miserable and needs comforting.

Learning control

Your baby is gradually gaining control of his body. When you place the child on his stomach he will be able to lift his head, keeping his nose and mouth free to breathe. If held by you in a sitting position, your baby will be able to hold his head up for about a minute, and if you touch his hand with a rattle your baby will jerk his hand toward the object. This is the first stage of learning when he reaches out to grab hold of something.

Six to eight week check-up

The ages at which check-ups take place vary depending on your doctor's system and the individual needs of the child. But in general, you can expect your baby to have his first check-up sometime between six and eight weeks old. Of course, each practitioner is an individual, and

Immunization

Your baby should be given the first round of immunizations for diphtheria, tetanus, and whooping cough (DTP), polio and Hib. After the immunization your child may feel a bit off-color for up to 24 hours and may even run a temperature. Rarely, a convulsion may occur as a result of the fever, but this is over quickly and has no lasting effect. It is also quite normal for the skin around the site of the injection to become red and sore or slightly swollen. If you are at all worried about your child's reaction, contact your doctor immediately.

Learning head movements

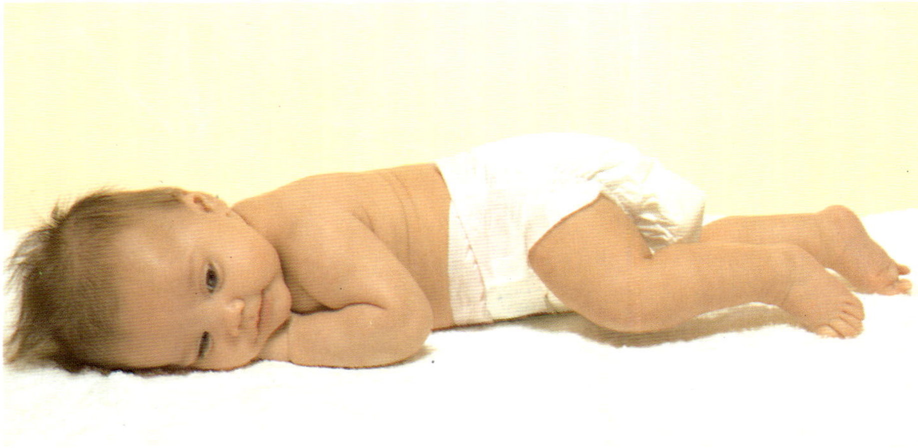

1 *At this stage of development, your baby is gaining control of her body. When lying on her stomach, with her arms supporting her, she can start to lift her head.*

2 *As she maneuvers herself into position, she pushes hard with her legs and starts to put her weight on her arms.*

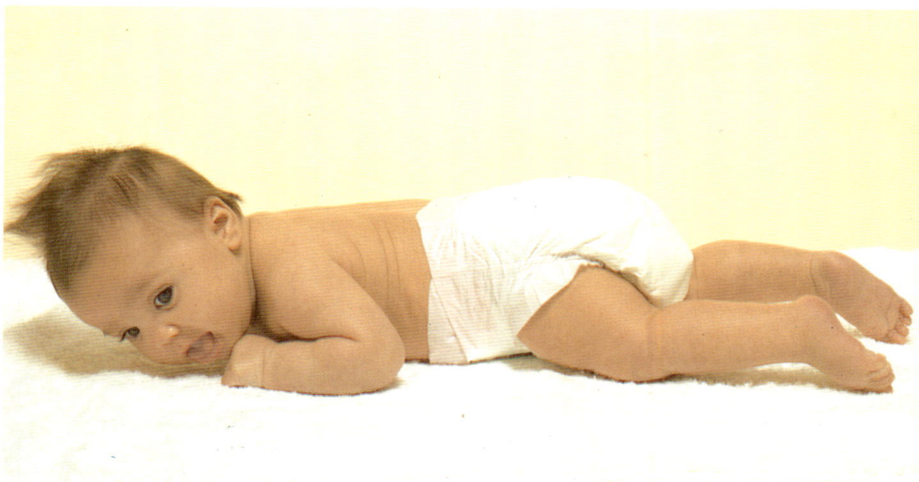

3 *As she raises her head, pushing up with her arms, she will find she can hold it up, keeping her nose and mouth free to breathe.*

Make sure you allow enough time to play and have fun with your baby, so that you can really get to know her.

approaches to care will inevitably vary. Nevertheless, the aim of any check-up is to detect any potential problems early, to prevent illnesses, and to promote your baby's good health. If the check-up detects any early signs of delayed development, or health or behavior problems, treatment can be begun at once. A number of routine check-ups take place between now and when your child reaches school age. They are all important because the check-ups are designed to reveal hidden disabilities as well as more obvious ones.

This early check-up will probably include measuring your baby's weight, length and head circumference and noting the changes that have occurred since birth. You will probably be asked questions about how your baby is feeding and sleeping. General progress will be assessed and the doctor may also carry out a series of tests to evaluate your baby's head control, use of hands, vision, hearing, and social interaction. You may be given some guidance about what you should expect during the next month in relation to feeding, sleeping, and also general development. You may also be asked questions about how you, the baby, and the rest of the family are managing with your new baby at home. This is the time to voice any concerns or problems that you might have or that have been particularly worrying you.

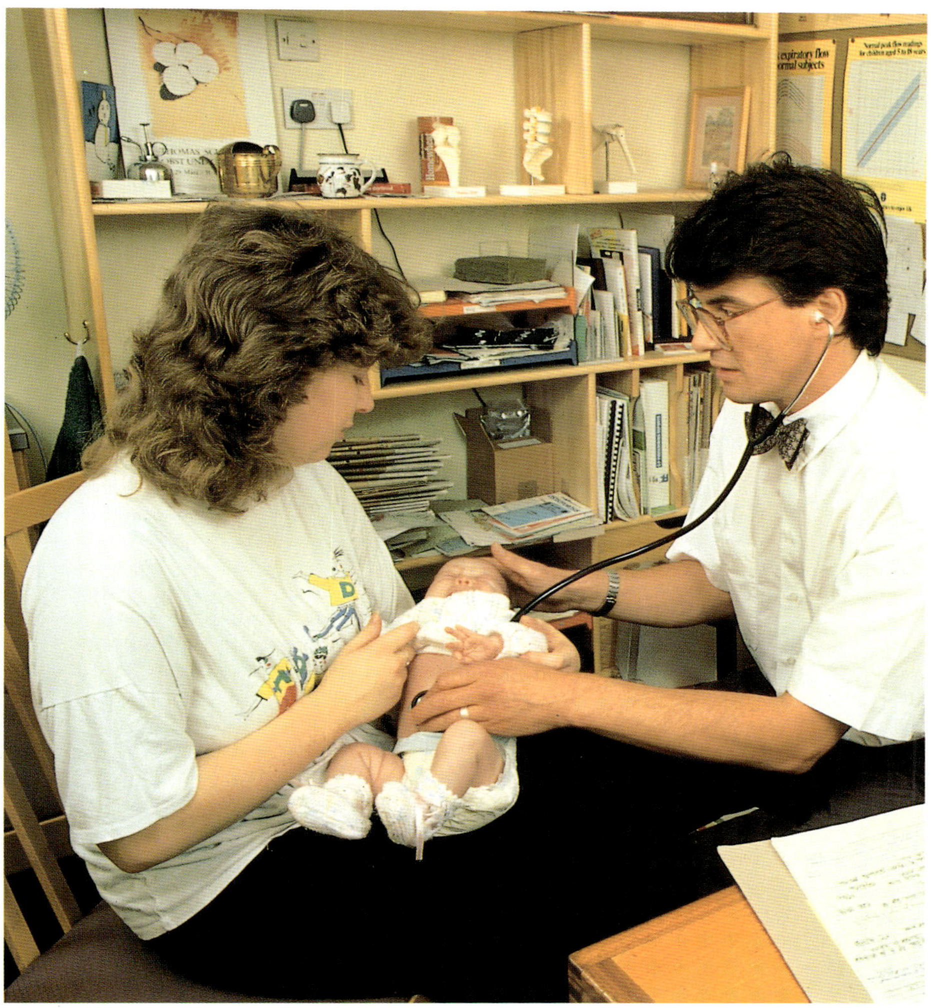

At six to eight weeks your baby will probably be given a check-up to see if everything is functioning normally. Any early problems should be detected.

THREE MONTHS

Your baby will probably have begun to control her head movements, so that when held in a sitting position she can keep her head up for several seconds before it drops forward. As her neck strengthens your baby will be able to look around and turn her head to watch something moving within 6–8 in.

Below: As you pull your baby up at this age, he will now be in more control of his head movements.

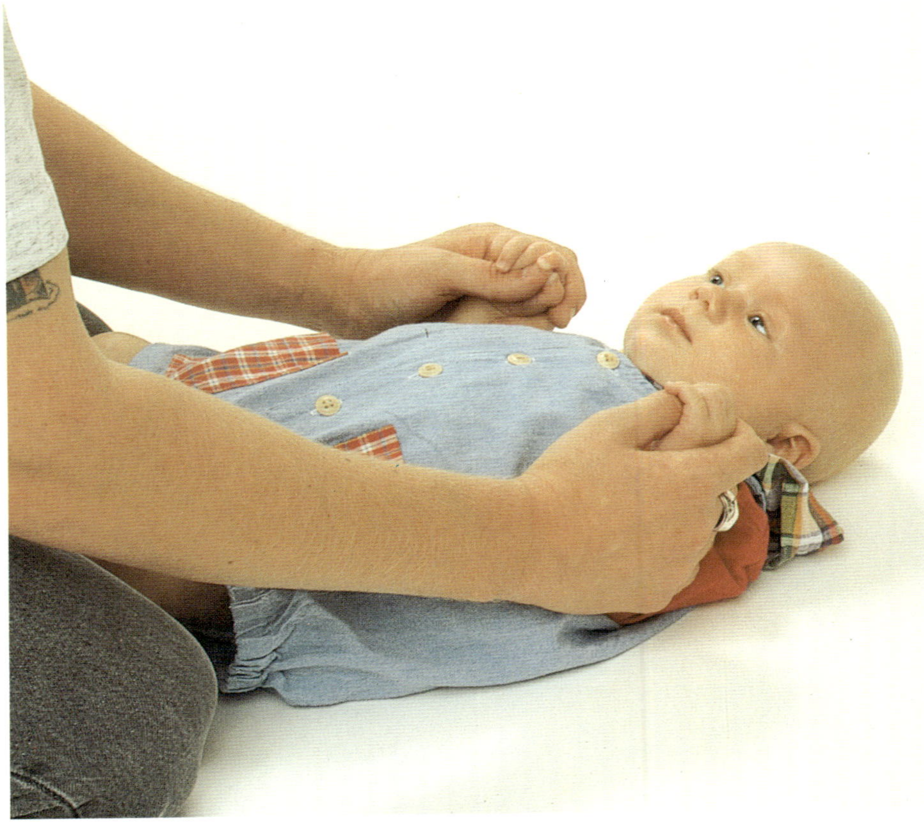

EARLY LEARNING

As babies begin to understand their own body, they will spend hours studying and moving their fingers. Their hands have opened out now and they can clasp and unclasp them, pressing the palms together. Babies enjoy playing with them and may even be able to hold a small toy for a few seconds. When your baby is lying down you will probably notice that her arms and legs make a lot of

Below: When your baby lies on the floor, he will often raise his head for several seconds before it drops forward.

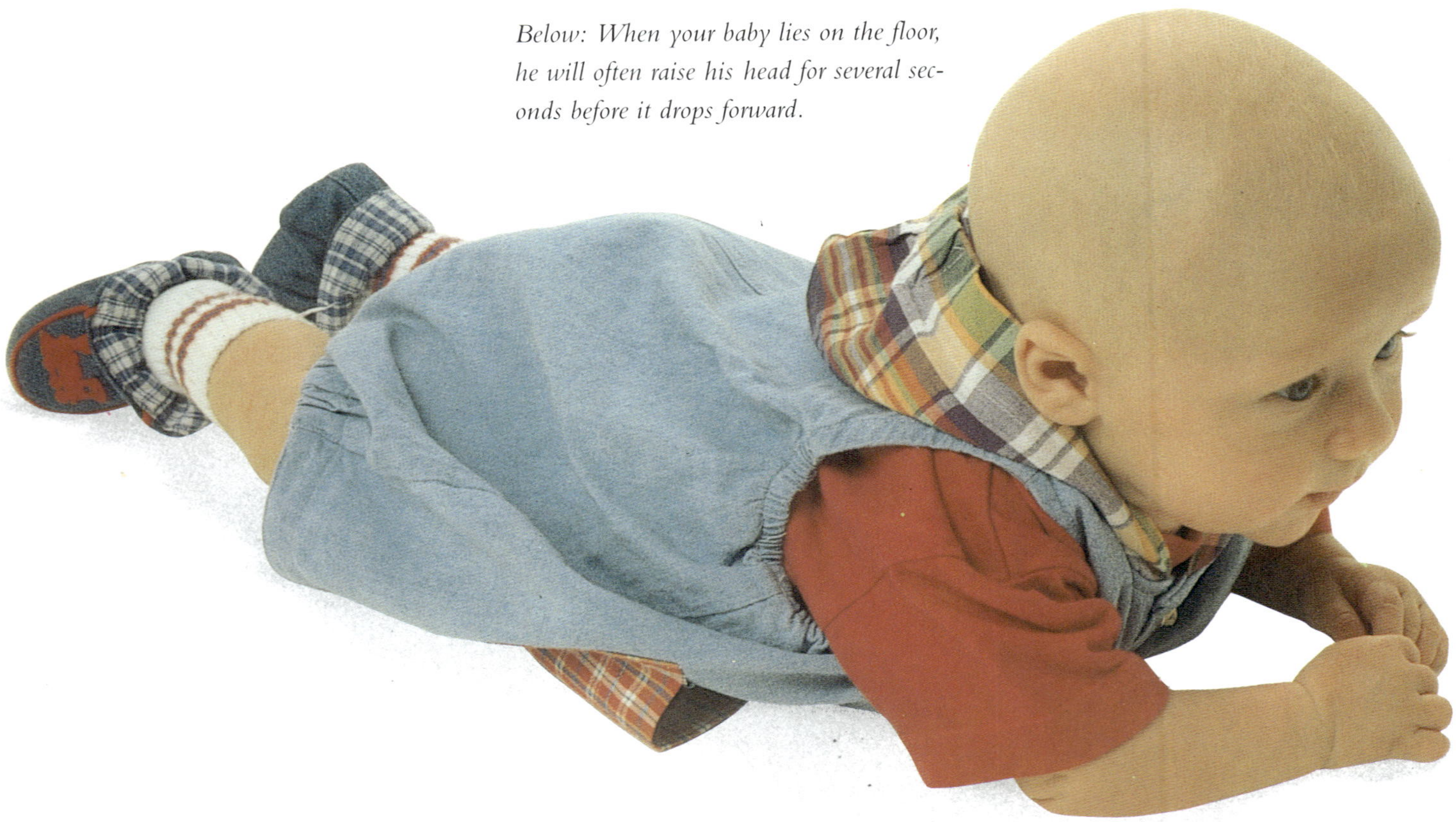

Below: As your baby sits up, he can hold his head steady more easily because his neck has strengthened.

Bottom: Your baby will be fascinated by any toys in bright, primary colors that are hung over her crib.

Milestones

Your child may be able to:

- Smile and coo when she sees you.
- Control her head.
- Show anticipation when food is on the way by licking her lips.
- Enjoy looking at brightly colored objects such as a mobile hanging over the crib.
- Play with her hands.
- Hold a small toy for a few seconds

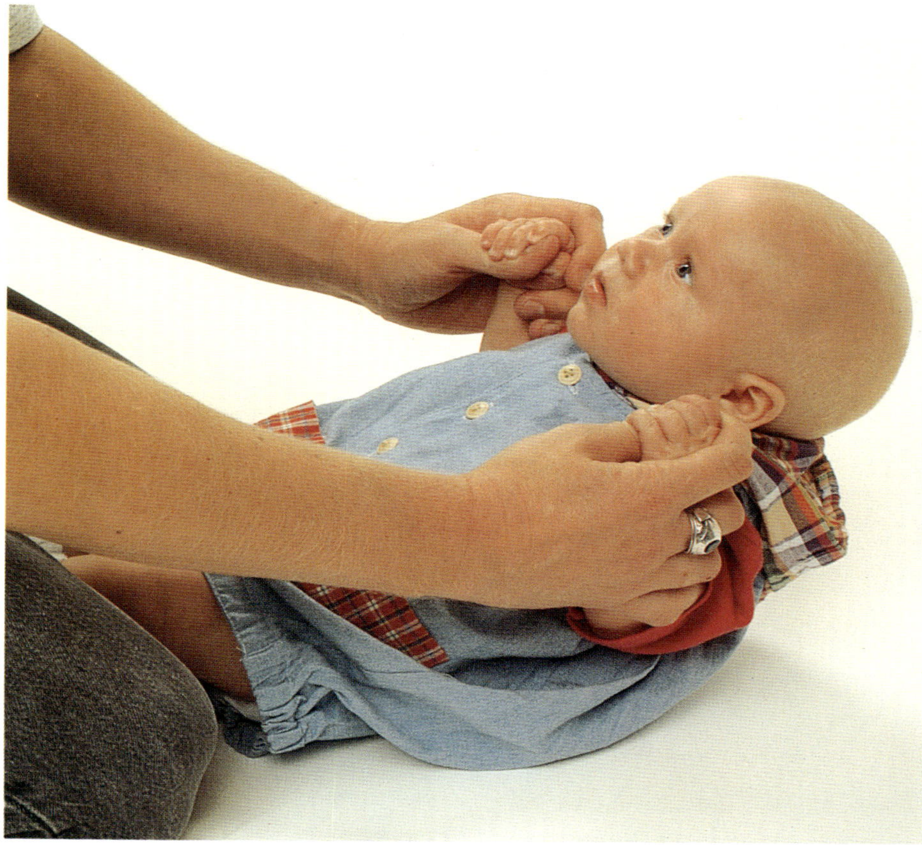

movement. A child will kick vigorously, usually with alternate legs, but occasionally with both legs together.

The first smiles are reflexive, but they very quickly become social and the baby will smile at you in response to your smile or voice. The smiles will come in clusters, four or five at a time, followed by a pause of maybe half a minute before the next cluster. The baby will also respond vocally when you speak to her. Talk

to your baby and she will answer you back in her own way, using her lips and tongue as she coos and tries to imitate you. She uses her whole body to express the way she feels, making excited movements when pleased, expressing happiness and delight with gurgles and squeals. When she is angry, uncomfortable, or lonely she will tell you by crying loudly and even angrily. To encourage your baby, you should respond to her behavior with exaggerated gestures and praise, using a slow singsong voice and lots of repetition.

A baby will react to familiar situations and will show excitement when she recognizes preparation for things that she enjoys. She responds with obvious pleasure to friendly handling, especially when it is accompanied by play and a friendly voice. Bathtime and other caring routines, where she has your undivided attention for quite a while, are likely to become her favorite times of the day.

Left: Plastic stacking toys in bright colors will soon attract the attention of your inquisitive baby who will try to grasp hold of them.

Below: Lying on his back, your young baby will enjoy kicking vigorously with alternate legs and sometimes with both legs together.

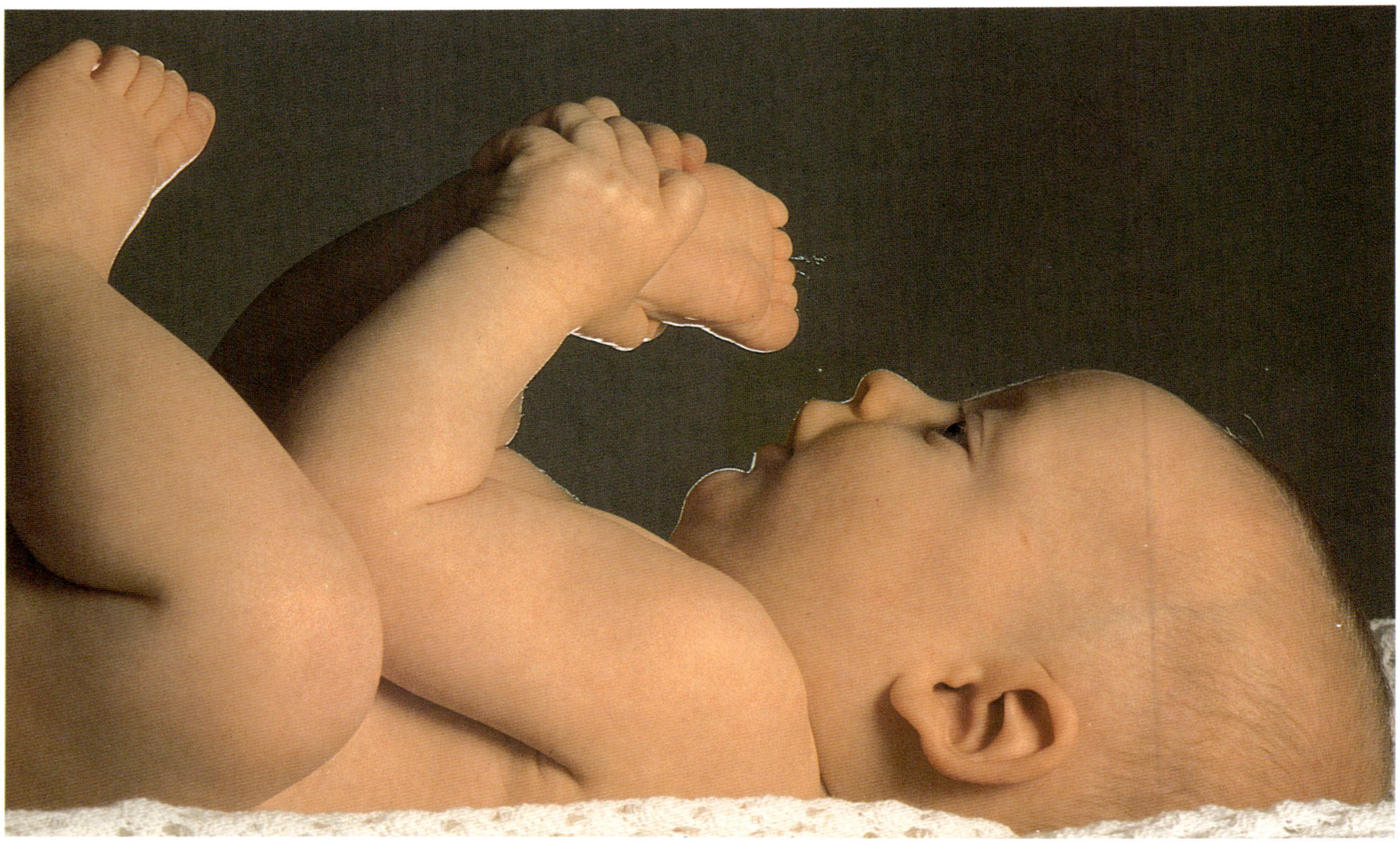

If you haven't already done so, introduce a regular bedtime routine now so that your child starts to realize that a bath, a story, and a cuddle are a prelude to being put into the crib to sleep. By about three months many babies begin to sleep for long periods at night. If your baby has started to sleep through the night you will probably find that she needs less sleep during the day and that her daytime sleep is not as deep as it was. You may find that your baby is more easily disturbed by household noises now. Encourage her to stay awake during the day by stimulating her with different toys and by playing and talking with her.

Immunization

At three to four months your baby will have the second round of immunizations for diphtheria, tetanus, and whooping cough (DTP), polio and also Hib.

Your baby is now using her whole body to show her feelings, and will start to recognize her favorite toys.

FOUR MONTHS

Your baby is developing rapidly. He is awake for much longer and during these waking periods will want to be sociable and will respond with delight to conversations with you and enjoy playing simple games.

You can encourage your baby's development by spending time responding to these early attempts at sociability. Make a point of showing your baby different objects and talk about them. Your baby will also enjoy seeing and talking to himself in a mirror. Place the mirror about 6–8 in away so that he can keep his image in focus.

Motor development and learning progress at the same rate between four and five months. Hand and eye coordination is being learned and your baby may be able to reach out and grasp an object. He will try hard to learn how to sit because he will have discovered that sitting up gives him a different view of the world. At first he will need you to help him balance, but as his confidence grows he will learn to adjust his legs and to use his hands to keep himself upright.

Milestones

Your child may be able to:

- Lift his head up 90° when he is on his stomach.
- Raise himself up a little way, supported by the arms, when lying on his stomach.
- Laugh out loud.
- Hold his head steady when he is held upright.
- Roll over in one direction.
- Reach out for an object.

STARTING ON SOLIDS

Although babies can get all the nourishment they require from breast milk or formula during their first six months, you may want to start to introduce solids at around four months. A baby needs to be able to have control over his head before you begin to offer him solids. Even strained or purèed first foods should not be given until he can hold his head upright when he is sitting propped up. Chunkier foods

At four months your baby will try to sit up with your help.

As your baby gains control over his head he will be able to hold it at different angles.

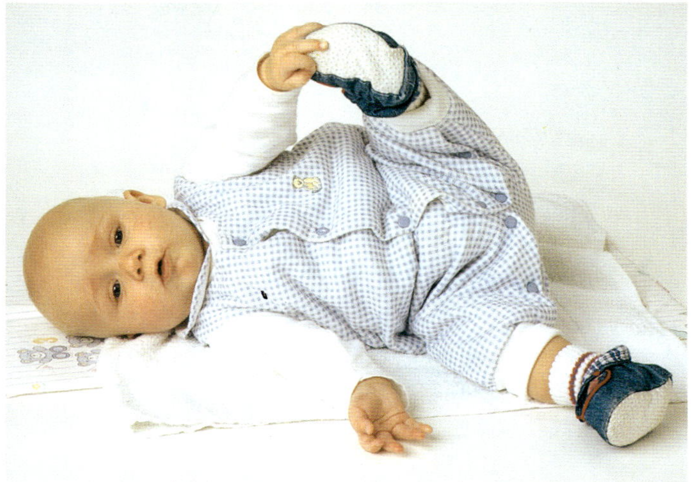

As he gets more active your baby will probably start to learn how to roll over in one direction. First, he will grab his foot with his hand and lift that leg up.

He'll then push down this leg, and helped by his bottom arm, roll his body over in one direction.

When your baby is lying flat on his stomach, he will now be able to raise his head up 90° and support himself more sturdily on his arms.

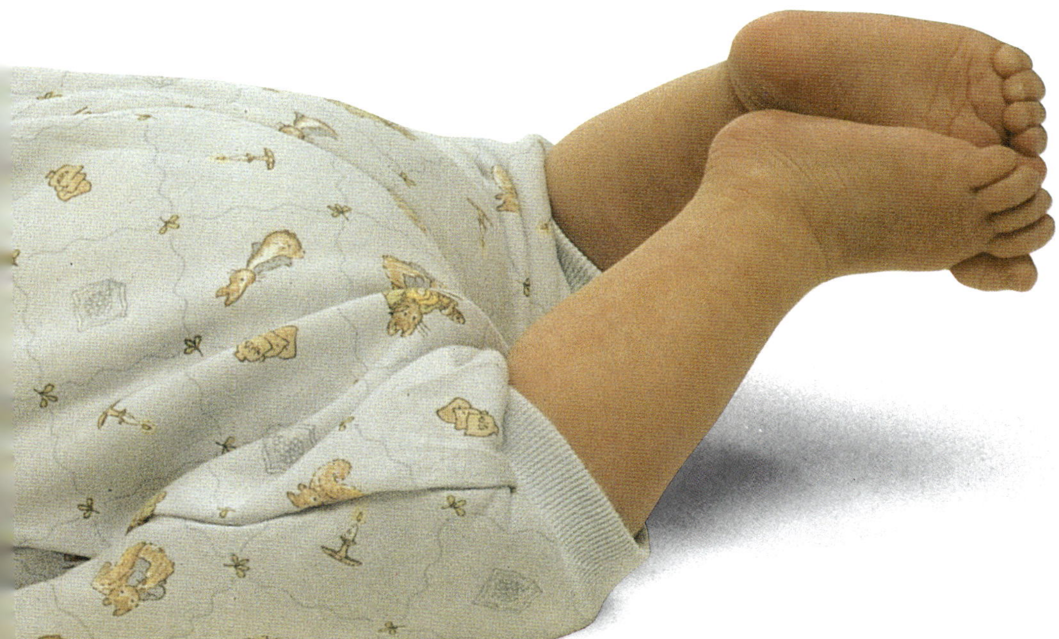

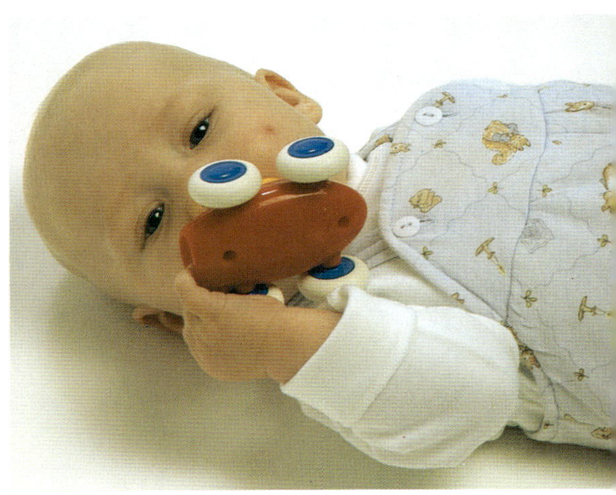

Your baby will now start to reach out for interesting toys and often try to put them in his mouth.

A young baby is fascinated by mirrors, but at distances she can only make out vague shapes.

If you place your baby 6–8in away from a mirror, she will be able to focus on her image and talk to herself.

that require chewing should not be introduced until your baby can sit up alone, which is not usually until about seven months.

First solids are little more than tasters that get a baby used to the idea of sucking from a spoon rather than from the breast or bottle. To be able to do this the tongue thrust reflex, which the baby was born with, must have disappeared. This is the reflex that causes the tongue to push any foreign matter out of the mouth and prevents very young babies from choking.

If the food offered is pushed straight back out of the mouth by the tongue and this happens several times, the reflex is still there and the baby is not ready for solids. To be able to eat from a spoon your baby also needs to be able to draw in his lower lip.

Another fairly obvious sign that your baby is ready for solids is if he shows any interest in the food that you are eating. If your baby watches intently while you eat and shows excitement or tries to grab your food, then he is probably telling you that he is now ready for more grown-up food himself. If you are unsure about when to start weaning your baby, remember to ask your doctor for advice.

THUMB SUCKING

Your baby will suck anything he can get into his mouth and now that he has some control over his hands, his fingers and thumbs will be preferred and he will suck them for pleasure and also for comfort. He may suck his whole hand, or one or two fingers, or he may prefer his thumb. This is quite normal and is not a sign of emotional distress, nor will it, at this age, damage the alignment of permanent teeth. If your baby is breast-fed you need to make sure that he isn't sucking his thumb to compensate for suckling he is no longer getting at the breast; otherwise there is no harm if you let your child suck his thumb. Most children grow out of this habit naturally over the next year or two, although a child who uses sucking his thumb as reassurance to get to sleep may take a little longer to break the habit. This is nothing to worry about.

Immunization

At four months your baby will have the third immunizations for diphtheria, tetanus, whooping cough (DTP), Hib and polio.

You can now give some solids to your baby if she can hold her head upright and if food isn't rejected by her tongue.

Your baby will try to stand with help, but he shouldn't put too much weight on his legs.

FIVE MONTHS

Your baby's grasp of basic concepts is growing and she is thinking much faster. It is thought that a baby when she is first born will take between five and 10 minutes to get used to something new; by three months a baby may take between 30 seconds and two minutes and by six months she will take only 30 seconds.

Your baby will begin to learn about cause and effect by carrying out simple experiments, such as throwing a toy out of her carriage. Initially she will believe that it has

Milestones

Your child may be able to:

- Hold her head steady when upright.
- Keep her head level with her body when pulled into the sitting position.
- Pay attention to a small object.
- Squeal with delight.
- Be able to say some vowel-consonant combinations such as "ah-coo".

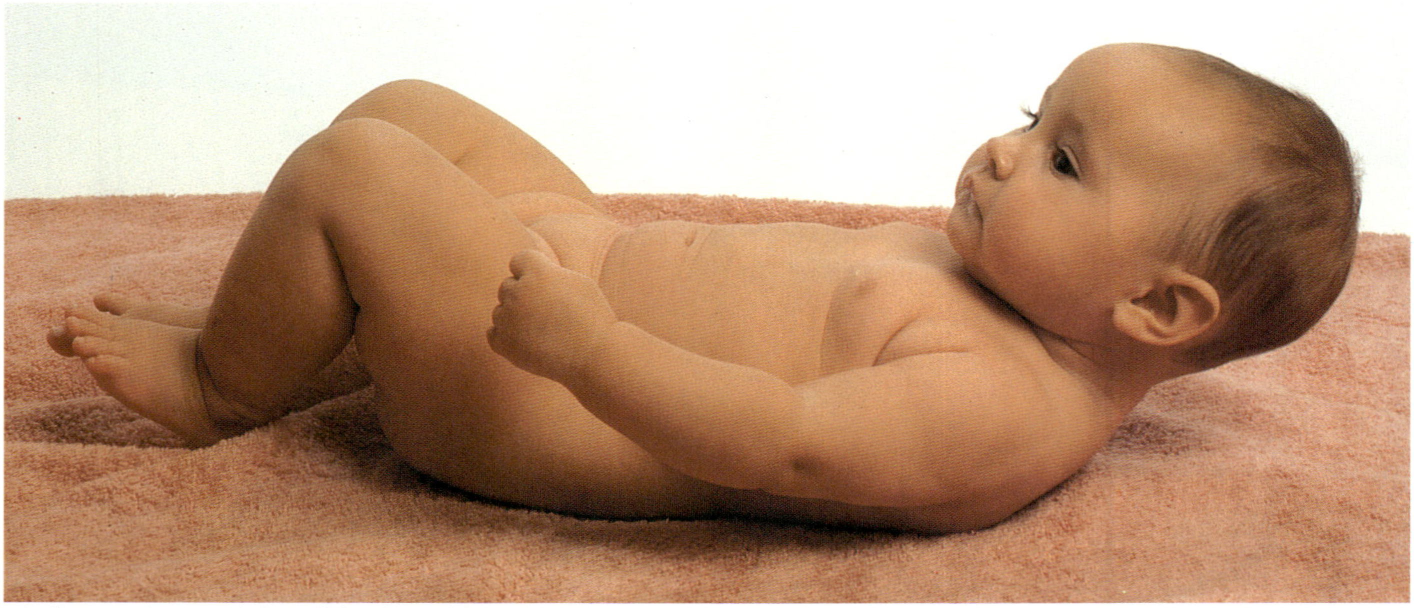

At five months, your baby will be able to lift her head up from a lying position and hold it steady.

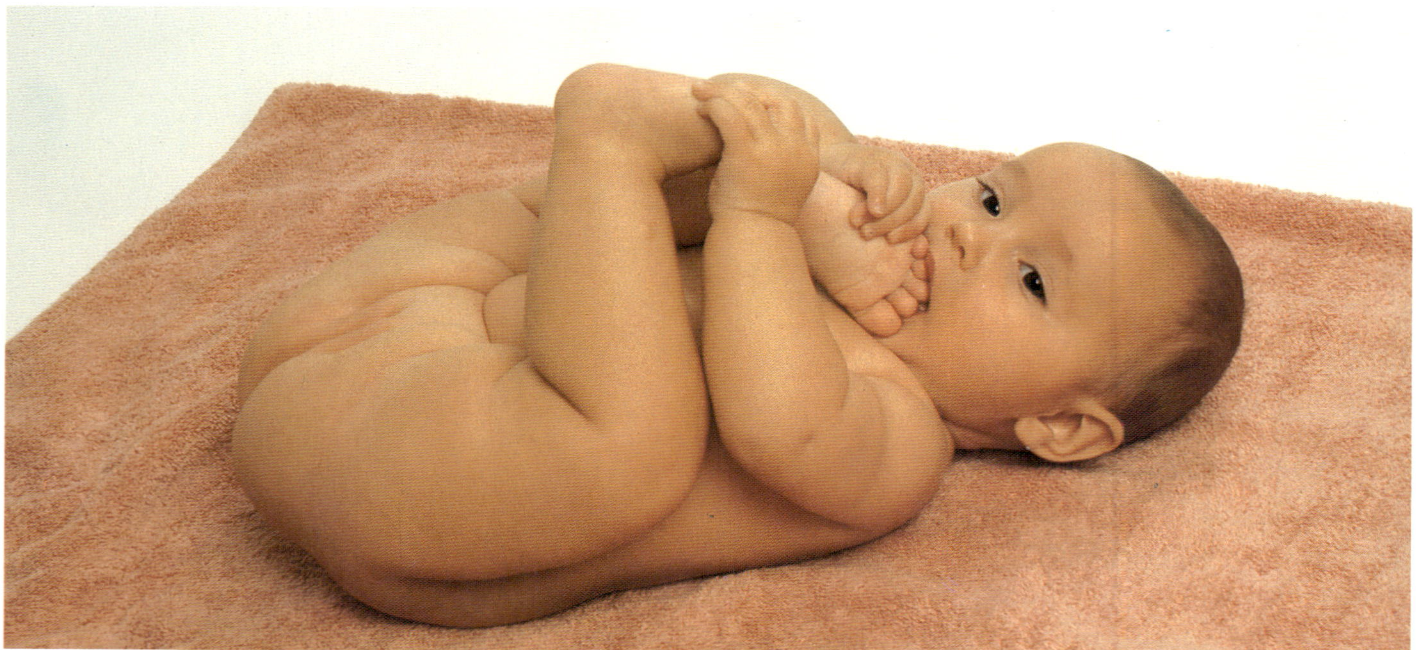

She will love to suck things, and will often put her hands or feet in her mouth.

Your baby's head movements are now getting much steadier as she gains more control.

vanished and won't understand where it has gone. If you pick up the toy and return it she will be both puzzled and delighted. She will do the trick again and again until she begins to realize that, by dropping the toy and getting it back, she is beginning to take control of her world by making things happen.

You can encourage your baby with her experiments by playing games such as peek-a-boo, or hiding an object that was in front of her and then making it reappear again. At this age your baby won't attempt to recover what you have hidden because she thinks that the object no longer exists because she can't see it. It will be several months before she learns that this really isn't the case and starts looking for the hidden object herself.

TEETHING

There is no fixed time for your baby to start teething, but on average a baby's first tooth appears sometime

between now and seven months. Babies teethe differently, with some experiencing a lot of discomfort and others hardly seeming to notice their first teeth coming through. It is thought that tooth eruption follows hereditary patterns, so if you or your partner teethed especially early or late your baby may do the same.

Teething symptoms often precede the tooth itself by several weeks or even months, and vary from child to child. Drooling is often the first sign that teeth are on their way and this can start as early as 10 weeks. Excessive drooling can cause a dry skin rash or chapping on the chin and around the mouth, which should be treated with a mild skin cream. Biting is another indication of teething. Your baby may start chewing on anything she can get into her mouth as the counterpressure from chewing on a hard object helps relieve the pressure under the gums. Rubbing her gums with your finger may bring relief or you can give her something to chew on such as a chilled teething ring or a cloth-wrapped ice cube.

Delight your growing baby with different types of toys to keep her interested and fully stimulated.

Inflammation of the tender gum tissue often occurs when a tooth is coming through so your baby is likely to have red, sore gums before a tooth erupts. Ear pulling and cheek rubbing may also be a sign of teething as pain can travel along the nerve pathways to these areas. This is particularly common when the molars are coming through. If your child seems to be in pain you can give her the recommended dose of acetaminophen. However, never attribute illnesses such as diarrhea, fever, or earache to teething: if you are concerned seek medical advice.

Your baby will often prefer a simple toy like this rattle as it is easier for her to manage and play with.

SIX MONTHS

Your child is beginning to show a greater interest in what is going on around him. He will turn his head quickly to familiar voices and will examine things that interest him for longer periods.

YOUR BABY TAKES CONTROL

Your baby is rapidly becoming more mobile and will probably be able to pull himself into the sitting position if both hands are held. When lying on his stomach, your baby may find that kicking will push him along, usually backward at first. If he becomes frustrated because he can't get to where he wants to go, don't be too eager to help him. You can encourage him by placing a toy just out of reach, or by placing your hands against the soles of his feet so that when he kicks he has something to push against. If you pick him up and place him where he wants to go he will not learn how to achieve this for himself.

The baby's ability to reach and grasp is becoming more accurate and you can help him improve these skills by passing objects in such a way that he has to reach up or down or to the side for them. Toys strung across his crib or playpen will allow him to practice using these skills. The baby will hold objects in the palm of his hands, and will be able to pass them from one hand to the other. You can encourage him by giving him two toys simultaneously, one in each hand, so that he has to reach out with both hands. If you offer him a rattle, shake it to make a noise as you hand it to him; he will reach for it immediately and then shake it deliberately to make the same noise.

Visually your baby is keenly aware of everything that is going on around him and will move his head and eyes eagerly in every direction to which his attention is attracted. He will follow what you are doing, even if you are busy on the other side of the room. His eyes now

Milestones

Your child may be able to:

- Laugh, chuckle, and also squeal aloud and scream with annoyance at things he doesn't like.
- Use his whole hand to grasp objects and pass them from one hand to the other.
- Move his eyes in unison and turn his head and eyes toward something that attracts him.
- Play happily with his feet as well as his hands.
- Manipulate small objects.

Immunization

At six months your baby will have the third set of injections, DTP, Hib, and an oral polio vaccine.

Right and opposite: If you have a very active baby it is best not to put her in her high chair at meal times until her food is ready to eat or has cooled, as she will only get restless and may have a temper tantrum because she can't easily move around. A quieter baby will probably be quite happy to sit in her chair and play for a while with a stimulating toy that you have given her.

move in unison so if your child appears to be cross-eyed (with an eye turned inward or outward all the time) he should see an eye specialist.

If your baby drops a toy within his field of vision he will watch until it reaches its resting place. Toys falling outside his visual field will be ignored or forgotten.

Your child is now very chatty and will vocalize tunefully both to himself and others in a singsong manner using vowel sounds and single and double syllables such as "a-a," "adah" and "er-leh." He laughs, chuckles, and squeals with delight when playing and will express anger or annoyance with loud screams.

INTELLIGENCE

Assessing a child's IQ (intelligence quotient) when he is very young is difficult, and the motor development tests that can be used to evaluate IQ in the first year do not usually correlate well with a child's IQ later on. Intelligence can be influenced by many factors, including stimulation, health and diet as well as social aspects such as poverty. Even trauma can play a part. At this stage in your child's development you can encourage his physical, social, and intellectual growth by raising him in a stimulating environment and spending time playing, reading, and talking to him.

It is hard to predict how fast your baby will develop, but she will be stimulated by your talking and playing with her.

Always buy toys that suit the age of your baby. This one has bendy projections that he can easily grasp.

Once you have helped your baby to sit up, she will often sit quite happily and watch you as you move around the room.

SEVEN MONTHS

Learning to move from one place to another is a huge achievement for your baby and one that will give her a whole new perspective on the world. How this locomotion is achieved will vary from baby to baby. Some crawl on all fours, others creep by wriggling on their stomachs, others roll their way from one place to another. Some push themselves backward, which can be very frustrating for them. It is thought that the children who walk the earliest are those who have crawled first or those who have gone straight from sitting to standing. Bottom shufflers and creepers tend to walk a bit later. However, there is little to suggest that a crawler who becomes an early walker is any brighter than a creeper who walks a little later.

Your baby will be able to take some weight on her legs now and she may even be able to stand while you hold her in an upright position. Over the next couple of months she will probably learn to pull herself up from sitting, and then she will practice standing alone.

At seven months your baby will be able to sit up and turn at the waist. She may also like to suck her thumb.

Your baby is developing a mind of her own and will often try to wriggle free when picked up or held.

DEXTERITY

Your baby may start to show a preference for using her right or left hand at this age. Offer her a toy held straight in front of her and see which hand she uses to reach for it. If your baby regularly uses the same hand she is beginning to show a preference, but this is by no means a final choice. Very often the hand she uses at seven months is not the same as the one she prefers at nine months

Milestones

Your child may be able to:

- Put weight on legs when upright.
- Sit with minimal support.
- Look for a dropped object.
- Babble combining vowels and consonants such as "ga-ga," "ma-ma" and "da-da".
- Feed herself with finger foods.
- Begin to crawl.

Your baby is now very much on the move and will be beginning to crawl everywhere quite quickly.

Your baby will hold toys in both hands with much more dexterity now. She will also still enjoy sucking them.

Try and talk to your baby as much as you can as he will reply with babble that mixes both vowels and consonants.

or a year. Once your baby is able to use two hands in a coordinated way, give her something that needs one hand to hold it and another to make it work – a pot with a lid that comes off is ideal – and see which hand she uses for which action. This will give you a better idea of whether your baby is likely to be left- or right-handed, although her final choice may not be made until she reaches two years of age.

You may notice that your baby no longer grasps things in the center of her palm to hold them. She now uses her fingers and thumb so that her grip has become very much more refined. Now that she can operate her fingers and thumb independently, rather than using them as a rake, she can pick up an object as small as a raisin to examine it.

You can encourage the baby by allowing her to feed herself. Give her a bowl and spoon and let her get on with it. At first it is a good idea for you to have a spoon too, so that you can give her the occasional mouthful while she is still figuring out how to get the food from the

bowl, onto the spoon and into her mouth. Finger foods will help your baby learn how to get food into her mouth using her fingers.

At around the time your baby starts to show hand preference her language also starts to become more fully developed and she will babble a lot more using both vowel sounds and consonants. Her cries also change to include both low- and high-pitched sounds and she will start to make different movements with her tongue and mouth.

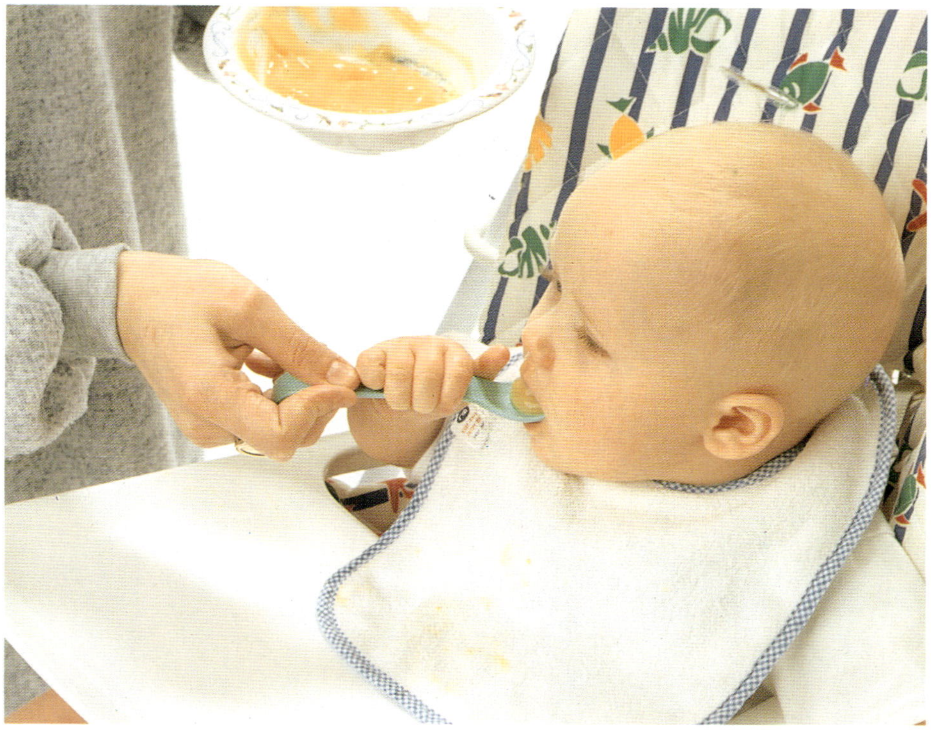

As his hand movements improve, your baby will start to grasp toys, such as blocks, with his fingers and thumb.

You can encourage your baby to eat solids by encouraging him to hold the spoon and to feed himself.

EIGHT MONTHS

By eight months your baby will probably have started to be selective about the people with whom he is sociable. The outgoing friendliness of the earlier months may have been replaced by a certain wariness, especially of strangers. If you leave your baby with someone he doesn't know he may now burst into tears, whereas before he would have been perfectly happy, as long as he was being entertained and was warm and comfortable. This newfound wariness of strangers often occurs at about the same time that your baby is making a surge in his development. About a month after this, your baby may start to show distress, sometimes known as separation anxiety, when you leave the room. This distress at being separated from you or your partner will probably peak at around 15 months and then gradually subside.

If your baby does suffer from separation anxiety it can be misery for both of you. The best way of easing his distress is to leave him in a familiar environment with, if possible, a well-known person or relative. Favorite and familiar toys can also be a source of comfort.

When you are leaving your baby to go out, try to leave quickly without making a fuss and keep your goodbyes down to a minimum.

As the bond grows stronger between you and your child, he will appreciate as much attention as you can give him.

Milestones

Your child may be able to:

- Stand up while holding on to something firmly.
- Get himself into a sitting position from his stomach.
- Pick up a small object with his hand such as a raisin.
- Turn round in the direction of a familiar voice.
- Move himself toward an out-of-reach toy.

DISCOVERING GENITALS

It is normal for your baby to start to show an interest in his genitals at around this age. This interest is an inevitable and healthy part of your baby's development in the same way that his fascination with his fingers and toes was earlier. There is no harm, either physical or psychological, in your baby handling his genitals and you should never make your child feel bad or think about punishing him because he is doing so.

A boy is capable of having an erection from before birth; this is simply the normal response to the touch of a sensitive organ. A baby girl has clitoral erections from a very young age too, although these are much less obvious.

INTRODUCING BOOKS

From eight months onward, your baby's behavior will become more flexible and he will begin to use his own initiative in a relationship. He will give you toys as well as taking them and may even start playing simple games with you. For the first time he will want to share his interest in an object with another person. This is a good time to introduce him to books which you can sit and read together. At first he will only be interested in the rhythm and sound of the words and the color and pattern of the pictures in the book. By speaking slowly in a singsong manner, putting exaggerated emphasis in the right places, and encouraging your child to join in with simple sounds such as "moo" when he sees the picture of a cow, you will make reading a shared, enjoyable experience.

DEVELOPMENTAL CHECK

At between six and nine months your baby will be given another development check by your doctor.

Your baby will happily respond to your games and will often try playful actions like grabbing your hair.

Left: As the grasping action is much more developed, your child will enjoy handling and playing with stacking toys. He may need guidance from you as to the order the shapes go in, and which color should go next

Opposite: A car or any toy with wheels is likely to be a particular source of interest for your baby. He may just want to sit and play with it, and only go after it if you join in and spend time pushing it back and forth to him.

She will be looking to see how your baby is developing and also checking that nothing has been missed in any previous health checks. Your baby's pelvis and legs will be examined to make sure there is no congenital dislocation of the hips. If your baby is a boy his testicles will be checked to make sure they are well down in the scrotum. A distraction test for hearing may be carried out. This involves making a noise for two seconds with something like a bell or rattle out of your baby's sight to see whether he turns toward the sound. His eyes will be checked to see that there is no sign of a potential problem. You will probably be asked if your baby has ever had any breathing problems such as wheezing, and his heart and lungs may be checked with a stethoscope. He may also be weighed and his height measured. Finally, the circumference of his head may be checked.

If you are worried about any part of your child's development you should talk about your concerns now with your doctor. She will be able to help with any questions you may have and can also offer advice if you are experiencing problems with feeding your child or with his sleeping.

NINE MONTHS

A nine-month-old baby is capable of showing a wide range of emotions from happiness to fear, anger, and sadness and she will use these as a means of expressing feelings at any given moment. Your child needs you to be in tune with her feelings and to understand what she is trying to express, otherwise she will become frustrated and unhappy. She may begin to show signs of early independence, but she will still want the reassurance of knowing that you are nearby and ready to help out if required.

Your baby is now constantly on the move and will use her hands to help push her forward as she crawls along.

MOVEMENT

Your baby can now sit alone for 10–15 minutes at a time and will be able to lean forward to pick up a toy without falling over. She can also turn her body and will stretch out for something at her side. She will spend time manipulating a toy with her hands and is able to pass the toy from one hand to the other, turning it as she does so. She uses a pincer grasp, using her finger and thumb, to pick up small items. She will poke at things with a forefinger and may even start to point. You will notice that she still cannot put down a toy she is holding. She will still drop it or press it against a hard surface to release it. If she drops a toy she will look where it has fallen, even if it has completely disappeared from view.

Your child is now very active and she will begin to move herself

As she moves along she will be distracted if you call out her name, and might even topple over as her balance is still unsteady.

As she pushes forward with her arms, her legs will move back and forth to propel her along.

Milestones

Your child may be able to:

- Look for an object that she dropped out of view.
- Pull herself into a standing position.
- Pick up small objects using her finger and thumb.
- Enjoy games such as pat-a-cake.
- Wave goodbye.
- Cruise around the furniture.

across the floor either by crawling, or by shuffling or rolling if she can't yet crawl. She will try pulling herself to standing while holding onto something and may manage to hold herself upright for a few moments before sitting down with a bump. She won't be able to lower herself in a controlled way into a sitting position. If you hold her in a standing position she will probably make purposeful stepping movements with alternate feet as though she is practicing walking.

ACTIVITY

You will notice that your child is becoming a lot more vocal now. She will shout for your attention, stop, listen for your response, and, if she doesn't get it, she will shout again. She will hold long conversations with you, babbling in a loud, tuneful way using strings of syllables such as "dad-da," "ma-ma," "aga-aga," over and over again. She not only uses this babble as a means of interpersonal communication to show friendliness or annoyance, but also as

After crawling for a while, your baby may try to push herself up, but will not be able to balance properly yet.

a way of amusing herself. She likes to practice imitating adult sounds, not just talking but also smacking her lips, coughing and making "brrr"-type noises.

By now your baby will be able to bite and chew her food well and she will be able to feed herself with some finger foods. She will probably try to grasp hold of the spoon as she is being fed. Let her have her own play spoon so that she can continue to practice feeding herself between the mouthfuls of food you are giving to her.

Your baby will probably enjoy games such as "peek-a-boo" and looking for something that you've half hidden while she watched. She will be delighted when she discovers the item and will show it to you with great glee. You may even be able to get her to look for something that you've completely hidden, but she won't necessarily be able to find it and this may cause her some distress and even annoyance.

If your baby seems at all worried by these first simple games you will need to encourage her to take part in them by responding to all her efforts with obvious surprise or

All toys will be held firmly now by your baby, who will use a pincer grasp with her finger and thumb.

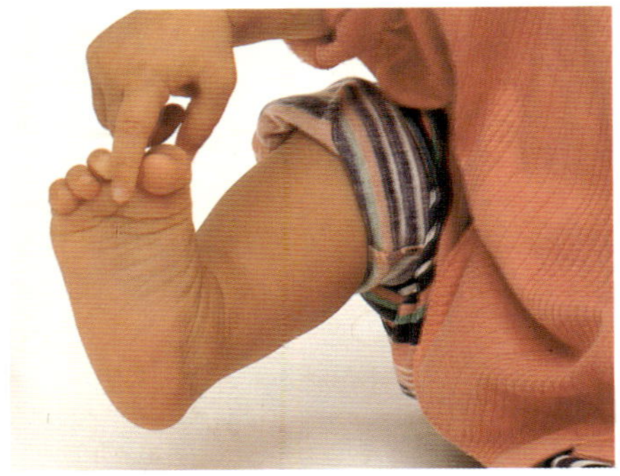

Your baby's fascination with her toes will continue and she will often be found playing with them.

Right: As bonding with her father continues, your baby will enjoy being lifted up in the air and other games with him.

delight. She will be happy when you show her how much you enjoy her cleverness because she will enjoy your approval.

As your baby starts to become more confident, the games to play will become more adventurous. She will let you know when she is ready to progress to the next stage.

Below: Your baby will not play with an older brother at this stage, but she will be interested in toys he is showing her.

Standing up will be a problem unless there is a support nearby. If he lets go he will sit down with a bump.

TEN MONTHS

You will probably have discovered by now that your child has a sense of humor. At 10 months, your baby will not only enjoy playing games with you but will also rock with laughter at some of his own antics. For example, he will enjoy splashing in the bath and this will become even more fun if he gets you wet too. The more you protest the more he will enjoy splashing you. You may also find some of the things you do make your baby laugh uproariously. Appearing around a door saying "boo" can make him squeal with laughter and he will enjoy this game over and over again. Your baby may also enjoy teasing you in return by offering you a toy and then snatching it back before you can take it.

Traditional nursery rhymes and games can give your child endless fun. Try saying: "Round and round the garden, like a teddy bear, one step, two step, tickly under there!" as you run your fingers around his palm, then up his arm and end with a tickle. Another favorite is Humpty Dumpty. Build up to a climax at the point Humpty is going to fall off the wall and pretend to let your baby fall

Your child is now developing rapidly and will be trying to stand. He won't be able to do it on his own and will need your support.

He might try a few faltering steps, but can't easily manage these and will need to hold on to one of your hands as he moves forward.

Milestones

Your child may be able to:

- Move around the furniture.
- Understand the word "no", but not necessarily obey it.
- Stand alone for a few seconds.
- Use the word "dada" to get his father's attention.
- Hold a feeder cup to drink from it.
- Roll a ball back to you.

Supports, such as a chair, will be used by your child to pull himself up as he learns to stand.

too. The baby has probably reached what is sometimes known as the joint-attention stage. This is when a child is able to concentrate on more than one thing at a time. You can encourage this by pointing out things while also giving your baby some information. For example, you can show your child a cat, then tell him that when a cat speaks it says "meow." Later, when he sees a cat again, you can ask him what the cat says. This is a great way of sharing knowledge and making learning fun.

ESTABLISHING ROLES

Along with this sense of humor, new mobility, and the desire to share with you, comes a real talent for getting into trouble. Your baby's curiosity will lead him into all sorts of dangers and you will need to be constantly on your guard so that he isn't allowed to hurt himself at any time. Your baby, on the other hand, may see thwarting your efforts at keeping him out of mischief as a great way of getting a response from you. For the first time since your child was born you may begin to think about using some form of discipline to deter him from getting in trouble.

Discipline doesn't mean rules and punishment, it means teaching the concept of right and wrong. It will be a long time before your child fully grasps the idea of what is involved, but by teaching him now, through your example and guidance, you will be helping him toward eventual self-control and showing him that he needs to have respect for other people.

It is important to remember that a baby cannot be bad because babies and toddlers do not know right from wrong. They learn about their world through experimentation, and by observing and testing adults. Introducing the concept of things being right or wrong at this early age is the first step to helping your child develop from a naturally self-centered baby to a much more sensitive and caring child. The most effective discipline is neither uncompromisingly rigid nor too permissive. Either of these extremes can leave a child feeling unloved.

You need to set limits and standards that are fair and enforce them firmly, but lovingly. Never threaten to withdraw love from your child as this will badly effect his self-esteem and it is important that he knows he is loved even when you don't approve of his behavior.

Don't spank your child. Spanking has been shown not to be an effective way to discipline a misbehaving child. It has many negative aspects including teaching the child violence and that using force is the best way of ending a dispute or getting what you want.

Opposite: A container with various slots for different shapes will keep a child amused as he tries to figure out which one should go in the right hole.

A young baby will use a low stool for support as he moves around.

If a stool is at the right level, your baby may use it as a means of pulling himself up, and as a table to leave some of his toys there in easy reach.

ELEVEN MONTHS

Many babies speak their first word at around 11 months, although some speak as early as nine months and others don't say a word until well after a year. This is a remarkable achievement when you consider that not very long ago your child didn't even know how to smile. These first words take the longest to learn and you will need to be patient while you wait for your child to produce another new one. Sometimes these first words are learned as infrequently as one a month from now on, until your child has a vocabulary of around 10 words. After this the rate usually increases quickly, but this stage isn't reached until around 15 months of age.

DEVELOPING SPEECH

You can help your child to build up her vocabulary by saying the names of things in which she expresses an interest. By now she can probably point at items that she wants because she will have already discovered that pointing is an effective means of communicating with you. When you pick up the item and hand it to the child you probably tell her what

Milestones

Your child may be able to:

- Say the word "mama" to attract your attention.
- Stand on her own.
- Take her first steps.
- Respond to a simple command that isn't accompanied by gestures.
- Say her first word other than "mama" and "dada".

At 11 months your child will be much more responsive and will start reacting to simple questions and commands.

it is. For example, your child points at an apple, you pick up the apple and hand it to her saying something like: "You want this apple?" By doing this you are teaching your child new words; although she may not remember them right away, in time each word will become part of her vocabulary.

Don't worry if you are the only person who can understand your baby's first words. It is not unusual for others outside the family to be baffled by the way a baby speaks. It may well be two or three years before your child can be easily understood outside the immediate family. It is important not to keep correcting your child's pronunciation. This will undermine her confidence and she may become worried about trying to use new words. However, don't revert to using her wrongly pronounced words simply because they sound really cute. If you imitate her errors, the child will continue using the incorrect words for much longer than she would otherwise have done.

MOBILITY

Your baby may have started to pull herself up onto her feet; she may even be walking by holding onto the furniture. Don't be tempted to rush out and buy shoes at the first sign of walking because the child doesn't need shoes yet, in fact they would not be good for her feet at this stage. A child needs to wear shoes when she is walking confidently and her feet will need protection when she goes outside.

Learning to walk is a matter of trial and error. You can't really do anything to help your child apart from making sure that the area she is learning to walk in is as safe as possible. But even when you have removed all the obvious hazards in your child's path you need to stay close at hand to make sure that she doesn't hurt herself.

A child is bound to experience falls while mastering the art of walking and your reaction to these mishaps can color your child's

r developing baby will now start to share things and will happily hand you such as a ball.

Even though she now has some teeth, your baby will still like the sensation of putting different objects in her mouth.

Right: Your baby will be particularly responsive playing games now. If you keep hiding a toy and then making it re-appear it will keep her happily amused for quite a while.
Below left and right: Your child will enjoy standing upright with some help from you. Provided she can hold on to something with one hand, she will eagerly pick up toys from the floor to show you, wave around or suck.

response to them as well. If you rush over in a panic every time she stumbles and demand to know if she is all right she may well shed more tears than she would if she'd really hurt herself. This over-reaction on your part may also make her lose her sense of adventure and make her afraid of attempting other normal physical development hurdles. By remaining calm and reacting with an "up you get, you're all right" sort of attitude, your child is likely to deal with minor tumbles in a matter-of-fact way.

Left: By pushing a baby walker, your baby can walk happily around the room. Keep an eye on her so that you can help if she gets stuck in a corner. It takes time for a child to learn how to walk backward. Below: A child will place her favorite toys on a low-level table and play with them there. When she is bored she may just leave them and go off to do something else more interesting.

TWELVE MONTHS

You are the parent of a year-old child. One by one all the skills that will make your baby a self-dependent and integrated member of society are being perfected. You are both teacher and observer. And now the changes come very quickly indeed.

Growing skills

If your baby isn't actually walking he should be well on his way to doing so by the end of the first year. He will probably be able to pull himself to his feet and navigate by holding onto the furniture. He will certainly be crawling, bottom shuffling, or rolling, and he will be able to get around at quite some speed. He will be able to sit for long periods and can now get into the sitting position from lying flat.

Your baby's grasp is now more refined and he will be able to pick up small objects using the thumb and the tip of the index finger. He will drop and throw toys deliberately and enjoy watching them as they fall. If a toy rolls out of sight he may look for it. He uses both hands to hold toys, but he may start to show a preference for using one hand rather than the other. When your child wants to show you something he will point using his index finger. He's curious and will want to explore everything, so make sure that your home is a safe place. This doesn't mean restricting your baby to such an extent that he becomes frustrated. Try to compromise by leaving some safe cabinets for him to get into and locking the others.

When the baby is outside he will watch people, animals, or cars with prolonged, intent regard. He will be able to recognize familiar people or animals from around 20 ft and will probably greet them vocally with great enthusiasm. The child responds to his own name and can understand other words such as the names of

Milestones

Your child may be able to:

- Indicate what he wants in other ways instead of crying.
- Stand on his own.
- Walk a little way unaided.
- Wave goodbye to you, close relatives and friends.
- Say "mama" and "dada" with discrimination.
- Roll a ball back to you.

Immunization

At 12 months your baby will receive his or her second to last battery of injections. Measles, mumps and rubella vaccine (MMR) is given now, along with Hib and a tuberculosis vaccine (thankfully just a skin prick).

At 12 months your child will be able to let you know what he wants by pointing or reaching toward an object.

All children vary when they first start walking, but your child may well be taking his first few steps now, so you should give him every encouragement.

family members. He may be able to understand simple instructions such as "give it to Mommy," and he may even do as you ask.

You may find that your baby holds out his arm or leg when you ask him to while you are bathing or dressing him. You will see through his actions that he can understand much of what you say even though he can't yet express himself verbally. He babbles to himself and to you, making a lot of speech-type sounds and if he hasn't already said his first word then he soon will.

EATING HABITS

Your baby will be joining in family meals and will probably be eating a mashed-up version of whatever everyone else eats. He is still too young to eat spicy or seasoned food, so remove his portion before adding salt and pepper and other seasoning. He enjoys finger foods but will want to imitate others at mealtimes by using a spoon. It will be difficult for him to get food onto the spoon and then the spoon into his mouth, so he may well revert to using his fingers after a few attempts.

Your child will be able to drink from a feeder cup by himself and will probably be able to drink from an ordinary cup with your help, but he's still too young to manage this on his own. If you are weaning, or are about to wean your baby off his bottle or the breast, you may want to start giving him cows' milk as his main drink. This should only be introduced into your baby's diet after the age of one year and you should always give him whole, pasteurized milk. Skim milk has too much protein and sodium content for babies and should probably not be introduced into your child's diet before the age of two or even older. Part-skim milk can be given from two years; ask your pediatrician for guidance on the matter.

Your baby may be reluctant to give up the bottle because it may be a source of emotional comfort, but it is recommended that a child stops drinking from a bottle at around a year because of the adverse effect it can have on his teeth. If you don't feel that he is ready to give up his bottle completely, try to limit the number of times he has a bottle each day. Encourage him to drink from a trainer cup at meal times and offer him a bottle between meals and at bedtime. When you give a bottle during the day, fill it with water rather than juice or milk, because this will help reduce your child's interest in it. Insist that he drinks from it while sitting in an adult's lap and when he wants to get down take the bottle from him. Don't allow him to take his bottle to bed or to walk around with it. By restricting the use of a bottle like this you will limit the amount of potential harm it can do to his teeth.

Your baby may have as many as four or five teeth and you should

Toys such as a cuddly, soft panda will soon become a strong favorite with your child as he will enjoy its furry texture.

When your child has a favorite cuddly animal he will love to carry it around, hug and squeeze it, and may want to take it with him wherever he goes.

have been cleaning them from the time they appeared. These first teeth can be cleaned with a soft baby toothbrush and a pea-sized amount of children's toothpaste. If your baby is cutting teeth and is cranky, offer him a cold teething ring or a cloth-wrapped ice cube.

YOUR CHILD AND OTHERS

Even though he is confident and outgoing with you, your baby may still be wary of strangers. He may also suffer from shyness. This is an inherited trait which he will have got from either you or your partner, even though neither of you may appear to display the trait yourselves. Shyness can be modified, but it is rarely possible to eradicate it altogether. If you build up your child's confidence with praise and encouragement this will help him to feel more comfortable with others and this may eventually help diminish any shyness.

It is possible that what you consider to be shyness is actually just a normal lack of sociability. At this age your child is not ready to make friends, and he probably won't be until he is at least three years old. Until then the social limit will probably be parallel play, which is when he plays side by side with another child. Don't try to force your child to play with others – pushing him may make him withdraw from social situations completely.

Don't expect a child to share his toys at this age. Right now the only things that matter are his own needs and desires. Other children are seen as objects not people. If he displays aggressive behavior toward other children, like biting or hitting, you need to respond immediately by removing him from the scene of the incident. Explain calmly why he shouldn't have behaved like that, then give him something to play with or point out a new object to distract him and change the subject. Of course he won't really understand what you are saying but, if you use this approach every time it happens, he will eventually understand that hitting and biting other people are just not acceptable behavior.

Opposite: Although your child will be perfectly happy when being held by you, he may be shy and withdrawn with other people he doesn't know.
Below: Your baby will interact quite happily with his father and will keep experimenting with touch.

UNDERSTANDING YOUR CHILD'S DEVELOPMENT

SIGHT AND VISION

Although your baby practiced the blinking reflex by opening and closing her eyes while she was in the womb, the first time she actually uses her eyes for seeing is at the moment of birth. As soon as she is born she is capable of distinguishing objects and most colors; but she is only able to focus on items that are 8–12 in away. These things will look slightly fuzzy and be lacking in definition and, since the images from the retinas of the eyes haven't merged yet, your baby's world will appear as if seen through two separate tunnels.

A newborn is very sensitive to bright lights and will blink and screw up her eyes if a light is shone in her face. Movement will attract a baby from birth and you may notice that yours actively seeks out moving objects. She will probably show a preference for an object that has a highly contrasting pattern rather than one which is just a solid block of color. As your baby begins to control her eye movements she will start tracking moving objects, and it is then that her eyes will begin to start working together.

A newborn baby's vision will be fairly limited and initially he will only be able to see a fuzzy image of you.

YOUR BABY'S WORLD

At first your face will be of more interest to your child than anything else. It is thought that a baby is born with a simple mental template of the human face and will actively search out and stare at any human face during the first couple of months. When she is first born, whether she is able to recognize you by your individual features is open to debate, but she will certainly know the general shape of your head and hairline and by two months will have started to recognize your features.

Your baby will soon become interested in other things and by six to eight weeks she will be concentrating on details, scanning faces and objects so that she can take in as

much information as possible. At this age she may find it hard to disengage her attention when she is watching something and she may need you to distract her before she can remove her gaze. But by three to four months the pathways in the brain for voluntary action begin to take over and your baby starts to disengage her attention on her own.

By three months a baby can perceive colors fully, with all their different shades, and will be able to focus at different distances and to see things in 3D. From seven to eight months as she begins to interpret what she

Your young baby will become fascinated by different objects and will become difficult to distract from whatever is capturing her attention.

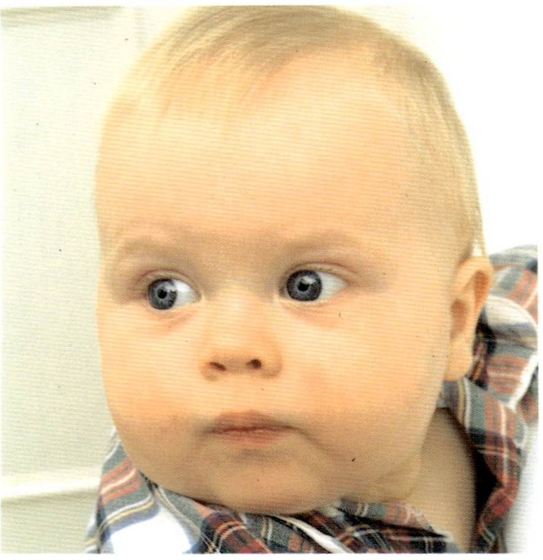

Left: If your baby spots a colorful object ahead of her when she is crawling, she will go and investigate it.

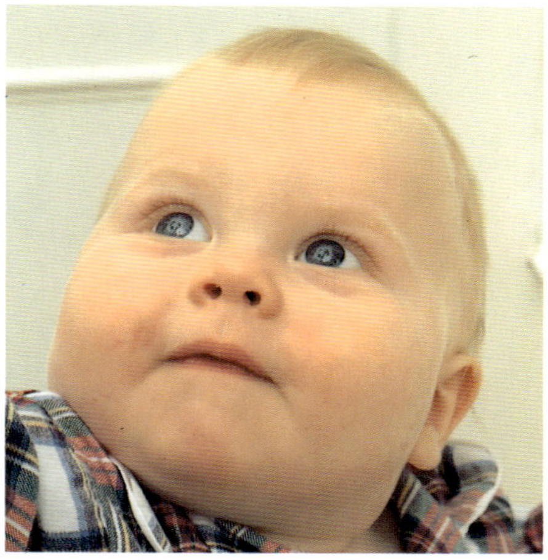

As your baby's eyesight improves, he will intently watch everything that is going on around him (top and above).

Your baby's eyes will follow a moving object which is held within his range of vision.

sees, your baby starts to realize that things don't necessarily cease to exist just because she can't see them anymore. A toy dropped over the edge of the high chair will be looked for; she will also enjoy playing "peek-a-boo" because she knows now that you will definitely reappear.

Learning the size and shape of things and understanding that something that looks small at a distance is in fact the same size close up takes some time for a baby to understand. She will also have to learn that a toy stays the same shape even when it appears different when

How you can help

- Give your baby plenty of stimulating things to look at.
- Hold an item within her range of vision and move it slowly in an arc so that she can follow it with her eyes.
- Play games like "peek-a-boo" and "hide-and-seek" with a toy or by hiding under a large cloth or blanket.
- Check that your child doesn't have crossed eyes. If you are concerned, talk to your doctor.

looked at from the side, top, or bottom. It will take your baby around two years to have good vision and to be able to see as clearly as an adult does.

Crossed eyes

Many babies are born with what may appear to be slightly crossed eyes and this often remains until they have learned to control the muscles around the eyes. It is quite difficult for a baby to hold both eyes in line with each other to focus on an object, and you may notice that when your baby stares at you one of her eyes wanders out of focus. A wandering eye usually rights itself by the time a baby reaches six months old, but you should always point it out to your doctor as it may be necessary for your child's eyes to be checked thoroughly by a specialist.

True crossed eyes occur when the eyes never focus together on an object and, rather than moving together and then one wandering off, they are often out of alignment with each other.

Crossed eyes need to be treated from an early age so you must talk to your doctor as soon as you notice it in your child.

A brightly colored mobile, moving in the breeze and suspended or held from above, will delight your child and keep him amused for a long time.

HEARING

During the last three months in the uterus a baby will have been hearing a variety of different noises. By the time a baby is born, he will already be familiar with his mother's voice, the beating of her heart, and the sound of the amniotic fluid in which he has been floating. His ability to hear at birth is almost as good as an adult's. His hearing threshold, however, is lower so your baby will be startled by loud, unfamiliar noises, although he will probably sleep happily through a constant loud sound such as a blaring television or loud music.

A very young baby will prefer to hear rhythmic noises that may not seem soothing to you: the noise of a washing machine or dryer, the hum of the vacuum cleaner or hair dryer. These will probably reassure him and may even lull him to sleep, perhaps because he remembers hearing such sounds before birth and he finds them both comforting and familiar.

Your own child will quickly associate you and your voice with comfort – it is thought that an infant of only a few days old can actually recognize his mother's voice. Your baby will respond to all the human voices he hears and will turn toward the sound of people talking and appear to listen intently. If he is being spoken to in the exaggerated, high-pitched tone, and rhythmic singsong manner known as "motherese" that adults often instinctively adopt for babies, you will notice that your baby pays particular attention. He may even lose interest if the speaker reverts to a normal tone.

It is through hearing others speak that your baby will eventually learn to form the words that will make up early vocabulary. He will start to understand what is being said long before he can actually make the noises himself; if he has a hearing defect this knowledge and the eventual ability to speak will be affected. As your baby gets older he will start looking for the source of the different sounds that he hears and will respond with obvious pleasure to familiar voices, words, and tunes.

How you can help

- When the baby is very young, try not to let him become startled by sudden noises which make him cry.
- Talk to your child, using "motherese," the high-pitched, singsong voice that babies find appealing.
- Introduce him to many different sounds from an early age.
- Let him sleep where he is happiest rather than insisting that he should be in a quiet room on his own.

HEARING TESTS

At your baby's first development check, at between six and eight weeks, your doctor will want to know whether you have any concerns about your baby's hearing and

From an early age your baby will respond to your voice and be interested in toys you are showing him.

He will turn toward any new or interesting noise that you make with a toy even if it is coming from behind him.

how he responds to your voice at home. You should mention if there is a close family history of hearing problems. If there is any concern at all, your baby can be referred to a specialist.

At around four months, your baby will have his next development check and this will include a screening test of your baby's hearing carried out by your doctor. By now the response to sounds should be obvious, turning his head when you speak to him and responding to different noises of varying pitch and intensity. Both ears will be tested to identify anything previously missed.

If your child is deaf or partially deaf, his speech may not progress past the babbling stage and you may notice that he becomes quieter as he gets older. Any concerns about your child's hearing should be discussed with your doctor as soon as they occur.

Your baby will study your expression and listen intently to your voice before trying to imitate you.

SMELL, TASTE, TOUCH

SMELL

Newborn babies are very sensitive to smell and can remember certain smells almost from the moment they are born. They recognize their parents' natural smell and a breast-fed baby can distinguish the smell of her mother's milk from that of any other woman's just a few hours after birth. In fact, your baby will start sucking in her sleep if she smells your milk.

A bottle-fed baby will quickly learn to identify her own mother's smell and the smell of any other family members who also feed her. The smell of people who are familiar to her will help your baby distinguish between family members and people strange to her.

As your baby grows, certain smells will become associated with specific things, just as they do for adults. For example, food smells will suggest mealtimes and perhaps happy social occasions, while the smell of bath preparation and baby powder will become associated with bathtime and bed. Smells that your baby finds unpleasant will make her turn her head away even when she is only a few days old.

Your baby will use her sense of smell with her other senses to learn about the world around her.

From a young age, a baby has a highly developed sense of smell and she will delight in a sweet-smelling flower.

Taste is very important to a baby and she will experiment with the sensation of sucking her toys.

From the moment he is born, your baby will be able to react to bitter tastes and show a preference for sweet foods.

How you can help

- Spend time cuddling and talking to your baby so that she really gets to know you.
- Offer your child a wide variety of tastes once she is old enough to take solids, but avoid foods that are seasoned or spicy.
- Don't encourage your child to have a sweet tooth.
- Remember that a young baby cannot control her temperature as well as an older child, so you need to keep a constant check on her to make sure she isn't too cold or if she is becoming overheated.
- Your baby's skin is very sensitive so check that her clothes aren't tight or rubbing her skin.

TASTE

Smell and taste are intrinsically linked so it is no surprise that a baby is born with the ability to differentiate between tastes. From birth your baby's taste buds can detect sweet, sour, bitter, and salty. When offered any of these tastes she will give a definite and consistent reaction to each one. Her taste buds will become more refined with age, but even as a newborn baby she will show appreciation for sweet flavors and grimace when experiencing salty or bitter tastes.

All babies seem to be born with a preference for a sweeter taste, probably because breast milk is slightly sweet and it is important that she likes its flavor. This natural preference for sweet things won't harm your baby's teeth provided that you don't indulge her by giving her sweetened juice to drink, or adding sugar to her food when you start to wean her. When you start to introduce solids into your baby's diet it is better to encourage her to eat bland foods at first and then savory foods and to keep sweet things to a minimum. Your baby will quickly develop her own tastes and you can help by giving her a varied diet once she is old enough to take solids.

By the time your child is around a year old she will use her experience of the different foods she has tried to help her distinguish between the more subtle flavors. For example, one brand of apple sauce will taste slightly different to another and at a year old your child will be able to taste the difference.

TOUCH

Your baby uses touch immediately after birth. This provides her with a means of finding out about her new environment through the textures that her skin comes into contact with, like her clothes, your clothes, and skin. Your baby can also feel through her skin whether her environment is warm or cold, wet or dry. She feels pain and discomfort and, because a young baby has more sensitive skin than an adult, you need to treat her gently.

As she matures, your baby will use touch in different ways to help her learn. Touch-sensitive nerve endings are concentrated at the end of the fingertips and around the lips, and a young baby will use her hands and mouth for exploring new objects. Gradually, after a few weeks touch will also become associated with feelings and your baby will start to connect the feeling of your nipple in her mouth or your arms around her and associate them with warmth and security. One of the most important sensory experiences for your baby is through her tongue and mouth so that sucking is not only a means of obtaining nourishment, but is also

Your young baby will reach out and touch different objects, such as this furry panda, to get used to the different sensations.

a great source of comfort for her.

When you undress your baby you may notice that she becomes increasingly tense as you remove each layer of clothes and she may actually cry when you remove the garment nearest to her skin, usually her undershirt. This is not because you are being clumsy, but because she physically misses the feel of her clothes against her skin. She should stop crying as soon as you dress her again.

Between two and three months your child begins to use touch as a means of exploring and she will use her hands to hit out at things that are near her. By around five months she will have mastered hand and eye co-ordination and will learn by feeling and putting things in her mouth.

BONDING

Touch plays an important part in the main bonding process. This is the formation of a close emotional relationship between you and your baby which will provide her with the love, comfort, and security that she wants. Although your baby is born with a deep-rooted psychological need to have a close interaction with you this doesn't always happen immediately. A child's bonding with her mother is often a gradual process which may not be fully completed until the baby is a few months old.

At a few months old a young baby will react to bright toys such as this octopus which has different materials on the undersides of its legs. He will enjoy the feel of the soft textures.

TALKING

Your child is born with the potential to learn to speak and a receptiveness to the influences that will help him communicate. A baby starts to learn about language while he is still in the womb, which is when he first begins to identify the voice of his mother. As a newborn he will prefer his mother's voice to any other because it will already be familiar and he will quickly associate it with warmth, comfort, and feeding. A newborn baby's brain is tuned to pick out the texture, pattern, and rhythm of language and he will pay more attention to voices talking than any other sounds he hears. From the moment he is born your baby understands speech sounds in a way that allows him to segment the speech he hears into sound units.

Even a very young baby will be receptive to the sound of his mother's voice because he will have heard it in the womb.

Before he can speak fluently a baby has to go through distinct stages of development. In the beginning your baby's vocal skills will consist of cries and burps. The inability to speak in the early months does not actually hinder a baby's ability to become a talker. He uses this time to learn how to control his mouth and his tongue. You may notice that from a very early age your baby will move his mouth a lot, pushing his lips forward and backward in a kind of rhythm.

Conversations

One of the skills your baby has to acquire before speech is the ability to interact with people. Your baby begins to learn about this process very early on and by three months he will already be using communicative gestures. Try raising your eyebrows to him and then watch as he imitates you. This is the first stage of learning about holding a conversation. These gestures will be accompanied by different noises as your baby begins to develop control over dozens of separate muscles that are involved in making speech sounds. When your baby coos and gurgles at you he is learning to coordinate tongue movements while taking air in. When you respond to these early noises you will instinctively use a high-pitched, rhythmic singsong tone, repeating words in such a way that you capture your baby's attention.

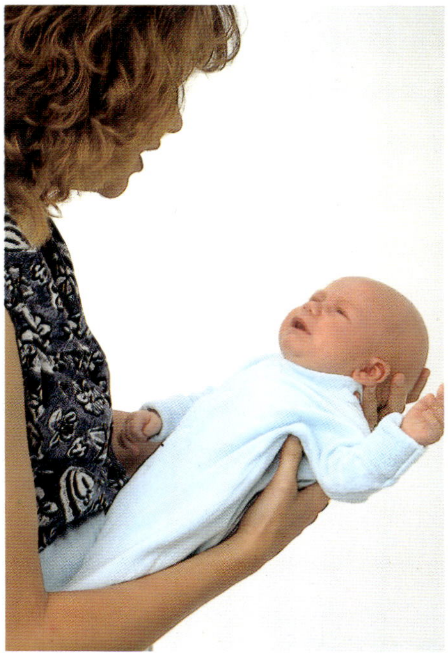

Talk to your baby when you hold him as he will find the sound of your voice soothing and comforting.

By around five or six months, your child will be concentrating on one-syllable words such as "ba" or "ma" which he will repeat over and over again, often when he is on his own. This use of early sounds is known as babbling, and is not yet being used as a form of communication. This is your baby's way of learning how to make new sounds. Soon after he has learned to babble you will notice that your baby starts to use his eyes to communicate with you and to direct your attention toward something that he wants. This communication is soon followed by what is called declarative pointing: pointing as a form of interacting, rather than just as a basic means of asking you to pass him

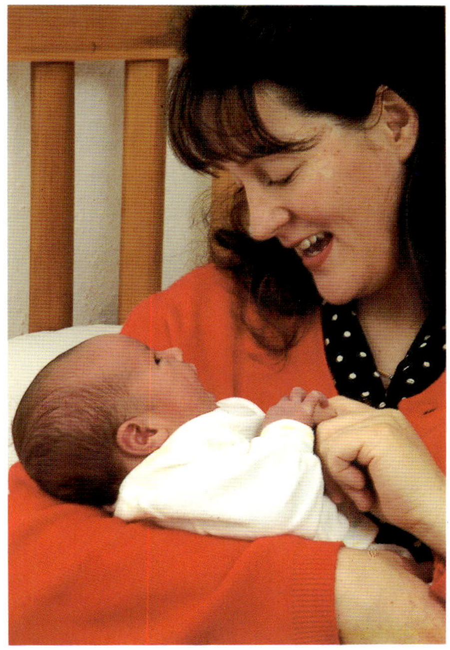

If you speak to your new baby in a high-pitched, singsong voice you will immediately get his attention.

Even at the young age of eight weeks your baby will respond to your voice and attempt to smile at you.

something he can't reach for himself.

After a month or two your baby's babbling will start to flow like speech, rising and falling as if he were holding a conversation. Although he is still not able to form words, he will understand simple words that are made clear, for example, "bottle" when you point to his feeding bottle. Understanding more than he is able to say will continue throughout baby- and toddlerhood until he can speak fluently.

FIRST WORDS

By the end of his first year your baby will probably produce his first word. It may not seem recognizable as a word to you, but it will be a sound that he uses for one specific object, for example, "ine" for when he wants an orange. It is certainly no accident that "Mama" and "Dada" are often among the first recognizable words that a new baby says, because first words are simple and are associated with things that are special to a child.

Once speech has begun with your baby, he will continue to produce a handful of new words each month with the majority of this early communication being simple nouns or proper names.

How you can help

- Always respond to your baby's attempts at communicating with you.
- Don't be embarrassed to use high-pitched speech; it is the language your child likes best.
- Talk to your baby as you go about your daily routine and remember to speak clearly using simple words.
- Be consistent, using the same words for the same thing every time.
- Look at simple picture books with your baby. By telling him what is in each picture you will be increasing his understanding of words.

A mother can help her child learn to talk properly by repeating words and by pointing out objects and saying the word.

As your baby investigates colorful items, such as a yellow flower, you can talk to him about it, telling him which are the petals, leaves and stem.

SOCIAL BEHAVIOR

A newborn baby doesn't appear very sociable to the outside world because she doesn't smile or respond verbally until some weeks after birth. But her parents' reactions to the baby's ordinary behavior lead to the development of social mannerisms. For example, gas may cause your baby to appear to smile at an early age and you respond by smiling back. Your baby will eventually realize that this movement of her mouth makes you react in this way and so will use it deliberately in the future. It is this early, simple form of communication that is the basis for your child's social development.

All babies' early social learning comes from imitating the people with whom they have the most contact, generally their mother and father. A newborn of only a few hours can imitate some adult gestures such as poking her tongue out or yawning. This ability to imitate is one of the most important tools your baby has to help her learn about life.

Through imitation your baby will eventually start communicating. You will speak to her and she will respond with "coos" and will wriggle her body in delight. This first stage of conversation will eventually develop into the ability to talk and listen. These early conversations often start during feeding, because the rhythm of feeding initiates your baby into the basics of dialogue. A baby sucks in her mother's milk in bursts with pauses in between. It is during these pauses that her mother usually fills in the gap by talking happily to her.

Imitation becomes choice

Social interaction between you and your baby becomes increasingly intentional on her part during the first two months of life, with much of your baby's behavior geared toward making you react. These early conversations and the ability to imitate are just two ways of getting you to respond; the other very effective way is crying. Initially, your baby's cries are a reflex to pain, hunger, or discomfort. But crying assures a baby of adult response, especially her mother's. Her cries will increase her mother's heart rate and, if breastfeeding, her mother will automatically start producing milk. Within a few weeks a baby will have learned to expect certain reactions to her crying, such as being fed or picked up.

At around six weeks your baby will learn to smile properly, another social skill which she will be able to use to her advantage. Although her

When young babies are placed together, they don't play with each other as they haven't yet learned how to interact. Instead they will just play on their own.

If you put two or three babies together in a playpen they will not play together as they haven't learned how to socialize.

first smiles are simply facial grimaces, your response will be such that she soon discovers that by using her facial muscles in this way she is guaranteed to get you to smile back. A baby will quickly learn to repeat an action if she gets a positive reaction. However, if she regards the response she receives as negative she is less likely to repeat the action.

By three months your baby will be able to show her enjoyment of people and surroundings. She will respond to friendly adults and will generally not mind who is with her as long as they are paying attention to her. Your baby will enjoy activities such as having a bath and often show pleasure when she realizes that bathtime has arrived. Feeding will be a great source of emotional pleasure and your baby will study your face unblinkingly while she feeds.

At around four months your baby will cry more deliberately. She will probably pause after crying to see if anyone is coming in response, before crying again. She has learned that crying brings attention and this new ability to manipulate is the beginning of some exciting discoveries.

CHANGING BEHAVIOR PATTERNS

Somewhere after six months your child may change from a social, happy baby, who will go to anyone and reward complete strangers with smiles, to one who overnight has become wary of people she doesn't know. Your baby has reached the stage when she needs time and space to handle each new sight and sound; and a stranger may present her with too many new, unfamiliar things to be taken in at one time. This new wariness leads to what is known as stranger anxiety. It often manifests itself as loud protestations when your baby is about to be separated from you. She is at the stage of development when she is becoming increasingly sensitive to change and appears to be suddenly more dependent. She may try to avoid upsetting or stressful events by crying, clinging to you, or turning away from what is upsetting her. Toward the end of her first year she may start to use objects such as a favorite blanket, bottle, or thumb for comfort.

As your baby will feel safe with you, try to show her different toys and items to interest her and attract her attention.

A baby will sit with her brother because he is familiar. She will be interested in his toys but won't play with him.

Over the next six months your baby will probably show an increasing reticence with strangers but will be very responsive to people with whom she is familiar. She may become very clingy so that any separation from you is accompanied by real distress. This attachment may cause you problems, but it is in fact an important stage of development. Your baby now recognizes individuals as people and is beginning to develop selective, permanent relationships. She will use these relationships as a safe base from which to explore the world. Now that she is getting older, your baby will use her developing vocal skills to create noise – this guarantees the attention that gives her the reassurance she needs. She may use mimicry to make you laugh and the more you show your appreciation the more she will repeat the antic that is amusing you. This is her first real control over her social environment.

By the time she is a year old, your child will probably have grasped the idea that she exists as an entity. She may even begin to use a word or sound to describe herself as a means of expressing this. Her social skills, however, are still very limited and she will show little interest in anyone outside her immediate circle of well-known people. Other children hold very little appeal for your child at this age and are more likely to be treated as inanimate objects rather than playmates.

It will be another year or two before your child has enough social understanding to develop friendships with other toddlers.

Your baby will sit quite happily on your knee, but may be wary of moving to his grandmother who is less familiar to him.

A baby will soon learn to recognize his older sister and will happily let her help him to stand up.

How you can help

- Encourage your baby to imitate you by exaggerating your responses to her actions.
- Smile at your baby to let her know how pleased you are when she smiles at you.
- If she becomes wary of strangers don't force her to be sociable.
- When you have to leave your baby, say goodbye quickly; don't prolong the parting.

MOBILITY

All babies go through the same stages of mobility, but how fast they move from one to another varies considerably. Your baby may walk independently before he is a year old, or he may be content to shuffle along on his bottom or hands and knees until well after this. Your baby's mobility takes place in a set order, starting at his head and working down to his toes. He won't be able to sit upright or crawl until he can hold up his head, and he won't be able to walk until he can move his body along, either by crawling or doing a bottom shuffle.

Finally, your baby will learn to control his arms and legs before gaining control of his hands and feet. At each stage it will take time for the movements he has learned to progress from being awkward, rather clumsy and uncoordinated to the smooth, controlled movements he will ultimately achieve.

MAKING PROGRESS

A newborn baby has no control over his head, which will flop around if left unsupported. By about eight weeks, control of the head and neck begins and you may notice your baby practicing lifting his head and holding it for a few seconds before letting it flop down again. At around three months most babies are able to hold their heads up steadily so that they can look around and examine the world about them.

The next stage in mobility comes when your baby starts to roll around, first from side to back and then, a few weeks later, from back to side. The way a baby rolls is highly individual and your baby will roll when he's ready and in his own way. Rolling is another way of practicing control over his body and your baby will do it over and over again until he's mastered what to him is a new movement. The result of this movement will change your baby's view of the world and once he has discovered this, rolling becomes a new function: a means of getting closer to something that he wants.

Your baby will have been using his legs to push with since he was born, but the first stepping movements he made were a

How you can help

- Hold your baby upright so that he can bounce his legs up and down on your lap to help strengthen his muscles.
- Sitting a little way away from your baby, persuade him to come to you. Do this to encourage both crawling and walking.
- Once he can sit upright, you can help your baby learn to balance by placing toys slightly out of reach so he has to stretch out for them.
- To get your baby to twist around, place a toy behind him and then support him as he turns.
- Push-along toys will encourage your baby to crawl and walk.

All babies' first movements will be uncoordinated, but they soon learn a basic crawl and to sit upright unaided.

When your baby is placed on his stomach at a few months old he will attempt to crawl.

He will lift up his arms and legs in the swimming motion that is the prelude to crawling.

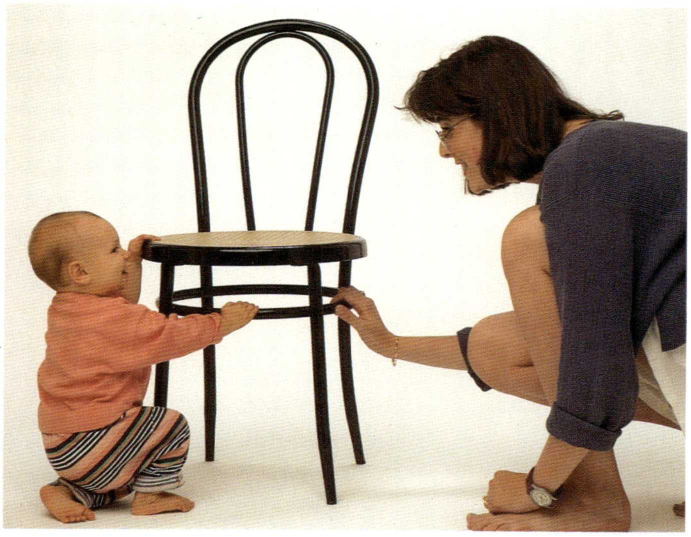

Before she's a year old, your baby will start to stand and balance holding on to a chair if you hold it steady for her.

She will grasp firmly on to the bottom part of the chair and start to pull herself up. Try to encourage her as much as possible.

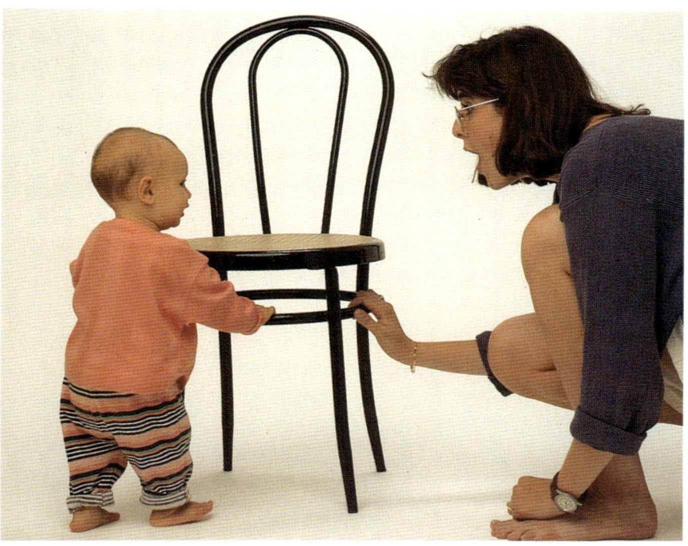

As she straightens into an upright position, she will need support from the chair you are holding.

Now that she is standing confidently, she will start to look around her to see what else is going on in the room.

As your baby starts to crawl, he will move toward interesting toys.

When he is nearer the toys, he will probably reach out for them.

reflex action. At around four months if you put your baby down on his abdomen, he will be able to lift his shoulders, arms, and legs off the floor and move them in a swimming-type motion, and by around five and a half months your baby should be able to sit with some support, his back straight and shoulders braced. By around six months he will probably be able to support himself in a crawling position, although he won't be able to go anywhere just yet. By seven months he will be able to sit upright using his arms for support. Once he has done this he will quickly learn to sit unaided, and he will also enjoy standing and bouncing around vigorously while you hold him.

By eight or nine months he will have learned to control his movements and he will be able to move his arms and legs in order to propel himself either backward or forward. Once he has mastered this he will be off and it will only be a matter of time before he starts trying to stand up on his own. By about nine months he will be able to sit and reach in front, upwards, to the side and behind him without falling over.

As soon as he has learned to crawl at around nine months he will be ready to start pulling himself up into a standing position using you, or the furniture, for support. At this stage he will not have mastered sitting down so when he wants to sit he will simply let go and land on the floor with a resounding bump. He probably won't be able to control his sitting movement until he is 11 to 12 months old.

Before he's a year old your baby will start to navigate all around the furniture, taking little sideways steps. Once he can move around like this with some confidence he will let go with one hand. As soon as he is able to let go with his remaining hand, perhaps to cross a gap in the furniture, he will begin to gain the confidence to walk on his own – unaided.

Your baby's first steps on his own will be very wobbly and ungainly, with his feet placed wide apart to help him balance. But once he becomes more mobile his legs will straighten and he'll become steadier on his feet.

By eight or nine months your baby will be able to crawl around on the floor.

Your baby will try to stand with your help.

Lift him up supporting his arms.

Once up, he will need your hand to balance.

A baby walker can help a child to take her first steps and practise walking.

Other types of baby walker can be sat in and propelled along by your child's feet.

A young baby will enjoy a baby bouncer, but make sure it is firmly attached.

Once crawling your baby will go all over.

Your child's first steps are often wobbly and his movements may seem awkward.

PLAY

Introduce your baby to games by teaching him nursery rhymes that involve parts of his body, such as his toes.

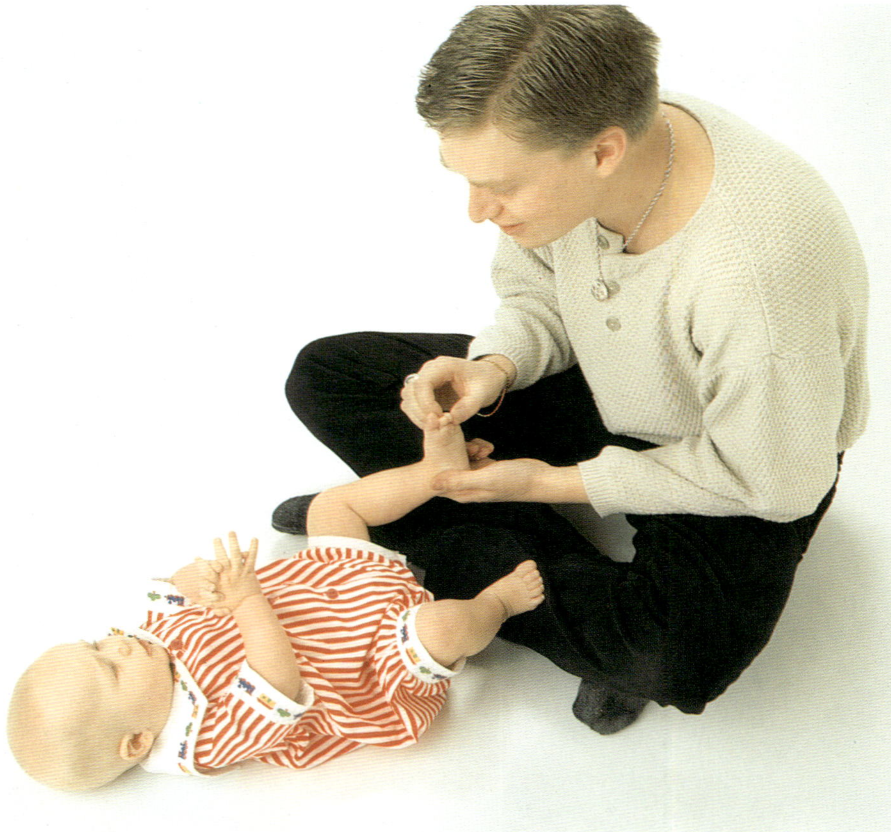

A baby is born with the potential to learn and play. She can see, hear, and feel. She is aware of her environment and will respond from birth to brightly colored, moving objects and to sounds. She learns all the time and play is one of the ways in which she develops new skills, while toys are the play tools that she uses to stimulate herself at each stage of development. Toys don't have to be elaborate; your child will invent her own games and use everyday objects as toys when she is young. Watching you and trying to imitate your voice and facial expressions will provide hours of entertainment in the early months. Ultimately, the toy that a child enjoys and plays with most will give her the greatest learning experience, and in the first weeks of life this "toy" will be you.

Your child will change very rapidly during the first year so that a toy that entertains her at two months will not appeal to her when she is a year old. As she develops, your child will need different stimuli and the choice of toys for each stage of development should reflect these different needs. It is also very important that the toys you give a child are appropriate to this age. A toy designed for a younger child will be boring, while a toy for an older child may be too complicated and may even be dangerous if it contains small pieces on which a young baby could choke.

Your child will be fascinated by nursery rhymes that involve actions that use his hands.

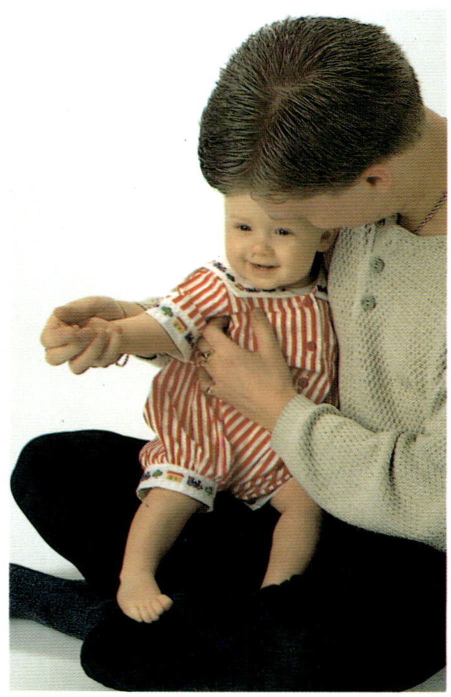

If the finale of the nursery rhyme includes tickling your baby, he will associate it with fun and ask for it again.

Birth to three months

During the first few months, your baby is developing her basic senses – touch, sight, and sound. She needs

As your child develops she will start to enjoy playing games with you such as "peek-a-boo."

As you teach her the game, she will enjoy "hiding" behind the chair and peeking out at you from behind the legs.

Games to play

- Gently bounce your baby up and down on your knee in rhythm to a nursery rhyme.
- Play "so big," asking "how big is – ?" and helping him spread his arms in response.
- Use her toes to play "this little piggy went to market".
- Take your baby as your partner and dance around the room with her in your arms.

You can buy your baby many expensive toys, but she'll still enjoy playing with simple kitchen utensils. Always make sure they have no sharp edges.

toys that will stimulate these senses and give experience of colors, textures, materials, and shapes. A good first toy is a mobile, hung where your baby can study it at leisure. It doesn't have to be expensive – one made from pictures cut from a magazine and suspended from a coat hanger will be just as effective as one you buy. Once your baby begins to wave her hands around and tries to swipe at things, she will enjoy toys that make a noise or that react to her actions, a rattle for example. This will give your child a sense of control as well as encouraging the development of manual skills and hand and eye coordination.

An activity center or "busy box" is ideal for babies around nine months as they will love to push the buttons and manipulate all the different shapes and knobs.

A newborn baby's hands are usually held closed in fists, but she will gradually relax them so that if you place an object in her open palm she will close her hand around it for a few seconds. The strong grasp reflex she was born with will have disappeared so that she will probably drop the object within a few seconds. By the age of two or three months she will try reaching out to touch things. These first grasping movements are important steps towards learning hand-eye coordination.

Once your baby is old enough to sit in a bouncing seat she will be able to see more of the world around her and her hands will be free to explore. A toy fastened across the front of the seat will encourage her to bring her hands forward to try and hit it to make it move. Once she has done this, she will want to do it again and again; gradually she sees that she is responsible for making this happen and her movements become more deliberate.

As she starts to move around, your baby will get pleasure from pushing a baby walker. She will also enjoy trying to put plastic shapes in the right holes on the walker.

A newborn is acutely aware of sounds and will already have become familiar with your voice while in the womb. Talking and singing to your baby from the time she is born will encourage her to listen and help her develop her own speech later. As she gets older, hold her on your lap and try having a conversation with her. Say something, then wait until your baby makes a noise in response. Her response will be slow at first so allow her plenty of time. These conversations will help her learn about taking turns, listening, and copying – all essential parts of communication. Once your baby has got used to life outside the womb, she will find touch and the freedom to move her limbs exciting. Different textures will give her new sensations of touch, so offer her various things to feel that will give her experience of rough, soft, silky, or smooth textures. Bathing and changing times will provide an opportunity for your baby to explore touch and sensation. She will like the feeling of not being hampered by nappies and clothing and should enjoy the sensation of warm water next to her skin. Try tickling her gently, blowing raspberries on her abdomen, and kissing her toes when she is undressed.

THREE TO SIX MONTHS

As your baby grows and her movements become more controlled, she will reach out for things and take them in her hands. Her grip becomes stronger and she will be able to hold a wider variety of items. This means that she will start to experience the difference between things that are light and heavy, soft and hard. Her curiosity will be endless and every object will be a plaything. She may prefer to use her mouth rather than her hands to explore things at this age, so it is important to make sure that she can't get hold of anything which could do her any harm.

Your baby will probably play happily for short periods on her own, but she needs you to encourage her. When you play with your baby get her to do things for herself; allow her to use her hands and eyes to work out what she wants to do with the toy she is holding. It is better to give your child only a few selected items to play with at this age because she won't be able to concentrate on more than one thing at a time. A stimulating, inviting environment is important for all creative play. Toys that are piled up in a jumble are not as inviting to a child as toys which are laid out for her in an attractive, inviting way.

SIX TO TWELVE MONTHS

Once your baby has learned to support herself sitting up and has started to make her first attempts at moving around, she will want toys that she can manipulate. This is the ideal time to give your child an activity centre with lots of different knobs and handles for her to twist and turn. By around seven or eight months she will want to find out what things can do and will bang objects on the ground or table to find out if they make a noise or wave them in the air to see what happens. As her manipulative skills develop she will learn that she can use her hands and arms simultaneously and will start to bang things together. She will be able to reach out to you with both arms when she wants to be picked up. It takes a while longer for her to learn how to let go of items she is playing with, but you can encourage her by giving her an object, then holding out your hand and asking for it back. Once she's

A young baby will enjoy being read to from a simple board book and will be interested in touching the pages. She will soon learn how to recognize the book's pictures.

Your child will often put different things in her mouth to investigate them.

got the hang of this game she will keep you busy for hours!

As she becomes more mobile, your baby will want to be into everything and her natural curiosity could lead her into danger, so you need to pay constant attention to safety. One of your baby's favorite pastimes will be emptying things out of containers. She will take things out of cupboards with just as much enjoyment as she will empty shapes out of a shape sorter. Once she has emptied a container she will want to examine the contents in great detail and will bang things together and may put them in her mouth before discarding them and moving on to the next object. When she has mastered this she will soon learn that she can put things back into the container and will spend hours tipping things out and putting them back again. She will try doing this with different objects and may discover that some of them don't fit. As your child plays she will be learning about the nature of the objects, how they behave, and their relative size and shape.

Water play can be introduced now and your baby will enjoy filling and emptying plastic measuring cups while she is having her bath. Give her toys that have different sizes of holes in them so that she can spend time sprinkling or pouring the water from one container into another.

Once your baby has started to crawl, give her toys that roll and move when they are pushed along so that she can go after them. Later, as she starts taking her weight on her legs, you can encourage her and help her balance with sturdy push-along toys, such as a block-filled truck.

A baby walker will help your child to walk and some double as an activity center.

This will give her something to hold on to until she feels confident enough to let go and walk unaided.

BOOKS

It is never too early to introduce your baby to books. Start at an early age with brightly colored cloth books that your baby can chew as well as handle, or simple board books. At first she will enjoy these books as objects to be explored but, if you sit her on your knee and talk to her about the pictures in the book, she will soon learn to recognize them. Encourage her involvement by making the noises of any animals pictured in the books and then getting her to do the same.

Games to play

- "Pat-a-cake, pat-a-cake, baker's man" is a rhyme to which your baby will enjoy clapping. When you get to "prick it and pat it and mark it with ..." use your baby's own initial and then her name when you come to "put in the oven for ...".
- Blowing bubbles using either a bubble solution and a wand or dish-washing liquid and your hands.
- "Peek-a-boo": use your hands to cover your face; then later hide and seek: hide objects under a soft cloth for your baby to find.
- Hold your baby's hands securely and rock her gently backwards and forward while singing "Row, row, row the boat ...".
- Sit your baby on your knee facing toward you and hold her firmly by the hands as you bounce her in time to "Humpty Dumpty." When you get to the big fall allow your baby to drop through your knees while holding her firmly.

By just giving your baby one toy at a time to play with, she will be able to concentrate on it more fully.

PART FOUR

COOKING FOR BABIES AND TODDLERS

A baby has specific nutritional requirements, very different from those of an adult. Many new parents are apprehensive of their ability to cater for their baby's needs – especially when children have a mind of their own, and can reject the carefully chosen and prepared food. This section sets out to explain the latest guidelines for feeding babies and young children. It explains clearly which are the highly nutritious foods, packed with the protein and vitamins that an active child needs, and warns against foods that do not provide enough calories or that may cause allergic reactions.

We all know commercially prepared food can be bad for us and it is sometimes hard to judge how much salt and sugar has been added. Home-cooked food is delicious, and can be just as quick to make. This section is packed with recipes, each fully illustrated and set out clearly, step by step. Many recipes have been specially created to work for the entire family with only a little adaptation. The same basic ingredients and methods of preparation can be tailored to create three meals: for a baby, a fussy toddler, and for two hungry parents. This section is also packed with tips to help make meals a calm, pleasant time, where you can relax and enjoy your family's company.

INTRODUCTION

Part Four, Cooking for Babies and Toddlers, aims to explain all you need to know about feeding your young family. Set out in three easy-to-use sections, it is packed with over 200 recipes, all beautifully illustrated with color pictures – from first purées to tempting toddler meals then moving on to food for all the family.

In the very early days all a baby needs is milk, but as it grows so too will its nutritional needs. By four months most babies will have doubled their birth weight and will be ready to begin mini-mouthfuls of smooth purée.

Although this marks an exciting time in your baby's development it can also cause immense worry for a new parent. We all want to provide the best for our child and what better start in life than to begin laying the foundations for a healthy diet? But what do you do if your child just refuses to eat? This section has practical tips that may provide some of the answers.

If your child has any food allergies or sensitivities, read each recipe to make sure that it doesn't contain a problem ingredient.

FIRST FOODS

Section one covers everything you need to know about introducing those first spoonfuls of smooth puréed foods: including when to begin weaning, the signs to look out for, what foods to serve and when, basic equipment, plus sound nutritional advice, helpful

guidelines on food preparation and masses of colorful and exciting recipes to tempt your baby.

You will almost certainly find that health professionals, friends, relatives and magazines will offer you differing, perhaps contradictory, advice. Some will be genuinely useful, while some turn out to be outdated or inappropriate: the difficulty is sorting through the well-meaning confusion to find something reliable. This book draws upon current dietary information to provide helpful advice on feeding your baby.

FOOD FOR TODDLERS

In the second section we move on to feeding an energetic toddler. By this stage your baby will probably have tripled its birth weight and will have begun to feed itself and may be developing strong likes and dislikes. Many young children go through a stage of extreme food fads, causing frustration and worry for parents. Again we have included down to earth tips and practical advice on coping with a fussy eater plus lots of easy and approachable recipes to tempt your child.

FAMILY MEALS

In the third section the recipes have been devised to feed the whole family from one basic set of ingredients prepared at the same time. With step by step instructions we illustrate how to mash food for your baby, make a mini-meal for your fussy toddler and how, by adding a few extra ingredients, to simultaneously transform this simple meal into something more exciting for Mom and Dad.

Above and below: *Start with simple vegetable purées. At about four to six months, you will find that babies begin to take an interest in the food by themselves!*

FOOD AND YOUR CHILD

Childrens' nutritional needs are very different from our own. Forget about low fat, high fiber diets. Young children require nutrient-dense foods to meet their rapid levels of growth. Requirements for protein and energy are high in proportion to the child's size. Tiny tummies mean children are unable to eat large quantities of food while at the same time they are usually very active. Their appetites can vary enormously, but the range of foods that they will eat may also be very limited. So it is vital that the foods which are eaten contain a variety of nutrients, in combination with calories, whilst still fitting in with family meals. High fiber foods can be very filling without providing sufficient levels of protein, vitamins and minerals.

For young children fat is the major source of dietary calories: both breastmilk and infant formula contribute about 50% of calories as fat. As your child progresses to a mixed diet, the proportion of calories supplied by fat decreases and is replaced by carbohydrates. But it is important that the calories are provided by fat up to the age of two, as too many carbohydrates may be too bulky for a young child.

Adequate calories are necessary to sustain growth. Fat is a very useful source of calories and the main source of the fat soluble vitamins, A, D, E and K, while also providing essential fatty acids that the body cannot make itself. It is best to obtain fat from foods which contain other essential nutrients: whole milk, cheese, yogurts, lean meat and small quantities of oily fish.

Try to include a portion of carbohydrates in every meal once your child is over nine months: for example bread, potatoes, rice or pasta. Encourage young children to

Below: *Babies are easily encouraged to take pleasure in their food, however simple.*

eat a variety of fruits and vegetables. As with adults, try to keep salt intake to a minimum; fried foods or very sugary foods should be generally discouraged and served only as a special treat.

As children approach school age they should gradually be pushed towards a diet that is lower in fat and higher in fiber, in line with the guidelines for adults.

Snacks are also important as young children require high calorie levels and cannot meet this requirement in three meals a day. Try to encourage healthy snacks such as mini ham sandwiches, cubes of cheese or wedges of apple instead of chocolate chip cookies.

Obviously eating a healthy, well-balanced diet is essential for any age group, but social skills are also important. Our children learn from us and so it is also vital to eat together as a family, if not every day, then as often as possible, so that young children can discover not only how to behave at the table but also that eating is a sociable and enjoyable experience.

We do hope this book will make family meal times fun for the entire family and help to minimize any problems and anxieties you may come up against when feeding your baby and toddler.

Above and below: *Giving their child the best possible start in life is the main concern of any parent, but good food planning is easy to achieve.*

FIRST FOODS

Introducing your baby to the delights of solid food heralds the beginning of a new and exciting stage in your baby's development. Although it will be a few months yet before your baby will be able to share in family meals fully, the foods that you give your baby now are vitally important not only for

their nutritional benefits but also in laying down the first foundations for a healthy diet through childhood and beyond. Start your baby with baby rice which is barely warm and only slightly thicker than milk – then move to bland vegetable purées.

Weaning to Solids

Most babies are ready to begin those first few mini-mouthfuls of puréed foods at around four months and almost all babies will be eating solid food by six months. By this age babies need the extra energy, protein, iron and other essential nutrients that are found in solids in order to help them develop and grow. Your baby will also be progressing from sucking to biting and chewing – as many breast-feeding mothers find out!

Remember that every baby has individual needs, so don't be surprised if your baby seems ready for solids earlier or later than other babies of the same age. Don't feel pressured by friends with young babies, or helpful relatives. Be guided by your own baby.

WHAT TO LOOK OUT FOR

- if your baby still seems hungry after nursing
- wants feeding more frequently
- starts waking at night after some weeks of sleeping through
- shows a real interest in the foods that you are eating
- seems more restless

If your baby is showing some or all of these signs then she is probably ready to begin solids. Check with your pediatrician; a few large and very hungry babies may show these signs earlier than four months, but the majority of babies should not be given solid foods before four months as their digestive systems can't cope.

Be guided as well by any family history of allergies, eczema or asthma. Studies suggest that babies who are fed on breast milk or formula somewhat longer are less likely to develop these complaints.

In the early days of weaning, your baby is not dependent on solid food

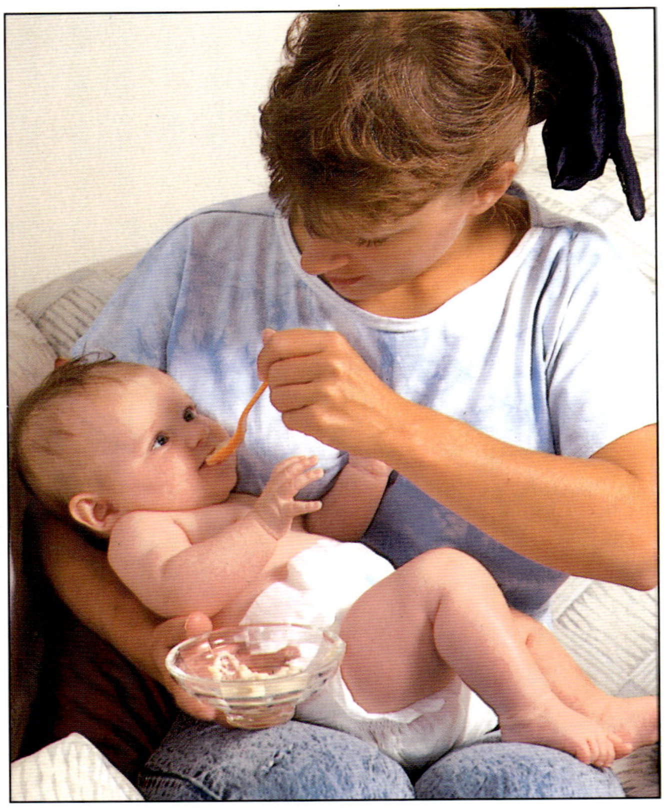

Left: *When the signs are right, start your baby with a few mouthfuls of puréed food. Your baby will feel most comfortable seated on your lap at this stage, and adopting one of the positions you have used for breast feeding will enhance security and confidence.*

Below: *If you have any doubts or worries about the right time to try purées and solids, your pediatrician will be able to help.*

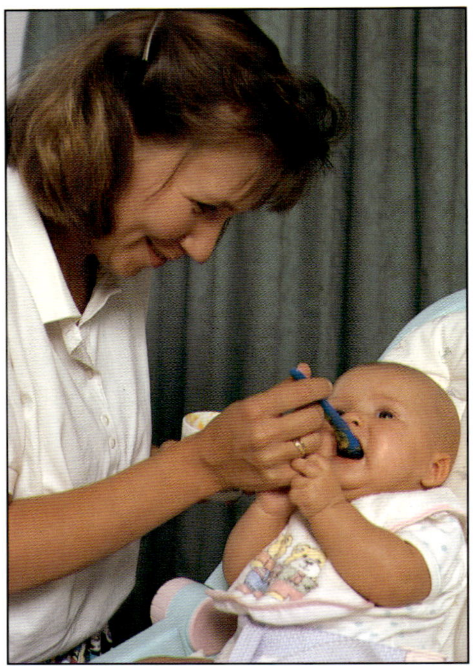

Above: *Your baby will very quickly take an interest in your hand and the spoon, and will play as she eats.*

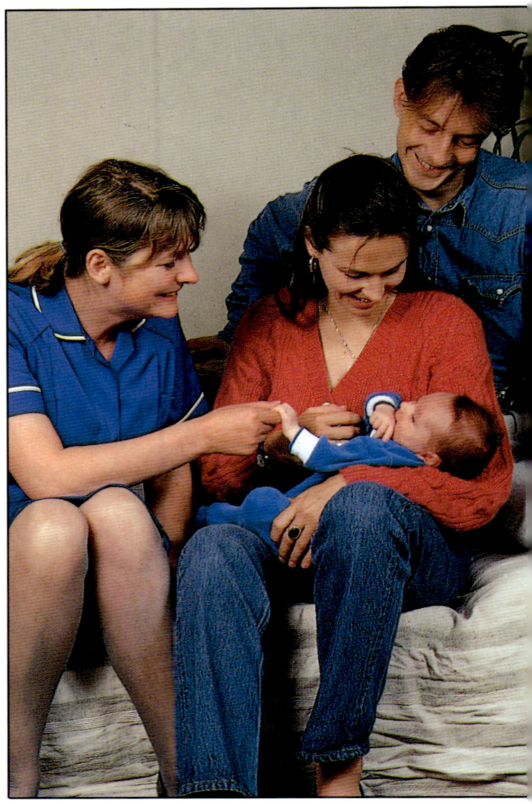

for the supply of nutrients as this is still met by milk or formula. Don't worry if she only takes a taste of food – the actual experience of taking food off a spoon is the important thing. However, by six months the baby's body store of nutrients has been used up and solid foods are crucial for supplying all the vital minerals and vitamins your baby needs.

WHAT ABOUT NURSING?

During the early stages of weaning, solids are given in addition to the normal feedings of breast milk or formula. As mixed feeding continues your baby will naturally cut down on the number of milk feedings, although milk will remain an important part of a child's diet.

Up to six months your baby should be having at least four milk feedings a day and by age one your baby needs at least 1 pint whole milk a day. Milk will still be contributing 40 percent of the energy she uses up.

More and more health professionals are now recommending that children should not be given cows' milk as their main drink until after 12 months, due to low levels of iron and vitamins C and D. Mothers are sometimes advised to go on to fortified formula when breastfeeding has finished. Small amounts of cows'

Above: *Bottles are a wonderful aid, but try to wean your baby off them by age one, or the sucking habit can be difficult to break.*

Above: *Every baby is different. There is no need to be worried if your baby seems ready for solids earlier or later than other babies.*

milk may be used in cooking from six months, but it is better to use formula.

Whole cows' milk can be given to children between one and two, while part-skim milk can be gradually introduced to those over two providing the child eats well. Skim milk should not be given to children under five.

Only give pasteurized milk to children. Long-life milk is a useful standby for holidays and traveling as it doesn't need to be refrigerated, although once opened treat as whole pasteurized milk.

Some people prefer to give goats' or sheeps' milk feeling it is less allergenic and offers additional nourishment, although this cannot be substantiated. Goats' milk is deficient in folic acid and must not be given to babies under six months. Boil goats' milk before use, as it may be sold unpasteurized.

WEANING FROM BREAST OR BOTTLE

You can go on breastfeeding your baby, as well as giving solid food, for as long as you wish. But many mothers are quite relieved when their baby is happy to try a feeder cup or bottle along with their lunch-time "solid" meal.

Once solids become established the number of daytime milk feedings naturally decreases with just the special morning and evening comfort feedings continuing until you and baby are ready to stop.

Whether bottle or breast and bottle feeding, try to wean your baby off the bottle completely by the age of one. Otherwise your baby may find it difficult to give the bottle up and comfort sucking on a nipple can be a hard habit to break.

Once your baby can sit up and is settled into three meals a day then you can introduce a lidded feeding cup – initially at one meal a day, then at two and so on. But do make sure to cuddle your baby while giving a drink so that the baby still enjoys the closeness and security of being with mother or father. There may be a few setbacks when your baby is teething or unwell, but be guided by your baby.

Above: *It won't all happen at once: a mixed period of feeding with breast, bottle and simple solids is perfectly natural and healthy.*

Introducing Solid Food

Many parents find that around late morning, after their baby's morning nap, is the best time to introduce solids. Baby is happy and nicely hungry without being frantic. Offer a small milk feeding to take the edge off her immediate hunger and make her feel secure, and then go on to offer solid food. Finish with the rest of the milk feeding or "second side."

Above: *At about six months your baby will be ready to sit safely in a highchair. You should always use a strap.*

SITTING COMFORTABLY

In the early days sit baby on your lap, protect her with a bib and yourself with a dish towel and hold the baby tightly so she feels secure. As you and baby become more confident about feeding then you may prefer to strap her into a portable car seat or baby chair. Most babies will be unable to sit in a highchair until six months or so.

FIRST SPOONFULS

First foods should be very smooth and mild in taste. Rice cereal is often the most successful because its milky taste and soft texture seem vaguely familiar to the baby. Begin by trying a teaspoonful of rice cereal, add a little previously boiled water, expressed breast milk or formula as the package directs, and mix to make a smooth runny purée, slightly thicker than milk. Test the temperature on the edge of your lip; it should be just lukewarm – too hot and you may put baby off solids completely. Offer tiny amounts on the end of a sterilized teaspoon. Learning to eat from a spoon is quite a skill and your baby may start by spitting out the food until she has mastered the technique of taking food off the spoon and transferring it to the back of her mouth. Go at your baby's pace and don't try to hurry things. If your baby seems reluctant, then abandon the feeding and go back to breast or bottle feeding. You could try solids again a few days later – there's plenty of time. Never force-feed and never add solid foods to a baby's bottle as it can lead to choking which can be dangerous.

Once your baby has accepted the idea of eating from a spoon continue with a midday meal of rice cereal or

Above: *First rice cereal will be barely warm, and only very slightly thicker than milk.*

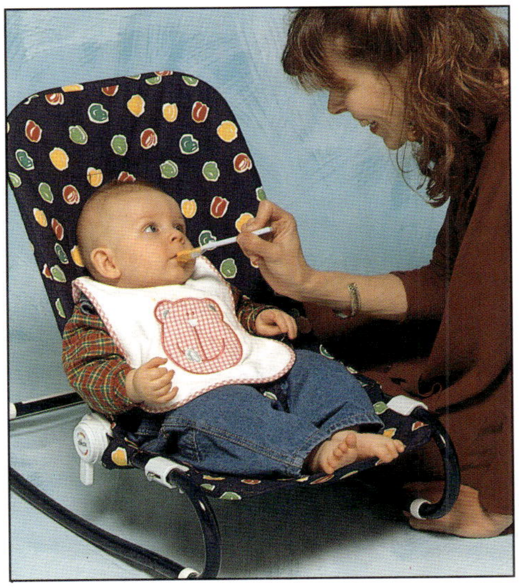

Left: *A good interim stage between lap feeding and the highchair is a baby chair on the floor, or even a portable car seat.*

SPOON FEEDING FOR THE FIRST TIME

1 Sit your baby on your lap in a familiar position. Always test the temperature of the food.

2 Offer the spoon to your baby. Go slowly and if the spoon or food is rejected try again another day.

3 When your baby has taken its first solid food, sit quietly for a little while in an upright position.

puréed potato for a week or two to give her digestive system a chance to adjust to the new food.

After that, you could gradually introduce puréed carrot, parsnip and rutabaga, or applesauce or puréed pears. As always be guided by your baby: this is a slow process so don't try to hurry your baby if she is not ready or you will run the risk of putting her off altogether.

After three to four weeks your baby may be ready to try two mini meals a day. Increase the amount of food to 2 tsp, even 3 tsp at each meal if your baby seems ready. You may be able to slightly reduce the amount of formula or breast milk you use to make the purée so that it is not quite so liquid.

If your baby likes the flavor, then offer it again for a few meals before introducing a new taste. If your baby spits out the food with obvious distaste then go back to rice cereal or try mixing the new flavor with a little rice cereal so that it is milder and more palatable.

Try to follow your baby's appetite and pace; most babies will stop when they have had enough. Don't be tempted to persuade your baby to finish off those last few spoonfuls. It's a bad habit to make or encourage anyone to clear the plate if they are full. If you do it with a baby, she'll probably be sick!

Adopt a feeding schedule to suit you both. In the early days it may be easier to give baby breakfast before older children get up, or after they're at school, when the house is quieter.

Six to eight weeks into solid feeding and your baby will probably be ready for three small meals a day. But again be guided by her needs and appetite, so don't introduce a third meal until you feel she is really ready. Aim to feed your baby at roughly equal time intervals that will eventually coincide with as many family meals as possible.

TIPS
- Be guided by your baby and your pediatrician.
- Sterilize all equipment before use.
- Don't force your baby if she doesn't seem ready for solids.
- Maintain milk feedings and offer plain boiled water or very diluted fruit juice as well.
- Try one taste at a time and continue with this until your baby is accustomed to it. If she doesn't like it, don't offer it for a few days.
- Remember, babies don't mind repetition, they've been living on milk for months!

Above: *Over the weeks you can build up the diet from rice cereal to items like puréed carrot, parsnip, apple or pear, gradually leaving more texture as your baby seems ready.*

EQUIPMENT

Choose a small plastic spoon, preferably with a shallow bowl that is gentle on your baby's gums. Look out for packs of weaning spoons in pharmacies or baby-care shops. If you don't want to buy a lot of equipment right away you may find it useful to mix small quantities of rice cereal in the sterilized cap of a bottle. Alternatively, use a small china ramekin or plastic bowl. Plastic bowls with suction feet or stay-warm linings are also perfectly adequate and will be useful later on when baby gets bigger. All equipment must be sterilized first and water must be previously boiled and cooled before use.

Below: *This dish and the spoon with the shallow bowl would be the perfect starter set.*

Top left, above, left and below: *Any small dish, or even the lid off a baby bottle, can be used for mixing and feeding so long as it is thoroughly sterilized.*

Below: *Bib*

Left: *Bowl with stay-warm lining.*

Below: *Your baby will graduate from bottles with nipples to cups and beakers with tight-fitting lids. There is a variety of types, but you will find one the toddler likes.*

FEEDING TWINS

Probably the easiest way is to sit each child in their car or baby seat, side by side, and offer food from one bowl. Twins can get rather frustrated if you have to keep picking up different bowls and spoons. Try to be adaptable and if you find a way that works then stick with it. Encourage finger foods slightly earlier: perhaps a tiny ham sandwich, or cooked broccoli floret or carrot stick.

Wait until each child has finished their main course before offering dessert as the slow eater will be distracted and want to go on to dessert too.

Caring for twins can be exhausting so you may find serving sandwiches for lunch an easier option and this will give you a chance to eat something too. Serve a cooked main meal for dinner.

DRINKS

Although your baby will need less milk for nourishment, she will still need something to drink, especially in hot weather. Always offer at least two drinks during the day along with a drink with every meal.

You can give:

- milk – breast milk, formula or, at over one year, whole cows' milk
- cooled boiled water
- well-diluted pure unsweetened fruit juice.

Above: *Dilute juices with boiled water.*

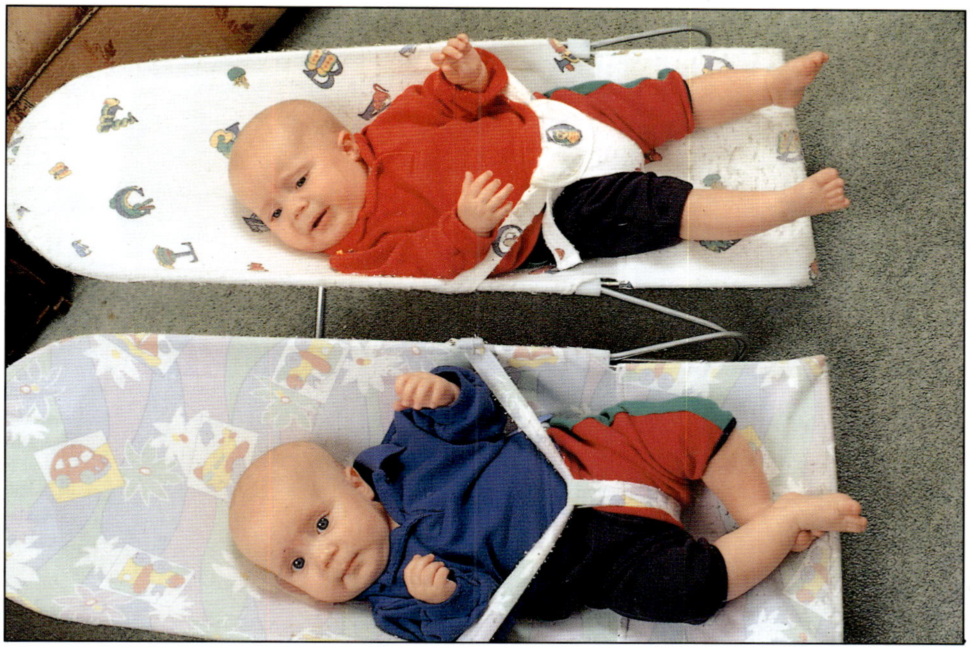

You can stop boiling the water for baby's drinks when you stop sterilizing her feeding equipment, but always make sure you allow the tap to run for a while before using. Never use water from the hot tap for drinks.

If you have a water softener make sure that you use a tap connected directly to the main water supply and independent of the water softener. Artificially softened water is not recommended as salts are added during the softening process. Check with your pediatrician before giving a baby bottled water as the mineral content varies and you will need to choose a low-mineral brand such as those labeled "spring water." As a general rule, bottled water is not really necessary unless you are vacationing somewhere where it is unsafe to drink the water.

Some fruit drinks contain a lot of added sugar, so check the label for sucrose, glucose, dextrose, fructose, maltose, syrup, honey or concentrated fruit juice. If you do give concentrated drinks to your baby make sure you dilute them correctly and do not give them too often. Pure fruit juices contain no added sugar. At first, dilute them one part juice to three parts water. The amount of water can be reduced as the child matures. Offer drinks at the end of meal times once your baby is settled into three meals a day.

Never allow a baby to use a bottle of juice as a comforter or go to sleep with a bottle in his mouth as this can result in serious tooth decay.

Above: *Feed twins side by side, alternating servings between the two.*
Below: *Drinks fill up the baby's tummy – so offer drinks* after *food.*

Food Preparation

At this first stage it is vital that whatever solid food you offer should be smooth and soft in texture. Puréeing foods is very simple and there are plenty of gadgets available to make it even easier. For ease and speed, an electric blender is by far the best. You may be able to buy a blender attachment for your mixer or look out for a freestanding blender unit. Prices vary considerably so it's worth shopping around. A food processor works well, but make sure the food is blended to a very fine purée before offering it to your baby, since processors can miss the odd lump, especially when processing small quantities. A hand-held electric multimixer is another useful gadget with the bonus of reducing washing up by mixing foods directly in the serving bowl. If you prefer to purée food by hand, then a strainer or hand mill are both perfectly adequate and are much cheaper alternatives.

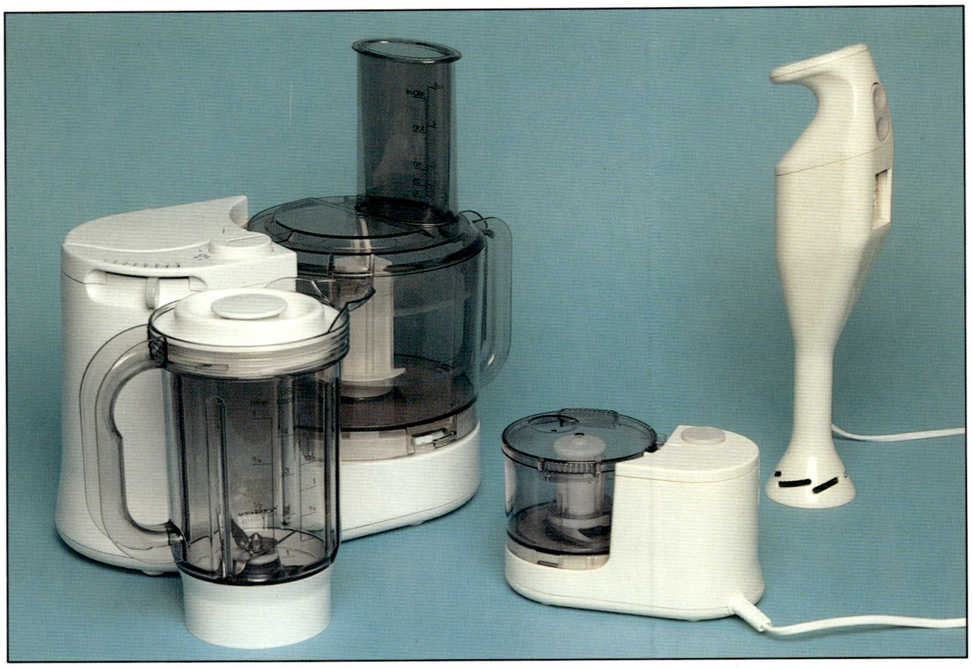

Above: *There is a huge range of brand-name food processors and blenders on the market, many of which have attachments for puréeing.*

Left: *The basics – manual mashers, or a strainer – take longer but will do the job just as well.*

Above: *A blender will make perfect purée in seconds. This is the right tool for making large batches.*

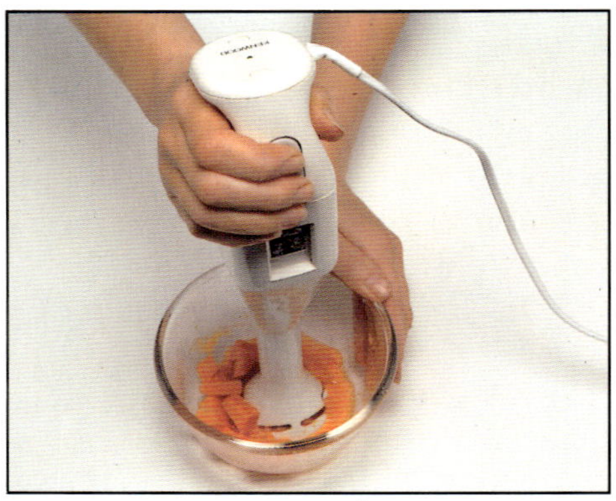

Above: *This hand-held blender takes a little longer, but the results are just as reliable. They are easy to clean and store.*

Above: *Making purée manually the old-fashioned way – with strainer and spoon – is time-consuming but highly satisfying.*

FOOD HYGIENE

Young babies can easily pick up infections so it is vitally important that all equipment be scrupulously cleaned before use.

- Always wash your hands before handling food or feeding equipment.

Above: *Rule one* – always *wash your hands before feeding your baby or handling food.*

- All items such as bottles and containers used for freezing or storing baby food, feeding spoons and serving bowls should be sterilized in the usual way, by boiling in a saucepan of water for 25 minutes, or by using a steam sterilizer. Larger items such as a strainer, knife, saucepan, blender or masher or plastic chopping board should be scalded with boiling water.

Above: *Scald larger objects with boiling water to sterilize.*

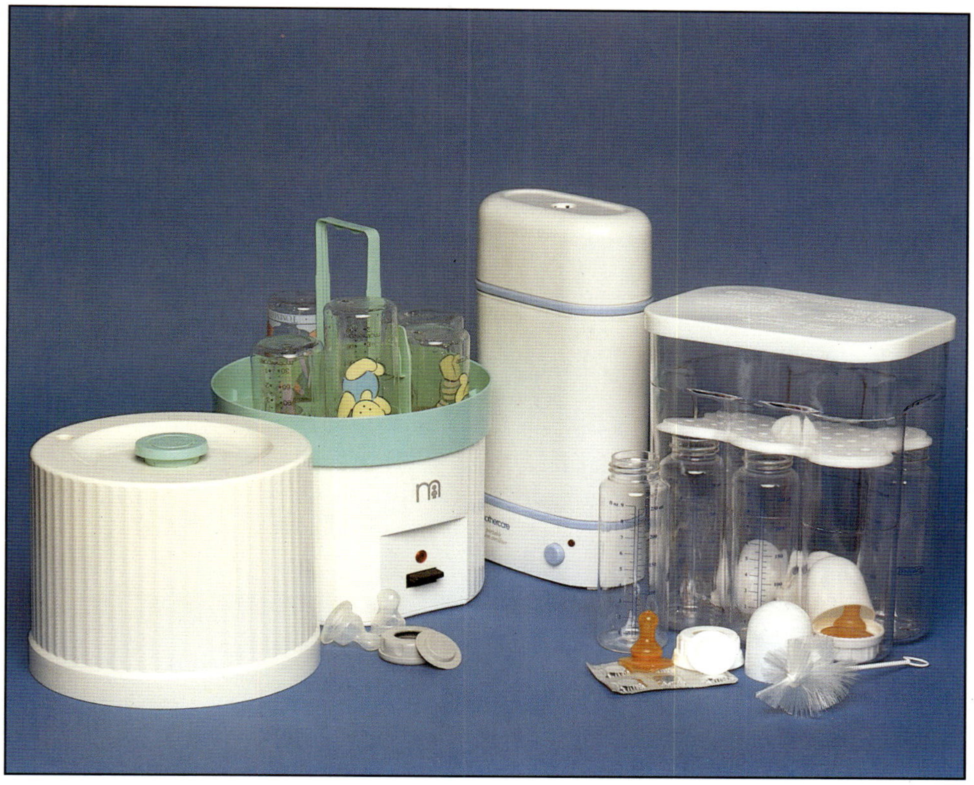

Above: *There is a wide range of sterilizing equipment to choose from. This group, all specially designed for bottles and nipples, comprises two steam sterilizing units that operate electrically and a traditional container (see right) that holds the bottles efficiently in cold water sterilizing solution.*

Right: *Always keep the surfaces around where your baby eats scrupulously clean.*

SOLUTION STERILIZER

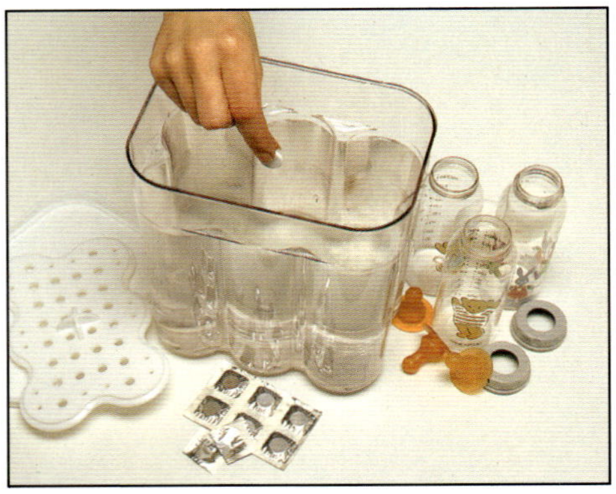

1 Fill the sterilizer to the required height with cold water, and add sterilizing tablets or liquid.

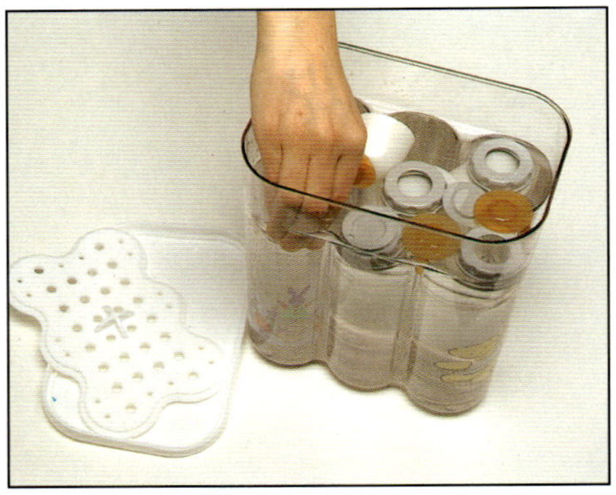

2 Pack the items to be sterilized into the container. Bottles will fit into the spaces provided.

3 Make sure no air gets trapped in the container – or these pockets will not be properly sterile. Push everything down with the "float."

4 Place the lid on and leave for the length of time specified in the instructions. Rinse everything afterwards in boiling water.

STEAM STERILIZER

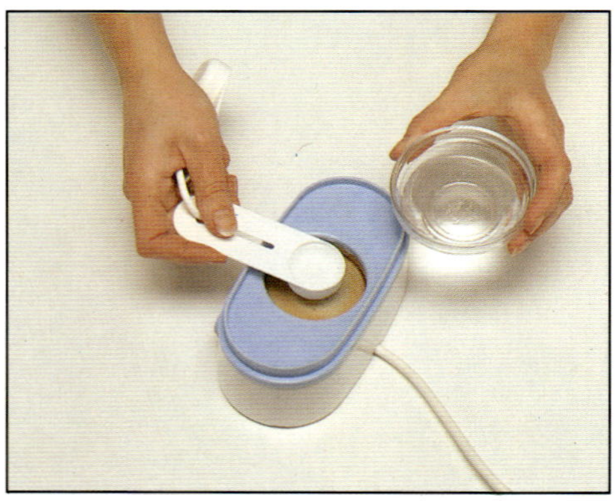

1 Measure the specified amount of water into the base of the steamer as directed in the manufacturer's instructions.

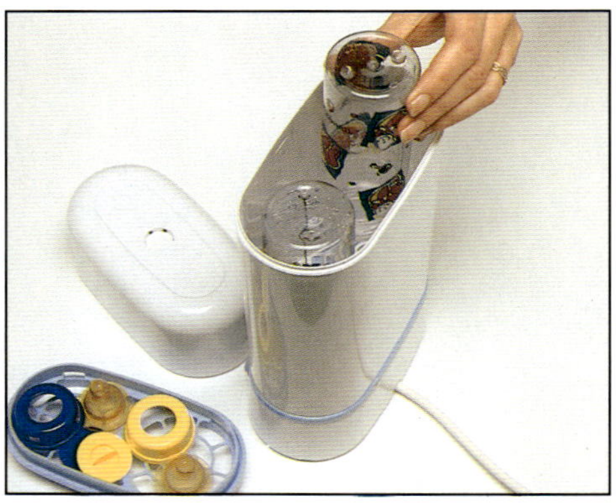

2 Pack the bottles and nipples into the container: steamers have less capacity for dishes or bowls, which will need to be boiled separately.

- Sterilize all baby equipment until she is six months; milk bottles, nipples etc. should be sterilized until she goes on to a cup.

Above: *Boiling in water for 25 minutes is still the simplest method of sterilizing.*

- Never use equipment used for the family pet when preparing baby food. Keep a can opener, fork and dish specifically for your pet and make sure other members of the family are aware of this.
- Once cooked, cover all baby food with a lid or plate and transfer to the refrigerator as soon as possible. Food should not be left for longer than 1½ hours at room temperature before refrigerating or freezing.

Above: *Always cover baby food at all times – even when stored in the refrigerator.*

STERILIZING IN THE MICROWAVE

Microwave ovens are not suitable for general day-to-day sterilizing without special equipment, and many health authorities and mother and baby experts specifically recommend against using the microwave for this purpose.

However microwave sterilizing units can be purchased for sterilizing bottles, and where used, the manufacturer's instructions should be followed closely.

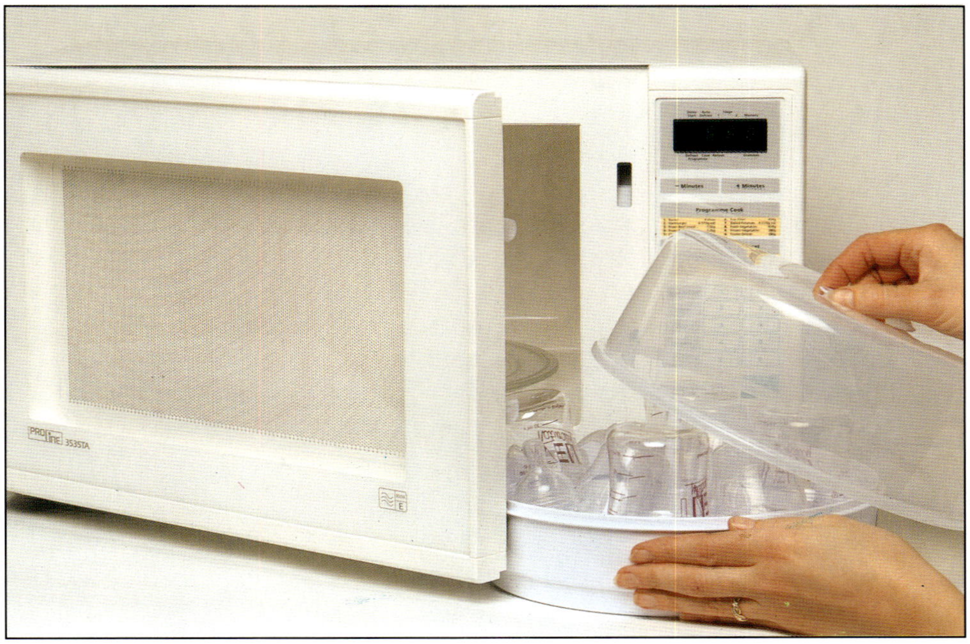

Right: *This sterilizing unit is specially made for microwave use.*

BATCH COOKING

Cooking for a tiny baby can be very frustrating. Those tiny spoonfuls of super-smooth purée so lovingly and hygienically prepared, offered with such hope and spat out so unceremoniously can leave you feeling quite indignant.

Save time by cooking several meals in advance. Freeze mini portions in ice-cube trays, great for those early days when you need only one cube for lunch and flexible enough for later weeks when your baby's appetite has grown to two or three cubes per meal.

Spoon the mixture into sterilized ice-cube trays and freeze until solid. Press the cubes into a plastic bag or container, seal, label and return to the freezer. Keep batches of food in the same bag so flavors don't get mixed.

Recycle yogurt containers, cottage cheese containers with lids, small plastic containers with lids or use disposable plastic cups and cover with plastic wrap. Sterilize using sterilizing fluid or tablets. Cover all prepared foods and label clearly so you know what they are and when they went into the freezer.

Most foods should be used within three months if stored in a freezer at 0°F. Defrost plastic containers in the refrigerator overnight. Ice cubes can be left to defrost at room temperature in a bowl or on a plate, loosely covered with plastic wrap.

BATCH COOKING TIPS

1 It is just as quick (and very much cheaper in the long run) to make a larger batch of purée as a smaller quantity for a single meal.

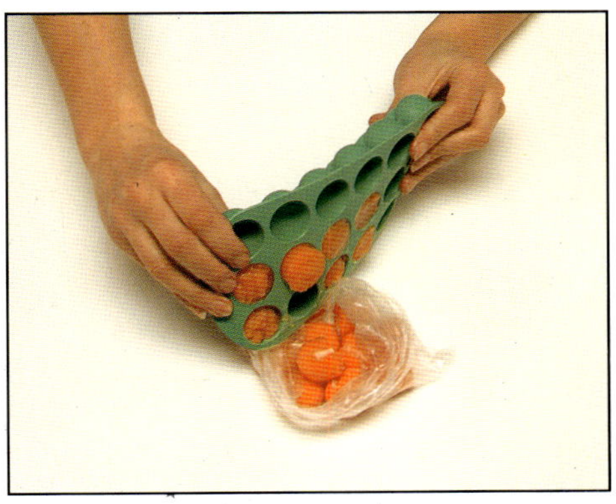

2 Freeze in meal-sized portions in sterilized ice-cube trays: these can later be turned out into freezer bags for storing.

3 Make sure the bags are carefully labeled and dated. Keep only for the period specified in your freezer handbook.

STAGE 1: FIRST TASTES – AROUND FOUR MONTHS

THE FIRST SOLIDS ARE A STEPPING-STONE TO INTRODUCING YOUR BABY TO REAL FOOD SO SHE BECOMES FAMILIAR WITH ALL SORTS OF DIFFERENT TASTES AND TEXTURES.

ALTHOUGH MILK IS STILL PROVIDING YOUR BABY WITH ALL HER NUTRITIONAL NEEDS THESE EARLY FOODS WILL BE THE GROUNDS ON WHICH LATER EATING HABITS ARE BUILT, SO IT IS IMPORTANT THAT THIS IS A HAPPY, POSITIVE EXPERIENCE. IT IS IMPORTANT TO BUILD ON GOOD FOUNDATIONS.

BEGIN BY OFFERING ONLY A TEASPOONFUL OF VERY SOFT RUNNY PURÉE ONCE A DAY, GRADUALLY BUILDING TO 2–3 TSP AND THEN SLOWLY ON TO TWO AND THREE MEALS A DAY.

Suitable Foods

FOODS TO INCLUDE

- rice cereal mixed with water, breast milk or formula.
- mild-tasting vegetable purées – beginning with potato then carrot, parsnip, or rutabaga purée.
- mild, naturally sweet fruit purées made with apples or pears.

FOODS TO AVOID

- highly spiced foods
- salt as this causes the kidneys to overwork. Avoid seasoning with salt or adding bouillon cubes, bacon and salami to foods
- cows' milk (give breast milk or formula feedings instead)
- foods containing gluten found in wheat, oats, rye and barley (check package labels)
- eggs
- meat, fish, poultry
- citrus fruits – can result in allergic reactions in some babies
- nuts, either whole or ground
- honey
- fatty foods

Right: *Adult favorites – but these must be avoided at this age, even as treats.*

Note: If you have a family history of allergies, your doctor may also advise you to avoid other foods as well. Do check with him.

Above: *A world of foodstuffs opens up over the months: but introduce them gradually, and at the right time.*

Baby Rice

Mix 1–3 tsp rice cereal with cooled boiled water, breast milk or formula as the package directs. Cool slightly and test before serving.

Left: *Plain rice cereal will be the staple for your baby for the first few weeks of solids – then gradually add flavor and variation.*

Vegetable Purées

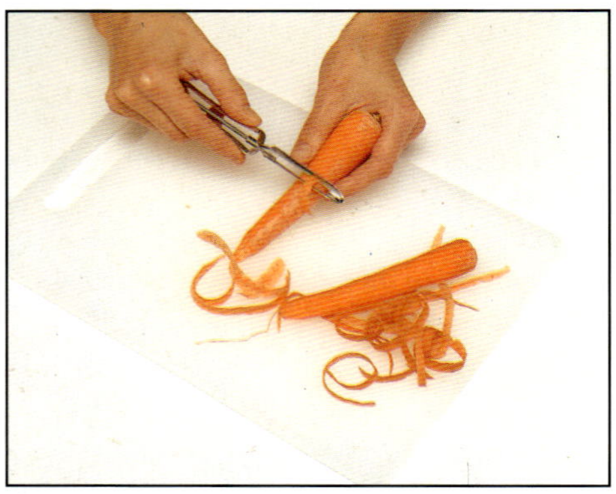

1 Peel 4oz potato, parsnip, carrot or rutabaga and dice.

2 Steam over a saucepan of boiling water for 10 minutes, until soft.

3 Press through a strainer, mix with 4–5 tbsp formula or breast milk depending on the vegetable used. Spoon a little into a bowl, test on a spoon and cool if needed. Cover the remaining purée and transfer to the refrigerator as soon as possible. Use within 24 hours.

• To microwave, put the vegetable or vegetables in a microwave-proof bowl with 2 tbsp formula or breast milk. Cover with plastic wrap, pierce and cook on High (100%) for 4 minutes. Let stand for 5 minutes, then press through a strainer and mix with 2–3 tbsp formula or breast milk. Cool and serve as described above.

Right: *This lovely selection of simple but satisfying vegetable purées illustrates that these bland foods need not lack color and variation, and can be made very attractive to the infant.*

Fruit Purées

Makes: ½ cup

1 Peel, quarter and core 1 eating apple or 1 ripe pear.

2 Thinly slice and put in a small saucepan with 1 tbsp water, formula or breast milk. Cover and simmer for 10 minutes until soft.

• **To microwave:** place the apple or pear in a microwave-proof bowl with water, formula or breast milk. Cover with plastic wrap, pierce and cook on High (100%) for 3 minutes. Let stand for 5 minutes then press through a strainer. Cool and serve as above.

3 Press through a strainer. Spoon a little purée into a serving bowl, test on a spoon and cool if needed. Cover, transfer to the refrigerator, and use within 24 hours.

Top: *Pear (top) and apple purée will bring a smile to any baby's face (above).*

Melon purée

Strawberry purée

Left: *These tasty purées will encourage even reluctant eaters to take solids regularly.*

Warning: *Soft berry fruits should be introduced at around five to six months at the earliest. Do so in very small portions as some infants may have allergies and always strain the purée carefully to remove berry pips.*

Right: *When your baby is ready to start taking solids at around four to five months old, start with a teaspoon and build gradually to two and finally three meals a day.*

Stage 2: Around Five to Six Months

By now your baby may be taking solids at two or three meals each day. Increase the variety of foods offered and start to combine food tastes. Baby purée can be a slightly thicker coarser texture, but make sure there are no pits or bones. Always choose the best, freshest ingredients and make sure utensils are scrupulously clean.

Suitable Foods

FOODS TO INCLUDE

- wider selection of vegetables including fresh or frozen peas, corn, cauliflower, broccoli, cabbage, spinach, celery, mushrooms, leeks
- poultry
- mild tasting fresh or frozen fish – sole, cod, haddock, trout
- small quantities of very lean red meat
- small quantities of split legumes – peas, red lentils and very well cooked or canned whole legumes – chickpeas, beans
- more interesting fruits – banana, apricots, peaches, plums, strawberries, raspberries, melon (Warning: offer tiny amounts of soft berry fruits as some children may be allergic to them.)
- gluten-free cereals – rice, cornstarch
- small quantities of cocoa

Above: *Every day brings a new taste: these young gourmets can't wait!*

Chickpeas

Cocoa

Split peas

Cornstarch

Lentils

Rice

FOODS TO AVOID

- gluten-based cereals, wheat flour and bread
- cows' milk and milk products
- eggs
- citrus fruit
- nuts, ground or whole
- fatty foods
- chilies and highly spiced foods

Below: *Even super-healthy adult foods such as whole wheat bread and oranges should still be avoided at this stage.*

Reheating, Freezing and Using a Microwave

REHEATING BABY FOOD

Reheating food sounds straightforward but it is vitally important that these rules are followed as tepid food provides the perfect breeding ground for bacteria, especially if left uncovered in a warm kitchen and reheated several times.

- Don't reheat food more than once. It is a health risk.
- If you have a large batch of baby food then reheat just a portion in a saucepan and leave the remaining mixture in a covered bowl in the refrigerator. If your baby is still hungry then reheat a little extra again with the remaining mixture left in the refrigerator.
- Reheat small quantities of baby food in a sterilized heat-proof container, covered with a saucer or small plate and put into a small saucepan half filled with boiling water. Or spoon larger quantities straight into a saucepan, cover and bring to a boil.
- Make sure food is piping hot all the way through to kill any bacteria. Food should be 158°F for a minimum of 2 minutes. Remove from the heat and allow to cool. Test before serving to baby.

1 Reheat small quantities in a sterilized bowl, covered with a dish or aluminum foil.

2 Place the bowl into a pan half filled with boiling water. Make sure the food is cooked through.

3 For larger quantities, put the food straight into the pan and bring to a boil.

FREEZING

When using a freezer for storing homemade baby foods, use up the foods as soon as possible as the texture preferred by the child will change very quickly as the child develops.

Keeping a well-stocked freezer of basics can be a lifesaver: there is nothing worse than going shopping with little children, especially when they're tired, and freezing will save you trip after trip.

Make sure to always label foods so you know exactly when they went into the freezer and double check storage against this handy list of dates:

Food	Storage time
Meat and poultry	
Beef and lamb	4–6 months
Pork and veal	4–6 months
Ground beef	3–4 months
Sausages and sausage meat	2–3 months
Ham and bacon	3–4 months
Chicken and turkey	10–12 months
Duck and goose	4–6 months
Fish	
White fish	6–8 months
Oily fish	3–4 months
Fish portions	3–4 months
Shellfish	2–3 months
Fruit and vegetables	
Fruit with or without sugar	8–10 months
Fruit juices	4–6 months
Most vegetables	10–12 months
Mushrooms and tomatoes	6–8 months
Dairy produce	
Cream	6–8 months
Butter, unsalted	6–8 months
Butter, salted	3–4 months
Cheese, hard	4–6 months
Cheese, soft	3–4 months
Ice cream	3–4 months
Prepared foods	
Ready prepared meals, highly seasoned	2–3 months
Ready prepared meals, average seasoning	4–6 months
Cakes	4–6 months
Bread, all kinds	2–3 months
Other yeast products and pastries	3–4 months

* *Chart published by kind permission of the Food Safety Advisory Centre*

USING A MICROWAVE

Health advisers do not recommend using a microwave for reheating as the food heats up unevenly but if you decide to microwave baby food then make sure you stir the food thoroughly after cooking. Let the dish stand for 2–3 minutes before stirring again so that "hot spots" are well stirred into the mixture, and always check the temperature before serving. Choose the type of dish carefully as some pottery dishes can get very hot; plastic or pyrex dishes are the most successful in the microwave, heating food quickly but staying relatively cool themselves.

Top: *All parents will find the microwave incredibly helpful and time-saving. It can be used for heating milk and drinks (for toddlers – not newborns), for defrosting, reheating and cooking preprepared foods.*

1 Cover dish with plastic wrap, pierce and place in oven.

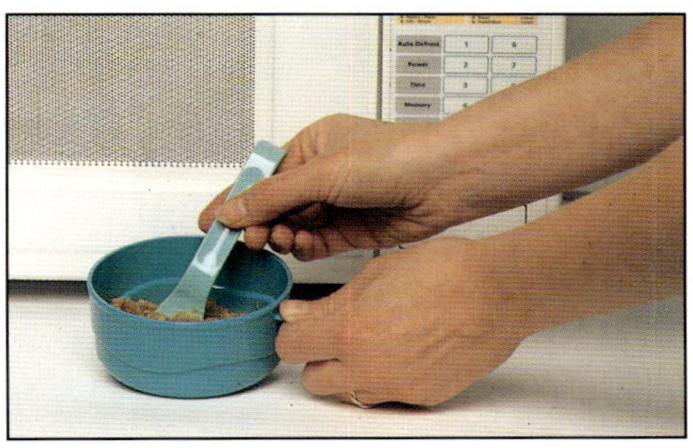

2 When cooked, remove and stir.

MICROWAVING TIPS

- Never warm milk for a newborn or young baby in the microwave.
- For older children warm milk in a bottle without the nipple or an uncovered feeder beaker for 30–45 seconds. Stir well and always test the temperature of the milk (*not* the temperature of the container) before serving to make sure that the milk is an even and comfortable temperature. Do also seek advice from your pediatrician.
- To defrost ice cubes of baby food, press three into a baby dish, cover with plastic wrap and thaw in the microwave on Defrost (30%) setting for 1 to 2 minutes. Stir well then re-cover and microwave on High (100%) for 1 minute. Stir well to avoid hot spots then test the temperature.

Root Vegetable Purée

Makes: 2½ cups
4oz carrot
4oz parsnip
4oz rutabaga
4oz potato
1¼ cups formula

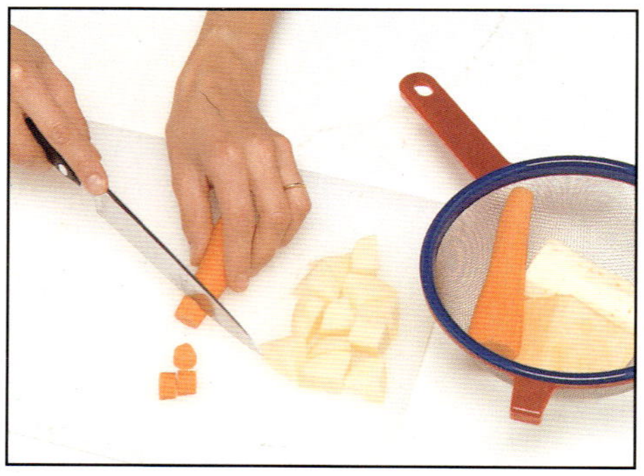

1 Trim and peel the carrot, parsnip, rutabaga and potato and place in a colander. Rinse under cold water, drain and chop.

2 Place the chopped vegetables in a saucepan with the formula then bring to a boil, cover and simmer for 20 minutes or until they are very soft.

3 Purée or strain the vegetables until they are smooth.

4 Spoon a little into a bowl. Test the temperature and cool if necessary, before serving.

5 Cover the remaining food and refrigerate as soon as possible. Use within 24 hours.

- Suitable for freezing.

TIP
Thin the purée with a little extra formula if your baby prefers a very soft purée.

Mixed Vegetable Purée

Makes: 2½ cups
4oz carrot
6oz potato
4oz broccoli
2oz green cabbage
1¼ cups formula

1 Peel the carrot and potato, rinse, chop and place in a saucepan. Wash the broccoli and cabbage and cut the broccoli into florets, the stems into slices and shred the cabbage finely.

2 Add the formula to the carrot and potato, bring to a boil then cover and simmer for 10 minutes.

3 Add the broccoli stems and florets and cabbage and cook, covered, for 10 minutes until all the vegetables are tender.

4 Purée or strain the vegetables until smooth.

5 Spoon a little into a bowl. Test the temperature and cool if necessary, before serving.

6 Cover the remaining food and refrigerate as soon as possible. Use within 24 hours.

- Suitable for freezing.

Carrot and Lentil Purée

Makes: 2½ cups

- 12oz carrots
- 6oz potato
- ¼ cup red lentils
- ½ tsp ground coriander
- 1¼ cups formula

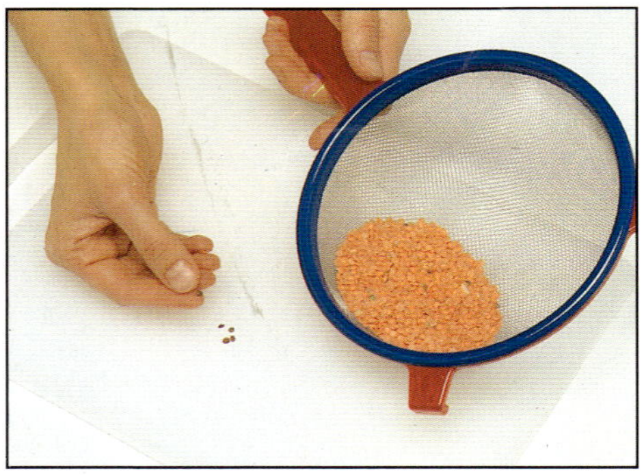

1 Trim and peel the carrots and potato and then chop into small cubes and place in a saucepan. Rinse the lentils thoroughly, discarding any black pieces.

2 Add the lentils, coriander and formula to the pan and bring to a boil, then cover and simmer for 40 minutes, until the lentils are very soft. Add a little extra boiling water if necessary.

TIP
The mixture thickens on cooling so any remaining mixture will need to be thinned slightly with a little formula before reheating for the next meal.

3 Purée or strain the vegetable and lentil mixture until smooth.

4 Spoon a little into a bowl. Test the temperature and cool if necessary, before serving.

5 Cover the remaining purée and refrigerate as soon as possible. Use within 24 hours.

- Suitable for freezing.

Red Bell Pepper and Rice Purée

Makes: 2½ cups
¼ cup long grain rice
1¼ cups formula
3oz red bell pepper
3oz zucchini
2oz celery

1 Place the rice and formula in a saucepan, bring to a boil and simmer, uncovered, for 5 minutes.

2 Discard the core and seeds from the bell pepper and trim the zucchini and celery. Place the vegetables in a colander and rinse under cold water then chop them into small pieces.

3 Add the vegetables to the rice mixture, bring to a boil, cover and simmer for about 10 minutes or until the rice is soft.

- Suitable for freezing.

4 Purée or strain the rice and vegetable mixture until smooth.

5 Spoon a little into a bowl. Test the temperature and cool if necessary, before serving.

6 Cover the remaining food and refrigerate as soon as possible. Use within 24 hours.

Parsnip and Broccoli Purée

Makes: 2½ cups
8oz parsnips
4oz broccoli
1¼ cups formula

1 Trim and peel the parsnips and place in a colander with the broccoli. Rinse the parsnips and broccoli under cold water. Chop the parsnips and cut the broccoli into florets, slicing the stems.

2 Put the parsnips in a saucepan with the formula, bring to a boil, then cover and simmer for about 10 minutes.

3 Add the broccoli and simmer for 10 minutes more, until the vegetables are soft.

4 Purée or strain the vegetable mixture to make a completely smooth purée.

5 Spoon a little into a bowl. Test the temperature and cool if necessary, before serving.

6 Cover the remaining food and refrigerate as soon as possible. Use within 24 hours.

- Suitable for freezing.

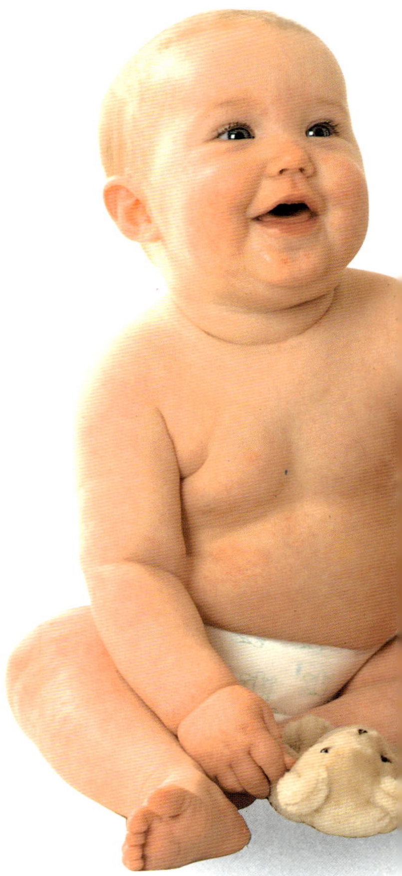

Turkey, Carrot and Corn Purée

Makes: 2½ cups
6oz potato
6oz carrot
4oz boneless, skinless turkey breast
⅓ cup frozen corn
1¼ cups formula

1 Trim and peel the potato and carrot, rinse under cold water and then chop into small cubes.

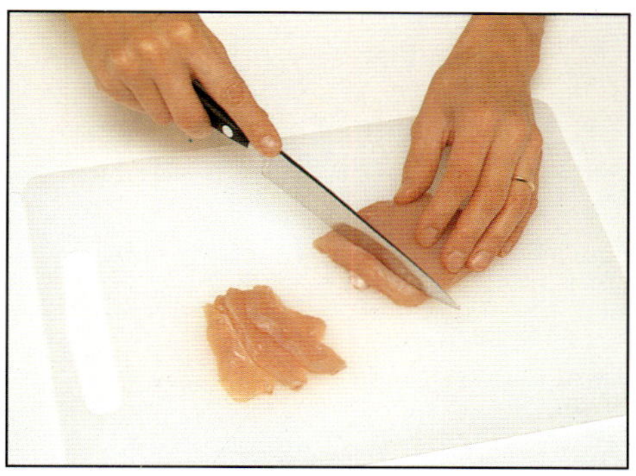

2 Rinse the turkey and cut into thin strips. Place in a small saucepan with the potato and carrot.

3 Add the corn and formula. Cover and simmer for 20 minutes, until the turkey is cooked. Purée or strain the mixture until completely smooth.

4 Spoon a little into a bowl. Test the temperature and cool if necessary, before serving.

5 Cover the remaining food and refrigerate. Use within 24 hours.

- Suitable for freezing.

TIP
Bring the turkey and vegetable mixture to a boil in a flameproof casserole and transfer to a preheated 350°F oven and cook for 1¼ hours if preferred.

Chicken and Parsnip Purée

Makes: 2½ cups

12oz parsnips

4oz boneless, skinless chicken breast

1¼ cups formula

1 Peel the parsnips, and trim the woody tops and bottoms. Rinse and chop roughly.

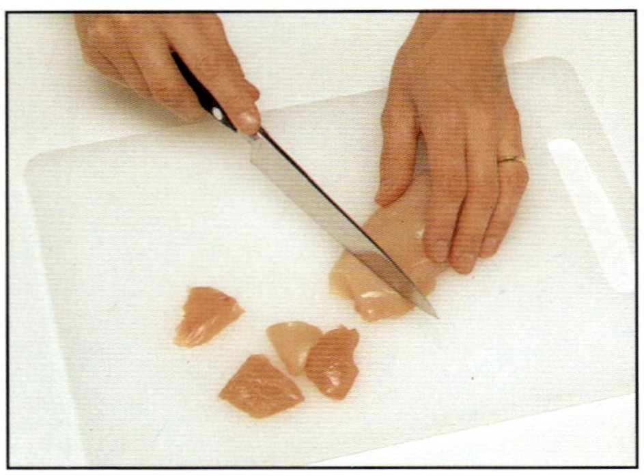

2 Rinse the chicken under cold water and cut into small pieces.

3 Place the parsnips, chicken and formula in a saucepan. Cover and simmer for 20 minutes or until the parsnips are tender.

4 Purée or strain the chicken and parsnip mixture until smooth.

5 Spoon into a bowl. Test the temperature and cool if necessary, before serving.

6 Cover the remaining food and refrigerate as soon as possible. Use within 24 hours.

- Suitable for freezing.

TIP
For a very smooth purée, drain all the liquid into a blender and add half the solids, blend until smooth then add the remaining ingredients. If using a food processor, add all the solids and a little liquid, process until smooth then add the remaining liquid.

Chicken and Leek Purée

Makes: 2½ cups
2oz leek
10oz potatoes
4oz boneless, skinless chicken breast
1¼ cups formula

1 Halve the leek lengthwise and rinse under running water to remove any dirt or grit.

2 Peel the potatoes and cut into dice. Rinse the chicken and cut into pieces and thinly slice the leek.

3 Place the vegetables and chicken in a saucepan with the formula.

4 Bring the mixture to a boil, cover with a lid and simmer gently for 20 minutes, until the potatoes are just tender. Purée or strain the mixture until it is completely smooth.

5 Spoon a little into a bowl. Test the temperature and cool if necessary, before serving. Use within 24 hours.

- Suitable for freezing.

TIP

You can vary the texture of this recipe depending on how you purée the mixture. A fine strainer produces the finest consistency, then a food processor, while a food mill gives the coarsest texture. Starchy vegetables thicken and bind the purée together. Any root vegetable can be used here, but make sure it is thoroughly cooked before blending.

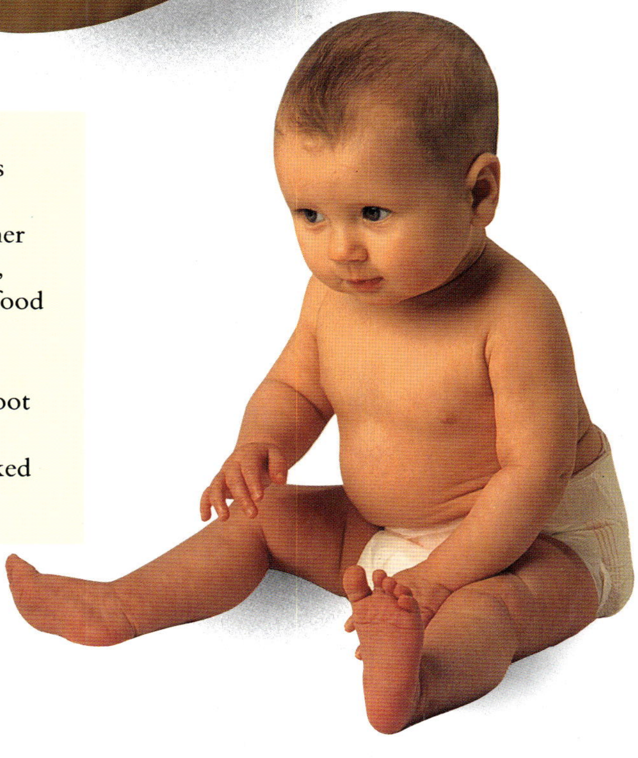

Fish and Zucchini Purée

Makes: 2½ cups
10oz potatoes
6oz zucchini
4oz trout fillet
1 cup formula

1 Peel the potatoes, trim the zucchini and rinse under cold water. Dice the potatoes and cut the zucchini into slices.

2 Place the vegetables in a saucepan. Rinse the trout and arrange on top, then pour over the formula. Bring to a boil, cover and simmer for 15 minutes, until the potatoes and fish are cooked.

3 Lift the trout out of the pan and peel off the skin. Break it into pieces with a knife and fork, checking carefully for any bones.

4 Purée or strain the fish, the vegetables and the liquid until quite smooth.

5 Spoon a little into a bowl. Test the temperature and cool if necessary, before serving.

6 Cover any remaining food and refrigerate as soon as possible. Use within 24 hours.

- Suitable for freezing.

Cod and Corn Purée

Makes: 2½ cups

12oz potatoes
3½oz frozen cod
¼ cup frozen peas
2 tbsp frozen corn
1¼ cups formula

1 Peel and rinse the potatoes and cut into even-sized pieces. Place in a saucepan with the fish, peas, corn and formula.

2 Bring to a boil, cover and simmer for 15 minutes until the potatoes are very tender.

3 Lift the fish out of the pan and break into pieces with a knife and fork, checking carefully and removing any small bones.

4 Purée or strain the fish, vegetables and cooking liquid until completely smooth.

5 Spoon a little into a bowl. Test the temperature and cool if necessary, before serving.

6 Cover the remaining purée and refrigerate as soon as possible. Use within 24 hours.

- Suitable for freezing.

Apple Ambrosia

Makes: 1¼ cups
1 eating apple
1oz rice cereal
1¼ cups formula

1 Quarter, core and peel the apple. Slice and place in a saucepan with the cereal and formula.

2 Bring to a boil then simmer gently for 10–12 minutes until the cereal is soft, stirring occasionally with a wooden spoon.

3 Purée the apple and cereal mixture until completely smooth.

4 Spoon a little into a bowl. Test the temperature and cool if necessary, before serving. Cover the remaining purée and refrigerate as soon as possible. Use within 24 hours.

VARIATION
Chocolate Pudding
Cook the cereal as above but without the apple. Stir 1oz milk chocolate chips and 1tbsp superfine sugar into the hot cereal and then purée until smooth. Spoon into small dishes and cool as necessary.

Fruit Salad Purée

Makes: 1½ cups

1 nectarine or peach
1 eating apple
1 ripe pear
1oz fresh or frozen raspberries or strawberries

1 Halve the nectarine or peach, discard the pit then peel and chop. Quarter, core and peel the apple and pear and slice thinly.

2 Put the prepared fruits, the raspberries or strawberries and 1 tbsp water in a saucepan. Cover and simmer for 10 minutes until the fruit is soft.

3 Strain the mixture, or process and then press through a strainer to remove the berry seeds. Discard the seeds.

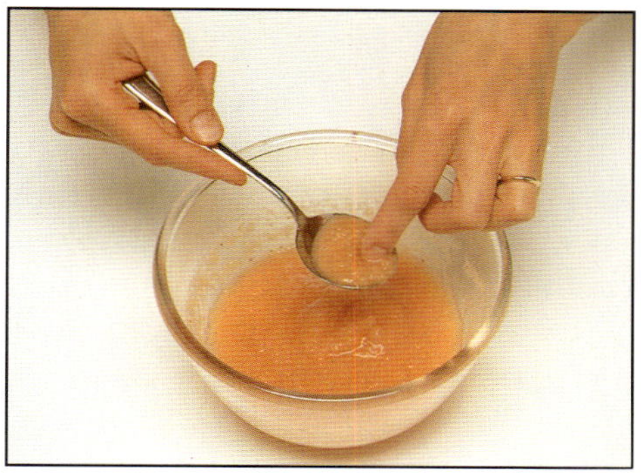

4 Spoon a little into a baby bowl. Test the temperature and cool if necessary, before serving.

5 Cover the remaining purée and refrigerate as soon as possible. Use within 24 hours.

- Suitable for freezing.

TIP
Babies tend to eat smaller quantities of dessert so it is best to freeze purée in a sterilized ice cube tray. Transfer the cubes to a plastic bag once frozen.

VARIATION
Peach Melon Purée
To make ¾ cup, take 1 ripe peach and ¼ ripe canteloupe melon. Peel and halve the peach, discard the pit and cut up the fruit. Scoop the seeds out of the melon and cut away the skin. Roughly chop the melon into pieces.

Purée or strain the fruit until completely smooth. Spoon a little into a bowl and serve.

STAGE 3: SIX TO NINE MONTHS

BABY PURÉE CAN BE PROCESSED OR MASHED BUT STILL NEEDS TO BE FAIRLY SOFT. A FEW SMALL BITS CAN BE INTRODUCED, BUT BE GUIDED BY YOUR BABY AND ADJUST THE TEXTURES AS REQUIRED. AS ALWAYS, DON'T RUSH THINGS AND GO AT YOUR BABY'S PACE.

IF YOU LIKE, LET YOUR BABY HOLD A SECOND SPOON WHILE YOU ARE FEEDING HER TO HELP DEVELOP COORDINATION. THIS IS THE FIRST STEP TOWARD SELF-FEEDING.

ALL THE RECIPES FROM THE PREVIOUS SECTION CAN STILL BE MADE FOR YOUR GROWING BABY; JUST ADJUST THE TEXTURE SO THAT FOODS ARE SLIGHTLY COARSER.

Suitable Foods

FOODS TO INCLUDE

- wheat-based foods, pasta, bread – first fingers of toast or bread sticks
- breakfast cereals such as oatmeal or Wheatina made up with cows' milk
- cows' milk and dairy foods, e.g. yogurt, cottage cheese, mild Cheddar and Edam cheese
- red meat, but make sure you trim off fat and gristle
- hard-boiled egg yolk
- citrus fruits
- fingers of cooked carrot, broccoli
- smooth peanut butter

Above: *At six to nine months your baby will be delighted to try pasta and cheese.*

FOODS TO AVOID

- egg white
- whole or chopped nuts
- canned fish in brine
- organ meats – liver, kidney
- chilies and other very spicy foods
- salty foods
- sugary foods

Right: *There is still a wide range of fatty, salty and spicy foods that must be avoided.*

Choosing a Highchair

There is a surprisingly wide choice of highchairs available in a range of finishes, colors and price levels so make sure you shop around before you buy.

Three-in-one type

Elevator type

CONVERTIBLE CHAIRS

Designed for babies between four weeks and six months, these chairs can convert from a highchair into a swing and some models into a baby chair and rocker too. It is best to buy one of these when the baby is very young so that you get maximum use from it. The only disadvantage may be the space required for the frame. The ease in converting from one type of chair to another varies from model to model, so you would be well advised to practice in the shop before buying. Most chairs have white painted frames.

THREE-IN-ONE CHAIRS

Various designs on the market convert into a separate chair, chair and table or highchair. Some simply clip apart while others require a little help with a screwdriver. There are good rigid structures available with a wide range of decorative seat patterns. They are available in wood or white finishes. The low chair is suitable for children up to four years old if used without the tray.

ELEVATOR CHAIRS

These slightly more expensive chairs convert from a highchair to a low chair. Some models have adjustable tray settings to fit a growing child. The frames are mostly available in white metal, with attractive seating.

TIPS

- For maximum use of a highchair, buy a booster cushion for the early days when your baby first begins to use the chair. Adjust the tray position as well, if possible.
- Check that the highchair is easy to clean – dried-on cereal can be impossible to clean off. Look out for possible dirt traps on the seat or around the tray fixing.
- Make sure that the chair is sturdy and rigid – it will need to withstand considerable wear.

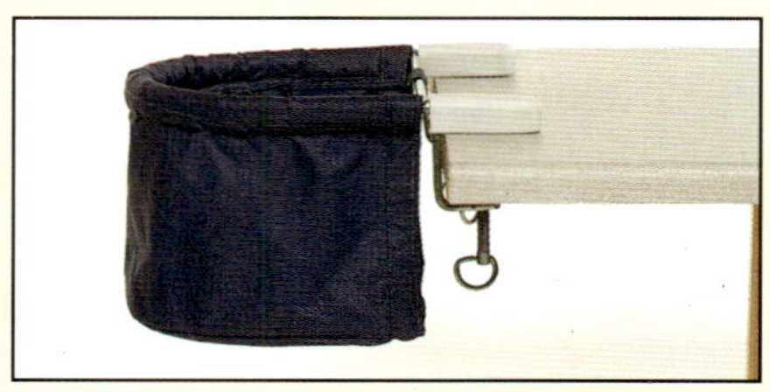

Above: *A portable clip-on chair.*

- If using a clip-on highchair make sure that the table is suitable and will be able to withstand the weight of your child. Never, in any circumstances, fix onto glass.

FOLDING CHAIRS

These less expensive chairs, available in wood or white finishes, usually fold up in a scissor movement. Some can be folded crosswise for packing into the trunk of the car. Before buying, check how easy they are to fold out and up and make sure the frame is rigid when opened out.

Folding type

1 Undo the tray catches by pressing both sides at once, and fold the tray upward.

2 Undo the side catches that keep the frame rigid so the chair can scissor in two.

3 This allows you to fold the chair over onto itself: the design is incredibly neat and compact.

4 It is now ready for storing, putting out of the way, or popping into the trunk of the car.

COUNTRY-TYPE CHAIRS

These are sturdy wooden high chairs usually with a wooden tray and attractive cottage-style spindle features. The seat can be hard for baby so it is best to buy a fitted chair cushion.

PORTABLE CHAIRS

There are two main types available:

- a very simple cloth tie, useful for visiting friends or eating out as it will fold up and fit in a bag. However, it is not really suitable for everyday use as the child is literally tied on to the chair and so cannot reach the table to feed himself.
- clip-on seats where the frames are placed under and over the edge of a dining table. Check that the table is strong enough and is not likely to overbalance before you put your baby in the chair.

TIPS

- Always use a safety harness. Although most highchairs have a three-point lap strap you will probably have to buy straps that will go around your baby's body and clip onto the chair. It is amazing how quickly a baby learns to wriggle out of a highchair when you're not looking.
- Never leave a child in a highchair unattended.

Above: *Always strap your baby in tightly.*

Shepherd's Pie Mash

Makes: 2½ cups

2 tomatoes
¼ onion
8oz potato
2oz button mushrooms
4oz lean ground beef
1 cup water
1 tbsp ketchup
pinch of dried mixed herbs

1 Make a cross cut in each tomato, put in a small bowl and cover with boiling water. Let stand for 1 minute and then drain and peel off the skins. Cut into quarters and scoop out the seeds.

2 Finely chop the onion, chop the potato and slice the mushrooms.

3 Fry the beef in a dry skillet. Brown for 5 minutes, stirring continuously.

- Suitable for freezing.

4 Add the tomatoes, potato, mushrooms and onion and cook for 3 minutes more. Stir well to blend all the flavors together.

5 Add the water, ketchup and herbs. Bring to a boil then reduce the heat, cover and simmer for 40 minutes until the meat and vegetables are tender.

6 Process or mash the meat and vegetables just enough to give the desired consistency.

7 Spoon a little into a bowl. Test the temperature and cool if necessary, before serving.

8 Cover and refrigerate as soon as possible. Use within 24 hours.

Braised Beef and Carrot Mash

Makes: 2½ cups

6oz potato
8oz carrots
¼ onion
6oz stewing beef
1¼ cups water
pinch of dried mixed herbs

1 Preheat the oven to 350°F. Peel and chop the potato, carrots and onion and place in a flameproof casserole.

2 Rinse the beef, cut away any fat and gristle and cut into small cubes using a sharp knife.

3 Add the meat, water and herbs to the casserole, bring to a boil and then cover and cook in the oven for 1½ hours or until the meat is tender and the vegetables are soft.

4 Process or mash the ingredients to the desired consistency and spoon a little into a bowl. Test the temperature and cool if necessary, before serving.

5 Cover any unused food and refrigerate as soon as possible. Use within 24 hours.

- Suitable for freezing.

TIP
Replace the carrots with any other root vegetable such as parsnip or rutabaga, if wished.

Lamb and Vegetable Mash

Makes: 2½ cups
4oz potato
4oz carrot
4oz rutabaga
2oz leek
4oz boneless lamb
1¼ cup water
pinch of dried rosemary

1 Peel the potato, carrot and rutabaga, rinse and chop into small cubes. Halve the leek lengthwise, rinse and slice. Place all the vegetables in a saucepan.

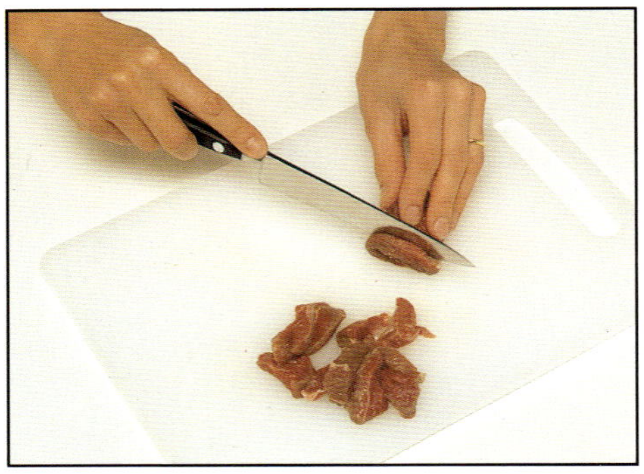

2 Rinse the lamb under cold water and chop into small pieces, discarding any fat.

3 Add the meat to the pan with the water and rosemary. Bring to a boil, cover and simmer for 30 minutes or until the lamb is thoroughly cooked.

4 Process or mash the ingredients to the desired consistency.

5 Spoon a little into a bowl, test the temperature and cool if necessary, before serving.

6 Cover the remaining food and refrigerate as soon as possible. Use within 24 hours.

- Suitable for freezing.

Lamb and Lentil Mash

Makes: 2½ cups

4oz boneless lamb
4oz rutabaga
1 celery stalk
2 tbsp red lentils
1 tbsp ketchup
1½ cups water

1 Rinse the lamb under cold water, trim off any fat and chop into small pieces. Peel the rutabaga, place in a colander with the celery and rinse with cold water. Chop into cubes and place in a saucepan.

2 Put the lentils in a strainer and rinse under cold water, picking out any black pieces. Add to the pan with the lamb and ketchup.

3 Add the water, bring to a boil, then cover and simmer for 40 minutes or until the lentils are soft. Add extra water during cooking if necessary, then process or mash to give the desired consistency.

4 Spoon a little into a bowl, test the temperature and cool if necessary, before serving.

5 Cover the remaining food and refrigerate as soon as possible. Use within 24 hours.

- Suitable for freezing.

VARIATION
Substitute green lentils or split peas for the red lentils and a small zucchini for the celery stalk.

Pork and Green Bean Mash

Makes: 1⅞ cups

- 4oz boneless, lean pork
- 4oz potato
- 4oz carrot
- 3oz green beans
- pinch of dried sage
- 1½ cups water

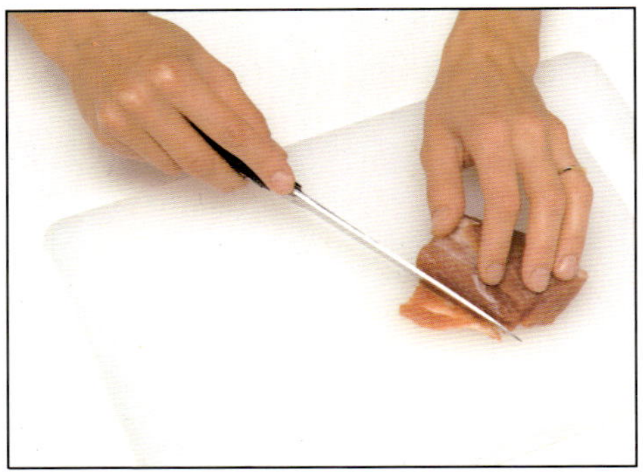

1 Rinse the pork under cold water, trim away any fat and gristle and chop into small cubes.

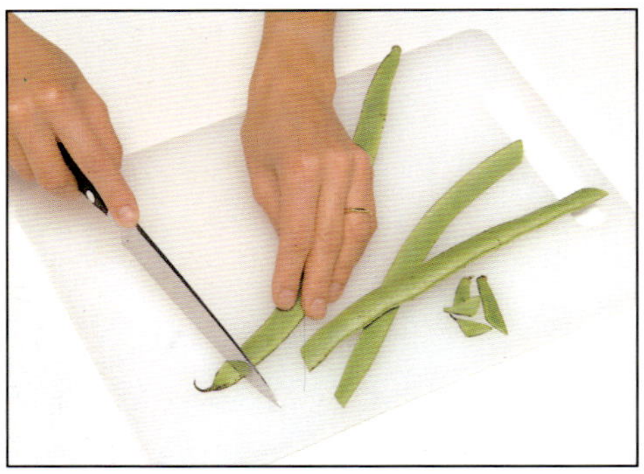

2 Peel the potato and carrot, trim the beans, rinse and chop.

TIP
Sugar peas or broccoli make tasty substitutes for green beans. Look for ready prepared diced pork in the supermarket. Cut the meat into smaller pieces and make sure to remove any gristle before cooking.

3 Put the pork, potato and carrot in a saucepan with the sage and water. Bring to a boil, cover and simmer for 30 minutes.

4 Add the beans and cook, covered, for 10 minutes more until all the vegetables are tender.

5 Process or mash to the desired consistency, then spoon a little into a bowl. Test the temperature before serving.

6 Cover and refrigerate as soon as possible. Use within 24 hours.

- Suitable for freezing.

VARIATION
Instead of the pork, use any lean meat in this recipe, such as chicken or turkey. Add broad beans, with the outer skins removed, in place of the green beans.

Pork and Apple Mash

Makes: 2½ cups
6oz boneless, lean pork
6oz potato
6oz rutabaga or parsnip
¼ onion
½ eating apple
1¼ cups water
pinch of dried sage

1 Preheat the oven to 350°F. Rinse the pork under cold water, trim away any fat and gristle then chop into small pieces. Peel and chop the vegetables. Peel, core and chop the apple.

2 Put the meat, vegetables, apple, water and sage in a flameproof casserole, cover and bring to a boil stirring once or twice.

3 Cover and cook in the oven for 1¼ hours until the meat is tender, then process or mash to the desired consistency.

4 Spoon a little into a bowl, test the temperature and cool if necessary, before serving.

5 Cover the remaining food and refrigerate as soon as possible. Use within 24 hours.

- Suitable for freezing.

TIP
The mixture can be cooked in a saucepan on the stove for 40 minutes if preferred.

Fish and Rice Mash

Makes: 2½ cups

¼ cup long grain rice
2 tbsp frozen peas
1½ cups formula
3oz frozen cod
2 hard-boiled egg yolks

1 Place the rice, peas, formula and fish in a saucepan, bring to a boil, cover and simmer for 15 minutes, until the fish is cooked and the rice is soft.

2 Lift the fish out of the pan and break into pieces with a knife and fork, checking for bones.

3 Stir the fish into the rice mixture and add the egg yolks.

TIP
Peas can be quite difficult to mash. Check the mixture before serving as whole peas are difficult for a baby to chew.

4 Mash with a fork to the desired consistency. Alternatively blend in a food processor, blender or press through a strainer.

5 Spoon a little into a bowl, test the temperature and cool if necessary, before serving.

6 Cover the remaining food and refrigerate as soon as possible. Use within 24 hours.

- Suitable for freezing.

Mediterranean Vegetable Mash

Makes: 2½ cups
3 tomatoes
6oz zucchini
3oz button mushrooms
4oz red bell pepper
4 tsp ketchup
1 cup water
pinch of dried mixed herbs
1½oz small pasta

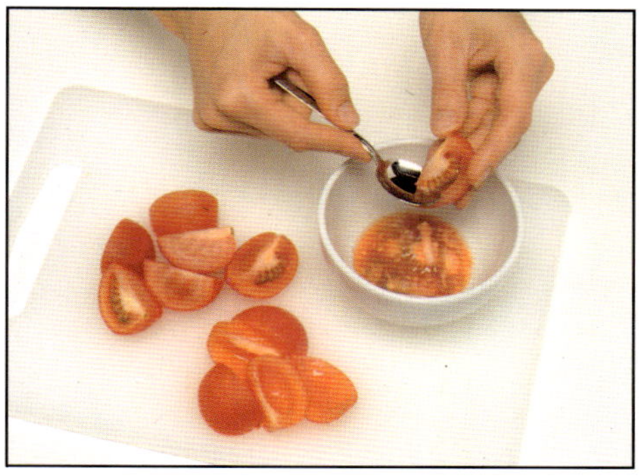

1 Make a cross cut in each tomato, put in a small bowl and cover with boiling water. Leave for 1 minute then drain and peel off the skins. Cut into quarters and scoop out the seeds from the tomatoes.

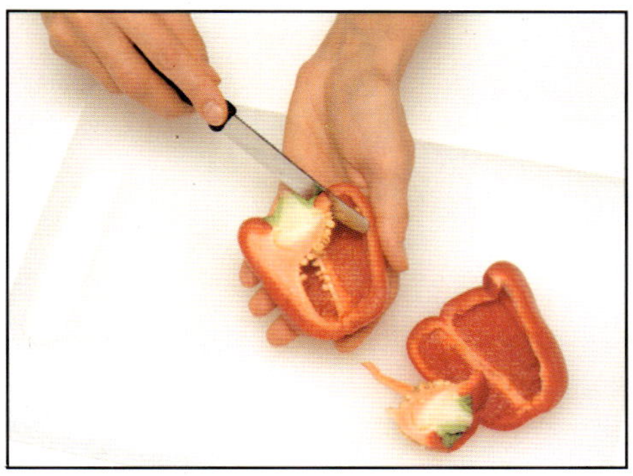

2 Trim the zucchini and mushrooms and cut away the core and seeds from the bell pepper.

3 Rinse and slice the zucchini and mushrooms. Chop the pepper.

4 Put the vegetables in a saucepan with the ketchup, water and herbs. Cover and simmer for 10 minutes or until tender.

5 Meanwhile cook the pasta in boiling water for 8–10 minutes until tender. Drain.

6 Mix the vegetables and pasta together and process or mash.

7 Spoon a little into a bowl, test the temperature and cool if necessary, before serving.

8 Cover the remaining food and refrigerate. Use within 24 hours.

- Suitable for freezing.

TIP
For adventurous eaters add ½ clove crushed garlic at Step 3.

Pasta and Vegetable Mash

Makes: 2½ cups

- 4oz carrot
- 2oz Brussels sprouts
- 1oz green beans
- 2 tbsp frozen corn
- 2oz small pasta
- 1½ cups formula
- 2oz mild Cheddar cheese

1 Peel the carrot, discard any discolored outer leaves from the sprouts and trim the beans. Rinse and then chop into pieces.

2 Place the vegetables, corn, pasta and formula in a saucepan, bring to a boil and then simmer, uncovered, for 12–15 minutes until the pasta is cooked.

TIP
Vary the vegetables depending on what you have available.

3 Grate the cheese and add to the vegetables, stirring until the cheese has completely melted.

4 Process or mash just enough to give the desired consistency, then spoon a little into a bowl. Test the temperature and cool if necessary, before serving.

5 Cover the remaining food and refrigerate as soon as possible. Use within 24 hours.

- Suitable for freezing.

Apple and Orange Custard

Makes: 1 cup
2 eating apples
1 tsp grated orange zest and 1 tbsp orange juice
1 tbsp instant vanilla custard
1 tsp superfine sugar
⅔ cup formula

1 Quarter, core and peel the apples. Slice and place the apples in a saucepan with the orange zest and juice.

2 Cover and cook gently for 10 minutes, stirring occasionally until the apples are soft.

3 Blend the instant custard and sugar with a little of the formula to make a smooth paste. Bring the remaining formula to a boil and stir into the custard mixture.

4 Return the custard to the pan and slowly bring to a boil, stirring until thickened and smooth.

5 Process or mash the apple to the desired consistency. Add the custard and stir to mix.

6 Spoon a little into a bowl, test the temperature and cool if necessary, before serving.

7 Cover the remaining food and refrigerate as soon as possible. Use within 24 hours.

- Suitable for freezing.

Orchard Fruit Dessert

Makes: 1⅞ cups

- 1 ripe pear
- 8oz ripe plums
- 1 tbsp superfine sugar
- 1 tbsp instant vanilla custard
- ⅔ cup formula

1 Quarter, core, peel and slice the pear. Wash the plums, then cut in half, pit and slice.

2 Put the fruit in a saucepan with 1 tbsp water and 2 tsp of the sugar. Cover and cook gently for 10 minutes until soft.

3 Blend the instant custard, remaining sugar and a little of the formula to a smooth paste.

4 Bring the remaining formula to a boil and gradually stir into the custard mixture. Pour the custard back into the pan and bring to a boil, stirring, until it is both thickened and smooth.

5 Process or mash the fruit to the desired consistency and stir in the custard. Spoon a little into a bowl, test the temperature and cool if necessary, before serving.

6 Cover the remaining custard and refrigerate as soon as possible. Use within 24 hours.

- Suitable for freezing.

Peach Melba Yogurt

Makes: ¾ cup
1 ripe peach
1oz fresh or frozen raspberries
1 tbsp confectioner's sugar
4oz plain yogurt

1 Halve the peach, discard the pit then peel and slice. Place in a saucepan with the raspberries and 1 tbsp water.

2 Cover and cook gently for 10 minutes until soft.

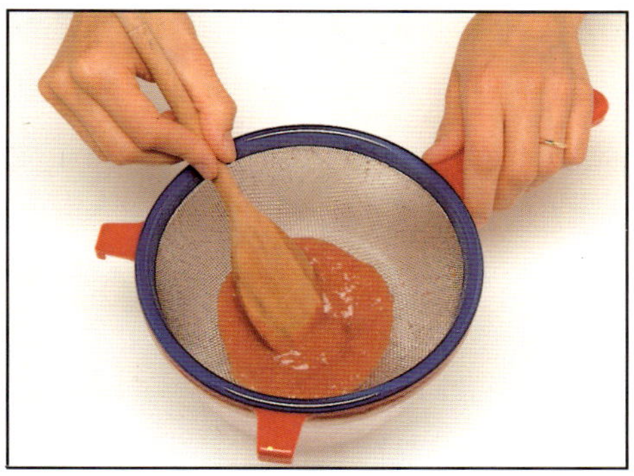

3 Purée and press through a strainer to remove the pips.

TIP
The finished dessert is not suitable for freezing although the sweetened fruit purée can be frozen successfully in sections of an ice cube tray. Defrost cubes of purée and mix each cube with about 1 tbsp yogurt.

4 Set aside to cool then stir in the sugar and swirl in the yogurt. Spoon a little into a baby dish.

5 Cover the remaining food and refrigerate as soon as possible. Use within 24 hours.

VARIATION
Bananarama
To make a single portion, use ½ a small banana and 1 tbsp of plain yogurt. Mash the banana until smooth and add the yogurt. Stir to mix and serve immediately. Do not make this dessert in advance, as the banana will discolor while standing.

STAGE 4: NINE TO TWELVE MONTHS

GRADUALLY PROGRESS FROM GROUND TO CHOPPED OR ROUGHLY MASHED FOOD. BY NOW YOUR BABY WILL BE ABLE TO JOIN IN WITH FAMILY MEALS AND EAT A LITTLE OF WHAT YOU ARE EATING. ENSURE THAT YOUR BABY IS EATING THREE MAIN MEALS AND TWO TO THREE SNACK MEALS PER DAY. YOUNG CHILDREN DEVELOP AT AN INCREDIBLY FAST RATE AND SO NEED TO EAT LITTLE AND OFTEN TO SUSTAIN ENERGY AND GROWTH LEVELS.

AGAIN FOODS FROM THE PREVIOUS SECTIONS CAN STILL BE SERVED TO YOUR BABY; JUST ADJUST THE TEXTURES AS NECESSARY.

Suitable Foods

FOODS TO INCLUDE

- whole eggs
- finely ground nuts
- more flavorings – bouillon cubes if part of a family-size casserole
- greater selection of finger foods – slices of peeled fruit (such as apple or pear), cooked carrot sticks and cucumber sticks, small cubes of cooked chicken
- selection of foods from the four main food groups

Left: *Finger foods – such as chopped vegetables and fruit pieces – come into their own at this age, and children love to help themselves.*

Apple, carrot and cucumber

Whole egg

Above: *Inquisitive children love the time when they can join the family at the table.*

FOODS TO AVOID

- keep salt to a minimum and omit if possible
- sugar: add just enough to make the food appetizing without being overly sweet
- honey
- fat: trim visible fat off raw meat, grill rather than fry
- organ meats – liver, kidney

Below: Though now a very small list, there are still some foods it is important to omit.

Bouillon cubes

Ground nuts

I can feed myself!

Encouraging your baby to feed herself can be a truly messy business. Some babies are interested from a very early age and those little fingers seem to move like lightning grabbing the bowl or the spoon you're using to feed them with. While foods are still finely puréed, give your baby a second spoon to play with, leaving you more able to spoon in the real lunch.

As your baby grows offer her a few finger foods to hold and hopefully eat, while you continue to feed from a spoon. Cooked carrot sticks, broccoli and cauliflower florets are soft on a young mouth and easy to chew. As your baby grows you can introduce bread sticks and toast fingers.

Encourage your baby to pick up foods and as her coordination improves and she gets the idea, more food will actually go where it is intended. Try to cut down on the mess by rolling up your baby's sleeves and covering clothes with a large bib, preferably with sleeves.

Above: *A bib with sleeves.*

Remove any hair bands and have a wet washcloth at the ready.

Although it is tempting not to allow a baby to feed herself, try not to be frustrated by the mess. Babies who are encouraged to feed themselves will probably be more adventurous later on and you will probably find there is less mess than

TEACHING YOUR BABY TO FEED ITSELF

1 Cover your baby well – this can be very messy! Give her a spoon of her own to play with.

2 While you are feeding your baby, allow her to play with the food – with her hands or the spoon.

3 Let your baby use the cup and spoon by herself. Don't worry about spillage – there are bound to be lots of slips at this stage.

4 Keep tissues or a damp washcloth available and clean as you go. Be patient and take things slowly.

with a baby who is always spoon fed and keeps grabbing at the bowl. In addition, she will be able to join in your family meals and also give you the chance to eat your own meal before it goes cold.

Left: *It is a real delight when your baby can begin to feed independently. Not only can you start to eat with your baby, and relax a little more, but she will also enjoy setting her own pace and eating her meal in the order she chooses. At this stage the family can usually return to eating together around the table as a group.*

WHAT TO DO IF YOUR CHILD CHOKES

- Don't waste time trying to remove food from your baby's mouth unless it can be done easily.
- Turn your baby, head down, supporting her head with your forearm and slap firmly between the shoulder blades.
- If this does not work, try again.
- Don't hesitate to call your doctor or emergency services if worried.

Above: *Don't be afraid to take quick, firm action in an emergency.*

COPING WITH THE MESS

As babies grow so too does the amount of mess! It can seem incredible how just a few tablespoons of lunch can be spread across so many surfaces and so many items of clothing.

- Choose a large bib. Fabric bibs with a plastic liner are the most comfortable for babies to wear when tiny, moving on to a plastic pelican-style bib to catch the spills as they grow older. Check the back of your baby's neck as these can rub.
- If you plan to feed your baby in the dining room, then protect the carpet with an old sheet, pieces of newspaper or plastic tablecloth or drop cloth. It is vital to take this with you if visiting friends.
- Give your baby a second spoon or small toy to play with so that she doesn't make a grab for the spoon you are using.

Above: *A hard plastic "pelican" bib.*

Above: *A plastic tablecloth or drop cloth on the floor will avoid carpet stains.*

FINGER FOODS

Finger foods are not only fun to eat but help your baby's coordination. Snacks play an important part in a young child's diet as appetites may be small, but energy and growth needs are great. Choose foods that are nutrient dense and avoid sweet sugary snacks such as chocolate cookies.

Above: *Your baby can eat at her own pace until she is full.*

TIPS

- Always make sure baby is comfortable either on your lap or strapped into a baby chair or highchair.
- Check the temperature of the food and make sure it is not too hot.
- Change the texture of the food: some babies like quite wet mixtures, some hate lumps, some like a few lumps for interest, others prefer food they can pick up – tiny ham sandwiches, thick slices of grilled fish finger, even picking up peas and corn.
- Encourage your baby to feed herself; don't worry about mess – your baby is still learning – but just mop up sticky hands and face at the end.
- Try to keep calm. If your baby keeps spitting food out, you may find it less upsetting to offer store-bought food rather than homemade so you don't feel you've been wasting your time cooking.
- Try not to let your baby see you're upset or angry. Even a one-year-old can sense the power she can have over you.
- If solid meals are well established, give her a drink at the end of the meal so that she is not filled up with milk before she begins.
- Avoid cookies and sweets as your baby will soon learn that if she makes a fuss when the main dish is offered, then dessert will soon follow.
- Remember no baby will starve herself. Continue offering a variety of food and don't despair.

Above: *Give drinks at the end of the meal, or they will fill her up before she eats.*

Coping with a fussy eater

All children are fussy eaters at some stage. If mealtimes are always calm and plates always clean then your family must be one in a million. Even very young children learn the power they have over their parents and mealtimes give them a great opportunity to exercise it. Here are some common problems and advice on how to deal with them.

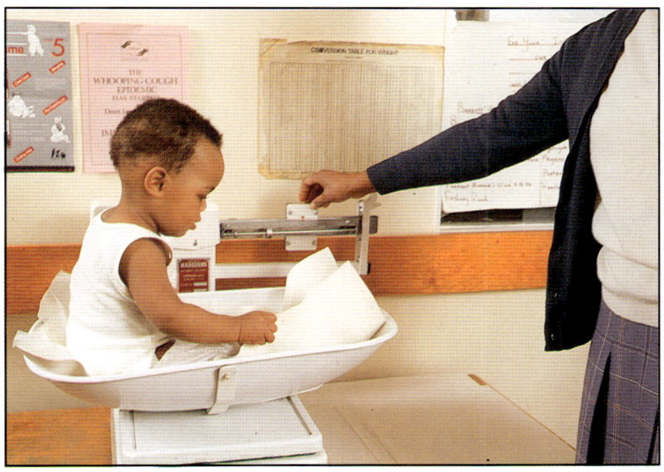

Above: *Don't worry when you encounter resistance in feeding: there never has been a baby that likes all foods, all the time.*

Left: *If you have serious anxieties, see your doctor and get your baby's weight checked regularly.*

BABY SPITS OUT FOOD

You may be trying to wean your baby too soon or possibly she simply doesn't like the taste of the food. If you started with baby rice then go on to potato or parsnip purée or a little applesauce mixed into the baby rice. If that fails, your baby may simply not be ready for solids just yet. Try again in a week or two's time.

BABY APPEARS TO GAG

Some babies just cannot cope with solids at first and may seem distressed and almost gag on the food. Try thinning down the food with a little more breast milk, formula or water, since the food may be too thick. Alternatively, you may be putting too much food on the spoon; try offering the baby a little less. If neither of these seems to help, stop solids and breast or bottle feed as usual, giving her plenty of reassuring cuddles. Try again in a few days' or weeks' time. If your baby is nearly six months old then don't hesitate to ask your doctor for advice.

BABY SEEMS TO HAVE A SMALL APPETITE

Babies' appetites, like adults', vary enormously. Don't force feed your baby; if she's been eating well and then turns her head away or starts spitting it out, it's a pretty clear indication that she's had enough, even if the amount does seem very small to you. Resist the temptation to encourage the baby to clean the plate: it is never helpful to force children of any age, and can be extremely counterproductive. If you're worried, talk to your pediatrician and regularly check your baby's weight.

Going Vegetarian

Above: *Raising your child as a vegetarian takes special planning and care.*

A vegetarian diet can provide all the necessary nutrients for health and vitality, but it is important to balance the baby's diet to ensure that she receives adequate supplies of protein, vitamins D and B12, calcium and iron.

The basic guidelines are the same as for weaning any other baby; introduce flavors slowly and be guided by your baby. The biggest differences are obviously in the type of foods offered. Instead of obtaining protein from meat and fish, your baby will receive it from other protein-rich food. These include eggs, legumes, split lentils and grains, finely ground nuts or nut creams, sunflower seed spread, milk and dairy products and vegetarian cheese where available.

Vegetarians need to make sure that sufficient iron is included in their baby's diet. If she is over six months, offer prune juice, puréed apricots, molasses, refined lentils and cereals, particularly fortified breakfast cereals. Green vegetables and well-mashed beans, if over eight months, are also a good source of iron. Vitamin C aids absorption of iron from plant sources so make sure you serve fresh green vegetables or fruit in the meal. Your doctor may also feel it beneficial for your baby to take vitamin drops.

If you plan to bring the baby up as a vegan and so omit dairy products and eggs from the diet, then it is vital to consult your doctor or dietician.

Vegetarian diets tend to be bulky and lower in calories than a diet containing meats so make sure you include foods that are protein and calorie rich, with little or no fiber, such as eggs, milk and cheese. These can be mixed with smaller quantities of vegetables, fruit and cereals. Fiber-rich foods can also be difficult for a child to digest as many nutrients may pass straight through.

To ensure your baby is getting the correct amount of vitamins, minerals and food energy her diet should include foods from the four groups on the opposite page:

Oranges

Carrots

Cucumber

Grapes

Cereals and grains: rice around four months; pasta, bread, oats, and breakfast cereals from six months.

Fruit and vegetables: begin with potato, carrot, apple and pear around four months, progressing to stronger-flavored foods as your baby develops.

Dairy produce: including milk, cheese and yogurt from six months. *Note:* Make sure cheese is rennet-free. If you are unsure, ask the delicatessen assistant, or check the package if pre-packed.

Beans and legumes: split peas and cooked lentils from five or six months. Gradual introduction of tofu, smooth peanut butter, hard-boiled egg yolks from six months. Well cooked mashed dried beans and peas and finely ground nuts from nine months. Do not give whole nuts to the under fives.

To make sure your baby is thriving and happy, irrespective of the type of diet, make sure you check your baby's weight at regular intervals at the pediatrician's.

Lentils

Split peas

Baby lentils

The Importance of a Varied Diet

Once your baby progresses to more varied fruit and vegetable purées, you are really beginning to lay down the foundations for a healthy eating pattern and sound nutritional habits that will take your baby through childhood and into adult life.

It is vitally important to include portions of food from each of the four main food groups per day. But do make sure that the types of food you choose are suitable for the age of your child.

Left: *Your baby is now at the age where the diet can and should be as diverse as any adult's. Variety is crucial for health reasons, and also has the benefit of allowing you many options for tempting and maintaining the kind of interest in all types of food that will ensure that good eating habits develop for the future.*

Group 1: *Cereals, bread, potatoes, rice and pasta*

Group 2: *Fruit and vegetables* – bland tastes to start, such as potato, rutabaga and parsnip, then stronger flavors

Group 3: *Meat and meat alternatives* – meat, poultry, fish, eggs, legumes (peas, beans and lentils), tofu, finely ground nuts

Group 4: *Milk and milk products* – milk, including soya milk, cheese, yogurt (plain at first, then flavored)

There are two more food groups that add palatability to the diet as well as contributing energy.

Group 5: *Sugars*

Group 6: *Fats and oils*

It is not recommended you add sugar to baby foods or give lots of sugary drinks, particularly in the early days of weaning. Many of us have an inherent need for sweetness but to cater to this without building in bad habits try and include foods in the diet that are naturally sweet. Choose eating apples instead of very tart cooking apples, mix bananas or ripe apricots with sharper-tasting fruits.

For those foods that are very tart try and add 1 tsp sugar per portion, so they become palatable without being overly sweet. Given the choice your baby would prefer sweet flavors to savory so make sure you include a good range of tastes in the diet. Too much sugar or sweetened foods or drinks at this stage could lead to tooth decay before the teeth are even through.

Try to avoid offering cookies as a mid-morning or afternoon snack. Try to encourage your baby to eat:

- a piece of banana
- a plain bread roll
- a few triangles of toast
- a milky drink
- a small container of yogurt

Watch the amounts of fat and oil you include in the diet. Avoid frying especially when preparing first foods as young babies have difficulty digesting such foods. As your baby develops, you can spread toast fingers with a little butter or margarine or offer a few oven-baked "fries" as easy-to-hold finger foods. Maintain the milk feedings and introduce whole cows' milk after one year as the main drink of the day. Don't be tempted to serve skim milk as the valuable fat-soluble vitamins A and D will be lost, and your baby may not get the energy needed for growth.

Above: *A piece of fruit or chopped vegetable is always preferable to a cookie.*

HOMEMADE OR MANUFACTURED FOODS?

Most mothers use a combination of the two. Store-bought baby foods are convenient and often easier to use if going out for the day or until your baby's meals coincide with the rest of the family. Jarred baby foods can be useful in the very early days when baby is eating only a teaspoon of food at each meal. On the other hand, homemade foods can be batch cooked or made with some of the ingredients from the main family meal and are often less trouble than you would expect. Added to this is the satisfaction of knowing your baby has eaten a wholesome meal and hopefully is acquiring a taste for home cooking.

Left: *Don't always assume that all homemade foods are better and more nutritious than all manufactured foods. There are now some excellent products available for purchase that can save you time and effort and add hugely to your repertoire without any loss of dietary values.*

Lamb and Couscous

Makes: 3⅓ cups
4oz carrot
4oz rutabaga
¼ onion
6oz boneless lamb
1 tsp oil
2 tsp tomato or vegetable paste
2 tbsp currants or raisins
1¼ cups water
2oz couscous

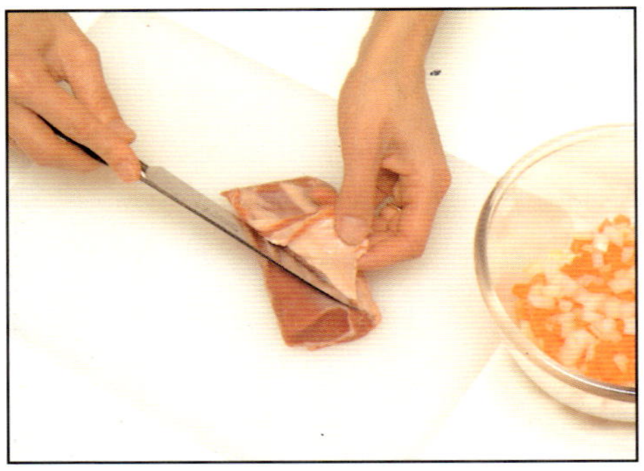

1 Peel the carrot, rutabaga and onion, rinse and chop. Rinse the lamb, trim off any fat, and chop.

2 Heat the oil in a saucepan, and sauté the lamb until browned.

3 Add the vegetables, cook for 2 minutes then stir in the paste, currants and water. Cover and simmer for 25 minutes.

4 Rinse the couscous in a strainer. Cover and steam the couscous over the lamb pan for 5 minutes.

5 Chop or process the lamb mixture to the desired consistency. Fluff up the couscous with a fork and add to the lamb mixture stirring well.

6 Spoon a little into a bowl, test the temperature and cool if necessary, before serving.

7 Cover the remaining food and refrigerate as soon as possible. Use within 24 hours.

- Suitable for freezing.

TIP
Vegetable paste can be found in some specialty stores. Otherwise substitute tomato paste.

Paprika Pork

Makes: 2½ cups

6oz boneless, lean pork
3oz carrot
6oz potato
¼ onion
¼ red bell pepper
1tsp oil
½ tsp paprika
⅔ cup baked beans
⅔ cup water

1 Preheat the oven to 350°F. Rinse the pork under cold water, pat dry with paper toweling and carefully trim away any fat or gristle. Cut the pork into cubes.

2 Peel the carrot, potato and onion. Cut away the core and remove any seeds from the pepper. Put into a colander, rinse under cold water then chop into small pieces.

3 Heat the oil in a flameproof casserole, add the pork and sauté for a few minutes, stirring until browned. Add the vegetables, cook for 2 minutes then add the paprika, baked beans and water.

4 Bring to a boil, then cover and cook in the oven for 1¼ hours until the pork is tender.

5 Chop or process the mixture to the desired consistency, then spoon a little into a bowl. Test the temperature and cool if necessary, before serving.

6 Cover the remaining food and refrigerate as soon as possible. Use within 24 hours.

- Suitable for freezing.

TIP
If using a food processor, drain off most of the liquid. Process then stir in the liquid until the desired texture is reached.

Chicken and Celery Supper

Makes: 2½ cups
6oz chicken thighs, skinned and boned
¼ onion
8oz carrots
3oz celery
1 tsp oil
2 tsp tomato or vegetable paste
1 cup water

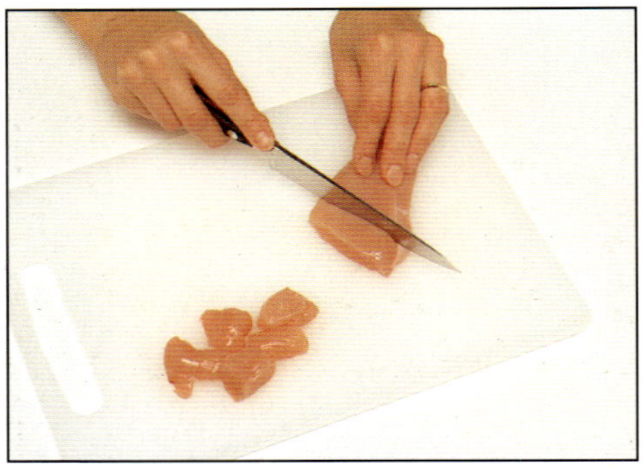

1 Rinse the chicken under cold water, pat dry, trim off any fat and cut into chunks.

2 Peel, trim and rinse the vegetables and cut into dice.

3 Heat the oil in a saucepan, add the chicken and onion and sauté for a few minutes, stirring until browned. Add the carrots, celery, paste and water. Bring to a boil, cover and simmer for 20 minutes until tender.

4 Chop or process the mixture to the desired consistency. If using a food processor, process the solids first and then add the liquid a little at a time.

5 Spoon a little into a bowl, test the temperature and cool if necessary, before serving.

6 Cover the remaining food and refrigerate as soon as possible. Use within 24 hours.

- Suitable for freezing.

TIP
For extra flavor, add homemade broth instead of the water, or use a bouillon cube, but make sure it is low in sodium.

Cauliflower and Broccoli with Cheese

Makes: 2½ cups

- 6oz cauliflower
- 6oz broccoli
- 6oz potato
- 1¼ cups formula
- 3oz mild Cheddar cheese

1 Rinse the vegetables, then break the cauliflower and broccoli into florets. Slice the tender stems but cut out and discard any woody core from the cauliflower. Peel and chop the potatoes into cubes.

2 Place the vegetables and formula in a saucepan, bring to a boil, cover and simmer for 12–15 minutes until quite tender.

3 Grate the cheese and add to the vegetables stirring until the cheese has melted.

4 Process or mash the mixture to the desired consistency, adding a little extra formula if necessary.

5 Spoon a little into a bowl, test the temperature and cool if necessary, before serving.

6 Cover the remaining food and refrigerate as soon as possible. Use within 24 hours.

- Suitable for freezing.

Noodles with Broccoli and Ham

Makes: 2½ cups
4oz broccoli
2oz thinly sliced ham
2oz Cheddar cheese
1¼ cups formula
2oz noodles

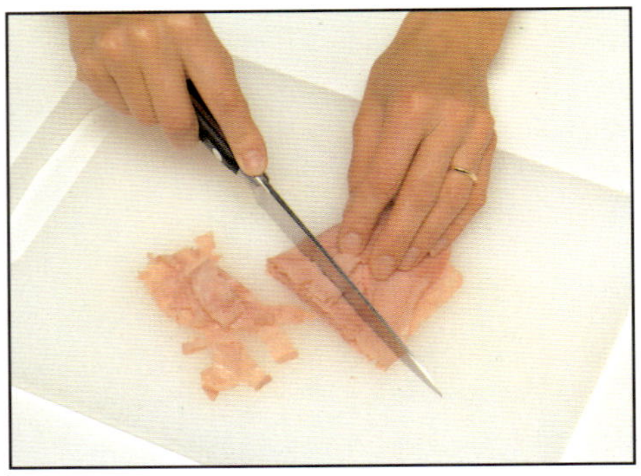

1 Rinse the broccoli and cut into small florets, chopping the stalks. Chop the ham and grate the Cheddar cheese.

2 Pour the formula into a saucepan, bring to a boil and add the noodles. Simmer, uncovered, for 5 minutes.

3 Add the broccoli and cook for 10 minutes until tender.

TIP
Pasta swells on standing so you may need to thin the cooled leftover mixture with extra formula before reheating.

4 Add the ham and cheese to the broccoli and noodles, stirring until the cheese has melted.

5 Chop or process the mixture to the desired consistency and then spoon a little into a bowl. Test the temperature and cool if necessary, before serving.

6 Cover the remaining food and refrigerate as soon as possible. Use within 24 hours.

- Suitable for freezing.

Lentils and Vegetables

Makes: 2½ cups

¼ cup red lentils
¼ onion
½ tsp ground coriander
¼ tsp turmeric
1½ cups water
3oz potato
3oz carrot
3oz cauliflower
3oz green cabbage

1 Rinse the lentils under cold water, discarding any black bits.

2 Peel and chop the onion, then add to a saucepan with the lentils, spices and water. Bring to a boil, cover and simmer for 20 minutes.

3 Peel and chop the potato and carrot. Finely chop the cabbage and break the cauliflower into small florets.

4 Stir the vegetables into the pan. Cook for 12–15 minutes.

5 Chop or process to the desired consistency, adding a little extra boiled water if necessary.

6 Spoon a little into a bowl, test the temperature and cool if necessary, before serving.

7 Cover the remaining food and refrigerate as soon as possible. Use within 24 hours.

- Suitable for freezing.

Fish and Potato Mash

Makes: 1⅞ cups

8oz potato
2oz leek
2oz button mushrooms
3oz frozen cod
1 cup formula
2oz Cheddar cheese, grated

1 Peel the potato, halve the leek and trim the mushrooms. Place all the vegetables in a colander and rinse well with cold water, drain, then chop the vegetables.

2 Place the vegetables in a saucepan with the frozen fish and formula. Bring to a boil, cover and simmer for 15 minutes, until the fish is cooked and the potatoes are tender when pierced with a knife.

3 Lift the fish out of pan with a slotted spoon and break into pieces with a knife and fork checking carefully for bones.

4 Return the fish to the pan and stir in the grated cheese. Chop or process the mixture to give the desired consistency.

5 Spoon a little into a bowl, test the temperature and cool if necessary, before serving.

6 Cover the remaining food and refrigerate as soon as possible. Use within 24 hours.

- Suitable for freezing.

Fish and Bell Pepper Rice

Makes: 1⅞ cups
2oz celery
2oz red bell pepper
1¼ cups water
¼ cup long grain rice
2 tsp ketchup
3oz frozen cod

1 Trim the celery and discard the core and seeds from the pepper. Rinse and chop the vegetables.

2 Bring the water to a boil in a saucepan and add the vegetables, rice, ketchup and fish.

3 Bring back to a boil, then reduce heat, cover and simmer for 15 minutes, until the rice is tender and the fish is cooked.

4 Lift the fish out of the pan with a slotted spoon. Use a knife and fork to check for bones.

5 Stir the fish back into the pan and then chop or process.

6 Spoon a little fish mixture into a small bowl, test the temperature and cool if necessary, before serving.

7 Cover the remaining food and refrigerate as soon as possible. Use within 24 hours.

- Suitable for freezing.

Chocolate Pudding

Makes: 2
1 tsp cocoa
1 tsp superfine sugar
⅔ cup formula or milk
1 egg

1 Preheat the oven to 350°F. Blend the cocoa and sugar with a little of the formula in a small bowl to make a smooth paste. Stir in the remaining formula and then pour the mixture into a saucepan.

2 Bring just to a boil. Beat the egg in a bowl then gradually stir in the hot formula, mixing well to a smooth consistency.

3 Strain the mixture into two ramekin dishes to remove any egg solids.

4 Place the dishes in a roasting pan or shallow cake pan. Pour boiling water into the pan to come halfway up the sides of the dishes.

5 Cook in the oven for 15–20 minutes or until the custard has set. Leave to cool.

6 Refrigerate as soon as possible. Serve one pudding and use the second within 24 hours.

Vanilla Custards

Makes: 2

1 egg

1 tsp superfine sugar

few drops vanilla extract

⅔ cup formula or milk

1 Preheat the oven to 350°F. Using a fork, beat the egg, sugar and vanilla extract together in a bowl.

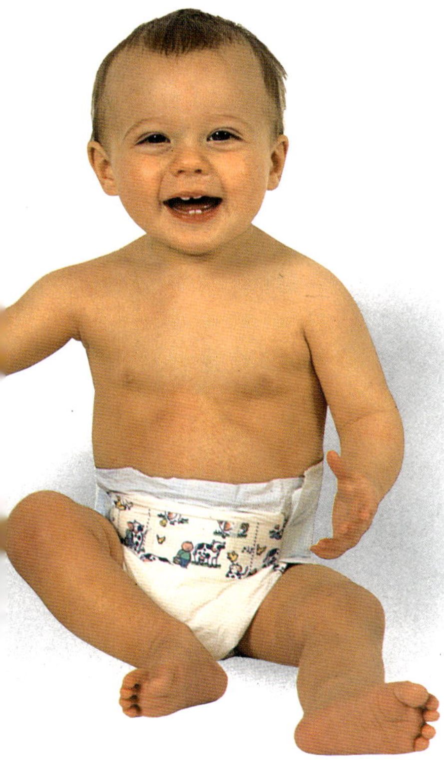

2 Pour the formula into a small saucepan and heat until it is just to a boil.

3 Gradually stir the formula into the egg mixture, whisking or beating until smooth.

4 Strain into two ramekin dishes and place in a roasting pan. Add enough boiling water to come halfway up the sides of the dishes.

5 Bake for 15–20 minutes or until the custard has set. Cool and serve as for **Chocolate Pudding**.

Flavored Bread Sticks

Makes: 36

oil, for greasing
5oz pizza dough mix
flour, for dusting
1 tsp Marmite (yeast extract)
1 egg yolk

1 Brush two baking sheets with a little oil. Put the pizza mix in a bowl, add the quantity of water as directed on the package and mix to make a smooth dough.

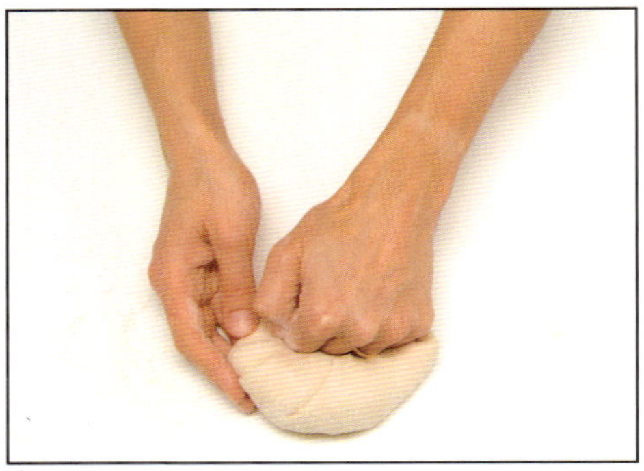

2 Knead on a lightly floured surface for 5 minutes until smooth and elastic.

3 Roll out to a 9in square. Cut into 3 × ½in strips, twisting each to give a corkscrew effect. Arrange on the baking sheets, spaced slightly apart.

4 Mix the Marmite and egg yolk together and brush over the bread sticks. Loosely cover with oiled plastic wrap and leave in a warm place for 20–30 minutes to rise.

5 Meanwhile preheat the oven to 425°F. Bake the bread sticks for 8–10 minutes until well risen. Loosen but let cool on the baking sheet.

6 Serve one or two sticks. Store the rest in a plastic container for up to three days.

- Suitable for freezing up to three months in a plastic bag.

French Toast

Makes: 16
2 slices bread
1 egg
2 tbsp formula or milk

1 Trim the crusts off the bread, then cut each slice in half.

2 Beat the egg and milk in a shallow dish and dip the bread, one slice at a time, into the egg until coated on both sides.

3 Heat a little butter and oil in a frying pan. Add the bread and fry until browned on both sides.

4 Cool slightly, cut into fingers and serve as finger food or as part of a meal.

Cheese Sticks

Makes: 42

- oil, for greasing
- 1½ cups all-purpose flour
- 6 tbsp butter or margarine, cut into pieces
- 4oz Cheddar cheese, grated
- 1 egg, beaten

1 Preheat the oven to 400°F. Brush two large baking sheets lightly with the oil.

2 Place the flour in a bowl, add the butter or margarine and rub in until the mixture resembles fine breadcrumbs. Stir in the grated Cheddar cheese.

3 Reserve 1 tbsp beaten egg and then stir the rest into the pastry mixture. Mix to a smooth dough, adding water if necessary.

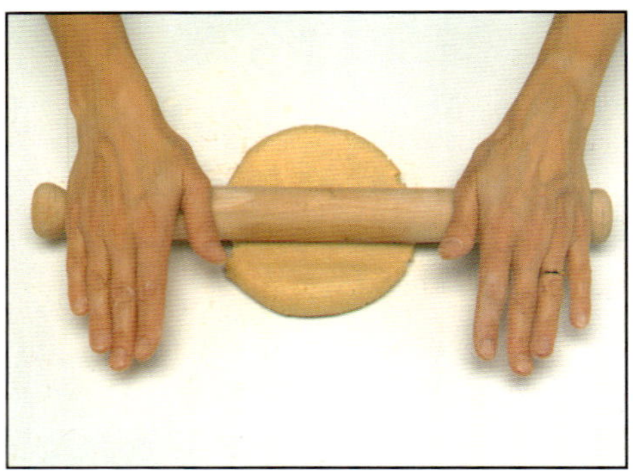

4 Knead lightly and roll out on a floured surface to a 12 × 8in rectangle. Brush with the remaining egg.

5 Cut the pastry into 3 × ½in strips and place on the baking sheets, spaced slightly apart.

6 Bake the cheese sticks in the oven for 8–10 minutes until golden brown. Loosen but let cool on the baking sheets.

7 Serve one or two sticks and store the rest in a plastic container for up to 1 week.

- Suitable for freezing up to three months in a plastic container, layered with wax paper.

TIP
Begin making these with mild cheese and as your child gets more adventurous change to stronger flavored cheese.

Mini Cupcakes

Makes: 26
4 tbsp soft margarine
¼ cup superfine sugar
⅓ cup self-rising flour
1 egg

1 Preheat the oven to 350°F. Separate 26 paper mini muffin cups and place on a large baking sheet, spaced slightly apart.

2 Put all the ingredients for the cakes into a mixing bowl and beat together well until smooth.

3 Divide the mixture among the cups and cook for 8–10 minutes until well risen and golden.

4 Transfer the cakes to a wire rack and leave to cool completely, then peel the paper off one or two cakes and serve.

5 Store the remaining cupcakes in a plastic container for up to three days.

• Suitable for freezing up to three months in a plastic container.

TIP
Cut a cupcake in half crosswise and spread one half with a little sugar-free jelly. Replace the top half and serve to baby.

Sugar Cookie Shapes

Makes: 60

oil, for greasing

1 cup all-purpose flour

3 tbsp cornstarch

¼ cup superfine sugar

½ cup butter

extra superfine sugar, for sprinkling (optional)

1 Preheat the oven to 350°F. Brush two baking sheets with a little oil.

2 Put the flour, cornstarch and sugar in a bowl. Cut the butter into pieces and rub into the flour until the mixture resembles fine breadcrumbs. Mold to a dough with your hands.

3 Knead lightly and roll out on a floured surface to a ¼in thickness. Stamp out shapes with small cookie or petits fours cutters.

4 Transfer to the baking sheets, sprinkle with extra sugar, if using, and cook for 10–12 minutes until pale golden. Loosen with a knife and let cool on the baking sheets, then transfer to a wire rack.

5 Offer one or two shapes and store the rest in plastic containers for up to one week.

TIP

These cookies will keep well in the freezer for three months. Pack in rigid plastic containers and thaw in a single layer. If preferred, freeze the cookies before baking. Wrap well to prevent them taking up flavors from other food.

FOOD FOR TODDLERS

Once your child has reached 12 months he or she will be enjoying a varied diet and eating habits and their personal food preferences will be developing. It is now vitally important to lay the foundations of a good and well balanced eating regimen.

This is a time when food fads may also develop. Try to weather this period of fussy eating – all children will experience it at some time, and even good eaters will go through a picky stage. Hopefully the fad will go as quickly as it comes, but while it lasts mealtimes can become a nightmare.

Coping With a Fussy Eater

We all have different sized appetites whatever our age, and young children are no exception. Children's appetites fluctuate greatly and often decrease just before a growth spurt. All children go through food fads; some just seem to last longer and be more difficult than others.

A toddler's appetite varies enormously and you may find that she will eat very well one day and eat hardly anything the next. Be guided by your toddler and try to think in terms of what the child has eaten over several days rather than just concentrating on one day.

At the time, it can be really frustrating and worrying. Try not to think of the food that you have just thrown away but try to think more of the long term. Jot down the foods that your child has actually eaten over three or four days or up to a week. You may actually be surprised, it's not just juice and chips after all!

Once you have a list you may find a link between the foods your child eats and the time of day. Perhaps your child eats better when eating with the family, or when the house is quiet. If you do find a link then build on it. You might find that your child is snacking on chocolate, doughnuts, soft drinks or fries when out with friends, and that fussiness at home is really a full tummy. Or it may be that by cutting out a milky drink and a cookie mid-morning and offering a sliced apple instead, your child may not be so full come lunch time. Perhaps you could hide the cookie box once visitors have had one, so that tiny hands can't keep reaching for more.

If your toddler seems hungrier at breakfast then you could offer eggy bread, a grilled sausage or a few banana slices with her cereal.

Above: *Don't panic about food rejection. Be patient and keep a journal listing what your child actually does eat.*

Right: *Fresh, healthful snacks will preserve the appetite for main meals.*

Although this all sounds obvious, when rushing about caring for a toddler and perhaps an older child or new baby, life becomes rather blurred and it can be difficult to stand back and look at things objectively.

REFUSING TO EAT

A child will always eat if she is hungry although it may not be when you want her to eat. A child can stay fit and healthy on surprisingly little. Providing your child is growing and gaining weight then don't worry, but if you are concerned, ask your doctor for advice. Take the lead from your child, never force feed a child and above all try not to let meal times become a battleground.

MAKING MEAL TIMES FUN

Coping with a fussy eater can be incredibly frustrating. The less she eats the angrier you get and so the spiral goes on as your toddler learns how to control meal times. To break this vicious circle, try defusing things by involving your child in the preparation of the meal. You could pack up a picnic with your child's help, choosing together what to take. Then go somewhere different to eat, it could be the back yard, the playground or even the car. Alternatively, have a dolls' or teddies' tea party or make a camp under the dining table.

Even very young children enjoy having friends for dinner. If your child is going through a fussy or non-eating stage, invite over a little friend with a good appetite. Try to take a back seat and don't make a fuss over how much the visiting child eats.

Above: *Changing the scene and breaking routine can help a lot.*

Below: *Making the meal a special event can distract the child from any eating worries.*

Above: *Getting your child to help you cook the food will encourage them to eat it, too.*

Above: *Children are more likely to eat with friends of their own age around them.*

10 TIPS TO COPE WITH A FUSSY EATER

1 Try to find meals that the rest of the family enjoys and where there are at least one or two things the fussy child will eat as well. It may seem easier to cook only foods that your child will eat but it means a very limited diet for everyone else and your child will never get the chance to have a change of mind and try something new.

2 Serve smaller portions of food to your child.

3 Invite her friend with a hearty appetite to dinner. A good example sometimes works but don't comment on how much the visiting child has eaten.

4 Invite an adult who the child likes for supper – a grandmother or friend. Sometimes a child will eat for someone else without any fuss at all.

5 Never force feed a child.

6 If your child is just playing with the food and won't eat, quietly remove the plate without fuss and don't offer dessert.

7 Try to make meal times enjoyable and talk about what the family has been doing.

8 Try limiting snacks and drinks between meals so your child feels hungrier when it comes to family meal times. Alternatively, offer more nutritious snacks and smaller main meals if your child eats better that way.

9 Offer drinks after a meal so that they don't spoil the appetite.

10 Offer new foods when you know your child is hungry and hopefully more receptive.

Above: *Remember to give drinks after the meal, not before.*

EATING TOGETHER

Eating together as a family should be a happy part of the day, but can turn into a nightmare if everyone is tired or you feel as though the only things your children will eat are fries.

There is nothing worse than preparing a lovely supper, setting the table and sitting down with everyone and then one child refuses to eat, shrieks her disapproval or just pushes the food around the plate. However hard you try to ignore this behavior, the meal is spoiled for everyone, especially if this is a regular occurrence. It's not fair on you or anyone else.

If you feel this is just a passing phase, then you could try just ignoring it and carry on regardless. Try to praise the good things, perhaps the way the child sits nicely at the table or the way she holds a knife and fork. Talk about the things that have been happening in the day, rather than concentrating on the meal itself. Try to avoid comparing your child's appetite with more hearty eaters. With luck, this particular fad will go away.

However, if it becomes a regular thing and meal times always seem more like a battleground than a happy family gathering, perhaps it's time for a sterner approach.

First steps

- Check to see if there is something physically wrong with your child. Has she been ill? If she has, she may not have recovered fully. If you're worried, then ask your doctor.
- Perhaps your child has enlarged adenoids or tonsils which could make swallowing difficult, or perhaps she has a food allergy, such as coeliacs disease – an intolerance to gluten – which may be undiagnosed but which would give the child tummy pains after eating. Again, check with your doctor.
- Is your child worried or stressed? If your family circumstances have changed – a new baby perhaps, or if you've moved recently – your child may be unhappy or confused.
- Is your child trying to get your attention?

Above: *Good seating of the right height will contribute to comfort and relaxation.*

Secondly
Look at the way in which you as a family eat. Do you eat at regular times? Do you sit down to eat or catch snacks on the run? Do you enjoy your food or do you always feel rushed and harassed? Children will pick up habits from their parents – bad as well as good. If you don't tend to sit down to a meal or you have the habit of getting up during meal times to do other jobs, then it's hard to expect the child to behave differently.

Finally
Talk things over with all the family. If you all feel enough is enough, then it's time to make a plan of action. Explain that from now on you are all going to eat together where possible, when and where you say so. You will choose the food, there will be three meals a day and no snacks. Since milk is filling and dulls the appetite, milky drinks will only be given after a meal; during the meal water or juice will be provided.

It is vitally important to involve all the family in this strategy so that there is no dipping into the cookie jar or raiding the pantry for chips after school. Make sure that the fussy eater is aware of what is going to happen and give a few days' notice so that the idea can sink in.

Once you have outlined your strategy, work out your menus and

stick to them. Include foods your child definitely likes, chicken or carrots for instance, and obviously avoid foods your child hates although you could introduce some new foods for variety. Set yourself a time scale, perhaps one or two weeks, and review things after this period has elapsed.

PUTTING THE PLAN INTO ACTION
Begin your new plan of action when all the family is there to help, such as a weekend, and stick to it. Make a fuss of the plans so it seems more like a game than a prison sentence. Add a few flowers to the table or a pretty cloth to make it more special.

Begin the day with a normal breakfast but give the fussy eater the smallest possible portion. If the child eats it up then offer something you know your child likes, such as an apple, a few raisins or a fruit yogurt. As the days progress, offer a cookie or chocolate milk as a treat.

Give plenty of encouragement and praise, but be firm if the child acts up. If she behaves badly, take her to a different room or to the bottom of the stairs and explain that the only food is that on the table. Sit down with the rest of the family, leaving the fussy eater's food on the table and try to ignore the child.

If the child changes her mind just as you're about to clear the table, then get the other members of the family to come back and wait until the fussy eater has finished.

Continue in this way with other meals. Don't be swayed if your child says she will eat her food watching TV or if she wants her dessert first. Explain that she must eat just like everyone else or go without.

If she begins to cry, sit her down in another room and return to the table. This is perhaps the hardest thing of all.

After a few days, there should be a glimmer of progress. Still offer tiny portions of food, followed by foods that you know your child will eat as a treat. Keeping to a plan like this is hard, but if all the family sticks together and thinks positively, then it is possible. Keep to the time span you decided, then suggest you all go to your local pizza or burger restaurant and let the fussy eater choose what she likes.

A Balanced and Varied Diet

Give your child a selection of foods in the four main food groups daily:

Breads, grains, and cereals: include three to four helpings of the following food items per day – breakfast cereals, bread, pasta, potatoes, rice.

Fruit and vegetables: try to have three or four helpings per day. Choose from fresh, canned, frozen or dried.

Meat and/or alternatives: one to two portions per day – meat – all kinds, including hamburgers and sausages, poultry, fish (fresh, canned or frozen), eggs (well-cooked), lentils and legumes (for example baked beans, red kidney beans, chickpeas), finely chopped nuts, smooth peanut butter and tofu.

Dairy foods: include 1 pint of milk per day or a mix of milk, cheese and yogurt. For a child who starts refusing milk, try flavoring it or using it in custards, ice cream, rice pudding or cheese sauce. A carton of yogurt or 1½oz of cheese have the same amount of calcium as 5oz of whole milk.

THE IMPORTANCE OF BREAKFAST

Breakfast is a vitally important start for any young child. Count back: your child may have had dinner at 5 o'clock the previous day and if she misses breakfast at 8 o'clock she will not have eaten for 15 hours. Allow time to sit down and don't hurry your child. Offer milk and cereals, fresh orange juice diluted with a little water, a few slices of fruit and half a piece of toast preferably spread with smooth peanut butter or cream cheese.

Above: *Cereals and grains, like bread, pasta and rice.*

Above: *Fruit and vegetables, including frozen, dried and canned goods.*

Above: *Meat and meat alternatives, like legumes and nuts.*

Above: *Dairy foods such as milk, cheese and yogurt.*

Toast

Sliced pears

FATS

As adults we are all aware of the need to cut down on our fat consumption, but when eating together as a family, bear in mind that fat is a useful source of energy in a child's diet. The energy from fat is in concentrated form, so that your child can take in the calories she needs for growth and development before her stomach becomes overfull. Fat in food is also a valuable source of the fat-soluble vitamins, A, D, E and K, as well as essential fatty acids that the body cannot make by itself.

In general, fat is best provided by foods that contain not just fat but other essential nutrients as well, such as dairy products, eggs, meat and fish. Whole milk and its products such as cheese and yogurt, and eggs contain the fat-soluble vitamins A and D, while sunflower oil, nuts and oily fish are a good source of various essential fatty acids.

Cut down on deep frying and broil or oven bake foods where possible. All children love chips and fries but do offer them as a treat rather than a daily snack.

Above: *Offer sweets and chocolate only as treats – give fruit and vegetables as snacks.*

Above: *A good mixture of the four basic food types will provide maximum energy and vitality for growing children.*

FRUIT AND VEGETABLES

Fresh fruit and vegetables play an essential part in a balanced diet. Offer fresh fruit, such as slices of apple or banana, for breakfast and dinner, and perhaps thin sticks of raw carrot and celery for lunch. Instead of cookies and chips, offer your child raisins, ready-to-eat apricots, carrots and apple slices if she wants a mid-morning or afternoon snack. Keep the fruit bowl within easy reach so your child may be tempted to pick up a banana as she walks through the kitchen.

SNACKS

Young children cannot eat enough food at meal times to meet their needs for energy and growth and snacks can play a vital part in meeting these needs. However offer chocolate cookies and chips only as a treat. They contain little goodness and are bad for the teeth. At meal times keep sweets out of sight until the main course has been eaten.

LUNCH SPECIALS

NOW THAT YOUR BABY HAS PROGRESSED FROM PURÉED TO CHOPPED FOOD YOU CAN BEGIN TO COOK MORE GROWN-UP LUNCHES. TRY TO INTRODUCE A RANGE OF FOODS TO GIVE A BALANCED DIET AND A VARIETY OF TASTES ALTHOUGH DON'T BE DISHEARTENED IF THERE ARE A FEW SETBACKS ALONG THE WAY.

Sticky Chicken

Serves 2–4

- 4 chicken drumsticks
- 2 tsp oil
- 1 tsp soy sauce
- 1 tbsp smooth peanut butter
- 1 tbsp ketchup
- small baked potatoes, corn and tomato wedges, to serve

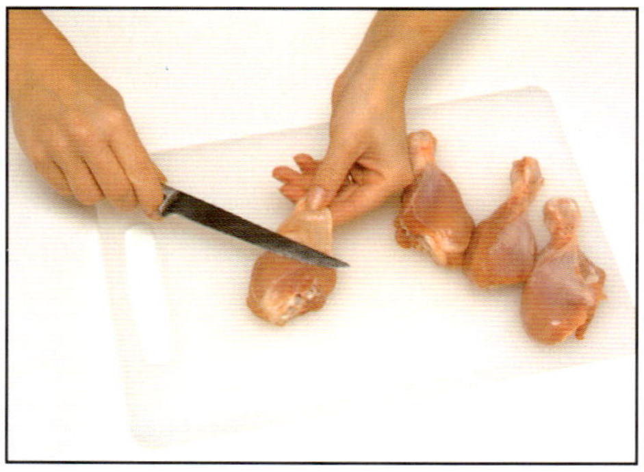

1 Preheat the oven to 400°F and line a small shallow baking pan with foil. Rinse the drumsticks under cold water, pat dry and peel off the skin. Make three or four slashes in the meat with a sharp knife and place in the pan.

2 Blend the remaining ingredients and spread thickly over the top of the chicken drumsticks. Cook in the oven for 15 minutes.

3 Turn the drumsticks over and baste with the peanut butter mixture and meat juices.

TIP
If more convenient, use the peanut butter and ketchup mixture over chicken thighs or kabobs instead.

4 Cook for 20 minutes more or until the juices run clear when the chicken is pierced with a knife.

5 Cool slightly, then wrap a small piece of foil around the base of each drumstick. Arrange on plates and serve with small baked potatoes, hot corn and tomato wedges.

Coriander Chicken Casserole

Serves 2

- 2 chicken thighs
- ¼ small onion
- 1 small carrot, about 2oz
- 1 small piece rutabaga, about 2oz
- 1 tsp oil
- ½ tsp ground coriander
- pinch of turmeric
- 1 tsp all-purpose flour
- ⅔ cup chicken broth
- salt and pepper (optional)
- mashed potatoes and peas, to serve

1 Preheat the oven to 350°F. Rinse the chicken under cold water, pat dry and trim away any excess skin if necessary. Chop the onion, carrot and rutabaga.

2 Heat the oil in a skillet, add the chicken and brown on each side. Add the vegetables.

TIP
Chop the meat for very young toddlers. Serve older children the whole thigh to make them feel more grown up, then help with cutting.

3 Stir in the spices and flour, then add the broth and a little salt and pepper, if desired. Bring to a boil then transfer to a casserole.

4 Cover and cook in the oven for 1 hour. Spoon onto serving plates or into shallow dishes, cool slightly and serve the chicken casserole with mashed potatoes and peas.

Chicken Parcels

Serves 2

- 1 boneless, skinless chicken breast, about 5oz
- 1oz Cheddar cheese
- 1 slice lean ham, cut into 4 strips
- 1 tbsp oil
- new potatoes, broccoli and carrots, to serve

1 Rinse the chicken under cold water, pat dry and cut in half crosswise. Place each half between two pieces of plastic wrap and flatten with a rolling pin until each piece is about 4in square.

2 Cut the cheese in half and place a piece on each scallop. Wrap the chicken around the cheese to enclose it completely.

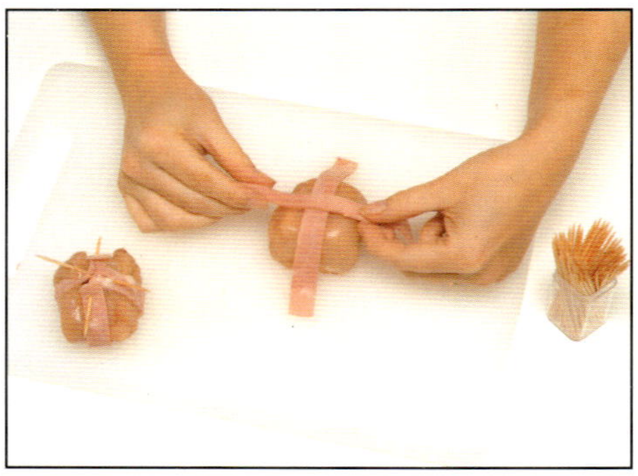

3 Arrange two pieces of the ham crosswise over each of the parcels, securing them underneath with toothpicks. Brush the chicken parcels with oil.

TIP
You could wrap the parcels with small slices of bacon in place of the ham, if you prefer.

4 Place on a piece of foil and chill until ready to cook.

5 Preheat the broiler. Cook the chicken for 10 minutes, turning once, until browned. Remove the toothpicks, cool slightly, then arrange on two plates and serve with new potatoes, steamed broccoli florets and sliced carrots.

Peppered Beef Casserole

Serves 2

- 4oz lean chuck or round steak
- 1/4 small onion
- 1/4 small red bell pepper
- 1/4 small yellow bell pepper
- 1 tsp oil
- 2 tbsp canned red kidney beans, drained and rinsed
- 1 tsp all-purpose flour
- 2/3 cup beef broth
- 1 tbsp ketchup
- 1 tsp Worcestershire sauce
- 3 tbsp couscous
- a few drops of oil
- 3 tbsp frozen peas
- salt and pepper (optional)

1 Preheat the oven to 350°F. Rinse the chuck steak under cold water and pat dry. Trim away any fat and cut into small cubes. Chop the onion, remove the seeds and core from the peppers and cut into small cubes.

2 Heat the oil in a small skillet or saucepan, add the beef and onion and brown on all sides, stirring frequently.

3 Add the peppers and kidney beans, then stir in the flour, broth, ketchup, Worcestershire sauce and a little salt and pepper if desired.

4 Bring to a boil, stirring, then transfer to a casserole dish, cover and cook in the oven for about 1½ hours, or until the meat is tender.

5 Just before serving place the couscous in a bowl, cover with boiling water and let soak for 5 minutes. Drain into a strainer and stir in a few drops of oil.

6 Bring a saucepan of water to a boil, add the peas, and place the strainer of couscous over the pan. Cover and cook for 5 minutes.

7 Spoon the casserole onto two plates or dishes. Fluff up the couscous with a fork, drain the peas and spoon onto the plates. Cool slightly before serving.

Lamb Stew

Serves 2

4oz boneless lamb
¼ small onion
1 small carrot, about 2oz
½ small parsnip, about 2oz
1 small potato
1 tsp oil
⅔ cup beef broth
pinch of dried rosemary
salt and pepper (optional)
crusty bread, to serve

1 Rinse the lamb under cold water and pat dry. Cut away any fat from the meat and cut into small cubes. Finely chop the onion, then dice the carrot and parsnip and cut the potato into slightly larger pieces.

2 Heat the oil in a medium-size saucepan, add the lamb and onion and brown. Add the carrot, parsnip and potato and sauté the lamb and vegetables for 3 minutes more, stirring frequently.

3 Add the broth, dried rosemary and a little salt and pepper, if desired. Bring to a boil, cover and simmer for 35–40 minutes or until the meat is tender and moist.

4 Spoon the stew into shallow bowls and cool slightly before serving with crusty bread.

Mexican Ground Beef

Serves 3–4

- ¼ small onion
- 1 strip red bell pepper
- ½ small zucchini, about 2oz
- 4oz lean ground beef
- 1 small garlic clove, crushed
- 3 tbsp canned baked beans
- 3 tbsp beef broth
- 1 tbsp ketchup
- 18 corn chips
- ¼ cup grated Cheddar cheese
- green salad, to serve

1 Finely chop the onion, dice the zucchini, then deseed and dice the pepper.

2 Sauté the onion and ground beef in a medium-size saucepan, stirring until browned all over.

3 Stir in the remaining ingredients and bring to a boil, stirring. Cover and simmer the mixture for 15 minutes, stirring occasionally.

4 Place the corn chips on plates, spoon on the mixture and sprinkle the grated cheese over the top. Serve with a green salad.

Lamb and Celery Casserole

Serves 2

- 4oz lamb fillet
- ¼ onion
- 1 small carrot, about 2oz
- 1 celery stalk
- 1oz button mushrooms
- 1 tsp oil
- 2 tsp all-purpose flour
- ¾ cup beef broth
- bay leaf
- salt and pepper (optional)
- mashed potatoes and baby Brussels sprouts, to serve

1 Preheat the oven to 350°F. Rinse the lamb under cold water and pat dry, then trim off any fat and cut into small cubes. Chop the onion and carrot, then rinse the celery and mushrooms, pat dry and slice thinly.

2 Heat the oil in a skillet, add the lamb, onion and bay leaf and sauté until the lamb is browned, stirring frequently. Add the remaining vegetables and sauté for 3 minutes more until they are softened and lightly browned.

VARIATION
For a more unusual flavor, substitute fennel for the celery. Its slight aniseed taste goes particularly well with lamb.

3 Stir in the flour, then add the broth, and a little salt and pepper, if desired. Bring to a boil, then transfer to a casserole, cover and cook in the oven for 45 minutes or until the meat is tender.

4 Spoon the casserole onto plates discarding the bay leaf. Cool slightly then serve with mashed potatoes and tiny Brussels sprouts.

Shepherds' Pie

Serves 2

½ small onion
6oz lean ground beef
2 tsp all-purpose flour
2 tbsp ketchup
⅔ cup beef broth
pinch of mixed herbs
slice rutabaga, about 2oz
½ small parsnip, about 2oz
1 medium-sized potato, about 4oz
2 tsp milk
1 tbsp butter or margarine
½ carrot
3 tbsp frozen peas
salt and pepper (optional)

1 Preheat oven to 375°F. Finely chop the onion and place in a small saucepan with the ground beef and sauté over low heat, stirring, until the ground beef is evenly browned.

2 Add the flour, stirring, then add the ketchup, broth, mixed herbs and seasoning, if desired. Bring to a boil, cover and simmer gently for 30 minutes, stirring occasionally.

3 Meanwhile, chop the rutabaga, parsnip and potato and cook for 20 minutes until tender. Drain.

4 Mash with the milk and half of the butter or margarine.

5 Spoon the beef mixture into two 1 cup ovenproof dishes. Place the mashed vegetables on top fluffing them up with a fork. Dot with butter or margarine.

6 Place both the pies on a baking sheet and cook for about 25–30 minutes until browned on top and bubbling.

7 Peel and thinly slice the carrot lengthwise. Stamp out shapes with small cookie cutters. Cook in a saucepan of boiling water with the peas for 5 minutes. Drain and serve with the shepherds' pies. Remember that baked pies are very hot when they come out of the oven. Always allow to cool slightly before serving to children.

Tuna Cakes

Serves 2–3

1 large potato, about 8oz
pat of butter or margarine
2 tsp milk
1 tsp lemon juice
3oz can tuna
3 tbsp frozen corn, defrosted
flour, for dusting
1 egg
4 tbsp ground almonds
2oz green beans
½ carrot
6 frozen peas
1 tbsp oil
salt and pepper (optional)

1 Peel and cut the potato into chunks and then cook in a saucepan of boiling water for about 15 minutes until tender.

2 Drain the potato and mash with the butter or margarine, milk, lemon juice and a little salt and pepper, if desired. Drain the tuna and stir into the potato with the defrosted corn.

3 Divide the mixture into six and pat each portion into a fish shape with floured hands.

4 Beat the egg in a dish and place the ground almonds on a plate. Dip the fish cakes into the egg and then into the almonds making sure they are completely covered. Place on a floured plate and chill until ready to cook.

5 Trim the beans, peel and cut the carrot into sticks a little smaller than the beans. Cook in a pan of boiling water with the peas for about 5 minutes.

6 Meanwhile heat the oil in a skillet, and fry the fish cakes for 5 minutes until golden brown and crisp, turning once.

7 Drain and arrange on serving plates with pea "eyes" and bean and carrot "seaweed." Cool slightly before serving.

Fish and Cheese Pies

Serves 2

- 1 medium-sized potato, about 5oz
- 1oz green cabbage
- 4oz cod fillets
- 2 tbsp frozen corn
- ⅔ cup milk
- 1 tbsp butter or margarine
- 1 tbsp all-purpose flour
- ¼ cup grated Colby cheese
- 1 tsp sesame seeds
- carrots and snow peas, to serve

1 Peel and cut the potato into chunks and shred the cabbage. Cut any skin away from the fish fillets and rinse under cold water.

2 Bring a saucepan of water to a boil, add the potato and cook for 10 minutes. Add the cabbage and cook for 5 minutes more until tender. Drain.

3 Meanwhile place the fish fillets, the corn and all but 2 tsp of the milk in a second saucepan. Bring to a boil then cover the saucepan and simmer very gently for 8–10 minutes until the fish flakes easily when pressed with a knife.

4 Strain the fish and corn, reserving the cooking liquid. Wash the pan then melt the butter or margarine in the pan. Stir in the flour then gradually add the reserved cooking liquid and bring to a boil, stirring until thickened and smooth.

5 Add the fish and corn with half of the grated cheese. Spoon into two small ovenproof dishes.

6 Mash the potato and cabbage with the remaining 2 tsp milk. Stir in half of the remaining cheese and spoon the mixture over the fish. Sprinkle with the sesame seeds and the remaining cheese.

7 Cook under a preheated broiler until the topping is browned. Cool slightly before serving with vegetable fish.

Fish Surprise

Serves 2

½ small zucchini, about 2oz
6oz smoked haddock
1 small tomato
pat of butter or margarine
pinch of dried mixed herbs
new potatoes and broccoli, to serve

1 Preheat the oven to 400°F. Tear off two pieces of foil, then trim and thinly slice the zucchini and divide the slices equally between the two pieces of foil.

2 Cut the skin away from the fish, remove any bones, cut into two equal pieces and rinse under cold water. Pat the haddock dry and place on top of the zucchini.

3 Slice the tomato and arrange slices on top of each piece of haddock. Add a little butter or margarine to each and sprinkle with mixed herbs.

4 Wrap the foil around the fish and seal the edges of each to make two parcels, then place the parcels on a baking sheet and cook in the oven for 15–20 minutes depending on the thickness of the fish.

5 To test for doneness, open up one of the parcels and insert a knife into the center. If the fish flakes easily then it is ready.

6 Cool slightly then arrange the parcels on plates and serve with new potatoes and broccoli.

Cowboy Hot Dogs and Beans

Serves 2

- 3 chicken or turkey hot dogs
- ¼ small onion
- 1 small carrot, about 2oz
- 1 strip red bell pepper
- 1 tsp oil
- 7oz can baked beans
- 2 tsp Worcestershire sauce
- fingers of toast, to serve

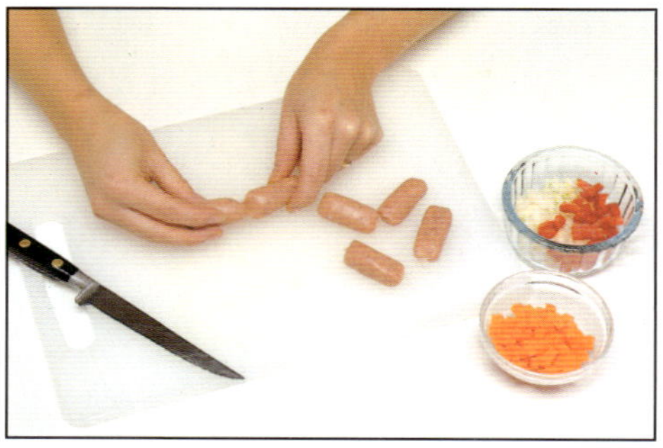

1 Cut each hot dog in half to make two small hot dogs.

2 Finely chop the onion, then dice the carrot and the pepper, discarding the core and seeds.

3 Heat the oil in a skillet, add the hot dogs and the chopped onion and brown.

TIP
Check the beans toward the end of cooking; you may need to add a little extra water.

4 Add the remaining ingredients and stir in 2 tbsp water. Cover and cook for 15 minutes or until the carrot is cooked.

5 Spoon onto serving plates or into dishes, cool slightly and serve with fingers of toast.

Mini Toad-in-the-Hole

Serves 2

- 3 breakfast-style sausages
- 1 tsp oil
- 4 tbsp all-purpose flour
- 1 egg
- 4 tbsp milk
- salt
- baked beans and green beans, to serve

1 Preheat the oven to 425°F. Press the center of each sausage with your finger, twist and then cut in half. Brush two 4in muffin pans with oil. Add the sausages and cook for about 5 minutes.

2 Place the flour, egg and a pinch of salt in a bowl. Gradually whisk in the milk, beating until a smooth batter is formed.

3 Pour into the pans, quickly return to the oven and bake for 15 minutes until risen and golden.

4 Loosen with a knife and turn out onto serving plates. Cool slightly and serve with baked beans and steamed green beans.

Pork and Lentil Casserole

Serves 2

- 6oz boneless rib pork chop
- ¼ small onion
- 1 small carrot, about 2oz
- 1 tsp oil
- 1 small garlic clove, crushed
- 1oz red lentils
- 6 tbsp canned crushed tomatoes
- 6 tbsp chicken broth
- salt and pepper (optional)
- rutabaga and peas, to serve

1 Preheat the oven to 350°F. Rinse the pork under cold water, pat dry, then trim off any excess fat and cut in half. Finely chop the onion and dice the carrot.

2 Heat the oil in a skillet, add the pork and onion and brown the pork on both sides.

3 Add the garlic, lentils and carrots and stir gently to mix.

4 Pour in the chopped tomatoes, broth and seasoning, if desired, and bring to a boil. Transfer to a casserole, cover and cook in the oven for 1¼ hours.

5 Spoon portions onto serving plates or shallow dishes and cool slightly. Serve with diced buttered rutabaga and peas.

TIP
Teaching a child to use a knife and fork can be frustrating. Rib pork chops are wonderfully tender when cooked in a casserole and very easy to cut with a child's knife.

Sticky Ribs and Apple Slaw

Serves 2

8oz short pork ribs
2 tsp oil
2 tsp ketchup
2 tsp Hoisin sauce
1 medium potato, scrubbed but not peeled
pat of butter or margarine

For the Apple Slaw

½ carrot
½ eating apple
1oz white cabbage
2 tsp golden raisins
2 tbsp mayonnaise
carrot slices, tomato wedges and celery sticks, to serve

1 Preheat the oven to 400°F. Rinse the pork ribs under cold water, pat dry and put on a roasting rack set over a small roasting pan. Mix the oil, ketchup and Hoisin sauce and brush over the ribs, reserving any extra mixture.

2 Pour a little boiling water into the base of the roasting pan. Prick the potato all over with a fork and then place in the oven with the ribs, preferably on the same shelf.

3 Cook for 1 hour, turning the pork ribs once during cooking and brushing with any of the remaining ketchup mixture.

4 Meanwhile peel the carrot and peel, quarter and core the apple. Coarsely grate the apple and carrot and finely chop the cabbage.

5 Place in a bowl with the raisins and mayonnaise and mix well.

6 Arrange the ribs on serving plates. Halve the baked potato and add a little butter or margarine to each half and serve with the pork ribs together with star-shaped carrot slices, celery sticks and tomato wedges and spoonfuls of coleslaw.

TIP

Check the temperature of the ribs before serving as they stay very hot for a surprisingly long time. Nothing will put a child off more than food that is very hot. Toddlers prefer their food to be lukewarm.

Mini Cheese and Ham Tarts

Makes 12

For the Pastry

1 cup all-purpose flour

4 tbsp margarine

For the Filling

½ cup Cheddar cheese

2 slices wafer thin ham, chopped

½ cup frozen corn

1 egg

½ cup milk

pinch of paprika

salt and pepper

carrot and cucumber sticks, to serve

1 Preheat the oven to 400°F. Place the flour in a bowl, add the margarine and rub in with your fingertips until the mixture resembles fine breadcrumbs.

2 Stir in 4 tsp water and mix to make a smooth dough. Lightly knead and roll out thinly on a floured surface.

3 Stamp out twelve 3in circles with a fluted cookie cutter, rerolling the pastry as necessary. Press into a muffin pan.

4 Grate the cheese, mix with the ham and corn and divide among the pastry cases.

5 Beat together the egg, milk, salt and pepper and pour into the tarts. Sprinkle with paprika.

6 Cook in the oven for 12–15 minutes until well risen and browned. Serve warm with carrot and cucumber sticks.

TIP

Encourage children to eat more vegetables by serving them with a yogurt dip flavored with tomato paste.

GOING GREEN

GETTING CHILDREN TO EAT MORE THAN A FEW FROZEN PEAS AND THE ODD CARROT CAN BE AN UPHILL BATTLE. ENCOURAGE THEM TO BE A LITTLE MORE ADVENTUROUS BY MIXING THEIR FAVORITE FOODS WITH SOME NEW VEGETABLES.

Pick-up Sticks

Serves 2

- 2in piece of leek
- 1oz green beans
- 1 strip red bell pepper
- 1 celery stalk
- 1oz bean sprouts
- 1 small carrot, about 2oz
- 1 tsp oil
- 1 tbsp ketchup
- 1 tsp soy sauce
- pinch ground ginger
- broiled breakfast sausages, to serve

1 Rinse the leek, beans, pepper, celery and bean sprouts. Peel the carrot. Halve any large beans and bean sprouts. Cut the remaining vegetables into thin strips.

2 Heat the oil in a skillet, add all the vegetables except the bean sprouts and sauté for 3 minutes, stirring all the time.

3 Add the bean sprouts, ketchup, soy sauce, ginger and 2 tsp water. Cook for 2 minutes more, stirring until the vegetables are hot.

4 Spoon onto serving plates and let cool slightly. Serve with broiled sausages.

TIP
Don't overcook the vegetables. They should be quite crisp, and firm enough for your child to pick up.

Saucy Spinach Pancakes

Serves 2–3

2oz fresh spinach, leaves only
2oz all-purpose flour
1 egg yolk
1¼ cups milk
1 tbsp margarine
1 tbsp all-purpose flour
¼ cup grated Colby cheese
1½oz thinly sliced ham, chopped
1½oz button mushrooms, thinly sliced
1 tbsp oil
tomato wedges and new potatoes, to serve

1 Wash the spinach leaves well in cold water and then place in a skillet, set over medium heat. Cover and cook gently for 2–3 minutes until the spinach has just wilted, stirring occasionally. Drain off any excess liquid, cool and chop finely.

2 Put the flour, egg yolk and a little salt and pepper, if desired, into a bowl. Whisk in half of the milk to make a smooth batter. Stir the spinach into the batter.

3 Melt the margarine in a saucepan, stir in the flour and then gradually stir in the remaining milk and bring to a boil, stirring continuously until smooth. Add the cheese, ham and mushrooms and stir to mix. Heat, cover and keep warm.

4 Heat a little oil in a skillet, pour off excess then add 2 tbsp pancake batter, tilting the pan so that the batter covers the base. Cook for a few minutes until browned, then flip over and cook the other side until golden. Slide the pancake onto a plate and keep warm.

5 Continue making pancakes until all the batter is used up.

6 Fold the pancakes into quarters then spoon a little of the ham mixture into each one. Arrange the pancakes on plates and serve with tomato wedges and new potatoes.

TIP
If offering spinach to your child for the first time make sure that the filling includes foods that you know are liked. Omit or add ingredients as necessary.

Broccoli and Cauliflower Bake

Serves 2
1 egg
3oz broccoli
3oz cauliflower
1 tbsp margarine
1 tbsp all-purpose flour
⅔ cup milk
⅓ cup grated Colby cheese
½ tomato
salt and pepper (optional)

1 Put the egg in a small saucepan of cold water, bring to a boil and cook for about 10 minutes until the egg is hard-boiled.

2 Meanwhile cut the broccoli and cauliflower into florets and thinly slice the broccoli stalks. Cook in a saucepan of boiling water for about 8 minutes until just tender.

3 Drain the vegetables and dry the pan. Melt the margarine, stir in the flour then gradually mix in the milk and bring to a boil, stirring until thickened and smooth.

TIP
Making a face or fun pattern can be just enough to tempt a fussy eater to try something new.

4 Stir two-thirds of the cheese into the sauce together with a little seasoning, if desired. Reserve two of the broccoli florets and stir the remaining vegetables into the sauce.

5 Divide the mixture between two heat-resistant shallow dishes and sprinkle with the remaining cheese.

6 Place under a hot broiler until golden brown.

7 Make a face on each dish with broccoli florets for a nose, a halved tomato for a mouth and peeled and sliced hard-boiled egg for eyes. Cool slightly before serving.

Potato Boats

Serves 2

2 small baking potatoes
2in piece leek
1oz button mushrooms
2 tsp oil
2 tbsp frozen corn
1 tbsp milk
pat of butter
½ zucchini, about 2oz, grated
1 carrot, about 2oz, grated
2 slices cheese
1 slice ham
salt and pepper (optional)

1 Preheat the oven to 400°F. Prick the potatoes with a fork and bake in the oven for 1 hour until soft. Alternatively, prick well and then microwave on a sheet of paper toweling on High (100%) for 7–8 minutes.

2 Halve the leek lengthwise, wash thoroughly to remove any grit and then slice thinly. Rinse the mushrooms, pat dry and thinly slice.

3 Heat 1 tsp oil in a skillet and sauté the leek, mushrooms and corn for about 3 minutes until softened, stirring frequently. Turn into a bowl and keep warm.

4 When the potatoes are cooked, cut in half and scoop the centers into the bowl with the leek and mushroom mixture. Add the milk, butter and a little salt and pepper if desired, and stir to mix. Pile the mixture back into the potato shells.

5 Reheat the remaining 1 tsp of oil and sauté the grated zucchini and carrot for 2 minutes until softened. Spoon onto two small plates and spread with a fork to cover the bottoms of the plates.

6 Arrange two potato halves on each plate. For sails, cut the cheese and ham into triangles and secure to potatoes with toothpicks. Cool slightly before serving.

Fat Cats

Serves 2

- oil, for greasing
- 7oz frozen puff pastry, defrosted
- a little flour, for dusting
- beaten egg, to glaze
- 2oz broccoli
- 2 tbsp frozen mixed vegetables
- 1 tbsp butter or margarine
- 1 tbsp all-purpose flour
- ½ cup milk
- 2 tbsp grated Cheddar cheese
- a little mustard and cress, chives, or sprouts, to garnish

1 Preheat the oven to 425°F and lightly brush a baking sheet with a little oil. Roll out the pastry thinly on a work surface lightly dusted with a little flour.

2 Using a shaped cookie cutter, stamp out four 5in cat shapes. Place two cats on the baking sheet and brush with egg.

3 Cut a large hole in the center of the two remaining cats and gently place the shapes on top of the other two cats.

Variation
Make this recipe using different shaped cookie cutters to cut out the pastry shapes. Get your child to choose his favorite.

4 Brush the tops with egg and cook for 10 minutes until the pastry is well risen and golden.

5 Meanwhile chop the broccoli and cook in a small saucepan of boiling water with the frozen vegetables for 5 minutes. Drain.

6 Dry the pan and melt the butter or margarine. Stir in the flour and then gradually add the milk. Bring to a boil, stirring all the time until thickened and smooth.

7 Reserve two peas and two pieces of carrot for garnish and then stir the remaining vegetables into the sauce with the grated cheese.

8 Enlarge the cavity in the center of each pastry cat by scooping out a little of the pastry. Spoon in the vegetable mixture and arrange on two serving plates. Garnish with halved peas for eyes, halved carrot strips for whiskers and red pepper noses. Add the garnish for grass. Cool slightly before serving.

Potato, Carrot and Zucchini Pancakes

Serves 2–4

1 small potato, about 4oz
½ carrot, about 1oz
½ zucchini, about 1oz
2 tsp light vegetable oil
breakfast-style sausages and baked beans, to serve

1 Grate the potato, carrot and zucchini into a bowl and mix together thoroughly.

2 Place several sheets of paper toweling on a surface and put the vegetables on top. Cover with more paper toweling and press down to soak up all the excess liquid.

3 Heat the oil in a large skillet and shape the vegetables to form eight rounds. Flatten slightly with a fork and fry four of the rounds for 5 minutes, turning once until the potatoes are cooked and the pancakes are golden brown on both sides.

4 Lift out of the pan and cook the remaining mixture. Cool slightly and serve with broiled sausages and baked beans.

Veggie Patties

Serves 2–4

1 large or 2 small potatoes, about 8oz
1 carrot, about 2oz
1oz broccoli
1oz Brussels sprouts
1 egg yolk
1 tbsp all-purpose flour
1 tbsp freshly grated Parmesan cheese
1 tbsp oil
salt and pepper (optional)
canned pasta circles, pieces of cucumber, strips of ham and ketchup, to serve

1 Cut the potato and carrot into chunks and cook in boiling water for 15 minutes until tender.

2 Meanwhile, cut the broccoli into small florets, chop the stem finely and thinly slice the Brussels sprouts. Rinse under cold water then add to the potatoes and carrots for the last 5 minutes of cooking.

3 Drain the vegetables thoroughly and then mash together. Add the egg yolk and a little salt and pepper, if desired, then mix well.

4 Divide into four and shape into patties with floured hands. Coat in flour and Parmesan cheese.

5 Heat the oil in a skillet, add the patties and fry for 5 minutes, turning once until golden brown. Cool slightly then serve with canned pasta, strips of ham, a few cucumber wedges and a little ketchup. Add a face with peas, carrot and cucumber.

TIP
To make a spider add cooked green bean legs, a red pepper mouth and yellow pepper eyes.

Vegetable Lasagne

Serves 2–3

¼ small onion
2oz carrot
2oz zucchini
2oz eggplant
1oz button mushrooms
2 tsp oil
1 small garlic clove, crushed
8oz can crushed tomatoes
pinch of mixed herbs
1 tbsp butter or margarine
1 tbsp all-purpose flour
⅔ cup milk
4 tbsp grated cheese
3 pre-cooked lasagne noodles
salt and pepper
mixed salad, to serve

1 Finely chop the onion and carrot, and finely dice the zucchini and eggplant. Wipe and thinly slice the mushrooms.

2 Heat the oil and sauté the vegetables for 3 minutes until softened. Add the garlic, tomatoes and herbs, then bring to a boil, cover and simmer for 5 minutes.

3 Melt the butter or margarine in a saucepan, stir in the flour. Add [illegible]lk and bring to a boil, stirring, [illegible]ed. Stir in half of the [illegible] a little salt and [illegible]

4 Preheat the oven to 350°F. Spoon one-third of the vegetable mixture into the base of an ovenproof dish, then add a little sauce. Add a noodle of lasagne then cover with half of the remaining vegetable mixture and half the remaining sauce.

5 Add a second noodle and top with the remaining vegetable mixture. Add a third noodle and top with the remaining cheese sauce. Sprinkle with the remaining cheese.

6 Cook for 50–60 minutes, checking after 30 minutes and covering loosely with foil if the topping is browning too quickly. Spoon onto serving plates and let the lasagne cool slightly. Serve with a little mixed salad.

Eggplant Bolognese

Serves 2

- 2oz eggplant
- 1 strip red bell pepper
- 1 strip yellow bell pepper
- 2in piece of leek
- 1 carrot, about 2oz
- 2 tsp oil
- 1 small garlic clove, crushed
- 2 tbsp frozen corn
- 2 tbsp red lentils
- 8oz can crushed tomatoes
- 1 cup vegetable broth
- pinch of dried herbs
- 2oz dried pasta shapes
- pat of butter or margarine
- 2 tbsp grated cheese (optional)
- salt and pepper

1 Rinse the eggplant, peppers and leek, peel the carrot and then finely dice all the vegetables.

2 Heat the oil in a medium-sized saucepan, add the diced vegetables and sauté for 3 minutes, stirring frequently, until they are slightly softened.

TIP
Sprinkle the diced eggplant with salt, leave to drain in a colander for 30 minutes, then rinse. This removes any bitter taste.

3 Add the garlic, corn, lentils, tomatoes, broth, herbs and a little salt and pepper.

4 Bring to a boil, cover and simmer for about 30 minutes, stirring occasionally and adding a little extra broth if necessary.

5 In the last 10 minutes of cooking, bring a pan of water to a boil and add the pasta. Cook for 10 minutes until tender.

6 Drain, toss in a little butter or margarine. Spoon onto plates and top with the eggplant bolognese. Sprinkle with cheese.

Quick Suppers

If you've had a day rushing around, then rustle up these quick and tasty toddlers' suppers – they all cook in 10 minutes or less. There is a wide variety of recipes to choose from. Remember the importance of fun presentation, to tempt your toddler to try new foods.

Speedy Chicken Pie

Serves 2

- 1 celery stalk
- 2 tbsp frozen corn, defrosted
- 2 tbsp mayonnaise
- ½ tsp ground coriander
- 3oz cold cooked chicken
- ½ small package plain potato chips
- 1 tbsp grated Colby cheese
- salt and pepper (optional)
- peas and broccoli, to serve

1 Preheat the oven to 425°F. Rinse the celery, slice thinly and place in a bowl with the corn, mayonnaise, ground coriander and a little salt and pepper, if desired. Dice the chicken, add to the bowl and mix well.

2 Spoon into a shallow ovenproof dish and level the surface.

3 Roughly crush the chips and sprinkle over the chicken. Top with the grated cheese and cook for 10 minutes until hot and bubbly.

4 Cool slightly then serve the pie with peas and broccoli.

Variation

Mexican Chicken Pie

Replace the ground coriander with ground cumin and replace the potato chips with about 2 tbsp crumbled plain tortilla chips.

Skinny Dippers

Serves 2

5oz boneless, skinless chicken breast
¼ cup grated Cheddar cheese
1 cup fresh breadcrumbs
1 tbsp butter or margarine
4oz frozen French fries
½ small carrot, sliced
½ small zucchini, cut in half lengthwise and sliced
3 tbsp ketchup

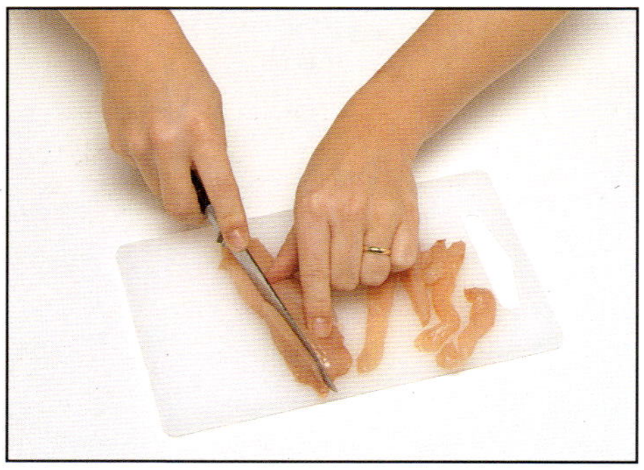

1 Rinse the chicken under cold water and pat dry with paper toweling. Cut into thin strips.

2 Mix the grated cheese and breadcrumbs on a plate. Melt the butter or margarine in a small saucepan or in a dish in the microwave on High (100%) for 20 seconds, then toss the chicken strips in the butter or margarine and roll in the breadcrumb mixture.

3 Arrange the chicken and fries on a foil-lined baking sheet. Preheat the broiler and bring a saucepan of water to a boil.

4 Broil the chicken for 6–8 minutes and the fries 8–10 minutes until well browned, turning once. When the chicken is ready, keep warm in a shallow dish while the fries finish cooking.

5 Cook the vegetables for 5 minutes in the pan of boiling water until tender.

6 Spoon the ketchup into two small bowls or ramekins and place in the center of two serving plates. Drain the vegetables and divide the vegetables, chicken and fries between the two plates. Allow to cool slightly before dipping into ketchup.

TIP
Keep a supply of fresh breadcrumbs in a sealed plastic bag in the freezer. There is no need to defrost, just take out as much as you need and use from frozen.

Sweet and Sour Chicken

Serves 2

- ¼ cup long grain white rice
- 1 carrot, about 2oz
- 1 zucchini, about 2oz
- 2 skinless chicken thighs
- 2 tsp oil
- 2 tbsp frozen peas
- 1 tsp cornstarch
- 1 tsp soy sauce
- 2 tsp ketchup
- 4 tbsp orange juice
- 1 egg, beaten

1 Cook the rice in boiling water for 8–10 minutes until tender.

2 Meanwhile, peel the carrot, trim the zucchini and cut both into thin strips. Bone the chicken and cut into small chunks.

3 Heat 1 tsp of the oil in a skillet, add the carrot, zucchini, chicken and peas and sauté for 5 minutes, stirring.

4 Blend the cornstarch with the soy sauce and then stir into the pan together with the ketchup and orange juice. Cook gently, stirring all the time, until the sauce is glossy and has thickened.

TIP
Make the meal into an occasion and serve the food in Chinese bowls with Chinese spoons – chopsticks may be a little too tricky to manage. All children love the idea of eating in a restaurant with a parent to wait on them.

5 Drain the rice thoroughly. Add the remaining oil to the rice together with the beaten egg and cook over gentle heat, stirring until the egg has scrambled.

6 Spoon the rice and sweet and sour chicken onto serving plates and cool slightly before serving.

Ham and Tomato Scramble

Serves 2

- 2 slices ham
- 1 tomato
- 1 small strip yellow bell pepper
- 2 eggs
- 1 tbsp milk
- 2 slices bread
- a little butter
- salt

1 Finely chop the ham. Halve the tomato, scoop out and discard the seeds then chop into small dice. Finely chop the strip of pepper.

2 Beat the eggs and milk together and season with a little salt. Toast the bread lightly.

3 Heat a small pat of butter in a saucepan, add the eggs, ham, tomato and pepper and cook gently, stirring all the time until cooked to taste. Cool slightly.

4 Butter the toast and cut into shapes with small fancy-shaped cookie cutters. Arrange on plates with the ham and tomato scramble.

TIP
If you don't have any special cutters then cut the toast into tiny triangles and squares with a knife.

Ham Salad Clown

Serves 2

- 2 slices ham
- 1 cherry tomato
- 2 slices apple
- 1 slice cheese
- 2 currants
- 2 slices hard-boiled egg
- a little mustard and cress, or chives, sprouts, or parsley
- 2 long slices carrot

TIP
Have fun varying the ingredients for the clown. Use cheese slices, radishes, peaches, raisins, lettuce and red pepper to change the appearance and features.

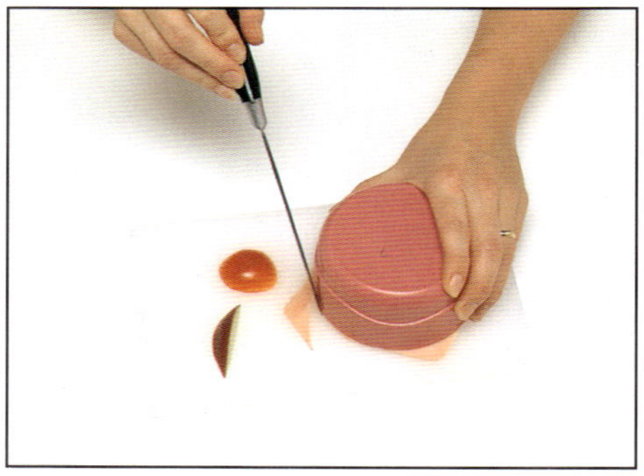

1 Cut two large rounds from the slices of ham using a cookie cutter or the top of a glass or other container as a guide. Arrange on two plates and add a halved tomato for a nose and slice of apple for a mouth, trimming if needed.

2 Cut out small triangles or stars of cheese with a knife for eyes, place on the ham and add halved currants for eye balls.

3 Halve the egg slices and add to the face for ears. Snip the mustard and cress for hair and use pieces of carrot for a collar.

Spanish Omelet

Serves 2

2 slices thinly sliced ham

1 strip red bell pepper

1 tbsp frozen peas

2oz frozen French fries

1 tsp oil

1 egg

salt and pepper (optional)

tomato wedges, to serve

1 Chop the ham and pepper. Mix the pepper and peas. Slice the French fries.

2 Heat the oil in a non-stick skillet, and sauté the fries for 5 minutes, stirring, until lightly browned. Add the pepper and peas and cook, stirring, for 2 minutes more. Stir in the chopped ham.

3 Beat together the egg, 2 tsp water and a little salt and pepper, if desired, and pour into the skillet, tilting it so that the egg mixture covers the base evenly.

4 Cook over medium-low heat for 2–3 minutes until the base of the omelet is set and browned. Loosen the edges and invert the skillet onto a plate to turn out the omelet. Then slide the omelet back into the skillet and cook the second side for a few more minutes until golden and cooked.

5 Cut the omelet into wedges, arrange on two plates and cool slightly. Serve with tomato wedges.

Pasta with Ham and Vegetables

Serves 2

- 2oz small pasta
- ½ cup frozen mixed vegetables
- 2 tbsp margarine
- 2 tbsp all-purpose flour
- ⅔ cup milk
- ½ cup grated Colby or Cheddar cheese
- 2 slices ham, chopped
- salt and pepper

1 Cook the pasta in a saucepan of boiling water for 5 minutes. Add vegetables and cook for 5 more minutes until pasta is tender. Drain.

2 Melt the margarine in a medium-size pan and stir in the flour. Gradually add the milk and bring to a boil, stirring, until the sauce is thickened and smooth.

3 Stir two-thirds of the grated cheese into the sauce and add the drained pasta and vegetables, the ham and a little salt and pepper.

4 Spoon into two shallow dishes and sprinkle with the remaining cheese. Cool slightly if necessary.

TIP
This recipe also works well if you use a 3½oz can tuna, drained, in place of the ham. You could serve the ham and vegetable sauce with rice, if you prefer.

Quickie Kabobs

Serves 2–3
1 tomato
3 slices ham
½ small yellow bell pepper
6 button mushrooms
6 small breakfast sausages
2 tsp ketchup
2 tsp oil
canned spaghetti, to serve

1 Preheat the broiler. Cut the tomato into six wedges and cut each slice of ham into two strips. Roll up each strip. Cut the pepper into six chunks, discarding any seeds. Wipe the mushrooms.

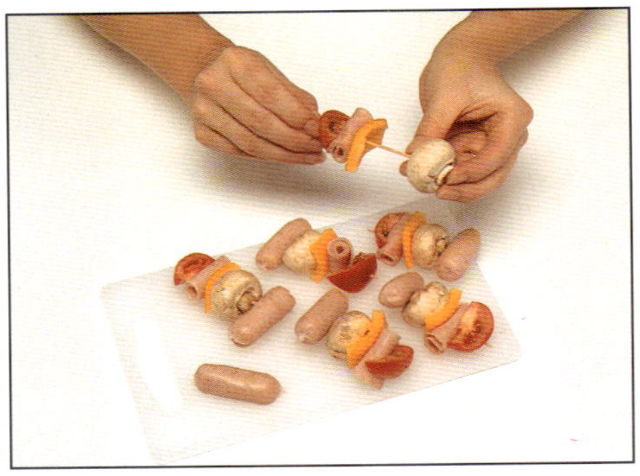

2 Make six kabobs by threading a tomato wedge, a ham roll, a piece of pepper, a mushroom, and a sausage onto six toothpicks.

TIP
Use two bacon slices, if preferred. Halve and roll up and use in place of the ham.

3 Line a broiling pan with foil and arrange the kabobs on top. Blend the ketchup and oil and brush over the kabobs. Broil for 10 minutes, turning once and brushing with the juices until the vegetables are browned and the sausages are thoroughly cooked.

4 Cool slightly then arrange on plates with canned spaghetti.

Sausage Wrappers

Serves 2
4 slices ham
2 tsp tomato relish or barbecue sauce
4 breakfast sausages
baked beans and grilled potato shapes, to serve

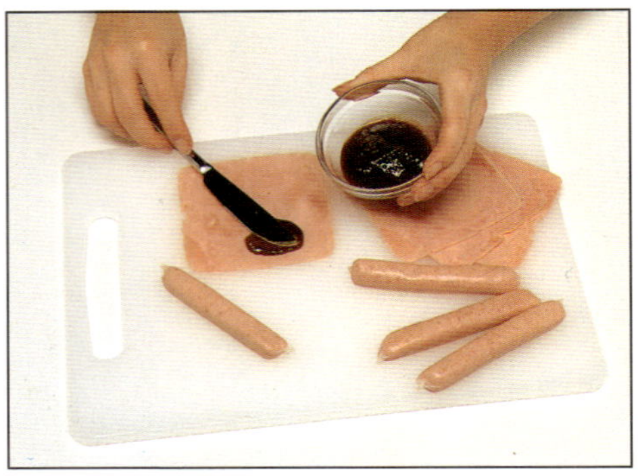

1 Spread one side of each slice of ham with relish or sauce.

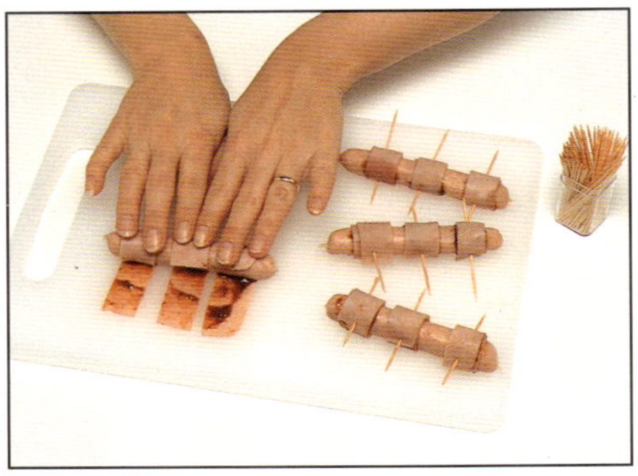

2 Cut each piece of ham into three thin strips and then wrap each sausage in three strips securing them in place with toothpicks.

3 Broil for 10 minutes, turning several times until the ham is browned and crisp.

4 Cool slightly then remove the toothpicks and serve the sausage wrappers with baked beans and grilled potato shapes.

TIP
Use four slices of bacon instead of ham, if preferred.

Corned Beef Hash

Serves 2

1 potato, about 6oz
2 tsp oil
2oz green cabbage
4oz corned beef
pinch of turmeric
1 tbsp ketchup
hard-boiled egg slices, to garnish

1 Dice the potato and cook in a saucepan of boiling water for 3–4 minutes until softened. Drain.

2 Heat the oil in a medium-size skillet, add the diced potato and fry for 3 minutes until golden.

3 Meanwhile, chop the cabbage and dice the corned beef.

4 Add the cabbage and turmeric to the pan with the potatoes and cook for 2 minutes. Stir in the corned beef and cook for 2 minutes.

5 Stir in the ketchup and spoon onto two plates. Cool slightly before serving. Garnish with the hard-boiled egg slices.

TIP
The hash can be garnished with tomato wedges, if liked.

Cannibal Necklaces

Serves 2

3 tbsp stuffing mix
4 tbsp boiling water
4oz lean ground beef
1 tsp oil
½ carrot
1 strip red bell pepper
1 strip green bell pepper
a little ketchup

1 Put the stuffing mix in a bowl and pour over the boiling water. Set aside for 5 minutes to soak.

2 Stir the ground beef into the stuffing mix and shape into 10 small balls with floured hands.

3 Preheat the broiler. Arrange the meat balls on a piece of foil on top of the broiling pan and brush lightly with a little oil. Broil for 7–8 minutes, until well browned, turning once during cooking.

4 Meanwhile thinly slice the carrot and cut the pepper into chunks, discarding the core and seeds.

5 Arrange the meat balls around the bottom edge of two serving plates. Leave spaces in between.

TIP
If you're feeling adventurous, liven up simple suppers by piping the child's initials onto the edge of the plate, the appropriate number for their age or even a short word like "hello."

6 Place carrot and pieces of red and green pepper between each meat ball and complete with a line and bow of ketchup for necklace strings. Pipe the ketchup with an icing bag if you prefer.

Beef and Mushroom Burgers

Serves 2

- ¼ small onion
- 1oz button mushrooms
- 4oz lean ground beef
- 4oz frozen French fries
- 2 hamburger buns
- 2 tsp ketchup
- 1 tomato
- salt and pepper (optional)

1 Finely chop the onion, wipe and chop the mushrooms. Place the ground beef in a mixing bowl, add the onion and mushrooms and a little salt and pepper, if desired, and mix together thoroughly. Alternatively, blend in a processor.

2 With floured hands shape two 3in burgers or press the mixture into a plastic hamburger press or upturned pastry cutter.

3 Preheat the broiler. Tear off two large pieces of foil. Fold up the edges and place on a broiling pan. Put the burgers on one piece and the French fries on the other.

4 Cook the burgers and fries for 10 minutes turning the food once. Remove from the broiler and keep warm. Split the hamburger buns in half and toast on one side.

5 Spread the bases of the buns with ketchup, slice the tomato and place on the buns. Top each with a burger and the second bun half. Cut in half and arrange on serving plates with the fries. Cool slightly if necessary before serving.

Four Fast Fish

Serves 2

4oz cod fillet
½ egg, beaten
4 tbsp fresh breadcrumbs
2 tsp sesame seeds
2 tsp oil
1 tbsp frozen peas
4 frozen corn niblets
1 carrot
canned spaghetti rings, to serve

1 Cut away and discard any skin from the fish and rinse. Pat dry and cut into four pieces.

2 Put the egg in a saucer and place the breadcrumbs and sesame seeds on a plate. Dip pieces of fish in egg and then in breadcrumb mixture to coat the fish.

3 Heat the oil in a skillet, add the fish and fry for 4–5 minutes, turning once, until the fish pieces are golden brown and cooked.

4 Meanwhile cook the peas and corn in a saucepan of boiling water for 5 minutes. Cut the carrot into long thin slices and then cut out fin and tail shapes and tiny triangles for mouths.

5 Arrange the pieces of fish on two plates with the carrot decorations, corn for eyes and peas for bubbles. Serve with warmed canned spaghetti rings.

TIP
You can freeze the uncooked breaded portions to provide a quick meal at a later date when you are pressed for time. Freeze them on a tray and then wrap them well to prevent the odor from tainting other food in the freezer.

Tuna Risotto

Serves 2
1 tsp oil
¼ onion, finely chopped
2oz long grain white rice
2oz frozen mixed vegetables
1 small garlic clove, crushed
2 tsp ketchup
3½oz can tuna in water
salt and pepper (optional)

1 Heat the oil in a small saucepan and sauté the chopped onion for about 3 minutes until softened.

2 Add the rice, mixed vegetables, garlic, ketchup and 1 cup water and a little salt and pepper, if desired.

TIP
If desired use cold leftover cooked chicken, lamb or beef in place of the tuna.

3 Bring to a boil and simmer uncovered for 10 minutes. Drain the tuna and add to the rice mixture, stirring to mix. Cook for 3–4 minutes, stirring occasionally, until the water has been absorbed by the rice and the rice is tender.

4 Spoon onto plates and cool slightly before serving.

Fish Finger Log Cabins

Serves 2
4 frozen fish fingers
1oz green cabbage
8 snow peas
2 frozen peas
1 strip green bell pepper
1 strip red bell pepper

1 Grill the fish fingers for 10 minutes, turning once until golden. Meanwhile finely shred the cabbage and cook in boiling water for 3 minutes. Add the snow peas and peas and cook for 2 minutes more. Drain well.

2 Arrange two fish fingers side by side on each plate. Trim the snow peas and use them to make a roof, slightly overlapping the edges of the fish fingers.

VARIATION
Sausage Log Cabin
Use four small broiled chicken or turkey hot dogs for each cabin. Make the roof from green beans and use shredded spinach for the grass.

3 Cut four windows from the green pepper and two doors from the red pepper and add to the log cabins, using peas as door handles. Arrange the shredded cabbage to look like grass.

TOAST TOPPERS

ALL CHILDREN, EVEN THE FUSSIEST OF DINERS, LOVE BREAD AND THERE IS NO QUICKER CONVENIENCE FOOD. INTRODUCE NEW TASTES WITH THESE SUPER-SPEEDY SNACKS.

Shape Sorters

Serves 2

4 slices bread
butter or margarine, for spreading
2 tbsp smooth peanut butter
½ cup grated Cheddar cheese
4 cherry tomatoes
3 slices cucumber

VARIATION
Pizza Shape Sorters
Spread the shapes with ketchup. Chop a tomato finely, and sprinkle over the shapes, then add some grated cheese. Broil until bubbling and golden.

1 Toast the bread lightly on both sides and remove the crusts. Stamp out shapes using square, star, triangle and round cookie cutters.

2 Spread the shapes with butter or margarine and then peanut butter. Place the shapes on a baking sheet and sprinkle with cheese.

3 Grill until the cheese is bubbly. Cool slightly, arrange on a plate and serve with tomato wedges and quartered cucumber slices.

Happy Families

Serves 2

3 slices bread
butter or margarine, for spreading
3 slices American cheese
2 slices ham
a little watercress
1 strip red bell pepper
½ carrot
small pieces of cucumber

1 Stamp out men and women shapes from the bread using small cutters. Spread with a little butter or margarine.

2 Stamp out cheese dresses using the woman cutter and trimming off the head. Press onto three of the bodies. Cut out cheese shirts and ham pants and suspenders. Add to the remaining shapes.

3 Snip off the leaves from the watercress and use for eyes. Cut tiny red pepper mouths and make necklaces and bow ties from the carrot and cucumber using flower cutters. Arrange on plates.

Eggy Bread Butterflies

Serves 2

4 small broccoli florets
8 peas
1 small carrot
1 slice Colby or Cheddar cheese
2 slices ham
2 slices bread
1 egg
2 tsp milk
1 tsp light vegetable oil
a little ketchup

1 Cook the broccoli florets and the peas in a saucepan of boiling water for 5 minutes. Drain well.

2 For each butterfly, cut four thin slices of carrot and cut into flower shapes with a small cookie cutter. Cut out four small squares from the cheese.

3 Cut four thin strips from the rest of the carrot for antennae. Roll up each piece of ham and arrange in the middle of two serving plates to make the two butterfly bodies.

4 Cut butterfly wings from the bread using a small knife.

5 Beat together the egg and milk and dip the bread in to coat both sides thoroughly. Heat the oil in a medium-size skillet and fry the bread until golden on both sides.

6 Assemble the butterfly, using the eggy bread for the wings and decorating with the carrot, cheese, broccoli and peas. Use a blob of ketchup for the head.

TIP
Vary the ingredients for butterfly decorations. Make a body from a broiled breakfast sausage if preferred.

Tuna Flowers

Serves 2–3

6 thin slices bread
1oz butter, plus extra if necessary
2 tsp all-purpose flour
5 tbsp milk
4 tbsp grated Colby or Cheddar cheese
3½oz can tuna, drained
4 tbsp frozen mixed vegetables, defrosted
½ carrot
6 slices cucumber, halved
a little watercress
salt and pepper (optional)

1 Preheat the oven to 400°F. Cut out six flower shapes from the bread using a 3½in scalloped cookie cutter. Flatten each piece slightly with a rolling pin.

2 Melt the butter in a saucepan or microwave. Brush a little over one side of each piece of bread and then press the bread, buttered side down, into sections of a muffin pan. Brush the second side of bread with a little more butter.

3 Bake in the oven for about 10–12 minutes until crisp and golden around the edges.

4 Stir the flour into the remaining butter (you should have about 2 tsp left). Gradually stir in the milk and bring to a boil, stirring until the sauce is thick and smooth.

5 Stir in 3 tbsp of the cheese, the tuna, the mixed vegetables and a little salt and pepper, if desired.

6 Heat through and then spoon into the baked bread cups and sprinkle with remaining cheese.

7 Arrange the tuna cups on serving plates. Cut the carrot into thin strips for flower stems and add to the plate with halved cucumber slices for leaves and watercress for grass.

Tic-tac-toe

Serves 2

- 8 green beans
- ¼ red bell pepper
- 6 slices spicy cooked sausage, such as chorizo
- 2 slices bread
- butter or margarine, for spreading
- 4oz Cheddar cheese

TIP
To vary the topping, use thin strips of carrot or ham for the grid, sliced sausage, turkey hot dogs or carrot for the O's, carrot, green pepper or cucumber for the X's.

1 Trim the beans, thinly slice the pepper, discarding any seeds, and thinly slice the sausage.

2 Cook the beans in boiling water for 5 minutes. Toast the bread lightly on both sides and spread with butter or margarine. Thinly slice the cheese and place on the toast.

3 Drain the beans and arrange four on each piece of toast to form a tic-tac-toe grid. Add X's made from pepper strips and O's from pieces of the sausage.

4 Grill the toasts until the cheese is bubbly. Arrange on plates and cool slightly before serving.

Stripy Cheese on Toast

Serves 2

- 2 slices bread
- butter or margarine, for spreading
- 2oz Cheddar cheese
- 2oz Colby cheese
- 2 cherry tomatoes, to serve

1 Toast the bread lightly on both sides then spread each slice with butter or margarine.

2 Thinly slice the cheese and then cut into strips about 1in wide. Arrange alternate colored cheese strips over the toast and broil the toasts until bubbly.

3 Cool slightly, then cut into squares, arrange on plates and serve with cherry tomato wedges.

TIP
Add a thin layer of ketchup or peanut butter underneath the cheese slices for a surprise flavor.

Speedy Sausage Rolls

Makes 18

8 slices multi-grain bread
8oz breakfast sausages
3 tbsp butter or margarine
carrot and cucumber sticks, to serve

1 Preheat the oven to 375°F. Trim the crusts off the bread and cut into slices just a little smaller than the sausages.

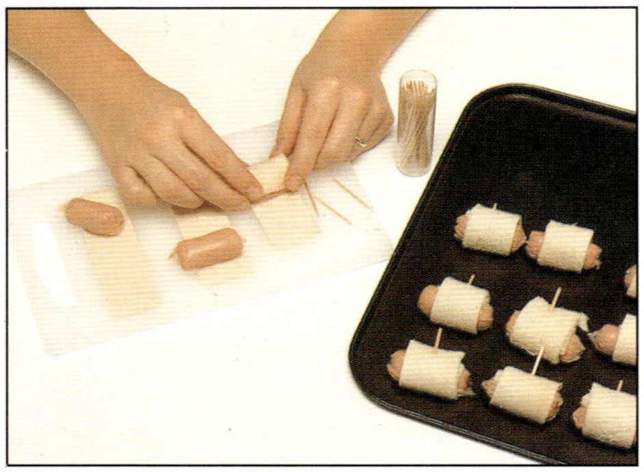

2 Wrap each piece of bread around a sausage and secure with a halved toothpick. Place the sausage rolls on a baking sheet.

3 Melt the butter or margarine in a small saucepan or in the microwave and brush over the prepared sausage rolls.

4 Bake in the oven for 15 minutes until browned. Cool slightly and remove the toothpicks. Arrange on a plate and serve with carrot and cucumber sticks.

TIP
If desired spread a little tomato relish or ketchup over the bread before wrapping around the sausages to give a sharper flavor. Spread the bread with a little mild, prepared mustard if the child likes it. If the bread is thickly cut, flatten it slightly with a rolling pin, before wrapping around the sausages.

Pizza Clock

Serves 3–4

8in ready-made pizza base

3 tbsp ketchup or pizza sauce

2 tomatoes

¾ cup grated cheese

pinch of dried marjoram

1 green bell pepper

1 large carrot

1 thick slice ham

1 Preheat oven to 425°F. Place the pizza base on a baking sheet and spread with ketchup or pizza sauce. Chop the tomatoes and scatter over the pizza with the grated cheese and marjoram.

2 Place directly on an oven shelf and bake for 12 minutes, until the cheese is bubbly. (Place a baking tray on the shelf below the pizza to catch any drips of cheese.)

3 Meanwhile halve the pepper, cut away the core and seeds and stamp out the numbers 3, 6, 9 and 12 with small number cutters. Peel and thinly cut the carrot lengthwise and stamp out the numbers 1, 2, 4, 5, 7, 8, 10 and 11. Arrange on the pizza to form a clock face.

4 Cut out a carrot circle. Cut two clock hands, each about 3in long from the ham. Arrange on the pizza with the round of carrot.

5 Place the pizza clock on a serving plate and arrange the numbers around the edge. Cool the pizza clock slightly before cutting into wedges and serving.

TIP
If preferred, make a smaller version of this using half a toasted English muffin. Top as above and broil until the cheese melts. Add ham hands and small pieces of carrot to mark the numbers.

Spotty Sandwiches

Serves 2

1 hard-boiled egg
2 tbsp mayonnaise
2 slices white bread
2 slices whole-wheat bread
a little mustard and cress or chives
½ small carrot
a little shredded lettuce

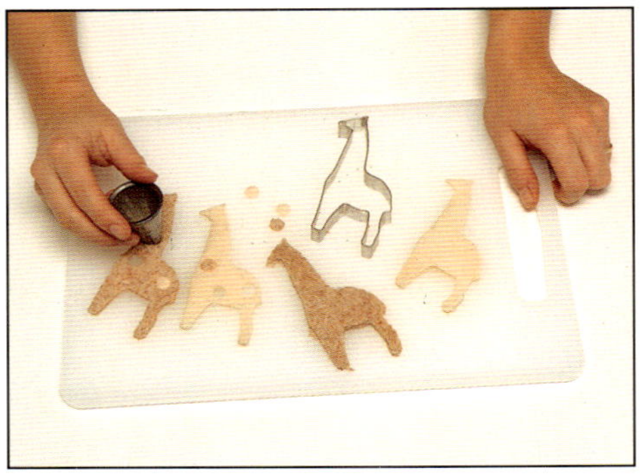

1 Peel and finely chop the egg, place in a small bowl and blend well with the mayonnaise.

2 Stamp out giraffe shapes from the whole-wheat and white bread using a cookie cutter.

3 Cut tiny rounds from each shape using the end of a metal piping tube and then replace the rounds with opposite colored bread circles.

4 Spread the egg mayonnaise over half of the shapes and top with the remaining shapes. Arrange on plates with snipped mustard and cress or chives for grass and shaped carrot slices for flowers.

Sandwich Snails

Serves 2

1 strip red bell pepper
small piece cucumber
1 tbsp frozen corn, defrosted
¼ cup grated Cheddar cheese
1 tbsp mayonnaise
1 slice bread
2 cooked breakfast sausages

1 Cut away any seeds from the pepper and cut out four small squares for the snails' eyes and cut four strips of cucumber for their antennae. Finely chop the remaining pepper and cucumber and mix with the corn, cheese and mayonnaise. Place in a bowl.

2 Trim the crusts off the bread, cut in half and overlap two short edges together to make a long strip. Flatten slightly with a rolling pin so that the bread bonds together.

VARIATION
For pasta snails, use large shell pasta instead of the bread and stuff with the corn mixture.

3 Spread the bread with the cheese mixture and roll up tightly. Squeeze together then cut in half crosswise to make two rounds.

4 Arrange each slice, cut side up, on two serving plates. Arrange the sausages for bodies, and use the cucumber strips for antennae and the red pepper squares for the eyes.

Strawberry Ice Cream

Makes 3¾ cups

- 1¼ cups heavy cream
- 15oz pre-prepared custard
- 1lb strawberries
- teddy bear graham crackers, to decorate
- strawberries, to decorate

1 Whip the cream until softly peaking then fold in the custard.

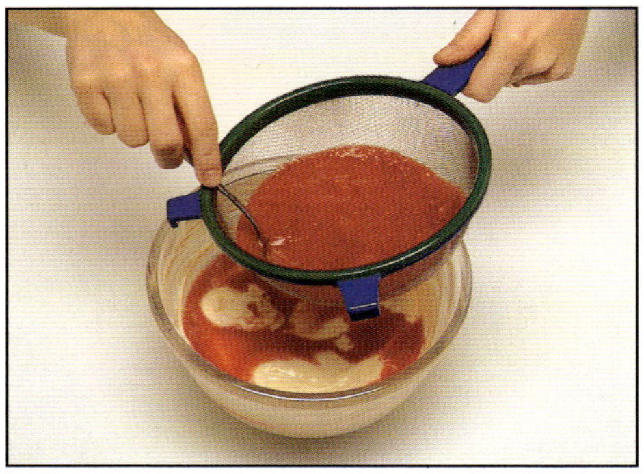

2 Hull the strawberries and then rinse and pat dry. Process or blend to make a smooth purée, then press through a strainer into the cream. Fold into the cream.

3 Pour the mixture into a plastic container and freeze the ice cream for 6–7 hours until half frozen.

4 Beat the ice cream with a fork or in a blender until smooth, then return the container to the freezer and freeze until solid.

5 Remove the ice cream from the freezer 10 minutes before serving so that it can soften slightly. Scoop into serving bowls and decorate each with graham crackers and extra fruit such as strawberries.

VARIATIONS

Strawberry Ripple Ice Cream
Purée and strain an extra 9oz strawberries and sweeten with 2 tbsp confectioner's sugar. Swirl this into the half-frozen ice cream at Step 4 and then freeze until solid.

Apricot and Chocolate Chip Ice Cream
Whisk 1¼ cups heavy cream, and fold in 15oz custard. Drain and purée the contents of a 15oz can apricot slices in natural juice and stir into the cream with the finely grated zest of 1 orange. Pour into a plastic container, freeze until slushy and then beat well. Stir in 3½oz package chocolate chips and freeze again until solid. Scoop into serving dishes and decorate the ice cream with orange segments and wafer cookies, if desired.

Raspberry Sorbet

Makes: 3¾ cups
2 tsp powdered gelatin
2½ cups water
1¼ cups superfine sugar
1½lb raspberries, hulled
grated zest and juice of ½ lemon

1 Put 2 tbsp water in a cup, sprinkle the gelatin over and set aside for a few minutes to soak.

2 Place the water and sugar in a saucepan and heat, stirring occasionally until the sugar has completely dissolved.

3 Bring to a boil and boil rapidly for 3 minutes. Remove from the heat, add the gelatin mixture to the syrup and stir until completely dissolved. Let cool.

4 Blend or process the raspberries to a smooth purée then press through a strainer into the syrup. Stir in lemon zest and juice.

5 Pour into a plastic container and freeze for 6–7 hours or until the mixture is half frozen.

6 Beat the sorbet with a fork or transfer to a food processor and process until smooth. Return to the freezer and freeze until solid.

7 Remove the sorbet from the freezer 10 minutes before serving to soften slightly, then scoop into dishes with a melon baller or small teaspoon.

VARIATION

Summer Fruit Sorbet

Follow the recipe up to Step 3. Put a 1¼lb package of frozen summer fruits into a second saucepan. Add 4 tbsp water, cover and cook for 5 minutes until soft, then purée and strain, add to the syrup and continue as above.

Yogurt Lollipops

Makes 6

5oz container strawberry yogurt
⅔ cup milk
2 tsp strawberry flavoring (for milk)

1 Mix the yogurt, milk and strawberry flavoring together.

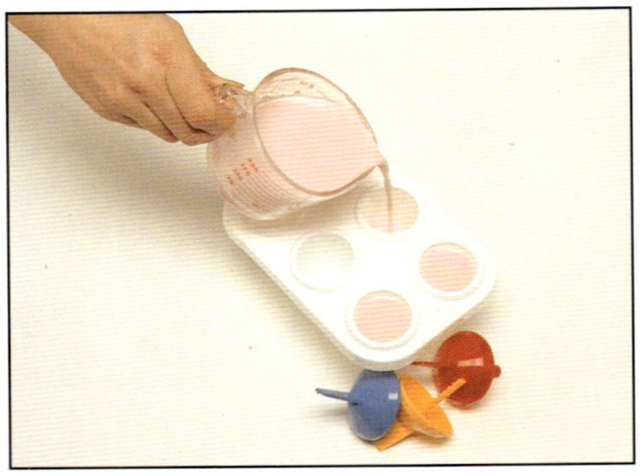

2 Pour the mixture into six small plastic popsicle molds. Add the popsicle sticks and freeze overnight.

3 Dip the molds into hot water, count to 15, then flex handles and remove. Serve at once.

TIP
Store lollipops for up to a week in the freezer. Make sure they are tightly covered as they can pick up other flavors in the freezer.

Jolly Jellies

Serves 4

3oz package strawberry Jell-o
2 ripe plums
6oz plain yogurt
4 candies
2 tsp colored jimmies

1 Make the Jell-o according to the package instructions and set aside to cool.

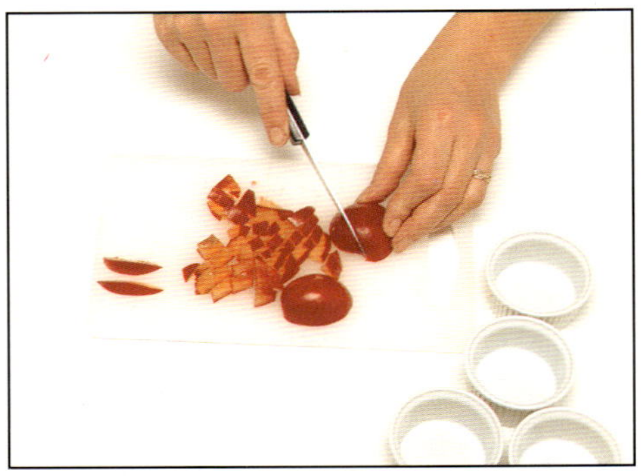

2 Halve the plums, cut away the pits and reserve four thin slices. Chop the remaining fruit and divide among four small dishes.

3 Stir the yogurt into the Jell-o and pour into the dishes. Chill in the refrigerator until set.

4 Decorate with sliced plums for mouths, candies for the eyes and colored jimmies for hair.

TIP
If you have a fussy eater who hates lumps, finely chop or purée the plums before adding to the Jell-o so that the child doesn't know it's not just Jell-o!

Pancakes

Serves 2–3

⅓ cup all-purpose flour
1 egg
⅔ cup milk
1 tbsp light vegetable oil
For the filling
1 banana
1 orange
2–3 scoops ice cream
a little maple syrup

1 Sift the flour into a bowl, add the egg and gradually whisk in the milk to form a smooth batter. Whisk in 1 tsp of the oil.

2 To make the filling, slice the banana thinly or in chunks. Cut the peel away from the orange with a serrated knife, then cut the orange into segments.

3 Heat a little of the remaining oil in medium-sized non-stick pan, pour off any excess oil and add 2 tbsp of the batter. Tilt the pan to evenly coat the pan and cook for a couple of minutes until the pancake is set and the underside is golden.

4 Loosen the edges with a knife then toss the pancake or turn with a knife. Brown the other side and then slide out onto a plate. Fold in four and keep warm.

5 Cook the rest of the batter in the same way until you have made 6 pancakes. Place two on each plate.

6 Spoon a little fruit into each pancake and arrange on serving plates. Top with the remaining fruit, a scoop of ice cream and pour over a little maple syrup. Serve at once.

Traffic Light Sundaes

Serves 6

½ package lime Jell-o
½ package orange Jell-o
½ package strawberry Jell-o
2 kiwi fruit
10oz can mandarin oranges
6 scoops vanilla ice cream, to serve
12 strawberries to decorate

1 Make up each batch of Jell-o in a separate bowl with boiling water according to the instructions on the package. Cool, then transfer to the refrigerator and allow to set.

2 Peel and slice the kiwi fruit, hull and rinse the strawberries and cut in half. Drain the mandarins.

3 Chop all of the Jell-o and divide the green Jell-o equally among six sundae glasses.

4 Add a little kiwi fruit and continue making layers using the orange Jell-o and mandarins and topping with the strawberry Jell-o.

5 Add half the strawberries, top with ice cream and decorate with the remaining strawberries. Serve immediately.

TIP
This is a great recipe for a party supper – simple but ever popular. For smaller numbers of children, halve the recipe to make three. Or for tiny children make up half-size sundaes in plastic cups.

Fruit-and-yogurt Jelly Roll

Serves 2

2 slices prepackaged jelly roll
4 tsp orange juice
1 small orange
2oz strawberries
5oz pre-prepared vanilla pudding
2 tsp plain yogurt
2 sugar flowers, to decorate

TIP
Use ⅔ cup leftover custard instead of pudding if you have it or make custard with custard powder and ⅔ cup milk.

1 Put a slice of jelly roll in the base of two ramekin dishes and spoon the orange juice over the top. Peel the orange and divide the segments between the dishes.

2 Hull, rinse and chop the strawberries. Place in dishes.

3 Spoon the pudding over the strawberries, top with yogurt and decorate with sugar flowers.

Baked Bananas

Serves 2

2 medium bananas
2 small scoops ice cream

1 Preheat the oven to 350°F. Separate the unpeeled bananas and put on a baking sheet. Cook for 10 minutes until the skins have blackened and the bananas feel soft.

2 Hold the banana in a dish towel, make a slit along the length of the banana and peel off the skin. Peel the second banana.

3 Slice and arrange each as a ring on a plate. Place a scoop of ice cream in the center of each plate.

TIP
For an adult version, slit the banana and spoon in a teaspoon or two of coffee cream liqueur, eat out of the skin with a teaspoon.

ABC·123

QUICK CAKES AND BAKES THE KIDS CAN MAKE

COOKING IS FUN AND THE EARLIER YOU LEARN THE MORE FUN IT IS. EVEN THE FUSSIEST EATER CAN BE AN ENTHUSIASTIC COOK, AND HELPING TO DECIDE WHAT TO COOK FOR DINNER CAN MAKE A CHILD MORE WILLING TO SIT DOWN WITH THE FAMILY AND HAND AROUND THEIR HOMEMADE GOODIES. LEARNING TO MEASURE INGREDIENTS, TO MIX, SPREAD AND SPOON OUT, ALL HELPS WITH COORDINATION AND ENCOURAGES A BASIC INTEREST AND LOVE OF FOOD.

Getting ready

- Find a large apron or cover the child's clothes with an old adult-sized shirt with the sleeves cut down.
- Always wash hands before you start to cook.
- Choose a sturdy chair for your child to stand on next to the work top or kitchen table. Or put a large cloth on the floor, set out bowls, ingredients, etc, and prepare the food sitting down.
- Make it clear to your child that only the adult opens the oven door and touches saucepans on the stove.
- Keep knives and scissors out of the way; provide blunt, round-ended scissors if required.

Orange and Apple Rockies

Makes 24

oil, for greasing
½ cup margarine
2 cups self-rising flour
1 large eating apple
2oz ready-to-eat dried apricots
2oz golden raisins
grated zest of 1 small orange
⅓ cup brown sugar
1 egg
1 tbsp milk
apple slices, to serve

1 Preheat the oven to 375°F and brush two baking sheets with a little oil. Rub the margarine into the flour with your fingertips until the mixture resembles fine breadcrumbs.

2 Peel, core and finely chop the apple, chop the apricots and stir into the flour mixture with the golden raisins and orange zest. Reserve 2 tbsp of the sugar and stir the rest into the mixture.

3 Beat the egg and milk, add to the flour mixture and mix until just beginning to bind together.

4 Drop spoonfuls, well spaced apart onto the baking sheet. Sprinkle with the reserved sugar and bake in the oven for 12–15 minutes. Transfer to a serving plate and serve warm or cold with apple slices.

TIP
Freeze any leftover rockies in a plastic bag for up to three months.

Date Crunch

Makes 24 pieces

8oz package oatmeal cookies
3oz pitted dates
⅓ cup butter
2 tbsp light maple syrup
3oz golden raisins
5oz milk or dark chocolate

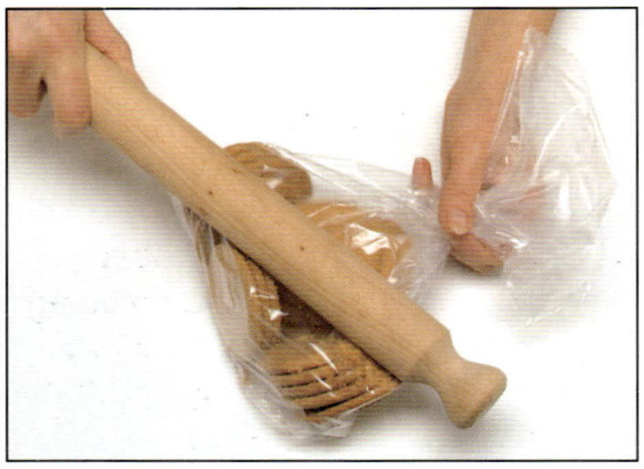

1 Line a 7in shallow pan with foil. Put the cookies in a plastic bag and crush roughly with a rolling pin. Finely chop the dates.

2 Gently heat the butter and syrup in a small saucepan until the butter has melted.

3 Stir in the crushed cookies, the dates and raisins and mix well. Spoon into the pan, press flat with the back of a spoon and chill for 1 hour.

4 Break the chocolate into a bowl, melt over hot water, and then spoon over the cookie mixture spreading evenly with a spatula. Chill until set.

5 Lift the foil out of the pan and peel away. Cut the cookie into 24 pieces and arrange on a plate.

TIP
For an alternative topping drizzle 3oz melted white and 3oz melted dark chocolate over the cookie to give random squiggly lines. Chill until set.

Chocolate Dominoes

Makes 16

oil, for greasing
¾ cup margarine
⅞ cup superfine sugar
⅔ cup self-rising flour
1oz cocoa, sifted
3 eggs
For the Topping
¾ cup butter, softened
1oz cocoa
3 cups confectioner's sugar
a few licorice strips and 4oz package M & M's, for decoration

1 Preheat the oven to 350°F. Lightly brush a 7 × 11in baking pan with a little oil and line the base of the pan with wax paper.

2 Put all the cake ingredients in a bowl and beat until smooth.

3 Spoon into the pan and level the surface with a spatula.

4 Bake in the oven for 30 minutes, or until the cake springs back when pressed with the fingertips.

5 Cool in the pan for 5 minutes, then loosen the edges with a knife and turn out onto a wire rack. Peel off the paper and allow the cake to cool.

6 Turn the cake onto a chopping board and cut into 16 bars.

7 To make the topping, place the butter in a bowl, sift in the cocoa and confectioner's sugar and beat until smooth. Spread the topping evenly over the cakes with a spatula.

8 Add a strip of licorice to each cake, decorate with M & M's for domino dots and arrange the cakes on a serving plate.

VARIATION
Traffic Light Cakes
Makes 16
To make Traffic Light Cakes omit the cocoa and add an extra 3 tbsp flour. Omit the cocoa from the icing and add an extra 3 tbsp confectioner's sugar and flavor with ½ tsp vanilla extract. Spread over the cakes and decorate with eight halved red, yellow and green candied cherries to look like traffic lights. Arrange the cakes on a serving plate.

Marshmallow Krispie Cakes

Makes 45

oil, for greasing
9oz bag toffees
4 tbsp butter
3 tbsp milk
4oz marshmallows
6oz Rice Krispies

1 Lightly brush an 8 × 13in roasting pan with a little oil. Put the toffees, butter and milk in a saucepan and heat gently, stirring until the toffees have melted.

2 Add the marshmallows and cereal and stir until well mixed and the marshmallows have melted.

3 Spoon into the pan, level the surface and let set. Cut into squares and serve.

Mini Muffins

Makes 24

1½ cups all-purpose flour
2 tsp baking powder
¼ cup soft light brown sugar
⅔ cup milk
1 egg, beaten
4 tbsp butter or margarine, melted
2oz candied cherries
2oz ready-to-eat dried apricots
½ tsp vanilla extract

1 Preheat the oven to 425°F and place 24 paper petits fours cups in the sections of two petits fours or mini muffin pans.

2 Place the flour, baking powder and sugar in a bowl and add the milk, egg and melted butter or margarine and stir thoroughly until the mixture is smooth.

3 Chop the cherries and apricots and stir into the muffin mixture with the vanilla extract.

4 Spoon the muffin mixture into the paper cups so they are about three-quarters full.

5 Cook for 10–12 minutes until well risen and browned. If you have just one pan cook in two batches.

TIP
For older children spoon the mixture into 12 medium-sized paper muffin cups. Muffins are best served warm from the oven. If they don't get eaten right away, they can be frozen for up to three months.

VARIATIONS

Chocolate Chip Muffins
Substitute 1oz cocoa for 2 tbsp flour. Omit the cherries, apricots and vanilla and add 2oz white and 2oz dark chocolate chips.

Orange and Banana Muffins
Substitute 2 small mashed bananas for ¼ cup milk. Omit the cherries, apricot and vanilla and add 1 tbsp grated orange zest.

Cupcake Faces

Makes 12

⅔ cup margarine
⅔ cup superfine sugar
1 cup self-rising flour
2 eggs

For the Topping

¼ cup butter
1 cup confectioner's sugar
pink food coloring
4oz package M & M's
2 red licorice bootlaces
12 candies
3oz plain chocolate

1 Preheat the oven to 350°F. Place 12 paper muffin cups in the sections of a muffin pan.

2 Put all the cake ingredients into a bowl and beat until smooth.

3 Divide the cake mixture among the cups and cook for 12–15 minutes until well risen and the cakes spring back when pressed with a fingertip. Let cool.

4 Meanwhile make the topping: beat the butter in a bowl, sift in the confectioner's sugar and beat the mixture until smooth. Stir in a little pink food coloring.

5 Spread the icing over the cakes. Add M & M eyes, short pieces of licorice for mouths and a candy nose.

6 Break the chocolate into pieces, melt in a bowl over a saucepan of gently simmering water and then spoon into a greaseproof paper piping bag. Snip off the tip and pipe hair, eye balls, glasses and mustaches onto the cakes.

7 Carefully arrange in a single layer on a serving plate and allow the icing to set before serving.

VARIATION
Alphabet Cakes

Make up a half quantity of cake mixture as above and spoon into 24 mini muffin or petits fours cups. Put into sections of a mini muffin or petits fours pan or arrange on a baking sheet close together and cook for 8–10 minutes then cool. Blend 2 cups sifted confectioner's sugar with 2 tbsp water until smooth. Add a little water if necessary to make a thick spoonable icing. Spoon 2 tbsp into a piping bag fitted with a small writing tube. Spoon half the remaining icing into a separate bowl and color pink. Color the remaining icing blue. Spoon the icing over the cakes, smooth the surface and pipe on letters of the alphabet. Let set.

Gingerbread People

Makes 24

- oil, for greasing
- 2 cups all-purpose flour
- 1 tsp ground ginger
- ¼ tsp ground cinnamon
- 1½ tsp baking soda
- 4 tbsp margarine
- ⅔ cup soft light brown sugar
- 3 tbsp light maple syrup
- 2 tbsp milk
- 3oz dark chocolate
- 2 packages M & M's

1 Brush two baking sheets with a little oil. Sift the flour, spices and baking soda into a bowl.

2 Place the margarine, sugar and syrup in a saucepan and heat until the margarine has melted.

3 Remove from heat and stir in the flour mixture and milk. Mix to a firm dough, chill for 30 minutes.

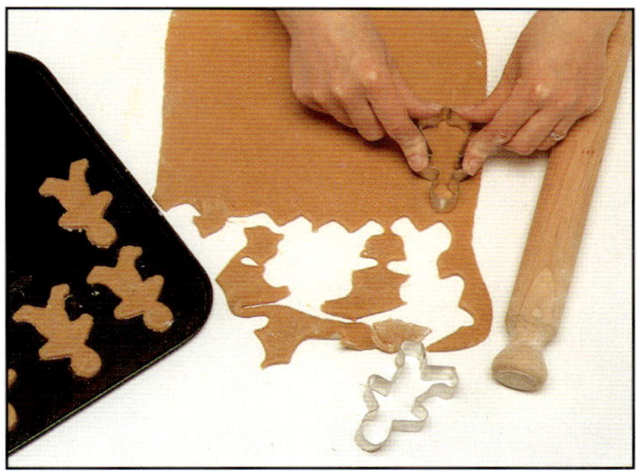

4 Preheat the oven to 325°F. Knead the dough lightly and roll out on a floured surface. Cut out gingerbread men and women with 3½in cutters. Place on the baking sheets, reroll the trimmings, stamp out more gingerbread people and continue until all the dough is used.

5 Cook for 10 minutes until golden and then set aside to cool and harden a little on the trays. Loosen while still warm.

6 Break the chocolate into a bowl and melt over hot water, then spoon a little chocolate over the gingerbread men for pants. Place on the baking tray to set.

7 Spoon the remaining chocolate into a piping bag fitted with a small writing tube and pipe faces on the gingerbread people and some swirls for petticoats on the women. Pipe two dots on all the people for buttons and stick on M & M's. Let set before serving.

TIP
Chocolate decorations soften cookies, so eat on the day or decorate as many cookies as you will eat and store the rest in a tin for up to four days. For a party, decorate people with clothes cut from colored ready-to-roll icing.

Bread Animals

Makes 15

oil, for greasing
2 × 10oz packages white bread mix
a few currants
½ small red bell pepper
1 small carrot
1 egg

1 Brush two large baking sheets with a little oil. Put the bread mixes in a large bowl and prepare as directed on the package with warm water.

2 Knead on a lightly floured surface for 5 minutes until the dough is smooth and elastic. Return the dough to the bowl, cover with oiled plastic wrap and leave in a warm place for ¾–1 hour until it has doubled in size.

3 Preheat the oven to 425°F. Knead the dough again for about 5 minutes and then divide into five equal pieces.

4 To make snakes, take one piece of dough, cut into three and shape each into a 6in snake, making a slit in one end for the mouth. Twist the snakes on the baking sheet. Insert two currants for eyes. Cut out a thin strip of pepper, cutting a triangle at one end for the forked tongue.

5 For hedgehogs, take another piece of dough and cut into three. Shape each into an oval about 2½in long. Place on the baking sheet and add currant eyes and a red pepper nose. Snip the dough with scissors to make the prickly spines.

6 For the mice, take a third piece of dough and cut into four pieces. Shape three pieces into ovals each about 2½in long and place on the baking sheet. Shape tiny rounds of dough for ears and wiggly tails from the fourth piece of dough. Press onto the mice bodies and use the currants for eyes.

7 Cut small strips of carrot and use for whiskers.

TIP
Give a portion of the prepared dough to your children, with some chopped dried fruits and allow them to create their very own bread animals.

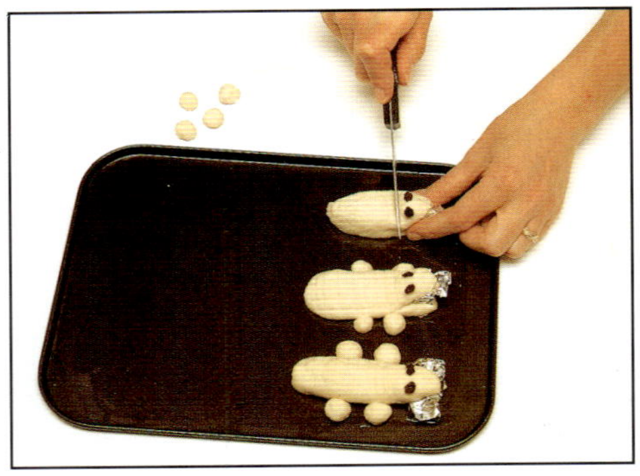

8 For the crocodiles, cut another piece of dough into three. Take a small piece off each and reserve. Shape the large pieces into 4in long "sausages." Make slits for the mouths and wedge open with crumpled foil. Add currant eyes. Shape the spare dough into feet and press into position. Make criss-cross cuts on the crocodiles' backs.

9 For rabbits, take the final piece of dough and cut into three. Take a small piece off each for tails. Roll the remaining pieces of dough into thick "sausages" 7in long. Loop the dough and twist twice to form the body and head of rabbit. Use the rest for tails.

10 Cover the shapes with oiled plastic wrap and leave in a warm place for 10–15 minutes. Brush with beaten egg and cook for 10–12 minutes until golden.

11 Serve warm or cold split and filled with ham or cheese.

Cheese Shapes

Makes 15

- oil, for greasing
- 3 cups self-rising flour
- pinch of salt
- ½ cup margarine
- 4oz Cheddar cheese
- 2 eggs, beaten
- 4 tbsp milk
- 2 tsp sesame seeds
- 2 tsp poppy seeds

1 Preheat the oven to 425°F.

2 Place the flour and salt in a bowl, add the margarine and rub in with your fingertips or an electric mixer until the mixture resembles fine breadcrumbs.

3 Grate the cheese, reserve 2 tbsp and stir the rest into the flour. Add three-quarters of the beaten eggs and milk to the flour and mix to a soft dough.

4 Knead the dough lightly and roll out thickly on a surface that has been dusted with flour.

5 Stamp out numbers with 3in cutters and arrange well spaced apart on two baking sheets. Reroll trimmings and stamp out more shapes to use up the pastry.

6 Brush the tops of the numbers with the reserved egg. Sprinkle five of the numbers with sesame seeds, five with poppy seeds and the remainder with grated cheese.

7 Cook for 12–15 minutes until well risen and browned. Cool slightly then arrange the cheese shapes on a plate and serve warm.

Marmite and Cheese Whirls

Makes 16

- oil, for greasing
- 9oz frozen puff pastry, defrosted
- flour, for dusting
- ½ tsp Marmite
- 1 egg, beaten
- 2oz Colby or Cheddar cheese, grated
- carrot and cucumber sticks, to serve

1 Preheat the oven to 425°F and brush a large baking sheet with a little oil.

2 Roll out the pastry on a floured surface to a large rectangle, about 14 × 10in.

3 Spread the pastry with Marmite, leaving a ½in border. Brush the edges of the pastry with egg and sprinkle the cheese to cover the Marmite.

4 Roll the pastry up quite tightly like a jelly roll, starting from a longer edge. Brush the outside of the pastry with beaten egg.

5 Cut the roll into thick slices and place on the baking sheet.

6 Cook for 12–15 minutes until the pastry is well risen and golden. Arrange on a serving plate and serve warm or cold with carrot and cucumber sticks.

TIP
Marmite is a yeast derivative high in B vitamins. Very popular in Great Britain, it is available here in specialty stores. Omit the Marmite and use peanut butter if preferred.

FAMILY MEALS

Eating together as a family takes on a new dimension as your family grows and there's a baby, fussy toddler and Mom and Dad to feed together. Rather than attempting to cook three different meals or to cook one very simple meal you know the children will like, opt instead to cook three meals

from one basic set of ingredients: a simple baby dinner, eye-catching meal for even the fussiest of toddlers and a spicy dinner for the grown-ups.

The recipes are aimed at a baby aged nine months and over, a toddler or small child aged eighteen months to four years and two adults.

Eating Together

Family meal times should be a pleasure but they can all too often turn into a battleground. Whatever family rules you have about table manners it's important that all the family knows about them and that you are consistent. What matters to some families may not be important to you. If you want your children to stay at the table until everyone has finished, make sure all the family understands this. Some parents may feel it's more relaxing if the children leave the table once they have finished, leaving the adults to eat the rest of their meal in relative peace. Whatever you decide, stick to it; don't be brow beaten by well-meaning grandparents or friends.

Try to eat together as a family at

Left: *Part of the fun of eating together is sharing the preparation, too. Children love helping in the kitchen, and this involves them in the meal from the very start.*

Below: *A relaxed but polite atmosphere will enhance enjoyment and consequently encourage good eating habits.*

least once a day, even if you don't all eat the same food, so that your toddler can learn how to behave by watching the rest of the family. Explain to other members of the family that you are all setting the baby an example – a great way to get everyone on their best behavior, whatever their age.

Above: *Setting the table is another task that children delight in, and another way to make them feel part of the family meal time.*

Below: *Even if the child is too young to have exactly the same food, sharing the table is important.*

It is never too early to encourage children to help: setting the table can become quite a game, especially if dolly or teddy has a place set too. Passing plates, bread and salt and pepper can be perilous to begin with but with a little practice becomes second nature. Transform a dull wet Monday dinner into a special occasion with a few flowers or candles (well out of reach of very tiny children) and pretty table mats and paper napkins for added decoration.

Try to avoid using a tablecloth with very young children as they can pull the cloth and everything with it onto the floor and themselves, with appalling consequences if there's a hot coffee pot or hot casserole dish. Similarly, beware of tiny hands reaching out from the highchair to grab a mug of hot coffee or snatch at a sharp knife.

Offer a variety of foods at each meal, some foods you know your toddler and baby will like and foods that you like too so that everyone is happy. Offer very tiny portions of foods that are new or ones that your child is not very fond of and encourage your child to have at least one mouthful.

Encourage baby to feed himself with easy-to-pick-up finger foods. This gives the adults a chance to eat their food too. Don't worry about the mess until you get to the end of the meal.

For added protection when your toddler is eating at the table, use a wipe-clean place mat and cover the seat of a dining chair with a towel or dish towel. Better still buy a thin padded seat cover that is removable and machine washable but will tie on to the seat securely.

Children cannot bear to eat foods that are too hot, not just because they may burn their mouths, but because of the frustration. Not being

able to eat when the food is there and they are hungry can lead to great outbursts of temper. Many children actually prefer their food to be just lukewarm. Cool broccoli quickly by rinsing with a little cold water. Spoon hot stews onto a large plate so they cool quickly and always test the temperature of foods before serving to a child.

TABLE MANNERS

Toddlers can be incredibly messy, but try not to be too fussy and just wipe sticky hands and faces at the end of the meal. Enjoyment is the key. If your child is eating her meal with enthusiasm rather than style, then that is the most important part at the beginning – table manners will come as your child becomes more adept with a knife and fork.

Be understanding and flexible, small children have a lot to learn when they begin to join in with family meals. An active toddler has to learn how to sit still – quite an art in itself – how to hold a knife and fork and how to drink from a cup and somehow watch what everyone else is doing and join in too.

The baby has to adapt to sitting up to the table in his highchair and waiting for an adult to offer him a spoonful of food. Not surprisingly there can be a few tantrums and accidents, not to mention mess. Try not to worry. Offer a few finger foods after a bowl of ground foods so that the baby can feed himself, giving you a chance to finish your own meal and tidy up.

Above: *Good manners and sharing provide the perfect atmosphere for good eating – and will aid digestion, too!*

Below and below right: *Never forget that food and eating are meant to be fun – don't discipline the child just for the sake of it, and don't impose adult rules too quickly.*

Left: *Unusual and varied environments, and the different types of food that go with them, provide huge additional pleasure, and will also help to familiarize your child with situations they will encounter later.*

TIPS

- Offer cubes of cheese at the end of a meal to help counteract the potentially harmful effects of any sugary foods eaten.
- Try to encourage children to eat more fruit. Cutting it into small pieces and arranging it on a plate can prove very inviting.
- Encourage children of all ages to drink whole milk, either cold, warm or flavored, as it is a valuable source of the fat-soluble vitamins A and D and the important mineral calcium, vital for healthy bones and teeth.
- If you reheat baby food in the microwave, make sure you stir it thoroughly and leave it to stand for a couple of minutes so any hot spots can even out. Always check the temperature before serving.
- Always make sure a baby is well strapped into a highchair and never leave children unattended while eating in case of accidents.
- Children love the novelty of eating somewhere different. If it's a nice day, why not have a picnic in the local park. If eating outside, pack children's food separately.
- Snacks can play a vitally important part in a young child's diet as their growth rate is so high it can be difficult to provide sufficient calories and protein at meal times alone.
- Make sure you coordinate main meals and snacks so that you serve different foods and so that the snacks won't take the edge off the child's appetite for the main meal of the day.
- Try to avoid candies or cakes and fatty chips.
- Offer slices of fresh fruit, a few raisins or dried apricots, squares of cheese, a fruit yogurt or milky drink, cream cheese or smooth peanut butter on toast.
- Make food fun and allow your child to choose where they eat the snack, e.g. in the camp in the garden or at the swings.

MEATY MAIN MEALS

TRYING TO PLEASE ALL THE FAMILY ALL OF THE TIME CAN BE A BIT OF A TALL ORDER, ESPECIALLY WHEN TRYING TO COOK TASTY MEALS ON A BUDGET. TRY THESE DELICIOUS NEW WAYS WITH QUICK-TO-COOK GROUND BEEF AND CHOPS, PLUS A SPEEDY STIR FRY, OR SLOW-COOK BEEF BOURGIGNON, BRAISED PORK OR LAMB CASSEROLE.

Mediterranean Lamb

- 3 rib lamb chops
- 12oz zucchini
- ½ yellow bell pepper
- ½ red bell pepper
- 3 tomatoes
- 1 garlic clove, crushed
- 1 tbsp clear honey
- few sprigs of fresh rosemary, plus extra to garnish
- 1 tbsp olive oil
- 7oz can baked beans
- salt and freshly ground black pepper
- crusty bread, to serve

1 Rinse the chops under cold water, pat dry, trim off any fat and place in the base of a broiling pan. Trim and slice the zucchini, cut away the core and seeds from the peppers and then rinse and cut into chunks. Rinse and cut the tomatoes into quarters and arrange the vegetables around the lamb.

2 Season two of the chops for the adults with garlic, honey, rosemary and salt and pepper, and drizzle oil over the vegetables.

3 Cook under a hot broiler for 12–14 minutes, turning once, until the lamb is well browned and cooked through and the vegetables are browned.

4 Warm the baked beans in a small saucepan. Drain and transfer the unseasoned chop to a chopping board and cut away the bone and fat. Thinly slice half the meat for the toddler and arrange on a plate with a few of the vegetables and 2–3 tbsp of the baked beans.

5 Chop or process the remaining lamb with four slices of zucchini, two small pieces of pepper, two peeled tomato quarters and 1–2 tbsp of baked beans, adding a little boiled water if too dry. Spoon into a dish for the baby and test the temperature of the children's food before serving.

6 For the adult's portions, discard the cooked rosemary. Spoon the pan juices over the chops and garnish with fresh rosemary. Serve with crusty bread.

TIP

Lamb varies hugely in price throughout the year. Depending on the season and price you may prefer to use lamb cutlets or loin chops. Allow two chops per adult and reduce the cooking time slightly as these chops are smaller. Do not give honey to young children. Use red currant jelly in place of honey for children and adults if preferred.

Lamb Casserole

- 12oz boneless lamb
- 1 onion
- 1 carrot
- 6oz rutabaga
- 1 tbsp light vegetable oil
- 2 tbsp all-purpose flour
- 1⅞ cups beef broth
- 1 tbsp fresh sage or ¼ tsp dried sage
- 2oz chorizo (optional)
- ½ eating apple
- 10oz potatoes
- 1 tbsp butter
- 8oz Brussels sprouts
- salt and freshly ground black pepper

1 Preheat the oven to 350°F. Rinse the lamb under cold water, pat dry, trim away any fat and then slice thinly. Peel and chop the onion, carrot and rutabaga.

2 Heat the oil in a large skillet and brown the lamb on both sides. Lift the lamb out of the pan, draining off any excess oil and transfer one-third to a small 2½ cup casserole dish for the children and the rest to a 5 cup casserole dish for the adults.

3 Add the vegetables to the pan and fry for 5 minutes, stirring until lightly browned.

4 Stir in the flour, then add the broth and sage. Bring to a boil, stirring, then divide between the two casserole dishes.

5 Peel and chop the chorizo if using, core, peel and chop the apple and add both to the larger casserole dish with a little seasoning.

6 Thinly slice the potatoes and arrange overlapping slices over both casserole dishes. Dot with butter and season the larger dish.

7 Cover and cook in the oven for 1¼ hours. For a brown topping, remove the lid and broil for a few minutes at the end of cooking until browned. Cook the Brussels sprouts in boiling water for 8–10 minutes until tender and drain.

8 Chop or process half the contents of the small casserole with a few sprouts for the baby, adding extra gravy if needed until the desired consistency is reached. Spoon into a baby dish.

9 Spoon the remaining child's portion onto a plate, add a few sprouts and cut up any large pieces. Test the temperature of the children's food before serving.

10 Spoon the adults' portions onto serving plates and serve with Brussels sprouts.

TIP

Traditionally, inexpensive stewing lamb would have been used for making a casserole. This cut does require very long slow cooking and can be fatty with lots of bones so not ideal for children. Boneless lamb is very lean, with very little waste and makes a tasty and healthier alternative.

Spicy Beef Sauté

- 12oz lean ground beef
- 1 onion, chopped
- 1 carrot, chopped
- 1 garlic clove, crushed
- 14oz can tomatoes
- pinch of dried mixed herbs
- 1oz small pasta
- 2oz creamed coconut
- 2oz button mushrooms
- 2oz fresh spinach leaves
- 1 tbsp hot curry paste
- salt and freshly ground black pepper
- boiled rice, warm naan or other Indian bread and a little grated Cheddar cheese (optional), to serve

1 Brown the meat and onion in a medium-sized dry saucepan, stirring continuously.

2 Add the carrot, garlic, tomatoes and herbs, bring to a boil, stirring, and then cover and simmer for about 30 minutes, stirring occasionally.

3 Cook the pasta in a small saucepan of boiling water for 10 minutes until tender. Drain.

4 Meanwhile place the coconut in a small bowl, add ½ cup of boiling water and stir until dissolved. Wipe and slice the mushrooms and wash and drain the spinach, discarding any large stalks.

5 Transfer one-third of the meat mixture to another saucepan. Stir the coconut mixture, curry paste and salt and pepper into the remaining meat mixture and cook for about 5 minutes, stirring.

6 Mash or process one-third of the pasta and the reserved meat mixture to the desired consistency for baby and spoon into a small dish.

7 Spoon the remaining pasta and reserved meat mixture into a small bowl for the older child.

8 Stir the mushrooms and spinach into the curried meat and cook for 3–4 minutes until the spinach has just wilted. Spoon onto warmed serving plates for the adults and serve with boiled rice and warmed bread. Sprinkle the toddler's portion with a little cheese, if desired. Test the temperature of the children's food before serving.

TIP

Weigh spinach after it has been picked over and stalks removed or, if you're short on time, buy ready prepared spinach.

If you can't get creamed coconut, use ½ cup coconut milk instead. Alternatively, soak 1 cup dried coconut in ⅔ cup boiling water for 30 minutes then strain and use the liquid.

Ground Beef Curry

- 3 medium baking potatoes
- 1 onion, chopped
- 12oz lean ground beef
- 1 garlic clove, crushed
- 2 tsp mild curry paste
- 2 tsp wine vinegar
- 6 tbsp fresh breadcrumbs
- 1 tbsp tomato paste
- 1oz raisins
- 1 tbsp mango chutney
- 1 medium banana, sliced
- 2 eggs
- 4 tsp turmeric
- ½ cup skim milk
- 4 small bay leaves
- 8oz broccoli, cut into florets
- 2 tbsp fromage frais or plain yogurt
- 7oz can baked beans
- salt and freshly ground black pepper

1 Preheat the oven to 350°F. Scrub the potatoes, insert a skewer into each and bake for 1½ hours until tender.

2 Place the chopped onion and 8oz of the beef in a saucepan and brown, stirring frequently.

3 Add the garlic and curry paste, stir well and cook for 1 minute, then remove from the heat and stir in the vinegar, 4 tbsp of the breadcrumbs, the tomato paste, raisins and a little salt and pepper.

TIP
Serve any leftover adult portions cold with salad.

4 Chop up any large pieces of mango chutney and stir into the meat mixture with the banana slices. Spoon into a 3¾ cup ovenproof dish and press into an even layer with the back of a spoon.

5 Place the dish on a baking sheet, cover loosely with foil and cook for 20 minutes.

6 Meanwhile mix the remaining beef with the remaining breadcrumbs, then beat the eggs together and stir 1 tbsp into the meat. Make eight small meatballs about the size of a grape for the baby. Form the remaining beef into a 3in patty using an upturned cookie cutter as a mold.

7 Blend the turmeric, milk and a little salt and pepper with the remaining eggs. Remove the foil from the ovenproof dish, and lay the bay leaves over the meat.

8 Pour the egg mixture over. Return to the oven for 30 minutes more until well risen and set.

9 When the adults' portion is ready, heat the broiler and cook the patty and meatballs until browned, turning once. The patty will take 8–10 minutes, while the meatballs will take about 5 minutes.

10 Cook the broccoli in boiling water until tender and drain.

11 Cut the adult portion into wedges and serve with baked potatoes topped with fromage frais or yogurt and broccoli.

12 Serve the toddler's patty with half a potato, warmed baked beans and a few broccoli florets. Serve the baby's meatballs with chunky pieces of peeled potato and broccoli. Spoon a few baked beans into a small dish for the baby. Test the temperature of the children's food before serving.

Moussaka

- 1 onion, chopped
- 12oz ground lamb
- 14oz can tomatoes
- 1 bay leaf
- 1 medium eggplant, sliced
- 2 medium potatoes
- 1 medium zucchini, sliced
- 2 tbsp olive oil
- ½ tsp grated nutmeg
- ½ tsp ground cinnamon
- 2 garlic cloves, crushed
- salt and freshly ground black pepper

For the Sauce

- 2 tbsp margarine
- 2 tbsp all-purpose flour
- 1 cup milk
- pinch of grated nutmeg
- 1 tbsp freshly grated Parmesan cheese
- 4 tsp fresh breadcrumbs

1 Brown the onion and ground lamb in a dry saucepan, stirring occasionally. Add the tomatoes and bay leaf, bring to a boil, stirring, then cover and simmer for 30 minutes.

2 Place the eggplant slices in a single layer on a baking sheet, sprinkle with a little salt and set aside for 20 minutes. Preheat the oven to 400°F.

3 Slice the potatoes thinly and cook in boiling water for 3 minutes. Add the zucchini and cook for 2 minutes until tender.

4 Remove most of the slices with a slotted spoon and place in a colander, leaving just enough for the baby portion. Cook these for 2–3 minutes more until soft, then drain. Rinse the vegetables and drain well.

5 Rinse the salt off the eggplant and pat dry. Heat the oil in a skillet and brown the eggplant on both sides. Drain.

6 Spoon 3 tbsp of the meat mixture into a bowl with the baby vegetables and chop or purée to the desired consistency.

7 Spoon 4 tbsp of the meat mixture into an ovenproof dish for the older child with four slices of potato overlapping over the top, then add a slice of eggplant and three slices of zucchini.

8 Stir the nutmeg, cinnamon, garlic and seasoning into the remaining meat mixture, and cook for 1 minute and then spoon into a 5 cup shallow ovenproof dish discarding the bay leaf.

9 Arrange the remaining potatoes overlapping on top of the lamb, and then add the eggplant slices, tucking the zucchini slices in between the eggplant in a random pattern.

10 To make the sauce, melt the margarine in a small saucepan, stir in the flour then gradually add the milk and bring to a boil, stirring until thickened and smooth. Add a pinch of nutmeg and a little salt and pepper.

11 Pour a little of the sauce over the toddler's portion then pour the rest over the adults' portion. Sprinkle the larger dish with Parmesan cheese and 3 tsp breadcrumbs, sprinkling the remaining breadcrumbs over the toddler's portion.

12 Cook the moussakas in the oven. The larger dish will take 45 minutes while the toddler's portion will take about 25 minutes. Reheat the baby portion, and test the temperature of the children's food before serving.

Chili con Carne

- 3 medium baking potatoes
- 1 onion, chopped
- 1lb lean ground beef
- 1 carrot, chopped
- ½ red bell pepper, cored, seeded and diced
- 14oz can tomatoes
- 2 tsp tomato paste
- ⅔ cup beef broth
- 3 small bay leaves
- 2 tbsp olive oil
- 4oz button mushrooms, sliced
- 2 garlic cloves, crushed
- 2 tsp mild chili powder
- ½ tsp ground cumin
- 1 tsp ground coriander
- 7oz can red kidney beans, drained
- 1½oz frozen mixed vegetables
- 1 tbsp milk
- pat of butter or margarine
- 4 tbsp fromage frais or plain yogurt
- 1 tbsp chopped fresh cilantro leaves
- salt and freshly ground black pepper
- green salad, to serve

1 Preheat the oven to 350°F. Scrub and prick the potatoes and cook in the oven for 1½ hours. Brown the onion and ground beef in a dry saucepan, stirring. Add the carrot and red pepper and cook for 2 minutes.

2 Add the tomatoes, tomato paste and broth and bring to a boil. Transfer one-quarter of the meat mixture to a 2½ cup casserole dish, add 1 of the bay leaves, cover with a lid and set aside.

3 Spoon the remaining meat mixture into a 5 cup casserole. Heat 1 tbsp of the oil in the same saucepan and sauté the mushrooms and garlic for 3 minutes.

4 Stir in the spices and seasoning, cook for 1 minute then add the drained red kidney beans and the remaining bay leaves and stir into the meat mixture. Cover and cook both dishes in the oven for 1 hour.

5 When the potatoes are cooked, cut into halves or quarters and scoop out the potato leaving a thin layer of potato on the skin.

6 Brush the potato skins with the remaining oil and broil for 10 minutes until browned.

7 Boil the frozen mixed vegetables for 5 minutes and mash the potato centers with milk and a pat of butter or margarine.

8 Spoon the meat mixture from the smaller casserole into an ovenproof ramekin for the toddler and the rest into a bowl for the baby. Top both with some of the mashed potato.

9 Drain the vegetables, arrange two pea eyes, carrot pieces for the mouth and mixed vegetables for hair on the toddler's dish.

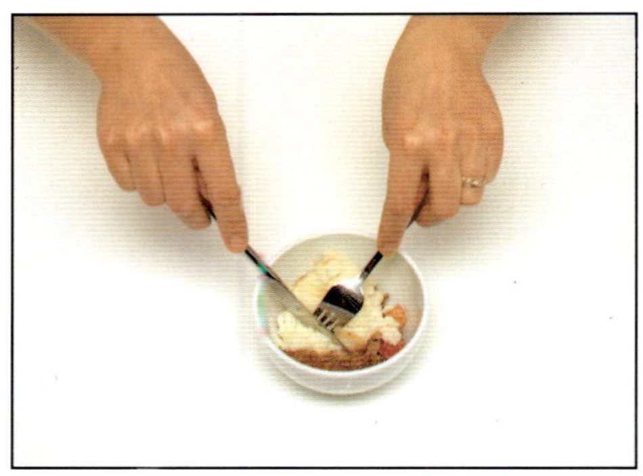

10 Spoon the remaining vegetables into a baby bowl and chop or process to the desired consistency. Test the temperature of the children's food before serving.

11 Spoon the adults' chili onto serving plates, add the potato skins and top with fromage frais or yogurt and chopped cilantro. Serve with a green salad.

Beef Bourguignon with Creamed Potatoes

- 1lb stewing beef
- 1 tbsp light vegetable oil
- 1 onion, chopped
- 2 tbsp all-purpose flour
- 1¼ cups beef broth
- 1 tbsp tomato paste
- small bunch of fresh herbs or ¼ tsp dried
- 2 garlic cloves, crushed
- 6 tbsp red wine
- 3oz shallots
- 3oz button mushrooms
- 2 tbsp butter
- 1lb potatoes
- 6oz green cabbage
- 2–4 tbsp milk
- salt and freshly ground black pepper
- a few fresh herbs, to garnish

1 Preheat the oven to 325°F. Trim away any fat from the stewing beef and cut into cubes.

2 Heat the oil in a skillet, add half of the beef and brown on all sides. Transfer to a plate and brown the remaining beef and the chopped onion.

3 Return the first batch of beef to the pan with any meat juices, stir in the flour and then add the broth and tomato paste. Bring to a boil, stirring, until thickened.

4 Spoon one-third of the beef mixture into a small 1¼ cup casserole dish for the children, making sure that the meat is well covered with broth. Add a few fresh herbs or half a dried bay leaf. Set the casserole aside.

5 Add the remaining herbs, garlic, wine and seasoning to the beef mixture in the skillet and bring to a boil. Transfer the beef to a 5 cup casserole dish. Cover both casserole dishes and cook in the oven for 2 hours or until the meat is very tender.

6 Meanwhile, cut the shallots in half if large, wipe clean and slice the mushrooms, then cover and set aside.

7 Half an hour before the end of cooking, sauté the shallots in a little butter until browned, then add the mushrooms and sauté for 2–3 minutes. Stir into the larger casserole and cook for the remaining time.

8 Cut the potatoes into chunks and cook in a saucepan of boiling, salted water for 20 minutes. Shred the cabbage, discarding the hard core, rinse and steam above the potatoes for the last 5 minutes.

9 Drain the potatoes and mash with 2 tbsp of the milk and the remaining butter.

10 Chop or process one-third of the child's portion with a spoonful of cabbage, adding extra milk if necessary. Spoon into a dish for the baby, with a little potato.

11 Spoon the remaining child's portion onto a plate for the toddler. Remove any bay leaf and cut up any large pieces of beef. Add potato and cabbage.

12 Garnish the adults' portion with fresh herbs and serve with potatoes and cabbage. Test the temperature of the children's food.

Braised Pork with Rice

- 3 pork spare rib chops, about 1¼lb
- 1 tbsp olive oil
- 1 onion, chopped
- 1 large carrot, chopped
- 2 celery stalks, thinly sliced
- 2 garlic cloves, crushed
- 14oz can tomatoes
- few sprigs fresh thyme or ¼ tsp dried thyme
- grated zest and juice of ½ lemon
- ⅔ cup long grain rice
- pinch of turmeric
- 4oz green beans
- pat of butter
- 4 tbsp freshly grated Parmesan cheese
- salt and freshly ground black pepper
- 1 or 2 sprigs parsley

1 Preheat the oven to 350°F. Rinse the chops under cold water and pat dry.

2 Heat the oil in a large skillet, add the pork, brown on both sides and transfer to a casserole dish.

3 Add the onion, carrot and celery to the skillet and sauté for 3 minutes until lightly browned.

4 Add half the garlic, the tomatoes, thyme and lemon juice and bring to a boil, stirring. Pour the mixture over the pork, cover and cook in the oven for 1½ hours or until tender.

5 Half fill two small saucepans with water and bring to a boil. Add ½ cup rice to one with a pinch of turmeric and salt, add the remaining rice to the second pan. Return to a boil, and simmer.

6 Trim the beans and steam above the larger pan of rice for 8 minutes or until the rice is tender.

7 Drain both pans of rice, and return the yellow rice to the pan and add the butter, Parmesan cheese and a little pepper. Mix together well and keep warm.

8 Dice one chop, discarding any bone if necessary. Spoon a little of the white rice onto a plate for the toddler and add half of the diced chop. Add a few vegetables and a spoonful of the sauce. Process the other half chop, some vegetables, rice and sauce to the desired consistency and spoon into a small bowl for the baby.

9 Spoon the yellow rice onto the adults' plates and add a pork chop to each. Season the sauce to taste and then spoon the sauce and vegetables over the meat, discarding the thyme sprigs if used. Finely chop the parsley and sprinkle over the pork with the lemon zest and the remaining crushed garlic.

10 Serve the adults' and toddler's portions with green beans. Test the temperature of the children's food before serving.

Pork Stir Fry

- 9oz pork fillet
- 1 zucchini
- 1 carrot
- ½ green bell pepper
- ½ red bell pepper
- ½ yellow bell pepper
- 7oz fresh bean sprouts
- 4 tsp light vegetable oil
- 1oz cashew nuts
- ⅔ cup chicken broth
- 2 tbsp ketchup
- 2 tsp cornstarch, blended with 1 tbsp cold water
- 1 garlic clove, crushed
- 2 tsp soy sauce
- 4 tsp yellow bean paste or hoisin sauce

1 Rinse the pork under cold water, cut away any fat and thinly slice. Halve the zucchini lengthwise and then slice thinly, thinly slice the carrot, and cut the peppers into thin strips, discarding the core and the seeds. Place the bean sprouts in a strainer and rinse well.

2 Heat 3 tsp of the oil in a wok or large skillet, add the cashews and sauté for 2 minutes until browned. Drain and reserve.

3 Add the sliced pork and stir fry for 5 minutes until browned all over and cooked through. Drain and keep warm.

4 Add the remaining oil and stir fry the zucchini and carrot for 2 minutes. Add the peppers and fry for 2 minutes more.

5 Stir in the bean sprouts, broth, ketchup and the cornstarch mixture, bring to a boil, stirring until the sauce has thickened.

6 Transfer 1 large spoonful of the vegetables to a bowl and 2–3 large spoonfuls to a plate for the children and set aside. Add the garlic and soy sauce to the pan and cook for 1 minute.

7 Chop or process four slices of pork with the baby's reserved vegetables to the desired consistency and spoon into a baby bowl. Arrange six slices of pork on the child's plate with the reserved vegetables. Spoon the vegetables in the wok onto two adult plates.

8 Return the remaining pork to the wok with the nuts and yellow bean paste or hoisin sauce and cook for 1 minute, spoon onto the adults' plates and serve immediately. Test the temperature of the children's food before serving.

Sausage Casserole

- 1lb large breakfast sausages
- 1 tbsp light vegetable oil
- 1 onion, chopped
- 8oz carrots, chopped
- 14oz can mixed navy and kidney beans in water, drained
- 1 tbsp all-purpose flour
- 1⅞ cup beef broth
- 1 tbsp Worcestershire sauce
- 3 tsp tomato paste
- 3 tsp brown sugar
- 2 tsp Dijon mustard
- 1 bay leaf
- 1 dried chili, chopped
- 3 medium baking potatoes
- 1 tbsp butter
- salt and freshly ground black pepper
- butter and sprigs of fresh parsley, to serve

1 Preheat the oven to 350°F. Prick and separate the sausages.

2 Heat the oil in a skillet, add the sausages and cook over high heat until evenly browned but not cooked through. Drain and transfer to a plate.

3 Add the chopped onion and carrots to the pan and sauté until lightly browned. Add the drained beans and flour, stir well and then spoon one-third of the bean mixture into a small casserole dish. Stir in ⅔ cup broth, 1 tsp tomato paste and 1 tsp sugar.

4 Add the Worcestershire sauce, remaining beef broth, tomato paste and sugar to the pan, together with the mustard, bay leaf and chopped chili. Season and bring to a boil, then pour the mixture into a large casserole dish.

5 Add two sausages to the small casserole dish and the rest to the larger dish. Cover both and cook in the oven for 1½ hours.

6 Scrub and prick the potatoes and bake on a rack above the casserole for 1½ hours until tender.

7 Spoon two-thirds of the child's casserole on to a plate for the toddler. Slice the sausages and give him or her two-thirds. Halve one of the baked potatoes, add a pat of butter and place on the toddler's plate.

8 Scoop the potato from the other half and mash or process with the remaining child's beans to the desired consistency for baby. Spoon into a dish and serve the remaining sausage slices as finger food.

9 Spoon the adults' casserole on to plates, halve the other potatoes, add butter and garnish with parsley. Test the temperature of the children's food before serving.

PERFECT POULTRY

WHATEVER THE AGE OF THE DINER, CHICKEN AND TURKEY ARE ALWAYS POPULAR. AVAILABLE IN A RANGE OF CUTS AND PRICES THERE'S SOMETHING TO SUIT ALL BUDGETS AND TASTES FROM A TASTY SALAD TO PAN-FRIED TURKEY, TANDOORI-STYLE MARINADE OR STUFFED CHICKEN BREASTS WITH PESTO, HAM AND CHEESE.

Chicken and Thyme Casserole

6 chicken thighs
1 tbsp olive oil
1 onion, chopped
2 tbsp all-purpose flour
1¼ cups chicken broth
few sprigs fresh thyme or ¼ tsp dried thyme

To Serve

12oz new potatoes
1 large carrot
¾ cup frozen peas
1 tsp Dijon mustard
grated zest and juice of ½ orange
4 tbsp fromage frais or plain yogurt
salt and freshly ground black pepper
few fresh thyme or parsley sprigs, to garnish

1 Preheat the oven to 350°F. Rinse the chicken thighs under cold water and pat dry.

2 Heat the oil in a large skillet, add the chicken and brown on both sides, then transfer to a casserole.

3 Add the onion and sauté, stirring until lightly browned. Stir in the flour, then add the broth and thyme and bring to a boil, stirring.

4 Pour over the chicken, cover and cook in the oven for 1 hour or until tender.

5 Meanwhile scrub the potatoes and cut any large ones in half. Cut the carrot into matchsticks.

6 Cook the potatoes in boiling water 15 minutes before the chicken is ready and cook the carrots and peas in a separate pan of boiling water for 5 minutes. Drain.

7 Take one chicken thigh out of the casserole, remove the skin and cut the meat away from the bone. Chop or process with some of the vegetables and gravy to the desired consistency. Spoon into a baby bowl.

8 Take a second chicken thigh out of the casserole for the toddler, remove the skin and bone and slice if necessary. Arrange on a plate with some of the vegetables and gravy. Test the temperature of the children's food before serving.

9 Arrange the remaining chicken thighs onto warmed serving plates for the adults. Stir the mustard, orange zest and juice, fromage frais or yogurt and seasoning into the hot sauce and then spoon over the chicken. Serve at once, with the vegetables, garnished with a sprig of thyme or parsley.

Tandoori Chicken

- 6 chicken thighs
- 5oz plain yogurt
- 1¼ tsp paprika
- 1 tsp hot curry paste
- 1 tsp coriander seeds, roughly crushed
- ½ tsp cumin seeds, roughly crushed
- ½ tsp turmeric
- pinch of dried mixed herbs
- 2 tsp light vegetable oil

To Serve

- 12oz new potatoes
- 3 celery stalks
- 4in piece cucumber
- 1 tbsp olive oil
- 1 tsp white wine vinegar
- 1 tsp mint jelly
- salt and freshly ground black pepper
- few sprigs of watercress, pat of butter and cherry tomatoes, to serve

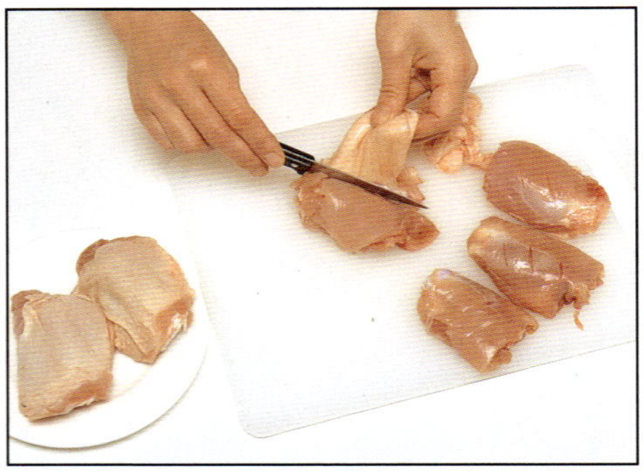

1 Cut away the skin from the chicken thighs and slash the meat two or three times with a small knife. Rinse under cold water and pat dry.

2 Place four thighs in a shallow dish, the other two on a plate. Place the yogurt, 1 tsp of the paprika, the curry paste, both seeds and almost all the turmeric into a small bowl and mix together. Spoon over the four chicken thighs.

3 Sprinkle the remaining paprika and the mixed herbs over the other chicken thighs and sprinkle the remaining pinch of turmeric over 1 thigh. Cover both dishes loosely with plastic wrap and chill in the refrigerator for 2–3 hours.

4 Preheat the oven to 400°F. Arrange the chicken thighs on a roasting rack set over a small roasting pan and drizzle oil over the herbed chicken. Pour a little boiling water into the base of the pan and cook for 45–50 minutes or until the juices run clear when the chicken is pierced with a skewer.

5 Meanwhile, scrub the potatoes and halve any large ones. Cook in a saucepan of boiling water for 15 minutes until tender.

6 Cut one celery stalk and a small piece of cucumber into matchsticks. Chop or shred the remaining celery and cucumber.

7 Blend together the oil, vinegar, mint jelly and seasoning in a bowl and add the chopped or shredded celery, cucumber and watercress, tossing well to coat.

8 Drain the potatoes and toss in a little butter. Divide the potatoes among the adults' plates, toddler's dish and the baby bowl. Cut the chicken off the bone for the toddler and arrange on a plate with half of the celery and cucumber sticks.

9 Cut the remaining chicken thigh into tiny pieces for the baby, discarding the bone. Add to the bowl with the cooled potatoes and vegetable sticks and allow baby to feed him- or herself. Add a few halved tomatoes to each portion. Test the temperature of the children's food before serving.

10 For the adults, arrange the chicken thighs on serving plates with the potatoes. Serve with the piquant salad.

Chicken Roll Ups

- 3 boneless, skinless chicken breasts
- 1 tsp pesto
- 1½oz thinly sliced ham
- 2oz Cheddar cheese
- 12oz new potatoes
- 6oz green beans
- 1 tbsp butter
- 2 tsp olive oil
- 1 tomato
- 6 pitted black olives
- 2 tsp all-purpose flour
- ⅔ cup chicken broth
- 1 tbsp crème fraîche or sour cream (optional)
- few sprigs of fresh basil (optional)

1 Rinse the chicken under cold water and pat dry. Put one chicken breast between two pieces of plastic wrap and pound with a rolling pin until half as big again. Repeat the process with the other two chicken breasts.

TIP
Depending on the age of your baby, you may prefer to omit the sauce and serve the meal as finger food, cutting it into more manageable pieces first.

2 Spread pesto over two of the chicken breasts and divide the ham among all three. Cut the cheese into three thick slices then add one to each piece of chicken. Roll up so that the cheese is completely enclosed, then secure with string.

3 Scrub the potatoes, halve any large ones and cook in a saucepan of boiling water for 15 minutes until tender. Trim the beans and cook in a separate pan of boiling water for 10 minutes.

4 Meanwhile, heat the butter and oil in a large skillet, add the chicken and sauté for about 10 minutes, turning several times, until well browned and cooked through.

5 Lift the chicken out of the pan, keeping those spread with pesto warm, and allowing the other one to cool slightly.

6 Cut the tomato into wedges and halve the olives. Stir in the flour and cook for 1 minute. Gradually stir in the broth and bring to a boil, stirring until thickened. Add the tomato and olives.

7 Snip the string off the chicken and slice the children's chicken breast thinly. Arrange four chicken slices on a child's plate with a couple of spoonfuls of sauce and a few potatoes and green beans. (Don't offer olives unless the child is a very adventurous eater.)

8 Chop or process the remaining cut chicken with 2 tbsp of the sauce, one or two potatoes and three green beans to the desired consistency. Test the temperature of the children's food before serving.

9 Arrange the remaining chicken on plates. Add the crème fraîche or sour cream to the pan, if using, and heat gently. Spoon over the chicken and serve with vegetables.

Pan-fried Turkey

3 large turkey cutlets
1 onion
1 red bell pepper, cored and seeded
1 tbsp light vegetable oil
1 tsp all-purpose flour
⅔ cup chicken broth
2 tbsp frozen corn
⅔ cup long grain white rice
1 garlic clove
1 dried chili
2oz creamed coconut
2 tbsp chopped fresh cilantro
fresh cilantro sprigs and lime wedges, to serve

1 Rinse the turkey cutlets under cold water, and pat dry. Chop one of the cutlets, finely chop one-quarter of the onion and dice one-quarter of the red pepper. Heat 1 tsp of the oil in a small frying pan and sauté the diced turkey and chopped onion until browned.

2 Stir in the flour, add the broth, corn and chopped pepper, then bring to a boil, cover and simmer for 10 minutes.

3 Cook the long grain rice in boiling water for 8–10 minutes or until just tender. Drain.

4 Meanwhile process or finely chop the remaining pieces of onion and red pepper with the garlic and chili, including the seeds if you like hot food.

5 Put the creamed coconut into a bowl, pour on 1 cup boiling water and stir until the coconut is completely dissolved.

6 Heat the remaining oil in a large skillet. Brown the turkey cutlets on one side, turn over and add the pepper paste. Sauté for 5 minutes until the second side of the turkey is also browned.

7 Pour the coconut milk over the turkey and cook for 2–3 minutes, stirring until the sauce has thickened slightly. Sprinkle with the chopped fresh cilantro.

8 Chop or process one-third of the children's portion with 2 tbsp of the rice until the desired consistency is reached. Spoon into a baby bowl.

9 Spoon the child's portion onto a child's plate and serve with a little rice. Test the temperature of the children's food before serving.

10 Spoon the rest of the rice onto warmed serving plates for the adults, add the turkey and sauce and garnish with cilantro sprigs and lime wedges.

VEGETABLE FEASTS

MORE AND MORE OF US ARE OPTING TO EAT LESS MEAT FOR EITHER HEALTH OR BUDGET REASONS. EATING LESS MEAT DOESN'T MEAN LOSING OUT ON FLAVOR: FAR FROM IT! CHOOSE FROM MEALS SUCH AS TOASTED CHEESE SANDWICHES, CHEESE AND VEGETABLE CRISP OR SLOW-COOKED SPICED MOROCCAN VEGETABLE STEW.

Toasted Cheese Sandwiches

- 2 slices thick bread
- 2 slices thin bread
- butter or margarine, for spreading
- 1 tsp Marmite or mild mustard
- 2 slices thinly sliced ham
- 1 garlic clove, halved
- 1 tbsp olive oil
- 7oz Cheddar cheese
- 1 tomato
- 6 pitted black olives
- 1 tbsp chopped fresh basil
- a few red onion slices
- cucumber sticks and green salad, to serve (optional)

1 Toast all the bread and spread the thin slices with butter or margarine. Spread one slice with Marmite or mild mustard and top this with ham.

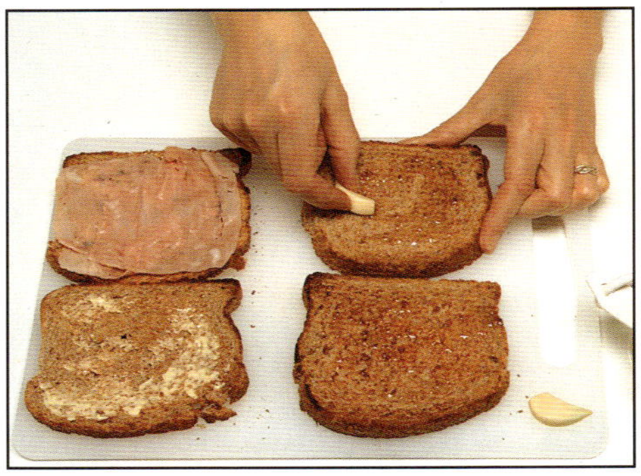

2 Drizzle the oil over the thick slices of toast then rub with the cut surface of the garlic.

3 Thinly slice the cheese and place over all of the pieces of toast.

4 Slice the tomato and halve the olives. Arrange on the thick toast for the adults, season with pepper and add basil and onion.

5 Broil until the cheese is bubbly. Cut the plain toasted cheese into tiny squares, discarding crusts. Arrange on a small plate for baby and allow to cool. Cut the ham and cheese toast into triangles and arrange on a plate. Add cucumber sticks to the toddler's portion and test the temperature before serving.

6 Slice the adults' sandwiches and arrange on plates with a green salad if desired, and serve.

Noodles with Tomato Sauce

- 5oz penne
- 1 onion
- 2 celery stalks
- 1 red bell pepper
- 1 tbsp olive oil
- 1 garlic clove, crushed
- 14oz can tomatoes
- ½ tsp superfine sugar
- 8 pitted black olives
- 2 tsp pesto
- ¼ tsp dried chili seeds (optional)
- ½ cup grated Cheddar cheese
- salt and freshly ground black pepper
- 2 tsp freshly grated Parmesan cheese, to serve
- green salad, to serve (optional)

1 Cook the pasta in salted boiling water for about 10–12 minutes until just tender.

2 Meanwhile chop the onion and the celery. Cut the pepper in half, then scoop out the core and seeds and dice the pepper finely.

3 Heat the oil in a large skillet, add the vegetables and garlic and sauté for 5 minutes, stirring until lightly browned.

4 Add the tomatoes and sugar and cook for 5 minutes, stirring occasionally until the tomatoes are broken up and pulpy.

5 Drain the pasta, return to the pan and stir in the tomato sauce.

6 Spoon 3–4 tbsp of the pasta mixture into a bowl or food processor and chop or process to the desired consistency for the baby. Spoon 5–6 tbsp of the pasta mixture into a bowl for the toddler.

7 Quarter the olives and stir into the remaining pasta with the pesto, chili seeds if using, and a little salt and pepper. Spoon into dishes.

8 Sprinkle the grated Cheddar cheese over all the dishes, and serve the adults' portions with the Parmesan cheese and a green salad, if wished. Test the temperature of the children's food before serving.

Zucchini Puff

- 4 tbsp butter
- ¼ cup all-purpose flour
- 2 eggs
- ½ tsp Dijon mustard
- 4oz Cheddar cheese
- salt and pepper

For the Filling

- 1 tbsp olive oil
- 12oz zucchini, sliced
- 1 small onion, chopped
- 4oz button mushrooms, sliced
- 8oz tomatoes, skinned and chopped
- 1 garlic clove, crushed
- 4 tsp chopped fresh basil

1 Preheat the oven to 425°F and grease a large baking sheet. Place the butter in a medium-sized saucepan with ⅔ cup water. Heat gently until the butter has melted then bring to a boil.

2 Remove the pan from the heat and quickly add the flour, stir well then return to the heat and cook for 1–2 minutes, stirring constantly until the mixture forms a smooth ball. Let cool for 10 minutes.

3 Beat the eggs, mustard and a little salt and pepper together. Cut 1oz of the cheese into small cubes and grate the rest.

4 Add 2oz of the grated cheese to the dough and then gradually beat in the eggs to make a smooth, glossy paste.

5 Spoon the mixture into a large pastry bag fitted with a medium plain tube. Pipe whirls close together on the baking sheet to make a 7in circular shape.

6 Pipe the remaining mixture into small balls for the baby and into the older child's initials.

7 Sprinkle the dough shapes with the remaining grated cheese.

8 Bake for 15–18 minutes for the small shapes and 25 for the ring, until well risen and browned.

9 Heat the oil in a frying pan, add the zucchini and onion and sauté until lightly browned. Add the mushrooms, fry for a further 2 minutes and then add the tomatoes. Cover and simmer for 5 minutes until the vegetables are cooked.

10 Spoon a little mixture into the baby's bowl or into a food processor and chop or process to the desired consistency. Serve with a few cheese balls and a little diced cheese.

11 Spoon a little onto a plate for the toddler, add a cheese initial and the remaining diced cheese. Test the temperature of the children's food before serving.

12 Transfer the cheese ring to a serving plate and split in half horizontally. Stir the garlic, basil and a little extra seasoning into the courgette mixture and heat through. Spoon over the bottom half of the cheese ring and add top half. Serve the puff immediately.

TIP

Beat the flour and butter mixture, cheese and eggs in a food processor if preferred.

ABC·123

Cheese and Vegetable Crisp

1 onion
8oz carrot
6oz rutabaga
6oz parsnip
1 tbsp olive oil
7½oz can red kidney beans
2 tsp paprika
1 tsp ground cumin
1 tbsp all-purpose flour
1¼ cups vegetable broth
8oz broccoli, to serve

For the Topping
4oz Cheddar cheese
2oz whole wheat flour
2oz all-purpose flour
2oz margarine
2 tbsp sesame seeds
1oz blanched almonds
salt and freshly ground black pepper

1 Preheat the oven to 375°F. Peel and coarsely chop the onion and peel and cut the carrot, rutabaga and parsnip into small cubes. Heat the oil in a large pan and sauté the vegetables for 5 minutes, stirring until lightly browned.

2 Drain the kidney beans and add to the pan with the spices and flour. Stir well, add the broth, then cover and simmer for 10 minutes.

3 Meanwhile make the topping. Cut a few squares of cheese for the baby and grate the rest. Put the two flours in a bowl, add the margarine and rub in with your fingertips until the mixture resembles fine breadcrumbs. Stir in the grated cheese and sesame seeds.

4 Spoon a little of the vegetable mixture into a 1¼ cup ovenproof dish for the toddler. Spoon the remaining mixture into a 3¾ cup ovenproof pie plate for the adults, leaving a little vegetable mixture in the pan for the baby. Season the adults' portion with a little salt and pepper.

VARIATION
Lentil and Herb Crumble
Substitute canned lentils for the red kidney beans. Instead of the paprika and cumin, use 2 tbsp chopped, fresh mixed herbs. Add more fiber and texture by replacing the all-purpose flour with rolled oats.

5 Spoon 3 tbsp of the topping over the older child's portion. Coarsely chop the almonds, add to the remaining topping with a little salt and pepper and spoon over the large plate. Bake in the oven for 20 minutes for the small dish, 30 minutes for the large plate, until golden brown on top.

6 Add ⅓ cup water to the baby's portion, cover and cook for 10 minutes, stirring occasionally, until the vegetables are very tender. Mash or process to the desired consistency and spoon into a bowl.

7 Cut the broccoli into florets and cook for 5 minutes or until tender; drain. Spoon the toddler's portion out of the dish and onto a small plate. Serve the broccoli to all members of the family, allowing baby to pick up and eat the broccoli and cubed cheese as finger food. Check the temperature of the children's food before serving.

Note: Never give whole nuts to children under 5 as they may choke.

Moroccan Vegetable Stew

- 1 onion
- 8oz carrots
- 8oz rutabaga
- 3oz prunes
- 4 tsp olive oil
- 15oz can chickpeas
- ½ tsp turmeric
- 2 tsp all-purpose flour, plus extra for dusting
- 2 garlic cloves, finely chopped
- 1⅞ cups chicken broth
- 1 tbsp tomato paste
- ¾in piece fresh gingerroot
- ½ tsp ground cinnamon
- 3 cloves
- 4oz couscous
- 8 green beans
- 2 frozen peas
- piece of tomato
- pat of butter or margarine
- salt and freshly ground black pepper
- sprig fresh cilantro, to garnish

1 Peel and chop the onion and peel and dice the carrots and rutabaga. Cut the prunes into chunks, discarding the pits.

2 Heat 3 tsp of the olive oil in a large saucepan, add the onion and sauté until lightly browned. Stir in the carrots and rutabaga and sauté for 3 minutes, stirring.

3 Drain the chickpeas and stir into the pan with the turmeric, flour and garlic. Add 1¼ cup of the broth, the tomato paste, and the chopped prunes. Bring to a boil, cover and simmer for 20 minutes, stirring occasionally.

4 Place three heaping spoonfuls of mixture in a bowl or food processor, draining off most of the liquid. Mash or process and then form the mixture into a patty with floured hands.

5 Chop or process two heaping spoonfuls of mixture and sauce to the desired consistency for the baby and spoon into a bowl.

6 Finely chop the gingerroot and stir into the remaining vegetable mixture with the cinnamon, cloves, remaining broth and seasoning.

7 Place the couscous in a strainer, rinse with boiling water and fluff up the grains with a fork. Place the strainer above the vegetables, cover and steam for 5 minutes.

8 Brown the patty in the remaining oil on both sides. Trim and cook the beans and peas for 5 minutes. Drain and arrange on a plate like an octopus with a piece of tomato for a mouth and peas for eyes.

9 Stir the butter or margarine into the couscous and fluff up the grains with a fork. Spoon onto warmed serving plates for adults, add the vegetable mixture and garnish with a sprig of cilantro. Check the temperature of the children's food before serving.

Cheese and Leek Quiche

- 1½ cups all-purpose flour
- 6 tbsp butter
- 1 carrot
- 2 slices ham
- 4in piece of cucumber
- mixed salad greens, to serve

For the Filling

- 2 tbsp butter
- 4oz trimmed leek, thinly sliced
- 3oz Stilton cheese, diced
- 1½oz Cheddar cheese, grated
- 3 eggs
- ¾ cup milk
- pinch of paprika
- salt and pepper

1 Put the flour in a bowl with a pinch of salt. Cut the butter into pieces and rub into the flour with your fingertips until the mixture resembles fine breadcrumbs.

2 Mix to a smooth dough with 6–7 tsp water, knead lightly and roll out thinly on a floured surface. Use to line a 7in pie pan, trimming around the edge and reserving the trimmings.

3 Reroll the trimmings and then cut out six 3in circles using a fluted cookie cutter. Press the pastry circles into sections of a muffin pan and chill all of the quiches.

4 Preheat the oven to 375°F. For the filling melt the butter in a small skillet and sauté the leek for 4–5 minutes, until soft but not brown, stirring frequently. Spoon into a bowl, stir in the diced Stilton, and then spread over the base of the large quiche.

5 Beat the eggs and milk together in a small bowl and season with salt and pepper.

6 Divide the grated Cheddar among the small quiche shells and pour some of the egg mixture over. Pour the remaining egg mixture over the leek and cheese quiche and sprinkle with paprika.

7 Cook the small quiches for 15 minutes and the large quiche for 30–35 minutes until well risen and browned. Leave to cool.

8 Peel and coarsely grate the carrot. Cut the ham into triangles for "sails". Cut the ham trimmings into small strips for the baby. Cut the cucumber into batons.

9 Place a spoonful of carrot, some cucumber, a small quiche and some ham trimmings in the baby dish. Spread the remaining carrot onto a plate for the older child, place the quiches on top and secure the ham "sails" with toothpicks. Serve any remaining quiches next day. Cut the large quiche into wedges and serve with the salad.

JUST DESSERTS

NO ONE CAN RESIST A DESSERT, ALTHOUGH LOOKING AFTER A YOUNG FAMILY MAY MEAN IT'S MORE OF A WEEKEND TREAT THAN AN EVERYDAY OCCURRENCE. SPOIL THE FAMILY WITH A SELECTION OF THESE TASTY HOT AND COLD TREATS FROM FRUITY BERRY PUDDING AND PLUM CRUMBLE TO CHOCOLATE AND TANGERINE TRIFLE OR ORANGE AND STRAWBERRY SHORTCAKES – ALL GUARANTEED TO GET THEM CLAMORING FOR SECONDS.

Bread and Butter Pudding

- 3 dried apricots
- 3 tbsp golden raisins
- 2 tbsp sherry
- 7 slices white bread, crusts removed
- ½ tbsp butter, softened
- 2 tbsp superfine sugar
- pinch of ground cinnamon
- 4 eggs
- 1¼ cups milk
- few drops of vanilla extract
- light cream, to serve

1 Chop two dried apricots and place in a small bowl with 2 tbsp of the raisins and the sherry. Set aside for about 2 hours. Chop the remaining apricot and mix with the remaining raisins.

2 Preheat the oven to 375°F. Lightly spread the bread with butter and cut one slice into very small triangles. Layer the triangles of bread in a ⅔ cup pie plate with the plain apricots and raisins and 1 tsp of the sugar.

3 Cut the remaining bread into larger triangles and layer in a 3¾ cup pie plate with the remaining fruits and all but 1 tsp of the remaining sugar, sprinkling the top with cinnamon. Put the last 1 tsp sugar in a small ramekin.

4 Beat the eggs, milk and vanilla together and pour into the ramekin and two pie plates.

5 Stand the ramekin in a large ovenproof dish and half fill with hot water. Cook the small pie plate and the ramekin for 25–30 minutes until the custard is just set, the larger pudding for 35 minutes until the bread is browned. Serve the adult portions with cream, if desired.

Berry Pudding

1¼lb cooking apples
¼ cup superfine sugar
2oz frozen or canned blackberries
For the Topping
4 tbsp butter or margarine
¼ cup superfine sugar
⅓ cup self-rising flour
1 egg
½ lemon, zest only
1 tbsp lemon juice
confectioner's sugar, for dusting
custard, to serve

1 Preheat the oven to 350°F. Peel and slice the cooking apples, discarding the core, and then place in a saucepan with the superfine sugar and 1 tbsp water. Cover and cook gently for 5 minutes until the apple slices are almost tender but still whole.

2 Half fill a ⅔ cup ovenproof ramekin with apple for the toddler and mash 2 tbsp apple for the baby in a small bowl.

3 Put the remaining apple slices into a 2½ cup ovenproof dish. Sprinkle the blackberries over the apple slices.

4 To make the topping, place the butter or margarine, sugar, flour and egg in a bowl and beat until smooth. Spoon a little of the pudding mixture over the toddler's ramekin so that the mixture is almost to the top of the dish.

5 Half fill three fluted paper baking cups with the pudding mixture.

6 Grate the lemon zest and stir with the juice into the remaining mixture. Spoon over the large dish, leveling the surface.

7 Put the small cakes, toddler and adult dishes on a baking sheet and bake in the oven for 8–10 minutes for the small cakes, 20 minutes for the ramekin and 30 minutes for the larger dish, until they are well risen and golden brown.

8 Dust the toddler's and adults' portions with confectioner's sugar and leave to cool slightly before serving with the custard. Warm the baby's apple mixture if desired and test the temperature before serving with the little cakes taken out of their paper cups.

TIP
If you can't get blackberries then use raspberries instead. There's no need to defrost before using as they will soon thaw when added to the hot apple.

Orange and Strawberry Shortcakes

6 tbsp all-purpose flour
4 tbsp butter
2 tbsp superfine sugar
grated zest of ½ orange
extra sugar, for sprinkling
For the Filling
6oz plain yogurt
1 tbsp confectioner's sugar
9oz strawberries
1 tsp Cointreau (optional)
2 sprigs of fresh mint

1 Preheat the oven to 350°F. Place the flour in a mixing bowl, cut the butter into pieces, and rub into the flour with your fingertips until the mixture resembles fine breadcrumbs.

2 Stir in the sugar and orange zest and mix to a dough.

3 Knead the dough lightly then roll out on a floured surface to ¼in thickness. Stamp out four 3½in flower shapes or fluted rounds with a cookie cutter and 12 small car, train or other fun shapes with novelty cutters, rerolling the dough as necessary.

4 Place on a baking sheet, prick with a fork and sprinkle with a little extra sugar. Bake in the oven for 10–12 minutes until pale golden, then let cool on the baking sheet.

5 For the filling, blend the yogurt with the sugar and wash and hull the strawberries. Pat dry. Reserve eight of the strawberries and process or blend the rest. Press through a strainer and discard the seeds.

6 For the adults, put 3 tbsp of the yogurt in a bowl and stir in the Cointreau, if using. Slice four strawberries and halve two, place on a plate and cover.

7 For the toddler, slice two of the strawberries and arrange in a ring on a small plate. Spoon 2 tbsp of yogurt into the center of the ring and serve with three of the small cookie shapes.

8 For the baby, stir 1 tbsp of the strawberry purée into the remaining plain yogurt and spoon into a small dish. Serve with one or two of the small biscuit shapes.

9 To complete the adults' portions, spoon the purée over two plates to cover completely.

10 Spoon the reserved yogurt over two biscuits, add the sliced strawberries and top with the other two cookies. Arrange on plates and decorate with halved strawberries and tiny sprigs of mint.

TIP
If you find shortbread difficult to roll out then chill for 20 minutes. Knead lightly and roll out on a surface dusted with flour, dusting the rolling pin too.

Warm Exotic Fruit Salad

oil, for greasing
2 tbsp brown sugar
1 ripe mango
1 kiwi
1 passionfruit
2 tbsp confectioner's sugar
12oz plain yogurt

1 Line a baking sheet with foil then trace two circles using a 1 cup ramekin, then trace another using a ⅔ cup ramekin. Lightly brush with oil. Sprinkle the sugar inside each marked circle in an even layer.

2 Broil the sugar discs for 2–3 minutes or until they have melted and caramelized. Let the discs cool on the baking sheet.

3 Slice the mango on either side of the central pit and then cut six thin slices for decoration, cutting away the skin. Cut the rest of the mango flesh from the pit, removing the skin, and finely chop one quarter, dividing between the baby bowl and a small ramekin. Coarsely chop the remainder and divide between the larger ramekins.

4 Peel the kiwi, cut in half lengthwise and then slice thinly. Reserve four half slices for decoration and divide the remaining fruit among the dishes, finely chopping the fruit for the baby and toddler. Cut the passionfruit in half and using a teaspoon scoop and place the seeds in the adults' dishes.

5 Stir the confectioner's sugar into the yogurt and mix 1 tbsp into the baby's portion. Spoon 2 tbsp yogurt over the toddler's dish and level the surface with a spoon.

6 Spoon the remaining yogurt into the other two ramekins, level the surface with a spoon and chill all of them until required.

7 When ready to serve, place the larger ramekins on two plates with the reserved mango and kiwi slices arranged around the sides. Peel the sugar discs off the foil and set on top of the adult and toddler portions. Serve immediately.

TIP
Traditionally the sugar topping on a brulée is made by sprinkling brown sugar over the top of the dessert and then broiling, or by making a caramel syrup and then pouring it over the dessert. Making the topping on oiled foil is by far the easiest and most foolproof way. Add the cooled sugar discs at the very last minute so that they stay crisp and you get that wonderful mix of crunchy sugar, velvety yogurt and refreshing fruit.

Plum Crumble

1lb ripe red plums
2 tbsp superfine sugar
For the Topping
1 cup all-purpose flour
4 tbsp butter, cut into pieces
2 tbsp superfine sugar
2 tsp chocolate chips
3oz marzipan
2 tbsp oatmeal
2 tbsp slivered almonds
plain yogurt or custard, to serve

1 Preheat the oven to 375°F. Wash the plums, cut into quarters and remove the pits. Place in a saucepan with the sugar and 2 tbsp water, cover and simmer for 10 minutes until just tender.

2 Drain and spoon six plum quarters onto a chopping board and chop finely. Spoon the plums into a small baby dish with a little juice from the saucepan.

3 Drain and coarsely chop six more of the plum quarters and place in a ⅔ cup ovenproof ramekin with a little of the juice from the saucepan.

4 Spoon the remaining plums into a 3⅔ cup ovenproof dish for the adults.

5 Make the topping. Place the flour in a bowl, rub in the butter and then stir in the sugar.

6 Mix 3 tbsp of the topping mixture with the chocolate chips then spoon over the ramekin.

7 Coarsely grate the marzipan and stir into the remaining topping with the oats and almonds. Spoon over the adults' portion.

8 Place the toddler and adult portions on a baking sheet and cook for 20–25 minutes until golden brown. Leave to cool slightly before serving. Warm the baby's portion if desired and check the temperature of the children's food before serving. Serve with plain yogurt or custard.

TIP

Ovens can vary in temperature: with convection ovens you may need to cover the adults' dish with foil halfway through cooking to prevent overbrowning.

Vary the fruits: cooking apples, peaches and pears also work well. If the plums are very tart you may need to add a little extra sugar.

Chocolate and Tangerine Trifle

½ chocolate jelly roll
3 tangerines
4 tsp sherry
2oz dark chocolate
1¼ cups ready-made custard
6 tbsp heavy cream
M & M's

1 Slice the jelly roll, halve one slice and put on a plate for the baby. Put a second slice into a ramekin for the older child and arrange the remaining slices in two dessert bowls for the adults.

2 Peel one tangerine, separate into segments and put a few on the baby plate. Chop the rest and add to the ramekin.

3 Peel the remaining tangerines, coarsely chop and add to the adults' bowls, sprinkling a little sherry over each.

4 Break the chocolate into pieces and melt in a bowl over a saucepan of hot water. Stir the melted chocolate into the custard.

5 Spoon 2 tbsp of the custard into a small bowl for the baby and arrange on the plate with the jelly roll and tangerines. Spoon a little more custard into the ramekin and then add the rest to the adult dishes, smoothing the surface.

6 Whip the cream until it just holds its shape. Add a spoonful to the ramekin and two or three spoonfuls each to the adults' dishes, decorating each dish with M & M's. Chill the trifles until serving.

TIP
Chocolate may be melted in the microwave in a microwave-safe bowl for 2 minutes on High (100%), stirring thoroughly halfway through cooking.

Some shops sell ready-made chocolate custard, buy this if available and you're short of time.

Vary the fruit depending on what is in season, sliced strawberries and orange or sliced banana and fresh or canned cherries also work well.

Apple Strudel

- 1lb cooking apples
- 2oz dried apricots
- 3 tbsp golden raisins
- 2 tbsp light brown sugar
- 2 tbsp ground almonds
- 1 tsp ground cinnamon
- 2 tbsp butter
- 3 sheets filo pastry, defrosted if frozen
- confectioner's sugar, to dust
- light cream, to serve

1 Preheat the oven to 400°F. Peel, core and chop the apples and place 5oz in a saucepan. Chop three apricots and add to the pan with 1 tbsp golden raisins, 1 tbsp sugar and 1 tbsp water. Cover and simmer for 5 minutes.

2 Chop the remaining apricots and place in a bowl with the remaining apples, raisins, sugar, ground almonds and cinnamon. Mix together well.

3 Melt the butter in a small saucepan or microwave in a microwave-safe bowl for 30 seconds on High (100%).

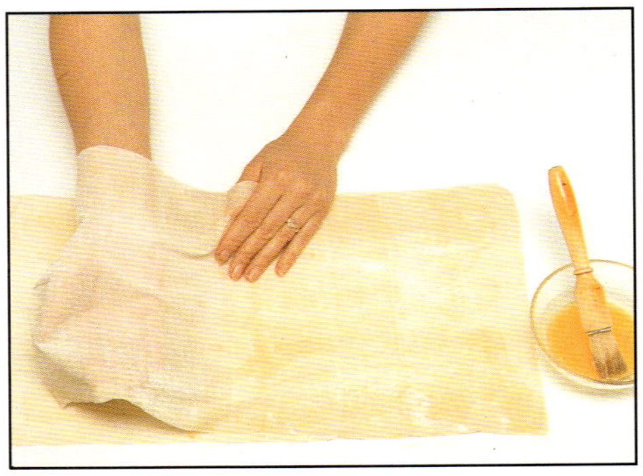

4 Carefully open out the pastry. Place one sheet on a work surface, brush with butter then cover with a second sheet of pastry and brush with more butter.

5 Spoon the uncooked apple mixture in a thick band along the center of the pastry.

6 Fold the two short sides up and over the filling and brush with butter. Fold the long sides up and over the filling, opening out the pastry and folding the pastry for an attractive finish. Place on a baking sheet and brush with a little butter.

7 Brush a little of the butter over half of the third pastry sheet then fold the unbrushed half over the top to make a square. Brush again and cut into three equal strips.

8 Put a spoonful of apple at the base of each strip then fold the bottom right-hand corner up and over the filling to the left side of the strip to make a triangle.

9 Continue folding the pastry to make a triangular pastry. Repeat with the other strips.

10 Transfer to a baking sheet and brush with the remaining butter. Bake for 10 minutes, and the adults' strudel for 15 minutes, until golden and crisp. Dust with confectioner's sugar and cool slightly.

11 Spoon the remaining cooked apple mixture into a baby dish. Mash the fruit if necessary. Transfer the toddler's portion to a plate. Slice the strudel thickly and serve with cream.

TIP
Filo pastry is usually sold frozen in 10oz packs or larger. Defrost the whole pack, take out as much pastry as you need, then rewrap the rest and return to freezer as soon as possible.

Strawberry Pavlova

- 2 egg whites
- 4oz superfine sugar
- ½ tsp cornstarch
- ½ tsp wine vinegar

For the Topping

- ⅔ cup heavy cream
- 9oz strawberries
- 2 chocolate chips
- green chuckles or gum drop

1 Preheat the oven to 300°F and line a baking sheet with non-stick baking paper.

2 Whisk the egg whites until stiff and then gradually whisk in the sugar 1 tsp at a time. Continue whisking until smooth and glossy.

3 Blend the cornstarch and vinegar and fold into the egg whites.

4 Spoon the mixture into a large pastry bag fitted with a medium-sized plain tube. Pipe six small dots for the baby and a snail for the older child with a shell about 2½in in diameter.

5 Pipe the remaining mixture into two 4in swirly circles and cook in the oven for 20–25 minutes or until firm. Lift the meringues off the paper and leave to cool.

TIP
For perfect meringues whisk the egg whites in a dry greasefree bowl. Remove any trace of yolk with a piece of shell and whisk until the peaks are stiff but still moist looking. Add sugar gradually and continue whisking until very thick. Meringues may be made 1–2 days in advance, if desired. Cover with wax paper and decorate just before serving.

6 Whip the cream until softly peaking and spoon over the two large meringues and the toddler's snail, reserving about 1 tbsp of cream for the baby.

7 Rinse, hull and slice the strawberries and arrange a few in rings over the snail. Place the snail on a plate and add chocolate eyes and a slice from a green chuckles or gum drop for the mouth.

8 Add some strawberries to the adult meringues then chop or mash a few extra slices and stir them into the reserved cream for the baby. Spoon into a small dish and serve with tiny meringues.

Poached Pears

- 3 ripe pears
- 1⅞ cup apple juice
- 1 tsp powdered gelatin
- few drops of green food coloring
- ½ small orange, peel only
- ½ small lemon, peel only
- 2 tsp chopped candied ginger
- 1 tsp clear honey
- 1 tsp cornstarch
- 1 red licorice bootlace
- 2 small currants
- 1 raisin or large currant
- ½ candied cherry

1 Peel the pears leaving the stems in place. Cut a small circle out of the base of two pears and tunnel out the cores with a small knife.

2 Halve the remaining pear, discard the stem, scoop out the core and then put them all in a pan with the apple juice. Bring to a boil, cover and simmer for 5 minutes, turning the pears once.

3 Lift out the pear halves and reserve, cooking the whole pears for 5 minutes more or until just tender. Remove with a slotted spoon and place on a serving dish reserving the cooking liquid. Finely chop one pear half and put into a small dish for the baby. Reserve the other half pear for the toddler.

4 Pour half of the reserved apple juice into a bowl, place over a pan of simmering water, add the gelatin and stir until completely dissolved. Transfer to a measuring cup and pour half over the chopped pear and chill.

5 Stir a little green coloring into the remaining gelatine mixture, pour into a shallow dish or a plate with a rim for the toddler, and chill.

6 Cut away the peel from the orange and lemon and cut into thin strips. Add to the remaining apple juice with the ginger and honey and simmer over a gentle heat for 5 minutes until the peel is soft.

7 Blend the cornstarch with a little water to make a smooth paste, stir into the pan then bring the mixture to a boil and cook, stirring, until thickened. Pour over the whole pears and let cool.

8 Place the toddler's pear, cut side down, on the green jelly. To make a mouse, add a piece of red licorice for a tail and two pieces for whiskers. Make two small cuts for eyes and tuck a currant into each slit. Add a raisin or large currant for the nose. Halve the cherry and use for ears. Serve slightly chilled with cream for the adults, if desired.

Peach Almond Tart

1½ cups all-purpose flour
6 tbsp butter
For the Filling
4 tbsp butter
¼ cup superfine sugar
1 egg
few drops of almond extract
⅔ cup ground almonds
2 tbsp apricot preserves
1 tbsp chopped candied citrus peel
14oz can peach slices in natural juice
1 tbsp slivered almonds
1 tbsp plain yogurt
confectioner's sugar, for dusting
crème fraîche or plain yogurt, to serve

1 Place the flour in a bowl, cut the butter into small pieces and rub into the flour with your fingertips until the mixture resembles fine breadcrumbs.

2 Stir in 6–7 tsp water and mix to a smooth dough. Knead lightly on a floured work surface and roll out thinly.

3 Lift the pastry over a rolling pin and use to line a 7in flan dish pressing down against the sides of the dish. Trim the top.

4 Reroll the trimmings and cut out twelve 2in circles with a fluted cookie cutter, pressing into sections of a mini muffin pan. Chill the pastry for 15 minutes.

5 Preheat the oven to 375°F. Line the large flan dish with wax paper and fill with baking beans. Cook in the preheated oven for 10 minutes then remove the baking beans and paper and cook the shell for 5 minutes more.

6 Meanwhile make the filling: cream together the butter and sugar in a bowl until light and fluffy. Beat the eggs and almond extract together then gradually beat into the creamed sugar. Stir in the ground almonds and set aside.

7 Divide the preserves among the small and large tarts, spread it into a thin layer in the large tart and sprinkle with candied peel. Spoon all of the almond mixture over the top and level the surface.

8 Drain the peaches and set aside three slices for the baby. Cut three slices into chunks and divide among six of the small tarts, leaving six with just preserves.

9 Arrange the remaining peaches over the top of the large tart and sprinkle with slivered almonds.

10 Cook the small tarts for 10 minutes and the large tart for 25 minutes until the filling is set and browned. Dust the large tart with confectioner's sugar and let cool.

11 Process or blend the reserved peaches for the baby. Mix with the plain yogurt and spoon into a small dish. Serve with two plain preserves tarts.

12 Arrange a few fruity tarts on a plate for the toddler. Cut the large tart into wedges and serve with crème fraîche or plain yogurt for the adults. Test the temperature of the children's tarts before serving.

Honey and Summer Fruit Mousse

- 2 tsp powdered gelatin
- 1¼lb bag frozen mixed berries, defrosted, or fresh berries, cleaned and trimmed
- 4 tsp superfine sugar
- 1¼lb container plain yogurt
- ⅔ cup whipping cream
- 5 tsp clear honey

1 Put 2 tbsp cold water in a cup and sprinkle the gelatin over making sure that all the grains of gelatin have been absorbed. Soak for 5 minutes, then heat in a saucepan of simmering water until the gelatin dissolves and the liquid is clear. Cool slightly.

2 For baby, process or blend 2oz of fruit to a purée and stir in 1 tsp sugar. Mix 3 tbsp plain yogurt with 1 tsp sugar in a separate bowl.

TIP

If you have a small novelty mold you may prefer to set the toddler's portion in this rather than a glass or plastic container.

Make sure the gelatin isn't too hot before adding to plain yogurt or it may curdle.

3 Put alternate spoonfuls of plain yogurt and purée into a small dish for the baby. Swirl the mixtures together with a teaspoon. Chill until serving.

4 For the toddler, process or blend 2oz fruit with 1 tsp sugar to a purée. Mix 4 tbsp plain yogurt with 1 tsp sugar then stir in 2 tsp fruit purée.

5 Stir 1 tsp gelatin into the fruit purée and 1 tsp into the yogurt mixture. Spoon the fruit mixture into the base of a glass and chill until set.

6 For the adults, whip the cream until softly peaking. Fold in the remaining plain yogurt and honey and add the remaining gelatin. Pour into two 1 cup molds and refrigerate until set.

7 Spoon the remaining yogurt mixture over the set fruit layer in the serving glass for the toddler and chill until set.

8 To serve, dip one of the dishes for the adults in hot water, count to 15, then loosen the edges with your fingertips, invert onto a large plate and, holding mold and plate together, jerk to release the mousse and remove mold. Repeat with the other mold. Spoon the remaining fruits and some juice around the desserts and serve.

Hot Fruit Salad with Ginger Cream

2 oranges
4 bananas
2oz pitted dates
2 tbsp golden raisins
2 tbsp butter
3 tbsp brown sugar
2 tbsp Cointreau or brandy
vanilla ice cream, to serve

For the Ginger Cream

⅔ cup heavy cream
1 tbsp chopped candied ginger
grated zest of 1 orange

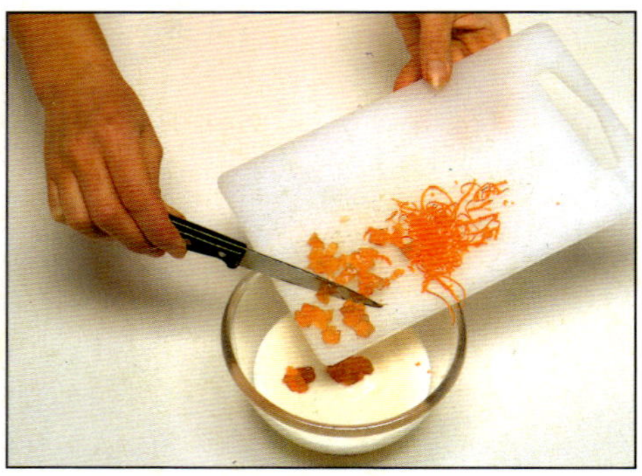

1 First make the ginger cream: whip the cream until it just holds its shape, then finely chop the ginger and stir into the cream with the orange zest. Spoon into a small serving dish.

2 Cut a slice off the top and bottom of each orange and cut the remaining peel and pith away in slices. Cut into segments.

3 Peel and slice the bananas. Coarsely chop the dates. Arrange a few orange segments, slices of banana, pieces of date and a few raisins on a plate for the baby.

4 Melt the butter in a skillet, add the remaining fruit and sauté for 2 minutes, then stir in the sugar and cook for 2 minutes, until lightly browned. Spoon a few pieces of fruit into a bowl for the toddler.

5 Stir the Cointreau or brandy into the pan, bring to a boil then quickly light with a match. Spoon the fruit into a serving bowl as soon as the flames subside. Serve the adults' flambéed fruit with ginger cream and the toddler's portion with ice cream. Test the temperature of the toddler's portion before serving.

TIP
Flaming dishes look so spectacular but are really very easy to do. The secret is to add the spirit to hot liquid, bring the liquid back to a boil then quickly light it with a match and stand back. The flames will subside in a minute or two. But if you are at all worried they can be quickly extinguished by covering the pan with a lid or baking sheet.

GLOSSARY OF PREGNANCY TERMS

ABORTION
The spontaneous or induced delivery of the fetus before the 28th week.

ABRUPTIO PLACENTAE
Part of the placenta peels away from the wall of the uterus in late pregnancy and often results in bleeding.

ALPHAFETOPROTEIN (AFP)
A protein produced by the fetus that enters the mother's bloodstream. A very high level can indicate neural tube defects of the fetus such as spina bifida, but it can also mean the woman is carrying more than one child.

AMNIOCENTESIS
A small amount of amniotic fluid is taken from the uterus through a needle inserted through the woman's abdomen and tested for chromosomal disorders such as Down's syndrome.

AMNIOTIC FLUID
The fluid surrounding the fetus in the uterus.

AMNIOTIC SAC
The bag of membranes that is filled with amniotic fluid in which the fetus floats during pregnancy.

ANALGESICS
Painkilling drugs which do not cause unconsciousness. The analgesics most commonly used during labor are meperidine hydrochloride (Demerol) and alphaprodine hydrochloride (Nisentil).

ANEMIA
A condition where the level of red corpuscles in the blood are abnormally low, which is treated with iron supplements.

APGAR SCORE
A simple test to assess the baby's condition after birth.

BEARING DOWN
The pushing movement made by the uterus during the second stage of labor.

BIRTH CANAL
See Vagina.

BLASTOCYST
The early stage of the developing embryo when it becomes a cluster of cells.

BRAXTON HICKS CONTRACTIONS
Contractions of the uterus which occur throughout pregnancy, but may not be felt until the last month or so. They feel like a painless, but sometimes uncomfortable, hardening across the stomach.

BREECH PRESENTATION
The position of a baby when he is bottom down rather than head down in the uterus.

CAESARIAN SECTION
Delivery of the baby through a cut in the abdomen and uterine walls.

CERVIX
The neck of the uterus or womb which is sealed with a plug of mucus during pregnancy. During labor, muscular contractions open up the cervix until it is about 4 in wide so that the baby can pass through it into the vagina.

CHLOASMA
Slight discoloration of the skin, usually on the face, which occurs during pregnancy and disappears within weeks of the birth.

CHORIONIC VILLUS SAMPLING
A screening test for genetic handicap which can be done as early as 11 weeks. Cells are taken from the tissue that surrounds the fetus and are then analyzed.

COLOSTRUM
A fluid that the breasts produce during pregnancy and immediately after the birth. It is full of nutrients and contains antibodies which will protect the baby from some infections.

CONCEPTION
The fertilization of the egg by the sperm and its implantation in the wall of the uterus.

CONGENITAL ABNORMALITIES
An abnormality or deformity that exists from birth. It is caused by a damaged gene or the effect of some diseases during pregnancy.

CONTRACTIONS
Regular tightening of the muscles of the uterus as they work to dilate the cervix and push the baby down the birth canal.

CROWNING
The moment when the crown of the baby's head appears in the vagina.

DEMEROL
A drug given during labor for pain relief and relaxation.

DILATION
The gradual opening of the cervix during labor.

DOPPLER
A method of using ultrasound vibrations to listen to the fetal heart.

ECTOPIC PREGNANCY
A pregnancy that develops outside the uterus, usually in the fallopian tube.

EDD
Estimated date of delivery.

EDEMA
Swelling caused by fluid retention.

ELECTIVE INDUCTION
Induction done for convenience rather than for medical reasons.

ELECTRONIC FETAL MONITORING
The continuous monitoring of the fetal heart.

EMBRYO
The name of the developing organism in pregnancy from about the 10th day after fertilization until the 12th week of pregnancy when it becomes known as a fetus.

ENGAGED
The baby's head is engaged when it drops down deep in the pelvic cavity so that the widest part is through the mother's pelvic brim. Another term for this is "lightening." Most babies are born head first and will have engaged before labor begins.

ENGORGEMENT
The breasts become congested with milk if long periods are left between feedings. This results in painful engorgement.

ENTONOX
Gas and oxygen, a short-term analgesic, now rarely used for inhalation during labor.

EPIDURAL
An anaesthetic that is injected into the fluid surrounding the spinal cord at the base of the spine to relieve pain but leave the mother fully conscious.

EPISIOTOMY
A small cut sometimes made in the perineum to enlarge the vagina if there is a risk of tearing when the baby's head is about to be born.

FALLOPIAN TUBES
Two narrow tubes about 4 in long which lead from the ovaries to the uterus.

FETUS
The developing baby from the end of the embryonic stage at about the 12th week of pregnancy, until the date of delivery.

FH
Fetal heart.

FMF
Fetal movement felt.

FOLIC ACID
A form of vitamin B that is important for the healthy development of the embryo. A daily supplement of 0.4mg should be taken before becoming pregnant and then until the 12th week of pregnancy.

FONTANELLES
The soft spots between the unjoined sections of the skull of the baby.

FORCEPS
An instrument sometimes used to assist the baby out of the birth canal.

FOREMILK
The first breast milk the baby gets when he begins to suck which satisfies his thirst before the hind milk comes through.

FUNDUS
The top of the uterus.

GAS AND AIR
See Entonox

GENETIC COUNSELING
Advice on the detection and risk of recurrence of inherited disorders.

GESTATION
The length of time between conception and delivery (usually around 40 weeks).

HEMOGLOBIN (HB)
The pigment that gives blood its red color and contains iron and stores oxygen.

HEMORRHAGE
Excessive bleeding

HEMORRHOIDS
A form of varicose veins around the anus.

HINDMILK
The calorie-rich breast milk that forms the foremilk during feed.

HORMONE
A chemical produced by the body to stimulate organs within the body, particularly those to do with growth and reproduction,

HUMAN CHORIONIC GONADOTROPHIN (HCG)
A hormone produced early in pregnancy by the developing placenta. Its presence in the urine is used to confirm pregnancy.

IMPLANTATION
The embedding of the fertilized egg in the wall of the uterus.

INCOMPETENT CERVIX
A weakened cervix that is unable to hold the fetus in the uterus for the full nine months. Sometimes a cause of late miscarriage or premature birth.

INDUCTION
The process of artificially starting off labor.

INTRAVENOUS DRIP
The infusion of fluids directly into the blood stream through a fine tube into a vein.

JAUNDICE
Neonatal jaundice often occurs in newborn babies because of the inability of the liver to successfully break down an excess of red blood cells.

LABOR
The process of childbirth.

LANUGO
A very fine covering of hair that appears all over the fetus during late pregnancy.

LIE
The position of the fetus in the uterus.

LIGHTENING
See Engaged.

LINEA NIGRA
A line of dark pigmentation that appears down the center of the abdomen on some women during pregnancy.

LOCHIA
Post-partum vaginal discharge

MECONIUM
The green matter passed from the baby's bowels during the first days after birth. Meconium in the amniotic fluid before delivery is usually a sign of fetal distress.

MISCARRIAGE
The loss of a baby before 24 weeks gestation.

MONITOR
Machine or instrument to measure the baby's heartbeat and breathing.

MOLDING
The shaping of the bones of the baby's skull as it passes through the birth canal.

MUCUS
A sticky secretion.

NAD
A medical term often used on medical records meaning "nothing abnormal detected."

NEURAL TUBE DEFECT
Development defect of the brain and/or spinal cord.

OBSTETRICIAN
Medical specialist in pregnancy and childbirth.

OVARY
Female organ responsible for production of sex hormones and eggs (ova).

OVULATION
The production of a ripe egg by the ovary, usually on a monthly basis.

PALPATION
Manual examination of the uterus through the wall of the abdomen.

PELVIC FLOOR
The muscles that support the bladder and the uterus.

PERINATAL
Period from before delivery until seven days after the birth.

PERINEUM
The area between the opening of the vagina and the anus.

PLACENTA
Also known as "afterbirth," this is the fetus's life-support system which is attached to one side of the wall of the uterus and to the baby by means of the umbilical cord. All the fetus's nourishment passes from the mother through the placenta while the fetus's waste products pass out through it.

PREMATURE OR PRETERM
A baby born before the 37th week.

PRE-NATAL
Before birth.

PRESENTATION
The position of the fetus in the uterus before and during the delivery.

PRIMIPARA
A woman who is having her first baby.

PROSTAGLANDIN
A hormone that stimulates the onset of labor contractions.

QUICKENING
The first movements of the fetus in the uterus.

ROOTING
The baby's instinctive searching for the mother's nipple

RUBELLA (GERMAN MEASLES)
A virus that can be dangerous if caught during the first three months of pregnancy.

SHOW
A vaginal discharge of blood-stained mucus that occurs before or during labor

STILLBIRTH
The delivery of a baby who has already died in the uterus after 28 weeks of pregnancy.

STRETCH MARKS
Silvery lines that may appear where the skin has been stretched during pregnancy.

TERM
The end of pregnancy – around 40 weeks from the date of conception.

TERMINATION
An artificially induced abortion before the end of 28th week of pregnancy.

TOXOPLASMOSIS
A parasitic disease spread by cat feces that can cause blindness in a baby.

TRIMESTER
Pregnancy is divided into three trimesters, each making one third of pregnancy.

ULTRASOUND SCAN
A way of screening the fetus in the uterus by bouncing high-frequency sound waves off it which build up a picture.

UMBILICAL CORD
The cord connecting the fetus to the placenta.

UTERUS (WOMB)
The hollow muscular organ in which the fertile egg becomes embedded.

VACUUM EXTRACTOR
An instrument sometimes used to pull the baby out of the vagina.

VAGINA
The birth canal through which the baby makes its way from the uterus.

USEFUL ADDRESSES

BIRTH DEFECTS

March of Dimes,
P.O. Box 2000,
White Plains,
NY 10602

National Down's Syndrome Congress,
1800 Dempster Street,
Park Ridge,
IL 60068-1146

The Spina-Bifida Association of America,
1700 Rockville Pike,
Suite 540,
Rockville,
MD 20852

BIRTHING CHOICES

Academy of Certified Birth Educators,
2001 East Prairie Circle,
Suite 1,
Olathe,
KS 66062
913-782-5116

American Academy of Husband-Coached Childbirth,
P.O. Box 5224,
Sherman Oaks,
CA 91413-5224
800-423-2397

American Foundation for Maternal and Child Health,
30 Beekman Place,
New York,
NY 10022
212-759-5510

Birthworks,
42 Tallwood Drive,
Medford,
NJ 08255
609-953-9380

Cesarean/Support, Education and Concern,
22 Forest Road,
Framingham,
MA 01701
617-738-6750

International Childbirth Education Association,
P.O. Box 20024,
Minneapolis,
MN 55420
800-624-4934

Positive Pregnancy and Parenting Fitness,
51 Saltrock Road,
Baltic,
CT 06330
203-822-8573

BREASTFEEDING

Human Lactation Center,
666 Sturges Highway,
Westport,
CT 06880
203-259-5995

La Leche International,
P.O. Box 1209,
Franklin Park,
IL 60131
708-455-7730

DEATH OF A BABY

Compassionate Friends,
P.O. Box 1347,
Oak Brook,
IL 60521

FERTILITY

American Fertility Society,
1209 Montgomery Highway,
Birmingham,
AL 35216
205-978-5000

Society for the Prevention of Human Infertility,
877 Park Avenue,
New York,
NY 10021
212-288-3737

Vanderbilt University for Fertility and Reproductive Research IVF Program,
D-3200 Medical Center North,
Nashville,
TN 37232

Women's Health and Fertility Branch, National Center for Chronic Disease Prevention and Health Promotion,
1600 Clifton Avenue, NE,
Atlanta,
GA 30333
404-329-3286

Yale Universtity Medical School, Department of Obstetrics and Gynecology,
333 Cedar Street,
New Haven CT,
C06510

GENERAL HEALTH

American College of Nurse/Midwives
1522 K. Street NW,
Suite 1000
Washington,
DC 20005
202-289-0171

American College of Obstetricians and Gynecologists,
409 12th Street SW,
Washington,
DC 20037
202-466-3825

Association of Reproductive Health Professionals,
2401 Pennsylvania Avenue, NW,
Suite 350,
Washington,
DC 20037
202-466-3825

Midwives Alliance of North America,
P. O. Box 1121,
Bristol,
VA 24203
615-764-551

National Women's Health Network,
1325 G Street, NW, LL,
Washington,
DC 20005
202-347-1140

Office on Women's Health,
200 Independence Avenue, SW,
Washington,
DC 20201
202-690-7650

GENETIC COUNSELING

Alliance of Genetic Support Groups,
35 Wisconsin Circle,
Suite 440,
Chevy Chase,
MD 20815
800-336-GENE

National Center for Education in Maternal and Child Health,
2000 15th Street N,
Suite 701,
Arlington,
VA 22201-26217
703-524-7802

National Society for Genetic Counselors,
233 Canterbury Drive,
Wallingford,
PA 19086
215-872-7608

National Network to Prevent Birth Defects,
Box 15309 SE Station,
Washington,
DC 20003
202-543-5450

MISCELLANEOUS

Center for the Study of Multiple Births,
333 East Superior Street,
Suite 463-5,
Chicago,
IL 606011

International Twins Association,
P.O. Box 77386, Station C,
Atlanta,
GA 30357

Parents Without Partners,
8807 Colesville Road,
Silver Spring,
MD 20910

Postpartum Support International,
215-295-3994
805-682-7529
(self-help organization for post-partum depression)

INDEX

Page numbers in italic refer to the illustrations

P

Q, R

S

T

ACKNOWLEDGEMENTS

Picture acknowledgements: Bubbles 78; /Jacquie Farrow 68, 262 br, 339 br; /Julie Fisher 11; /Nikki Gibbs 16 b, 80, 423 t; /Paul Howard 75 t; /Julia Martin 21 b, 85 (all 3); /S Price 327; /F Rombout 279 t; /Lois Joy Thurston 29 b, 47 t and r, 52, 64, 81, 273 t, 289, 319 tr, 422 b, 425 t; /Ian West 77 b, 338 t, 343 t; /J. Woodcock 29 t, 78; /Richard Yard 69; Greg Evans 332; Sally and Richard Greenhill 314 t; Lupe Cunha 18, 19, 21 t and b, 23, 26, 27 b, 33 t and b, 39 t, 52, 53 t, 61 bl and t, 61 r, 73 t, 82, 83 r and tr, 86, 87, 262 bl, 286-287, 292, 295 t, 308, 316, 325, 422 t; Lyons Waddell 311 t; PR Communications 54 (box); Reflections/Jennie Woodcock 315 b, 318 tr, 328-329, 331, 339 cr, 349, 378, 423 b, 424 bl, 424 br; Science Photo Library/BSIP Bajande 89 b; /Mark Clarke 60, 61 t, 72, 73 b, 74, 75 b, 79 r, 88 t and b, 89 t and b; /Custom Medical Stock 61 t, 89 t; /Simon Fraser 47, 73 b; /Will & Deni McIntyre 24 t, 25 b; /Joseph Mettis 72; /Petit Format/Nestle 16 t; /Chris Priest 36; 39; /Richard G Rawlins 15 tl, 24 t, 25 b, 35, 36; /Pascale Roche/Petit Format 88 t and b; /James Stevenson 20 br, 35 b, 47 bl; /Ron Sutherland 79 r; /Sheila Terry 21 t, 65, 83 bl; /Jonathan Watts 60; Carin Simon 80 r; Timothy Woodcock 262 t, 425

(Key: b – bottom, bl – bottom left, br – bottom right, r – right, t – top, tl – top left, tr – top right)

The publishers have tried to credit all agencies and photographers whose pictures appear in this book and apologize for any omissions.

ACKNOWLEDGEMENTS

The author and publisher would like to thank the many individuals who helped in the creation of the Pregnancy and Babycare sections of this book. In particular thanks are due to Bobbie Brown, Elsa Jacobi, Pauline Richardson, Mary Lambert and Jane Barret. Many thanks also go to everyone who modeled for special photography: Yvonne Adams and Martin; Ruth Auber and Bethany; Jo Bates and Lois; Amanda Bennet-Jones; Kim, Neil and Andrew Brown; Christine Clarke; Jacqueline Clarke and Cassia; Jocelyn Cusack and Beth; Sam Dyas and Colt; Patricia Gannon and Matthew; Nici Giles and Fergus; Yiota Gillis and Cameron; Sandra Hadfield and Annie; Louise Henriques and Joshua; Lynette Jones and Hugh and Rhys; Karen, Mark, Megan and Robert Lambert; Claire Lehain and Harriet; Lavinia Mainds and Polly; Pippa Milton and Oliver; Philippa Madden and Inca; Jackie Norbury; Jess Presland; Katey Steiner; Saatchi Spracklen and Niamh; Sophie Trotter and Archie; Josephine Whitfield and Lily May; Lucinda Whitrow and Hector. Thanks also to companies who loaned items and photographs: Blooming Marvellous Ltd (pages 36-37), Boots Children's Wear and Toys, Fisher-Price, Littlewoods Home Shopping, Maclaren Ltd and Mattel UK Ltd.

The author and publisher would also like to thank all those involved in the creation of the Cooking for Babies & Toddlers section of this book. In particular thanks are due to the Department of Health for reading and approving the section on food for babies; the National Dairy Council Nutrition Service; the Health Education Authority; Dr Nigel Dickie from Heinz Baby Foods; The British Diabetic Association; The Health Visitors Association; Broadstone Communications for their invaluable help in supplying the Kenwood equipment for recipe testing and photography; hand-painted china plates, bowls and mugs from Cosmo Place Studio, 11 Cosmo Place, London WC1N 3AP. Tel 0207 278 3374; Tupperware for plain-coloured plastic bowls, plates, feeder beakers and cups; Cole and Mason for non-breakable children's ware; Royal Doulton for Bunnykins china; Spode for blue and white Edwardian Childhood china.